Fifth edition

Your
Rights
in the
Workplace

by Attorney Barbara Kate Repa

edited by Attorney Amy Delpo

KEEPING UP TO DATE

To keep its books up to date, Nolo issues new printings and new editions periodically. New printings reflect minor legal changes and technical corrections. New editions contain major legal changes, major text additions or major reorganizations. To find out if a later printing or edition of any Nolo book is available, call Nolo at 510-549-1976 or check our Website at www.nolo.com.

To stay current, follow the "Update" service at our Website at www.nolo.com. In another effort to help you use Nolo's latest materials, we offer a 25% discount off the purchase of the new edition of your Nolo book when you turn in the cover of an earlier edition. (See the "Special Upgrade Offer" in the back of the book.)

This book was last revised in: November 2000.

FIFTH EDITION	November 2000		
EDITOR	Amy DelPo	PROOFREADER	Bob Wells
LEGAL RESEARCH	Ella Hirst	BOOK DESIGN	Jackie Mancuso
INDEX	Susan Cornell	COVER DESIGN	Toni Ihara
PRINTING	Bertelsmann Services, Inc.	PRODUCTION	Sarah Hinman

Repa, Barbara Kate.
    Your rights in the workplace / by Barbara Kate Repa.-- 5th ed.
      p. cm.
    Includes index.
    ISBN 0-87337-597-1
    1. Labor laws and legislation--United States--Popular works. 2. Employee rights--United States--Popular works. I. Title.

    KF3455.Z9 R47 2000
    344.7301--dc21   00-037215

QUANTITY SALES: For information on bulk purchases or corporate premium sales, please contact the Special Sales department. For academic sales or textbook adoptions, ask for ACADEMIC SALES, 800-955-4775. Nolo, 950 Parker St., Berkeley, CA, 94710.

ACKNOWLEDGMENTS

Many people gave their time, expertise and wise counsel to help make this tome possible.

Some of them merit special thanks, including:

Marcia Stewart, editor extraordinaire on the second edition, whose special brand of encouragement worked its way onto every page.

Amy DelPo, editor on this fifth edition, who cheerfully shoveled fodder and good karma my way—and judiciously spotted the antiques.

Ella Hirst, research maven and former relative, who never met a statute too elusive for her—and the book is much the better for it.

Jackie Mancuso, express designer, who made the innards look grand.

Susan Cornell, who took the index to new heights with her nitpicking mind.

Stanley Jacobsen, who worked tirelessly and pleasantly to keep the facts current—and provided an endless supply of blue M & Ms all along the way.

And finally, a heartfelt thanks to my beacons—Joel and Thomas.

DAN LACEY, one of the primary authors of the first edition of *Your Rights in the Workplace,* died in 1992. Some of his words live on here.

Contents

HEALTH INSURANCE

FAMILY AND MEDICAL LEAVE

PRIVACY RIGHTS

CHAPTER 7

HEALTH AND SAFETY

CHAPTER 8

ILLEGAL DISCRIMINATION

CHAPTER 9

SEXUAL HARASSMENT

LOSING OR LEAVING A JOB

CHALLENGING A JOB LOSS

UNEMPLOYMENT INSURANCE

CHAPTER

1

YOUR RIGHTS
IN THE
WORKPLACE

Maybe you're just curious. Or maybe you're the cautious type of soul who likes to think ahead and prevent a wrong before it happens. But the best bet is that you are reading this book because you already have a work-related problem:

- You were not hired for a job and you have good reason to suspect it was because of your race. Or your disability.
- Your employer promoted a less qualified person to fill a position you were promised.
- You want to know your legal rights if you consistently work overtime. Or if you want to take a leave to care for a sick parent. Or if you are called to serve on a jury.
- You have just been laid off and you're wondering if you have the right to get your job back. Or to get unemployment payments in the meantime. Or whether your employer owes you severance pay.

- You want to help evaluate a new job you've been offered. Or you want to find out your legal rights as a jobseeker.

This book will help you understand the legal rights that apply to your situation. It explains federal workplace laws—such as those guaranteeing your rights to be paid fairly and on time and to work free from discrimination. And it also explains the twists state law may place on your workplace rights—regulating, for example, both your right to smoke and to work in a smokefree place, or whether or not you are entitled to time off work to vote or to care for a sick child.

When pondering how to tackle a potential workplace problem, heed that noble adage: Simplify, simplify. Better still: Simplify. Woe unto the reader whose concerns span every chapter. First skim Chapter 2 on determining your legal employment status. Then proceed to the chapters that discuss the substance of your problem.

Also, be aware that there are many public and private agencies, groups and organizations that specialize in workplace issues, and many of them provide free—or low cost—counseling, support or referrals. You will find lists of such organizations peppered throughout the book, and a comprehensive listing in the Appendix.

A. Analyzing Your Options

If something is amiss in your workplace and you have turned to watercooler wisdom, commuter train tales or locker room skinny, you may have come away with the same urging: Sue.

For most people, that is bad advice. The courtroom is usually the worst place to resolve workplace disputes. Most of them can be handled more efficiently and much more effectively in the workplace itself—through mediation, arbitration or, most often, by honest conversation.

If you have suffered an insult, an injury or a wrong at work, you are probably feeling angry or hurt. If you have lost your job, you may be hurting financially, too. All of this is likely to cloud your ability to make well-reasoned decisions. So go slowly. Decide what you want to gain. If an apology from your employer would suffice, save yourself the time and expense of filing a legal action.

B. Talking It Over With Your Employer

Do not overlook the obvious: First try talking over your workplace problem with your employer. An intelligent discussion can resolve most wrongs—or at least get your differences out on the table. Most companies want to stay within the law and avoid legal tangles. So the odds are that your problem is the result of an oversight, a misunderstanding or a lack of legal knowledge.

Here are a few tips on how to present your concerns to your employer or former employer:

Know your rights. The more you know about your legal rights in the workplace—to be paid fairly and on time, to do your job free from discrimination and retaliation, to labor in a safe and healthy place—the more confident you will be in presenting your problem. This book offers a wealth of information about the basic laws of the workplace—and tells you where to turn if you need more specific information to clarify your rights.

Also, the book contains a number of charts summarizing state laws on various workplace rights, including, where the laws set them out, the penalties that may be imposed on employers who violate them. Your best course is probably not to sue your employer over a violation of a law requiring paid time off for jury duty or a single miscalculation of overtime pay. But knowing whether a particular transgression can be punished with a fine, a criminal conviction or an order to rehire you is the kind of self-interested information that can make your employer take your complaint more seriously in the bargaining process.

Stick to the facts. Keeping your legal rights firmly in mind, write a brief summary of what has gone wrong and your recommendation for resolving the problem. It often helps to have someone who is more objective, such as a friend or family member, review the facts of your workplace problem with you and discuss possible approaches to resolving it.

Check the facts again. The human memory is not nearly as accurate as we like to think it is—particularly when it comes to remembering numbers and dates. Before you approach your employer with a complaint about your pay, check to be sure your math is correct. If your beef is about a discriminatory remark, be sure you can quote it verbatim. Review all of your written records to make sure you have not overlooked a past event or pivotal memo.

Do not be overly emotional. Dealing with a workplace problem can be stressful. After all, if you are like most workers, you spend about half of your waking hours on the job. But you also know friends, relatives and acquaintances who are out of work—and who are having hard times finding new jobs.

Do not tolerate abuse. But if your job is on shaky ground, try not to jeopardize it further by losing your temper and getting fired as a result. A calm presentation of a complaint is always better than an emotional confrontation.

Remember the common wisdom that it is easier to find a new job while you still have your old one. At the very least, it's easier to blaze a new career trail if you leave no muddy tracks behind you.

Be discreet. Discussions of workplace problems are often very personal, and should take place privately—not in front of co-workers. Employment problems can be divisive not only for those involved, but for an entire workplace. You don't want to be justly accused of poisoning the workplace atmosphere or of filling it with disgruntled workers forming pro and con camps. Ask for an appointment to discuss your complaint privately with your supervisor or another appropriate manager. Give that person a chance to resolve your problem rationally and privately—and he or she will be more apt to see things your way.

C. Documenting the Problem

Most employers now heed the workplace mantra reinforced by thousands of court cases: Document, document, document. If your good working situation has gone bad—or you have recently been fired—you, too, must heed the call: Document all that happened. You are nowhere, legally, without evidence of how and when things went wrong.

A little bit of workplace paranoia may later prove to be a healthy thing. Even if everything seems fine now, take the extra seconds to make a paper trail. Collect in one place all documents you receive on the job: initial work agreements, employee handbooks, management memos, performance reviews. To be safe, keep your file at home, away from the office.

If you have what seems to be a valid complaint, it is crucial to gather evidence to bolster your claim. From the start, beware of deadlines for filing specific types of legal claims. The deadlines may range from a few weeks to a few years, but will likely signal that you will have to act quickly.

There are several kinds of evidence you should collect as soon as possible.

Company policies. Statements of company policy, either written or verbal, which indicate arbitrary or wrongful treatment—including job descriptions, work rules, personnel pamphlets, notices or anything else that either indicates or implies that company policy is to treat workers unfairly may be the most meaningful evidence you can amass.

Written statements by management. Statements by supervisors, personnel directors or other managers about you are also important. Save any written statements and note when and from whom you received them. If you have not received any written reasons for a job decision you feel is discriminatory or otherwise wrongful, make a written request for a statement of the company's reasons.

Verbal comments. In many cases, employers and their managers do not write down their reasons for making an employment decision. In such cases, you may still be able to document your claim with evidence of verbal statements by supervisors or others concerning unwritten company policy or undocumented reasons for a particular action involving your job.

Make accurate notes of what was said as soon as you can after the statement is made. Also note the time and place the statement was made, who else was present and the conversation surrounding it. If others heard the statement, try to get them to write down their recollections and have them sign that statement. Or have them sign your written version of the statement, indicating that it accurately reflects what they heard.

We're All in This Together

Co-workers may be reluctant to help you with your workplace complaint, whether by giving statements of their own experiences or by backing up your story of what has occurred. You may run into the same common reaction: "I don't want to get involved."

People may be afraid they will lose their own jobs or suffer in some other way if they pitch in and create bad blood with the company. You may be able to persuade them to help you by reassuring them that the law which prohibits the initial wrongful treatment also specifically prohibits the company or union from retaliating against anyone who helps in an investigation of your claim.

D. Considering Legal Action

Wipe the dollar signs from your eyes. While it's true that some workers have won multi-million dollar judgments against their employers, it's also true that such judgments are very few and very far between. There are several things to think about before you decide to launch a no-holds-barred legal challenge to your firing or wrongful workplace treatment.

Evaluate your motives. Answer one question honestly: What do you expect to gain by a lawsuit? Are you angry, seeking some revenge? Do you hope to teach your former employer a lesson? Do you just want to make your former employer squirm? None of these provides a strong basis on which to construct a lawsuit. If an apology, a letter of recommendation or a clearing of your work record would make you feel whole again, negotiate first for those things.

You will need good documentation. As this book stresses again and again, the success of your claim or lawsuit is likely to depend upon how well you can document the circumstances surrounding your workplace problem. If your employer claims you were fired because of incompetence, for example, make sure you can show otherwise by producing favorable written performance reviews or evidence that your employer circumvented the company's disciplinary procedures before firing you.

Before you discuss your case with a lawyer, look closely at your documentation and try to separate the aspects of your problem that you can prove from those you merely suspect. If you cannot produce any independent verification of your workplace problem, you will be in the untenable position of convincing a judge or jury to believe your word alone.

Taking action will require time and effort. You can save yourself some time and possibly some grief by using this book to objectively analyze your job loss or problem. If possible, do it before you begin talking with a lawyer about handling your case. Once again, the keys to most successful wrongful discharge lawsuits are good documentation and organized preparation—both of which must come from you.

Be mindful of the expense. Because many challenges to workplace problems are legal longshots, lawyers who specialize in this type of case often refuse to handle them. In fact, these days, many originally well-meaning employment lawyers have switched to where the money is: They represent employers.

So your initial search for legal help is likely to be frustrating. And if you do find a lawyer willing to take your case, you will probably have to pay dearly. If you hire a lawyer with expertise in wrongful discharge lawsuits and your case is less than a sure win, you can expect to deposit several thousands of dollars to pay for the lawyer's time if your lawsuit fails, plus thousands more to cover other costs.

CHAPTER

2

YOUR LEGAL EMPLOYMENT STATUS

As a worker, you may be labeled a variety of things—an independent contractor, a temporary, parttime, fulltime or permanent employee. The semantics can be befuddling. But the meaning behind the words is important. Most workplace laws protect only those workers who are legally defined as employees. You must first determine which legal category fits your work situation and responsibilities before you will know whether laws covering employees apply to you.

Beware, too, that within many workplace laws there are specific exceptions. For example, some laws exempt government employees from their protections, while some laws only cover public employees. Some laws exempt domestic workers. There is even a workplace law that specifically does not apply to those who work harvesting almonds. Some of these exceptions and exemptions seem spurious, some hard-hearted. But these intricacies point up the need to make sure that you are protected by a specific law before you assert some legal right or decide to take legal action against an employer.

A. Types of Employees

The Internal Revenue Service—because it routinely requires that money be withheld from the paychecks of employees—is the agency responsible for determining who is and who is not an employee, legally. If you have had dealings with the monolithic IRS, or even if you have used its allegedly simple forms for filing taxes, this news may not inspire much confidence in you.

Luckily, the IRS has demonstrated uncharacteristic restraint over the years by classifying workers into only a few categories: common law employees, independent contractors and statutory employees.

1. Common Law Employees

Most working people are common law employees. The IRS will most heavily weigh one fact in deciding whether to classify a worker as a common law employee: whether an employer retains the right to control both the type and method of work being done. (See Section B for a complete list of considerations the IRS uses in classifying workers.) The title that you have printed on a business card or a supervisor assigns to your work situation simply does not matter for legal purposes.

One strong indication that you are legally an employee is if the company you work for gives you a W-2 Form at the end of each calendar year. If your employer does not consider you to be a common law employee, it will either give you an IRS Form 1099-Miscellaneous to report your work income, or it will not report your income to the IRS at all.

Employers have specific legal obligations to their employees. For example, employers must:

- withhold state and federal income taxes and Social Security from paychecks
- pay unemployment insurance taxes, and
- pay for workers' compensation insurance.

In addition, many workplace laws—including those controlling wages and hours—protect employees, not other categories of workers. For example, most employees must be paid overtime at a rate of one-and-a-half times the regular rate for all hours worked beyond 40 in a week.

2. Independent Contractors

As in the employee category, the employer's control over the work is a key fact in determining whether a worker has the legal status of independent contractor. (See Section B.) The person or company paying for the work controls the outcome of the independent contractor's work. The independent contractor, however, retains control over how the work gets done.

Example: *Moira, a freelance writer, agrees to write a technical guide for new software being produced by the Dikus Company. The completed draft must be 40 double-spaced, typewritten pages and is due on February 1. Moira can use a word processor to complete the draft. If she's hearty—or possibly foolhardy—she can write the entire thing the evening of January 31. Because Moira controls the process and means by which she prepares the technical guide, she is legally considered an independent contractor.*

Another major earmark of independent contractors is that they offer services to the public at large, not just to one employer.

Example: *Jeffrey does machine repairs and gets most of his income from one company that operates several factories containing hundreds of machines. When a machine breaks down, a factory manager calls Jeffrey, who makes onsite repair calls. Sometimes, Jeffrey takes the machines to his shop and repairs them there. Other times, he fixes the machines at the factory. Jeffrey also advertises his services in the local telephone directory, from which he gets a few repair calls from other companies.*
Because he determines how to do the repairs and also offers his work to more than one company, Jeffrey is legally considered an independent contractor with every company for which he works—even the one that provides most of his income.

Most workplace rights guaranteed by law to employees are not guaranteed to people who work as independent contractors. In general, the relationship between independent contractors and the company or person paying for their work is covered not by the law of the workplace, but by state business codes and contract laws. From a legal standpoint, an independent contractor is just a one-person business and must live by the laws that govern all businesses, large or small. For example, an independent contractor who agrees to perform a task for a specific amount of money must fulfill that contract and cannot demand to be paid overtime rates for spending more than 40 hours in one week to complete that task.

Still, being an independent contractor holds great appeal for some workers. It offers flexibility in workhours and the chance to pick and choose assignments. And independent contractors are allowed to deduct, for tax purposes, 100% of their expenses that are related to self-employment—such as supplies and travel; most employees may deduct only business expenses exceeding 2% of their gross incomes.

In addition, many workers just like the sound of being an independent contractor. The term seems to imply that you are your own boss—and not under anyone else's thumb.

3. Statutory Employees

This category includes groups of workers—such as delivery people and some home workers—who might not seem to qualify as employees, but who have been designated by specific laws as being subject to tax withholding requirements imposed upon employees. Other specific legal obligations of employers are generally also spelled out in the statute that makes these workers employees (Internal Rev. Code §3121). An employer's control is irrelevant here. What matters most is the specific type of work being done.

Most of the laws defining statutory employees were passed in response to special interest political lobbying. For example, labor unions usually view independent contractors and people who work at home as threats to the work standards of unionized factories, so they exerted political pressure to keep as many home workers as possible under the wage and hour laws that govern employees.

Because of such piecemeal lobbying, there is no central logic to the statutory employee category. If the law labels you as one, you are one. There is little to be gained by trying to figure out why.

The most common types of workers who are statutory employees are discussed here.

- *Delivery drivers.* Drivers who deliver meat, vegetables, fruits, bakery products, or beverages other than milk, or who pick up and deliver laundry or dry cleaning, but who are legally agents of a company—authorized by the company to act on its behalf. These workers are most often paid on commission.

Example: *A bread truck driver who sells on commission to a customer route on behalf of only one bakery would typically be an agent of that bakery—and therefore, a statutory employee of the bakery. But a restaurant supply distributor who buys bread at wholesale prices and resells it at a profit would typically be considered neither an agent nor a statutory employee of the bakery that produced the bread.*

- *Life insurance agents.* Insurance sales agents whose main job is selling life insurance or annuity contracts, or both, primarily for one life insurance company.
- *Home workers.* People who work at home according to a company's explicit instructions on materials or goods that are supplied by the company and which must be returned to that company or to someone designated by that company.
- *Traveling salespeople.* People whose main job is to sell on behalf of a company and take orders from wholesalers, retailers, contractors, hotels, restaurants or other business establishments. The goods sold must be merchandise for resale or supplies for use in the buyer's business operation, as opposed to goods purchased for personal consumption at home.

    This category applies only to those whose main job is selling business-to-business. Because the IRS sets no firm statistical standards for this type of work, the definition of "main job" is not interpreted consistently. In general, this category is directed at traveling salespeople who might otherwise be considered independent contractors because their employers exercise so little control over their daily work activities.

Example: *Mary is an on-the-road salesperson for a roofing manufacturer that supplies building contractors. Because she works primarily out of her car and an office in her home, and visits the company's headquarters only twice a month, the company has very little control over how and when she does her work. Nevertheless, the IRS considers her to be a statutory employee.*

Statutory Nonemployees: A Rare Breed

The IRS has designated one additional category of rare worker: the statutory nonemployee. As is true for statutory employee, the category of statutory nonemployee lacks a central logic. It also has been specifically created through efforts by special interest lobby groups, and the rights and responsibilities that attach to the status are also made clear in the laws defining them (Internal Rev. Code §3121).

Statutory nonemployees live in a strange legal limbo as neither employees nor independent contractors. They are excluded from the protections of most workplace laws—and are treated as self-employed for federal income and employment tax purposes.

There are only three categories of statutory nonemployees recognized by the IRS:

* licensed real estate agents
* companion sitters—as long as they do not work for a placement service that pays or receives their salaries, and
* direct sellers—people who sell goods to a consumer who intends to use them personally—for example, a person who sells household vacuum cleaners through in-home demonstration; in addition, direct sellers must do their selling someplace other than in an established retail store or salesroom.

People working in these occupations are considered statutory nonemployees if:

* most payments for their services are directly related to sales, rather than to the number of hours worked, and
* their services are performed under a written contract providing that they will not be treated as employees for federal tax purposes.

B. Guidance in Determining Your Legal Status

In the past, the IRS used a rather grueling 20-factor test in evaluating whether a worker was an employee or an independent contractor. In response to complaints about the complexity of the system, the agency issued somewhat simplified guidelines several years ago. Workers are still railing against some of the new guidelines—pointing up that they do not reflect the reality of today's workplaces. So the IRS may change its rules yet again.

If your work situation now presents a close call as to whether you are an employee or independent contractor, take a closer look at the following facts—the most important of the ones that the IRS currently considers in determining your official status. Note that no one factor is determinative; the IRS will look at the whole relationship and weigh and balance the factors on either side.

⚠ One Size Does Not Fit All Here, Either

There is another possible twist in this worker status mélange. The rules for determining whether you will be classified as an employee or an independent contractor are different from the IRS rules discussed here if you are seeking a benefit administered by the states. For example, if you are most interested in whether you qualify for benefits such as workers' compensation (see Chapter 13) or unemployment insurance (see Chapter 12), you might want to double check the rules for classification with the local offices that administer those programs.

For a detailed discussion on the various tests applied to determine worker status, see *Hiring Independent Contractors* by Stephen Fishman (Nolo).

Instructions. An employee must comply with instructions about when, where and how to work. The requirement that a worker must obtain approval before taking certain actions is good evidence that he or she is an employee. But even if no instructions are given, it may be enough demonstration of employer control if the employer has the right to give instructions. Independent contractors must only deliver a finished product; how they produce it is up to them.

Training. An employee is trained to perform services in a particular manner. Independent contractors use their own methods and receive no training from those who pay for their services. A short orientation session—for example, about a new product line—might be given to all workers. It is not the sort of training that indicates employee status.

Investment. An employee invests in a job primarily by putting in time and labor. An independent contractor, however, typically makes significant money investments—for example, purchasing a truck or specialized computer system—to carry on business. The IRS recognizes, however, that some common types of independent contractor businesses—writing or consulting are good examples—simply do not require significant investments to operate.

Business expenses. Businesses usually incur a number of expenses: rent and utilities, tools and equipment, training, advertising, wages or salaries for assistants, licensing fees, insurance costs, postage, repairs and maintenance, supplies, equipment rental and travel expenses. Generally, the more of these expenses that the worker takes on, the more likely the IRS will dub the worker an independent contractor.

According to the IRS, an employee's business and travel expenses are paid by the employer. Unless their agreements specify otherwise, independent contractors are usually responsible for paying for their own expenses. Independent contractors have protested that this factor should not receive much weight. In reality, many independent contractors are reimbursed for expenses—travel, phone calls, even special supplies—without a fair inference that they are employees.

Method of payment. Employees are typically paid salaries or hourly wages. Independent contractors usually agree to perform a task for flat fees—although they are sometimes paid in installments. Note that workers have complained that this new IRS guideline is unrealistic, too. Many workers who are clearly independent contractors—computer graphics designers, training consultants, word processors—charge and get paid an hourly rate. For many, it is simply the most accurate method for both the worker and hiring agency to value the services.

Realization of profit and loss. Apart from their own job security, employees have little say or investment in whether a business rises or falls; their compensation is set and usually remains fairly constant. But independent contractors can realize a profit over and above or incur a loss well below what an employee might experience. The IRS finds this to be strong evidence that the worker, not the employer, controls the business—and so that worker is more apt to be labeled an independent contractor.

Working relationship. This last bit of guidance is the most nebulous—and most likely to change over time. The IRS now looks to factors that courts have found to be important in determining worker status. Most of them relate to how the worker and the business perceive their relation to one another.

In brief, these factors are summarized here.

- *Benefits.* Employees typically get benefits—including paid vacation and sick leave, health insurance, life or disability insurance and retirement plans. Independent contractors must typically pay for their own benefits or do without.

- *Written contracts.* Courts will look to the words in the documents that the worker and the business have signed—particularly those describing the work relationship.

- *Permanency.* An employee has a continuing relationship with an employer. However, a continuing relationship may exist where work is performed frequently, although at irregular intervals. An employee who is called in to work for only a few days each month is still an employee. Independent contractors may work for several different employers—often completing only a brief stint with each.

- *Discharge or termination.* An employee can be fired by an employer. An independent contractor cannot be fired as long as he or she produces a result that meets the specifications of the contract.

  An employee can quit his or her job at any time without incurring liability. An independent contractor usually agrees to complete a specific job and is responsible for completing it satisfactorily—or is legally obliged to make good for failure to complete it.

  But courts often have a hard task in sorting through reality here. It is often difficult to tell whether a worker was an employee who was fired for failing to perform work or an independent contractor who was fired for failing to produce what he or she contracted to produce.

- *Regular business activity.* An employee's services are integrated into the business operations because the services are important to the success or continuation of the business. Independent contractors are typically consulted only for short-term or occasional projects.

Where to Go for More Help

The IRS publishes a free pamphlet, "Employer's Supplemental Tax Guide," IRS Publication 15-A. While its aim is to spell out tax responsibilities for employers, it provides valuable information for employees who want to doublecheck their employer's tax treatment of them. To obtain a copy, call the IRS at: 800-829-3676. You can also read or download the publication directly from the IRS website at http://www.irs.gov.

C. Misclassified Workers

It is not disrespect for workers as much as it is love of money that compels many employers to classify employees as independent contractors.

When a worker is classified as an independent contractor, an employer need not pay:

- the customary half share of Social Security and Medicare tax, commonly called FICA
- federal and state unemployment taxes
- workers' compensation
- medical insurance
- vacation and holiday pay
- pension contributions, and
- other fringe benefits such as health club memberships.

Primarily, this means a loss in revenue for the Internal Revenue Service. The IRS is aware of the cheaters. It estimates that, each year, employers misclassify several million employees as independent contractors.

This does not sit well with the IRS, the government agency best known for its doggedness. In the last few years, it has stepped up efforts to ferret out misclassified workers through intensified audits of tax returns. According to a recent government investigation, small employers—those with less than $3 million in assets—are the most likely to offend.

Disingenuous employers may be forced to pay back unemployment, Social Security, Medicare and income taxes, interest, legal fees and penalties if they misclassify workers.

And there are consequences for the workers as well. They may be found liable for past due self-employment taxes—which can amount to a hefty 15.3% of their earnings. In addition, the time they lodged as ostensible independent contractors will not count toward eligibility for Social Security benefits—which may make for bleaker retirement years than planned.

If you suspect you have been misclassified as an independent contractor, you may get help from the IRS, which will issue a formal determination and will reclassify you if appropriate. To do so, complete Form SS-8, available from the nearest IRS office or from the IRS website at http://www.irs.gov. Then file the completed form with the appropriate District Director. You can get the address for filing by calling the IRS at: 800-829-1040 and providing the employer's nine-digit federal identification number. (See Section E.)

D. Common Worker Labels and the IRS

The following definitions cover what might be called conversational categories of work. These are tags that people and companies often give to various work relationships, but that are not really legal categories of work according to IRS rules. No matter what you, your employer or your associates call your job, it falls under one of the official categories of employment set out by the IRS. (See Section A.)

The following explanations offer some guidance on which legal category generally best fits a hard-to-place work situation.

1. Consultants and Subcontractors

In some areas of the United States, and within some industries, the terms consultant and subcontractor are frequently used to describe work relationships. However, the IRS does not recognize either one as a legal category of work. The business arrangements under which consultants and subcontractors work typically make them independent contractors.

2. Personal Service Contractees

Because some feel it has a flattering ring to it, people who work as independent contractors will say that they have a personal service contract with a company. But a personal service contract is more correctly defined as a written agreement between a company and an employee that spells out the terms of the employee's work and compensation over and above what is required by law.

For example, engineers with rare technical skills sometimes agree to leave one company for another only after their new employer promises, in a personal service contract, to employ them for several years—or to pay them the equivalent of the salary they would have received for those years if they are fired before their contract expires.

Many workplace specialists now recommend that you negotiate a personal service contract before taking a new job. It is a nice thought, but the truth is that very few working people have sufficient power on their side of the employment transaction to negotiate a personal service contract. And for many positions, such contracts are simply impractical or unnecessary.

Consequently, personal service contracts are rare except at the highest levels of corporate management, in professional sports and other forms of commercial entertainment and where an employee has unique skills or is required to move to a distant country—in essence, to give up a lifestyle completely for a time—to perform a job for a limited number of years before returning home.

If you are an employee but also have an individual contract that specifies such things as how much you will be paid, what hours you will be expected to work, what bonuses you will receive and how many years you will be employed, you are among the lucky. Such a contract does not, however, negate the fact that you are an employee. It merely gives you some extra rights—enforceable under contract law.

If you are working under an individual contract but are not legally an employee or statutory employee (as described in Section A), then you are either an independent contractor or statutory nonemployee, depending on the nature of the work.

3. Parttime Workers

There is no single, overriding definition of a parttime worker in workplace law. Some state workplace laws—and a number of individual employers—specify their own definitions of fulltime and parttime workers. Those identified as parttimers are on the rise, with many workers holding down a number of parttime positions simultaneously. But for the most part, it is merely contemporary American culture that defines fulltime work as 40 hours of work spread over a five-day period within a given week.

Therefore, describing a job as parttime does not change a worker's legal status. A worker who puts in fewer than 40 hours weekly who fits the description of an independent contractor is an independent contractor. And a person who works substantially fewer than 40 hours per week and whose work situation fits the description of an employee is an employee.

While some workplace benefits—such as vacation time and retirement fund contributions—may be reduced proportionately to the amount of time worked, parttime workers generally have the full arsenal of employee rights at their disposal.

4. Temporaries

On a typical day, more than 2.9 million jobs in America are filled by workers from services that specialize in temporary staffing. About 40% the temp workers are office support staff, about 25% are technical workers such as software designers and a growing proportion of them are doctors and lawyers and corporate executive officers.

Most people working through temporary services are legally employees of the services, not the companies to which they are assigned. The temporary services pay workers' wages, withhold taxes from their paychecks and contribute to programs such as Social Security, unemployment insurance and workers' compensation, just as any other employer would.

Many of the temporary services now also offer benefit programs such as health insurance, retirement plans and paid vacation and sick days to those they employ. But most temp workers do not have the luxury of these types of job benefits: About 92% have no health insurance, and 98% are not covered by a pension or tax-deferred retirement plan. And on the whole, temp workers earn between 15% to 20% less than permanent employees who do similar work at the same company.

And now, some additional potential pitfalls to the temping arrangement are emerging for both workers and those who hire them.

The cost can be prohibitive for many employers. Although an employer is generally saved from paying for insurance and other common benefits, some temp agencies exact hefty hiring premiums or hourly rates—charges that are usually not passed along to the worker while he or she is onboard. The theory is that this pricing structure will help ensure that a temporary worker stays temporary. But the reality is often that employers who balk at the high rates are precluded from trying temp arrangements, or they rush a project before a trial work relationship can truly be tested.

And for workers, an even greater peril may occur when the work lags on for several months or even years while they remain on the payroll as temporary employees. Nowhere is this abuse more common than in the burgeoning high tech industries. And arguably, nowhere is there more to lose—the most obvious loss being a stake in the ubiquitous and sometimes lucrative stock options.

Many workers have stopped taking it silently, banding together with other temporary co-workers to sue for the rights—and options—bestowed upon their co-workers who are deemed to have permanent status. So far, the majority of courts that have taken on the issue have ruled in the workers' favors, awarding them backpay and benefits, although there is still no judicial guidance about how long an employee can be on staff before he or she will be converted to permanent status. Decisionmakers have also been swayed by facts in addition to length of service. For example, the more similarly temps are treated to those in the permanent workforce—given similar workspaces and assignments and required to work similar hours—the more likely they will be classified as permanent.

When Temping Becomes a Permanent Fixation

There's a subculture around temping that helps explain why so many workers take the jobs—usually for lower pay, fewer benefits and less assurance of stability than their permanent counterparts in the working world.

According to the American Staffing Association (ASA), about one-third of those working as temps do so because of the flexibility of the arrangement. Temps are generally free to turn down assignments when they simply don't want to work. Some have used temping as a way to see the world, accepting short-term positions in towns and cities wherever they are needed.

And some extol the virtues of simplicity: Most temps are informally exempt from attending office meetings, jockeying for position and playing office politics.

Finally, a growing number of temporary workers use the experience as a way to get one foot in the door—a relatively risk-free way to check out an employer while being checked out as a potential employee. The hope is not far-fetched. According to ASA, 24% of companies that used temporary workers did so to test out individuals for permanent positions.

5. Leased Employees

Employee leasing allows companies to cut costs and simplify workforce management by paying another specialized company to hire and fire workers, for example, and to manage benefit programs. As the American workplace has grown more legally complex, employee leasing has become increasingly popular.

Like temporary workers, most leased workers are legally employees of the service firm supplying workers to the client company in which they work. The basic difference between leased workers and temporaries is that the leased employees are expected to be assigned to one job for a substantial amount of time—usually a year or more.

6. Job Shares

In some workplaces, two or more people share a job that requires 40 or more hours of work per week. For example, two workers might agree to work 20 hours each weekly, taking a prorated share of fringe benefits. The flexibility of the arrangement is good for the workers—allowing them time off work to pursue other interests or attend other obligations, while assuring them the security of enduring employment. The arrangement is also good for employers who want to promote employee satisfaction and save time and money in training a new employee to take over job duties.

But job sharing is not a legal category of work. Workers involved in job sharing are legally employees when all other aspects of their work situation fit the definition of an employee, and legally independent contractors when all other aspects of their work situation fit the definition of an independent contractor.

E. The Definition of Employer

There are far fewer legal permutations in the legal definition of employer than there are of employee. In most cases, there is little room for confusion over who hires, fires or signs the paychecks.

1. Who Is Responsible

Confusion over who is the legally responsible individual sometimes arises during workplace disputes. As a general rule, the term employer, as used in most workplace laws, includes all individuals that a company holds out to have authority to act and to make decisions—the owner of the business, the chief executive officer or the president. It may also include supervisors, managers and sometimes even other employees.

2. Employer Identification Numbers

The IRS and other government agencies need a way to track employees and employers by numbers, rather than by names. There are many thousands of Smiths in America, for example, but when keyed in by their individual nine-digit Social Security numbers, computers can easily distinguish them.

You, too, can refer to a government-assigned number if you want to be sure of your employer's identity. This may seem unnecessary. But many working people today who appear to be employed by one company are, in fact, employed by another. Look at the name badges of some service station attendants, for example. Although they are wearing uniforms done up in the colors of the oil company, their badges point out in small print that they are really working for an employee-leasing subsidiary of the oil company.

Some small, unincorporated employers use their personal Social Security numbers to identify their companies to the IRS. Larger employers, and all those that are incorporated, are assigned an Employer Identification Number (EIN) by the IRS. Each corporation is allowed to have only one EIN, so one number often is used by several divisions of a corporation that conducts business under different names.

Employment-related IRS forms such as the W-2 and the 1099-Miscellaneous include spaces in which the person or company paying you must note an identification number. That number is then used to track the records of the company and its employees within the IRS system.

Consequently, your employer's identification number is an important component of your employment status and history. Your true employer is the one assigned to the employer identification number that appears on your records.

There are a number of reasons why a less-than-honest employer might use an identification number other than its own. One typical example would be at a hazardous waste clean-up site, where workers think they are working for a well-heeled company but are technically being paid by a financially unsound subcontractor that is likely to go out of business about the time that it gets sued because of worker injuries.

Because of privacy laws, there is no official way to verify the validity of the employer identification number that your employer is using. Nevertheless, the IRS encourages people who suspect that an employer is using false or incorrect employer identification numbers—a tip from a disgruntled payroll office worker would be a typical reason—to report it to the criminal investigation department of their local IRS district office.

WAGES AND HOURS

The French writer Voltaire once pointed out that work spares us from three great evils: boredom, vice and need. Most of us can tolerate a little boredom, and some may even enjoy a small helping of vice. But need is something we would all rather avoid. Although most people like their jobs to be fun and fulfilling, what they likely want most is to be paid—fairly and on time—so that they can enjoy the other aspects of their lives.

A. The Fair Labor Standards Act

The most important and most far-reaching law guaranteeing a worker's right to be paid fairly is the federal Fair Labor Standards Act or FLSA (29 U.S.C. §§201 and following). The FLSA:
- defines the 40-hour workweek
- covers the federal minimum wage
- sets requirements for overtime, and
- places restrictions on child labor.

Basically, the FLSA establishes minimums for fair pay and hours—and it is the single law most often violated by employers. An employer must also comply with other local, state or federal workplace laws that set higher standards. So in addition to determining whether you are being paid properly under the FLSA, you may need to check whether the other laws discussed in this chapter also apply to your situation.

The FLSA was passed in 1938 after the Depression, when many employers took advantage of the tight labor market to subject workers to horrible conditions and impossible hours. One of the most complex laws of the workplace, the FLSA has been amended many times. It is full of exceptions and exemptions—some of which seem to contradict one another. Most of the revisions and interpretations have expanded the law's coverage, for example:
- requiring that male and female workers receive equal pay for work that requires equal skill, effort and responsibility
- including in its protections state and local hospitals and educational institutions
- covering most federal employees and employees of states, political subdivisions and interstate agencies, and
- setting out strict standards for determining, paying and accruing compensatory or comp time—time given off work instead of cash payments.

1. Who Is Covered

The FLSA applies only to employers whose annual sales total $500,000 or more, or who are engaged in interstate commerce.

You might think that this would restrict the FLSA to covering only employees in large companies, but in reality the law covers nearly all workplaces. This is because the courts have interpreted the term interstate commerce very broadly. For example, courts have ruled that companies that regularly use the U.S. mail to send or receive letters to and from other states are engaged in interstate commerce. Even the fact that employees use company telephones to place or accept interstate business calls has placed an employer under the FLSA.

2. Who Is Exempt

A few employers, including small farms—those that use relatively little outside paid labor—are explicitly exempt from the FLSA.

In addition, some employees are exempt from FLSA requirements, such as pay for overtime and minimum wages, even though their employers are covered.

a. Executive, administrative and professional workers

This is the most confusing and most often mistakenly applied broad category of exempt worker.

Above all, bear in mind that you are not automatically exempt from the FLSA solely because you receive a salary; the work you do must be of a certain type as well. However, watch for how and when your employer docks your pay. If you are called a salaried employee, for example, but you get a cut in pay if you miss work or you get a bonus for working more hours, the pay you receive may not legally be a salary—and you may be entitled to overtime and compensatory time for some of your working hours.

The requirements for executive workers are most rigorous. To qualify as an exempt executive, you must:

- be paid with a salary, so that compensation is not subject to reductions for quality and quantity of work
- use discretion in performing job duties
- regularly direct the work of two or more people
- have the authority to hire and fire other employees, or to order such hiring and firing
- be primarily responsible for managing others, and
- devote no more than 20% of worktime to other tasks that are not managerial. For certain retail and service companies, 40% of nonmanagerial time is allowed.

The definitions of administrative and professional employees are similar, but contain minor differences. For example, employees categorized as professionals must perform work that is primarily intellectual.

The definitions also change with the employee's salary level. For example, if the weekly salary of the executive, administrative or professional employee exceeds a certain minimum, fewer factors are required to qualify for the exemption.

They Can Barely Afford the Bleach for Their White Collars

The salary levels required for alleged managerial workers to be exempt from the FLSA—as low as $155 per week—are so out of sync with today's marketplace that they hardly qualify as requirements at all.

Even the higher-end salary tests, stuck at the same low rate of $250 since 1975, mean that a worker who earns only $13,000 in yearly salary could be exempt because of it. According to the U.S. General Accounting Office, by today's standards, that salary would be inflated to $40,000.

The impractical result of this outmoded law is that an astonishing number of workers—nearly one-third of the fulltime workforce—is exempt under the executive, administrative and professional categories often loosely dubbed white collar workers. Clearly, the law no longer comes close to accomplishing its original goal of protecting employees from being overworked and underpaid.

While reforms to the FLSA exemptions have long been urged by both employer and employee groups, none has yet made inroads on convincing Congress to correct its math.

Exemption Guidelines

The chart on the next page summarizes exemption guidelines for executive, administrative and professional employees. Be aware, however, that not all of the legal nuances appear in the chart. Unless you fit squarely into the simplified guidelines, your best bet is to dig further. Your state labor department can be helpful. (See the Appendix for contact details.)

Note that there's a long test and a short test for each category. If you meet all of the requirements of the short test, you are exempt and need not meet the long test.

The long test requirement that executives and administrators spend at least 80% of the workday in certain activities is reduced to 60% for employees who work in retail and service establishments. Further, the percentage test does not apply at all to an executive who is in charge of an independent business establishment or branch or who owns at least a 20% interest in the business.

Exemption Guidelines

Executive Exemption	Administrative Exemption	Professional Exemption
Short Test		
Primarily manages a business or department	Meets the first test described below under Long Test	Duties as described below under Long Test
Routinely supervises two or more employees	Work includes discretion and independent judgment	Duties need only include work requiring discretion and independent judgment
Earns salary of at least $250 per week	Earns salary of at least $250 per week	Earns salary of at least $250 per week
Long Test		
Primarily manages a business	Mainly performs office or non-manual work directly related to management policies	Primary duties include work acquired by a prolonged course of specialized intellectual study requiring advanced knowledge
	-or-	*-or-*
		Original and creative work stemming primarily from invention, imagination or talent
Routinely supervises two or more employees	Routinely exercises discretion and independent judgment	Work requires consistent exercise of discretion and judgment
Can hire, fire or promote workers	Routinely assists a proprietor or executive	Work is intellectual and varied, not routine
Routinely exercises discretion	Performs technical work under general supervision	
	-or-	
	Executes special assignments under general supervision	
Spends at least 80% of workday in above activities	Spends at least 80% of workday in above activities	Spends at least 80% of workday in above activities
Earns salary of at least $155 per week	Earns salary of at least $155 per week	Earns salary of at least $170 per week; does not apply to doctors and lawyers

Adapted from The Employer's Legal Handbook *by Fred Steingold (Nolo).*

The fine points of these exemptions are explained in a free booklet titled "Regulations Part 541: Defining the Terms—Executive, Administrative, Professional and Outside Sales." It is available from the nearest office of the Wage and Hour Division of the U.S. Department of Labor. Division offices are listed on the Department of Labor's website, http://www.dol,gov. You can also get them by telephoning the DOL at 202-693-4650.

b. Outside salespeople

An outside salesperson is exempt from FLSA coverage if he or she:
* regularly works away from the employer's place of business while making sales or taking orders, and
* spends no more than 20% of worktime doing work other than selling.

Typically, an exempt salesperson will be paid primarily through commissions and will require little or no direct supervision in doing the job.

c. Computer specialists

This exemption applies to computer system analysts and programmers who receive a salary of at least $170 a week or who, if paid by the hour, receive at least $27.63 an hour.

You will likely be exempt from the wage and hour laws as a computer specialist if your primary duties consist of such things as determining functional specifications for hardware and software, designing computer systems to meet user specs and creating or modifying computer programs.

d. Miscellaneous workers

Several other types of workers are exempt from the minimum wage and overtime pay provisions of the FLSA. The most common include:

- employees of seasonal amusement or recreational businesses
- employees of local newspapers having a circulation of less than 4,000
- newspaper delivery workers
- switchboard operators employed by phone companies that have no more than 750 stations
- workers on small farms, and
- personal companions and casual babysitters. Officially, domestic workers— housekeepers, childcare workers, chauffeurs, gardeners—are covered by the FLSA if they are paid at least $1,000 in wages from a single employer in a year, or if they work eight hours or more in a week for one or several employers. For example, if you are a teenager who babysits only an evening or two each month for the neighbors, you probably cannot claim coverage under the FLSA; a fulltime au pair would be covered.

e. Apprentices

An apprentice is a worker who's at least 16 years old and who has signed an agreement to learn a skilled trade. Apprentices are exempt from the requirements of the FLSA. But beware that your state may have a law limiting the number of hours you can work as an apprentice. State law may also require that as an apprentice, you must be paid a certain percentage of the minimum wage. Check with your state labor department for more information. (See the Appendix for contact details.)

Hold the Pickle, Hold the Law

Current U.S. Labor Department guidelines permit employers to pay executives weekly salaries less than the minimum wage for a 40-hour workweek. And because these poorly paid execs are exempt from the FLSA, they are also free to work an unlimited number of overtime hours. No extra charge.

This egregious practice came to light well over a decade ago when several Burger King assistant managers sued the fast food chain. The employees took issue with the corporate policy of requiring FLSA-exempt assistant managers to spend much of their 54-hour workweeks doing the same work as the people they supervised. The appeals court ruled, however, that if assistant managers were allowed to shun burger production duties, more hourly employees would be needed, breaking the restaurant's hourly labor budget (*Donovan v. Burger King Corp.*, 675 F. 2d 516 (2d Cir. 1982)).

The abuses continue. According to the most recent survey by the National Restaurant Association, one-quarter of fast food assistant managers earn less than $15,000 annually. But they have impressive titles.

Keep your eyes on the courts for hopeful signs, however. In a number of recent decisions, courts throughout the land have shown the aptitude to cut through the semantics of job titles and award workers the benefits due them.

- A Connecticut court recently ruled that homemaking maven Martha Stewart owed a former employee thousands of dollars in overtime pay. Renaldo Abreu alleged he washed cars, groomed dogs and performed many other work tasks on the television set of the "Martha Stewart Living" show. Stewart, however, labeled Abreu as an agricultural worker who was not entitled to any overtime pay. The court held this was not a Good Thing and that Stewart owed him more than $30,000 for the overtime hours he put in on the job.

- The U.S. Supreme Court held recently that poultry processor Tyson Foods was wrong when it lumped together its truckers, chicken catchers and forklift operators as agricultural workers—this in an attempt to prevent the workers from joining the Teamsters Union. The Court concentrated on the true nature of the work being performed.

- A Washington appeals court held that the United Parcel Service was not an airline as it claimed, while also claiming its employees were airline employees exempt from overtime pay entitlements. The court held simply that UPS began business as a trucking company and remained a trucking company; its air freight business did not convert it to an airline.

B. Rights Under the FLSA

The FLSA guarantees a number of rights, primarily aimed at ensuring that workers get paid fairly for the time they work. (See Sections G and H for an explanation of how to take action for FLSA violations.)

Independent Contractors Are Exempt

The FLSA covers only employees, not independent contractors (discussed in Chapter 2, Section A). However, whether a person is an employee for purposes of the FLSA generally turns on whether that worker is employed by a single employer, not on the Internal Revenue Service definition of an independent contractor.

The FLSA was passed to clamp down on employers who cheated workers of their fair wages. As a result, employee status is broadly interpreted so that as many workers as possible come within the protection of the law.

If nearly all of your income comes from one company, a court would probably rule that you are an employee of that company for purposes of the FLSA, regardless of whether other details of your worklife would appear to make you an independent contractor.

In early cases determining close questions of employment status, most courts found workers to be employees rather than independent contractors, and the scales remain tipped that way. Key realities cited by the courts: the relationship appeared to be permanent, the workers lacked bargaining power with regard to the terms of their employment (*Martin v. Albrecht*, 802 F.Supp. 1311 (1992)) and the individual workers were economically dependent upon the business to which they gave service (*Martin v. Selker Bros., Inc.*, 949 F.2d 1286 (1991)).

But workers' skill and pay levels can push courts to the opposite conclusion. Some courts are more likely to class workers with higher skills and higher pay as independent contractors rather than employees. In two cases hailing from Texas, for example, two groups of workers—pipe welders and topless dancers—who were classified as independent contractors claimed they were really employees under the labor laws and so should be entitled to overtime pay. The courts, apparently reasoning that welding pipes takes more skill than dancing topless, held that the welders were independent contractors, but the dancers were employees. (*Carrell v. Sunland Constr., Inc.*, 998 F.2d 330 (5th Cir. 1993); *Reich v. Circle C. Investments, Inc.*, 998 F.2d 324 (5th Cir. 1993).)

1. Minimum Wage

Employers must pay all covered employees not less than the minimum wage—currently set at $5.15 an hour.

Some states have established a minimum wage that is higher than the federal one—and you are entitled to the higher rate if your state allows for one. Employers not covered by the FLSA, such as small farm owners, are required to pay all workers the state minimum wage rate. (See the chart, State Minimum Wage Laws, in Section E.)

The FLSA does not require any specific system of paying the minimum wage, so employers may base pay on time at work, piece rates or according to some other measurement. In all cases, however, an employee's pay divided by the hours worked during the pay period must equal or exceed the minimum wage.

Many employers either become confused by the nuances and exceptions in the wage and hour law—or they bend the rules to suit their own pocketbooks. Whatever the cause, you would do well to doublecheck your employer's math. A few simple rules distilled from the law may help.

- *Hourly*. Hourly employees must be paid minimum wage for all hours worked. Your employer cannot take an average—or pay you less than minimum wage for some hours worked and more for others.
- *Fixed rate or salary*. Employees paid at a fixed rate can check their wages by dividing the amount they are paid in a pay period by the number of hours worked. The resulting average must be at least minimum wage.
- *Commissions and piece rates*. Your total pay divided by the number of hours you worked must average at least the minimum hourly wage rate.

a. Form of pay

Under the FLSA, the pay you receive must be in the form of cash or something that can be readily converted into cash or other legal forms of compensation, such as food and lodging. Your employer cannot, for example, pay you with a coupon or token that can only be spent at a store run by the employer. Employee discounts granted by employers do not count toward the minimum wage requirement.

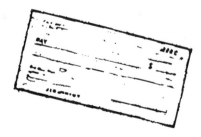

b. Pay for time off

Neither the minimum wage section nor any other part of the FLSA requires employers to pay employees for time off, such as vacation, holidays or sick days. Although most employers provide fulltime workers some paid time off each year, the FLSA covers payment only for time on the job.

However, some state laws mandate that employees get paid time off for jury duty (see Section E2), for voting (see Section E3) and for family and medical leave (see Chapter 5, Section B). And most state laws provide that if employers offer paid days off, employees are entitled to be paid for the portion they have already earned when they quit or are fired.

A Possible Cure for Sick Leave: PTO

The trend afoot in many workplaces is to give employees a certain amount of Paid Time Off, or PTO, without labeling it vacation, sick leave or personal leave; all three types of traditional time off are rolled into one figure.

For example, say your company's traditional system specifies that employees receive ten vacation days, seven sick days and three personal days. The system is revamped, creating a PTO bank for each employee that accrues at a rate of 12 hours a month. That's 18 days a year that employees can use however they want.

Proponents of PTO praise its flexibility, as it allows employees to claim and schedule time off from work when it best suits their needs. They also point out that PTO helps keep everyone more honest, as it obviates a worker's human tendency to fake a bout of the flu when his or her favorite team is playing a day game on the home field.

Many employers also claim that PTO relieves them of the meddlesome duties of tracking and policing workers' time off.

And there is often an unexpected advantage for employees who leave a job with PTO on their slates: Unlike personal or sick leave, employers must pay them for time that has accrued but not been taken.

c. Tips

When employees routinely receive at least $30 per month in tips as part of their jobs, their employers are allowed to pay only $2.13 an hour—and credit the tips received against the minimum wage requirement. However, the employer's offset may not exceed the tips the employee actually receives. (See Section B3b for more on tips as wages.) Also, the employee must be allowed to keep all of the tips he or she receives.

Example: *Alfonse is employed as a waiter and earns more than $10 per hour in tips. The restaurant's owner, Denis, may use those tips as a partial credit to reach the minimum wage requirement of $5.15 an hour. Denis is still required, however, to pay Alfonse at least $2.13 per hour on top of his tips for the first 40 hours worked in each week.*

During the two weeks or so following a negative review by a local newspaper columnist, the restaurant business slows to a crawl, and Alphonse's tips dip to $1 an hour. Denis must make up the full amount of minimum wage Alphonse is owed: $5.15 an hour.

d. Commissions

When people are paid commissions for sales, those commissions may take the place of wages. However, if the commissions do not equal the minimum wage, the FLSA requires that the employer make up the difference.

Example: *Julia, a salesperson in an electronics store, is paid a percentage of the dollar volume of the sales she completes. During one slow week, she averaged only $2 in commissions per hour. Under the FLSA, her employer must pay her an additional $3.15 for each hour she worked through the first 40 hours of that week, and more for any overtime hours.*

Finding Out More About the FLSA

FLSA exemptions for employers change often. Doublecheck any exemption your employer claims by calling the local U.S. Labor Department, Wage and Hour Division office, listed in the federal government section of your telephone directory and also available on the Department of Labor's website at http://www.dol.gov. Keep in mind, however, that the FLSA is so broadly written and so full of amendments and cross-references that it applies to most employers.

Most of the exemptions to FLSA coverage are listed in federal statute 29 U.S.C. §213. The most direct way to become familiar with these exemptions is to read about them in an annotated edition of the code, which is what your local law library is most likely to have. You can also find the letter of the law on the DOL's website, http://www.dol.gov. (See Chapter 18, Section E, for more information about how to do your own legal research.)

---

2. Equal Pay for Equal Work

Men and women who do the same job, or jobs that require equal skill and responsibility, must be compensated with equal wages and benefits under a 1963 amendment to the FLSA called the Equal Pay Act (29 U.S.C. §206). Be aware, however, that some payment schemes that may look discriminatory at first glance do not actually violate the Equal Pay Act. The Act allows disparate payments to men and women if they are based on:

- seniority systems
- merit systems
- systems measuring earnings by quantity or quality of production, such as a piece goods arrangement, or
- any factor other than sex—for example, salary differentials that stem from unequal starting salaries because of differences in experience levels.

Although the Equal Pay Act basically covers the same employers and employees as the rest of the FLSA, there is one important difference. The Equal Pay Act also protects against discriminatory pay arrangements for executive, administrative and professional employees—including administrators and teachers in elementary and secondary schools.

(Because the Equal Pay Act is enforced along with other anti-discrimination laws by the Equal Employment Opportunity Commission, illegal wage discrimination based on gender is discussed in detail in Chapter 8, Section C.)

3. Pay for Overtime

The FLSA does not limit the number of hours an employee may work in a week—except through some of the child labor rules (discussed in Section B5). But it does require that any covered worker who works more than 40 hours in one week must be paid at least one and one-half times his or her regular rate of pay for every hour worked in excess of 40.

The math is simple if you are paid solely an hourly salary.

Example: *Raymond works for a software shipping company at the wage of $8 per hour. When he works 50 hours in one week filling back orders in preparation for a national exhibition, Raymond must be paid $12 per hour for the last ten hours he worked that week.*

Jody, who is vice president of the software shipping company and Raymond's boss, also worked 50 hours the same week. Since Jody qualifies as an executive and so is exempt from the FLSA (see Section A2), she is not entitled to overtime pay but receives her regular weekly salary.

There is no legal requirement that workers must receive overtime pay simply because they worked more than eight hours in one day. Nor is there anything that requires a worker to be paid on the spot for overtime. Under the FLSA, an employer is allowed to calculate and pay overtime by the week—which can be any 168-hour period made up of seven consecutive 24-hour periods.

It is custom, not law, that determines that a workweek begins on Monday. However, the FLSA requires consistency. An employer cannot manipulate the start of the workweek to avoid paying overtime.

Also, because of the nature of the work involved, common sense—and the law—both dictate that some jobs are exempt from the overtime pay requirements of the FLSA.

The most common of these jobs include:
- commissioned employees of retail or service establishments
- some auto, truck, trailer, farm implement, boat or aircraft workers
- railroad and air carrier employees, taxi drivers, certain employees of motor carriers, seamen on American vessels, and local delivery employees
- announcers, news editors and chief engineers of small nonmetropolitan broadcasting stations
- domestic service workers who live in their employer's residence
- employees of motion picture theaters, and
- farmworkers.

And finally, some employees may be partially exempt from the Act's overtime pay requirements. The most common of this hybrid type is an employee who works in a hospital or residential care establishment who agrees to work a 14-day work period. However, these employees must be paid overtime premium pay for all hours worked over eight in a day or 80 in the 14-day work period, whichever is the greater number of overtime hours.

Is It a Bonus or a Bludgeon?

Some employers have tried to skirt the overtime pay requirements by labeling part of the pay received as a bonus. In fact, bonuses have a strict legal definition, being reserved only for money paid in addition to wages because of some extra effort you have made on the job, as a reward for loyal service or as a gift.

While the term bonus has a grand ring to it, be skeptical if you receive one too often. And take the time to do some math to discover whether the bonus is an apt description for the sum you receive—or a ploy to circumvent the laws requiring overtime pay.

Example: *Henri agrees to work for a weekly salary of $300. His employer makes no mention of the number of hours Henri must work to earn his pay. But the first week on the job, Henri puts in 40 hours and his paycheck totals the promised $300—$192 of it is labeled as wages and $108 is deemed a bonus. Henri is delighted to have received a bonus so new into the job.*

The second week on the job, Henri puts in 45 hours and receives a paycheck of $304. This time, the paystub shows he has received $192 in wages for the first 40 hours worked, $36 (5 hours at $7.20 per hour) for the hours worked over 40 and another bonus, this time for $72. Henri's employer has computed overtime based on the bonus: $72 divided by 45 hours, for an increase of $1.60—and pays half this rate, or an additional $4 for the five extra hours worked. Henri is again delighted to get a bonus in his paycheck. But he should not be. In truth, his regular rate of pay for the week is $6.67 per hour—$300 divided by 45 hours. Henri's employer owes him $316.85, not $304.

a. Piece rates and commissions

People who work on piece rates and commissions instead of by the clock have a more complicated task in calculating their rates of pay.

For piece rate workers, the regular wage rate may be calculated by averaging hourly piece rate earnings for the week. Calculating overtime is a bit trickier. Employees are entitled to an additional one-half times the regular rate of pay for each hour worked over 40, plus the full piecework earnings.

Example: *Max is an assembler in a photocopier factory who is paid a piece rate of 75 cents for each copier cover he installs. One week, he worked 40 hours and installed 400 covers, so his regular rate of pay for that week was $7.50 per hour (400 x .75, divided by 40).*

One of two alternatives may be used to determine Max's overtime pay:
- *Increase the piece rate by 50% during the overtime hours. For example, Max's employer could raise his piece rate to $1.13 per copier cover (150% of .75) for overtime hours.*
- *Estimate an average hourly wage and then use that estimated average to compute overtime.*

Keep in mind that if the U.S. Labor Department investigates the legality of your pay rate, it may require proof that any estimates used to calculate your pay are in line with the piece rate pay you actually earned over a substantial time— usually several months.

Revamping the Overtime System

Under current laws, the strict but confusing rules on overtime entitle about 75 million workers to overtime pay for hours they work over 40 in a week.

The notion of paying a premium for overtime workhours harkens back to the 1930s, when employers were encouraged to hire more workers rather than pay high rates to a select few.

But these days, a growing number of people claim that overtime pay is an anachronism.

Many employers, oblivious to or unmindful of overtime pay strictures, routinely deny workers the extra pay they have coming. Few of them get caught. The Labor Department currently collects only about $100 million a year in back overtime—a small drop in its oversize bucket.

But those that do get caught by the Department of Labor pay dearly. Employees lose their exempt status, which means they must be paid overtime— and they must be paid any overtime pay due them during the last two years.

Some employers unwittingly become liable for large overtime claims by putting conditions on exempt, salaried employees. Some courts have held, for example, that executive employees who are suspended without pay or docked for taking partial days off have been treated as nonexempt workers and so become entitled to overtime pay and other benefits guaranteed by the FLSA.

Many employees, citing increased difficulties over balancing time between work and personal lives, say they would prefer more flexibility over more take-home pay. Restructuring proposals which also have the support of many small business organizations include the plan to abandon the 40 hour workweek. If, for example, entitlement to overtime was based on a two-week, 80 hour work schedule, an employee would be free to work 75 hours in one week and a mere five the next without being entitled to overtime pay.

The methods for calculating and paying commissions vary tremendously. If you have questions about whether your employer is complying with the wage laws on piece rates and commissions, call or visit the nearest office of the Labor Department's Wage and Hour Division, listed in the government section of the telephone book.

b. Jobs involving tips

If you regularly work for tips, all of the tips you usually receive are not counted as part of your regular rate of pay when calculating overtime pay. Only the wage that your employer has agreed to pay you counts, and in most cases where people work for tips, that is the federal minimum wage. Of course, tip money that you receive beyond the minimum wage amount is still taxable to you as income.

Example: *Lisa works as a waitress for wages plus tips. Because she receives a substantial amount in tips, her employer is allowed to take a set-off against the minimum wage requirement, paying her a wage of just $2.13 per hour. Nevertheless, her regular rate of pay for calculating overtime pay under the FLSA standards is still the minimum wage of $5.15 per hour.*
One week, Lisa worked 41 hours—one hour of overtime. For that overtime hour, she must be paid $5.15, regardless of the tips she received during that hour.

c. Split payscales

If your job involves different types of work for which different payscales have been established, you must calculate your regular rate of pay for each category of work, then apply the appropriate rate to any overtime hours. The payscale that applies to the type of work you did during overtime hours is the one on which you calculate the time-and-a-half rule.

Example: *Matt works for a company that manages a large apartment complex. For landscaping work, he is paid $8 per hour. When he works as a guard with the company's private security force for the complex, Matt gets $6 per hour. For payroll purposes, his workweek begins on Monday.*
During one week in the spring, he worked eight hours a day, Monday through Friday, for a total of 40 hours with the landscaping crew. But the landscaping crew does not work on weekends, and Matt needed some extra money, so he worked eight hours on Saturday with the security patrol. He took Sunday off.
Because the FLSA's overtime pay rules take effect only after an employee works 40 hours in one week, the eight overtime hours Matt worked with the security force were at the security patrol rate of $6 per hour. His overtime pay for that week is $72 ($6 x 8 x 1½).

Exemption for Skills Training

Up to ten hours per week of otherwise payable time is exempt from the overtime rules in wage and hour law for some types of skills training. To qualify, the extra hours must be used to provide employees who have not graduated from high school or otherwise demonstrated that they have attained at least an eighth grade education with general training in reading and other basic skills. To qualify for this exemption, the training cannot be specific to the worker's current job, but must cover skills that could be used in virtually any job (29 U.S.C. §207(q)).

d. Multiple employers

No matter how many jobs you hold, the overtime pay rules apply to each of your employers individually. If in one week you work 30 hours for one employer and 30 additional hours for another, for example, neither one owes you overtime pay.

4. Compensatory Time

Most workers are familiar with compensatory or comp time—the practice of employers offering employees time off from work in place of cash payments for overtime. What comes as a shock to many is that the practice is illegal in most situations. Under the FLSA, only state or government agencies may legally allow their employees time off in place of wages (29 U.S.C. §207(o)).
Even then, comp time may be awarded only:
- according to the terms of a collective bargaining unit agreement (see Chapter 16), or
- if the employer and employee agree to the arrangement before work begins.

When compensatory time is allowed, it must be awarded at the rate of one-and-a-half times the overtime hours worked—and comp time must be taken during the same pay period that the overtime hours were worked.

Example: *John, a state employee, is paid a fixed salary every two weeks. His standard workweek is made up of five shifts, each eight hours long. During the first week of a pay period, John works 44 hours, earning four hours of overtime pay. During the second week of that pay period, he can take six hours off as comp time (4 hours x 1 1/2). In the second week of the pay period, he works only 34 hours, but is paid his full salary as though he had worked 40 hours.*

Many employers and employees routinely violate the rules governing the use of compensatory time in place of cash overtime wages. However, such violations are risky. Employees can find themselves unable to collect money due them if a company goes out of business or they are fired. And employers can end up owing large amounts of overtime pay to employees as the result of a labor department investigation and prosecution of compensatory time violations.

a. State laws

Some states do allow private employers to give employees comp time instead of cash. But there are complex, often conflicting laws controlling how and when it may be given. A common control, for example, is that employees must voluntarily request in writing that comp time be given instead of overtime pay—before the extra hours are worked. Check with your state's labor department for special laws on comp time in your area. (See the Appendix for contact information.)

b. Alternative arrangements

Employees who value their time off over their money may feel frustrated with the letter of the law preventing them from taking comp time. If you are in this boat, you may have a few options for getting an arrangement that feels like comp time but is still within the letter of the law.

You may be allowed to take time off by rearranging your work schedule. This is legal if:

- the time off is given within the same pay period as the overtime work, and
- you are given an hour and a half of time off for each hour of overtime worked.

One way is to subtract the time during a single workweek.

Example: *Josh, an editorial assistant at a publishing company, normally works eight hours a day, Monday through Friday. One week, Josh and some of the editors need to meet a deadline on a book due at the printer. So that week, Josh works 10 hours a day, Monday through Thursday. The publishing company gives Josh Friday off and pays him for a 40-hour week at his regular rate of pay. This is legal because Josh hasn't worked any overtime as defined by the FLSA; only the hours over 40 hours a week count as overtime hours.*

But you are not confined to an hour-for-hour trade. You can also take time-and-a-half pay in one week, then reduce your hours the next week so that your paycheck remains constant.

Example: *Christi works at Wholey Soles, a shop that specializes in handmade shoes, and earns $560 at the close of each two-week pay period. Because he needs to prepare an inventory of shoes to have on hand during a street fair, the shop's owner wants Christi to work longer hours one week. However, the owner doesn't want to increase Christi's paycheck, and Christi does not want to habitually work long hours. Christi works 50 hours the week before the fair, but takes 15 hours off the next week (10 hours of overtime x 1 1/2 per hour = 15 hours). Since Christi is paid every two weeks, Wholey Soles may properly reduce Christi's hours the second week to keep her paycheck at the $560 level.*

5. Restrictions on Child Labor

Minors under 18 years old may not work in any jobs that are considered to be hazardous—including those involving mining, wrecking and demolition, logging and roofing. The Secretary of Labor defines what jobs are deemed hazardous, and so out-of-bounds for young workers. To find out which jobs are currently considered hazardous for the purposes of the FLSA, call the local office of the U.S. Labor Department's Wage and Hour Division, located in the government section of your telephone book The Department of Labor's website, at http://www.dol.gov, has a listing of local offices—and also has information about child labor restrictions.

To encourage youngsters to stay in school rather than becoming beholden to the dollar too soon, there are additional restrictions on when and how long workers between ages 14 and 16 may be employed in nonhazardous jobs.

- They may work no more than three hours on a school day and no more than 18 hours in a school week.
- They may work no more than eight hours on a nonschool day and no more than 40 hours in a nonschool week.

- During the period that starts with the day after Labor Day and ends at midnight May 31, their workday may not begin earlier than 7 a.m. or end later than 7 p.m.
- From June 1 through Labor Day, their workday may not begin earlier than 7 a.m., but it can end as late as 9 p.m.

Some industries have obtained special exemptions from the legal restrictions on child labor. Youths of any age may deliver newspapers, for example, or perform in television, movie or theatrical productions.

The farming industry has been fighting the child labor restrictions as well as the rest of the FLSA ever since the law was first proposed in the 1930s, so less strict rules apply to child farmworkers. For example, children as young as 12 may work on their parents' farms. And workers as young as 10 years old may work for up to eight weeks as hand harvest laborers as long as their employers have obtained a special waiver from the U.S. Labor Department.

Watch for State Law Twists

Many states also have restrictions on child labor. A number of them are more restrictive than the federal law—requiring, for example, more frequent meal or rest breaks for younger workers. Check with your state labor department for specific laws that may apply to your situation. (See the Appendix for contact details.)

C. Calculating Your Pay

To resolve most questions or disputes involving the FLSA, you must first know the regular rate of pay to which you are legally entitled.

Whether you work for hourly wages, salary, commissions or a piece rate, the courts have ruled that your regular rate of pay typically includes your base pay plus any shift premiums, hazardous duty premiums, cost of living allowances, bonuses used to make otherwise undesirable worksites attractive, and the fair value of such things as food and lodging that your employer routinely provides as part of your pay.

Obviously, there is much room here for individual interpretation and arbitrary decisions. But the overriding concept is that everything that you logically consider to be a routine part of your hourly pay for a routine day is a part of your regular rate of pay.

The courts have often ruled that the regular rate of pay does not include contributions that an employer makes to benefit plans, paid vacations and holiday benefits, premiums paid for working on holidays or weekends and discretionary bonuses. And some employee manuals clarify what is included in your regular rate of pay by specifying that some benefit programs are regarded by the company to be extra compensation that is not part of an employee's regular pay.

The regular rate of pay for people who work for hourly wages is their hourly rate including the factors just mentioned.

For salaried workers, the hourly rate is their weekly pay divided by the number of hours in their standard workweek.

If you are paid a salary that covers a period longer than a week, it may be a bit trickier to compute your wage rate. Department of Labor regulations attempt to shed light on this by requiring that all salaries must be reduced to a weekly equivalent to determine the rate of pay.

If you are paid a monthly salary, for example, you can determine your weekly wage rate by multiplying your total monthly salary by 12 (the number of months in a year), then dividing that sum by 52 (the number of weeks in a year).

D. Calculating Workhours

When a work pay period begins and ends is determined by a law called the Portal-to-Portal Pay Act (29 U.S.C. §251). This amendment to the FLSA and several other workplace laws requires that an employee must be paid for any time spent that is controlled by and that benefits the employer.

This aspect of wage and hour law has generated a tremendous number of clashes—and cases in which the courts have attempted to sharpen the definition of payable time.

Worktime for which you must be paid includes all the time you must be on duty or at the workplace. However, the courts have ruled that on-the-job time does not include the time employees spend washing themselves or changing clothes before or after work, nor does it include time spent in a regular commute to the workplace.

Employers are not allowed to circumvent the Portal-to-Portal Pay Act by simply "allowing" you to work on what is depicted as your own time. You must be paid for all the time you work—voluntary or not. This issue has come up frequently in recent years because some career counselors have been advising people that volunteering to work free for a company for a month or so is a good way to find a new job. Although working for free may be legal in situations where the job being sought is exempt from the FLSA—for example, a professional fundraising position with a nonprofit organization—it is not legal when the job involved is governed by the Act. (See Section A2 for details on FLSA exemptions.)

For ease of accounting, employers are allowed to round off records of worktime to the nearest five-minute mark on the clock or the nearest quarter hour. But rounding off becomes illegal if it means employees will get paid for less time than they actually worked. In practice, this means that your employer will usually round your worktime up to add a few minutes each day to the time for which you are paid.

In calculating on-the-job time, most concerns focus on how to deal with specific questionable situations, such as travel time, time spent at seminars, meal and coffee breaks, waiting periods, on-call periods and sleeping on the job.

1. Travel Time

The time you spend commuting between your home and the place you normally work is not considered to be on-the-job time for which you must be paid. But it may be payable time if the commute is actually part of the job.

If you are a lumberjack, for example, and you have to check in at your employer's office, pick up a chainsaw and then drive ten miles to reach the cutting site for a particular day, your workday legally begins when you check in at the office.

Even if the commute is not part of your job, circumstances may allow you to collect for the odd trip back and forth. You can claim that you should be paid for your time in commuting only when you are required to go to and from your normal worksite at odd hours in emergency situations.

Example: *Ernest normally works 9 to 5 as a computer operator and is paid hourly. One day, about two hours after he arrived home from work, he got a call from his office notifying him that the computer was malfunctioning and that he was needed there immediately to help correct the problem. It took him one-half hour to drive back to the office, two hours to get the computer back on track and one-half hour to drive home again.*

The company must pay Ernest for three extra hours—two of them workhours and the third for the extra hour of commuting time required by the company's emergency.

When It's Unclear Whether You're Coming or Going

Questions about whether workers can be considered on the job while enroute to it or from it often make it to courtrooms when there is possible liability for an accident. For example, a worker who gets in a car crash on the way home from work may claim the employer should foot the bill for medical costs and property damages.

Courts and employers usually invoke the Going and Coming Rule, which generally absolves employers from liability by holding that an employee is "not acting within the scope of employment" when going to or coming from the workplace.

There are, however, specific exceptions to this rule. Courts have found employers liable where they:

- get some benefit from the trip—such as new clients or business contacts
- pay the employee for the travel time and travel expenses such as gasoline and tolls, and
- request that the employee run a special errand while traveling to or from work—such as volunteering to clean up after a company party—although carpooling with co-workers and taking classes as encouraged by an employer do not count here.

---

2. Lectures, Meetings and Training Seminars

Generally, if you are a nonexempt employee and your employer requires you to attend a lecture, meeting or training seminar, you must be paid for that time—including travel time if the meeting is away from the worksite.

The specific exception to this rule is that you need not be paid if:

- you attend the event outside of regular working hours
- attendance is voluntary
- the instruction session isn't directly related to your job, and
- you do not perform any productive work during the instruction session.

3. Meal and Break Periods

Contrary to the laws of gastronomy, federal law does not require that you be allotted or paid for breaks to eat meals.

However, many states have laws specifically requiring that employees be allowed a half hour or so in meal and rest breaks during each workday. (See the chart below.) Meal breaks of 30 minutes or more usually need not be counted as part of your payable work hours—as long as you are completely relieved of work duties during that time. Technically, however, if your employer either requires that you work while eating—or allows you to do so—you must be paid for time spent during meals. Also, you must be paid for break periods that are less than 20 minutes.

A number of state laws controlling meal and rest breaks contain interesting anachronisms. The law in New Mexico, for example, specifically protects only women workers. Louisiana law sets out complicated rest requirements for divers and tunnel and caisson workers. California, predictably, stands alone in exempting those who work in motion pictures.

And some state laws set work break restrictions that are hard to picture. New Hampshire law flexibly allows workers 30-minute meal breaks for every five hours of work—"except if it is feasible for the employee to eat while working." And Tennessee mandates an unpaid break every six hours—"except for workplaces that by their nature provide for ample opportunity to rest or take an appropriate break."

Additional Laws May Apply

If the chart below indicates that your state has no statute, this means there is no law that specifically addresses the issue. However, there may be a state administrative regulation or local ordinance that does control. Call your state labor department for more information. (See the Appendix for contact details.)

State Meal and Rest Break Laws

Alabama	No one 15 or younger shall be required to work five continuous hours without a meal or rest break of at least 30 minutes. Ala. Code §25-8-38(c)
Alaska	Employees under the age of 18 who work at least a six-hour shift have the right to take an unpaid 30 minute break after their first five hours of work. Does not apply to employees in fishing or farming or who work for a family member. Alaska Stat. §23.10.350
Arizona	No statute
Arkansas	No statute
California	Meal—30 minutes within five hours of starting work if workday is six hours or more. If less, waivable if a meal period occurs on a shift between 10 p.m. and 6 a.m., shelter and facilities shall be provided for consuming hot food and drink.
	Rest—ten minutes per four hour period. Compensated.
	Does not apply to motion picture, agricultural and household occupations. Cal. Code of Regs., tit. 8, §11010 and following
Colorado	Meal—30 minutes unpaid within five hours of starting work.
	Rest—ten minutes per four hours paid.
	Applies only to employees in retail, service, commercial support service, food and beverage and health industries. Wage Order No. 22
Connecticut	Meal—30 minutes per 7 1/2 hour workday; given after second hour and before last two hours. Does not apply to public school teachers—or to workplaces with fewer than five employees, where breaks would affect safety or disrupt special continuous operations. Conn. Gen. Stat. §31-51ii
Delaware	Meal—30 minutes for 7 1/2 hour workday; given after second hour and before last two hours. Does not apply to public school teachers—or to workplaces with fewer than five employees, where breaks would affect safety or disrupt special continuous operations. Del. Code Ann. tit. 19, §707
District of Columbia	No statute
Florida	Employees age 17 and under are entitled to a 30-minute break for every four hours of work. Does not apply to minors with high school diplomas, who are employed as domestic servants or by their parents, who are pages in the state legislature, who have a certificate of exemption from compulsory education or who receive a hardship or family emergency waiver from the school superintendent. Fla. Stat. Ann. §450.081
Georgia	No statute
Hawaii	Meal—45 minutes for state government employees only. Haw. Rev. Stat. §80—1
Idaho	No statute
Illinois	Meal—20 minutes for a 7 1/2 hour workday beginning no later than five hours into the work period. 820 Ill. Comp. Stat. 140/3
Indiana	No statute

Iowa	Employees under the age of 16 who work five or more hours are entitled to an intermission of 30 minutes. Iowa Code §92.7
Kansas	No statute
Kentucky	Meal—"Reasonable" break between three and five hours into the work period. Rest—ten minutes per four hours. Statute does not apply to railroad employees. Ky. Rev. Stat. Ann. §§337.355 and 337.365
Louisiana	Divers and tunnel and caisson workers who use compressed air must be given the following rest intervals between shifts, in the open air: 0–26 pounds, one hour; 26–33 pounds, two hours; 33–38 pounds, three hours; 38–43 pounds, four hours; 43–48 pounds, five hours; 48–50 pounds, six hours. La. Rev. Stat. Ann. §23:486
Maine	Meal—30 minutes per six hours of work for meals or rest. Does not apply if there are fewer than three employees on duty. Me. Rev. Stat. Ann. tit. 26, §§601 and 602
Maryland	Employees under the age of 18 get a 30-minute break every five hours. Md. Code Ann. Lab. and Emp. §3-210(a)
Massachusetts	Meal—30 minutes per six hour work period. Mass. Gen. Laws Ann. ch. 149, §100
Michigan	Minors who are employed more than five continuous hours must be given 30 minutes for a meal or rest break. Mich. Comp. Laws §409.112
Minnesota	Meal—Employer must allow "adequate time" to eat a meal during an eight-hour work period. Minn. Stat. Ann. §177.254 Rest—Employer must allow a "reasonable" amount of time in a four-hour period to use the restroom. Minn. Stat. Ann. §177.253
Mississippi	No statute
Missouri	No statute
Montana	No statute
Nebraska	All employees in assembly plants, workshops or mechanical establishments are required to have at least 30-minute lunch breaks without having to remain on the premises. Establishments that operate 24 hours a day are exempt. Neb. Rev. Stat. §48-212
Nevada	Meal—30 minutes per eight hours of work. Rest—ten minutes per four hours of work. Nev. Rev. Stat. Ann. §608.019
New Hampshire	Meal—30 minutes per five hours of work, except if it is feasible for the employee to eat while working and the employer allows him or her to do so. N.H. Rev. Stat. Ann. §275:30-a
New Jersey	Employees under the age of 18 are entitled to take a 30-minute break for every five hours of work. N.J. Stat. Ann. §34-2-21.4
New Mexico	Women's working hours are restricted to eight hours per day and 48 hours per week, except for domestic workers and workers in interstate commerce. Those employees must be given a 30-minute rest period, which is not counted as part of the working day. N.M. Stat. Ann. §§50-5-1 to 4

New York	Meal—Mercantile or similar establishments: 30 minutes; Factory: 60 minutes. If shift begins before 11 a.m. and extends past 7 p.m., an additional 20 minutes is given to factory and mercantile workers between 5 p.m. and 7 p.m. If shift is more than six hours long and begins between 1 p.m. and 6 a.m., mercantile employees must receive 45 minutes and factory employees 60 minutes at a point midway through the shift. N.Y. Labor Law §162
North Carolina	Minors are entitled to take a 30-minute break for every five hours of work. N.C. Gen. Stat. §95-25.5. State personnel are entitled to 30-minute meal breaks for each eight-hour shift. 25 N.C.A.C. ID 1936
North Dakota	Meal—30 minutes if shift is over five hours. By wage order. Commissioner of Labor sets the standards. N.D. Admin. Code §46-02-07-02
Ohio	No statute
Oklahoma	Employees under the age of 16 may take a one hour break for every eight hours of work and cannot work more than five consecutive hours without at least a 30-minute break. Okla. Stat. Ann., tit. 40, §75
Oregon	Meal—30 minutes for each work period of between six and eight hours within the 2nd and 5th hour worked. Or, if work period is more than seven hours, a break must be given between the third and sixth hour worked. Rest—ten minutes for every four hours worked. Or. Admin. Rules §839-020-050
Pennsylvania	Seasonal farmworkers and employees under the age of 18 are entitled to take a 30-minute break per five hours of work. 43 Pa. Cons. Stat. Ann., §46
Rhode Island	Meal—20 minutes per six hours of work. R.I. Gen. Laws §28-3-14
South Carolina	No statute
South Dakota	No statute
Tennessee	Meal—30 unpaid minutes for six hour work period, except in workplaces that by their nature provide for ample opportunity to rest or take an appropriate break. Tenn. Code Ann. §50-2-103
Texas	No statute
Utah	Minors must be allowed meal periods of 30 minutes after five hours of work—and ten minutes for rest every four hours. Utah Admin Code §296-126.092
Vermont	Employees must be afforded a reasonable opportunity to eat and use toilet facilities during work periods. Vt. Stan. Ann. tit. 21, §304
Virginia	No statute
Washington	Meal—30 minutes per five-hour work period. Rest—ten minutes per four-hour work period unless the nature of the work allows the employee to take intermittent rest breaks equivalent to ten minutes per four hours. Wash. Admin. Code 296-126-092
West Virginia	Meal—20 minutes per six hour work period. W.Va. Code §21-3-10a
Wisconsin	Meal—30 minutes close to usual meal time or near middle of shift. Shifts of more than six hours without a meal break should be avoided. Break mandatory for minors. Wis. Admin. Code, Ind. 74.02
Wyoming	No statute

4. Waiting Periods

Time periods when employees are not actually working, but are required to stay on the employer's premises or at some other designated spot while waiting for a work assignment, are covered as part of payable time. For example, a driver for a private ambulance service who is required to sit in the ambulance garage waiting for calls must be paid for the waiting time.

5. On Call Periods

A growing number of employers are paying on call premiums—or sleeper pay—to workers who agree to be available to be reached outside regular worktime and respond by phone or computer within a certain period. Some plans pay an hourly rate for the time spent on call; some pay a flat rate.

If your employer requires you to be on call but does not require you to stay on the company's premises, then the following two rules generally apply.

- On call time that you are allowed to control and use for your own enjoyment or benefit is not counted as payable time.
- On call time over which you have little or no control and which you cannot use for your own enjoyment or benefit is payable time.

Example: *Jack works in an office, 9 to 5, Monday through Friday, as a client services representative for a funeral director. His employer also requires him to be on call at all times in case a business question arises—and it furnishes him with a message beeper. Jack can spend his free time any way he wants. All his employer requires him to do is to call the office as soon as is convenient after his beeper registers a message, so Jack's on-call time is not payable time.*

Example: *Elizabeth is a rape crisis counselor with a social service agency. The agency that employs her must constantly have someone with her expertise available. During weekends when Elizabeth is the on-call counselor, she is allowed to stay at home but must remain near her telephone at all times. She cannot leave her apartment except in response to a rape report, and she cannot drink any alcohol. Practically speaking, she cannot even throw a little dinner party because, if a call were to come in, she would have to leave her guests immediately. Elizabeth's on-call time is not hers to control and enjoy, so it is payable time.*

Unless there's an employment contract that states otherwise, employers are generally allowed to pay a different hourly rate for on-call time than they do for regular worktime, and many do. The employer need only make sure that the employees are paid at least the minimum amount required under wage and hour regulations.

Example: *A hospital emergency room has a policy of paying medical technicians a high hourly rate when they are actually working on a patient, and just the minimum wage when they are merely racking up on-call time on the hospital's premises. If such a technician were to record 20 hours active time and 20 hours on-call time in one week, the FLSA requires only that he or she receive the minimum wage for the 20 on-call hours.*

The courts have generally approved such split-rate pay plans for the purposes of both the minimum wage and overtime requirements if there are marked differences in the types of work performed and the employer has clearly informed employees that different wages are paid for different types of work. (See Section B3 on split payscales.)

When Sleeper Pay Becomes an Employer's Nightmare

Most companies responding to a recent study indicated that they pay employees a premium—either a flat sum or hourly rate—for on-call work.

And a whopping 42% reported that they pay on-call pay to their employees who are otherwise considered exempt from wage and hour laws. While the pay practice sounds well meaning, it could be risky business for employers, especially those who compute and provide the extra compensation based on the number of on-call hours worked. It opens the possibility that exempt employees would in effect lose their exempt statuses—leaving the employer liable for past and future overtime pay.

Source: 1998 study by N.E. Fried and Associates, Inc., a compensation consulting firm based in Dublin, Ohio

---

6. Sleep Time

If you are required to be on duty at your place of employment for less than 24 hours at a time, the U.S. Labor Department allows you to count as payable any time that you are allowed to sleep during your shift of duty. If you are required to be at work for more than 24 hours at a time—for example, if you work as a live-in housekeeper—you and your employer may agree to exclude up to eight hours per day from your payable time as sleep and meal periods.

However, if the conditions are such that you cannot get at least five hours of sleep during your eight-hour sleep-and-eat period, or if you end up working during that period, then those eight hours revert to being payable time.

Example: *Bill works on an offshore oil rig for two days at a time. At the start of each shift, the boat takes him out to the platform and does not come back for him until two days later. Bill and his employer have an agreement that requires that Bill gets an unpaid eight-hour sleep period each day, so his payable time for each 48-hour period he spends on the platform totals 32 hours. During one of Bill's shifts, a storm blew up and caused so much trouble that he had to keep working through the night. That reduced one of his sleep periods to only two hours. Bill must be paid for the sleep period that was cut short, so his payable time at the end of that shift would be 40 hours, or 32 + 8 hours payable sleep time.*

E. State and Local Laws

Although the niggling matters of wage and hour requirements are not among the most scintillating workplace topics, disputes over either tend to hit employees hard and fast. In addition to broad controls over wages and hours that are set out in federal law, a number of state and local regulations are thrown into the fray. If your dispute involves a wage and hour issue, check all these sources of legal controls to get a clear picture of your possible rights and remedies. (See Section F for a discussion and state listing of wage garnishment laws.)

In particular, check the discussions of state laws and charts below on:

- minimum wages (Section 1)
- time off for jury duty (Section 2)
- time off for voting (Section 3)
- military leave (Section 4), and
- protections for filing wage and hour complaints (Section 5).

Pay Interval Laws: How Often Is Often Enough?

The question of how often you must be paid is most often addressed by state wage and hour laws. The FLSA states only that the pay period must be no longer than once a month, but state laws controlling pay intervals often require that most employees be paid at least every two weeks or twice a month.

Like state wage and hour laws, state laws governing how often you must be paid are complex, usually covering only certain types of companies and employees. If you have a question about how often you must be paid under your state's laws, contact the local office of your state's labor department. (See the Appendix for contact details.)

1. Minimum Wage Laws

All but a few states have laws specifying wage and hour standards. Some of these laws are virtually meaningless because they set standards less stringent than those set by federal law. Some state laws set lower minimum wages for groups of employees such as young workers or apprentices—and this is legally permissible.

On the other hand, some state wage rates are higher than those set by federal law. (See the chart below.) And in recognition that the federal minimum wage increases from time to time, a number of states specify that the state minimum is a certain amount above the current minimum wage. If the federal minimum increases, the state minimum will automatically rise. Alaska is a good example. Its minimum wage is 50 cents higher than the federal minimum. In addition, Alaska is one of the few states that does not allow tips to be used as a credit against its minimum wage.

Each state has its own rules for who is covered by its minimum wage law, and they are usually complex. The best way to determine whether your job is covered by a state wage and hour law that has a standard higher than the FLSA is to call the local office of your state's labor department. (See the Appendix for contact details.)

Whenever the FLSA sets a standard higher than one at the state or local level, the FLSA rules. When a state or local law sets standards higher than the FLSA, the state or local law is the one that applies.

Check Local Controls

In the last few years, some counties, cities and towns have also passed their own wage laws. Such local wage laws are still rare and controversial, but you may want to check with the law department of the county or municipality in which you work if you have reason to think that it has passed a wage and hour law covering your job.

Additional Laws May Apply

If the chart below indicates that your state has no statute, this means there is no law that specifically addresses the issue. However, there may be a state administrative regulation or local ordinance that does control. Call your state labor department for more information. (See the Appendix for contact details.)

State Minimum Wage Laws	
Alabama	No statute
Alaska	50 cents above federal minimum wage. Alaska Stat. §23.10.065
Arizona	No statute
Arkansas	$5.15. Fulltime students working 20 hours per week or less are entitled to only 85% of the minimum wage. Ark. Code Ann. §11-4-210
California	$5.75. 85% of minimum wage for learners during their first 160 hours of employment if they have no prior related experience and for minors if less than 25% of the employees are minors. Cal. Code Regs., tit. 8, §11000
Colorado	$5.15. By order of the Department of Labor and Employment, 1515 Arapahoe Street, Tower 2, Suite 400, Denver, CO 80202-2117; 303-620-4700. Authorizing statute: Colo. Rev. Stat. §§8-6-109 Minimum wage for minors may be 15% below the regular minimum wage unless the minor is married and living away from parents or guardians, or supports himself or herself or can show that his or her well-being is substantially dependent on being employed. Colo. Rev. Stat. §8-6-108.5

Connecticut	$6.15 or at least 1/2 of 1% above the federal minimum wage, whichever is higher. For employees under the age of 18, learners and beginners, the minimum wage for the first 200 hours of work is 85% of the regular minimum wage. Conn. Gen. Stat. §31-58j
Delaware	$6.15 or the federal minimum wage, whichever is higher. Del. Code Ann. tit. 19, §902(a)
District of Columbia	$6.15, or the federal minimum wage plus $1. D.C. Code Ann. §§36-220.1 and 36-220.2
Florida	No statute
Georgia	$3.25. Ga. Code Ann. §34-4-3
Hawaii	$5.25. Employees who receive tips can be paid 20 cents per hour less. Haw. Rev. Stat. §387-2
Idaho	$5.15. For tipped employees, 65% of minimum wage. For employees under 20 years old, $4.25 for first consecutive 90 days. Idaho Code §44-1502
Illinois	$5.15. For employees under the age of 18, minimum wage is 50 cents less. 820 Ill. Comp. Stat. 105/4
Indiana	$5.15 for employers who employ at least four employees. For employees under the age of 20, minimum wage for first 90 consecutive days is $4.25. Ind. Code Ann. §22-2-2-4
Iowa	$4.65 or federal minimum, whichever is greater. Iowa Code Ann. §91D.1
Kansas	$2.65. Kan. Stat. Ann. §44-1203
Kentucky	Federal minimum wage. For employees who earn more than $30 per month in tips, minimum wage is 50% of regular minimum wage so long as salary plus tips is at least equal to the minimum wage. Ky. Rev. Stat. Ann §337.275
Louisiana	No statute
Maine	Same as federal minimum wage. Employers can deduct up to 50% off the minimum wage for employees who receive tips. Me. Rev. Stat. Ann. tit. 26, §664
Maryland	At least the federal minimum wage. Employers can deduct up to $2.77 from minimum wage for employees who receive tips. Md. Lab. & Emp. Code Ann., §§3-413, 419
Massachusetts	$6. Set by the Labor and Industries Department, 100 Cambridge Street, Room 1100, Boston, MA 02202; 617-727-3465. Authorizing statute: Mass. Gen. Laws Ann. ch. 151, §1
Michigan	$5.15. Mich. Comp. Laws §408.384
Minnesota	$ 5.15 for employers grossing more than $500,000 per year. For others, $4.90. Minn. Stat. Ann. §177.24
Mississippi	No statute
Missouri	The federal minimum wage. Mo. Ann. Stat. §290.502
Montana	Federal minimum wage for businesses with gross annual sales of $110,000 or more. For others, $4.00. Mont. Code Ann. §§39-3-404; 39-3-409; Dept. of Labor & Industry Rules §24.16.15104

Nebraska	$5.15. The minimum wage for student learners is 75% of the regular minimum wage. Neb. Rev. Stat. §48-1203
Nevada	$5.15. Minimum wage for minors is 85% of regular minimum wage. Nev. Rev. Stat. Ann. §608.250
New Hampshire	$5.15. For tipped employees (except for domestic or farm labor, summer camp employees, newsboys, golf caddies and nonprofessional ski patrol), minimum wage is $2.38, or 45% of regular minimum wage, whichever is higher. For employees under the age of 16 or with less than six months experience, minimum wage is 75% of regular minimum wage. N.H. Rev. Stat. Ann. §279:21
New Jersey	Federal minimum wage. Law does not apply to car salespeople, parttime home childcare workers or workers under the age of 18 who do not have a special vocational school graduate permit. N.J. Stat. Ann. §34:11-56a4
New Mexico	$4.25. N.M. Stat. Ann. §50-4-22
New York	$5.15. N.Y. Labor Law §652
North Carolina	Federal minimum wage. Fulltime students, learners, apprentices and messengers entitled to 90% of regular minimum wage. N.C. Gen. Stat. §95-25.3
North Dakota	$5.15. For employees who receive tips, the minimum wage is $3.45. Commissioner of Labor sets the standards of minimum wages, hours of employment and conditions of employment. Labor Department, 600 East Boulevard, Bismarck, ND 58505; 701-328-2660. Authorizing statute: N.D. Cent. Code §34-06-03
Ohio	$4.25; 85% of regular minimum wage for students in cooperative vocational education programs approved by the board of education. Ohio Rev. Code Ann. §4111.02
Oklahoma	Not less than current federal minimum wage. Okla. Stat. Ann. tit. 40, §197.2
Oregon	$6.50. Or. Rev. Stat. §653.025
Pennsylvania	The federal minimum wage. Employees under the age of 18, seasonal employees, employees under the age of 21 at summer day camps, golf caddies, switchboard operators at small phone companies, farm laborers, domestic servants in private homes and news delivery workers are not covered under the minimum wage law. 43 Pa. Cons. Stat. Ann., §333.104, 105
Rhode Island	$6.15. R.I. Gen. Laws §28-12-3
South Carolina	No statute
South Dakota	$5.15. Statute does not apply to employees under the age of 18, babysitters or outside salespeople. S.D. Codified Laws Ann. §60-11-3
Tennessee	No statute

Texas	$3.35, except that an employer may pay only 60% of the minimum wage if the employee's earning or productive capacity is impaired by age, physical or mental deficiency, or injury; or if the person is over 65 years old. Lower wages may not be paid to agricultural piece rate workers. Statute does not apply to employees under the age of 18 who are not graduates of high school or a vocational training program, employees under the age of 20 who are students in high school or in a vocational training program, employees under the age of 21 who are disabled and who are clients of vocational rehabilitation and are in a school-work program, amusement parks or recreational establishments that operate less than seven months out of the year, dairy and livestock production workers, inmates, patients and clients of state mental health facilities. Tex. Labor Code Ann. §§62.051 and following; §62.155 and following
Utah	$5.15 for employees 18 and older; does not apply to waitressing, personal attendants, domestic employees, seasonal employees of nonprofit camping, religious or recreational programs, prisoners, livestock or harvest laborers, agricultural employees who worked less than 13 weeks during the prior year, registered apprentices or students employed by the school they are attending, employees of seasonal amusement parks. Set by the Industrial Commission of Utah, but may not be more than the federal minimum wage. Industrial Commission of Utah, 160 East 300, 3rd Floor, P.O. Box 146600, Salt Lake City, UT 84114-6600; 801-530-6921. Authorizing statute: Utah Code Ann. §34-40-103
Vermont	$5.75 until 12/31/00; $6.25 after 1/1/01 or the federal minimum wage, if it is higher. Not applicable to state employees, retail or service establishments, amusement or recreational facilities, hotels, restaurants, certain hospitals, public health centers or nursing homes. Vt. Stat. Ann. tit. 21, §384a
Virginia	Not less than the federal minimum wage. Va. Code Ann. §40.1-28.10
Washington	$4.90. Wash. Rev. Code Ann. §49.46.020
West Virginia	$5.15. Training wage of $4.25 for employees under age 20 for first 90 days. W.Va. Code §21-5C-2(a)
Wisconsin	$5.15. Minimum wage for employees under 20 years old during their first 90 days of employment is $4.25. Minimum wage for adult agricultural workers is $4.05, for minor agricultural workers the wage is $3.70. Minimum wage for employees who receive tips is $2.33. Set by wage order of the Dept. of Industry, Labor and Human Relations Regulations, P.O. Box 7946, Madison, WI 53707; 608-266-6860. Authorizing statute: Wis. Stat. Ann. §104.02
Wyoming	$1.60. Wyo. Stat. §27-4-202

2. Time Off for Jury Duty

Most states have some specific requirements that apply to employees who are called to serve on juries. Most of these laws fall under the broad rubric of wage and hour controls.

Some employers doggedly resist the idea of allowing employees time off from the workplace—and apply subtle or not-so-subtle pressure on them to do what they can to squirm out of jury service. Employees are easy targets for this form of coercion, since most of us prefer to think of ourselves as indispensable workers. Recognizing this, many state laws contain an anti-discrimination twist—baldly stating that employees called to serve on juries may not be fired for doing so. And a few laws broadly restrict employers from attempting to intimidate employees not to serve on juries.

A number of state laws impose picayune obligations on employees before they can claim legal protections. California protection, for example, applies only if an employee has given advance notice of the jury summons. In Tennessee, you must show the summons to your employer the day after you receive it.

A few states have gone through gyrations in an attempt to reach a balance between the court systems that sorely need jurors to serve and the reality of workplaces that need to remain productive. Illinois, for example, protects nightshift employees, who cannot be required to work nights and do jury duty during the day. And Michigan specifies that the number of hours of jury duty plus worktime must not exceed employees' regular number of working hours for that day.

But these days, when employees labor under the fear of losing their jobs and employers labor under the pressure of increasing their bottom lines, the issue of taking time off for jury duty looms ever larger. The two major concerns are:

- whether employers must pay employees who are called as jurors, and
- what the penalties are for employers who violate statutes setting out obligations for employees on jury duty.

a. Pay requirements

Unless employee handbooks or other published policies state otherwise, employees are not generally entitled to be paid by their employers for time off work spent responding to a summons or serving on a jury.

However, a number of states are exceptions to this rule. State laws that set out some qualified rights to payment include: Alabama, Alaska, Colorado, Connecticut, Hawaii, Kentucky (for teachers and state employees), Louisiana, Massachusetts, Nebraska, New Jersey, New York, Ohio (state employees) and

Tennessee. (See Section 2c below for additional restrictions and requirements in these state laws.)

b. Penalties for employer violations

Most of the statutes specify what penalties can be imposed upon employers who do not live up to their legal rights and responsibilities when it comes to employee-jurors.

However, unless you have an exceptionally high tolerance for legal minutiae, you will not likely want to end up in court because an employer has violated your rights to time off for jury duty. But as a practical matter, laws that set out penalties for employers who violate them can speak more loudly during your negotiations to resolve a wrong. Some laws specifically allow discharged employees to file lawsuits for back wages. Presumably, employees would be free to file such lawsuits even in states with laws that are mum on the issue. A few state laws specify that an employee who is fired specifically for taking jury duty must be reinstated.

Many states make a violation a misdemeanor, so that employees who are discriminated against or fired in violation of a jury duty law need only complain to the district attorney or other local prosecuting authority, who will decide whether to prosecute the case. A prosecutor who is successful and creative should be able to get back pay and even reinstatement for employees who are fired. But keep reality in mind. Prosecutors are not required to bring charges—and in areas where serious crime is rampant, a district attorney may well decide to put his or her energy elsewhere.

South Carolina is an example of a state with a harsh consequence: Employers who fire an employee because of jury duty are liable for up to one year of the discharged employee's salary, or the difference between the original and the lessened salary if the employee is demoted. But New York's law is the toughest on employers who break jury duty laws; it leaves the employer open to criminal contempt charges.

Ignoring the Jury Duty Laws: 'Not One of His Smarter Management Decisions'

A Texas employer was arrested recently after firing a worker who insisted on honoring her civic duty of responding to a call for jury duty.

Jennifer Sutton, an executive assistant at Dallas-based computer company Affiliated Computer Services, claims she reminded her boss, Warren Edwards, about the jury duty summons several times in advance. She even confided that she was looking forward to serving on a jury for the first time.

Edwards response was to give her a reprimand and an additional work assignment, which she came to work to finish early on the morning her jury duty was to begin. He then demanded she stay to finish the task.

"I was in tears and told Mr. Edwards that I needed to go to jury duty," Sutton recalls. "He said for me to pack up my stuff, consider this my last day, that I was fired." The verbal pink slip was delivered ten days before Christmas.

Sutton's tale so incensed District Judge John M. Marshall that he issued a warrant for Edwards' arrest and ordered Dallas deputies to bring him in at once.

"I made it clear to him that this was not one of his smarter management decisions," opined the judge.

"It was a mistake," a computer company official later conceded of the firing.

Sutton seconded that emotion, refusing the company's offer of another job. Her final demand was getting her former job back—or six months of pay.

The final settlement terms are undisclosed. But the story of the ill-decided firing was writ large in newspapers nationwide.

c. State laws on jury duty

The chart below summarizes state laws on jury duty. If you wish to read the complete text of the law, you can track it down through the citation at the end of each entry. (See Chapter 18, Section E for help.)

Additional Laws May Apply

If the chart below indicates that your state has no statute, this means there is no law that specifically addresses the issue. However, there may be a state administrative regulation or local ordinance that does control. Call your local court administrator or your state labor department for more information. Also, consider talking to the judge who is overseeing the case for which you have been called. He or she might have something to say about your employer not giving you time off to do your civic duty—and might be able to point you to a law or regulation that can help.

State Laws on Jury Duty

Alabama	Employees may not be fired for taking time off to serve on a jury. A fulltime employee is entitled to usual pay less any compensation received from the court for service. Ala. Code §12-16-8 Penalty: Employees may recover actual and punitive damages. Ala. Code §12-16-8.1
Alaska	Public employees may not be fired or penalized for taking time off to serve on a jury and are entitled to paid leave for their absence from employment. Alaska Stat. §39.20.270 Private employers cannot penalize employees for serving on a jury but are not required to pay the employees during their leave. Alaska Stat. §9.20.037
Arizona	Employees may not be fired for serving on a jury. Employers are not required to pay employees when absent from employment for jury service. Ariz. Rev. Stat. Ann. §21-236 Penalty: Violation of this law is a Class 3 misdemeanor, which carries a fine of up to $500.
Arkansas	City, county and school employees may not be fired for taking time off to serve on a jury. Ark. Stat. Ann. §21-12-304 Employees may not be fired for taking time off to serve on a jury—and cannot be required to use sick leave or vacation to cover time off spent serving on a jury. Ark. Stat. Ann. §16-31-106 Penalty: Violation of this law is a Class 3 misdemeanor, which carries a fine of up to $1,000.
California	Employees may not be fired or discriminated against for taking time off to serve on a jury, but employees must give employers a reasonable amount of advance notice. Cal. Lab. Code §230 Penalty: Violation of this law is a misdemeanor; employee has one year to file a complaint with the Division of Labor Standards Enforcement of the Department of Industrial Relations, and is entitled to reinstatement plus lost wages and benefits.

Colorado	Employees may not be fired for taking time off to serve on a jury. Regular employees, including parttime, temporary and casual workers, are entitled to regular wages up to $50 per day for the first three days of jury service. Colo. Rev. Stat. §13-71-126
	Penalty: Violation of this law is a Class 2 misdemeanor, which carries a fine of $250 to $1,000, a prison sentence of three to 12 months or both. An employee may file a civil lawsuit and be awarded triple damages and reasonable attorneys' fees. Colo. Rev. Stat. §§13-71-133 and 13-71-134
Connecticut	Employees may not be fired for taking time off to serve on a jury. Conn. Gen. Stat. Ann. §54-247a
	Fulltime employees are entitled to be paid their regular wages by their employer for the first five days of jury service. Conn. Gen. Stat. Ann. §51-247a
	Penalty: Violation of this law is criminal contempt, which carries a fine of up to $500, imprisonment of up to 30 days or both. An employee who is discharged may bring a civil action for reinstatement and recovery of lost wages up to 10 weeks; an employer who does not pay may be liable for triple damages and reasonable attorneys' fees.
Delaware	An employer cannot fire, threaten or coerce an employee who responds to a summons or serves as a juror. Del. Code Ann. tit. 10, §4515
	Penalty: A fine of up to $500, six months of imprisonment or both.
District of Columbia	An employer cannot fire, threaten or coerce an employee who responds to a summons or serves as a juror. D.C. Code Ann. §11-1913
	Penalty: Violation of this law is criminal contempt, punishable by a fine of up to $300, 30 days of imprisonment or both for a first offense; a fine up to $5,000, imprisonment of up to 180 days or both for a second offense.
Florida	Employees may not be fired for taking time off to serve on a jury. Fla. Stat. §40.271
	Regular employees, including parttime, temporary and casual workers, who continue to receive their regular wages are not entitled to be compensated by the court for the first three days of jury duty. Employers are not required to pay jurors during absence. Fla. Stat. §40.24
	Penalty: Violation of this law is contempt of court; employer may also be liable for compensatory and punitive damages and reasonable attorneys' fees.
Georgia	An employer may not discharge, discipline or otherwise penalize an employee who responds to a judicial summons, including a jury subpoena. Ga. Code Ann. §34-1-3
Hawaii	Employees may not be fired for taking time off to serve on a jury. Haw. Rev. Stat. §612-25
	Public employees may not be fired for taking time off to serve on a jury and are entitled to paid leave during their absence from employment. Haw. Rev. Stat. §79-14
	Penalty: Violation of this law is a petty misdemeanor, which carries a fine of up to $1,000.

Idaho	Employees may not be fired for taking time off to serve on a jury. Idaho Code §2-218 Penalty: Violation of this law is criminal contempt, which carries a fine up to $300; within 60 days of being fired, an employee may bring a civil action for reinstatement, three times the amount of damages lost and attorneys' fees.
Illinois	Employees may not be fired for taking time off to serve on a jury. Nightshift employees cannot be required to work while they do jury duty during the day. All employees are required to give their employers copies of the jury summons within 10 days of receiving them. 705 Ill. Comp. Stat. 310/10.1 Penalty: Violation of this law may be civil or criminal contempt; employers may also be liable for damages for loss of wages and benefits.
Indiana	It is a misdemeanor to dismiss an employee or to deprive an employee of benefits, or to threaten to do either, because an employee has responded to a jury summons or served on a jury. Penalty: Employers may be liable for lost wages and attorneys' fees and required to reinstate employees who have been fired. Ind. Code §35-44-3-10
Iowa	Employees may not be fired for taking time off to serve on a jury. Iowa Code §607A.45 Penalty: A violation of this law is contempt; within 60 days of being fired, a former employee may bring a civil action to recover attorneys' fees, up to six weeks of wages and to be reinstated.
Kansas	Employers may not discharge or threaten to discharge employees who serve as jurors. Kan. Stat. §43-173 Penalty: Employers may be liable for attorneys' fees and damages for lost wages and other loss of benefits and be required to reinstate employees who have been fired.
Kentucky	Employees may not be fired for taking time off to serve on a jury. Ky. Rev. Stat. §29A.160 Teachers and state employees must be granted leave with pay while serving on a jury—minus any compensation for serving on a jury. Ky. Rev. Stat. §161.153 Penalty: Within 90 days of being fired, a former employee may bring a civil action for lost wages, attorneys' fees and reinstatement with full seniority and benefits; damages recovered may not exceed lost wages.
Louisiana	Employees may not be fired for taking time off to serve on a jury. Regular employees get one day of paid leave for either responding to a summons or serving on a jury. La. Rev. Stat. Ann. §23:965 Penalty: Employers may be fined $100 to $1,000 and required to reinstate employees who have been fired.
Maine	Employees may not be fired or deprived of health insurance coverage for taking time off to serve on a jury. Me. Rev. Stat. Ann. tit. 14, §1218 Penalty: A violation of this law is a Class E crime.

Maryland	Employees may not be fired for taking time off to serve on a jury. Md. Cts. and Jud. Proc. Code Ann. §8-105
Massachusetts	Employees may not be fired for taking time off to serve on a jury. Regular employees, including part-time, temporary and casual workers, are entitled to regular wages for the first three days of jury service. However, a court may excuse an employer from the obligation to pay the employee if it finds that "extreme financial hardship" would result. In that case, the court must compensate the employee for up to $50 per day for the first three days of service. Mass. Gen. Laws Ann. ch. 234A, §§48 and 49
Michigan	Employees may not be fired or disciplined for taking time off for jury service. Penalty: An employer who forces an employee to work hours which, when added to jury duty time, exceed the number of hours that the employee usually works, is guilty of a misdemeanor and may be punished for contempt of court. Mich. Comp. Laws 600.1348
Minnesota	Employees may not be fired for taking time off to serve on a jury. Minn. Stat. Ann. §593.50 Penalty: A violation of this law is criminal contempt, which carries a fine of up to $700, imprisonment for up to six months or both.
Mississippi	Employers may not intimidate employees to keep them from jury service. Miss. Code Ann. §13-5-23 Penalty: A violation of this law is contempt of court and an interference with the administration of justice.
Missouri	An employer cannot fire, discipline or take any adverse action against an employee on account of receiving or responding to a jury summons. Mo. Ann. Stat. §494.460
Montana	No statute
Nebraska	Employees may not be fired or otherwise penalized for taking time off to serve on a jury and are entitled to regular pay during absence from employment less any compensation received from court. Neb. Rev. Stat. §25-1640 Penalty: Violation of this law is a Class IV misdemeanor.
Nevada	Employers may not fire or threaten to fire employees for responding to jury summons. Employees must give their employers at least one day of notice of the intended absences. Nev. Rev. Stat. §6.190 Penalty: A violation of this law is a misdemeanor. In addition, the employee may sue for lost wages, reinstatement, damages equal to the lost wages and punitive damages up to $50,000.
New Hampshire	Employer may not retaliate against an employee who performs jury service. N.H. Rev. Stat. Ann. §500-A:14 Penalty: A violation of this law is contempt of court; former employees have up to one year to bring civil actions for lost wages and reinstatement.

New Jersey	Fulltime state, county, local and mass transit employees who serve on juries are entitled to regular pay less any pay received for being a juror. N.J. Stat. Ann. §2B:20-16
	Employers may not penalize, threaten or coerce employees who attend jury service. N.J. Stat. Ann. §2B:20-17
	Penalty: Violation of this law is a disorderly persons charge; former employees may bring actions for economic damages and reinstatement within 90 days of being fired.
New Mexico	Employees may not be fired for taking time off to serve on a jury. N.M. Stat. Ann. §38-5-18
	Penalty: Violation of this law is a petty misdemeanor. §§38-5-19
New York	An employee who receives a summons and gives notice to an employer may not be discharged or penalized. Employers with more than 10 employees must pay the first $40 of the employee's daily wages for up to three days of jury service.
	Penalty: Violation of this law is criminal contempt. N.Y. Judiciary Law §519
North Carolina	An employer may not discharge or demote an employee who was called to perform jury duty. N.C. Gen. Stat. §9-32
	Penalty: Fired employees have up to one year to sue for reasonable damages and for reinstatement.
North Dakota	An employer who fires or in any way penalizes an employee because the employee receives a jury subpoena or serves on a jury is guilty of a misdemeanor.
	Penalty: Fired employees may sue for reinstatement and back wages. N.D. Cent. Code §27-09.1-17
Ohio	Employees may not be fired for taking time off to serve on a jury. Ohio Rev. Code Ann. §2313.18
	State employees are entitled to paid leave when summoned for jury duty. Ohio Rev. Code Ann. §124.135
	Penalty: Violation of this law is contempt of court.
Oklahoma	Employees may not be fired for taking time off to serve on a jury. Okla. Stat. Ann. tit. 38, §35
	Penalty: Violation of this law is a misdemeanor. Employers are liable for up to $5,000 in lost earnings, mental anguish and the costs of securing suitable employment. Okla. Stat. Ann. tit. 38, §34
Oregon	Employees may not be fired for taking time off to serve on a jury. Or. Rev. Stat. §10.090
Pennsylvania	Employees may not be fired for taking time off to serve on a jury. The statute does not protect employees of retail or service businesses with fewer than 15 employees or employees of manufacturing businesses with fewer than 40 employees. 42 Pa. Cons. Stat. Ann. §4563
	Penalty: Violation of this law is a summary offense.
Rhode Island	Employees may not be fired or otherwise disadvantaged for taking time off to serve on a jury. R.I. Gen. Laws §9-9-28
	Penalty: Violation of this law is a misdemeanor.

South Carolina	Employers may not dismiss or demote an employee for serving on a jury. Penalty: Employers are liable for up to one year of the discharged employee's salary or the difference between the original and the lessened salary of demoted employees. S.C. Code Ann. §41-1-70
South Dakota	Employees may not be fired for taking time off to serve on a jury. S.D. Codified Laws Ann. §§16-13-41.1 and 16-13-41.2 Penalty: Violation of this law is a Class 2 misdemeanor.
Tennessee	An employer with five or more employees may not discharge an employee for serving on a jury or responding to a summons, provided that the employee shows the summons to the employer the day after receiving it. Employees are entitled to regular pay less any jury pay received. Statute protects only permanent employees and parttime employees who have worked more than six months. An employer who discharges an employee in violation of the law is guilty of a misdemeanor. Tenn. Code Ann. §§22-4-108 and 39-16-514 Penalty: Violation of this law is a Class A misdemeanor, which is punishable by a fine of up to $2,500, up to 12 months of imprisonment or both.
Texas	Employees may not be fired for taking time off to serve on a jury. Texas Code Ann. Civil Prac. & Remedies Code §122.001
Utah	Employees may not be fired for taking time off to serve on a jury. Utah Code Ann. §78-46-21 Penalty: Violation of this law is criminal contempt, punishable by a fine up to $500, six months of imprisonment or both.
Vermont	Employees may not be fired for taking time off to serve on a jury. Vt. Stat. Ann. tit. 21, §499 Penalty: A fine up to $200.
Virginia	Employees summoned to jury service shall not be discharged or discriminated against or be forced to use sick leave or vacation time; they must give employers reasonable notice of the absence. Penalty: Violations are Class 3 misdemeanors. Va. Code §18.2-465.1
Washington	Employers must give employees leave to serve as jurors. Penalty: A violation of this law is a misdemeanor and employees may sue for reinstatement. Wash. Rev. Code Ann. §2.36.165
West Virginia	Employers may not discriminate against, threaten or discharge employees who respond to summons for jury duty. W.Va. Code §§52-3-1 Penalty: Violation of this law is civil contempt, punishable by a fine of $100 to $500.
Wisconsin	Employers may not be fired or otherwise penalized for taking time off to serve on a jury. Wis. Stat. Ann. §756.255 Penalty: Employers may be fined up to $200; employees may be entitled to full restitution, including reinstatement and backpay.
Wyoming	Employees may not be fired, threatened or coerced for taking time off to serve on a jury. Wyo. Stat. §1-11-401 Penalty: Employers may be liable for up to $1,000 damages plus reasonable costs and attorneys' fees; former employees have six months to sue for reinstatement and damages.

3. Time Off for Voting

Another set of state laws that falls under the broad category of wage and hour controls regulates the time off employers must allow for employees to vote.

Some state laws set out a specific amount of time that employees must be allowed off from work to cast their ballots. In some states, the time off must be paid; not in others. And most state laws prohibit employers from disciplining or firing employees who take time off work to vote.

Finally, some states impose hardball restrictions on employees who want to claim protection under the voter laws. In Maryland and Oklahoma, for example, employees may be required to show proof that they actually cast a ballot before they can claim the time off. In California, Iowa and Wisconsin, employees must give their employers previous notice that they intend to take time off work to vote.

Additional Laws May Apply

If the chart below indicates that your state has no statute, this means there is no law that specifically addresses the issue. However, there may be a state administrative regulation or local ordinance that does control. Call your local board of elections or your state labor department for more information.

State Laws on Voting

Alabama	No statute
Alaska	Employees may not be fired for taking two hours off without loss of pay unless the employee has two nonwork hours to vote. Alaska Stat. §15.56.100
Arizona	Employees may not be fired for taking three hours off without loss of pay unless the employee has three nonwork hours to vote. Ariz. Rev. Stat. Ann. §16-402
Arkansas	Employers must change work schedules to allow employees to vote. No specific amount of time off is required. Ark. Stat. Ann. §7-1-102
California	Employees may take enough time off work to vote if they do not have enough time to vote outside of working hours. Up to two hours may be taken without loss of pay. Employees must give two workdays' prior notice. Cal. Elec. Code 14000
Colorado	Employees cannot be fired for taking two hours off without loss of pay unless the employee has three nonwork hours to vote. Colo. Rev. Stat. §1-7-102
Connecticut	No statute
Delaware	No statute

District of Columbia	No statute
Florida	It is a misdemeanor to discharge or threaten to discharge an employee for voting or not voting. Fla. Stat. §104.081
Georgia	Employees cannot be fired or disciplined for taking two hours off of unpaid time unless the employee has two nonwork hours to vote. The employee must give the employer reasonable notice. Ga. Code Ann. §21-2-404
Hawaii	Employees cannot be fired for taking two hours off without loss of pay unless they have two nonwork hours to vote. Hawaii Rev. Stat. §11-95
Idaho	No statute
Illinois	Employees cannot be fired for taking two unpaid hours off to vote. 10 Ill. Comp. Stat. 5/7-42
Indiana	No statute
Iowa	Employees may take as much time off as will, when added to nonworking time, give the employee three consecutive hours during which the polls are open. The time taken from work is paid, but the employee must apply for the leave in writing and the employer designates the period of time to be taken off. Iowa Code §49.109
Kansas	It is a misdemeanor for an employer to refuse to give an employee two hours leave with pay in order to vote. However, if the polls are open before or after work, the employee is entitled to take only as much time off as will constitute a two-hour block. Kan. Stat. Ann. §25-418
Kentucky	Employees cannot be fired for taking off four unpaid hours to vote. Ky. Rev. Stat. §118.035
Louisiana	No statute
Maine	No statute
Maryland	Employees cannot be fired for taking two hours off without loss of pay unless they have two nonwork hours in which to vote. Employee must furnish proof that they have voted. Md. Ann. Code art. 33, §24-26
Massachusetts	Manufacturing, mercantile and mechanical employees must be given time off for the first two hours the polls are open without loss of pay. Mass. Gen. Laws Ann. ch. 149, §178
Michigan	No statute
Minnesota	Employees cannot be fired for taking time off to vote and must be given an unspecified amount of morning time without loss of pay for this purpose. Minn. Stat. Ann. §204C.04
Mississippi	No statute
Missouri	Employees cannot be fired for taking three hours off to vote without loss of pay. Statute does not apply if the employee has three successive nonworking hours while the polls are open. Mo. Ann. Stat. §115.639
Montana	No statute

Nebraska	Employees may take time off to vote without penalty or loss of pay, unless they have two consecutive nonworking hours while the polls are open. Neb. Rev. Stat. §32-922
Nevada	Employees cannot be fired for taking up to three hours off, depending upon where they live in relation to the polling place, without loss of pay unless they have enough time during nonwork hours to vote. Nev. Rev. Stat. §293.463
New Hampshire	No statute
New Jersey	No statute
New Mexico	Employees cannot be fired for taking two hours off without loss of pay unless they have two hours before or three hours after work to vote. N.M. Stat. Ann. §1-12-42
New York	Employees cannot be fired for taking up to two hours off without loss of pay unless they have four hours of nonwork time to vote. Employers must post these provisions in a conspicuous place in the workplace not less than ten days before the election. N.Y. Elect. Law §3-110
North Carolina	No statute
North Dakota	Employers are encouraged to grant employees time off to vote. No specific requirements are mandated. N.D. Cent. Code §16.1-01-02.1
Ohio	Employees cannot be fired for taking a reasonable amount of time off to vote without loss of pay. Ohio Rev. Code Ann. §3599.06
Oklahoma	Employees cannot be fired for taking two hours off to vote without loss of pay, unless the employee has three nonwork hours in which to vote. If the worksite and the polling place are at a distance, employers must grant "sufficient time" in which to vote. Employees must present proof of having voted. Does not apply to school board or bond elections. Okla. Stat. Ann. tit. 26, §7-101
Oregon	No statute
Pennsylvania	No statute
Rhode Island	No statute
South Carolina	No statute
South Dakota	Employees may not be fired for taking two hours off without loss of pay unless they have two nonwork hours to vote. S.D. Codified Laws Ann. §12-3-5
Tennessee	An employee may be absent for a reasonable period, up to two hours, to vote, unless there are three hours during which the polls are open and the employee is not at work. Tenn. Code Ann. §2-1-106
Texas	It is a misdemeanor for employers to refuse to allow employees to be absent from work to vote, or to threaten employees for attending the polls. Employees are not entitled to time off if they have two nonwork hours in which to vote. Tex. Elect. Code §276.004
Utah	Unless an employee has three or more hours of nonwork time in which to vote, he or she cannot be fired for taking paid time off. Employees must request time off before election day. Utah Code Ann. §20A-3-103
Vermont	No statute

Virginia	No statute
Washington	Employers must arrange employees' work schedules so that they will have a reasonable amount of nonwork time, up to two hours, in which to vote. If a work schedule cannot be arranged to give an employee two free hours (not counting meal and rest breaks), the employer must grant up to two paid hours leave. Paid leave applies only if, during the time between when the employee is informed of his or her work schedule and election day, there is insufficient time to apply for an absentee ballot. Wash. Rev. Code Ann. §49.28.120
West Virginia	Employees cannot be fired for taking three hours off without loss of pay unless they have three nonwork hours to vote. W. Va. Code §3-1-42
Wisconsin	An employee is entitled to up to three hours unpaid leave to vote, but must notify the employer first. The employer may designate which hours are to be taken off. Wis. Stat. Ann. §6.76
Wyoming	Employees cannot be fired for taking one hour, other than meal time, without loss of pay to vote, providing they actually vote. This law does not apply to employees who have three or more consecutive hours off work while the polls are open. Wyo. Stat. §22-2-111

4. Time Off for Military or National Guard Duty

Most states have laws requiring employers to give time off for National Guard or state militia members or reservists to serve. A number of laws set a minimum amount of paid or unpaid time off that must be given. Some apply only to public employees, some to both public and private. And most laws include a provision preventing discrimination against employees who take military leave.

When leave is required, the employer must usually reemploy service member employees without loss of benefits, status or reduction in pay. These reemployment guarantees usually contain a number of additional conditions. Typical rights and restrictions are that:

- the employee must not have been dishonorably discharged
- the employee must present proof that he or she has satisfactorily completed service
- the employee must request reinstatement within a specified time

- if the employee is not able to do the job he or she left, the employer must offer an appropriate substitute position, and
- the employer need not reinstate the serviceperson if changes in the workforce have made that unreasonable.

In a few states—including Louisiana, New Mexico, North Dakota and Utah—job protections for returning servicepeople are nearly bulletproof: They cannot be fired except for cause for a specified time after returning to the workplace.

State Laws on Military Leave	
Alabama	Active members of the Alabama National Guard or any reserve of the armed forces are entitled to up to 168 working hours of paid leave of absence. Ala. Code §31-2-13(a). But *White v. Associated Industries of Alabama, Inc.*, 373 So. 2d 616 (Ala. 1979) held this statute unconstitutional as applied to private employers.
Alaska	Public employees are entitled to 16 1/2 days of paid leave if they are members of the reserves and are called to training, duty or a search and rescue mission. Alaska Stat. §39.20.340 Private employers must grant unpaid leaves of absence to state militia members called to active service. Alaska Stat. §26.05.075
Arizona	Employers may not discriminate against employees because of membership in the National Guard or other state or federal military forces or for absence from work for military duty. Employers must allow National Guard members an unpaid leave of absence for active duty or training. State employees can take up to 30 days paid leave in a two year period for National Guard training. Ariz. Rev. Stat. Ann. §§26-167 and 26-168
Arkansas	Fulltime state employees may not be fired or discriminated against for membership in the military reserves. Ark. Stat. Ann. §21-3-306 Public employees who are National Guard members or reservists must receive 15 days of paid leave for training or other official duties per year. If called to active duty in an emergency situation, they must receive 30 days of paid leave. Unused portions of the paid leave may be carried over to the next year, but the total days available per year shall not exceed 30 days. Ark. Stat. Ann. §21-4-212 National Guard or militia members who are called to active duty by the governor are entitled to the same reemployment rights, benefits and protections as those afforded employees who are called to active duty in the U.S. forces. Ark Stat. Ann. §12-62-413
California	Employers may not discriminate against employees on account of membership in state or federal military forces. Employees who are members of the National Guard or reserves are entitled to 17 days leave for active military duty for training. Public employees who are members of the National Guard or the U.S. reserves are entitled to 30 days of paid leave and 180 days of unpaid leave per year for training and duty. Cal. Mil. & Vet. Code §§394 through 395.9

Colorado	Public employees who are members of the National Guard or federal reserves are entitled to 15 days of unpaid leave per year for military training. If required to serve more than 15 days, they are entitled to take leave without pay and to be reinstated. Colo. Rev. Stat. §28-3-601 and 602 Private, nontemporary employees who are members of the National Guard or federal reserves are entitled to 15 days off without pay per year for training, and are entitled to return to their jobs provided they are still qualified to fill the positions. Colo. Rev. Stat. §28-3-609
Connecticut	Employees who are members of the military reserves or National Guard are entitled to paid leave for up to 30 days for training or active duty. Conn. Gen. Stat. Ann. §27-33
Delaware	State and school employees may take up to a 3 year leave of absence for service in the armed forces or National Guard. Del. Code Ann. tit. 14, §1327; tit. 29, §5105
District of Columbia	Employees may take up to 15 or 22 days of paid leave per calendar year, depending on the type of military service. This applies to members of the armed forces and the National Guard. District employees serving in the D.C. National Guard may take an unlimited amount of paid leave. D.C. Code Ann. §1-613.3
Florida	Employees cannot be fired or penalized for active service in the National Guard. Fla. Stat. §250.482 Public employees get 17 days paid leave per year for reserve and National Guard training and unpaid leave when called to duty. Fla. Stat. §115.07
Georgia	Public employees ordered into military duty are entitled to 18 days of paid leave per year. National Guard members called to active duty are entitled to 30 days of paid leave. Public employees attending service school may take up to six months unpaid leave. Ga. Code Ann. §38-2-279 Privately employed employees who are ordered into military service are entitled to reinstatement provided they are still qualified to do the job, present proof of completion of military duty and request reemployment within 90 days of discharge. Employees attending service school for a maximum of six months are entitled to reinstatement if they request reinstatement within 10 days. Reinstatement is not required if the employer's circumstances have so changed as to make rehiring impossible or unreasonable. Ga. Code Ann. §38-2-280
Hawaii	Private employees are entitled to unpaid leaves of absence for National Guard duty. Hawaii Rev. Stat. §121-43 Public employees with at least 6 months of service are entitled to 15 days of paid leave per year for National Guard or reserves duty. Hawaii Rev. Stat. §79-20
Idaho	All employees are entitled to 15 days of unpaid leave per year for serving in National Guard or military reserves. Idaho Code §46-224 Public employees who leave their employment, voluntarily or not, to perform military duty are entitled to reinstatement or, if reinstatement is not possible, placement in a state job with similar seniority. The employee must have been honorably discharged and have served four or fewer years. The request must be made within 90 days of discharge or within one year of discharge from

	hospitalization. An employee who is disabled as a result of military service must be placed in an appropriate job. Idaho Code §65-511
Illinois	Employees may not be fired, discriminated against or threatened because they are members of the state militia or the United States armed forces. It is also unlawful to attempt to dissuade employees from enlisting in military service. 20 Ill. Comp. Stat. 1805/100
Indiana	An employee who is a member of the U.S. reserves and who is called for training is entitled to 15 days of leave without pay per year. The employee must give notice, as soon as practicable, of the dates of departure and return and, upon presenting proof of his or her satisfactory completion of training, is entitled to reinstatement. Ind. Code Ann. §10-5-9-2-1 to 2
Iowa	Employees may not be fired, discriminated against or penalized for membership in the National Guard or military reserves. Employer must give leaves of absence for training or service and must reinstate the employee if he or she presents evidence of satisfactory completion of service and is still qualified to do the job. Iowa Code §29A.43
Kansas	Employees may not be fired or punished for absence for National Guard service. Kan. Stat. Ann. §48-222
Kentucky	Employees cannot be fired or discriminated against for service in National Guard or active militia. Ky. Rev. Stat. §38.460 An employer must grant a member of the National Guard leave without pay to perform active duty or training. Ky. Rev. Stat. §38.238
Louisiana	Any employee who gave advance notice and who is absent from employment due to service in the uniformed services is entitled to reemployment if the cumulative leave is less than five years. The employee may not be discharged except for cause within one year of reemployment. Employers are excused if their circumstances have changed so that reemployment is unreasonable or impossible, or if an undue hardship would result. La. Rev. Stat. Ann. §29:410 Employees cannot be discriminated against for duty in state militia or state National Guard and are entitled to unpaid leaves of absence for such service and to be reinstated to their former position after the leaves. Employees may not be discharge except for cause within one yearof reinstatement. La. Rev. Stat. Ann. §29:38 Public employees are entitled to 15 days of paid leave per year for fulfilling military reserves or National Guard duty. La. Rev. Stat. Ann. §42:394
Maine	Employees cannot be fired or penalized for membership in National Guard or state military reserves. Public employees are entitled to paid leave while on annual training duty. Me. Rev. Stat. Ann. tit. 37-B, §342.5
Maryland	Employees cannot be fired or penalized for taking time off for duty in the state militia. Md. Ann. Code art. 65, §32A Public employees may take up to 15 days paid leave annually for training and unlimited paid leave for active duty under the authority of the Governor. Md. Ann. Code art. 65, §42
Massachusetts	Employees may not be fired or denied employment for membership in National Guard or the reserves. Mass. Gen. Laws Ann. ch. 33, §13 Fulltime employees must be given 17 days per year of unpaid leave of absence for military training. Mass. Gen. Laws Ann. ch. 149, §52A

Michigan	Employees cannot be fired, hindered or dissuaded from performing duty as a member of the U.S. reserves, the National Guard or state naval militia. Statute applies to enlistments as well as those already enlisted. Mich. Comp. Laws §32.271-274
Minnesota	Employees cannot be fired for being members of military. Minn. Stat. Ann. §192.34 Public employees are entitled to 15 days per year of paid leave for National Guard or reserves active duty or training and are entitled to leave without pay if called to extended duty. Minn. Stat. Ann. §§192.26 and 192.261
Mississippi	Any person in the federal reserves or state military reserves who leaves a fulltime position for duty or training is entitled to leave without pay and reinstatement upon receiving a discharge that is anything but dishonorable. Applies only if the employee is still qualified to do the job. Miss. Code Ann. §33-1-19 Public employees in state or federal armed forces are entitled to reinstatement and 15 days of leave with pay for training. Miss. Code Ann. §33-1-21
Missouri	Employees cannot be fired or threatened for membership in the state militia or U.S. armed forces or hindered or prevented from performing their militia service. Mo. Ann. Stat. §41.730 Public employees who are in the reserves or the state militia get 15 days of leave with pay per year for service or training. Mo. Ann. Stat. §105.270 Public employees are entitled to extended leaves without pay for federal or state military service or training without loss of position or benefits. Mo. Ann. Stat. §41.942
Montana	Members of the state militia may not be deprived of employment, or an employment benefit, due to their membership in the militia. Mont. Code §10-1-603 Public employees who have been employed for at least six months get 15 days paid leave of absence for military or state militia duty. Mont. Code Ann. §10-1-604
Nebraska	Permanent pubic employees who are members of the National Guard or reserves are entitled to an unpaid leave of absence for up to four years during active duty. All employees who are members of the National Guard or reserves are entitled to 15 days with pay per year for training or duty. If the governor declares a state of emergency, employees called to active service get additional leave and are entitled to be paid the difference between their regular pay and their service pay. Neb. Rev. Stat. §55-160 to 161
Nevada	Employers cannot fire or discriminate against employees because of National Guard duty or membership. Nev. Rev. Stat. §§412.1393 and 412.606
New Hampshire	Employers cannot fire employees because of membership in or absence from work due to performance of duty in the National Guard. N.H. Rev. Stat. Ann. §110-B:65
New Jersey	Employees may not be deprived of employment or prevented from being hired because of membership in the armed forces or because of performing a military duty. Employees may not be dissuaded from joining the military through threats to their employment. N.J. Stat. Ann. §38A:14-4

New Mexico	Employers cannot fire employees because of membership in the National Guard. N.M. Stat. Ann. §§20-11-6 and 20-4-6 Public and private employers must give members of the reserves or National Guard unpaid leaves of absence during active duty. Such employees cannot be fired except for cause within one year of their return to work. N.M. Stat. Ann. §§28-15-1 to 28-15-3
New York	It is the policy of the state of New York that employers should not discriminate against nor refuse to employ employees who are subject to military duties, but there are no specific remedies for those discriminated against, nor are there penalties for those employers who discriminate. N.Y. Mil. Law §318 Public and private fulltime employees are entitled to unpaid leaves of absence when called for active or inactive duty or training. Employees must apply for reemployment within ten days of completion of service. N.Y. Mil. Law §317
North Carolina	Employers cannot fire employees because of National Guard duty, and must reinstate the employee if he or she is still qualified to do the job (an employee who is not qualified must be placed in another position for which he or she is qualified), unless restoration would be unreasonable due to the employer's changed circumstances. N.C. Gen. Stat. §127A-202 Employers cannot fire employees because of emergency state militia or reserves duty. N.C. Gen. Stat. §127B-14
North Dakota	Public employees cannot be fired for performance of National Guard, military reserves or federal service duty. Employees who have been employed for at least 90 days must be granted 20 days of paid leave when ordered to active service and 30 days of paid leave per year for full or partial mobilizations. Such employees may not be fired for one year from the date of reinstatement except for cause. N.D. Cent. Code §37-01-25 and 25.1
Ohio	Public employees must be granted leave to be inducted into military service. If they are not accepted, they must be reinstated. No public employer may discriminate against or discharge any person because of membership in the National Guard, state militia or US reserves. Ohio Rev. Code Ann. §5903.02
Oklahoma	Employers cannot hinder or prevent employees who are members of the National Guard from performing their military duty. Okla. Stat. Ann. tit. 44, §208 Public employers must give a leave of absence when a service member is called to active or inactive duty and 20 days of paid leave per year for training. If the leave extends beyond 20 days, the state and its political subdivisions may elect to make up the difference between the employee's regular pay and the National Guard pay. Okla. Stat. Ann. tit. 44, §209
Oregon	Public employees cannot be discharged for performing military duty. They are entitled to reinstatement to the same or similar positions. Statute does not cover leaves over four years-five years if the orders are from the federal government. Or. Rev. Stat. §408.240 Any employee who is a member of the state militia who is called to active service must be granted a leave without pay. Or. Rev. Stat. Ann. §399.230 Public employees are entitled to 15 days of paid leave for training per year. Or. Rev. Stat. §408.290

Pennsylvania	Employers cannot fire or discriminate against employees because of performance of military duty in the National Guard or reserves. Pa. Cons. Stat. Ann. tit. 51, §7309 In the event of war, armed conflict, a draft or an emergency declared by the president or the governor, employees who enlist or are drafted into active service and reservists called to duty are entitled to unpaid leaves. Pa. Conn. Stat. Ann., tit. 51, §7302(A) Public employees who are members of the National Guard are entitled to 15 days of paid leave for training and active duty. Pa. Cons. Stat. Ann. tit. 51, §4102
Rhode Island	Employers cannot fire or discriminate against employees for duty in the National Guard or reserves. R.I. Gen. Laws §§30-11-2 and 30-11-6 Employees who are National Guard members are entitled to unpaid leave for training periods and active military service. R.I. Gen. Laws §30-11-3 An employee who enters the land, naval or air forces and is honorably discharged, must be reinstated to his or her position or one of similar seniority if the employee is still qualified to do the job and makes the request within 40 days of discharge. The statute does not apply if the employer's circumstances have so changed so that it would be unreasonable to force compliance. R.I. Gen. Laws §§30-21-1 through 30-21-7
South Carolina	Private and public employers cannot fire employees for membership or performance of duty in National Guard. S.C. Code Ann. §§25-1-2310 and 2320 Public employees who are members of the National Guard or U.S. Reserves are entitled to up to 15 days paid leave for training or active service and an additional 30 days if called to serve in an emergency. S.C. Code Ann. §8-7-90
South Dakota	Fulltime employees who are members of the National Guard or reserves are entitled to 15 days per year of unpaid leave of absence for training or when called to active duty. S.D. Codified Laws Ann. §33-17-15
Tennessee	It is a felony for an employer to refuse employment or terminate an employee because he or she is a member of the National Guard, or to terminate employment because the employee is absent while attending any prescribed drill or training. Tenn. Code Ann. §58-1-604
Texas	Private employers cannot fire a permanent employee who is called to active service in the state militia. Tex. Gov't Code Ann. §431.006 Public employees are entitled to 15 days of paid leaves of absence per year for training or duty in the state militia or armed forces reserves. Tex. Govt. Code Ann. §431.005
Utah	Employers cannot fire employees who are members of the National Guard or U.S. reserves and must grant them up to five years of leaves of absence for service. Public employees may not be discharged within one year of return except for cause. State employees are entitled to 15 days per year with pay for training and instruction. Utah Code Ann. §§39-1-36, 39-3-1 and 39-3-2
Vermont	Employers cannot fire fulltime employees who are members of the U.S. reserves for engaging in military training and must grant them 15 days of unpaid leave per year. Vt. Stat. Ann. tit. 21, §491

Virginia	Employers cannot fire nor refuse to hire members of the National Guard, nor may they dissuade employees from joining the Guard. Va. Code §44-98 Public employees who are members of the reserves, National Guard or state naval militia are entitled to 15 days per year of paid leave for the performance of military duties. Va. Code §44-93
Washington	Employers cannot fire fulltime employees for military service and must grant an unpaid leave of absence when employees are called to active duty or training in the National Guard, armed forces reserves or U.S. public health service. An employer does not have to re-employ a returning employee if circumstances have changed so much that it is impossible or unreasonable to do so. Wash. Rev. Code Ann. §73.16.033
West Virginia	Employees in the National Guard are entitled to the same reemployment rights guaranteed to members of the U.S. Reserves by applicable federal law. W. Va. Code §15-1F-8 Public employees are entitled to 30 days paid leave per year for training or active duty. Employees called to active duty by the president are entitled to an additional 30 days of leave. W.Va. Code §15-1F-1
Wisconsin	Employers must grant fulltime employees up to four years of unpaid leave for enlistments, inductions and orders to active service in the U.S. reserves or National Guard. Wis. Stat. Ann. §§45.50 and 45.51
Wyoming	Employers cannot fire, refuse to hire, hinder or penalize employees for performing duty or enlisting in the uniformed services. Wyo. Stat. §19-11-104 Public employees are entitled to 15 days of unpaid leave per year for National Guard or U.S. reserves training or duty. Wyo. Stat. §19-11-108

5. Penalties for Retaliation

A whopping majority of the states have laws that specifically protect from retaliation employees who file complaints or testify in investigations controlled by the wage and hour statutes. Most of these laws simply provide that employees cannot be fired for filing wage and hour complaints. Several protect those who testify at a wage and hour dispute on their own behalf or on behalf of another employee.

A number of laws pack a wallop for employers who violate the laws' strictures. In Alaska, for example, violators can be fined up to $2,000 and jailed for up to 20 days—and each day of a violation counts as a separate offense.

Additional Laws May Apply

If the chart below indicates that your state has no statute, this means there is no law that specifically addresses the issue. However, there may be a state administrative regulation or local ordinance that does control. Call your state labor department for more information. (See the Appendix for contact details.)

State Laws Prohibiting Retaliation	
Alabama	No statute
Alaska	An employer may not discriminate against or discharge an employee who has complained, instituted a proceeding or testified in a proceeding regarding the minimum wage act. Violations are a fine of $100 to $2,000, 10 to 20 days in jail or both. Each day a violation occurs constitutes a separate offense. Alaska Stat. §§23.10.135 & 140
Arizona	Employees cannot be fired or discriminated against for serving on or testifying before a wage board. Ariz. Rev. Stat. Ann. §23-329 An employer may not discriminate against anyone who has opposed, made a charge, testified or participated in a hearing of an alleged violation of the Arizona Civil Rights Act (Ariz. Rev. Stat. Ann. §§41-1401 and following). Ariz. Rev. Stat. Ann. §41-1464
Arkansas	It is a misdemeanor to retaliate against an employee who complains, testifies or participates in proceedings instituted by the Department of Labor with respect to equal wages for males and females. Ark. Code Ann. 11-4-608
California	Employees cannot be fired for asserting rights under the jurisdiction of the Labor Commissioner. Cal. Lab. Code §98.6 Employees cannot be fired for refusing to work hours in excess of those permitted by the Industrial Welfare Commission. Cal. Lab. Code §1198.3
Colorado	Employers cannot fire or otherwise discriminate against employees for participating in any wage and hour proceeding. Colo. Rev. Stat. §8-6-115 It is a misdemeanor to threaten, blacklist or in any way discriminate against an employee who has complained about a violation of the state wage law or who has instituted a proceeding concerning the state wage law. Colo. Rev. Stat. §8-4-124
Connecticut	Employees may not be disciplined in any manner for reporting violations of minimum wage laws. Conn. Gen. Stat. §31-69
Delaware	Employees may not be fired for participating in a proceeding under wage payment and collection law. Del. Code Ann. tit. 19 §1112

District of Columbia	Employees may not be fired for filing a complaint or participating in a proceeding to enforce the minimum wage law. D.C. Code Ann. §36-220.9
Florida	No statute
Georgia	No statute
Hawaii	Employees may sue employers if they are fired for reporting a violation of law to a public agency. Haw. Rev. Stat. §378.62
Idaho	Employees cannot be fired or discriminated against for participating in proceedings under the minimum wage law. Idaho Code §44-1509
Illinois	An employer may not discharge or discriminate against any employee who testifies, cooperates or brings a complaint to a wage board; or who serves as a member of a wage board. 820 Ill. Comp. Stat. 125/15 A whistleblower under the Prevailing Wage Act may not be discriminated against or discharged. 820 Ill. Comp. Stat. 130/11b
Indiana	Employees may not be fired for participating in an action to recover wages under the state wage and hour law. Ind. Code Ann. §22-2-2-11
Iowa	Employees cannot be fired for participation in wage and hour proceedings. Iowa Code §91A.10(5)
Kansas	An employer who discharges or discriminates against an employee who has filed a complaint, participated in proceedings or initiated proceedings with respect to the wage board shall be fined $250 to $1,000. Kan. Stat. Ann. §44-1210
Kentucky	Employees cannot be fired for exercising rights under wage and hour law. Ky. Rev. Stat. §337.550
Louisiana	Employees may not be fired or in any way discriminated against for testifying regarding enforcement of any labor laws. Criminal penalties are a fine of $100 to $250, 30 to 90 days in jail or both. La. Rev. Stat. Ann. §23:964
Maine	An employer who discharges or otherwise discriminates against an employee who makes a complaint concerning minimum wages is subject to a $50 to $200 fine. Me. Rev. Stat. tit. 26 §671
Maryland	An employer may not discharge an employee because that employee made a complaint to the commissioner of labor or an authorized representative that the employee has not been paid in accord with the minimum wage law. Md. Labor and Emp. Code §3-428 An employer may not discharge or otherwise discriminate against an employee who makes a complaint to the commissioner of labor or any person regarding equal pay for equal work or any subject that relates to equal pay for equal work. Md. Labor and Emp. Code §3-308
Massachusetts	No employee may be penalized by an employer for seeking rights under the wage and hours law. Mass. Gen. Laws Ann. ch. 149 §148A

Michigan	Employees may not be fired for protesting violations or participating in proceedings regarding the state minimum wage law. Mich. Comp. Laws 408.395
Minnesota	Employers may be fined $700 to $3,000 for firing or discriminating against employees who testify or complain about minimum wage violations. Minn. Stat. Ann. §177.32(2) Employees cannot be fired or discriminated against for testifying or filing a complaint about violations of the Minnesota Labor Relations Act. Minn. Stat. Ann. §179.12(b)
Mississippi	No statute
Missouri	An employer may not discharge or in any way discriminate against an employee who has complained, testified or caused a proceeding to be instituted regarding the minimum wage law. Mo. Ann. Stat. §290.525(7)
Montana	No statute
Nebraska	Employers may not fire or discriminate against any employee who attempts to enforce the state law mandating equal pay for men and women. Neb. Rev. Stat. §48-1221(4)
Nevada	Employees cannot be threatened, discriminated against or fired for testifying in any proceeding or investigation concerning wages and hours laws. Nev. Rev. Stat. §608.015
New Hampshire	No statute
New Jersey	An employer who fires or in any way discriminates against an employee who complains, institutes a proceeding or testifies regarding wage law violations will be guilty of a disorderly person offense and fined $100 to $1,000, and ordered to reinstate the employee or to correct any discriminatory action. Further penalties may be imposed. N.J. Stat. Ann. 34:11-56a24
New Mexico	No statute
New York	Employers cannot fire or in any way discriminate against employees who complain to them or to the Labor Commissioner about violations of state labor laws. N.Y. Lab. Law §215 Employers cannot fire or in any way discriminate against employees because of complaints under the state Minimum Wage Act. N.Y. Lab. Law §662
North Carolina	Employers cannot fire or take any retaliatory action against employees who, in good faith, file or threaten to file a wage claim. N.C. Gen. Stat. §95-240 and 95-241(a)(1)(b)
North Dakota	An employer may not discharge or in any way discriminate against an employee who has testified or is about to testify in any proceeding relative to hours and wages. N.D. Century Code §34-06-18
Ohio	An employer may not discharge or discriminate against an employee for filing a complaint, lodging a claim or for testifying in any proceeding regarding the wage laws. Ohio Rev. Code §4111.13(B)

Oklahoma	It is a misdemeanor for any employer to discharge or penalize an employee who files a complaint, institutes an investigation or testifies in any proceeding relative to the minimum wage law. Okla. Stat. Ann. tit. 40 §199
Oregon	Employers cannot fire employees because of filing a wage claim. Penalties include actual damages not less than $200, but not reinstatement. Or. Rev. Stat. §652.355
Pennsylvania	An employer who discharges or in any way discriminates against an employee who testifies in any proceeding under the wage laws may be fined from $500 to $1,000 or, if the fine is not paid, may be imprisoned from 10 to 90 days. 43 Pa. Cons. Stat. Ann. §333.112
Rhode Island	An employer may not discharge or discriminate against an employee for reporting a violation of the wage laws to the Department of Labor. R.I. Gen. Laws §§28-14-18
South Carolina	No statute
South Dakota	Employers may not fire or otherwise discriminate against employees for wage complaints. S.D. Codified Laws Ann. §60-11-17.1
Tennessee	Employees who invoke the state's equal pay laws for women and men are protected from retaliation. Tenn. Code Ann. §50-2-202(c)
Texas	No statute
Utah	Employers may not discharge or threaten to discharge an employee who files a complaint or testifies in proceedings to enforce the state wage laws. Utah Code Ann. §34-28-19
Vermont	An employer may not discharge or in any way discriminate against an employee who has served or is about to serve on a wage board or has testified or is about to testify before a board or because the employer thinks an employee is about to serve or testify. Vt. Stat. Ann. tit. 21 §394
Virginia	No statute
Washington	An employer who discharges or discriminates against an employee who files a complaint, institutes a proceeding or has testified or is about to testify before a wage board is guilty of a gross misdemeanor. Wash. Rev. Code Ann §49.46.100(2)
West Virginia	Employers who fire or otherwise discriminate against employees for wage complaints are guilty of a misdemeanor and may be fined from $100 to $500. W. Va. Code §21-5C-7
Wisconsin	Employers cannot fire, threaten or discriminate against employees who testify or are about to testify before wage complaint proceedings or investigations. Violators are liable for a fine of $25 for each offense. Wis. Stat. Ann. §104.10
Wyoming	No statute

F. Payroll Withholding and Deductions

Since the end of the Depression of the 1930s, the right and responsibility of employers to withhold a portion of your pay has become a virtually undisputed part of American culture. The laws that created the income tax and Social Security programs, for which funds are withheld, typically authorize payroll withholding to finance those programs.

But a growing number of additional deductions are now also authorized.

1. What Can Be Deducted or Withheld

In addition to Social Security and local, state and federal taxes, an employer may also make several other deductions from minimum wages: costs of meals, housing and transportation, loans, debts owed the employer, child support and alimony, payroll savings plans and insurance premiums. As in most other workplace laws, there are exceptions to these rules. There are often limitations on how much may be withheld or deducted from a paycheck.

a. Meals, housing and transportation

Employers may legally deduct from an employee's paycheck the "reasonable cost or fair value" of meals, housing, fuel and transportation to and from work.

But to deduct any of these amounts from a paycheck, an employer must show that it customarily paid these expenses and that:

- they were for the employee's benefit
- the employee was told in advance about the deductions
- the employee voluntarily accepted the meals and other accommodations against minimum wage.

Example: *Bob accepted a job as a guide at a remote wilderness ski resort after the employer told him that the job paid $10 per hour plus room and board. But when he got his first paycheck, Bob saw that charges for housing and meals had been deducted from his pay. And the charges were so high that he really was earning only $3 per hour, far less than the minimum wage.*

Asking around among other employees at the resort, Bob learned that the exorbitant meal charges were billed to his payroll account by a catering service owned by the resort owner's brother-in-law. Bob's employer had violated several of the FLSA's rules governing noncash compensation, so Bob filed a complaint with the U.S. Labor Department's Wage and Hour Division.

Additional Guidance on Payroll Withholding

The Internal Revenue Service rules for payroll withholding and reporting vary greatly among the legal categories of work: employee, statutory employee, statutory nonemployee and independent contractor. (See Chapter 2, Section A.)

You can obtain a detailed explanation of those rules free by calling the IRS forms distribution center at 800/829-3676 and requesting Publication 15-A, entitled "Employer's Supplemental Tax Guide." This booklet is also available at your local IRS office, and can be downloaded from the agency's website at http://www.irs.gov. The guide provides a thorough employers' eye view of requirements for classifying workers and withholding required.

State and local payroll withholding taxes usually parallel the IRS rules, but the taxing authorities in your state and city should be able to provide you with publications outlining their payroll withholding rules.

b. Loans

An employer that has loaned you money can withhold money from your pay to satisfy that loan. However, it is illegal to make any such deduction if it would reduce your pay to below the minimum wage.

Example: *Bruce works 40 hours a week at $6 per hour making deliveries for an auto parts store. He is paid each Saturday. One Monday morning, the battery in his car went dead. His employer authorized Bruce to replace his car's battery with a new one out of the store's stock—if he agreed that the price of the new battery, $100, would be deducted from his pay.*

However, it took three weeks for the store to be fully paid for the battery. Under the FLSA, Bruce's employer could legally deduct no more than $34 per week from his gross pay to cover the battery. To deduct more would drop Bruce's pay rate to below the required minimum of $5.15 per hour.

c. Debts and wage garnishments

If you owe someone money and do not pay, that person might sue you and obtain a court judgment against you. If you do not pay the judgment, the creditor may try to collect by taking a portion of your paycheck until the judgment is paid in full. This is called a wage attachment or wage garnishment. Except in a few situations—student loans, child support, alimony and taxes—a creditor must sue you and obtain a court judgment before he or she can garnish your wages.

A wage garnishment works simply. Once the creditor has a judgment, he or she delivers a copy of it to a sheriff or marshal, who in turn sends a copy to your employer. Your employer must immediately:

- notify you of the garnishment
- begin withholding a portion of your wages, and
- give you information on how you can protest the garnishment.

Protesting is straightforward. You file a paper with the court and obtain a hearing date. At the hearing, you can present evidence showing that your expenses are very high and that you need all of your paycheck to live on. The judge has the discretion to terminate the wage garnishment or let it remain.

A federal law, the Consumer Credit Protection Act (15 U.S.C. §1673), prohibits judgment creditors from taking more than 25% of your net earnings through a wage garnishment to satisfy a debt. A few states offer greater protection, however. In Delaware, for example, judgment creditors cannot take more than 15% of your wages.

The Consumer Credit Protection Act also prohibits your employer from firing you because your wages are garnished to satisfy a single debt. If two judgment creditors garnish your wages or one judgment creditor garnishes your wages to pay two different judgments, however, you can be fired. Again, some state laws offer employees stronger job protection. In Washington, for example, an employer cannot fire you unless your wages are garnished by three different creditors or to satisfy three different judgments within a year. In Connecticut, you cannot be fired unless your employer has to deal with more than seven creditors or judgments in a single year.

For more information on debts, getting sued and wage garnishments, see *Money Troubles: Legal Strategies to Cope With Your Debts,* by Robin Leonard (Nolo).

There are several types of statutes that prohibit employers from retaliating against an employee for being subject to a wage garnishment. (See the chart below.) They differ in how many garnishments an employee is allowed per year and still have his or her job protected.

Most state laws have a general provision protecting from employer retribution employees who have their wages garnished. Some states prohibit retaliation if the employee has one garnishment per year; some laws apply to more than one garnishment. To heap on a little legal intrigue, many state statutes simply do not specify whether the protection extends to one garnishment per year or to multiple garnishments for one debt or to something else. If you run up against this confusion, contact your state's consumer protection agency for help.

Another type of anti-retribution for wage garnishment statute is one that applies to cases in which income is withheld to satisfy child support obligations. (See also Section F1e.) Employers may not fire employees merely because they are subject to this type of order, regardless of the quantity of garnishments.

Of course, none of these statutes prohibit firing for just cause. They only prohibit firing an employee solely because of the wage garnishment.

Additional Laws May Apply

If the chart below indicates that your state has no statute, this means there is no law that specifically addresses the issue. However, there may be a state administrative regulation or local ordinance that does control. Call your state labor department for more information. (See the Appendix for contact details.)

State Laws on Wage Garnishments	
Alabama	Employees may not be fired and individuals may not be denied employment for having wages garnished for child support obligations. Violators will be charged with contempt. Ala. Code §30-3-70
Alaska	Employees may not be disciplined or fired and individuals may not be denied employment for having wages assigned for child support obligations. Violators will be fined up to $1,000. Alaska Stat. §25.27.062(f)
Arizona	Employees may not be discriminated against, fired or disciplined and individuals may not be denied employment because of wage assignment to provide child support obligations. Ariz. Rev. Stat. §23-722.02(B)
Arkansas	Employees may not be fired or disciplined and individuals may not be denied employment for having a wage assignment for child support obligations. Violators will be fined up to $50 per day. Ark. Stat. Ann. §9-14-226
California	Employees may not be fired for having one wage garnishment. Cal. Lab. Code §2929b Employees may not be fired, disciplined or discriminated against in hiring because of an order to withhold wages for child support. Employers may be fined up to $500 for violating the law. Cal. Family Code §5290
Colorado	Employees may not be fired for having wages garnished. Colo. Rev. Stat. §13-54.5-110 Employees may not be fired, disciplined or discriminated against in hiring because of a notice to withhold income for child support. Colo. Rev. Stat. §14-14-111.5(4)(i)

Connecticut	Employees may not be fired for having wages garnished unless they have more than seven in one calendar year. Conn. Gen. Stat. Ann. §52-361a(j) Employees may not be discriminated against, fired or disciplined and individuals may not be denied employment because of wage garnishments for child support. Employers who violate the law may be fined up to $1,000. Conn. Gen. Stat. Ann. §52-362(j)
Delaware	Employees may not be fired for having wages garnished. Del. Code Ann. tit. 10 §3509 Employers who violate the law may be fined up to $1,000, imprisoned up to 90 days or both for the first offense; each subsequent offense carries a penalty of a fine up to $5,000, one year in prison or both. An employer who refuses to hire someone because of such a wage attachment may be fined up to $200 for each offense. Corporations are subject to criminal charges. Del. Code Ann. tit. 13 §513(b)(10)
District of Columbia	Employees may not be fired for having wages garnished. D.C. Code Ann. §16-584 Employers who refuse to hire individuals or who discriminate against or fire employees because of wage garnishments for child support may be fined up to $1,000. D.C. Code Ann. §30-519
Florida	Employees may not be disciplined because of a garnishment order for alimony or child support. Employers who violate the law may be held in contempt. Fla. Stat. §61.12(2)
Georgia	Employees may not be fired for having one wage garnishment. Ga. Code Ann. §18-4-7 Employees who voluntarily assign a portion of their wages for child support payments may not be fired. Ga. Code Ann. §19-11-20
Hawaii	Employees may not be fired for having a wage assignment for child support obligations. Haw. Rev. Stat. §378-25 Employees may not be fired and individuals may not be denied employment for having wages garnished. Haw. Rev. Stat. §378-32(1)
Idaho	An employer may not discharge an employee on the basis of a creditor's garnishment order. Idaho Code §28-45-105 An employer may not fire or discipline an employee or refuse to hire an individual because of an income withholding order for child support. Employees may sue for double the amount of lost wages and other damages resulting from a violation; employers may be fined up to $300 and be ordered to reinstate or hire the individual. Idaho Code §32-1211
Illinois	An employee may not be discharged because of a single garnishment. 735 Ill. Comp. Stat. 5/12-818 An employee may not be fired, discriminated against in hiring or penalized in any way because of an income withholding order for child support. 750 Ill. Comp. Stat. 5/706.1(E)(4)
Indiana	Employees may not be fired for having wages garnished. Ind. Code Ann. §24-4.5-5-106

Iowa	Employees may not be fired or disciplined for having wages garnished. Iowa Code §252D.10
Kansas	Employees may not be fired for having wages garnished. Kan. Stat. Ann. §60-2311
	Employees may not be fired or disciplined and individuals may not be denied employment because of an order to withhold wages for child support. Employers who violate the law may be fined up to $500 and attorneys' fees. Kan. Stat. Ann. §23-4, 108(j)
Kentucky	Employees may not be fired for having one wage garnishment. Ky. Rev. Stat. §427.140
	Employees may not be fired or disciplined and individuals may not be denied employment because of an order to withhold wages or wage assignment for child support. Ky. Rev. Stat. §405.465(7)
Louisiana	Employees may not be fired for having one wage garnishment. An employee may be discharged for having three or more garnishments for unrelated debts in a two-year period. La. Rev. Stat. Ann. §23:731(C)
	Employees may not be fired, disciplined or otherwise penalized for having income withheld for child support. La. Rev. Stat. Ann. §46.236.3(J)
Maine	Employees may not be fired for having wages garnished. Me. Rev. Stat. Ann. tit. 14, §3127-B(6)
	Employers who fire, discipline or discriminate against an employer or who refuse to hire an individual because of withholding orders for child support may be fined up to $5,000. They may also be liable for compensatory and punitive damages, plus attorneys' fees and costs. Me. Rev. Stat. Ann. tit. 19A, §2306(7)(D)
Maryland	Employees may not be fired for having one wage garnishment in a year. Md. Com. Law Code Ann. §15-606
	Employees may not be fired, refused a promotion or retaliated against and individuals cannot be denied employment because of a withholding order for child support. Md. Family Law Code Ann. tit. 10, §127(c)
Massachusetts	Employees may not be fired or disciplined and individuals cannot be denied employment because of a withholding order for child support. Employers who violate the law may be fined $1,000 and may be liable for the employee's lost wages and benefits. Mass. Ann. Laws ch. 119A, §12(f)(2)
Michigan	Employees may not be fired for having one or more garnishments. Mich. Comp. Laws §§600.4015 and following
	Employees may not be fired, refused a promotion or penalized and individuals cannot be denied employment because of an income withholding order for child support. Employers who violate the law must reinstate the employee with backpay and may be fined up to $500. Mich. Comp. Laws §552.623

Minnesota	Employees may not be fired or disciplined for having wages garnished. Minn. Stat. Ann. §571.927
	Employees may not be fired or disciplined and individuals cannot be denied employment because of a wage or salary withholding order for child support. Minn. Stat. Ann. §518.611 (Subd. 5)(c)
Mississippi	Employees may not be fired, disciplined or otherwise penalized and an individual may not be refused employment for having wages garnished for child or spousal support obligations. Miss. Code Ann. §93-11-111(9)
Missouri	Employees may not be fired or disciplined for having one wage garnishment. Mo. Ann. Stat. §525.030(5)
	Employees may not be fired or disciplined and an individual shall not be denied employment for having wages assigned for child support obligations. Mo. Ann. Stat. §452.350(9)
Montana	Employees may not be fired or discriminated against and an individual may not be denied employment for having wages assigned for child support obligations. Employers who violate this law may be fined from $150 to $500 and required to reinstate the employee and pay backpay. Mont. Code Ann. §40-5-422
	An employer may not fire an employee because of a garnishment of wages. Mont. Code §39-2-302
Nebraska	Employees may not be fired for having one wage garnishment. Neb. Rev. Stat. §25-1558(6)
	Employees may not be discriminated against in hiring or be fired, demoted or disciplined for having wages assigned for child support obligations. Employers who violate this law may be fined up to $500 and required to reinstate the employee and pay backpay. Neb. Rev. Stat. §43-1725
Nevada	Employees may not be fired or disciplined for having wages garnished. Nev. Rev. Stat. §31.298
	Employees may not be fired or disciplined and an individual may not be refused employment because of an order to withhold income for child support. Employers who violate the law must hire or reinstate the employee with no loss of pay or benefits, are liable for support payments not withheld and will be fined $1,000. If an employee takes the complaint to court and wins, the employer is liable for costs and attorneys' fees of at least $2,500. Nev. Rev. Stat. §31A.120
New Hampshire	Employees may not be fired or disciplined and individuals may not be denied employment for having wages garnished for child support obligations. Employers who violate this law may be fined up to $1,000. N.H. Rev. Stat. Ann. §458-B:6(VII)

New Jersey	Employees may not be fired for having one or more wage garnishments. N.J. Stat. Ann. §2A:17-56.12
	Employees may not be fired or disciplined and individuals may not be denied employment for having income withheld for child support obligations. Employers who violate the law may be liable for compensatory damages, including costs and lost income. N.J. Stat. Ann. §2A:17-56.11(a)
New Mexico	Employees may not be fired, disciplined or otherwise penalized and an individual may not be denied employment for having wages garnished for child support obligations. N.M. Stat. Ann. §40-4A-11
New York	Employees cannot be fired, laid off or denied promotions and individuals cannot be denied employment because of past or pending wage garnishments. Employers who violate this law may be liable for six weeks of lost wages and forced to reinstate or hire the individual. If the violation is against someone with an income deduction order for child support, the employer may be fined up to $500 for a first offense and up to $1,000 for additional offenses. N.Y. Civ. Prac. L. & R. §5252
North Carolina	Employees may not be fired or disciplined and individuals may not be denied employment for having wages garnished for child support obligations. Employers who violate this law may be fined $100 for a first offense, $500 for a second offense and $1,000 for a third offense. N.C. Gen. Stat. §110.136.8(e)
	Employees may not be fired for having wages garnished to pay debts owed a public hospital. N.C. Gen. Stat. §131E-50
North Dakota	Employees may not be fired for having wages garnished, and within 90 days, may sue for twice the amount of wages withheld, plus reinstatement. N.D. Cent. Code §32-09.1-18
	Employers who fire or in any way penalize an employee whose wages have been ordered withheld for child support may be sued for reinstatement, lost wages and attorneys' fees. N.D. Cent. Code §§14.09-09.3
Ohio	An employer who discharges an employee because of a child support deduction order is subject to a fine of $50 to $200 and ten to 30 days in jail. Ohio Rev. Code §§2301.39 and .99
	No employer may discharge an employee on the basis of one garnishment in any 12-month period. Ohio Rev. Code §2716.05
Oklahoma	An employer may not fire, suspend, refuse to promote or discipline an employee because of a wage assignment. An employer who does becomes liable for all lost wages and benefits, plus reinstatement. Okla. Stat. Ann. tit. 56 §240.2(D)(18)
	Employees may not be fired for having wages garnished, unless there are more than two in a year. Okla. Stat. Ann. tit. 14A, §5-106
	An employer may not fire, suspend, refuse to promote or discipline an employee because of a wage assignment for child support. Okla. Stat. Ann. tit. 12, §1171.3(E)(15)

Oregon	Employees may not be fired for having wages garnished. Or. Rev. Stat. §23.185(5)
	An employer may not fire or discriminate against an employee or refuse an individual employment because of an order to withhold wages for child support. Employers who violate the law may be liable for compensatory damages and a fine up to $1,000. Or. Rev. Stat. §25.363(3)(A)
Pennsylvania	Employees may not be fired or disciplined for having wages garnished for child support obligations. Employers who violate the law may be held in contempt and fined or jailed. 23 Pa. Cons. Stat. Ann. §4348
Rhode Island	An employer who discharges or discriminates against an employee because of a garnishment for child support shall be liable for all damages, a $100 fine and an order of reinstatement. R.I. Gen. Laws §15-5-26
South Carolina	Employees may not be fired for having wages garnished for consumer debt. S.C. Code Ann. §37-5-106
	Employees may not be fired, discriminated against in hiring or penalized for having wages garnished for child support. S.C. Code Ann. §§20-7-1315(F)(9) and (I)(1)
South Dakota	Employers who fire, discipline or penalize an employee or refuse to hire an individual because of a garnishment order for child support are guilty of a petty offense. S.D. Codified Laws Ann. §25-7A-46
Tennessee	Employees may not be fired or disciplined because of having wages garnished for child support. Tenn. Code Ann. §36-5-501(h)
Texas	Employees may not be fired or disciplined nor may they refuse to hire an individual for having wages garnished for child support obligations. Tex. Fam. Code Ann. §158.209
Utah	Employees may not be fired for having one wage garnishment. Utah Code Ann. §70C-7-104
	An employer who discharges, refuses to employ or takes disciplinary action against an employee because of an order to withhold wages for child support is liable for the amount of the garnishment plus costs, interest and attorneys' fees not to exceed $1,000. Utah Code Ann. §62A-11-316
Vermont	No employer may discharge an employee because of garnishment or the trustee process. Any firing within 60 days of trustee process is presumed to be in retaliation, entitling the former employee to reinstatement, back wages, damages and court costs. Vt. Stat. Ann. tit. 12 §3172
	Employees may not be fired or disciplined for having wages assigned for child support. Employers who violate the law may be fined up to $100. Vt. Stat. Ann. tit. 15 §790

Virginia	Employees may not be fired for having wages garnished for one debt. Va. Code §34-29(f)
	No employer shall fire or discipline an employee or refuse to hire an individual because of a withholding order for child support. An employer who violates this law may be fined up to $1,000. Va. Code Ann. §20-79.3.A(9)
	No employer may fire an employee because of a voluntary assignment of earnings to settle a support debt or lien or an order to withhold. Va. Code Ann. §63.1-271
Washington	Employees may not be fired for having wages garnished, unless the employee has three or more on separate debts within a year. Wash. Rev. Code Ann. §6.27.170
	No employer may discharge or discriminate against an employee, or refuse to hire an applicant, because of an assignment of earnings for child support. Violations of the statute subject the employer to double the amount of lost wages, damages, costs and attorney fees and a civil penalty of not more than $2,500 per violation, plus court orders to rehire, reinstate or to hire. Wash. Rev. Code Ann. §§26.18.110(8) and 74.20A.230
West Virginia	Employees may not be fired or receive any reprisals for having wages garnished for a consumer credit sale or loan. W.Va. Code §46A-2-131
	Employees may not be fired or discriminated against, nor applicants not hired, for having wages garnished for spousal or child support obligation. Employers who violate the law may be fined from $500 to $1,000. W.Va. Code §48A-5-3(r)
Wisconsin	Employers may not take any adverse action against employees for having wages garnished. Those who violate this law may be fined up to $500 and made to reinstate and pay backpay. Wis. Stat. Ann. §812.43
	Employees may not be fired or disciplined, nor may job applicants be refused, for having wages garnished for child support. Wis. Stat. Ann. §767.265(6)(c)
Wyoming	Employees may not be fired for having wages garnished. Wyo. Stat. §1-15-509
	Employees may not be fired, disciplined or penalized for having wages garnished for child support obligations. Wyo. Stat. §20-6-218

d. Student loans

The federal Emergency Unemployment Compensation Act of 1991 extended unemployment insurance for Americans who are out of work (20 U.S.C. §1095a). A rider to that bill authorizes the U.S. Department of Education or any agency trying to collect a student loan on behalf of the Department of Education to garnish up to 10% of a former student's net pay if he or she is in default on a student loan.

The Department of Education does not have to sue you before garnishing your wages. But at least 30 days before the garnishment is set to begin, you must be notified in writing of:

- the amount the Department believes you owe
- how you can obtain a copy of records relating to the loan
- how to enter into a voluntary repayment schedule, and
- how to request a hearing on the proposed garnishment.

The law includes only one specific ground upon which you can object to the garnishment: that you returned to work within the past 12 months after having been fired or laid off.

e. Child support and alimony

The federal Family Support Act of 1988 (102 U.S. Stat. §2343) requires that all new or modified child support orders include an automatic wage withholding order. If child support is combined with alimony and paid as family support, the wage withholding applies to the payment. It is not required for orders of alimony only.

In an automatic wage withholding order, a court orders you to pay child support; then the court or your child's other parent sends a copy of the order to your employer. At each pay period, your employer withholds a portion of your pay and sends it on to the parent who has custody.

In most states, where there is not an automatic wage attachment, employers must withhold wages if you are one month delinquent in paying support. But an employer cannot discipline, fire or refuse to hire you because your pay is subject to a child support wage withholding order. If an employer does discriminate against you, the employer can be fined by the state. (See Section F1c for specific state law provisions.)

f. Back taxes

If you owe the IRS and do not pay, the agency can grab most—but not all—of your wages. The amount that you get to keep is determined by the number of your dependents and the standard tax deduction to which you are entitled.

If the IRS wants your wages, it sends a wage levy notice to your employer, who must immediately give you a copy. On the back of the notice is an exemption claim form. You should fill out, sign and return this simple form to the IRS office that issued it within three days after you receive it. Your employer should not pay anything to the IRS until you have your chance to file your exemption claim.

If you do not file the claim form, your employer must pay you only $116 per week and give the rest to the IRS. An employer who ignores the IRS wage levy notice and pays you anyway is liable to the IRS for whatever amounts were wrongly paid. Once the wage levy takes effect, it continues until either the taxes are paid in full or the collection period expires—ten years from when the taxes are assessed.

Most state and some municipal taxing authorities also have the power to seize a portion of your wages—and some act even more quickly than the IRS does when you owe back taxes. State laws vary, however, as to the maximum amount of wages that the state can take. In California, for example, the state taxing authority cannot take more than 25% of your net pay.

2. What Cannot Be Deducted or Withheld

Only a few things are off-limits for an employer to deduct from an employee's paycheck:
- the value of time taken for meal periods (see Section D3)
- the cost of broken merchandise
- tools and materials used on the job
- required uniforms, and
- cash register shortages and losses due to theft.

The History of Payroll Withholding

The Social Security Act of 1935, a part of President Franklin D. Roosevelt's New Deal, was the first law to sink its teeth firmly into the typical paycheck. Intended only to save industrial and commercial hourly workers of the Depression era from poverty in old age, the original Social Security program required employers to withhold a mere 1% of workers' pay.

Since then, the Social Security Act has been amended many times. The age of eligibility has been lowered from 65 to 62, and coverage has been extended to people unable to work because of physical disabilities, government employees, self-employed people and a number of other groups not covered by the original Act. Consequently, the amount withheld from most wages to pay for Social Security programs now is more than 7%.

The federal income tax, the other major cause of paycheck shrinkage, was created when the 16th Amendment to the U.S. Constitution was passed in 1913. The original federal income tax rates ranged from 1% to 7% of annual income above $3,000—a lot of money back then.

To pay for World War II, however, the government raised the income tax rates so dramatically that the tax on the top income level bracket hit a record of 94% in 1944 and 1945. The minimum income subject to taxation was lowered so that most working people were for the first time subject to some income tax.

Politicians, hoping to assuage the public angst over paying a large yearly lump sum, decided to lessen the trauma by making employers withhold the income tax, little by little, from workers' pay each week.

By the 1970s, employees had become so accustomed to having large sums of money withheld from their pay that most states and cities—as well as nongovernment groups such as health insurance companies and pension fund managers—instituted additional withholding programs.

Today, it is common for employees to have more than a third of their pay withheld by their employers on behalf of government, with still more withheld to finance private benefit plans.

G. Enforcing Your Right to Be Paid Fairly

Your first step in enforcing your right to be paid fairly should be to decide whether your complaint involves a violation of a law, or is simply a matter of disagreement or misunderstanding between you and your employer.

If, for example, your employer refused to pay you time-and-one-half for five hours of overtime that you worked, then the issue would be covered by the FLSA. But if you had been working under the impression that you would get a raise every year—a matter not covered by the FLSA—and your employer will not give you one, then the issue is left for you to resolve with your employer, without the clout that a law can lend.

Once you have refined your complaint, try discussing it with your employer or former employer before filing any official action. Some companies have dispute resolution programs—usually outlined in their employee manuals—that can help you resolve a pay dispute without resorting to legal action. (See Chapter 18, Section A.)

H. Filing a Complaint or Lawsuit

If your complaint involves what you believe is a violation of the FLSA—for example, you have not been paid fairly or on time—contact your local office of the Wage and Hour Division of the U.S. Department of Labor, listed in the federal government section of the telephone directory and available on the agency's website at http://www.dol.gov.

If you call, visit or write to your local Wage and Hour Division office, workers there will take down the information you provide and transcribe it onto a complaint form. You can request one of these forms and fill it out yourself. But since the staff members are familiar with which details are legally pertinent, they usually prefer to fill it out themselves. They will probably ask you to provide photocopies of documents relevant to your dispute, such as pay stubs.

Review the completed complaint form and attached documents to be sure they are correct and as complete as possible. If you are assigned to a staff person who seems particularly unsympathetic or unhelpful, calmly and politely ask to speak with someone else. Also, keep in mind that a huge dollop of patience is required. The process—from filing a complaint through investigation and the final outcome—typically takes from one to three years.

Once your complaint has been put together, U.S. Labor Department investigators will take over the job of gathering additional data which should either prove or disprove your complaint.

If the thought of reporting your employer to the authorities frightens you, take some comfort in knowing that Labor Department investigators must keep the identities of those who file such complaints confidential. Also, it is illegal for an employer to fire or otherwise discriminate against an employee for filing a complaint under the FLSA, or for participating in a legal proceeding related to its enforcement. Many state laws also provide protection for employees who file state wage and hour complaints. (See Section E5.)

Where the federal investigators find violations of the FLSA, the action that they then take will depend upon the severity of the violations and whether or not the employer appears to have been violating the law willfully.

When the violations are severe and apparently willful, the Labor Department may ask the Justice Department to bring criminal charges against the employer. Government lawyers will handle the matter for you. If convicted, a first-time violator of the FLSA may be fined by the courts; subsequent convictions can result in both fines and imprisonment.

If the violations are not too severe, or if the Labor Department investigators feel the infractions were not willful, one of the following steps may be taken:

- The Labor Department may set up and supervise a plan for your employer to pay back wages to you and anyone else injured by the violations.
- The Secretary of Labor may file a lawsuit asking the court to order your employer to pay you the wages due, plus an equal amount as damages. The court may also issue an injunction or order preventing your employer from continuing the illegal behavior.
- You may file your own lawsuit under the FLSA to recover the wages you're owed, plus other damages, attorney fees and court costs. You will probably need to hire a lawyer to help with this type of lawsuit. (See Chapter 18, Section D.)

When You Cannot Sue Under the FLSA

You cannot file an FLSA lawsuit if your employer has already paid back wages to you under the supervision of the Labor Department. This amounts to an incentive system for employers: An employer who cooperates in correcting any violations discovered by the Wage and Hour Division investigators must pay only the back wages that are due. An employer who refuses to cooperate by paying back wages stands the chance of having to pay double the wages, plus your attorney's fees and costs, plus the cost of its own defense.

You cannot bring a lawsuit under the FLSA if the Secretary of Labor has already done so on your behalf. And if you file a lawsuit and then the Secretary of Labor files a lawsuit over the same violations, your right to sue ends and the Labor Department takes over.

I. Violations of State and Local Laws

The laws of each state and municipality specify which branch of government is responsible for enforcing state and local wage and hour laws, and what remedies—criminal, civil or both—are available. In most states, the Labor Department is authorized to take action on your behalf to recover unpaid wages. (See the Appendix for contact information.)

If you are dissatisfied with the action taken by the government agency responsible for enforcing state or local wage and hour laws, consider resolving your problem in small claims court. Because of the relatively small amounts of money typically involved, disputes over wages, commissions or other forms of compensation can often be pursued quickly and inexpensively in small claims courts without requiring help from a lawyer.

For a complete explanation of small claims court—from preparing a case through collecting a judgment—see *Everybody's Guide to Small Claims Court,* by Ralph Warner (Nolo).

Despite sweeping reforms proposed and reproposed by politicians, health insurance remains an expensive necessity. Long term treatment of a medical condition or even a short hospital stay is likely to quickly bankrupt most Americans. To help foot the bills, most employers offer their employees some type of group insurance plan.

The specifics of insurance coverage are dictated by the terms of individual policies. This chapter discusses the broader state and federal legal controls on health insurance and will help you evaluate whether any insurance you have meets the minimum legal standards.

A. No Legal Right to Coverage

While many workers feel insurance coverage is an entitlement, in reality, offering health insurance to employees is purely voluntary—a matter of tradition, not law. This truth flies in the face of many firmly held beliefs about workplace benefits. But in fact, there is no federal law that requires employers to provide or pay for health insurance coverage for all current employees, or even fulltime employees. Over eight million employed workers have no health insurance. And millions more are underinsured.

No federal legal scheme requires every employer to offer insurance coverage. However, an employer who promises to provide health insurance—in an employee manual, for example—must follow through on the promise. And benefits must be provided without discriminating against any employee or group of employees. That includes employees who are statistically more likely to incur high medical costs. For example, federal laws specifically provide that women workers and older workers must be provided with the same coverage as other workers. (See Chapter 8, Sections C and E.) One grand exception to this general rule is that many state laws now allow employers to offer health plans that offer higher premiums to smokers. (See Chapter 7, Section E.)

In recent years, some companies have discontinued or cut back on insurance coverage they offer employees, simply because of the expense. The legal rule emerging is that of evenhandedness: Employers cannot offer insurance coverage to some employees and deny it to others.

But because health insurance is a job benefit that is not regulated by law, employers are otherwise free to fashion a plan of any stripe. They may:
- require employees to contribute to the cost of premiums
- offer reduced reimbursement or pro rata coverage to parttime employees
- limit options to one insurance plan or offer a variety of choices, or
- give employees a sum of money earmarked for insurance coverage that may be applied to any chosen plan.

As anyone who has read the fine print on a health insurance policy can attest, insurers, too, place conditions on the coverage they provide. The most nettling of these limitations is on preexisting conditions. Under these provisions, if you have had a recent illness or have a chronic medical condition, you may be denied coverage, be made to wait a specific time period until your condition will be covered or be forced to pay high premiums for specialized coverage. The greatest headway on doing away with the preexisting condition denial of coverage has been made in the federal law requiring continuing coverage for former employees. (See Section C3.)

Traditionally, employers that have provided healthcare coverage have done so through an indemnity or reimbursement plan which pays the doctor or hospital directly, or reimburses the employee for medical expenses he or she has already paid. Blue Cross/Blue Shield is a traditional type of plan.

While traditional coverage allowing employees to seek out their preferred medical provider is still widely used, a growing number of employers today provide coverage through the alternatives of a health maintenance organization (HMO) or a preferred provider organization (PPO).

An HMO is comprised of hospitals and doctors who provide specified medical services to employees for a fixed monthly fee. Within the HMO service area, covered employees must use the HMO hospitals and doctors unless it's an emergency or they receive permission to go elsewhere.

A PPO is a network of hospitals and doctors who agree to provide medical care for specified fees. Often the network is put together by an insurance company that also administers it. Employees usually can choose between using the network's hospitals and doctors or going elsewhere.

There are two main categories of employee health insurance: coverage for current employees and coverage for former employees.

But Wait — There's More

Insurance—and all its crafty permutations—has insinuated itself into many aspects of workplace law. You will find discussions of other insurance-related issues peppered throughout the book, including:

- privacy issues, such as employers' access to medical records (see Chapter 6, Section A)
- coverage for unemployed workers provided by state unemployment insurance programs (see Chapter 12)
- coverage for sick or disabled workers provided by state workers' compensation programs (see Chapter 13), by the Social Security disability system (see Chapter 14) and by private and state disability programs (see Chapter 10, Section K)
- coverage or time off provided for family and medical leave (see Chapter 5), and
- continuing coverage after retirement (see Chapter 15).

B. Coverage for Current Employees

No law mandates insurance coverage in every workplace. But employees can take some insurance aid and comfort from a number of state laws—and from a new federal law imposing some fundamental fairness in coverage.

1. State Laws

A few states, counties and cities now require some employers to provide health insurance coverage for some employees who work there. For example, Hawaii requires employers to provide coverage to employees earning a set amount per month or more (Haw. Rev. Stat. §393-11).

In addition, some state laws require that employers who offer insurance to employees must provide certain minimum coverage. The state requirements vary considerably, but typical minimums include coverage for medical and surgical benefits, treatment of mental illness, alcoholism and drug abuse and preventative testing such as mammograms and PAP smears. Check with your state's health commissioner to find out whether there is any minimum mandated coverage in your area.

Some states impose additional restrictions on workplace health insurance. For example, a growing number of them make it illegal for employers to fire employees because they file a legitimate claim against their company's health insurance.

Why Many Employers No Longer Pay

For many people, the greatest shock involved in finding their first job or securing a new one comes from learning that few employers pay all the costs of health insurance anymore—and that a growing number of employers do not pay anything at all.

The sad truth is that America's healthcare costs are so out of control that most companies are no longer willing or able to pay for them. In recent years, U.S. healthcare costs have been rising at nearly three times the rate of inflation.

2. The Health Insurance Portability Act

The Health Insurance Portability and Accountability Act, a federal law that took effect in July of 1997, should make it easier for employees to change jobs without losing insurance coverage—and to get coverage in the first place.

The law's biggest promise is to improve the portability of health insurance coverage. But in addition, it purports to:

- take aim against healthcare discrimination, fraud and abuse, and
- promote the use of medical savings accounts.

a. Increased portability

Group insurers now face limits when attempting to limit enrollment because of preexisting medical conditions.

Under the new law, for example, pregnancy is no longer considered a preexisting condition—and newborns or newly adopted children cannot be excluded if they are enrolled within 30 days of birth or adoption.

The maximum amount of time a group health insurance plan, HMO or self-insured plan may exclude someone on the basis of a preexisting condition is 12 months. This exclusion period is reduced by the amount of time an employee previously had continuous coverage through other private insurance or public insurance programs.

Insurers must offer individual coverage to a person who loses group coverage if the individual:

- was continuously covered for 18 months under a group health plan
- has exhausted COBRA coverage (see Section C), or
- is ineligible for coverage through government programs such as Medicare or Medicaid.

b. Discrimination protection

Group health plans and employers cannot deny coverage for an individual and his or her dependents based on health status, physical or mental medical condition, claims experience, genetic information, or disability or domestic violence.

The Inspector General and U.S. Attorney General are charged with establishing a program to coordinate federal, state, and local programs to control health plan fraud and abuse—and criminal penalties can now be imposed for defrauding any health benefits program.

c. Medical savings accounts

The Medical Savings Account (or MSA) program offers tax advantages for employees whose sole health coverage is a high-deductible catastrophic health plan; employees can't also be covered by basic health insurance with small deductibles and co-pay requirements. Only self-employed workers and those who work at places with 50 or fewer workers during the past two years may participate.

The catastrophic health insurance policy under this program must satisfy a number of guidelines.

If you qualify and secure a catastrophic policy, your employer can make a tax-free contribution each year to your MSA of up to 65% of the deductible for an individual or 75% for a family.

You can use your MSA to pay for medical expenses not covered by the catastrophic insurance.

Example: *Radiant Corporation, a company employing 45 people, buys a cata-strophic health insurance policy for each of its employees. For Stan, who has a family, the deductible is $4,000. Radiant contributes $3,000 to Stan's MSA. Stan's wife is injured in a car accident and incurs $10,000 in medical expenses. Stan's MSA pays $3,000 of the deductible; Stan uses $1,000 from his bank account to pay the rest. The $3,000 that Radiant paid into Stan's MSA is a tax-deductible business expense for Radiant and is tax-free to Stan.*

Unused money stays in your MSA, earning tax-free income. For younger employees, there are penalties if money is removed for purposes other than medical care, but at age 65, an employee can remove the balance in his or her account for any reason, without penalty. During the test period, the program will be available only to the first 750,000 participants each year.

It is still too soon to tell whether MSAs will meet their lofty goals of encouraging better healthcare at lower costs. Critics fret that beckoning refunds will cause consumers to forego preventative and routine medical care. And they fear that people with high medical expenses will end up paying more than ever.

C. Coverage for Former Employees

A federal workplace law, the Consolidated Omnibus Budget Reconciliation Act, or COBRA (29 U.S.C. §1162), requires your employer to offer you—and your spouse and dependents—continuing insurance coverage if:

- you lose insurance coverage because your number of workhours is reduced, or
- you lose your job for any reason other than gross misconduct. Because the law is still relatively new, the courts are still grappling with the question of how egregious the workplace behavior must be to qualify as gross misconduct. So far, courts have ruled that inefficiency, poor performance, negligence or errors in judgment on the job are not enough. There must be some deliberate, wrongful violations of workplace standards to qualify as gross misconduct.

COBRA was intended to extend access to group health insurance coverage to people who would otherwise be totally unprotected—and unlikely to be able to secure coverage on their own. The law applies to all employers with 20 or more employees. Under the law, employers need only make the insurance available; they need not pay for it. Employers may charge up to 102% of the base premium for continued coverage—the extra 2% thrown in to cover administrative costs.

Those covered under COBRA include:

- all individuals who are or were provided insurance coverage under an employer's group plan, and
- those individuals' beneficiaries—who typically include a spouse and dependent children.

1. Continuing Coverage

Qualified employees and former employees may elect to continue coverage up to 18 months after they quit or are fired or get laid off, or after a reduction in hours that makes them ineligible for coverage. Those who become disabled, however, can get COBRA coverage for 29 months—until Medicare payments typically kick in.

No one can choose to enroll in an insurance plan upon becoming ineligible for workplace coverage. COBRA extends only to those already enrolled when their health insurance coverage ceases.

In addition, COBRA provides that covered individuals must be given the right to convert to an individual policy at the end of the continuation period—although that coverage is usually significantly more expensive.

Insurance From Continuing or Former Employment

Medicare is a federal government program that assists older and some disabled people with their medical costs. Many people who are eligible for Medicare continue to work and have health insurance through their own or their spouse's employer.

And many other people keep their job-related health insurance after they retire, as part of their retirement benefits package, although they usually have to pay much more than a current employee.

Employment-based health plans require you to sign up for Medicare when you turn 65, but most of them will cover you in conjunction with Medicare. The health benefits or human resources office at your work or union can explain the details of coordinating coverage.

Just because you are eligible for a work-related health plan, however, does not mean that you have to continue with it. You may find that Medicare plus an additional limited policy—often called medigap—or Medicare through a health maintenance organization (HMO) provides you with better coverage at a better price than does your work's medical insurance combined with Medicare benefits.

Even if you decide not to participate in the regular health plan offered in your workplace, your employer's insurance company may offer you a different policy with limited coverage for some services Medicare does not cover at all, such as prescription drugs, dental care or hearing aids. Compare such a policy with the medigap policies and managed care plans discussed in this chapter to see which one offers you the best coverage for your money.

Adapted from Social Security, Medicare and Pensions: Get the Most Out of Your Retirement and Medical Benefits, *by Joseph L. Matthews with Dorothy Matthews Berman (Nolo).*

2. Coverage for Dependents

Beneficiaries or dependents may also elect to continue coverage for 18 months.
However, they may opt to have coverage continued for up to 36 months if any of the following occur:

- the covered employee dies
- they are divorced or legally separated from the covered employee
- a minor dependent child turns 18 or otherwise ceases to be considered a dependent under the plan, or
- they become disabled and eligible for Social Security disability insurance benefits. (See Chapter 14.)

3. Preexisting Conditions

COBRA addresses the most common health insurance bugaboo: denial of coverage for preexisting conditions.

Under COBRA, coverage must be offered regardless of any preexisting medical conditions. And importantly, if an employee obtains new employment with coverage that contains exclusions or limitations for any such conditions, the former employer may not terminate coverage before the end of the COBRA coverage period. However, the employer may end coverage if a beneficiary such as a spouse is covered by another group health plan—as long as there is no significant gap in benefits.

Coordination Is Key for Some Plans

Many group insurance plans contain coordination of benefits (COB) provisions in which two policies provide overlapping coverage—a common situation for families with two working spouses. A COB provision establishes a hierarchy for determining which policy provides primary coverage and which provides secondary coverage.

Most COBs provide that if the primary insurer's obligation is less than the amount of the total bill, the insured can then submit a claim to the secondary insurer, asking for coverage for the amount not paid. If only one policy has a COB provision, the policy that does not have a COB clause is primarily responsible for paying; if the same person is covered as an employee and a dependent, the employee policy coverage is primary.

In addition, for coverage of children of two working parents covered by insurance, most states now follow the Birthday Rule. That rule provides that the parent who has a birthday earlier in the year is the one whose insurance will cover the children.

4. Enforcing COBRA

COBRA provides for a number of fines for employers and health insurance plan administrators who violate its requirements. However, the Act has so many complexities that no one can agree on exactly what circumstances release an employer from its requirements. And, frustratingly, there is no one place you can call to get help if you think your rights under COBRA have been violated. Parts of the law are administered by the U.S. Labor Department and other parts fall under the Internal Revenue Service—and the two agencies frequently refer COBRA complaints back and forth to each other.

If you have a COBRA-related question or complaint, you can try calling your local office of either of those agencies, but neither has a track record of actively enforcing COBRA requirements. Your employer is required to provide you with an explanation of your COBRA rights when you are enrolled in a group healthcare plan covering 20 or more employees. However, these materials are seldom well written or easy to understand.

In general, COBRA can be enforced only through an expensive lawsuit. That means that it typically can be used only by large groups of former employees who have been denied their rights to continue group health insurance coverage—and who can share the expense of hiring a lawyer and filing a lawsuit to enforce that right. (See Chapter 10, Section H.)

Getting More Help

If you need advice or run into problems claiming COBRA benefits, contact the Older Women's League; 666 Eleventh Street, NW, Suite 700; Washington, DC 20001; 202-783-6686. The organization also assists younger women and men.

He Also Hurts Who Sits and Waits

A recent study by the healthcare industry released the predictable information that the top three concerns of working Americans were:
- being unable to afford medical care
- losing health insurance and other benefits because of a job change, and
- having enough income if unable to work for an extended period due to illness or injury.

On a painful note of reality, the study also revealed that the average waiting time in a doctor's office was 24 minutes and 32 minutes in an emergency room.

And more of the same fear and loathing will come at a high price in the future. Healthcare experts estimate that annual healthcare spending in the U.S. will be $1.8 trillion dollars in the year 2000 and $16 trillion in the year 2030.

Source: Source Book of Health Insurance Data for 1997-1998, *published by the Health Insurance Association of America (HIAA).*

D. State Laws on Insurance Continuation

Because COBRA generally cannot be enforced by any means other than a complex and expensive lawsuit, state laws that give former employees the right to continue group health insurance coverage after leaving a job are often a better alternative.

State laws often provide interesting twists that make it easier to get continued coverage. California, for example, provides for three months of group insurance coverage in addition to COBRA coverage, although in most states, you must choose one or the other. A number of states—including California—provide special insurance protections for older workers, who are most likely to suffer in a staff cut. And in Washington, the spouse and children of a worker who is fired even after severe misconduct may be entitled to continued coverage. (See the chart below.)

To be eligible for continued coverage, most state laws require that an employee must be covered for a certain time—three months is common—just before being terminated. In nearly all instances, any continuation of coverage will be at your expense—just as it would be under COBRA.

However, the specific requirements of these laws and how they are enforced vary tremendously. For more specific information, contact your state's insurance department, or read the controlling laws at a local law library. (See Chapter 18, Section E.) In addition, the plant closing laws of a few states also may give you the right to continue group health insurance coverage. (See Chapter 10, Section H.)

Additional Laws May Apply

If the chart below indicates that your state has no statute, this means there is no law that specifically addresses the issue. However, there may be a state administrative regulation or local ordinance that does control. Contact your state insurance commission or state labor department for more information. (See the Appendix for state labor department contact details.)

State Health Insurance Continuation Laws	
Alabama	No statute
Alaska	No statute
Arizona	No statute
Arkansas	Former employees and their dependents have the right to continue group insurance coverage for 120 days after the coverage would have ended because of a change in employment status. Employees must request continued coverage within ten days of the change of employment status. Employees, who must have had consistent coverage for three months before the change in employment status, are responsible for paying the premium. Ark. Stat. Ann. §23-86-114
California	Former employees and their dependents, including widows and widowers and divorced spouses, have the right to continue group insurance coverage for 90 days after termination, which shall run consecutive to any COBRA continuation benefits. Cal. Health & Safety Code §§1373.621 and 1373.6
	An employee whose group coverage terminates may convert to individual coverage without having to establish proof of eligibility, as long as the

employee was continuously covered for the preceding three months. The employer must notify the employee of this benefit within 15 days of termination of the group plan, and the employee must request continued coverage within 30 days of COBRA termination or 31 days of group plan termination. Cal. Health & Safety Code §1373.6

Employers whose insurance plans are subject to COBRA shall also offer coverage beyond the COBRA maximum to employees who are at least 60 years old and have worked for that employer for at least five years. Cal. Health & Safety Code §1173.621

Colorado	Former employees who had been covered for at least six months by group health insurance and their dependents have the right to continue that coverage for 18 months. Employees must apply for continued coverage within 31 days of termination. Employers must give employees written notice postmarked at least ten days after termination. If the employer does not provide timely notice, the employee has the right to coverage if payment is made within 60 days after termination. Colo. Rev. Stat. §10-16-108
Connecticut	Employees who are terminated and their eligible dependents have the right to continue group health insurance for 104 weeks after the coverage would have ended, provided they were continuously covered for six months before termination. If the employment has ended due to the employee's death, the employee's surviving spouse, former spouse or dependents may continue the coverage for up to 36 months. Employers must give notice of the right to continued coverage within ten days. The person who wants continued coverage must notify the employer of his or her election within 30 days. Conn. Gen. Stat. 38a-538
Delaware	No statute
District of Columbia	No statute
Florida	Former employees who were terminated and had been covered by group health insurance for at least three months and their eligible dependents have the right to convert the coverage to an individual policy. Employees must apply for converted coverage within 63 days after termination of the group policy. Fla. Stat. §627.6675
Georgia	Former employees and their eligible dependents who have been covered by group health insurance for at least six months have the right to continue coverage for three months after the end of employment. Ga. Code Ann. §33-24-21.1 and 21.2
Hawaii	Every policy for group life insurance must provide for the conversion to an individual policy upon termination of employment. The employee need not prove insurability. The conversion does not apply to disability or other

	supplementary benefits. The employee must apply within 30 days of termination. Haw. Rev. Stat. §431:10D-213(8)
Idaho	No statute
Illinois	Former employees and their dependents who were terminated and had been covered by group health insurance for at least three months have the right to continue group coverage unless they are covered by another group plan or by Medicare. Employees must request continued coverage within ten days of being terminated or of receiving notice of their right to continued coverage, whichever is later. The continued coverage need not include dental, vision, prescription drugs or other benefits other than hospital and major medical. 215 Ill. Comp. Stat. 5/367e
Indiana	An employee who loses coverage under a small employer's health plan, who has worked for that employer for at least one year and has been covered for at least three months, may continue the coverage for one year. The request must be made within 30 days of termination. Employers must notify employees within ten days of the date they become eligible for continued coverage. Ind. Code Ann. §27-8-15-31
Iowa	Former employees who were terminated have the right to continue group health insurance for nine months, but some types of coverage such as prescription drug benefits are excluded. Employees must have been covered by the employer during the three months prior to termination and must request continued coverage within ten days of receiving notice of their right to continued coverage. Continued coverage need not provide dental or vision benefits. Iowa Code Ann. §509B.3
Kansas	Former employees who were continuously covered for three months and their dependents are entitled to continued group health insurance coverage for six months after the end of employment. Employees must apply within 31 days after termination. At the end of the six-month period, the insurer must offer a comparable policy to former employees and their dependents who do not have other coverage. The insurer must also provide reasonable notice of this option at least once during the six-month period—and those who wish to continue coverage must apply for it within 31 days of receiving the notice. Kan. Stat. Ann. §40-2209(I)
Kentucky	Former employees and eligible dependents who had been covered by group health insurance for at least three months have the right to continue that coverage for 18 months. Those who wish to continue coverage must apply for it within 31 days of receiving the notice of its termination. Ky. Rev. Stat. Ann. §304.18-110
Louisiana	Former employees and their dependents can continue their health insurance for 12 months if they were continuously insured for three months prior to termination and are not eligible for another group plan. Continued coverage does not have to cover vision, dental and other benefits other than hospital

and major medical. La. Rev. Stat. Ann. §22:215:13

A deceased employee's surviving spouse who is 50 years old or older can continue group health coverage. La. Rev. Stat. Ann. §22:215.7

Maine	Former employees and their dependents who have been covered by group health insurance for three months can continue group coverage for one year or until they become eligible for another group plan or for Medicare. Former employees have 31 days from termination to elect continued coverage. Me. Rev. Stat. Ann. tit. 24-A, §2809-A
Maryland	Former employees and their divorced or surviving spouses and their dependents who were involuntarily terminated and had been covered for at least three months can continue coverage for 18 months. They have 45 days from the date of termination to elect continued coverage. Md. Code Ann. [Ins.] §15-409 Former employees and their dependents who were involuntarily terminated and had been covered for at least three months can continue coverage for six months. Md. Ann. Code [Ins.] §15-412
Massachusetts	Employee and dependents, or surviving spouse and dependents, may continue coverage for 39 weeks if employment is terminated due to the employee's death or because the employee is fired. If employment is terminated because of a plant closing, coverage may continue for 90 days. Failure to pay premiums on time acts as a waiver of the right to extended coverage. Mass. Gen. Laws Ann. ch. 175 §110G; ch. 176A, §8D; ch. 176B, §6A; ch. 176G, §4A
Michigan	No statute
Minnesota	Former employees who quit or were terminated for reasons other than gross misconduct or who have become ineligible for coverage due to a reduction in force have the right to continue group health coverage for themselves and their families for 18 months after it would otherwise end or until they become covered by another group plan, whichever comes first. Employers must notify eligible people within ten days of termination of the group plan, and the person has 60 days—from the date of termination or notice, whichever is later—to elect continued coverage. Minn. Stat. Ann. §62A.17
Mississippi	Former employees and their dependents are entitled to continued coverage for up to 12 months as long as the employee was continuously covered for the three months prior to termination. The continued coverage is for hospital and major medical benefits only. The employee must apply for continued coverage on or before the day that the group plan coverage terminates. Miss. Code Ann. §83-9-51
Missouri	Former employees who have been covered by a group health plan for at least three months have the right to continue that insurance for up to nine months after it would otherwise end. Employees are not entitled to continued coverage if they are eligible for Medicare or another group plan. Continued coverage benefits may be limited to hospital and major medical. Continued

	coverage must be requested within 31 days of termination. Mo. Ann. Stat. §376.428
Montana	If an employee's health insurance coverage ends because employment has terminated, the employer has gone out of business or the employer has left the plan without substituting a new one, an employee who has worked at least three months and his or her dependents are entitled to continued group or individual coverage. Continued coverage must be requested within 31 days of termination. No maximum coverage period is specified. Mont. Code Ann. §§33-22-508 to 510
Nebraska	Former employees are entitled to continue group health insurance for six months after being involuntarily terminated; termination due to a labor dispute is not considered involuntary. The employer must notify the employee of the right to continued coverage within ten days of termination, and the employee then has ten days to make the election. A surviving spouse and dependents of an employee who dies are entitled to one year's continuation. Neb. Rev. Stat. §44-1640 to 1643
Nevada	Former employees and their dependents are eligible for continued coverage if the employee was covered for the three months before termination. Employees must notify employers if they want continued coverage within 31 days of termination of the group plan. Nev. Rev. Stat. §§689B.120 Former employees of employers with fewer than 20 employees who have been covered by a group health plan for at least three months are entitled to continue coverage for 18 months. Eligible dependents are entitled to continue coverage for 36 months, as long as the dependents were covered under the policy for the preceding 12 consecutive months. Employees must notify employer if they want continued coverage within 60 days of the day they become eligible. No coverage if employee voluntarily quits. No continued coverage for vision and dental care. Nev. Rev. Stat. Ann. §§689B.245 and 689B.246
New Hampshire	Former employees and eligible dependents are entitled to group health plan continuation if employee is terminated or dies. Coverage continues for 29 months if termination is due to disability, 36 months for spouse upon separation or divorce or if the employee dies, and 18 months in all other situations. Available only if the employee has been insured for 60 days and applies within 31 days of termination. Employer must notify employee of right to continued coverage within 15 days of termination. N.H. Rev. Stat. Ann. §415.18(VII)
New Jersey	Former employees and eligible dependents are entitled to continuation of group health coverage if termination is due to total disability and they have been covered for three months or until they become eligible for other group coverage. N.J. Stat. Ann. §17B:27-51.12
New Mexico	Former employees have the right to continue group health insurance coverage for up to six months after it would otherwise end. Covered family members may convert to individual policies upon the former employee's death or divorce. The employer must notify the terminated employee of the right to

continued coverage, and the employee must exercise this right within 30 days of notification. N.M. Stat. Ann. §59A-18-16

New York

Former employees and their dependents who have been insured under the policy for at least three months have the right to continue group health coverage. Conversion is also available to the spouse and dependents of a deceased employee, or to the former spouse who loses coverage due to divorce from the employed spouse. Employers must notify employees of the right to continued coverage within 15 days before or after termination, and employees must apply within 45 days of termination.

Employees who convert at age 60 or later and have been insured for at least two years under the group policy have protected maximum premium costs. N.Y. Ins. Law §3221(e) to (i)

If the policy covers hospital, surgical and medical expenses only, continued coverage is available for up to 18 months for the former employee and 36 months for dependents. This type of continued coverage must be requested within 60 days from termination or notice, whichever is later. N.Y. Ins. Law §3221(m)

North Carolina

Former employees and their eligible dependents are entitled to continue group health plan coverage for 18 months if they have been covered by the plan for at least three consecutive months immediately preceding termination. Employers must notify employees of their right to continued coverage as part of the exit process, and the employee must request continued coverage within 31 days from termination. N.C. Gen. Stat. §58-53-25 to 55

North Dakota

Former employees who had been covered by group health insurance for at least three consecutive months immediately preceding termination have the right to continue that coverage for 39 weeks. The employee must request continued coverage within ten days of termination or of notice of the right to such coverage, whichever is later. An employee who is covered by Medicare is not entitled to continued coverage. The continued coverage need not include dental, vision, prescription drugs or other benefits besides hospital, surgical and major medical. N.D. Cent. Code §26.1-36-23

Ohio

Former employees who have been covered continuously during the three months prior to termination who were terminated involuntarily have the right to continue group health insurance coverage for six months after termination. The continued coverage need not include supplemental benefits such as dental, vision and mental health. The employer must notify the terminated employee of the right to continued coverage, and the employee must elect coverage within 31 days of termination or, if the employer notified the employee prior to termination, within ten days of termination or notice, whichever is earlier. Ohio Rev. Code. Ann. §1751.53, 1751.01(B)

Oklahoma

Former employees and spouses are entitled to continue group health coverage for 30 days after termination. If the employee has been covered by the plan for at least six months and is suffering from a medical condition that began prior to termination, then basic medical coverage continues for three months

	and major medical coverage continues for six months. Okla. Stat. Ann. tit. 36, §§4502.1 and 4509
Oregon	Former employees and eligible dependents who have been covered by a group health insurance plan for least three months are entitled to continuation of coverage for six months after the end of employment. The employer must notify the employee of the right to continued coverage. The employee must request it within ten days of termination or notice, whichever is later, but no later than 31 days after termination. Continued coverage need not cover benefits besides hospital and medical. Or. Rev. Stat. §743.610
Pennsylvania	An employee and his or her eligible dependents whose coverage has been terminated for any reason, who has been continuously covered for the preceding three months, is entitled to convert to an individual policy. The insurer may elect, however, to offer a separate converted policy for dependents. An employer must notify an employee of the right to converted coverage within 15 days before or after termination, and the employee must apply within 31 days of termination. If the employer does not give notice within 15 days, the employee may have additional time to apply, but never more than 90 days after the notice was given. 40 Pa. Stat. Ann. §756.2
Rhode Island	Former employees who were terminated due to an involuntary layoff or death have the right to continue group health insurance coverage for themselves and their dependents for up to 18 months after it would otherwise end. Employees must elect continued coverage within 30 days of termination. R.I. Gen. Laws §27-19.1-1
South Carolina	Former employees who have been covered by a group health insurance plan for at least six months are entitled to continue coverage for at least six months after employment ends. Upon termination, the employer must clearly advise the employee of the right to continue insurance. S.C. Code Ann. §38-71-770
South Dakota	Former employees and their dependents who have been covered by a group health insurance plan for at least six months have the right to continue that coverage for up to 18 months after it would otherwise end. Employers must notify employees of the right to continued coverage within ten days of termination, and employees must request continued coverage within 30 days of notice. S.D. Codified Laws Ann. §§58-18-7.5 and following Dependents of a deceased employee may continue coverage for 36 months. S.D. Codified Laws Ann. §§58-18-7.12
Tennessee	Former employees who had been covered by group health insurance for at least three months have the right to continue that group coverage for up to three months after it would otherwise end. The employee is required to pay the premium in advance and must make the first payment no more than 31 days after termination. Employees eligible for other group coverage or for Medicare are not entitled to continued coverage. At the end of the continua-

tion period, the individual is entitled to a health insurance policy issued by the insurer. Tenn. Code Ann. §56-7-2312

Texas	Former employees and their dependents who have been covered by a group health insurance plan for at least three months and who are not terminated for cause are entitled to continue coverage for six months.
	Employers must notify employees of the right to continued coverage, and employees must make the election with 31 days of termination or notice, whichever is later. Continued coverage is not available if the employee is eligible for a similar plan or for Medicare. Tex. Rev. Civ. Stat. Ann. Insurance, art. 3.51-6(d)(3)
Utah	Former employees who have been continuously covered by a group health insurance plan for at least six months prior to termination are entitled to continue coverage for six months after the end of employment.
	Employees must apply within 60 days of termination. Employees who acquire other group coverage or Medicare are not eligible for continued coverage. Employees are also eligible for a converted policy for an additional six months after the six months of continued coverage end. Utah Code Ann. §§31A-22-703 to 714
Vermont	Former employees who have been covered by a group health insurance plan for at least three months preceding termination are entitled to continue such coverage for six months unless terminated for misconduct or could be covered by other arrangement or by Medicare. The employee must request continued coverage within 30 days of termination. The continued coverage only has to provide hospital and medical benefits. Vt. Stat. Ann. tit. 8 §§4090a through 4090g
Virginia	Former employees and their dependents who have been covered by a group health insurance plan for at least three months immediately preceding termination may either continue coverage for 90 days after employment ends or convert to an individual policy at the employer's option. Employers must notify employees of their right to a converted policy within 15 days of termination, and the employee must apply within 31 days of termination. Va. Code Ann. §§38.2-3541 and 3416
Washington	Former employees are entitled to continue group health insurance benefits for a period of time and at a rate upon which the employer and employee have agreed. When the continued policy terminates, the employee must be allowed to convert to an individual policy unless the employee was terminated because of misconduct—in which case the spouse and children must still be given the right to convert. Employees must apply for continued coverage within 31 days of termination. Wash. Rev. Code Ann. §§48.21.250 through 48.21.270

West Virginia	Former employees who have been involuntarily laid off are entitled to continue group health benefits for 18 months. W.Va. Code §33-16-3(e)
Wisconsin	Former employees and their minor children who had been covered by group health insurance for at least three months have the right to continue coverage or convert it to an individual policy. If the former employee chooses group coverage, it will continue indefinitely and cannot be terminated unless the former employee moves out of state or becomes eligible for similar coverage.
	Employers must give employees notice of this option within five days of the coverage terminating; employees must apply within 30 days of receiving notice. Wis. Stat. Ann. §632.897
Wyoming	Employees and their families who have been continuously covered by a policy not subject to COBRA for three consecutive months preceding employment termination may continue for 12 months. Thereafter, the employee and family may convert to an individual policy. The employee must apply for continued coverage within 31 days of termination.
	Employees who are eligible for Medicare or other hospital or medical coverage are not entitled to continued coverage. The continued coverage need not include dental, vision or other benefits other than hospital and major medical. Wyo. Stat. §26-19-113

E. Individual Health Insurance

Even if your state does not have a law that gives you the right to continue group healthcare coverage after employment ends, it may have a law that requires health insurance companies to offer you the option of converting your group policy to individual coverage. Among the states offering this conversion option are California, Florida, Hawaii, New Mexico, New York, Pennsylvania, Tennessee, Utah, Washington, Wisconsin and Wyoming.

Individual coverage typically is much more expensive than group coverage—and the coverage limits are usually much lower than those offered under group coverage. For example, a group health insurance policy often will not have any limit on total benefits paid during your lifetime, while individual coverage often limits total lifetime benefits to $500,000. However, laws that give you the right to convert to individual health coverage usually do not require you to lose your job to be eligible.

If your employer cancels your group healthcare coverage but continues to employ you—an increasingly common situation—these laws can give you the right to convert to individual coverage until you can find a better insurance deal, or a job with better health insurance benefits. You can usually find the laws guaranteeing you the right to convert group health insurance coverage to individual coverage among the statutes governing your state's insurance industry. Some states have a consumer complaint section in their insurance departments that can help you with this.

F. Utilization Review

If your health insurance coverage provider has joined the swelling ranks of those who use a process called utilization review, you may get caught in the crossfire of one of the greatest workplace legal feuds on record if you become ill.

The idea behind utilization review is simple: By having an objective eye, usually an independent agency, take a look at your medical problem and approve or disapprove the things your doctor recommends, insurance companies can cut down on treatments that are unnecessary and expensive. The savings can then be passed along to the employers and employees who are finding it ever more difficult to pay for health insurance coverage.

Most physicians hate utilization review—for different reasons. Some feel the pain in their purses: Any process that prevents doctors from prescribing treatment significantly reduces the charges they can bill to your insurance company. And a number of doctors view utilization review as nettlesome bureaucratic padding—too often staffed with decisionmakers who know little about medical practice. But employers like utilization review. So lawyers have found a lucrative place for themselves in the middle of that opinion clash—routinely filing lawsuits on behalf of doctors, employers and their insurance companies.

Utilization Review and Insurance Coverage

Unless the legal feud over utilization review is settled, you should be particularly careful in making sure you understand what role it would play in your healthcare coverage if you became ill and needed to file a claim.

Here are some questions to ask to help you evaluate coverage.

- Does my health insurance coverage include a provision for utilization review?
- If so, who will perform the review? Will it be someone on the company's staff? Someone on the insurance company's staff? An outside agency?
- What kind of professional credentials are required of the people who would review my doctor's recommendations for treating me?
- What methods does my health insurance coverage use to enforce its utilization review decisions? For example, some health insurance plans merely compile lists of doctors whose charges are habitually high, and then try to talk them into exercising restraint. Others use more aggressive tactics, such as reducing by 25% the fees paid to doctors who fail to obtain permission from the insurance company before performing a treatment on a patient.
- Do I have the option of electing to participate in a health insurance plan that doesn't include utilization review? If so, will it cost me more to be covered by that plan?
- If my doctor or I disagree with a decision made by a reviewer, would I have the option of rejecting the utilization reviewer's decision?

Having this information is not likely to keep you completely out of the utilization review feud, but at least you will understand what is happening to you and what options you have if you get caught in it.

CHAPTER

5

FAMILY AND MEDICAL LEAVE

The typical American household has changed dramatically in the decades since the 1950s, when most American families were rigidly organized around a wage-earning father and a housekeeping, stay-at-home mother.

The workforce, too, has changed dramatically as women, single parents and two-paycheck couples have entered in droves.

And due to the astronomical costs of medical care, more workers are yoked with the responsibility for providing at least some of the care for sick or injured family members and aging parents.

There have been some additions to workplace legal rights that recognize these grand changes. But by and large, legislation has limped far behind societal shifts.

A. The Family and Medical Leave Act

The most sweeping federal law to help workers with the precarious balance between job and family is the Family and Medical Leave Act, or FMLA (29 U.S.C. §§2601 and following). Under the FMLA, an employee is eligible for up to 12 weeks of unpaid leave during a year's time for the birth or adoption of a child, family health needs or the employee's own health needs.

The employer must not only allow an employee to take the leave, but must allow the employee to return to the same or a similar position to the one he or she held before it. And during the leave, the employer must continue to make the same benefit contributions, such as paying insurance policy premiums, as the employee was receiving before going on leave. However, the FMLA does not require that employers pay any benefits that are not generally provided to employees—and seniority and pension benefits need not accrue during an employee's leave.

Employers who violate the Act, including its provisions against retaliating against those who take advantage of its protections (see Section 4), may be required to pay backpay, damages, attorneys' and expert witnesses' fees—and importantly, for the cost of up to 12 weeks of caring for a child, spouse or parent.

1. Who Is Covered

The FMLA applies to all private and public employers with 50 or more employees —an estimated one-half of the workforce.

To take advantage of this law, an employee must have:
- been employed at the same workplace for a year or more, and
- worked at least 1,250 hours—or about 24 hours a week—during the year preceding the leave.

Early Returns Show Tepid Results

The Family and Medical Leave Act is a newish law. Before it took effect in July of 1993, critics blasted that the law portended doom for small businesses forced to keep unproductive workers on staff. Supporters heralded the measure as the first real taste of family values palatable to workers of every political stripe.

But in its short history, the law has delivered neither gloom nor glory. No one is quite sure why—and pollsters, for once, have avoided the issue of why no one showed up for the revolution.

In February of 1998, on the FMLA's fifth anniversary, Secretary of Labor Alexis Herman declared victory: "The past five years have proven that this law has worked exactly as it was intended," she said. "Millions of American workers have gained precious time to be with their families during medical emergencies. At the same time, their employers have not experienced the effects that some who opposed the law feared."

Herman's view of the glass is half full.

The Department of Labor, responsible for enforcing the law, investigated 6,000 FMLA complaints during its first five years or so in existence. About 90% of those were settled, usually after a quick call from the DOL explaining how to comply. Agency officials claim they have completed investigating and acting on about 95% of the complaints filed; it has taken legal action for violations in only 16 cases.

But there are also other, more confounding numbers: The median length of time away from work for those taking leave under the law in its early years was 10 days. And, most tellingly, only about 3.6% of all employees actually took leave under the law.

So reality seems to show that it is not errant employers who are responsible for the law's lackluster effect. The key fact is that the leave is unpaid—meaning that many workers cannot afford to take advantage of it. Among women who took time off for family care during the FMLA's first 18 months, one in eight was forced to go on public assistance to make ends meet.

Interestingly, a number of employees say they would hesitate to take the proffered leave because of more subtle psychological pressures: Others would view them as less serious workers. In a workplace that gives the greatest glories to those who have put in the most hours, perceived slackers do not make the grade.

2. Restrictions on Coverage

Anticipating that some of the leave provisions in the FMLA might cause a hardship for smaller and some specialized employers, Congress included a number of exceptions to its coverage. Some of the exceptions sound rather harsh, and would likely result in fractionating some workplaces—providing some employees with benefits that others are blanketly denied. So to maintain morale and encourage company loyalty, many employers opt to adopt uniform standards for all employees rather than adhere slavishly to the exceptions allowed.

a. 50 employees within 75 miles

Companies with fewer than 50 employees within a 75-mile radius are exempt from the FMLA. This means that small regional offices of even the largest companies may be exempt from the law's requirements. However, the magic number of 50, for purposes of the FMLA, is computed by adding up all the employees on the payroll, so that those already on leave and those who work erratic schedules are tallied into the final count.

When Counting Employees, Use Both Hands

In a departure from most other federal workplace laws, the FMLA may extend coverage to workers by including contingent workers among those counted to meet the 50-employee threshold for coverage.

Workers generally cut out of other workplace benefits who may be able to take advantage of the FMLA include temp workers who customarily are placed with employers through agencies. The FMLA regulations specify that temp agencies and the workplaces accepting the workers may be considered their joint employers. The two must generally split duties under the FMLA. The temp agency is charged with informing workers about benefits, providing leave and returning the worker to his or her job after a leave. The employer accepting the temp's services must also accept the temp back after a leave and cannot discriminate against a temp who has taken a leave. Time spent working at the temp agency and for the employer can be added to meet the FMLA requirement of 1,250 workhours—an especially important twist if an employer decides to hire the temp.

Example: *Macrotech, a computer software firm, has only 20 employees. It contacts the Placeright Agency, a mid-sized temp agency, to provide 10 more programmers to help deliver a new software program. Since Macrotech and Placeright together have over 50 employees, both now must comply with FMLA requirements.*

The expansive counting requirements of the FMLA may also extend coverage to other work arrangements. This includes:

- small corporate employers or joint venturers that share control over a business where the combined employee total is at least 50 employees, and
- business owners who buy out a business that was covered by FMLA regs in the past.

While small business owners loudly protested that this broad interpretation of the counting requirement was nothing more than a sleight of hand that would thwart their abilities to do business, their cries fell on the Department of Labor's selectively deaf ears.

b. The highest paid 10%

The law allows companies to exempt the highest paid 10% of employees. This exception recognizes the theory that in many companies, the highest paid employees are the executives, the leaders and the managers—the most essential to be around to keep workplaces running smoothly. Employers may choose to provide these employees with unpaid leave, however, and many do—recognizing that the standard is broader than the reality of most workplaces. For example, in a smallish workplace of 100 employees, it is highly unlikely that ten workers will be deemed top-level executives.

c. Teachers and instructors

Those who work as schoolteachers or instructors are partially exempt from the FMLA—that is, they may be restricted from taking their unpaid leave until the end of a teaching period, commonly a quarter or semester, to avoid disrupting the continuity of the classroom. Teaching assistants and school staff, however, are fully covered under the FMLA.

d. Two spouses, one employer

Unless their need for leave is due to a personal medical problem, spouses who work for the same employer must aggregate their 12 weeks of leave time—that is, together, they are entitled to a total of 12 weeks off.

Congress defends this exception in the FMLA as a way to counter an employer's unwillingness to hire a married couple. In reality, it forces a couple to choose who should be the caregiver in the family. Note, however, that because of the loophole allowing time off for medical problems, if a woman qualifies for a pregnancy leave, her husband may be entitled to family leave to care for her.

Scheduling Time Off

Theoretically, an employee and employer are required to agree in advance on scheduling leave time to be taken under the FMLA. The law requires the employee to give at least 30 days of notice for "foreseeable medical treatment."

But the reality is that the FMLA provides time off from work for events that are often unpredictable and impossible to schedule—birth, adoption, sudden illness. In cases of medical emergencies, premature births or surprise adoption placements, employee leave is allowed—even without the employer's advance approval.

3. Reasons for Time Off

The FMLA established what was long-awaited in the workplace: a federal standard guaranteeing many workers the right to leave for the birth or adoption of a child and to care for their own or a family member's serious health condition.

When Is a Benefit Not a Benefit?

Your employer can count your accrued paid benefits—vacation, sick leave and personal leave days—toward the 12 weeks of leave you are allowed under the FMLA. If you use three weeks of vacation, for example, and another week of sick leave, you are left with only eight weeks of protected job leave under the FMLA.

To ease the strain, however, many employers let employees decide whether to include paid leave time as part of their family leave allotment.

a. Birth, adoption or foster care

The FMLA states that all covered employees must be given 12 weeks of unpaid leave for the birth, adoption or foster placement of a child, as long as that leave is taken within a year of the child's arrival. Also, if the leave is for a new child, it must be taken in a 12-week chunk; whereas a leave for medical problems may be scheduled more flexibly.

Motherhood in the Land of the Free, Home of the Knave

According to the United Nations' International Labor Organization, paid maternity leave is required in more than 120 countries.

Leading the list is the Czech Republic, with 24 weeks. Notably absent from the list are Australia, New Zealand and the United States—which allow 12 weeks of unpaid leave annually.

b. Health problems

The law is targeted so that workers can provide adequate care for children under 18 who are ill or injured, and for those 18 and older who cannot take care of themselves because of a physical or mental disability. Leave is available to care for an employee's son or daughter—which is broadly defined to include biological, adopted or foster children, stepchildren and legal wards. Also covered are children for whom employees stand in the place of parents—such as cases in which a grandparent, aunt or uncle has complete caretaking responsibilities.

The FMLA also provides for time off for health problems—physical and psychological—that affect either the employee or his or her spouse or parents. The required care need only limit the employee's ability to work or the employee's family member's ability to carry on with daily activities.

In the FMLA, the definition of spouse is limited to "a husband or wife, as the case may be"—overtly banning unmarried partners from the Act's coverage. In-laws are not included in the definition of parents.

The FMLA's definition of a medical condition entitling an employee to take a leave is quite liberal. It includes, for example, time off to care for a parent or spouse who has Alzheimer's disease or clinical depression, has suffered a stroke, is recovering from major surgery or is in the final stages of a terminal disease. It also covers employees who need time off to recover from the side effects of a medical treatment—including chemotherapy or radiation treatments.

However, the employee's or family member's health condition or medical treatment must require either an overnight stay in the hospital or a three-day absence from work. For example, a one-time health problem that is expected to require a short recovery period, such as orthodontic treatments, is not covered under the FMLA.

Also excluded are ailments not deemed to be serious health conditions—colds, flu, earaches, upset stomachs, minor ulcers, headaches other than migraines and routine dental or orthodontia visits. Regimens of over-the-counter medications, bed rest, fluids and exercise popularly ordered by doctors are not within the law's contemplation. Nor does the law cover requests for time off for routine physical, eye or dental exams—except when required to diagnose a serious illness. In fashioning the law, Congress presumed, rightly or wrongly, that most workplace sick days or personal leave policies would be sufficient to cover these situations.

If Your Employer Doubts Your Word

The cautious Congress that fashioned the FMLA took special care to guard against employees' potential abuse of the leave time policy.

And so the law includes a means of routing out cheaters.

If your employer doubts that you or yours has a serious health condition that requires you to take a leave, your employer may request that the condition be certified—that is, that a physician, psychologist, mental health counselor or other healthcare worker vouch for the condition in writing.

An employer who doubts even that confirmation can request, but is required to pay for, a second—and a third—medical opinion of the condition.

---

4. Penalties for Retaliation

By passing the FMLA, Congress intended to signal that employers must foster employees' needs to preserve both family and job. As in other workplace laws prohibiting unfair practices, the FMLA prohibits employers from demoting or firing an employee solely because he or she took a legally sanctioned leave.

The law also provides that an employer may not use either a carrot or a stick in handling leave requests. That is, an employee may not be promised a raise or promotion as an inducement not to take a leave; nor may an employee be denied a raise or promotion because of taking a leave.

5. Returning to Work

When you return to work after taking a family leave, the FMLA requires that you be returned to your old position or to an equivalent one.

This is a strict requirement and, according to the Department of Labor, the single provision employers violate most often. Congress has intimated that it is not enough that the position to which you are returned be "comparable" or "similar." It has stated that the "terms, conditions and privileges"—including the security of the position within the company—must be the same as the previous position.

Example: *A credit manager, responsible for supervising several employees, took a leave from her position due to pregnancy. When she returned to work, she was given a job with the same pay, the same benefits and the same office as her previous position, but she no longer had a job title, she supervised fewer employees—and a fourth of her worktime was to be spent in clerical work. Focusing on the diminished responsi-*

bility and authority, a court held that the new position was not equivalent under the terms of the FMLA (Kelley Co., Inc. v. Marquardt, 493 N.W. 2d 68 (1992)).

6. If You Do Not Return to Work

An interesting twist in the law provides that if an employee does not return to work after an FMLA-sanctioned leave, the employer may seek return of the benefits paid while he or she was away.

Although it has not yet been questioned in court, this recapture provision seems to be a mistake in the law, as it enables employers to set off benefit amounts from an employee's final paycheck or from a severance award. However, the setoff most often involves health insurance premiums, which the employer usually pays directly to the insurer.

7. Enforcing Your Rights

You must file a claim under the FMLA within two years after an employer violates the Act—or within three years if the violation is willful. Since the law is fairly new, it is still unclear what conduct will be considered willful, but retaliation is likely to be such an offense.

As mentioned, employers found to violate the FMLA may be liable for a number of costs and benefits, including:

- wages, salary, employment benefits or other compensation an employee has lost
- the cost of providing up to 12 weeks of care for a baby or ill family member
- reasonable attorneys' and expert witness fees, and
- interest on the amounts described above.

The employee may also win the right to be promoted or reinstated to a particular job.

The FMLA is now enforced by the U.S. Department of Labor, much the same as the Fair Labor Standards Act, which controls work hours and wages. (See Chapter 3, Section H.) If you have specific questions about the FMLA, contact the Department of Labor at: 800-959-3652; TDD: 800-326-2577.

From the Horse's Mouth: What to Do If You're Denied Leave

The Department of Labor, the federal agency responsible for enforcing the FMLA and investigating violations of it, recommends that you take the following commonsense steps if you are denied family and medical leave to which you are entitled.

- **Write down what happened.** Write down the date, time and place. Include what was said and who was there. Keep a copy of these notes at home. They will be useful if you decide to file a complaint against your company or to take legal action.
- **Get emotional support from friends and family.** It can be very upsetting to feel treated unfairly at work. Take care of yourself. Think about what you want to do. Get help to do it.
- **Talk to your union representative.** If you belong to a union, your union representative can help you file a grievance if you are denied family leave.
- **See what your company can do to help.** Your company may have a way for you to make a complaint. For instance, some companies offer ways to resolve problems, such as mediation. Check your employee handbook for procedures that may be available.
- **Find out if other workers have been denied leave.** Talk with anyone else who had the same problem. Join with them to try to work out the problem.
- **Keep doing a good job and keep a record of your work.** Keep copies at home of your job evaluations and any letters or memos that show that you do a good job at work. Your boss may criticize your job performance later on in order to defend what he or she did to you.
- **File a complaint.** Remember, the law has a time limit on how long you can wait to file a complaint against your company. You can file a complaint even if you do not work for your employer anymore. You can file a complaint through your local U.S. Department of Labor Wage and Hour office. Look in the telephone book under the heading Federal Government.
- **Contact community resources.** If you and several other workers are being denied rights to leave by the same boss, you may be able to file a formal complaint as a group. Call a women's or disability rights group. You may be able to help other people in the future.
- **Find out more about your legal rights.** You do not need a lawyer to file a legal claim. But you may want to call a free legal service or a lawyer who specializes in job rights. Call the state bar association or the women's bar association. They can refer you to lawyers, and can help you figure out the pros and cons of taking legal action, including the time and the cost of such action.

Many women have fought unfair treatment and have improved their worklives. The first step is to know your rights under the law. Laws give you and your co-workers the right to join together to try to get better treatment at work.

You can also win money in court because of illegal treatment. The Family and Medical Leave Act can give workers their jobs back, the wages they should have been paid and sometimes promotions or payment for legal costs.

Where to Get Help
- Women's Bureau, U.S. Department of Labor, Washington, DC 20210; 800-827-5335; TDD: 800-326-2577
- Wage and Hour Division Employment Standards Administration, U.S. Department of Labor. Check your local telephone listing under the heading Federal Government.
- Office of Federal Contract Compliance Programs Employment Standards Administration, U.S. Department of Labor, Washington, DC 20210; 202-219-9475.

Adapted from the U.S. Department of Labor Website: http://www.dol.gov

B. State Laws on Family Leave

The majority of states now have leave laws, but their provisions differ wildly—leaving a patchwork of protections, benefits and loopholes that are often confusing to both employers and employees.

1. Choosing Federal or State Protections

If your state also has some incarnation of a family leave law, you are free to seek benefits under the federal FMLA or your state law—whichever law offers you the greatest benefit. If you have a baby one year, you may use the leave allotted you by the state; if you become ill the next year, you may be entitled to benefits guaranteed by the FMLA. However, several states have recently amended their laws to provide that state and federal coverage cannot be piggybacked; you must choose coverage under one law or the other.

> ### Leaves With Pay
>
> In general, state family leave laws only require employers to grant an employee a leave without pay. Paid leaves are uncommon, but some companies—typically very large ones or very small ones that regard their employees as family members—do provide at least partial paid leave.
>
>   Check with your supervisor well before you anticipate needing a leave to determine your workplace's policy on paid leaves. Make sure that you fulfill all the requirements for receiving your regular pay during the time that you're away from work—such as giving your employer adequate notice of your need to take such a leave.

2. State Laws

State laws governing family leaves differ greatly as to:
- the size of workplace covered—varying from 4 to 100
- the reasons allowed for time off—some states provide leaves for birth and adoption only; others also provide it for family members' illnesses; the District of Columbia seems to allow leave to care for roommates and other unrelated residents
- who is covered—a number of states specify that an employee must have worked for one employer for a minimum time before being entitled to a-leave
- the length of leave allowed
- the length of notice that an employee must give before taking a leave
- whether or not benefits must be continued and at whose expense
- whether or not an employee is entitled to the same or an equivalent position after returning to work—in some states, this is required only if proper advance notice has been given

- how rights to parental leaves are divided when both parents are employed by the same company, and
- how the laws can be enforced.

A quickly growing trend is for states to allow employees to take paid time off to donate organs, tissue or bone marrow for transplant. A few states—including California, Illinois, Louisiana, Minnesota, North Carolina and Vermont—also provide that parents must be given a certain amount of unpaid leave to attend a child's school conferences.

On their faces, many state laws are more liberal than the federal law. But many state laws are rife with large loopholes, too. For example, the family leave laws in a number of states—including Montana, Tennessee and Vermont—provide that an employer is free to replace a worker who has taken leave if the time off would burden the workplace.

Additional Laws May Apply

If the chart below indicates that your state has no statute, this means there is no law that specifically addresses the issue. However, there may be a state administrative regulation or local ordinance that does control. Call your state labor department for more information. (See the Appendix for contact details.)

State Family and Medical Leave Laws	
Alabama	Employees of certain state and local educational agencies may use sick leave to attend to the death or illness of a family member or individual with a close personal tie. Statute applies to bus drivers and employees of state or local Board of Ed, Institute for the Deaf & Blind, Youth Services Dept, School of Fine Arts, School of Mathematics & Science, State Senate, State House of Reps, Lt. Governor, organizations participating in the Teacher's Retirement System. Ala. Code § 16-1-18.1
Alaska	Public employers with 21 or more employees must grant any employee who has worked fulltime for six months or halftime for one year 18 weeks of unpaid leave per 12-month period for pregnancy, childbirth or adoption, or 24 months for care of a family member during a serious illness. Employees who take such leave must be restored to their same or comparable position. Alaska Stat. §§23.10.500, .550
Arizona	No statute
Arkansas	Public employees can use sick leave to care for a sick parent or guardian, spouse, child, sibling, grandparent or in-law. Ark. Code Ann. §21-4-206
	School district employees may use sick leave to care for a sick spouse, child, parent or other relative in the household. Ark. Code Ann. §6-17-1304

California	It is an unfair employment practice for an employer to refuse to grant a leave of up to four months for a female employee who is disabled as a result of pregnancy, childbirth or related medical conditions. Cal. Gov't Code §12945
	Employees who have worked for at least one year and have done 1,250 hours of work during the previous year may take up to 12 working weeks in any 12-month period for family care and medical leave, with reemployment guaranteed. Applies only to employers with more than 50 employees. Does not apply to an employer with fewer than 50 employees within 75 miles of the employee's worksite. Cal. Gov't Code §12945.2
	A government employer may not refuse to hire and may not discharge or discriminate against any person who has exercised his or her rights to family and medical leave. Cal. Gov't Code §19702.3
	Employers with 25 or more employees working at the same location must grant parents, guardians or custodial grandparents up to 40 hours per school year—but not more than eight hours per calendar month—to participate in the school activities of a child in grades K through 12, as long as the employee gives reasonable advance notice. Employer may require verification from the school. Cal. Labor Code §230.8
	Employers may not discharge or discriminate against employees who are called to attend their children's schools following suspension. Employees must give reasonable advance notice. Cal. Labor Code §230.7
Colorado	Employer policies applying to leaves for biological parents must also be extended to adoptive parents. Colo. Rev. Stat. §19-5-211
	Employees in the state personnel system may take two days per year of paid leave to donate organs, tissue or bone marrow for a transplant. Colo. Rev. Stat. 12-34-101.5
Connecticut	Employers with at least 75 employees are required to give 16 weeks of unpaid leave—or to allow employees to substitute paid vacation, personal or sick leave—within any two-year period. Applies to employees who have worked for at least one year and for at least 1,000 hours during the year prior to the requested leave.
	Leave may be for birth or adoption of a child or for care of a child, spouse or parent during serious illness. Employees must give the employer 30 days of notice—or as much notice as is possible. Employees must be allowed to return to either their original or equivalent jobs. Employers may request certification by a health care provider. Conn. Gen. Stat. Ann. §§31-51kk-pp
	State employers must give 24 weeks of unpaid leave within any two-year period.
	Leave may be for birth or adoption of a child or for care of a child, spouse or parent during serious illness. Employees who take such leave must be allowed to return to either their original or equivalent jobs. Employees must provide written certification from a physician before going on leave and must submit a signed statement that they intend to return to work. Conn. Gen. Stat. Ann. §5-248a

Delaware	State employees who have been employed fulltime for at least one year may take six weeks unpaid leave for the adoption of a child. Del. Code Ann., tit. 29, §5116
	Parttime or fulltime state employees and their spouses may use sick leave for the birth of a child or adoption of a pre-kindergarten-age child. Del. Code Ann., tit. 29, §5120
	Public school employees may take five days of paid leave for the death of an immediate family member or one day paid leave for the death of a near relative. This leave is in addition to any other sick leave or vacation. School employees can use their sick leave to attend to an immediate family member who is seriously ill. If the absence is more than five days, a doctor's certification is required. Del. Code Ann., tit. 14, §1318
District of Columbia	An employee who has worked with a company of at least 20 employees for at least one year, and who has worked at least 1,000 hours during the previous 12-month period, must be granted up to 16 weeks of unpaid leave during any 24-month period in connection with the birth or adoption of a child or serious illness of a family member. Family member includes a child who lives with the employee and for whom the employee assumes parental responsibility. It also includes a person with whom the employee shares and maintains a residence. If the necessity of taking such leave is foreseeable, the employee must give the employer a reasonable amount of advance notice. The employer may request certification by a healthcare provider. Employees who take such leaves must be restored to either their original or equivalent jobs. D.C. Code Ann. §§1301-1305
Florida	Career service state employees are entitled to up to six months unpaid time off for parental or family leave if needed to attend to a serious family illness, a condition that poses imminent danger of death or any mental or physical condition that requires constant in-home care. Fla. Stat. §110.221
Georgia	No statute
Hawaii	Employers with at least 100 employees must grant employees an unpaid leave of up to four weeks per calendar year for the birth or adoption of a child or for the care of a child, spouse or parent during a serious illness. The employer may require certification by a healthcare provider. Employees who take such leave must be restored to their same or comparable positions. Haw. Rev. Stat. §§398-1 to 11
Idaho	No statute
Illinois	Township employees (60 Ill. Comp. Stat. 1/100-5), highway commissioners' employees (605 Ill. Comp. Stat. 5/6-201.20) and town tax assessor employees (35 Ill. Comp. Stat. 200/2-65) are entitled to maternity leaves as developed by their employers.
	All employers must give an employee up to eight hours during each school year to attend their child's classroom activities and conferences that cannot be scheduled during nonworking hours. The employee must first exhaust all vacation and compensatory time and must give the employer 7 days of notice except in an emergency. 820 Ill. Comp. Stat. 147/15

Indiana	No statute
Iowa	Employers with at least four employees must grant employees who are disabled by pregnancy, childbirth or related medical conditions an unpaid leave for the duration of their disabilities, up to a maximum of eight weeks. An employee must give advance notice—and an employer may require medical certification before granting leave. Iowa Code Ann. §216.6
Kansas	No statute
Kentucky	An employer of any size must grant up to six weeks of unpaid leave to an employee who has adopted a child under seven years old. Ky. Rev. Stat. Ann. §337.015
Louisiana	Employers with more than 25 employees must allow up to six weeks of disability leave and must grant additional leaves for a "reasonable period of time" not to exceed four months. La. Rev. Stat. Ann. §§23:341, 342 An employer may grant up to 16 unpaid hours per year for an employee to attend or participate in school conferences and activities of a child for whom the employee is the legal guardian if those activities cannot be scheduled during nonworking hours. Employees must give reasonable notice and schedule the time off so that it does not unduly disrupt the employer's operations. La. Rev. Stat. Ann. §23:1015 Employers with 20 or more employees at one site must give employees up to 40 hours of paid leave per year for the purpose of donating bone marrow. La. Rev. Stat. Ann. §40:1299.124
Maine	An employee who has worked at least 12 consecutive months with a company employing at least 15 people at the worksite must be granted up to ten consecutive weeks of unpaid leave in any two-year period for the birth of a child, the adoption of a child 16 years old or younger or to care for a family member during illness. The same benefits apply to employees of the state and of the city or town agencies with 25 or more employees. Unless prevented by medical emergency, employees must give at least 30 days of notice before taking leave; returning employees must be restored to either their original or equivalent jobs. Me. Rev. Stat. Ann. tit. 26, §§843, 844
Maryland	An employer who provides leave with pay to an employee following the birth of a child shall provide the same leave to an employee who adopts a child. Md. Lab. and Emp. Code Ann. §3-802 Permanent state employees on sick or maternity leave must be allowed to apply for or to receive promotions. Employees must return to work within 120 days of receiving notice. Md. State Personnel and Pensions Code Ann. §2-303 All permanent state employees may use paid sick leave in case of death or illness in the immediate family, birth or adoption of a child or a family member's medical appointment. In addition, an employee may use up to 30 days of paid sick leave to care for a child immediately after birth or adoption. Md. State Personnel and Pensions Code Ann. §9-501 and 505

	All state employees, including temporary employees, may take up to seven days of paid leave in any 12-month period to serve as a bone marrow donor; up to 30 days of paid leave in any 12-month period to serve as an organ donor. Md. State Personnel and Pensions Code Ann. §9-1106
Massachusetts	Employers of at least six employees must grant those who have completed their probationary periods or have worked fulltime for at least three months up to eight weeks of unpaid leave for the birth or adoption of a child under 18 or the adoption of a child under 23 if the child is mentally or physically disabled. Mass. Gen. Laws Ann. ch. 149, §105D
Michigan	No statute
Minnesota	An employer with 21 or more people must grant employees who have worked for the company an average of 20 hours per week for at least 12 months up to six weeks of unpaid leave for the birth or adoption of a child. During the leave, the employer must offer the employee the option of paying for continuing group healthcare insurance coverage. Employees must be returned to either their original or equivalent jobs, unless they would have been laid off during leave. Minn. Stat. Ann. §§181.940 and following
	An employee may use paid sick leave to care for a sick child. Minn. Stat. Ann. §181.9413
	An employer must grant up to 40 hours with pay to enable an employee to donate bone marrow. Minn. Stat. Ann. §181.945
	An employee is entitled to 16 hours of leave per year to attend school conferences or classroom activities that can't be scheduled during nonworking hours; employee may use vacation or other paid leave. Minn. Stat. Ann. §181.9412
Mississippi	All state employees may use major medical leave to care for an ill or injured family member, including a foster child. Employees must first use accrued personal or compensatory leave.
	An employee may use up to three days of major medical leave if there is a death in the immediate family without having to first use personal leave. Miss. Code Ann. §25-3-95
Missouri	Public employees who are adoptive parents have the same rights as biological parents to take time off without pay and vacation time to arrange for the adoption itself or for care, but only if the adoptive parent is the person primarily responsible for the care of the child. A stepparent may use sick leave or vacation or take leave without pay to care for a sick stepchild. Mo. Ann. Stat. §105.271
Montana	An employer of any size may not dismiss an employee who becomes pregnant, or refuse to allow a reasonable unpaid leave for pregnancy, or refuse to allow accrued disability or other leave benefits for a pregnancy leave. Employees also cannot be required to take pregnancy leave for an unreasonable period of time. Employees who take pregnancy-related leaves must be returned to their original jobs or equivalents unless, in the case of a private employer, the employer's circumstances have so changed as to make it unreasonable or impossible to do so. Mont. Code Ann. §49-2-310 and §49-2-311

Nebraska	Any employer, including a government agency, that permits an employee to take a leave of absence for the birth of a child must give the same leave to adoptive parents. Neb. Rev. Stat. §48-234 Employers are encouraged to grant paid leaves of absence to employees donating bone marrow. Neb. Rev. Stat. §71-4820
Nevada	The same leave policies that apply to other medical conditions must be extended to female employees before and after childbirth, or after a miscarriage. Nev. Rev. Stat. §613.335
New Hampshire	Employers must allow female employees to take leave for period of temporary disability resulting from pregnancy, childbirth or related condition. When the employee is able to return to work, she must be restored to the same or a comparable position unless the employer's business necessity makes this impossible or unreasonable. N.H. Rev. Stat. Ann. §354-A:7y
New Jersey	Employers of at least 50 employees must grant to those who have worked for at least 12 months, and who have worked at least 1,000 hours in the preceding 12 months, up to 12 weeks of unpaid leave in any 24-month period for the birth, adoption or care during the serious illness of a child under 18 years old, or one older than 18 who is incapable of self-care or a parent or a spouse. The employer may require certification by a healthcare provider. Employees who take such leaves must be restored to either their original or equivalent jobs. An employer may deny leave if the employee is among the seven highest-paid employees or is in the highest 5%, whichever is greater, and if substantial and grievous economic injury to the business would result. The employer must notify the employee of the intent to deny leave upon determining that denial is necessary. If leave has commenced, the employee must return within ten days. Family Leave Act, N.J. Stat. Ann. §§34:11B-1 to B16
New Mexico	No statute
New York	If an employer permits leave for the birth of a child, then leave must be granted for adoption. N.Y. Labor Law §201-c An employer with 20 or more employees must grant an employee up to 24 hours leave to donate bone marrow and may not retaliate against an employee who requests a leave for this purpose. N.Y. Labor Law §202-a
North Carolina	An employee who is a parent, guardian or who acts in place of a parent may take up to four hours per year without pay to be involved in the child's school—including a public or private school or daycare. The hours taken must be at a mutually agreed-upon time; the employer may require 48 hours notice for the request and may require verification that the employee actually attended or was involved. No retaliatory action may be taken against an employee who exercises rights under this law. N.C. Gen. Stat. §95-28.3
North Dakota	State employees, but not employees of subdivisions of the state, may take unpaid leave to care for a newborn child or to care for a child, spouse or parent with a serious health condition. The amount of leave depends on the average number of hours per week the employee works, up to a maximum of four months per year. Employees may also take up to 40 hours per year of sick leave to care for a sick parent, spouse or child.

	Employees must give employers reasonable notice before taking leave. Employers may require certification by a healthcare provider. N.D. Cent. Code §§54-52.4-01 and following
Ohio	Permanent state employees are entitled to up to six weeks leave for the birth or adoption of a child—the first 14 days are unpaid; the next four weeks are paid at 70% of base pay. Employees may choose to work or to use sick or vacation leave for the first two weeks or to supplement the reduced pay. Adoptive parents may choose a $2,000 payment instead of the leave benefit. Ohio Rev. Code Ann. §124.136
	Fulltime permanent state employees are entitled to three paid days' bereavement leave for a death within the employee's immediate family. Ohio Rev. Code Ann. §124.387
Oklahoma	No statute
Oregon	Employers with 25 or more employees must grant up to 12 weeks of leave per year to employees who have worked for at least 180 days immediately before the leave.
	Leave is permitted to care for: an infant, a newly adopted or placed child under 18, a family member with a serious health condition or a sick child. Women may take an additional 12 weeks for any condition or disability related to childbirth or pregnancy.
	Employers may require 30 days of notice as well as an explanation and medical certification of leave. Employees must be restored to their original positions even if the employer has filled the positions while they were on leave; if a position no longer exists, an employee must be given an equivalent position either at the original jobsite or at one within 20 miles. Or. Rev. Stat. §659.470 to 494
	Employees may take up to 40 hours of leave for a bone marrow donation procedure. Or. Rev. Stat. §659.358
Pennsylvania	No statute
Rhode Island	Employers with 50 or more employees must grant those who have worked for them for at least 12 consecutive months up to 13 weeks of unpaid leave in any two calendar years for the birth or adoption of a child or for the care of a family member during illness. Employees who take such leaves must be restored to either their original or equivalent jobs. R.I. Gen. Laws §§28-48-2 and 28-48-3
South Carolina	All permanent fulltime state employees may use up to eight days of sick leave to care for members of their own or their spouse's immediate families. S.C. Code Ann. §8-11-40
	State employees may use up to six weeks of sick leave to care for an adopted child after placement. S.C. Code Ann. §8-11-155
	All private and government employers with more than 20 employees at one site may grant paid leaves of absence to employees for donating bone marrow. S.C. Code Ann. §44-43-80

South Dakota	State employees may use up to 40 hours of accumulated sick leave per year for the death of or to care for a member of the immediate family. S.D. Admin. Code §55:01:22:02:04
	State employees who have worked at least 12 months may take up to 12 weeks of unpaid leave, sick leave, personal leave or vacation leave to care for a newborn, adopted or foster child or to care for a spouse, child or parent who has a serious health condition. S.D. Admin. Code §55:01:22:08:02
Tennessee	Companies with 100 or more employees must grant up to four months of unpaid leave for pregnancy or childbirth to any fulltime female employee who has worked at least 12 consecutive months. If the employee gives the employer at least three months advance notice of her intent to take such a leave or if a medical emergency makes the leave necessary, she must be restored to her original job or its equivalent upon returning to work. The employer must allow an employee who takes such a leave to continue benefits such as healthcare insurance, but the employer is not required to pay for the benefits during the leave period.
	Reinstatement rights do not apply if the employee uses the time to actively pursue other employment opportunities or work fulltime or parttime for another employer. Tenn. Code Ann. §4-21-408
Texas	State employees may use sick leave to care for a sick family member or an adopted foster child. Tex. Gov't Code §661.202
	State employees are entitled to paid emergency leave because of a death in the family. Tex. Gov't Code §661.902
	State employees with children in pre-kindergarten through 12th grade may take up to eight hours of sick leave per calendar year to attend school conferences. Tex. Gov't Code §661.206
	State employees who have worked less than one year or fewer than 1,250 hours during the year prior to leave are eligible to take 12 weeks of parental leave for the birth of a child or the adoption or placement of a foster child who is less than three years old. Tex. Gov't Code §661.913
Utah	No statute
Vermont	Companies with 15 or more employees must allow employees who have worked with them an average of at least 30 hours per week, for at least one year, to take up to 12 weeks of unpaid leave per year for pregnancy, childbirth, the adoption of a child under the age of 16 or the serious illness of the employee or a family member. The employee must provide the employer with written notice of intent to take such a leave and of its anticipated duration. The employee must be allowed to use accrued vacation or sickness leave for up to six weeks of leave. The employee must also be given the option of continuing benefit programs at his or her own expense. After returning from such a leave, the employee must be restored to his or her original job or its equivalent—unless the employer can demonstrate that the employee performed unique services and hiring a permanent replacement worker, after giving notice to the employee, was the only alternative to preventing substan-

tial and grievous economic injury to the employer's business.

An employee who does not return to the job after taking such a leave for reasons other than the serious illness of the employee must refund to the employer any compensation paid during the leave, except payments for accrued vacation or sickness leave. Vt. Stat. Ann. tit. 21, §472

Employees may also take up to four hours of unpaid leave in a 30-day period but not more than 24 hours in 12 months, to participate in a child's school activities, to take a family member to a medical or professional appointment or to respond to a family member's medical emergency. Vt. Stat. Ann., tit. 21, §472a.

Virginia	No statute
Washington	Employers with 100 or more employees, including political subdivisions of the state, and the state, must grant up to 12 weeks of unpaid leave during any two-year period in connection with the birth or adoption of a child or to care for a child under the age of 18 who is terminally ill. The employee must provide the employer with at least 30 days of advance notice in most situations. Employees who take such leaves must be restored to their original or equivalent jobs. If circumstances have changed to the point that no equivalent job is available, the employee must be given any vacant job for which he or she is qualified. An employer may limit or deny family leave to either the highest paid 10% of the employees or 10% designated as key personnel. Wash. Rev. Code §§49.78.010 and following
	Employees may use sick leave to care for a sick child. Wash. Rev. Code §49.12.270
	Employers who provide parental leave to employees to care for a biological newborn child must provide the same leave to adoptive parents and stepparents of children under the age of six—and to men as well as women. Wash. Rev. Code §§49.12.350 and .360
West Virginia	Fulltime state or county board of education employees who have worked at least 12 consecutive months are entitled to 12 weeks of unpaid leave, after using up available personal leave, for the birth or adoption of a child; or to care for a child, spouse, parent or dependent who has a serious medical condition. The employer may require verification from the healthcare provider. The Parental Leave Act, W.Va. Code §§21-5D-1 to 9
Wisconsin	Employers with 50 or more employees must grant employees who have been with the company one year and worked 1,000 hours up to six weeks of unpaid leave for the birth or adoption of a child and up to two weeks for the care of a parent, child or spouse with a serious health condition. This leave, when combined with any other family-related leave, may not exceed a total of eight weeks within a 12-month period. The employee must give notice of the leave and the employer may require certification by a healthcare provider. Statute specifically prohibits discharge of or retaliation against anyone who exercises a practice permitted under the Family and Medical Leave Act, and provides a complaint procedure in the Department of Industry, Labor and Human Relations. Wis. Stat. Ann. §103.10
Wyoming	No statute

Changing Your Mind

A common sore point with employers is that some employees officially state they are taking a parental leave of only a few months, but then decide to become fulltime parents and quit their jobs outright.

This strategy is particularly popular among employees who are having their first baby because, at the very least, it seems to allow the option of going back to a job after experimenting with a few months of stay-at-home parenting.

But this strategy is far from new—and most employers have seen it before. Many companies now require employees who take paid parental leaves and then decide to leave their jobs permanently to pay back compensation received during the leave. And the FMLA specifically allows employers to recover the cost of maintaining health insurance coverage from employees who do not return after a leave. (See Section A6.)

To enforce this type of policy, employers usually need you to sign an agreement in which you agree to make such a repayment, so be careful to read and understand anything you sign in connection with any paid leave that is granted to you.

3. Anti-Discrimination Provisions

Some state laws also forbid workplace discrimination on the basis of gender. In states that have no specific family leave laws, anti-discrimination laws often can be used to establish a right for parents to take time off from work for pregnancy and childbirth.

The anti-discrimination laws of most states include marital status among the factors that may not be used as the basis for work-related discrimination. Some states, such as Alaska, for example, go a step further, protecting even unmarried couples by specifically listing parenthood as an illegal basis for discrimination. (See the chart in Chapter 8, Section B, for a listing of state anti-discrimination laws.)

4. Enforcing Your Rights

Anti-discrimination laws often can be applied to such leaves only through slow-moving complaints to the Equal Employment Opportunity Commission or through complex and expensive lawsuits. But in general, state laws that grant family leaves offer a clear basis for enforcing the right to take such a leave.

But most often, the most direct and constructive way to exercise your right to take a family leave is to know your rights and to make sure your employer is aware of both your plans and the law well before you take a leave. Nearly all state family leave laws have been enacted recently and your employer may be sincerely unaware of them.

If you have made your employer aware of your right to take such a leave and the employer refuses to comply, the options available to you will vary with the situation.

- If your problem seems to be merely a matter of disagreement over interpretation of the law, suggest to your employer that a mediator or arbitrator help settle the dispute. (See Chapter 18, Section A.)
- If your state is listed in this chapter as having a specific leave law, you may be able to have a state agency intervene in your case. To find the appropriate state agency, start with the one responsible for overseeing your state's anti-discrimination law. (See Chapter 8, Section B.)
- If your case involves a violation of Title VII of the Civil Rights Act, you can file a complaint with the Equal Employment Opportunity Commission (EEOC). If the EEOC decides not to take action in your case, you may be able to file a federal lawsuit on your own. (See Chapter 8, Section A.)
- If your state has no agency to enforce its law, you may be able to file a lawsuit on your own behalf. (See Chapter 8, Section A.) In some states, those who sue under family leave laws are allowed to collect punitive damages, court fees and the cost of hiring a lawyer to help.

When Parents' Rights Are Parents' Wrongs

According to many experts, the next wave of legal reform in the workplace is likely to be championed by an unexpected source: workers who have no children.

The backlash, ironically, may first be felt most strongly in companies that attempted to provide the most accommodations for workers. Corning, Inc., a large optical fiber and ceramics company based in New York, is one good example: The company recently began providing a number of innovative benefits for workers—childcare programs, childcare counseling, flexible work schedules for parents. "After the first couple of years, people who didn't have young children started quietly saying, 'What about us? Does my personal life count?'" recalls Sonia Werner, a workplace consultant at Corning. Corning recently righted its shortsightedness by offering flexible work schedules to workers who have no children, changing the name of its Family Support Program to Work Life and offering employee seminars in assertiveness training and other general concerns.

The murmurs of resentment are becoming louder in many other workplaces, too. Many workers who feel the sting—and nearly two-thirds of U.S. workers do not have children under age 18—say this form of discrimination takes more subtle forms, so it is often more difficult to document, speak up about and correct. But an increasing number of childless workers are beginning to voice their grievances, including that they are customarily treated differently than their co-workers who have children. The childless say they are:

- expected to work more hours
- made targets for frequent transfers and out-of-country assignments
- forced to absorb extra work to cover for parents who arrive late or leave early to drop off and pick up their children
- deprived of paid benefits such as childcare and counseling offered only to traditional families, and
- exclusively called upon to cover weekend and after-hours assignments.

Some companies are beginning to get the message. For example, Quaker Oats, a food company based in Chicago, recently began to offer workers a more equitable benefits program, as masterminded by a team of workers in various ages and stages holding various positions throughout the company. Quaker's new Flexplan gives an additional $300 to employees who claim no dependents on company-reimbursed insurance coverage. Their employees can opt to take the $300 in cash, or as an investment to their 401k plans—or they can use it to buy other employee benefits, such as vacation time.

C. The Pregnancy Discrimination Act

Additional workplace rights for new parents come from the Pregnancy Discrimination Act, or PDA (92 Stat. §2076), passed in 1978 as an amendment to Title VII of the Civil Rights Act of 1964. This federal law widely prohibits many types of discrimination. The PDA outlaws discrimination based on pregnancy, childbirth or any related medical condition.

Working Mothers Are Here to Stay

Even the most stalwart ostrich might be willing to concede that women continue to face a lopsided level of discriminatory treatment on the job.

Many people believe that the heart—or the womb—of the matter are antiquated images of both the U.S. workforce and the nature of pregnancy. Even in this day and this age, the term Working Mother still prompts strong reactions ranging from awe to disdain.

But figures show that moms on the job are the norm, not the aberration.

More than two-thirds of American women work for pay.

At least 80% of women who now work for pay are of childbearing age.

Of these women, 93% are likely to become pregnant at some point in their working lives

Source of statistics: Equal Rights Advocates, 2000

1. Who Is Covered

Like other provisions of Title VII, the PDA applies to all workplaces that:

- engage in some type of interstate commerce—today, broadly construed to include all employers that use the mails or telephones, and
- have 15 or more employees for any 20 weeks of a calendar year. (See Chapter 8, Section A, for more on Title VII protections.)

2. Available Protections

The PDA specifies that pregnant employees—and those recovering from an abortion—who need time off from work must be treated the same as other temporarily disabled employees. For example, a company that allows employees to return to work with full seniority and benefit rights after taking time off for a surgical operation and recovery must similarly reinstate women who take time off because of a pregnancy.

On the flip side, this law may also help sanction the denial of a benefit to a pregnant worker if that benefit has been denied any other temporarily disabled worker. If it is company policy, for example, to suspend seniority rights and benefits for employees who require extended medical leave, those work benefits must also be denied to pregnant workers on leave.

Also, while the PDA bars discrimination based on pregnancy, unlike the Family and Medical Leave Act (see Section A), it does not require an employer to provide a pregnant employee with leave—and does not guarantee job security while a worker is out on leave.

The protections in the Act sound sensible and absolute. But in truth, employers routinely shirk their legal duties when dealing with pregnant workers. The EEOC, charged with enforcing complaints of pregnancy discrimination on the job, reports that the number of charges of this wrong increased by a third from 1992 to 1998. And with 20 million new pregnancies likely among working women in the decade kicked off by the year 2000, the problems and complaints are not likely to shrink without more definitive legislation, stronger workplace policies or both.

a. Forced leaves

The PDA bars mandatory maternity leaves—and those that are prescribed for a set time and duration. The focus instead is on whether an individual pregnant worker remains able to perform her job. And a pregnant woman cannot be required to take a leave from work during her pregnancy as long as she remains able to do her job.

Example: *Jody's pregnancy is proceeding without problems, and she has no difficulty performing her job as an office manager. Even though she is a week past her delivery due date according to her doctor's calculations, her employer cannot force her to take off work in anticipation of labor.*

b. Hiring and promotion discrimination

In addition, an employer cannot refuse to hire or promote a woman solely because she is pregnant—or because of stereotyped notions of what work is proper for a pregnant woman to do or not to do.

Example: *Marsha is the most qualified applicant for a job, but is six months pregnant during her job interview. The company cannot choose another applicant simply because it does not want to find a replacement for Marsha when she takes a leave to give birth.*

c. Insurance discrimination

The PDA also states that an employer cannot refuse to provide healthcare insurance benefits that cover pregnancy if it provides such benefits to cover other medical conditions.

Example: *The Dumont Company provides complete hospitalization insurance to spouses of female employees, but has a $500 cap on childbirth coverage for spouses of male employees. This policy is illegal under the PDA.*

The sole exception here is that an employer need not pay for health insurance benefits for an abortion—except where the life of the pregnant woman would be endangered if the fetus is carried to term or where there are medical complications following the abortion.

3. Men's Rights to Leaves

Under Title VII, an employer must grant men the same options for taking leaves from their jobs to care for children as it grants to women. To do otherwise would constitute illegal discrimination based on gender.

Example: *Steven works for a company that provides a 12-week unpaid leave for women who give birth to or adopt a child. If his employer refuses to allow Steven to take such a leave to adopt a child, he can file a complaint against his employer under Title VII, alleging gender discrimination.*

For details about who is covered by Title VII and how to file a complaint under it, see Chapter 8, Section A. But first read Section B of this chapter to see if your state offers a more direct approach. Also, see the Appendix for organizations that provide information on work and family issues.

Childcare Problems Affect Both Moms and Dads

A recent survey of 500 working parents found that both mothers and fathers, regardless of how much they earn or how many kids they have, have missed work because of childcare problems.

Statistics on the workdays parents missed because of childcare problems in an isolated month:

6% of parents had missed work 1 day

5% of parents had missed work 2 days

3% of parents had missed work 3 days, and

4% of parents had missed work 5 or more days.

Some state legislatures are beginning to heed the cry of this reality, proposing clauses in their leave laws that forbid discrimination. Washington is a forerunner in the effort. A clause added in 2000 to the state's parental leave statute states simply: An employer must grant the same leave upon the same terms for men as it does for women.

Source of statistics: Study by the University of Cincinnati, 1999

D. Balancing Work and Family: Other Ways to Cope

Some companies help employees juggle work and family responsibilities in various ways, including:

- allowing employees to work parttime or to share a job (see Chapter 2, Section D)
- allowing employees to put in some of their work hours at home
- allowing flexible onsite work hours
- allocating dependent care spending accounts
- providing specific childcare benefits, including emergency care programs, onsite care centers, employer-arranged discounts with local care providers, and
- providing additional assistance to employees, such as counseling and seminars on work and family issues.

If you feel that one of these options is feasible in your workplace and would make your life more manageable, talk with your employer. Better still, come to the talk armed with success stories of similar set-ups in local companies.

1. Work at Home Agreements

These days, many jobs use computers as essential tools. And computers can easily be transported or hooked up to communicate with the main worksite from various locales. Many other kinds of work are also portable and may lend themselves well to work at home arrangements for employees.

These arrangements often involve an agreement between the worker and the company—best if it is in writing—that spells out who is responsible for any legal liabilities that arise from the work at home arrangement and how worktime will be measured.

For example, a work at home agreement may specify that you are responsible for any damage that occurs to a company-owned laptop computer while it is being used in your home. Most homeowners' and renters' insurance policies do not automatically cover business equipment, so you may have to purchase additional coverage.

Also, check the agreement against the wage and hour laws (discussed in Chapter 3) to make sure that neither you nor your employer would be breaking the Fair Labor Standards Act through your work at home plan. In general, if you are not an exempt employee, the wages and hours provisions of the Act still apply even when you are working at home.

Whose Child Is This?

According to a recent AT&T study of working parents, 73% of men and 77% of women with children under 18 said they take time at work to deal with family issues. And 25% of men and 48% of women reported that they spend "unproductive time at work because of childcare issues." Indeed, some workplace specialists posit that filling in for childcare arrangements that have run awry is the biggest source of employee absenteeism and lack of workplace productivity.

Still, employers have done little to pitch in. Very few offer incentive compensation earmarked for childcare. And fewer still provide the solution for which parents clamor loudest: onsite childcare facilities.

Many businesses are hesitant to establish their own childcare facilities simply because they represent a grand departure from business practices as usual. Others fear reprisals from the appearance of inequality—offering a service that cannot benefit workers without children.

And some cite start-up difficulties—picayune state regulations requiring separate kitchen facilities and per child minimums on everything from space to caretakers to supervisors of caretakers.

But where the experiment has been tried—Stride Rite Corporation in Boston and Nyloncraft of Indiana were among the trendsetters—it has, by most accounts, succeeded. Employee turnovers, absenteeism and tardiness plummet and peace of mind and company loyalty escalate. As one human resources director at a bank put it, their childcare center is good for the bottom line: "Not only is this an excellent recruitment tool, but a phenomenal retention tool."

2. Flexible Workhours

In many urban workplaces, where rush hour commuting makes for immense amounts of downtime, 9 to 5 workdays are all but extinct. In fact, a growing number of employers everywhere are putting less credence in the rigid Monday to Friday, 9 to 5 workweek and allowing employees to adopt more flexible work schedules.

When this idea was newer, it was referred to by the high-tech appellation of flextime. Flextime is not a reduction in hours, but simply a shift in the times employees are required to clock in and out of work. An increasingly popular flextime option, for example, is the ten-hour/four-day workweek, as it gives employees at least the illusion of a three-day weekend. Since flextime employees usually maintain 40-hour workweeks, they lose no benefits—such as healthcare coverage or vacation time—in the bargain.

3. Counseling and Other Benefits

Many employers now make employee counseling an integral part of their discipline procedures. That is, fewer employees are surprised by being fired from a company, since more have had the option of getting some form of counseling first—to improve their work performances, to help them conquer drug or alcohol abuse problems, to help raise awareness about potential sexual harassment.

And more enlightened employers now also offer employees a number of seminars and workshops more indirectly related to the workplace—workshops on building self-esteem, dealing with long-term healthcare for aging parents and First Aid and CPR certification. These educational workshops not only train employees in more valuable skills, they also have the more nebulous value of improving morale.

At some workplaces, employees have taken the initiative in setting up their own workshops during lunchtimes or after work hours. Volunteers from local special interest groups—the Red Cross, stress management groups, battered women's shelters, self-defense trainers—are often available to present the training free or at a very low cost.

Breastfeeding at Work:
A Whole New Meaning to Eating at Your Desk

Pediatric guidelines recently released urge that mothers can boost the health and development of their babies if they breastfeed them for at least a year. But for many moms who must return to work, the urging is unrealistic. In fact, in the United States, only about 12% of fulltime working mothers keep nursing for five months or longer.

Very few employers provide working mothers the time or place to nurse on the job. Some fear flack from other employees, who may decry that lactating moms would receive preferential treatment on the job. Others decry the possibility, labeling workplace breastfeeding with a range of epithets from Unprofessional to Abhorrent.

If some breastfeeding backers get their way, it may one day be the law. For example, a bill recently introduced in Congress, the New Mothers' Breastfeeding Promotion and Protection Act of 1998, sought to make it illegal to discriminate against working mothers who breastfeed on the job. The bill proposed unpaid breaks of up to one hour each workday so that women could express milk. And it offered tax credits for employers who set up nursing stations, provide breast pumps or hire lactation consultants. While the bill garnered 41 cosponsors, it was not passed.

But breastfeeding moms have legions of supporters outside Congress, many of them organized into groups such as World Alliance for Breastfeeding Action (WABA). Guided by the declaration that: "Today's babies are tomorrow's workers," WABA offers steps that employers and employees can undertake together to make workplaces Mother-Friendly.

1. Gather the facts.

Find out what is needed. Then make a situation analysis. Look at your workplace to see what facilities already exist to enable mothers to breastfeed at work.

Next, look at possible barriers; remember, these can often be removed with little cost. Often there are barriers of the mind more than barriers in fact.

2. Generate understanding and commitment.

Talk to other decisionmakers about the costs of labor in your company and the benefits of a mother-friendly workplace. Expect skepticism. But do also expect that support comes from unlikely places, and don't rely on stereotypical images to anticipate where objection and support will come from. Be patient and remember that time is an ally; attitudes change with knowledge and others have gone before with demonstrable success.

3. Establish a working group to develop a specific approach.

Once you have commitment from your corporate decisionmakers, working in a representative and supportive group reinforces the idea.

The group must be rigorous about recognizing any problems and quickly taking remedial action. Often, this is as simple as chatting with a supervisor to allow 5-minutes extra break time for a mother, which she will make up at the end of the day.

4. Evaluate.

At the end of the pilot project, the group and the decisionmakers evaluate feedback about acceptance of the program. Some policy and practice adjustments may be made. Most will have already been made during the pilot stage.

5. Implement and publicize.

With renewed corporate commitment, announce and implement your company's permanent commitment to a workplace that supports mothers and families.

CHAPTER

6

PRIVACY RIGHTS

Technology has made it easier to pry into people's lives and psyches—through computerized recordkeeping, drug and alcohol testing, videotaping and audiotaping. And that has caused more workers to want to protect something of themselves, to jealously guard their rights to privacy, to be left alone at work.

Theoretically, at least, employers sit on the other side of the fence. They are understandably concerned about stomping down on wrongdoing and waste in the workplace, such as drug and alcohol abuse, theft, incompetence and low productivity. And usually, their concerns center on finding and keeping the best qualified employees. To that end, most employers want to learn as much as possible about what goes on and who spends time in a workplace.

While there are some legal controls on what an employer and prospective employer can find out about you and on how they can use that information, there are still many ways an employer can invade your privacy—for example, by requiring you to take a drug test under some circumstances. But there are also some subtle limits on the extent to which your privacy can be invaded. In general, employers are entitled to intrude on your personal life no more than is necessary for legitimate business interests.

Most abuses of privacy rights occur when people are not aware of the legal constraints and how to enforce them. This chapter covers these legal constraints and outlines some of the most profound current workplace privacy issues: access to personnel records, medical and psychological testing and use of credit checks and surveillance during work.

A. Your Personnel Records

Your employer is required by law to keep some tabs on you—including information on your wages and hours, workplace injuries and illnesses and tax withholding, as well as records of accrued vacation and other benefits. That information is usually gathered together in one place: your personnel file. Your file will usually contain little information you did not know or provide to your employer in the first place.

But personnel files can sometimes become the catch-alls for other kinds of information—references from previous employers, comments from customers or clients, employee reprimands, job performance evaluations, memos of management's observations about an employee's behavior or productivity. When employment disputes develop, or an employee is demoted, transferred or fired, the innards of his or her personnel file often provide essential information—often unknown to the employee—about the whys and wherefores.

A federal law, the Privacy Act (5 U.S.C. §552a), limits the type of information that federal agencies, the military and other government employers may keep on their workers.

However, private employers have a nearly unfettered hand when it comes to the kind of information they can collect. The laws in a few states restrict the information in personnel files. Michigan, for example, bars employers from keeping records describing an employee's political associations (Mich. Stat. Ann. §17.62 (8)). And employers in Minnesota may not retaliate with any information intentionally left out of a personnel file (Minn. Stat. Ann. §§181.960 to .965).

While many states now have some type of law regulating personnel files for private employers (see the chart below), most of these laws control not the content of the files, but:

- whether and how employees and former employees can get access to their personnel files
- whether employees are entitled to copies of the information in them, and
- how employees can contest and correct erroneous information in their files.

1. Getting Access to Your File

The best way to find out what a company knows about you, or what it is saying about you to outside people who inquire, is to obtain a copy of the contents of your personnel file from your current or former employer.

In some states, the only way you would get to see those files is while collecting evidence after filing a lawsuit against the employer or former employer. And even then you might be in for a legal battle over what portions of the files are relevant to the case. But in many states, you have the right to see the contents of your personnel file without filing a lawsuit. For example, Oregon law gives employees the right to a copy of any documents an employer uses in making a workplace decision—including promotions, raises or firings. But beware that a number of states limit what documents you have the legal right to see. In California, Nevada and Wisconsin, for example, employees need not be shown references from past employers. And those three states in addition to Michigan, New Hampshire and Washington limit employees' access to their files if employers are investigating them for a possible crime or other misconduct. The rationale behind this is to protect incriminating evidence from being destroyed.

State laws on employee access to personnel records generally cover technical matters, such as when your request must be made and how long the employer has to respond. Before you request your file, read the law on procedures for your state. In general, you must make your request to see your personnel files in writing to your employer or former employer as soon as you decide that you want to see them. If you send your request by certified mail, you will be able to prove when the request was submitted, should you need that evidence later.

If you live in a state that does not have a specific law ensuring you access to your personnel records, all is not lost. If you wish to see and copy your personnel files, ask to do so. If you meet with resistance, make a more formal request in writing. If that request is denied, and you genuinely believe your records may contain information that is critical to your position, you may need to consult with an expert such as a private investigator or experienced attorney.

Forcing an Employer to Keep Your Secrets

Employers are supposed to collect only information about you that is job-related. And only those people with a proven need to know are supposed to have access to your personnel file. For example, your employer cannot tell your co-workers the results of a drug screening test you were required to take. But the truth is that employers frequently give out information about their employees to other people—other employers, unions, police investigators, creditors, insurance agents.

Job applicants or employees who wish some personal information to remain private—address and phone number, for example, if they fear physical violence at the hands of a former spouse—should request in writing that the information be kept confidential. That request may end up being worth little more than the paper it is written on. But it may also be the strongest evidence of an employer's negligence should problems develop later.

Additional Laws May Apply

If the chart below indicates that your state has no statute, this means there is no law that specifically addresses the issue. However, there may be a state administrative regulation or local ordinance that does control. Call your state labor department for more information. (See the Appendix for contact details.)

State Laws on Employee Access to Personnel Records	
Alabama	No statute
Alaska	Employees have the right to see their personnel files and make a copy of them. Alaska Stat. §23.10.430
Arizona	No statute
Arkansas	Public employees have right of access to their personnel and evaluation records. Ark. Code Ann. § 25-19-105(c)(2)
California	All employers must make a copy of the employee's personnel file available where the employee reports to work and must permit the employee to inspect it when he or she asks to see it. The employee must make the inspection request at "reasonable times"—which are set by the Labor Commissioner.
	Does not apply to letters of reference or records relating to the investigation of a possible offense. Cal. Lab. Code §1198.5

Colorado	No statute
Connecticut	Employees have the right to see their personnel files and to insert a written rebuttal of information with which they disagree. Conn. Gen. Stat. Ann. §§31-128b and 128e
Delaware	Employees have the right to see their personnel files and to insert written rebuttals of information with which they disagree. Employees must inspect files at work during regular business hours and may not take any copies of the file off the premises. Employers may require employees to submit written requests, to view files on their own time and in the presence of a company official and may limit inspections to once a year.
	Employers who deny access or who retaliate against employees for making complaints are subject to fines of $1,000 to $5,000 for each violation. Del. Code Ann. tit. 19 §§730 through 735
District of Columbia	Employees of The District of Columbia have the right to review their personnel records, to insert rebuttal information and to request the removal of information that is irrelevant or more than three years old. D.C. Code Ann. §1-632.5
Florida	No statute
Georgia	No statute
Hawaii	No statute
Idaho	School district employees have the right to review and obtain copies of their personnel files—except for letters of recommendation—and to attach rebuttals to any material in the file. Idaho Code §33-518
Illinois	Employers with five or more employees must allow them to see and make copies of their personnel files at least twice a year and must make the files available seven working days after receiving the request. The exceptions are: letters of reference, testing documents and investigatory records concerning possible criminal conduct of the employee, which could harm the employer. Employees may insert written rebuttals of any information with which they disagree. 820 Ill. Comp. Stat. 40/0.01 to 40/13
Indiana	No statute
Iowa	Employees have the right to see and copy personnel files, including performance evaluations and disciplinary records, but not references. Iowa Code §91B.1
Kansas	No statute
Kentucky	No statute
Louisiana	Current or former employees, or their designated representatives, have a right to get access to employers' records of employee exposure to toxic substances, medical records and analyses using employee records. La. Rev. Stat. Ann. §23.1016
	State employees are allowed access to their entire personnel files—and they may rebut any information with which they disagree. La. Rev. Stat. Ann. §§17:1235 and 1237

Maine	Employees have the right to see and make copies of their personnel files, including workplace evaluations. Me. Rev. Stat. Ann. tit. 26 §631
Maryland	No statute
Massachusetts	Employees have the right to see their personnel files and to insert rebuttals of any information with which they disagree. Employees may take court action to expunge any information that the employer knows, or should have known, was incorrect. Does not apply to employees of private colleges or universities who are tenured, on tenure track or who have positions or responsibilities similar to those in tenure track positions. Violators can be punished by a fine of $500 to $2,500. Mass. Gen. Laws Ann. ch. 149 §52C
Michigan	Employees have the right to see and make a copy of their personnel files—except for employee references—and to insert rebuttals of any information with which they disagree. If an employer is investigating an employee for criminal activity that may cause loss to the employer's business, that information must be kept in a separate file. When the investigation ends or after two years, whichever comes first, the employee must be told of the outcome and, if no disciplinary action is taken, the investigation file must be destroyed. Mich. Comp. Laws §§423.501 to 512
Minnesota	Employees have the right to see their personnel files and to insert rebuttals of any information with which they disagree. Does not apply to public employers. A former employee may inspect once within the year following termination. An employer may not use in any retaliatory way any information intentionally left out of the personnel record. Minn. Stat. Ann. §§181.960 to 965
Mississippi	Public employees are permitted access to their personnel records. Miss. Code Ann. §25-1-100
Missouri	Teachers and school administrators must be given copies of evaluations maintained in their personnel files. Mo. Ann. Stat. §§168.128 and 168.410
Montana	No statute
Nebraska	Employees of counties with more than 300,000 inhabitants have access to their personnel records. Neb. Rev. Stat. §23-2507
Nevada	Employees who have been employed at least 60 days have the right to see and copy any records that the employer used to confirm the employee's qualifications, or as the basis for any disciplinary action. If those records contain incorrect information, the employee may notify the employer of the errors in writing. The employer is required to correct the challenged information if the employer decides it is false. However, the employee may not inspect confidential reports from past employers or reports from an investigative agency regarding the employee's violation of any law. Nev. Rev. Stat. §613.075

New Hampshire	Employees have the right to see and copy their personnel files and to insert rebuttals of any information with which they disagree. Employers may not disclose information that relates to a government security investigation or information regarding an investigation of the employee if that disclosure would prejudice law enforcement. N.H. Rev. Stat. §275:56
New Jersey	No statute
New Mexico	No statute
New York	No statute
North Carolina	Employees have access to records of their exposure to toxic substances. N.C. Gen. Stat. §95-143. School, community college and state employees and their authorized representatives have access to personnel records except for letter of reference. N.C. Gen. Stat. §§115C-32, 115D-29 and 126-24
North Dakota	State employees, but not those of political subdivisions, must be given the opportunity to read information regarding their performance or character before it is placed in their files. Anonymous entries are not permitted. Employees have the right to answer any material in the file, and they may copy the information at their own expense. Employers may maintain separate performance notes to use in employee evaluations or in disciplinary actions. N.D. Cent. Code Ann. §54-06-21
Ohio	Employees have the right to copies of medical reports furnished to employers. Ohio Rev. Code §4113.23 Public employees have the right to review records of their exposure to toxic substances. Ohio Rev. Code §4167.11
Oklahoma	An employee is entitled to a copy of a report of a required medical examination. Okla. Stat. Ann., tit. 40, §191
Oregon	Employees have the right to see and copy any documents used by the employer in making work-related decisions, such as promotions, wage increases or termination. Or. Rev. Stat. §652.750
Pennsylvania	Employees have the right to see the personnel files that contain their qualifications for employment, promotion, additional compensation, termination or disciplinary action. They do not have access to letters of reference or any criminal investigation records. The files may not be copied or removed. Employers may require employees to submit written requests, to view files on their own time and in the presence of a designated company official and may limit access to once a year. 43 Pa. Cons. Stat. Ann. §§1321 through 1323
Rhode Island	Upon submitting a written request at least seven business days in advance, employees have the right to see their personnel files up to three times per year. The files may not be removed, but the employees may request that specific documents be copied. Employers do not have to allow employees to review letters of reference, criminal investigation records, managerial records or confidential reports from prior employers. R.I. Gen. Laws §§28-6.4-1 and 28-6.4-2
South Carolina	Employees have the right to review records of their exposure to toxic substances. S.C. Code Ann. §14-15-100

South Dakota	Public employees have the right to review their personnel records. S.D. Codified Laws §3-6A-31
Tennessee	State employees have the right to review their personnel records and to make copies at their own expense. Tenn. Code Ann. §8-50-108
Texas	Government employees have access to all information in their personnel files. Tex. Gov't Code Ann. §552.101
	Teachers must receive written copies of all evaluations placed in their personnel files and are entitled to submit written rebuttals. Tex. Educ. Code Ann. §21.352
	If a negative document is placed in the personnel file of a firefighter or police officer, the employer must notify him or her, give him or her a copy upon request and allow him or her to file a written response. Tex. Local Gov't. Code Ann. §143.089
Utah	Public employees have the right to examine and make copies of their personnel files. Utah Code Ann. §§67-18-1 and following
Vermont	Public employees have access to all information in their personnel files. Va. Code Ann. §2.1-342.01 (A)(4)
Virginia	Public employees may have access to their personnel files. Vt. Stat. Ann. tit. 1, §317(7)
Washington	Employees have the right to see their personnel files at least once a year and to insert written rebuttals of any information with which they disagree. A former employee retains the right of rebuttal or correction for two years. Does not apply if employee is subject to criminal investigation or if the records have been compiled in preparation for an impending lawsuit. Wash. Rev. Code §§49.12.240 to 260
West Virginia	No statute
Wisconsin	Employees have the right to see and copy their personnel files up to twice a year, and to insert rebuttals of any information with which they disagree. Does not apply to records related to a criminal investigation or a pending claim or to letters of reference.
	If an employer thinks that disclosing medical records would be detrimental to an employee, the employer may instead disclose them to a physician designated by the employee. Wis. Stat. §103.13
Wyoming	Public employees may see personnel records containing their application information, performance ratings and scholastic achievements. Wyo. Stat. 16-4-203 (d)(iii)

2. Criminal Records

According to recent statistics collected by the Bureau of Justice, approximately one-third of the workforce has a criminal record, most commonly including theft. Despite this high proportion of workers with criminal records, many feel they are approached with wariness, or even subjected to abject discrimination, by employers who learn of their histories.

Arrest and conviction records are public records available to anyone, including an employer, who has the wherewithal and incentive to search for them. These records are also kept by a number of agencies—police, prosecutors, courts, the FBI, probation departments, prisons, parole boards. These recordkeepers are theoretically barred from releasing this information to anyone other than other criminal justice agencies and a few types of specialized employers such as those who help manufacture controlled substances or run childcare or eldercare facilities. In reality, however, slips of the tongue are made and persistent employers can generally find the ways and means to get their eyes on the information.

Most states now have laws that specifically bar employers and prospective employers from getting access to records of arrests that did not lead to convictions. And a number of states—including California, Michigan and Rhode Island—forbid employers from even asking job applicants about such arrests.

Still, there are many exceptions to this Don't Ask, Don't Tell rule for specific categories of workers, including most bank employees, securities industry and commodities workers and nuclear power employees.

And states are especially mindful of the need and right to do thorough background checks when employees and volunteers will be working closely with children or adults who are ill or elderly and may be considered vulnerable. Many statutes specify that those working in schools, adult care homes, nursing homes, home care agencies and facilities for those with mental and physical disabilities may—and often must—be subjected to criminal background checks before being allowed on the job.

Whatever the state of the law, the reality is that employers customarily bend and trample on the rules against asking about former arrests and convictions. And in most states, private employers can check—and are often duty-bound to check—the conviction records of prospective employees. Since most records of criminal convictions are freely open to the public, there is usually little a job applicant or employee can do to stop an employer from discovering them.

Expunging Your Past

Many states have laws that allow individuals to expunge, or seal, their criminal records. When a record is expunged, it is usually not available to anyone other than criminal justice agencies and the courts. If your criminal record has been expunged, you are generally allowed to deny that you have had one when a prospective employer asks about it.

But states have varying policies on this. In Massachusetts, for example, an employer that asks about criminal history must include on the application a statement that an applicant with a sealed record is entitled to answer "no record" regarding the underlying offenses. But in Ohio, an employer may question an applicant regarding an expunged record if the underlying incident relates to the type of job you are seeking.

Some states extend the expungement privilege only to a first arrest that did not result in a conviction. Other states are more generous, allowing a conviction for a petty offense to be expunged if probation was successfully completed. Some states limit the procedure to juvenile records. Usually, the request to seal your record will be granted only if you have remained clear of any contacts with the criminal justice system for a specified period of time following your arrest or conviction.

The bottom line: Only small potato crimes can be easily expunged from your record—not the ones likely to derail you from most jobs. Records of truly serious offenses cannot be sealed and are with you for life.

Additional Laws May Apply

If the chart below indicates that your state has no statute, this means there is no law that specifically addresses the issue. However, there may be a state administrative regulation or local ordinance that does control. Call your state labor department for more information. (See the Appendix for contact details.)

State Laws on Employee Arrest & Conviction Records	
Alabama	Applicants for a job or volunteer position with a public or private school who have unsupervised access to children under 19 must sign a statement that they have not been convicted of a crime that relates to their fitness to teach or to be responsible for children. Those who fail to reveal prior convictions or to submit to an investigation may be denied employment. Employers will conduct state and federal background checks of applicants. Current employees will not be subject to background checks unless their behavior

causes a reasonable suspicion that a background check is warranted.
Employees and applicants may contest the criminal history background information. They may also request that a disqualifying decision be reversed, provided it
is not based on a conviction for a sex crime or a crime against a child, elderly
person or a person with disabilities. Ala. Code §§16-22A-1 and following.

Alaska

The state can release information concerning past convictions if less than ten
years have passed since the person was released from prison. Sealed criminal
justice records cannot be released except for criminal justice employment
purposes. Alaska Stat. §12.62.160, .180

Arizona

Those employed by schools, in programs for schools or for developmentally
disabled adults and in domestic violence shelters must have valid fingerprint
clearance cards—which are issued after a local, state and federal criminal
history background check is conducted. They must also certify that there are
neither pending charges nor previous convictions for violent or sex crimes or
drug related offenses. Ariz. Rev. Stat. Ann. §§15-1330, 15-534, 36-425.03,
36-594.01 and 36-3008

Other employers may obtain arrest or conviction records only if there is a
compelling business reason for doing so. Arizona Attorney General, Civil
Rights Division, "Guide to Pre-Employment Inquiries under the Arizona Civil
Rights Act."

Enforcing agency: Civil Rights Division, 1275 West Washington Street,
Phoenix, AZ 85007, 602-542-5263

Arkansas

Private investigators and security officers must provide a verified statement
disclosing any convictions of a felony, Class A misdemeanor, violent crime or
crime involving moral turpitude. Ark. Code Ann. § 17-40-327

California

Employers may not ask prospective employees to disclose information regarding
an arrest or detention which did not result in conviction. They also may not ask
regarding a referral to a diversion program. Employers may not seek or use as a
condition of employment any such information, but may inquire as to an arrest
for which a current or prospective employee is out on bail or their own recogni-
zance. Law enforcement and criminal justice agencies are exempt.

Employees and applicants for positions at health facilities and for jobs
involving access to drugs and medications may be asked questions regarding
certain arrests. Does not apply to applicants for public concessions. Cal. Lab.
Code §432.7

Employers may not inquire about convictions involving marijuana that were
earlier than January 1, 1976. Cal Labor Code §432.8

Colorado

Employers may not require the disclosure of sealed arrest records if the
employee was acquitted, no charges were filed or the case was dismissed.
Does not apply to pleas or convictions for any type of offense, driving under
the influence of drugs or alcohol, sexual assault, indecent exposure, incest or
child prostitution. Colo. Rev. Stat. §24-72-308

Connecticut

Information about the arrest record of an applicant may not be made available
to anyone other than the personnel department or the person in charge of
employment. Conn. Gen. Stat. Ann. § 31-51i

Delaware	Records of an arrest that resulted in a dismissal or an acquittal, that have been ordered expunged by a court, do not have to be disclosed for any reason as an arrest. Does not apply to applicants to law enforcement agencies. Del. Code Ann. tit. 11 §§4371 to 4374
District of Columbia	Healthcare and community residence facilities and hospice and home care agencies must conduct criminal background checks on all unlicensed personnel, including volunteers. Those convicted of felonies may be denied employment. Records of background checks are confidential and may not be released to anyone but the mayor or the mayor's designee during an investigation or inspection of the facility. The facility must destroy an employee's criminal records one year after employment ends. D.C. Code Ann. §32-1352
Florida	A background screening or security check is required by law for employees of childcare facilities, nursing homes and home healthcare and developmentally disabled service agencies. Applicants and employees must undergo statewide and local criminal record checks, and people in positions of trust must undergo checks of juvenile and federal records as well. The employer may give the information to any other employer who requests it. Fla. Stat. Ann. §§435.01 to 435.11, 400.215, 402.302, 110.1127 Counties and municipalities may not enact legislation that requires routine background checks of public employees; however, license requirements that include background screening are lawful. Fla. Stat. §125.581
Georgia	The Department of Human Resources can obtain records of a job applicant's convictions if the job duties would include the care, treatment or custody of clients or if obtaining the information is otherwise necessary for the safety of clients, other employees or the general public. The Department of Human Resources may not release this information to other people or agencies. Ga. Code Ann. §49-2-14
Hawaii	The state may not disqualify someone for employment or for a license, permit or certificate solely on the basis of a conviction for a crime but may consider it if it relates to the person's possible job performance. Does not apply to the issuance of a liquor license nor for employment in healthcare, youth care or detention facilities. Haw. Rev. Stat. §831-3.1(a) Employers may inquire into an applicant's conviction record if it bears a rational relationship to the duties and responsibilities of the job and if the employer has made a conditional offer of employment. The state can disseminate records of convictions only, and not of arrests that did not lead to convictions, expunged convictions, convictions for which no jail sentence was possible and misdemeanor convictions that are more than 20 years old. Haw. Rev. Stat. §§378-2.5; 831-3.1(a)
Idaho	Board and care facilities for adults with mental and developmental disabilities and agencies that provide personal care services must conduct criminal background checks on employees. Idaho Code §§39-3342 and 39-5604
Illinois	Employers, employment agencies and labor organizations may not inquire about or use arrest information or a criminal history record that has been ordered sealed or expunged as a basis to refuse to hire or take any adverse employment action against a current or prospective employee.

	However, the state, school districts and certain private organizations can use information from the Department of State Police in evaluating qualifications of applicants or prospective employees. 775 Ill. Rev. Stat. 5/2-103; 20 Ill. Comp. Stat. 2630/3
Indiana	The state can release to prospective employers information on arrests or charges—including information on volunteers with child service agencies or with public and private schools. Ind. Code Ann. §5-2-5-1 and following
	Applicants for taxicab driver or for massage therapist licenses may be required to submit fingerprints for investigation. Ind. Code Ann. §5-2-5-14
	A person may petition to limit access to state criminal history data if more than 15 years have elapsed since a conviction or a discharge from prison, probation or parole. Ind. Code Ann. §35-38-5-5
Iowa	No statute
Kansas	Employers can require applicants to sign releases allowing them to access the applicant's criminal history record for the purpose of determining the applicant's fitness for employment. Kan. Stat. Ann. §22-4710
Kentucky	A person cannot be disqualified from public employment based on a misdemeanor for which no jail sentence can be imposed. For other types of misdemeanors and felonies, the hiring agency can consider the nature and seriousness of the crime and the relationship of the crime to the job duties.
	If employment is denied based on a criminal record, the applicant must be given notice, a hearing and the opportunity to reapply upon rehabilitation. This law does not apply to lawyers and police. Ky. Rev. Stat. §§335B.010 and following
Louisiana	Applicants cannot be disqualified from a license, permit or certificate, required to practice a trade or profession, on account of a prior criminal record unless it is a felony conviction that directly relates to the position or occupation sought. This does not apply to doctors, dentists, nurses, pharmacists, funeral directors, lawyers, private investigators, architects or engineers—professions which have separate licensing requirements. La. Rev. Stat. Ann. §37:2950
	An employer of a nonlicensed person hired to perform nursing care or health-related services must ask the state police to do a criminal record check. The applicant must be told about the check before he is offered the job. All information received must be kept confidential and destroyed one year after employment ceases. La. Rev. Stat. Ann. §40:1300.51 to 1300.56
Maine	When granting an occupational license, state licensing agencies may consider both convictions involving dishonesty and those that directly relate to the trade or occupation for which the license is sought. State boards of medicine, psychology, social work and criminal justice will consider convictions for sexual misconduct.
	An agency may refuse to grant or may suspend a license because of a person's criminal history only if it determines that the person has not been sufficiently rehabilitated; it is up to the applicant to prove that he or she is worthy of public trust. An agency that denies a license based on criminal history must state the reason in writing.

If more than three years have passed since the applicant was released from prison—ten years for healthcare, criminal justice and social workers—the licensing agency cannot consider the conviction; however, if the conviction is for an offense that would be grounds for disciplinary action against a licensee, there is no time limit. Me. Rev. Stat. Ann. tit. 5 §§5301 to 5303

Maryland	Employers or educational institutions may not require job applicants to disclose information regarding criminal charges that have been expunged. Md. Code Ann. art. 27, §740
Massachusetts	An applicant for public employment may not be disqualified on account of information in sealed criminal records. Any employer who asks about criminal history must include, on the application, the advice that an applicant with a sealed record is entitled to answer "no record" regarding prior convictions, court appearances or arrests. Mass. Gen. Laws. Ann. ch. 276, §100A
Michigan	Employers, employment agencies and labor organizations may not request, make or maintain records regarding arrest or detention that did not result in conviction. Applicants and employees are free to withhold information that is within their civil rights to withhold. This does not apply to felony charges prior to conviction or dismissal or to public law enforcement agencies. Mich. Comp. Laws §37.2205a
Minnesota	A person seeking public employment, or a license or a certificate from the state necessary for an occupation or a profession, cannot be disqualified because of a prior conviction unless it directly relates to the position or occupation. Records of arrest that did not lead to conviction, expunged conviction or misdemeanor conviction not subject to a jail sentence cannot be disclosed to an employer. Does not apply to law enforcement, fire protection, lawyers, doctors, schools or childcare providers. Mich. Stat. Ann. §§364.01 and following
Mississippi	Employers of those providing childcare must obtain sex offense criminal history information—including arrests and charges even if the person was not convicted or prosecuted—for every employee or volunteer. People with specific prior sex offenses may not be hired. Miss. Code Ann. §§43-20-8 and following
Missouri	Those applying for positions or licenses involving caring for children or the elderly must submit to criminal history background checks. Every child or elder care worker hired beginning January 1, 2001, must register with the Family Care Safety Registry and consent to background check information being released. Mo. Ann. Stat. §210.485.1 and following
Montana	No statute
Nebraska	Applicants for any civil service position must disclose a criminal history and submit a full set of fingerprints for state and federal identification. Neb. Rev. Stat. §19-1831
	Employees of licensed foster care, child care and developmentally disabled adult care facilities must undergo investigations of their criminal histories. Neb. Rev. Stat. §71-1903 and 1912; 83-1217 and 1217.01

Nevada	Employers may inquire if applicants have been convicted of felony or a misdemeanor, but must inform them that conviction does not necessarily disqualify them. *Nevada Equal Rights Commission Pre-Employment Inquiry Guide* Enforcing agency: Equal Rights Commission, 2450 Wrondel Way, Suite C, Reno, NV 89502, 702-688-1288
New Hampshire	All job applicants and volunteers with schools or school administrations must submit notarized criminal history records releases and complete sets of fingerprints. Convictions of violent felonies and sex crimes are valid grounds not to hire—and local school governing bodies may adopt policies refusing employment to applicants convicted of any felony. All criminal history information is confidential; schools must destroy information immediately if an applicant has no criminal record, or within 30 days if an applicant has been convicted of a felony or a sex crime. N.H. Rev. Stat. Ann. §189:13-a
New Jersey	In addition to federal and state employers, any private employer or volunteer supervisor may request criminal conviction and arrest information from the state Bureau of Identification to determine a person's qualifications for work. Requests must be accompanied by a set of fingerprints or the person's Social Security number and date of birth. Employers who are required by federal or state law to perform criminal history background checks will also be given information on arrests. Employers must keep the information confidential. New Jersey Administrative Code §§ 13:59 to 13:59-1.6 Public and private employers that operate schools, daycare facilities or youth centers must perform state and federal criminal history record checks for all applicants—including school bus drivers—who will regularly come into contact with students under 18 years old. Applicants with specified convictions may not be hired unless they can present proof of rehabilitation. Does not apply to volunteers. N.J. Stat. Ann. §§18A:6-4.15 and .16, 18A:6-7.1 to 7.4, 18A:39-19.1
New Mexico	An employer must conduct a nationwide criminal records check of all employees of childcare and detention facilities. N.M. Stat. Ann. §§32-A-15-1 to 4 State employers and licensing authorities can consider applicants' felony convictions and misdemeanor convictions for crimes involving moral turpitude but the convictions are not an automatic bar to employment. A person's license can be suspended or revoked if he or she is convicted of a felony or a misdemeanor involving moral turpitude if the crime directly relates to the employment, trade or business. N.M. Stat. Ann. §§28-2-3 and 4
New York	Public employers and private employers with more than ten employees may not deny employment to an applicant who has one or more past criminal convictions unless there is a direct relationship between the past offense and the employment or license sought. Employment may also be denied if, in light of the applicant's record, the job or license would involve an unreasonable risk to property or the safety and welfare of individuals or to the general public. Does not apply to crimes where forfeiture of a license is part of the penalty. N.Y. Correction Law §752 and following

North Carolina	Criminal record checks are required for job applicants and those employed at adult care homes, nursing homes, home care agencies, Department of Health and Human Services and charter schools. N.C. Gen. Stat. §§114-19.6, 115C-238.29K, 131D-40, 131E-265
North Dakota	Employees of licensed early childhood facilities are subject to criminal record screening. People who have been convicted of child abuse or neglect and who have not been sufficiently rehabilitated are disqualified from employment. N.D. Cent. Code §50-11.1-04 Teaching certificates can be revoked if a criminal conviction has direct bearing on the person's ability to serve as a teacher. N.D. Cent. Code §15-36-15 Criminal background checks are required on applicants for jobs in the gaming industry. N.D. Cent. Code §53-06.1-06
Ohio	An employer may question applicants regarding only those convictions that have not been sealed by court order, unless the question bears a direct and substantial relationship to the position sought. Ohio Rev. Code §2953.33
Oklahoma	Employers, educational institutions and local and state government agencies may not question a prospective employee, in any job application or interview, about a criminal record that has been expunged. Okla. Stat. Ann. tit. 22 §19(F) Every owner or administrator of a child care facility or home must arrange for a criminal history investigation, conducted by the Oklahoma State Bureau of Investigation, for every applicant or, if the applicant has lived in the state less than one year, by the appropriate agency in the previous state of residence. Sex crimes requiring registration under the Sex Offenders Registration Act bar employment. Okla. Stat. Ann. tit. 10 §404.1
Oregon	Employers may seek criminal offender information after first advising the current or prospective employees that such information is being sought. The Department of State may inform the employer of the date of arrest, offense, arresting agency, court of origin, disposition and sentence. Or. Rev. Stat. §181.557 to .560 Employers may not discriminate against an applicant because of a juvenile record that has been expunged by law. Or. Rev. Stat. §659.030
Pennsylvania	Felony and misdemeanor convictions may be considered only to the extent that they relate to an applicant's suitability for the job. Employers must notify applicants in writing if the decision not to hire is based on criminal history. 18 Pa. Cons. Stat. Ann. §9125
Rhode Island	Employers may not inquire of prospective employees whether they have ever been arrested or charged with a crime, but may ask about convictions. Does not apply to law enforcement. R.I. Gen. Laws §28-5-7(7) Prospective employees who have had a conviction of a crime expunged may state that they have never been convicted of a crime. Law enforcement applicants, applicants for the bar, teachers applying for certificates and operators or employees of early childhood educational facilities are excepted. R.I. Gen. Laws §12-1.3-4

South Carolina	Local school districts must obtain a state criminal history before hiring a teacher. S.C. Code Ann. §59-26-40(M)
South Dakota	Applicants for positions with public or private schools or child welfare agencies must submit to criminal background investigations. S.D. Codified Laws Ann. §§13-10-12 and 23-5-12.1
Tennessee	All job applicants and volunteers with the Department of Mental Health and Developmental Disabilities, child care agencies and youth service organizations and institutions must submit to criminal history records checks. Tenn. Code Ann. §§33-1-209, 37-1-414, 71-3-507 Counties and municipalities may require all job applicants to submit to criminal history records checks. SB 2557 (5/9/00)
Texas	State criminal record history information is available to numerous specified employers—including state agencies, fire departments, hotels, schools, public housing, boards of medical and law examiners, child care and treatment facilities and licensing and regulatory agencies. Texas Code Ann. Government §§411.081 to .128 and Health and Safety §765.001 and following
Utah	No statute
Vermont	Criminal records are confidential and may be disclosed only to specifically designated people. Records of applicants for teaching positions with the school district or with an independent school may be disclosed with the signed release of the applicant. Juvenile court records may not be disclosed. Vt. Stat. Ann., tit. 16 §§251 to 260; tit. 33 §5536
Virginia	Employers, educational institutions and local and state governments may not require applicants to disclose expunged arrests or charges, and need not answer questions relating to them. Va. Code Ann. §19.2-392.4
Washington	Employers may request conviction records of current or prospective employees for these specified purposes only: employee bonding; pre-employment and post-employment evaluation of employees with access to money or items of value; or investigation of employee misconduct which may constitute a penal offense. Employers must notify the employee or prospective employee of the inquiry and make the record available. Employers who provide services to children or vulnerable adults or people with mental or physical disabilities may obtain conviction records for employees, applicants and volunteers. The information disclosed is limited to convictions for crimes against children or other people, and does not include expunged records. Wa. Rev. Code Ann. §§43.43.815 to .845
West Virginia	If an employee's or applicant's juvenile records have been expunged—at age 19 or when jurisdiction of the court over the individual has ceased, whichever is later—no employer may discriminate on the basis of those records against that individual with respect to employment or its terms or conditions. W.Va. Code §49-5-17
Wisconsin	Employers may not discriminate on the basis of an arrest or conviction record. Wis. Stat. Ann. §111.321

However, employers may ask about pending charges. Questions may be asked about past arrests or convictions if the position requires bonding. Employment may be denied based on pending charges or past record if the applicant is not bondable or if the circumstances substantially relate to the job or activity being offered. Wis. Stat. Ann. §111.335

Wyoming   Records of an applicant's criminal background can only be given to the state board of nursing or if someone voluntarily agrees to submit to a record check. Wyo. Stat. Ann. §§7-19-106 and following

---

Checking Up on Yourself

The FBI is charged with maintaining complete arrest records—or rap sheets—on every individual who is arrested. It may behoove you to look at the information in your file before an employer does.

You can obtain a copy of your FBI rap sheet by writing to:

Federal Bureau of Investigation
CJIS Division; ATTN: SCU, Mod. D-2
1000 Custer Hollow Road
Clarksburg, WV 26306

Along with your request, you must include: your name, date and place of birth and a set of rolled ink fingerprints obtainable at a local police department—along with an $18 certified check or money order payable to the United States Treasury. It will take about 20 working days to process your request.

You are allowed to correct inaccurate FBI records—although it requires substantial patience and good documentation.

---

3. Medical Records

Medical information about employees comes into the workplace a number of ways. It is volunteered by an employee who is calling in sick. It becomes general knowledge after filtering through the gossip mill. It is listed on the insurance application for a group policy, which your employer will likely have on file.

As a general legal rule, employers are not supposed to reveal medical information about employees unless there is a legitimate business reason to do so. Again, that nebulous standard, so often used as a fallback in workplace controversies, provides little guidance because it is so poorly defined.

If you are concerned about keeping your medical information confidential and out of the workplace limelight, you must take active steps to do so. If you confide any medical information about yourself to co-workers, ask them not to tell others. Inform all doctors who treat you that they should not reveal anything about your health or treatment to another person without getting a release, or written permission, from you first. (See Section B1 below for more on employee medical exams and records.)

4. Credit Information

This era of the computer is also the era of the ever-present personal credit rating. Credit bureaus—profit-making companies that gather and sell information about a person's credit history—have become a booming business. And the growing power and popularity of the computerized credit rating has found its way into the workplace, as well.

Many employers now use the same credit bureau files used by companies that issue credit cards and make loans to do routine credit checks on employees and job applicants. Unfortunately, there is very little you can do to prevent employers from evaluating your credit history in deciding whether to hire, promote or even continue to employ you.

a. Employers' access to your record

A federal law, the Fair Credit Reporting Act (15 U.S.C. §1681 and following), requires credit agencies to share their data only with those who have a legitimate business need for the information, and employers generally qualify. Employers are given broad access to an individual's credit report, which they can use to evaluate eligibility for "employment, promotion, reassignment or retention." In short, as far as your employer or prospective employer is concerned, your credit rating is an open book.

Credit bureaus typically track not only your bill-paying habits, but also all companies that have asked to see your credit rating when you apply for credit, insurance, a place to live or a new job. The result is that employers increasingly use credit bureau files to find out whether an employee is job hunting with other companies. And prospective employers may use a shaky credit report to conclude that it is risky to welcome you aboard.

However, an amendment to the Fair Credit Reporting Act gives you some rights to know how and whether a current or prospective employer is using credit information about you. It requires an employer to get your written permission before peeping at your credit report. And the words granting permission can't be buried deep within a job application form or other word-laden document; you have to sign separately to signal your approval.

While this sounds like strong stuff at first, the truth is that if you refuse to give approval to the employer's wondering eyes, you will leave the impression that you have something to hide—and that will likely kill your chances for getting or keeping the job.

Also, the amendment mandates that a prospective employer who rejects you for a job based "in whole or in part" on an item on your credit report must give you:

- a copy of the report before turning you down, and
- written instructions on how to challenge the accuracy of that report.

Again, while this smells at first whiff like strong consumer protection, the reality is that it is tough to track whether employers have followed the letter of the law. They remain free to claim that you were turned down for reasons entirely separate from the harsh marks on your credit report.

b. How to take action

Amendments to the Fair Credit and Reporting Act at least theoretically give you some idea of whether you are up against an employer marauding for credit information that might cause you to lose out on a job.

And an employer who uses your credit information against you is not only supposed to fess up to it, but must also give you the name, address and telephone number of the credit agency that provided the report about you. You are entitled to a free copy of the report from that agency.

You also have the right to correct any errors in credit reports compiled about you, and most experts recommend that you check and correct your file every few years, especially if you will be job hunting or applying for credit.

Call the nearest office of the Federal Trade Commission, listed in the federal government section of the telephone directory, for guidance on how to correct the report. If you suspect a misuse of your credit report, you may want to contact your state consumer protection agency or attorney general to see whether state laws give you additional avenues for action.

For more detailed information about how credit bureaus operate and how to deal with them, see *Money Troubles: Legal Strategies to Cope With Your Debts*, by Robin Leonard (Nolo).

B. Workplace Testing

Ostensibly, prospective employers and employees want the same thing: to match the best person with the most fitting job. But these days, there are a number of tests that purport to take the guesswork out of the process. Ploughing through the Information Age, many employers are quick to welcome outside evaluations of an individual's mental and physical fitness and integrity, and to believe in their results—often at the risk of sacrificing individual privacy rights.

Of Genes and Pink Slips

When it first became possible to test for the genetic risks of isolated diseases, the advance was widely hailed as a modern medical near-miracle, sure to improve preventative healthcare and treatment. People with the potential risk of contracting inherited conditions such as breast cancer, colon cancer and Huntington disease now commonly undergo genetic testing to gauge their chances. But the powerful information can also pose a triple-edged threat to tested workers' jobs, health insurance and privacy.

Some employers—about 10% and growing, according to a 1998 survey by the American Management Association—now routinely test employees for genetic predispositions to diseases.

Privacy experts warn that genetic test results will be misused to target and fire employees who may run up company health insurance costs or to deny them coverage. And without specific privacy controls on the evolving medical information, they claim the hardship of diagnostics can follow workers from job to potential job, hampering their chances at finding additional work.

For too many people, the fears are already a reality. The Council for Responsible Genetics has documented hundreds of cases in which healthy individuals have suffered insurance and other workplace discrimination based on predictive genetic information.

About half the states now have laws that either protect against genetic discrimination or prohibit the testing in employment or insurance decisions—and dozens more bills are pending. The next frontier is likely to be federal legislation curbing the use and abuse of genetic testing in the workplace.

1. Medical Examinations

A number of insurers require employees to undergo medical evaluations before coverage will begin. Beyond that, and often in addition to that, employers may require specific physical and mental examinations to ensure a qualified workforce. However, there are strict rules on when those exams can be conducted and who can learn the results.

Courts have also ruled that the constitutional right to privacy covers medical information and that honesty is the only policy when it comes to medical tests for prospective and existing employees. That is, employers must identify what conditions they are testing for—and get individual consent to perform the tests, first.

a. Examining job applicants

Employers may legally give prospective employees medical exams to make sure they are physically able to perform their jobs. However, timing is crucial. Under the federal Americans With Disabilities Act, or ADA (see Chapter 8, Section F), covered employers cannot require medical examinations before offering an individual a job. They are, however, free to make an employment offer contingent upon a person's passing a medical exam.

The ADA also requires that your medical history and exam results must be kept in a file separate from your other personnel records. Only a few individuals have the right to see your medical file:

- a supervisor who needs to know whether your medical condition or health requires that you be specially accommodated within the workplace
- First Aid or medical personnel who need to administer emergency treatment, and
- government officials who are checking to be sure your employer is complying with the ADA.

During the course of a medical exam, a company-assigned doctor may ask anything at all about an applicant's health and medical history. However, the final medical evaluation is supposed to include only a stripped-down conclusion: able to work, able to work with restrictions, not able to work.

b. Examining existing employees

Employees can be required to take a physical or psychological examination after they are hired only if there is a reason to believe they are jeopardizing the health and safety of the workplace. For example, several courts have opined that if an employee clearly appears to be homicidal or suicidal, then an employer may have the duty to require a psychological exam, or even inform co-workers of the condition, in the name of workplace safety.

Again, while an examining doctor or psychologist has freer reign to ask questions as part of the examination of these employees than of applicants, the final evaluation revealed to an employer is supposed to be succinct and free of detail: able to work, able to work with restrictions, not able to work.

2. Drug and Alcohol Testing

The abuse of drugs such as alcohol and cocaine has been widely publicized for many years—and many private employers now test for drug and alcohol use. The laws regulating drug abuse in the workplace and the testing of employees for such abuse, however, are relatively new and still being shaped by the courts. Currently, there is a hodgepodge of legal rules controlling drug testing—some in the Americans With Disabilities Act (see Chapter 8, Section F), some set out in specific state laws (see the chart below) and a number arrived at through court decisions.

Testing in workplaces is on the rise. Some of that is explained by the passage, in 1988, of the Drug-Free Workplace Act (102 Stat. §4181). That law dictates that workplaces receiving federal grants or contracts must be drug-free or lose the funding, although it does not call for testing or monitoring workers.

Work-related drug tests take a number of forms. Analyzing urine samples is the method most commonly used, but samples of a worker's blood, hair and breath can also be tested for the presence of alcohol or other drugs in the body. Typically, state laws set out the testing methods that must be used. Many statutes provide for retesting, at the employee's expense, following a positive test.

Metabolics of illegal substances remain in urine for various periods: cocaine for approximately 72 hours, marijuana for three weeks or more. Detectable residues apparently remain in hair samples for several months.

a. Testing job applicants

In general, employers have the right to test new job applicants for traces of drugs in their systems as long as:

- the applicant knows that such testing will be part of the screening process for new employees
- the employer has already offered the applicant the job
- all applicants for the same job are tested similarly, and
- the tests are administered by a state-certified laboratory.

Today, most companies that intend to conduct drug testing on job candidates include in their job applications an agreement to submit to such testing. If, in the process of applying for a job, you are asked to agree to drug testing, you have little choice but to agree to the test or drop out as an applicant.

b. Testing existing employees

There are a number of employees who, because of their specialized positions or type of work, can be tested more freely for drugs and alcohol use. For example, the Department of Transportation requires drug testing for some critical positions, such as airline pilots. In addition, courts have routinely approved random drug testing for employees with national security clearances, prison officers, employees at chemical weapons and nuclear power plants and police officers. Note, however, that while many laws allow that such employees be tested, they do not require automatic discharges if the results are positive. Many overly exuberant employers have used the fact of testing as a reason to give automatic pink slips.

But there are some legal constraints on testing existing employees in most private employment jobs for drug usage. Companies cannot usually conduct blanket drug tests of all employees or random drug tests; the testing must usually be focused on an individual. In some cases where employers have tested for drugs without good reason, the employees affected have sued successfully for invasion of privacy and infliction of emotional harm.

However, the courts have generally ruled that companies may test for drugs among employees whose actions could clearly cause human injury or property damage if their performances were impaired by drugs, and in cases where there is good reason to think that the employees are abusing drugs. For example, a bulldozer operator who swerved the machine illogically through a field crowded with workers could be the legal target of drug testing.

And a legal secretary found slumped at her desk who was unable to respond cogently to questions asked of her was also considered fair game for a drug test.

c. Challenging drug tests

As an employee, you can always refuse to take a workplace drug test, of course. But if you are fired because of your refusal, you may have little recourse. Your employer needs only to defend that he or she had good reason to believe that you were a safety hazard on the job, or that you seemed unable to perform the work required. You would be placed in the untenable position of proving that your employer knew no such thing. You may, however, be able to win your job back if you can show that you were treated differently from other employees in the same position.

If you have been given a drug test and unfairly suspended or demoted because of it, your best bet may be to argue that the testers did not meet with the strict requirements for form and procedure set out in your state law (see below). And note that employers are free to add safeguards to protect against specimen tampering—requiring those taking the test to remove their own clothing and don hospital gowns, or providing a test monitor who checks the temperature of the urine and adds dye to toilet water, as examples. However, a modicum of discretion is required; while most courts have found it reasonable to have a monitor listen as a urine test is administered, a number have found it an unreasonable invasion of privacy to watch.

In addition, many laws require employers to maintain workplace counseling and outreach programs before they can test employees. While most employers these days are too savvy to slip up on procedural details, many of the laws are so picky and detailed that it may be worth your while to wade through and see whether your test made the grade.

When Is a Suspicion Reasonable?

In most situations, an employer may test you for drugs only if there is a reasonable suspicion that you are using them. What suspicion is reasonable and what is not is in the eye and mind of the beholder, which makes it a slippery standard indeed.

But some statutes and courts have attempted to set some guidelines that may be helpful if you are targeted for a test and you believe your employer's suspicions are less than reasonable. A reasonable suspicion of drug use must generally be based on actual facts and logical inferences such as:

- direct observation of drug use or of physical symptoms including slurred speech, agitated or lethargic demeanor, uncoordinated movement and inappropriate response to questions
- abnormal conduct or erratic behavior while at work, or significant deterioration in work performance
- a report of drug use provided by a reliable and credible source that has been independently corroborated
- evidence that the employee has tampered with current drug test results
- information that the employee has caused or contributed to an accident at work, and
- evidence that the employee has used, possessed, sold, solicited or transferred drugs while working or at work.

d. State and local drug testing laws

As mentioned, a number of state courts have set out rulings defining when and why drug tests may be given. For example, a New Jersey court considering the issue held firmly that pre-employment testing of employees is an illegal invasion of their privacy (*O'Keefe v. Passaic Valley Water Comm'n*, 602 A. 2d 760 (1992)). In California, pre-employment testing was given a court's stamp of approval, but not blanket testing of current employees up for possible promotion (*Loder v. City of Glendale*, 14 Cal. 4th 846 (1997)).

In addition, a number of states and several municipalities have laws that regulate work-related testing for substance abuse. Those that do also specify the scientific procedures to which testing labs must adhere. And many of these laws provide ways of dealing with overbroad or abusive workplace drug testing that are simpler, quicker and less expensive than filing a lawsuit. Some states also require companies to distribute to employees written policies on drug testing and rehabilitation.

Laws in a growing number of states—including California, Florida, Georgia and Vermont—include a kinder, gentler twist, protecting employees who seek treatment for a substance abuse problem from being discriminated against or fired.

Ironically, workers in states that have laws regulating the timing and procedures of drug and alcohol testing may actually have more protections than those living in states that are mum on the topic. Employees living in such lawless states, for example, may generally be tested without advance notice.

Drug and alcohol testing laws vary tremendously and are changing rapidly. The best way to get up-to-date details on laws in your state is to research them at a library near you. (See Chapter 18, Section E.) Your state labor department may also have information on current testing laws. (See the Appendix for contact details.)

Additional Laws May Apply

If the chart below indicates that your state has no statute, this means there is no law that specifically addresses the issue. However, there may be a state administrative regulation or local ordinance that does control. Call your state labor department for more information. (See the Appendix for contact details.)

State Drug and Alcohol Testing Laws

Alabama	To qualify for a reduction in workers' compensation rates, an employer must require testing of all new hires and may perform tests on some applicants. Employers may test if there is a reasonable suspicion of illegal drug or alcohol use, may use regularly scheduled and random tests and must test if the employee is involved in an injury-causing accident at the workplace resulting in the loss of work time. However, if the drug test is based on reasonable suspicion, the employer must document in writing the circumstances forming the basis for the suspicion and provide the employee with a copy of this document upon request. An employee who tests positive has five days to explain the results to the employer.
	Employers must give employees and applicants written notice of their substance abuse policy, including the consequences for refusal to submit to a test, the resources available to employees with substance abuse problems and an employee's right to explain a positive test result.
	Employers must have an employee assistance program or provide a resource file on employee assistance programs. Ala. Code §§ 25-5-330-340
Alaska	School bus drivers must be tested for improper use of drugs or alcohol; random tests are allowed for them. Discipline or discharge is allowed for positive results. Alaska Stat. §14.09.025
Arizona	Employees are subject to random and scheduled tests for any job-related purpose. Employers must give all employees a copy of the written policy before conducting tests. The policy must give employees the right to obtain written test results and to explain positive results. Notice of test must state the consequences of a positive test or refusal to submit to testing. Employees must be given the opportunity to inform employers of prescription drugs or other medical information that might affect test. Does not apply to federal or state employees except for those who work in the state Department of Public Safety or Department of Correction. Ariz. Rev. Stat. Ann. §23-493 and following School district transportation employees are subject to testing if their supervisor has probable cause to believe that their job performance is impaired or they have an on-the-job accident. Ariz. Rev. Stat. Ann. §15-573
Arkansas	Employers with Drugfree Workplace Programs may test job applicants who have been given conditional offers of employment. They may also test employees in safety-sensitive positions such as those that involve carrying firearms, working with confidential information or performing life-threatening procedures; police officers, Department of Correction employees and people who work with delinquent minors.
	Other employees may be tested on reasonable suspicion of drug use. Ark. Code Ann. §§11-14-101 to 112
	No employee may be fired, disciplined or discriminated against on the basis of a single positive test result. An employee or applicant has five days after receiving written notice of test results to contest or explain them. The employer must pay for required tests; the employee must pay for others. Ark. Code Ann. §§11-14-105 to 107

California	Employers with 25 or more employees must reasonably accommodate any employee who enters an alcohol or drug rehabilitation program, unless the employee's current alcohol or drug use makes him or her unable to perform work duties or do a job safely—unless this would impose an undue hardship on the employer. An employer must make reasonable efforts to safeguard the privacy of an employee who is enrolled in a treatment program. Cal. Lab. Code §§1025 & 1026
Colorado	No statute
Connecticut	Job applicants may be required to submit to testing if informed in writing beforehand.
	Employers may require a drug or alcohol test when there is a reasonable suspicion that an employee is under the influence and his or her job performance is or could be impaired. Employers may test randomly when authorized by federal law, when the employee works in a dangerous or safety-sensitive occupation, or when the test is part of an employee assistance program in which participation is voluntary.
	Testing required for intrastate truck drivers after a reportable accident, with reasonable cause or on a random basis. Testing required for applicants for school bus driver positions. Conn. Gen. Stat. §31-51t through 51aa, 14-261b
Delaware	Testing required to certify school bus drivers; if there is a positive result, employee can request that the employer conduct further analysis. Del. Code Ann. tit. 21, §2708
District of Columbia	Random testing is required of employees who work in a Department of Corrections institution or have responsibility for the custody or care of inmates. Other Department of Corrections employees can be tested only upon reasonable suspicion or if they have been involved in a job accident involving a vehicle or resulting in personal injury or property damage, after being given 30 days notice and the opportunity to seek treatment. An employee who tests positive can request confirmation of the results by another lab; secondary test is at employee's expense. D.C. Code Ann. §24-448.1 to 448.4
Florida	Employers may test for drugs and alcohol upon reasonable suspicion that an employee is under the influence, as a pre-employment screening with advance notice, during routine fitness-for-duty examinations and as a follow-up to participating in a drug treatment program. Fla. Stat. Ann. §440.101
	Employers who do not have a written drug testing policy in place that has been disseminated to employees must give 60 days advance notice of testing. Employees who voluntarily seek treatment for substance abuse cannot be fired, disciplined or discriminated against, unless they have tested positive or have been in treatment in the past. Fla. Stat. Ann. §440.102
	State agencies may test job applicants and employees as part of routine fitness-for-duty examinations, based upon a reasonable suspicion of substance abuse or as a follow-up to a drug treatment program. A state employee who completes a rehabilitation program must be reinstated to the same or an equivalent position. Fla. Stat. Ann. §112.0455
	All employees have the right to explain positive results within five days. A

	positive result must be verified by a confirming test before the employer can take adverse action against the employee. All test results must be kept confidential and cannot be used in criminal proceedings against the employee. Fla. Stat. Ann. §§440.102; 112.0455
Georgia	State employees who are involved in dangerous work may be subject to random drug testing. Ga. Code Ann. §45-20-90 and 91
	A public employee who, prior to any arrest, tells an employer about illegal use of a controlled substance may keep his or her job if he or she enters a licensed treatment program and does not refuse to be tested. Ga. Code Ann. §45-23-3 to 23-9
	Applicants for state government jobs must submit to a drug test if the head of the agency has determined that the duties involved in that position warrant drug testing; employees in these jobs with high-risk positions, such as school bus drivers, may be tested at random. Positive results must be verified by a confirming test—and the applicant has the right to provide proof that use of the drug is legitimate. Ga. Code Ann. §45-20-110 and 111
	Under the Drugfree Workplace Act, the state may not enter into any contract with a private contractor unless the contractor certifies that the workplace or site is drugfree. The contractor must post this policy and report any employee convictions for illegal drug use to the state agency that is part of the contract. The statute does not establish drug testing by the contractor. Ga. Code Ann. §50-24-1 and following
Hawaii	All employers may test employees or job applicants for substance abuse as long as the following conditions are met: the employers pay all costs; the tests are performed by a licensed laboratory; the individuals tested are given a list of the substances they are being tested for and disclosure forms for the medicines and legal drugs they are taking; and the results are kept confidential. Haw. Rev. Stat. §329B-1 and following
Idaho	Private employers who institute drugfree workplace guidelines may fire employees who test positive for drugs or alcohol or who refuse to submit to testing. Such employees will be fired for misconduct and denied unemployment benefits. Idaho Code §§72-1701 and following
	Employers may test applicants or employees for drugs or alcohol as a condition for hiring or continued employment. Idaho Code §§72-1702
	An employee or prospective employee who receives notice of a positive test may request a retest within seven working days. If the retest results are negative, the employer must pay for the cost; if they are positive, the employee must pay. Idaho Code §§72-1706
Illinois	Employers may test applicants and employees for drugs and alcohol, especially when positions are safety-sensitive. 755 Ill. Comp. Stat. 5/2-104(C)(4)(3)(4)
	Applicants for school bus driver permits must be tested for drug and alcohol within 90 days of applying. Any applicant who tests positive for either drugs or alcohol may not receive a permit for three years after the test. 625 Ill. Comp. Stat. 5/6-106.1

Indiana	An employer may implement reasonable policies, including drug testing, designed to ensure that an employee is no longer using illegal drugs. Ind. Code Ann. §22-9-5-6
Iowa	Employers cannot request random drug testing of employees or require employees or job applicants to submit to drug testing as a condition of employment, pre-employment, promotion or change in employment status, except as part of a pre-employment or regularly scheduled physical examination under certain restrictions. An employer may require a specific employee to submit to a drug or alcohol test if there is a reasonable suspicion that the employee's faculties are impaired on the job or if the employee is in a position where such impairment presents a danger to the safety of others or if the impairment is a violation of a known rule of the employer. Random testing is prohibited. A positive test result must be verified by a confirming test. An employee who tests positive has the right to explain the results, and the results must be kept confidential. An employee cannot be fired after one positive test if he or she undergoes a substance abuse evaluation and, if recommended, substance abuse treatment. This law does not apply to peace or correctional officers. Iowa Code §730.5
Kansas	Applicants for jobs in law enforcement agencies that involve carrying a firearm, corrections agencies, mental health institutions, gubernatorial staff or appointed heads of state agencies can be required to take a drug test, after they are offered the job, as long as there is prior notice. Employees may be tested but only if there is reasonable suspicion of drug abuse. The results of drug tests are confidential. Kan. Stat. Ann. §§75-4362 and 4363
Kentucky	An employer may reject an applicant based on his or her drug or alcohol addiction. Ky. Rev. Stat. §207.140
Louisiana	Employers may require all job applicants and employees to submit to drug testing as long as certain procedural guidelines are followed and the specimens are collected with due regard for the individual's privacy. Employees have the right to review test results and to have a confirming test. Applicants must pay for any confirming test. Public employers can test applicants and employees if there is an accident or reasonable suspicion of substance abuse. Public employees in safety-sensitive positions are subject to random testing. La. Rev. Stat. Ann. §§49:1001 and following
Maine	Public and private employers may require an employee to submit to a drug test when there is probable cause to believe the employee is impaired. Random testing is permitted when substance abuse might endanger co-workers or the public, during a rehabilitation program, when returning to work after a positive test or when it is permitted by a union contract. Job applicants may be tested only if offered employment or placed on an eligibility roster. Employees and applicants cannot be denied employment, fired or reassigned without a confirmed positive test result, but may be suspended without pay pending test results. Employers must have employee assistance programs and

	a written policy approved by the state Department of Labor. Test results are confidential and cannot be used in criminal proceedings. Me. Rev. Stat. Ann. tit. 26, §§681-690
Maryland	Employers may require testing for alcohol or drug abuse of employees, contractors or other people for job-related reasons as long as certain procedural guidelines are followed. Employees must be informed of the right to have a sample tested at an independent laboratory at the employer's expense. Md. Code Ann. Health Law §17-214.1
Massachusetts	No statute
Michigan	No statute
Minnesota	Employers may require employees to submit to drug or alcohol testing if there is a written and posted testing policy and the test is performed by an independent, licensed laboratory. Random tests may be given only to employees in safety-sensitive positions. Employers may require a drug test as part of an annual routine physical examination after giving employees two weeks notice. Job applicants may be tested if they have been offered jobs and if testing is required of all applicants.
	Specific individuals may be tested when there is a reasonable suspicion that the employee is under the influence of drugs or alcohol, has violated rules against the use, possession or distribution of drugs or alcohol on the job, or has caused injury or accidents at work.
	An employee who tests positive has the right to explain the results and to obtain a confirming test at his or her personal expense. Test results are confidential and cannot be used in a criminal proceeding. Minn. Stat. Ann. §§181.950 to 181.957
	An employer may refuse to hire and may discipline or discharge an employee who refuses or fails to comply with the conditions established by a chemical dependency treatment or aftercare program. Minn. Stat. Ann. §181.938(3)(4)
Mississippi	Public and private employers may require employees to submit to drug or alcohol testing after the policy has been posted for at least 30 days and certain prescribed procedures are followed. Testing is authorized when there is a reasonable suspicion that an employee is abusing drugs or alcohol. Random testing is also authorized. Employers may also test as part of routine fitness-for-duty examinations or as part of the follow-up to a rehabilitation program. Employees who test positive have the right to contest or explain the results. Job applicants may be tested if they are warned when they apply for the job. Test results are confidential. Miss. Code Ann. §§71-7 and following
Missouri	No statute
Montana	No person may be required to submit to a blood or urine test unless the job involves hazardous work or security, public safety or fiduciary responsibilities. Employees subject to testing may be tested if the employer has reason to believe the employee's faculties are impaired by drug or alcohol use or that the employee contributed to a work-related accident involving injury or property damage. The employee has the right to a confirming test and to explain or rebut a positive test result. If the additional test results are negative,

	the employer must pay for them; if positive, the employee must pay. Mont. Code Ann. §§39-2-205 to 211
Nebraska	Employers with more than six employees may require employees to submit to drug or alcohol testing if certain screening procedures are met, including a confirming test of a positive result. Refusal to undergo a test can be grounds for discipline or discharge. Neb. Rev. Stat. §48-1901 and following
Nevada	Applicants for state jobs and state employees may be tested if the job involves public safety. Nev. Rev. Stat. § 284-406 and following
New Hampshire	No statute
New Jersey	The Board of Education can require drug testing of applicants who have received a conditional offer of employment. The Department of Education is responsible for developing guidelines for conducting the testing. N.J. Stat. Ann. §18A:16-2
New Mexico	No statute
New York	No statute
North Carolina	Public and private employers may test applicants and employees for the presence of controlled substances as long as they follow specified procedures, including preserving the test samples so that those examined may perform their own tests. N.C. Gen. Stat. §§95-230 to 235
North Dakota	School bus drivers are required to pass drug and alcohol screening tests. N.D.Cent. Code §15.1-07-20
Ohio	No statute
Oklahoma	Public and private employers are allowed to test applicants and employees as long as they adhere to procedures outlined in the Act and issue a written workplace policy. An applicant may be tested as long as all applicants are tested; and an employee may be tested if the employer has a reasonable suspicion that the employee has violated the written policy and after a work-related accident involving property damage or injury. Random testing is allowed for certain employees only, including peace officers and those whose jobs directly affect the safety of others. Routine testing can be done if part of fitness-for-duty exam and if all employees in the same classification are subject to routine testing. The employee must be given the opportunity to explain test results. No adverse action can be taken without a confirming test. The employer must provide an employee assistance program for drug or alcohol abuse. Test results are confidential and cannot be used in a criminal proceeding. Standards for Workplace Drug and Alcohol Testing Act, Okla. Stat. Ann. tit. 40, §§551-565
Oregon	Employers may not require any employee or job applicant to submit to any breathalyzer alcohol test unless there is a reasonable suspicion that the employee or applicant is under the influence of alcohol. Or. Rev. Stat. §659.227 When employees are tested for drugs, the laboratory must be licensed by the state and must follow certain procedural safeguards. Onsite screening tests are permitted, provided that the tests meet U.S. Food and Drug Administration

standards. Written notice of test results must be reported to the person from whom the specimen was obtained. Or. Rev. Stat. §438.401 and .435

Pennsylvania   No statute

Rhode Island   Public and private employers may require an employee to submit to drug or alcohol testing when there is reason to believe that the use of controlled substances is impairing the employee's ability to do the job, the test sample is provided in private, the testing is part of a rehabilitation program, positive results are confirmed by the most accurate method available, the employee is given reasonable notice that the test will be given and the employee is given a chance to explain the results.

Employers may not terminate employees because they test positive but may refer them to a substance abuse professional for assistance. Employers must keep test results confidential.

Pre-employment testing is permitted if an applicant has received a conditional job offer and the test sample is given in private. Public employers may not test applicants unless they are applying for jobs as law enforcement or correctional officers, firefighters or where federal law requires testing. R.I. Gen. Laws §28-6.5-1 and 5-2

South Carolina   An employer may establish a drug prevention program that must include testing of employees. The employer must distribute its substance abuse policy statement to employees before conducting any tests and must keep results confidential. Test results may not be used in a criminal proceeding. S.C. Code Ann. §41-1-15

South Dakota   No statute

Tennessee   All private and certain public employers have the option of participating in the Drugfree Workplace Program. Employers who choose to participate must post their drugfree workplace policy at least 60 days before conducting any drug or alcohol tests.

Employers must test applicants who have received a conditional offer of employment for drugs and may test for alcohol.

Employers may test employees for drugs and may test employees in safety-sensitive positions or upon reasonable suspicion for drugs or alcohol.

Employers may test employees for drugs or alcohol as part of a routine fitness-for-duty examination and after an accident resulting in injury.

Employees have the right to explain or contest the results. Employers can fire or refuse to hire someone who has a confirmed positive test. The results are confidential. Tenn. Code Ann. §§50-9-101 and following

Employees in security positions within the Department of Corrections may be required to submit to drug tests, but only if the supervisor has a reasonable suspicion, based on specific objective facts, that the employees' faculties are impaired and that this presents a clear and present danger to the safety of the employees, other employees or the security of the institution. If an employee tests positive, a confirming test must be done and the employee must be provided with a copy of the results. The employer must provide counseling and rehabilitation to employees who test positive. Tenn. Code Ann. §41-1-122

Texas	An employer with 15 or more employees who has a workers' compensation insurance policy must adopt a drug abuse policy and provide a written copy to employees. Tex. Lab. Code §411.091
	Employees in state-licensed home and community support agencies and in nursing and convalescent institutions may be tested for drugs and alcohol. Any person applying for services and anyone else requesting the information will be given a written statement of the institution's or agency's drug testing policy. Tex. Health and Safety Code §§142.007 and 242.0371
Utah	Private employers and public utility or transit district employers who test for drugs must have a written policy regarding the methods used, and management must submit to regular testing as well as employees. A confirmed positive test result may be used as grounds for suspension, discipline or discharge. Test results are confidential and cannot be used in any criminal proceeding. Utah Code Ann. §§34-38-1 to -15
Vermont	Public and private employers may require an employee to be tested for drugs or alcohol if there is a probable cause to believe the employee is using or is under the influence on the job, if the employer provides a rehabilitation program and if the employee who tests positive is given a chance to participate in a rehabilitation program rather than being fired. Applicants may be tested if advance notice is given and an offer of a job has been made. Employees who have already been through rehabilitation and who again test positive may be fired. Job applicants may be tested when they have been offered the job conditioned upon passing the test, if they are given advance notice of the test and the test is given as part of a comprehensive physical examination.
	Applicants and employees must be given the opportunity to retest samples that have tested positive. Vt. Stat. Ann. tit. 21, §511 and following
Virginia	No statute
Washington	Private employers who want a discount on their workers' compensation premiums may test applicants if advance notice has been given and a job has been offered. Employees may be tested upon reasonable suspicion of drug abuse, following a workplace accident, or at random. Employer must post testing policy and must offer an employee-assistance program to employees who test positive before terminating them.
	Employers can terminate employees who have a second confirmed positive test or refuse to participate in the employee-assistance program. Employees have the right to explain or contest the results. Random testing is allowed. Results are confidential and cannot be used in a criminal proceeding. Wash. Rev. Code §§49.82.010 and following
West Virginia	No statute
Wisconsin	No statute
Wyoming	No statute

3. Psychological Testing

A number of people who label themselves as Workplace Consultants claim they have developed series of written questions—integrity tests—that can predict whether a person would lie, steal or be unreliable if hired for a particular job. And a number of other alleged experts claim to have perfected personality tests that allow employers to tell in advance whether an individual is suited by temperament and talent to a particular position. Employers are drawn to these tactics because they seem to short-circuit the process of interviewing—during which conversation too often degenerates into chatty small talk that takes time and cuts into productivity.

Psychological tests are not a new idea. They were first developed during World War I to help the military decide how to assign soldiers to various jobs. Some legal cutbacks to personality and psychological testing in the workplace began in the 1970s, when employers were banned from questioning prospective employees about age, race or sex. The tests had a heyday again in the early '90s, shortly after lie-detector screening was curtailed by law. (See Section B4.) And today, legions of test publishers have cropped up online—most of which claim they can forecast everything from a potential employee's likelihood of being honest and hardworking to his or her absence and injury rate on the job. And they promise an analysis fast—often within 48 hours of receiving responses to test questions. Critics say that is a suspiciously tall order to fill so quickly. And there may be legal pitfalls to the tests as well. Despite the doubts that surround them, however, the employee screening tests remain popular with many employers, most of whom claim to temper their acceptance with a dollop of skepticism and to cast about for information in more subtle ways.

Today's prescreening questionnaires usually cover the forbidden topics in roundabout ways. For example, employers may glean information about marital and family status by asking applicants to give information about hobbies and other interests. And many employers—about 40% of them, according to the American Management Association—use these questionnaires in the process of screening applicants for job openings. But even that temptation has been curbed of late by a number of cases that send a clear warning: Psychological tests cannot be used as an excuse to discriminate against prospective employees—and they must be limited to job-related questions. Recently, these tests have been challenged as being discriminatory and as violating employees' rights of privacy.

A few states have enacted laws against some specific forms of psychological testing. In New York, for example, employers may not require that job applicants or employees take psychological stress evaluator tests (N.Y. Lab. Code §§733 to 739).

Target Learns What Not to Ask

The first major case to challenge psychological testing of job applicants yielded grand results: a $2 million settlement and a five-year ban on testing.

The settlement came in July 1993, in a class action brought by several people who had applied to the Target Stores chain for work as security guards. As part of the application process, they had been asked to respond to over 700 true/false statements including:

- I am very strongly attracted by members of my own sex.
- I have never indulged in unusual sex practices.
- I believe my sins are unpardonable.
- I believe in the second coming of Christ.
- I have had no difficulty starting or holding my urine.

About 30% of the 2,500 test takers did not get jobs with Target—either because of the answers they gave or because the results were deemed inconclusive.

But the test made even successful applicants queasy. Robert Marzetta worked at Target for a year before becoming one of the main plaintiffs in the case. He said that while he felt the test questions were "out of line" and made him "uncomfortable," he didn't object at exam time because he needed the job.

Sue Urry joined in the case because, she said, as a Mormon, she found the religious questions particularly offensive.

Another plaintiff, Sibi Soroka, also got a guard job. Soroka found the test questions so unsettling that he copied all 700 of them before turning in his answers—then went to the American Civil Liberties Union and a number of attorneys seeking help. He was on the job only about a month because, he said, "it's kind of difficult to work for a person you're suing."

Target argued that the test, the Rodgers Condensed CPI-MMPI, helped weed out the emotionally unstable from the pool of those who would be subjected to the stressful task of apprehending shoplifting suspects.

The applicants challenged the test as violating their privacy rights and the state Labor Code, which bans questions about sexual orientation.

They shared in the $2 million in wealth Target lost.

This headline-grabbing case also inspired hundreds of other workers around the nation to mount challenges to psychological tests they found offensive or intrusive. So far, the majority of courts have sided with the workers.

4. Lie Detector Tests

For decades, lie detectors, or polygraphs, that purport to measure the truthfulness of a person's statements by tracking bodily functions such as blood pressure and perspiration were routinely used on employees and job applicants.

Employers could—and often did—ask employees and prospective employees questions about extremely private matters such as sexual preferences, toilet habits and family finances, while a polygraph machine passed judgment on the truthfulness of the answers. Push the machine's needle too far by reacting to an offensive question and you could be labeled a liar and denied employment.

The federal Employee Polygraph Protection Act (29 U.S.C. §2001), passed in 1988, virtually outlawed using lie detectors in connection with employment. That law covers all private employers in interstate commerce, which includes just about every private company that uses the U.S. mail or the telephone system to send messages to someone in another state.

Under the Act, it is illegal for all private companies to:

- require, request, suggest or cause any employee or job applicant to submit to a lie detector test
- use, accept, refer to or inquire about the results of any lie detector test conducted on an employee or job applicant, or
- dismiss, discipline, discriminate against or even threaten to take action against any employee or job applicant who refuses to take a lie detector test.

The law also prohibits employers from discriminating against or firing those who use its protections.

While government employees are not protected by this law, they are generally protected from lie detector tests by civil service rules.

a. When lie detector tests can be used

The Employee Polygraph Protection Act allows polygraph tests to be used in connection with jobs in security and handling drugs, or in investigating a specific theft or other suspected crime. However, before you can be required to take such a test as part of an investigation of an employment-related crime, you must be given a written notice, at least 48 hours before the test, stating that you are a suspect. And there must be a provable, reasonable suspicion that you were involved in the theft or other conduct triggering the investigation.

The Act does not apply to employees of federal, state or local government, nor to certain jobs that handle sensitive work relating to national defense.

b. Limitations on the tests

In addition to the strict strictures on when and to whom the tests may be given, there are a number of restrictions on their format. Before a lie detector test can be administered, your employer must read to you and ask you to sign a statement that includes:
- a list of topics you cannot be asked about, including questions on religious beliefs, sexual preference, racial matters, lawful activities of labor organizations and political affiliation
- the information that you have the right to refuse to take the test
- the fact that you cannot be required to take the test as a condition of employment
- an explanation of how the test results can be used, and
- an explanation of your legal rights if the test is not given in keeping with the law.

While the test is being administered, you have the right:
- to stop it at any time, and
- to be asked questions in a way that is not "degrading or needlessly intrusive."

When the test is said and done, results can be disclosed only to the employer who ordered the test, the employee who was tested, a court or government agency or an arbitrator or mediator if there is a court order. The law specifically prohibits prospective employers from getting access to old test results.

c. How to take action

The Employee Polygraph Protection Act is enforced by the U.S. Department of Labor. If you have questions about whether the Act applies to your job or if you suspect that you have been subjected to illegal polygraph testing, call the office of the U.S. Labor Department's Wage and Hour Division nearest you. It is listed in the federal government section of the telephone directory under Labor Department.

There is no official form for filing a complaint. If, after discussing your situation with a Wage and Hour Division investigator, you decide to file a complaint, do so as soon as possible by writing a letter addressed to your local Wage and Hour Division office. Include such details as the name and address of the employer, when the incident occurred and the address and telephone number where an investigator can reach you. And keep a copy of your letter for your records.

If the Labor Department finds that your rights under the Act were violated, it can fine the employer up to $10,000 and issue an injunction ordering the employer to reinstate you to your job, promote you, compensate you for back wages, hire you or take other logical action to correct the violation.

If the Labor Department's action on your complaint does not satisfy you, you can file a lawsuit against the employer to obtain whatever compensation or other remedy would be appropriate. Move quickly, because the lawsuit must be filed within three years. You will probably need to hire an attorney to help you if you decide to file a lawsuit under this Act. (See Chapter 18, Section D.) But the law allows the court to grant you attorneys' fees and other costs if you win.

d. State laws on lie detector tests

Some states have laws prohibiting or restricting employers from using lie detectors in connection with employment, but most have been made obsolete by the federal anti-polygraph statute.

A few states' penalties are more strict than those provided under federal law. In New York, for example, an employer who uses polygraph tests illegally may be convicted of a misdemeanor and sentenced to up to one year in jail (N.Y. Lab. Code 189 §§733 to 739).

In addition, state coverage may be broader; while the federal law does not apply to state and local government employees, many of the state statutes do.

Some states have also expanded anti-polygraph laws to cover other types of tests that probe bodily functions in connection with employment. For example, it is illegal for employers in Oregon to require employees to submit to genetic screening or brainwave testing (Or. Rev. Stat. §659.227).

Note that the laws in a few states—including California, Hawaii, Maine and Nebraska—provide that an employee who volunteers to take a lie detector test may be given one. But such laws have safeguards, requiring that the tests be administered under approved and supervised conditions and that employees be clearly informed about how and why test results may be used.

Additional Laws May Apply

If the chart below indicates that your state has no statute, this means there is no law that specifically addresses the issue. However, there may be a state administrative regulation or local ordinance that does control. Call your state labor department for more information. (See the Appendix for contact details.)

State Lie Detector Testing Laws	
Alabama	State employees cannot be required to take a lie detector test as a condition of employment. Ala. Code §36-1-18.
Alaska	Employers cannot require an applicant or employee to submit to a polygraph or lie detection test as a condition of employment. Current or prospective police officers are excepted. Alaska Stat. §23.10.037
Arizona	No statute
Arkansas	No statute
California	Private employers cannot require employees or applicants to submit to lie detector tests as a condition of employment. Does not apply to public employers. Does not prohibit voluntary testing as long as employees' rights are explained in writing. Cal. Lab. Code §432.2
Colorado	No statute
Connecticut	Employers may not request or require employees or applicants to take polygraph exams as a condition of employment or dismiss or discipline them for refusing to take the tests. Those who violate this law may be fined $250 to $1,000 for each violation. Not applicable to Department of Corrections employees nor to police departments except for civilian employees. Conn. Gen. Stat. Ann. §31-51g
Delaware	Employers may not require employees or applicants to submit to lie detector tests and may not fire or discriminate against them for refusing to submit to such tests. Those who violate this law may be fined $1,000 to $5,000 for each violation. Does not apply to law enforcement applicant background checks. Del. Code Ann. tit. 19, §704
District of Columbia	Employers may not request or require an employee or applicant to submit to a polygraph or any lie detector test as a condition of employment. Those who violate this law may be fined $500, imprisoned for 30 days or both—and employers shall be liable for damages and reasonable attorneys' fees.

	Does not apply to employees of the federal government, foreign governments or law enforcement agencies. However, law enforcement employees shall not be denied employment based solely on the results of polygraphs; there must be independent corroboration of the results. D.C. Code Ann. §§36-801 to 803
Florida	No statute
Georgia	No statute
Hawaii	Employers cannot require an employee or applicant to submit to a lie detector test as a condition of employment. Employers may not terminate or otherwise discriminate against an employee or applicant for refusing to submit to an exam. Does not prohibit voluntary testing as long as the right of refusal is explained in writing. Does not apply to law enforcement agencies. Those who violate this law may be fined $100 to $1,000 for each violation. Haw. Rev. Stat. §378-29-3
Idaho	Private employers cannot require employees to take lie detector tests as a condition of being hired or of continuing employment. Does not apply to law enforcement agencies or to the federal or state government. Idaho Code §44-903, 904
Illinois	No statute
Indiana	No statute
Iowa	Employers may not request, require or administer a lie detection test as a condition of new or continued employment. Does not apply to law enforcement or corrections agencies. Iowa Code §730.4
Kansas	No statute
Kentucky	No statute
Louisiana	No statute
Maine	Employers cannot request, require, administer or suggest that an employee or applicant submit to a lie detection test as a condition of employment. However, an employee can voluntarily request a test, and an employer can refer to the results as long as the results are not used against the person for any reason. Does not apply to law enforcement agencies. Me. Rev. Stat. Ann. tit. 32, §7166
Maryland	Employers cannot require that employees or applicants submit to lie detector tests as a condition of employment. Those who violate this law may be fined up to $100. This law does not apply to federal government, Division of Corrections, law enforcement nor correctional officers. Md. Code Ann. Labor and Employment §3-702
Massachusetts	Employers cannot require or request employees or applicants, including police officers, to submit to lie detector tests as a condition of employment. Employers cannot fire or discriminate against them for refusing to take such tests. Those who violate this law may be fined from $300 to $1,000 for a first offense; second and subsequent offenses are punishable by a fine of up to $1,500, imprisonment of up to 90 days or both. Mass. Gen. Laws Ann. ch. 149 §19B

Michigan	Employers cannot require employees or applicants to submit to polygraph examinations as a condition of employment. If an employee or applicant voluntarily requests a polygraph, the employer must give him or her a copy of the statute before administering it. Mich. Comp. Laws §§37.201 and following
Minnesota	Employers may not request or require a polygraph or any test purporting to test an employee's or applicant's honesty as a condition of employment. Minn. Stat. Ann. §181.75
Mississippi	Applicants for patrol officer training may be required to submit to a lie detector test. Miss. Code Ann. §45-3-470
Missouri	No statute
Montana	Employers may not require employees to submit to polygraphs or any mechanical lie detection tests. Mont. Code §39-2-304
Nebraska	No employee or applicant may be required to take a lie detector test, but voluntary tests are allowed as long as they meet specified requirements. Violation of this statute is a Class III misdemeanor. Statute does not apply to law enforcement agencies. Neb. Rev. Stat. 81 §§1932 and 1933
Nevada	Private employers may not request or require employees or prospective employees to take lie detector tests, nor may they refer to, accept or use the results of a test to fire, discipline, discriminate against or threaten an employee. Does not apply to an ongoing investigation of an economic loss to the employer's business, if there is a reasonable suspicion that the employee is involved. Lie detector tests may be used in hiring when the job has a significant impact on the health or safety of the state or is in the security industry. Other exceptions are also included. Nev. Rev. Stat. §§613.480 and following
New Hampshire	No statute
New Jersey	An employee or prospective employee who is asked to submit to a lie detector test has the right to be represented by a lawyer. An employee who takes the test must be given a written copy of the results, which should not be disclosed to any other employer or other person. The law does not apply to manufacturers of controlled dangerous substances. N.J. Stat. Ann. §2C:40A-1
New Mexico	A peace officer under investigation may be ordered by a chief administrator to take a lie detector test, as long as all other reasonable investigative means have been tried and the employee is told why he or she is being ordered to take the test. N.M. Stat. Ann. §29-14-5
New York	An employer may not require an employee or applicant to take any psychological stress evaluator test, and it is unlawful to administer the test or to use the results of the test. Violations are misdemeanors. N.Y. Lab. Code §§733 and following
North Carolina	No statute
North Dakota	No statute
Ohio	No statute
Oklahoma	No statute

Oregon	Employers cannot require lie detector tests, psychological stress tests, genetic screening or brainwave tests. Or. Rev. Stat. §§659.225 and 659.227
Pennsylvania	Employers cannot require employees or applicants to take lie detector tests as a condition of employment. Does not apply to law enforcement or to dispensers of narcotic or dangerous drugs. 18 Pa. Cons. Stat. Ann. §7321
Rhode Island	Employers cannot request, require or subject any employee to a lie detector test. Written examinations are allowed as long as results are not the primary basis of an employment decision. Does not apply to law enforcement agencies. Employers who violate this law may be fined up to $1,000. R.I. Gen. Laws §§28-6.1-1 to 28-6.1-4
South Carolina	No statute
South Dakota	No statute
Tennessee	Employers may require an employee or applicant to submit to a polygraph test, but no personnel action may be based solely on the results. Tenn. Code Ann. §62-27-128
Texas	The Department of Public Safety may not discharge or discriminate against an officer for refusing to take a lie detector test. However, if there is a valid internal complaint or extraordinary circumstances, a peace officer may be required to take a polygraph exam. Texas Code Ann. Government §411.007(c) and §614.063 Municipal firefighters may be required to take lie detector tests under conditions similar to peace officers. Texas Code Ann., Local Gov. §143.124 and 313
Utah	No statute
Vermont	Employers cannot request, require or administer polygraph examinations to employees or applicants, nor fire or discriminate against them, for refusing to submit to such a test. Does not apply to law enforcement agencies, departments of public safety and sellers of precious metals, gems or jewelry; nor does it apply to an employer whose business includes manufacturing or selling regulated drugs—with respect to only those employees who come into contact with the drugs. Penalties are fines of $500 to $1,000, six months in jail or both. Vt. Stat. Ann., tit. 21, §494a-e
Virginia	An employer may require a prospective employee to take a polygraph examination, but may not question about sexual activities unless they resulted in a criminal conviction. The employee must be given the results of the test upon request. Law enforcement agencies and regional jails cannot require employees to submit to a lie detector test except during an internal administrative investigation into allegations of misconduct or criminal activity and cannot discharge or demote employees solely on the basis of the test results. Va. Code Ann. §§40.1-51.4:3 and 4:4
Washington	Employers cannot request or require an employee or applicant to submit to a lie detector test as a condition of employment or continued employment. Employers cannot fire, discipline or discriminate in any way for refusal to take such a test. Those who violate this law may be penalized $500, payable to the employee or prospective employee, in addition to damages and reasonable attorneys' fees.

	Does not apply to law enforcement applicants or applicants or employees in positions involving manufacturing, distributing or dispensing any controlled substance, or to people in sensitive positions involving national security. Wash. Rev. Code Ann. §§49.44.120 to 49.44.135
West Virginia	Employers may not request or require an employee or applicant to submit to a lie detector test as a condition of employment, nor can they use the results of a test administered by someone else. Employers cannot fire or discriminate against an employee or applicant for refusing to submit to such a test. Those who violate this law may be fined up to $500. Does not apply to those who manufacture, distribute or dispense controlled or prescription drugs, nor to law enforcement agencies or to the military; but results of a test given by an exempt employer cannot be the sole basis of hiring or firing an employee. W.Va. Code §§21-5-5a to 21-5-5d
Wisconsin	Employers cannot request or require an employee or applicant to submit to a lie detection test as a condition of employment, nor may they use the results of a test administered by someone else. Employers cannot fire or discriminate against an employee or applicant for refusing to submit to such a test, or for filing a complaint, testifying about or exercising their rights under this law. Those who violate this law may be fined up to $10,000. Does not apply to an employee who is suspected of involvement in theft, embezzlement or damage to employer's property, security personnel, or manufacturers and sellers of controlled substances. Wis. Stat. Ann. §111.37
Wyoming	No statute

5. AIDS Testing

The disease of Acquired Immune Deficiency Syndrome (AIDS) was first identified in 1981. Fairly early on, researchers isolated its viral cause, Human Immunodeficiency Virus (HIV), which suppresses the immune systems of those who carry it, making them easy targets for various other infections and diseases. But beyond that, no great strides have been made in treating AIDS symptoms, or in finding a cure. Many of those who have the HIV infection live nearly symptom-free. But ultimately, the disease is fatal—and spreading.

The impact on American workplaces has been and will continue to be enormous. Not only have hundreds of thousands of workers died, most of them suffered also from the reactions of others—irrational fear and ostracism—that play in tandem with the

AIDS epidemic: AFRAIDS. Many workplaces responded to the hysteria with more hysteria, developing intrusive policies of isolating workers suspected to have the disease. (See Chapter 8, Section G for a discussion of discrimination against HIV- and AIDS-infected workers.)

Another offshoot of this hysteria is the practice of testing employees for the HIV virus. While a number of courts have struck down state and local efforts to screen employees for HIV, the practice continues in many workplaces.

Legal Actions Against Privacy Violations

There are specific laws that forbid employers from being overly invasive. However, your most powerful weapon may be to file a lawsuit against your employer claiming invasion of privacy. And the most likely way to win such a case is to show that in the process of collecting information on you, the employer was guilty of one or more of the following.

Deception. Your employer asked you to submit to a routine medical examination, for example, but mentioned nothing about a drug test. However, the urine sample that you gave to the examining physician was analyzed for drug traces, and because drugs were found in your urine, you were fired.

Violation of confidentiality. Your employer asked you to fill in a health questionnaire and assured you that the information would be held in confidence for the company's use only. But you later found out that the health information was divulged to a prospective employer that inquired about you.

Secret, intrusive monitoring. Installing visible video cameras above a supermarket's cash registers would usually be considered a legitimate method of ensuring that employees are not stealing from the company. But installing hidden video cameras above the stalls in an employee restroom would probably qualify as an invasion of privacy in all but the highest security jobs.

Intrusion on your private life. Your employer hired a private detective, for example, to monitor where you go in the evening when you're not at work. When the company discovered that you are active in a gay rights organization, you were told to resign from that group or risk losing your job.

a. Types of tests

Although medical researchers may develop more methods of testing for the HIV virus, the test first approved for commercial use by the Food and Drug Administration in 1985 is still in use today. Basically, the test measures antibodies in the blood that are stimulated by the HIV virus. If a test is positive, indicating exposure to the deadly virus, a confirmation test is usually performed, which uses a more complicated system of weighing molecular weights found in the blood.

Importantly, there are a number of things the HIV antibody testing does not indicate.

Tests do not identify people who have AIDS. AIDS is defined by the Center for Disease Control (CDC), and the definition is still evolving. Currently, an individual is considered to have AIDS if he or she has any of the AIDS-related diseases specified by the CDC and has a T-count—or number of infection-fighting white corpuscles—of less than 200 in a cubic milliliter of blood.

Also, tests do not identify every person carrying the AIDS virus. The tests are aimed at measuring the antibodies stimulated by HIV, so they do not work effectively on individuals who have been exposed to the virus but have not developed antibodies to it—a period which usually takes about eight weeks, but may take up to a year or more.

b. Legal controls on testing

Originally, HIV blood tests were fashioned to screen blood, not people. But when prospective employees and employees are subjected to testing, the reality is that people are being screened—and sometimes labeled as unfit workers.

A federal law, the Americans With Disabilities Act (see Chapter 8, Section F), prohibits testing job applicants to screen out people with HIV or AIDS. Once an applicant is offered a job, however, the legal constraints on testing become a bit murkier. To avoid singling out any individual or group, which would be illegal discrimination, an employer would have to test all employees. Even then, to justify giving employees an HIV test, an employer would have to show that the test is necessary to determine fitness to hold a job. This would be nearly an impossible task, as many people infected with HIV show no symptoms of ill health.

States are just beginning to enact laws regulating employers' uses of HIV tests. Alabama, California, Florida, Hawaii, Iowa, Maine, Massachusetts, Minnesota, Montana, New Jersey, New Mexico, Vermont, Washington and Wisconsin all have laws setting some bounds on employers.

Wisconsin's law is the most restrictive and the most comprehensive, with an interesting qualifier. That law provides that unless the state epidemiologist and Secretary of Health and Social Services declare that individuals with HIV infections provide a "significant risk" of transmitting it to others in the workplace, employers are prohibited from:

- soliciting or requiring as a condition of employment that any employee or applicant take an antibody test
- affecting the terms, conditions or privileges of employment or terminating the employment of any employee who obtains an antibody test, and

- entering an agreement with an employee or applicant for any pay or benefit in return for taking an antibody test (Wis. Stat. Ann. §3103.15(2)a and b).

Test results may not be used to determine suitability for insurance coverage or employment according to the laws in a number of states, including Florida (Fla. Stat. §381.6065). And Massachusetts bans employers from requiring employees to take a test as a condition of employment (Mass. Gen. Laws ch. 111, §70f).

In addition, a number of cities have enacted ordinances that put additional limits on how and when employers may test for HIV and AIDS. A strict law in San Francisco, for example, states that employers cannot test for AIDS unless they can show that the absence of AIDS is an essential employment qualification (San Francisco Police Code §§3801-16).

This area of the law is changing very rapidly. Doublecheck your local, state and federal law for recent changes. A local clinic, support group or AIDS hotline may be able to provide you with the most up-to-date local information. A number of organizations also offer information on the HIV virus, AIDS and resources on AIDS in the workplace. (See the Appendix for organization contact details.)

If a Co-Worker Has HIV Infection or AIDS

If someone you know has HIV infection or AIDS, you may feel anxious. That's a normal reaction. People with HIV infection or AIDS also feel anxious about their health and about how coworkers will treat them.

Be supportive of coworkers with HIV infection or AIDS. If you have a close relationship, you can let the person know you are concerned and offer support.

- Most people with HIV infection or AIDS are able to function normally and independently. They want to live and work without being singled out or harassed. They need your understanding and sensitivity.
- Let the person with HIV infection or AIDS decide whom to tell about their situation. Do not spread rumors or gossip about someone with HIV infection or AIDS.
- People infected with the virus have damaged immune systems. Be careful not to expose them to your colds or coughs. Even a minor cold can be dangerous to someone with HIV infection or AIDS.
- Your co-workers may have a spouse, family member, life partner or close friend with the virus. Be supportive of them.

Source: National AIDS Fund, 1999

C. Surveillance and Monitoring

We recently arrived at the place we long feared: Technological advances have made it easy for Big Brother—and anyone else who wants to join him—to watch us. In truth, most employers cannot properly be painted as paranoid Peeping Toms. And the law does require that most workplace monitoring— listening in on telephone calls, audiotaping or videotaping conversations— must have some legitimate business purpose. Other than that, however, there are very few federal legal controls protecting workers from being watched and listened to while at work.

Some states set their own bounds on how much prying you must tolerate. For example, several states—including Connecticut, Georgia, Ohio, Virginia and Wisconsin—have laws specifically restricting searches and surveillance of employees, and some of those laws are quite powerful.

In Connecticut, for example, an employer that repeatedly uses electronic devices such as video cameras or audiotape recorders to monitor employees in restrooms, locker rooms or lounges can be charged criminally and sentenced to jail for 30 days (Conn. Gen. Stat. §31-48b 1987).

1. Telephone Calls

In general, it is legal for employers to monitor business-related telephone calls to and from their own premises—for example, to evaluate the quality of customer service. However, a federal law, the Electronic Communications Privacy Act, or ECPA (18 U.S.C. §§2510 to 2720), puts some major limitations on that right. The ECPA restricts individuals and organizations, including employers, from intercepting wire, oral or electronic communications.

Under the Act, even if a call is being monitored for business reasons, which is perfectly legal, if a personal call comes in, an employer must hang up as soon as he or she realizes the call is personal. An employer may monitor a personal call only if an employee knows the particular call is being monitored—and he or she consents to it.

While the federal law seems to put some serious limits on employers' rights to monitor phone calls, some state laws have additional safeguards. A number of them require, for example, that not only the employee but the person on the other end of the phone must know about and consent to the call being monitored.

> ### Caught Red-Lipped, She Got Away
>
> The first test of the ECPA's bounds questioned an employer's right to secretly monitor workplace calls.
>
> In the case, Newell and Juanita Spears, owners of a liquor store, tape recorded and listened to the telephone calls of an employee they suspected of helping rig a burglary of the store. They first warned the employee, Sibbie Deal, to stop making personal calls and that her calls might be monitored. The Spearses recorded about 22 hours of phone calls. While the tapes mentioned not a peep about the burglary, they did reveal that Deal sold a keg of beer at cost in violation of store policy—and that she carried on long and salacious phone calls with her boyfriend while store customers presumably listened and waited.
>
> The Spearses fired Deal—first playing her a snippet of the tapes to explain their beef. The court held that the Spearses had violated the EPCA by taping and playing her calls and that warning her they might monitor the calls did not qualify as consent (*Deal v. Spears,* 980 F.2d 1153 (8th Cir. 1992)).

2. Voicemail

While much business communication these days takes place through messages left on voicemail systems, the law is still unclear on how much privacy employees can expect these messages to retain.

The ECPA appears to protect them. It states that an employer may be liable for obtaining, reading, disclosing, deleting or preventing access to an employee's voicemail messages that are in "electronic storage." But given the true workings of voicemail systems, this clarifies little. It is not yet known, for example, whether the ECPA—widely denounced as an awkward and muddled piece of legislation—prohibits employers from listening to messages that employees have listened to but not deleted from their systems.

3. Computers

Nearly every workplace in America today conducts some part of its business on computers, and many businesses have become slavish to them. While hailed by many as timesavers and aids to efficiency, computers have lent a new murkiness to workplace privacy laws.

a. Computer files

It is unsettled whether and when the files you create on a workplace computer are legally protected from others' snooping eyes. Generally, employers who claim a right to rummage through employees' computer files must show they have a valid business purpose for doing so. Employees often counter this by claiming that they had a valid expectation of privacy—a logical, reasonable belief that others would not retrieve and read the files.

Some employers have attempted to clear up the question of what is and is not considered private about workplace computers by writing specific policies spelling out that employees are forbidden from using one another's computers. In other places, employers have established elaborate password systems for employees to use to log on to computers and store files on them. It is still unclear, however, whether either of these approaches will create an expectation of privacy in an employee's work computer that will be given credence by the courts.

b. E-mail

While it is unclear whether the Electronic Communications Privacy Act applies to voicemail messages, its application to electronic mail, or e-mail, systems is murkier still. The Act, which originally served to limit wiretapping, took effect in 1986, before business e-mail systems became the commonplace animals they are today.

Prying Into a McLove Affair

When Michael Huffcut and Rose Hasset became smitten a few years ago, they also became what many couples in the first throes of romance are: sappy and careless. Huffcut worked as a regional supervisor at a McDonald's in Elmira, New York. Hasset held a management track position at a McDonald's 60 miles up the road in Binghamton. When the two weren't able to share happy meals together, they kept in touch by phone.

Harry Harvey, another McDonald's manager, intercepted messages the lovers left on each other's voicemail systems at work. He then relayed them to Fred Remillard, operator of a dozen of the fast food franchises, who directed Harvey, an alleged friend of the Huffcut family, to play the torrid tapes to Huffcut's wife, Lisa.

Presumably, that angered both of the Huffcuts, in their ways. But when Michael complained that his bosses were wrong to spy on him, he was fired.

Michael and Lisa Huffcut each sued McDonald's for $1 million, claiming, in addition to a violation of privacy rights, that Remillard intentionally inflicted emotional anguish, embarrassment and loss of reputation and income on them. McDonald's defended that there was a legitimate business purpose behind the monitoring—and that Huffcut had no reasonable expectation of privacy in his voicemail, since he should have known it might have been monitored.

Unfortunately for those hoping for some legal guidance on the boundaries of workplace eavesdropping rights, the case did not make it to court.

The Huffcuts and McDonald's reached an out-of-court settlement in March 1996, the terms of which remain undisclosed. Their lawyer coyly admitted only that: "The case has been resolved to the satisfaction of Mr. and Mrs. Huffcut."

There is no shortage of happy endings to the story. Rose Hasset was recently promoted to store manager.

Some experts now posit that whether your e-mail messages are protected from your employer's gaze may depend on what kind of system is in your workplace. If the system is accessible to the public—that is, if customers, vendors or contractors can use it—it is likely that your employer may not retrieve and read your messages without your written consent. It is considered to be more like a telephone, so more apt to be protected by the ECPA. If, however, the system is totally internal to the company, your employer likely has no limits to reading and copying what is on your screen. The natural extension is that you can be disciplined or fired if your employer does not like what he or she finds.

The question of legality aside, the truth is that many employers now routinely monitor e-mail messages that their employees send and receive. Some e-mail systems copy all messages that pass through them; others create backup copies of new messages as they arrive on the system servers. Workers who logically assume their messages are gone for good when they delete them are very often wrong.

Cases now working through the courts challenging employers' rights to monitor e-mail messages contain some novel arguments. For example:

- Two customer service reps were fired after their supervisor discovered sexually suggestive messages on their e-mail systems. The former workers argued that they were wrongfully singled out because they were not the ones who wrote the messages; they were only on the receiving end.
- An employer conducting a routine audit of computer programmers' e-mail messages found that two of them were revealing trade secrets to a competitor. The programmers sued for wrongful termination.
- An administrative assistant walked into her manager's office as he was perusing print-outs of employees' e-mail messages. When she questioned him about the practice, he told her to "mind her own business." She was fired shortly afterward—and she sued, claiming the termination was in retaliation for catching her boss in the act of spying.
- A technical writer was fired after he sent a number of e-mail messages demeaning to gays. He sued, claiming his employer violated his right to free expression.

A word to the wise: Treat your e-mail system at work as you should your business phone. Strictly limit your communications with family and friends. And do not send a message if you would be uncomfortable having a co-worker or your employer read it.

c. Internet use

The next gasp of complaints about employers monitoring computer use on the job is likely to settle on employees' Internet habits. And some former employees have already felt the sting when hit with evidence of site surfing that is hard to pass off as work-related. For example, one fellow was recently fired on his third day of work at a large CPA firm after being confronted with company records that revealed repeated trips to a pornography Website.

The wisdom quickly emerging is to save personal surftime for your home computer.

4. Mail

Whether or not an employee has the right to expect privacy in the mail he or she receives at work depends for the most part on company custom and policy. In most workplaces, one or more individuals routinely sort and distribute the mail—and most mailings related to work matters range from the boring to the mundane. An employer may inadvertently, or even purposely, open most such mail without incurring any legal liability.

However, sometimes mail arrives addressed to an individual worker that is also marked "Personal" or "Confidential"—or sometimes with the overkilling warning "Personal and Confidential." An employer who opens such mail, or directs or sanctions another person in the workplace to do so, must usually have a compelling business reason to open it. If the employer cannot demonstrate a compelling reason—for example, that there was important, time-sensitive business information in the envelope, and the employee to whom it was addressed was on a month-long vacation—then the employer may be guilty not only of being rude, but of invading the addressee's privacy.

5. Audiotaping and Videotaping

As the number of lawsuits over workplace disputes has grown, so has an alarming trend: Employers and employees intent on bolstering their claims have begun to record one another in the hope of capturing some wrongdoing on tape. There are a number of legal and practical problems with this approach to gathering evidence, however.

Federal law appears to allow any person involved in a conversation to tape it without the other person's knowledge or permission—as long as the recording is not made for the purpose of committing a crime, such as extortion. But a number of state laws have much stricter controls—generally requiring that everyone involved must consent before a conversation or an action can be taped.

Although our guts might tell us the opposite, audiotapes and videotapes also have questionable value as trial evidence. Before any jury would be allowed to hear or see a tape of a workplace scene, the tape would have to satisfy many picky rules designed to qualify and disqualify trial evidence.

Also, in real life, tapes rarely run to script. They often come out garbled or unclear. And they rarely hold up well out of context. What may feel like a damning conversation in which your boss blatantly admits you were fired because of your age may sound very different to those who do not know your boss or you.

A final reality is that if you have any desire to keep your job, confronting your employer with a tape immortalizing some perceived transgression is not the way to convince him or her that you make a loyal asset to the company.

All warnings said, the fact that you have an incriminating tape may make your employer more likely to quickly settle a complaint you lodge. It may make an investigating agency such as the Department of Labor or Equal Employment Opportunity Commission take a closer look at your file. It may make an attorney more inclined to take on your case. But the tactic is just as likely to backfire. You are in the best position to evaluate whether recording a workplace confrontation or other incident may be your best shot at getting strong evidence for later negotiations or a lawsuit—or is more likely to help you lose your job.

Who Is Watching and How

According to a recent survey, nearly three-quarters of major U.S. firms record and review employees' words and deeds on the job—including their phone calls, e-mail messages, Internet connections and computer files. And such corporate spying seems to be on the rabid increase; it has nearly doubled in the three years since 1997.

Some specific forms of monitoring and the percentage of those polled who engage in it:

Recording and reviewing telephone conversations, 11.5%

Storing and reviewing voicemail messages, 6.8

Storing and reviewing computer files, 30.8

Storing and reviewing e-mail messages, 38.1

Monitoring Internet connections, 54.1

Videotaping employee performance, 14.6

Most of the companies surveyed—88% of them—claim that they inform employees that they may be monitored in the workplace before doing so.

Source: Survey by the American Management Association, 2000

D. Searches and Seizures

Most employers would claim a legitimate desire to keep workplaces free of illegal drugs, alcohol and weapons. And most employees would claim that they have a right to expect that their personal belongings will remain safe from the groping hands of their employers.

The legal truth lies somewhere between. Employers are generally free to search through an employee's personal items kept at work—unless the employee reasonably expects that the spot in which those items are stored is completely private. An employer who searches an employee's private belongings such as a purse, briefcase, pockets or car must usually meet a higher standard and have a compelling reason to do so—such as the belief that work property is being stolen and hidden inside.

Example: *Thomas sold household appliances for a department store that provides each employee with a storage cabinet for personal belongings in a room adjacent to the employee lounge. The store's employee manual states that although the company does not provide locks for the cabinets and does not take responsibility for any thefts from the storage area, employees may bring in a lock of their own to secure their individual cabinet.*

One day while at work, Thomas was called to the manager's office, where he was confronted with a letter that had been written to him from his drug rehabilitation counselor. The manager said the letter had been found in his storage cabinet during a routine search by the company's security force, and that he was being fired because he had a history of drug abuse.

Thomas could likely win an invasion of privacy lawsuit against his former employer because, by allowing Thomas to use his own lock to secure his cabinet, the department store had given him a logical expectation of privacy for anything kept in that cabinet. His claim would be somewhat weaker if his former employer had furnished the locks and doled out the keys or combinations to them, because Thomas would then be on notice that others could get into his locker—defeating his claim to an expectation of privacy.

Another fact that weighs heavily in determining whether an employer's search is legal is its reasonableness in terms of length and scope. For example, an employer who suspected an employee of stealing foot-long copper piping might be justified in searching his or her work locker, but not purse or pockets.

E. Clothing and Grooming Codes

In general, employers have the right to dictate on-the-job standards for clothing and grooming as a condition of employment. Codes governing employees' appearance may be illegal, however, if they result in a pattern of discrimination against a particular group of employees or potential employees. This type of violation has most often been mounted in companies with different codes for male and female employees.

1. Dress Codes

Many companies have policies about uniforms to keep their employees looking uniform—a legal goal. There is nothing inherently illegal, for example, about a company requiring all employees to wear navy blue slacks during working hours.

Many employers provide workers with some or all of the clothing that they are required to wear on the job. A few companies even rent suits for their employees to assure that they will be similarly dressed.

Although generally legal, such systems can violate your rights if the cost of the clothing is deducted from your pay in violation of the Fair Labor Standards Act (FLSA). For example, it is illegal under the FLSA for an employer to deduct the cost of work-related clothing from your pay so that your wages dip below the minimum wage standard, or so that the employer profits on the clothing. (For details on the FLSA and how to file a complaint under it, see Chapter 3.)

A few states have attempted to address the concerns of employees who fear their uniform costs will cut into their earnings and have passed laws that prohibit employers from charging employees for required uniforms. But these laws are very narrow—and often do not apply to workers who need the economic boost the most, such as restaurant employees. Other laws erase the patina of generosity by imposing complicated schemes for when an employer may charge employees for cleaning a uniform. If you have questions about the legality of uniform charges, contact your local department of labor.

And sometimes, the legal lines on dress restrictions become blurry. Courts have held, for example, that an employer cannot require female employees to wear uniforms if it allows male employees to wear street clothes on the job. And some differences that seem to be gender-based—such as barring men from wearing earrings but allowing them for women—have been allowed to stand. The courts reason that the differences in dress codes are not discriminatory if they do not put an unfair burden on one gender or the other.

2. Grooming Codes

Most workplace grooming codes simply require that employees must be clean and presentable on the job—a reasonable request. And such codes are rarely challenged.

However, several lawsuits challenging workplace grooming codes have been waged by black men with Pseudofollicullitis Barbae, a race-specific skin disorder making it difficult to shave. Several individuals have successfully challenged companies that refuse to hire men with beards or that fire men who do not comply with no-beard rules.

Example: *Nelson, a black man, was advised by his physician not to shave his facial hair too closely because that would cause his whiskers to become ingrown and infected. Although Nelson took with him to a job interview a note from his doctor attesting to this problem, he was turned down for employment because the company where he had applied had a no-beard policy.*

Nelson filed a complaint against the company under his state's anti-discrimination laws on the basis of racial discrimination. Medical experts testified in his case that the condition which prevented Nelson from shaving usually affected only black men.

The court ruled in Nelson's favor, saying that the company's failure to lift its ban on beards despite Nelson's well-documented medical problem resulted in illegal workplace discrimination against black men. (See Chapter 8 for details on discrimination laws.)

F. Conduct Codes

Some employers have fashioned comprehensive behavior codes for their employees, setting out the bounds of workplace behavior they consider Professional. The dictate that gets caught in many workers' craws is the prohibition against dating others in the workplace, sometimes quaintly referred to as fraternizing. Others go a step further and prohibit married couples from working in the same place.

Such attempted controls over workers' personal relationships fly in the face of reality. Workplace experts claim that as many as 70% of all male and female workers have either dated or married someone they met at work. Those are far better odds than you have of meeting someone at a bar, party or other social gathering specifically engineered to be a meeting place.

But courts have been painfully slow to recognize the social reality of today's workplaces. During the last decade, employees have been fired for having extramarital affairs, for attending out-of-town conventions with someone other than a spouse, for dating and marrying co-workers. There are no clear guidelines but an appeal to common sense. Where that fails, and an employer's demands truly seem unreasonable, there may be no alternative but to sue.

1. Policies Against Marrying

Some employers think that nepotism—hiring a spouse or another relative—is an efficient way to recruit new workers and to keep them happy by surrounding them with loved ones. But others adamantly refuse to allow two spouses to be part of their workforce. They reason that married couples will be inconvenient at best, insisting on the same time off for vacations and holidays. At worst, they claim that being married will make workers less stable. For example, some police departments have argued that married troopers would not react objectively if a spouse got injured on the job—or that their credibility would be undermined if called to testify to support one another's actions.

Some such policies, however, may be on shaky legal ground. Nearly half the states explicitly prohibit public and private employers from discriminating based on marital status. (See Chapter 8, Section B.)

But whether or not your state prohibits marital status discrimination, the legality of no-spouse employment rules is still unclear. Courts called upon to decide the issue have been contradictory. Some have found that there is no business justification for preventing co-workers from marrying or working together. Other courts stick stridently to the letter of workplace policies, reasoning that employees are legally free to ban married workers on their premises.

When Cupid Aimed, They Should Have Ducked

Employees have just begun to fight back against codes they consider to damper and hamper their lives. In July 1993, a New York couple, Laural Allen and Samuel Johnson, sued the nation's largest retailer, Wal-Mart, after it fired them both for dating one another.

Allen was separated but not yet divorced from her husband when Johnson first spotted her in the sporting goods department, showing a hunting rifle to a customer. Allen and Johnson, both sales associates in an upstate New York branch of Wal-Mart, began dating shortly afterward. They were both fired when the store manager learned of the relationship.

Allen and Johnson sued, seeking $2 million each, claiming Wal-Mart discharged them wrongfully—and caused them emotional distress in the process.

Wal-Mart, a self-proclaimed champion of the "family unit," defended that the couple's behavior clearly violated the Fraternization Policy set out in the company handbook. This rule prohibits a "dating relationship between a married employee and another employee, other than his or her own spouse."

Allen and Johnson argued that Wal-Mart's policy violated a New York labor code provision which bans employers from discriminating against employees for legal recreational activities outside of work.

In an appeal of the case, the Supreme Court of New York refused to strike down Wal-Mart's policy. The court noted that the statute banning discrimination explicitly protects outside work activities such as sports, games, hobbies, exercise, reading and watching movies and television—but it makes no mention of dating.

However, the court seemed to be influenced by the fact that Allen was married to someone else when the Wal-Mart workers became involved. It concluded that its decision "in no way diminishes the statutory protection afforded social relationships between unmarried employees or married employees having no romantic interest or involvement with one another." (*New York v. WalMart Stores, Inc.*, 207 A.D.2d 150, 621 N.Y.S.2d 138 (1995).)

2. Policies Against Dating

Where the issue is prohibiting employees from dating rather than marrying, the law is even less clear. Few of the policies banning workers from dating have been challenged in court—most likely because the lovestruck workers were surreptitious about their strickenness or got annoyed enough to get jobs elsewhere or their love took a backseat to the stress of a court battle, ending the relationship.

To many, policies prohibiting co-workers from dating seem paternalistic and fly in the face of a cardinal law of human nature: Proximity Often Breeds Attraction. Those with the gumption to challenge such policies might base a legal claim on their right to privacy, freedom of association, wrongful discharge—or if the policies are enforced disproportionately against workers of a particular age, gender or race, they may claim a violation of civil rights.

A number of employers have adopted strict policies prohibiting supervisors from dating people they supervise, although these days, a growing number give the supervisor the option of being transferred rather than fired on the spot. While these strong anti-dating policies may be understandable given the relatively low legal threshold for a supervisor's conduct to be considered sexual harassment, they may be just as impossible to enforce. (See Chapter 9.) Consider the practical difficulty, for example, in determining exactly when two people have crossed the line between friendly and involved. Strict policies prohibiting liaisons between bosses and worker bees also would seem to encourage a double standard of behavior within the ranks of employees. Far better to remember that since workplace harassment is almost always about an abuse of power—not about romance gone sour—the focus should be on preventing intimidation.

CHAPTER

7

HEALTH AND SAFETY

Workers in the past 20 years have pushed strongly for laws to protect their health and safety on the job. And they have been successful. Several laws, notably the Occupational Safety and Health Act (OSHA), now establish basic safety standards aimed at reducing the number of illnesses, injuries and deaths in workplaces. Since most workplace safety laws rely for their effectiveness on employees who are willing to report on the job hazards, most laws also prevent employers from firing or discriminating against employees who report unsafe conditions to proper authorities.

Some of the currently contested workplace health and safety issues call into play two sides of an uneasy compromise. The debated issues mirror our own life choices, such as the debate between workers who smoke and those demanding protection from annoyances and illnesses caused by secondhand smoke. As more employers establish nonsmoking workplaces, a growing number of states have passed laws prohibiting discrimination against smokers. (See Section E.)

A. The Occupational Safety and Health Act

The main federal law covering threats to workplace safety is the Occupational Safety and Health Act, or OSHA (29 U.S.C. §§651 to 678). That law created the Occupational Safety and Health Administration (also called OSHA) under the U.S. Department of Labor to enforce workplace safety. And it created the National Institute for Occupational Safety and Health (NIOSH) to research ways to increase workplace safety. (See the Appendix for contact details.)

OSHA broadly requires employers to provide a safe workplace for employees—one that is free of dangers that could physically harm those who work there. The law implements this directive by requiring employers to inform employees about potential hazards, to train them in how to deal with hazards and to keep records of workplace injuries.

Sometimes, workplace dangers are caught and corrected during unannounced inspections by OSHA. But the vast majority of OSHA's actions against workplace hazards are initiated by complaints from employees or labor unions representing them.

Still more reform is needed. According to recent estimates, 6 million Americans are injured at work each year, and 6,000 workers actually die as a result of their injuries. In addition, 50,000 Americans die each year from illnesses caused by chemicals they were exposed to on while on the job.

States Have OSHA Laws, Too

About half the states now have their own OSHA laws. The legal requirements for workplace health and safety in the state laws are generally similar to the federal law. In some cases, the state laws are more strict. (See Section D, below.)

1. Who Is Covered

Unlike many other laws which cover only companies with a minimum number of employees, OSHA covers nearly all private employers engaged in interstate commerce. That includes nearly every employer that uses the U.S. Postal Service to send messages to other states or makes telephone calls to other states. Independent contractors are not specifically covered by the law. (See Chapter 2, Section A.)

OSHA does not apply to state and local governments. However, these employees have some protection if their state or local government has a safety plan. As an incentive to these employers, OSHA will fund half the cost of operating such a plan. Farms owned and operated by a family are the only significant private employers exempted from OSHA coverage.

For more information on the basics of the law, see "All About OSHA," a free pamphlet. You can download it from the agency's website at http://www.osha.gov. You can also order it by calling the Superintendent of Documents at 202-512-1800.

2. OSHA Requirements

The Occupational Safety and Health Act requires all private employers to maintain a workplace that is as safe and healthy for employees as is reasonably possible. Under OSHA, all employers are charged with this general safety duty. In addition, the law sets specific workplace safety standards for four major categories of work: General Industry, Maritime, Construction and Agriculture.

Safety regulations are usually concerned with preventing a one-time injury—falling from an unsafe ladder or tripping on an irregular walkway, for example.

The Act's health concerns are in preventing employee illnesses related to potential health dangers in the workplace—exposure to toxic fumes or asbestos, for example, and cumulative trauma such as carpal tunnel syndrome. (See Chapter 13, Section B, for more about Carpal Tunnel Syndrome.)

The law quite simply, but frustratingly, requires that employers protect workers from "recognized hazards." It does not specify or limit the types of dangers covered, so hazards ranging from things that cause simple cuts and bruises, to the unhealthy effects of long-term exposure to some types of radiation, are all arguably covered.

But proving the law was violated is not easy. Basically, to prove an OSHA violation, you must produce evidence that:

- your employer failed to keep the workplace free of a hazard, and
- the particular hazard was recognized as being likely to cause death or serious physical injury.

Under OSHA, the definition of a workplace is not limited to the inside of an office or factory. The Act requires that work conditions be safe no matter where the work is performed—even where the workplace is an open field or a moving vehicle.

In addition to the general duty to maintain a safe workplace, employers are required to meet OSHA's safety standards for their specific industries. Depending on the types of hazards and workplaces involved, the employer's responsibility for creating and maintaining a healthy and safe workplace can include such diverse things as informing workers about potentially hazardous substances and labeling them, upgrading or removing machinery that poses a danger, providing employees with special breathing apparatus to keep dust created by a manufacturing process from entering workers' lungs, improving lighting above work areas, providing emergency exits and fire protection systems, vaccinating against diseases that can be contracted at work or even tracking the effects of workplace conditions on employees' health through periodic medical examinations.

Finally, OSHA requires employers to display a poster explaining workers' rights to a safe workplace in a conspicuous spot. If the workplace is outdoors, the poster must be displayed where employees are most likely to see it—such as in a trailer at a construction site where workers use a timeclock to punch in and out.

These posters are supplied to employers by OSHA and commercial publishers. An employer's failure to display such posters is itself a violation of OSHA rules.

Plain Language, Plainly Needed

In the three decades since the Act took effect, the OSHA administration claims it has been "unwavering" in its mission "to assure so far as possible every working man and woman in the nation safe and healthful working conditions." And that mission statement is telling in and on itself: Lots of words. But no one is quite sure what they mean.

President Clinton trained the spotlight on OSHA's murkiness in a 1995 address urging major reforms to the law, in which he lamented that the OSHA was "too often driven by numbers and rules, not by smart enforcement and results." He also threw down the gauntlet, urging the agency to adopt plain language in its regulations and rulings. In response to that charge, OSHA issued a Plain Language poster August 9, 2000.

Put side by side, the old and new poster show that OSHA has done its penwork in making the new notice less clunky, more cogent, easier to understand.

The old language telling employees of their rights to complain read: *Employees or their representatives have the right to file a complaint with the nearest OSHA office requesting an inspection if they believe unsafe or unhealthful conditions exist in their workplace. OSHA will withhold, on request, names of employees complaining.*

The new language: *You have the right to notify your employer or OSHA about workplace hazards. You may ask OSHA to keep your name confidential.*

3. Injury and Illness Reports

Within eight hours of any workplace accident that results in the death of a worker or requires hospitalization of four or more workers, employers must report complete details to OSHA, including names of injured workers, the time and place of the accident, nature of the injuries and any type of machinery involved in the accident. All employees and former employees must be given access to this report upon request.

Companies employing ten or more people must also keep records of workers' work-related injuries and illnesses that have caused death or days off work, and post a report on those injuries and illnesses.

B. Enforcing OSHA Rights

If you believe that your workplace is unsafe, your first action should be to make your supervisor at work aware of the danger as soon as possible. If your employer has designated a particular person or department as responsible for workplace safety, inform the appropriate person of the danger.

In general, your complaint will get more attention if it is presented on behalf of a group of employees who all see the situation as a safety threat. And there is safety in numbers. An employer who becomes angry over a safety complaint is much less likely to retaliate against a group of employees than against an individual. (See Section B6.)

This Law Swings Both Ways

Although neither federal nor state OSHA laws cite employees for violations of their responsibilities, the laws generally require that workers comply with all standards, rules, regulations and orders issued under the Act. The unspoken inference here is that workers who do not hold up their end of the safety law bargain may jeopardize their own protections under health and safety laws.

Specifically, according to OSHA, an employee should:

- read the OSHA poster at the jobsite
- comply with all applicable OSHA standards.
- follow all employer safety and health regulations and wear or use prescribed protective equipment while working
- report hazardous conditions to the supervisor
- report any job-related injury or illness to the employer and seek treatment promptly
- cooperate with the OSHA compliance officer conducting an inspection if he or she inquires about safety and health conditions in the workplace, and
- exercise rights under the Act in a responsible manner.

While some of these responsibilities sound a bit nebulous, you should be prepared to show that you did your best to carry them out before claiming protection under any OSHA law.

1. Filing a Complaint

If you have not been successful in getting your company to correct a workplace safety hazard, you can file a complaint at the nearest OSHA office. Look under the U.S. Labor Department in the federal government section of your local telephone directory or find them on the agency's website at http://www.osha.gov under About OSHA.

You can request the proper complaint forms from any OSHA office. You also have the option of telephoning your complaint to your nearest OSHA office, where a compliance officer will complete the paperwork and then send you the completed version for your approval and signature. For more information about filing a complaint and to file one online, go to OSHA's Workers' Page at http://www.osha.gov/as/opa/worker/index/html.

If you request it, OSHA must keep confidential your identity and that of any other employees involved in the complaint. If you want your identity to be kept secret, be sure to check the section on the complaint form that states: "Do not reveal my name to the employer."

Once you have completed the complaint form, file it with the nearest OSHA office. You can do this in person, but if you send it in by certified mail, you will have proof that OSHA received it should it get mislaid in OSHA's offices. Keep a photocopy of your completed complaint form for your own files.

Upon receiving your complaint, OSHA will assign a compliance officer to investigate your case. The compliance officer will likely talk with you and your employer and inspect the work conditions that you have reported.

Time Off Under the FMLA

If your workplace injury requires an extended recovery at home or in a hospital, state and federal leave laws may not only protect your right to take time off work, but require that you be returned to your former position with continued insurance benefits. (See Chapter 5.)

Preventing Additional Injuries

Workplace hazards often become obvious only after they cause an injury. For example, an unguarded machine part that spins at high speed may not seem dangerous until someone's clothing or hair becomes caught in it. But even after a worker has been injured, employers sometimes fail—or even refuse—to recognize that something that hurt one person is likely to hurt another.

If you have been injured at work by a hazard that should be eliminated before it injures someone else, take the following steps as quickly as possible after obtaining the proper medical treatment.

- If you believe the hazard presents an immediate life-threatening danger to you and your co-workers, call OSHA's emergency reporting line at 800-321-6742.
- File a claim for workers' compensation benefits so that your medical bills will be paid and you will be compensated for your lost wages and injury. (See Chapter 13.) Workers' compensation claims can cost a company a lot of money; filing such a claim tends to quickly focus an employer's attention on safety problems. In some states, the amount you receive from a workers' comp claim will be larger if your injury was due to a violation of a state workplace safety law.
- Point out to your employer the continuing hazard created by the cause of your injury. As with most workplace safety complaints, the odds of getting action will be greater if you can organize a group of employees to do this.
- If your employer does not eliminate the hazard promptly, file a complaint with OSHA and any state or local agency that you think may be able to help.

2. How Complaints Are Resolved

A compliance officer who finds that the condition about which you complained poses an immediate danger to you and your co-workers can order your employer to immediately remove the danger from the workplace—or order the workers to leave the dangerous environment.

Where the danger is particularly urgent or the employer has a record of violations, OSHA may get tough by asking the courts to issue an injunction—a court order requiring the employer to eliminate workplace hazards.

Example: *A group of pipeline workers complained to OSHA that the earth walls of the excavation in which they were working were not well supported and could collapse on them. The OSHA compliance officer tried unsuccessfully to talk the employer into improving the situation. OSHA obtained a court injunction forbidding work to continue within the excavation until the walls were shored up with steel supports.*

If the danger is less immediate, the compliance officer will file a formal report on your complaint with the director of OSHA for your region. If the facts gathered by the compliance officer support your complaint, the regional director may issue a citation to your employer.

The citation will specify what work conditions must be changed to ensure the safety of the employees, the timetable that OSHA is allowing for those changes to be made—usually known as an abatement plan—and any fines that have been levied against your employer.

Example: *Leslie is a machine operator in an old woodworking shop that uses lathes that throw a large quantity of wood dust into the air inside the shop. The wood dust appeared to be a hazard to the employees who breathe it, and Leslie was unsuccessful in resolving the problem with the shop's owner. She filed a complaint with OSHA.*

OSHA studied the air pollution in the shop and agreed that it was a threat to workers' health. It ordered the shop's owner to install enclosures on the lathes to cut down on the amount of dust put into the air and filter-equipped fans throughout the shop to capture any wood dust that escapes from the enclosures. Because the lathe enclosures and fans needed to be custom designed and installed, OSHA allowed the shop's owner six months to correct the situation.

In the meantime, OSHA ordered the shop's owner to immediately provide Leslie and all the other people employed there with dust-filtering masks to wear over their mouths and noses. However, since OSHA regulations generally require employers to make the workplace safe and not just protect workers from an unsafe work situation, the masks are considered merely a temporary part of the long-term abatement plan.

An OSHA inspector who finds a workplace safety hazard or other violation will tell all affected employees about it and post a danger notice before leaving the workplace. This public notice of an unsafe condition is often the impetus an employer needs to take it seriously and correct it.

The Importance of Being Specific

Like many other government agencies, OSHA is a huge bureaucracy that is organized and operated according to computerized file numbers. The best way to get prompt service and accurate information from OSHA is to be as specific as possible. In your dealings with OSHA, be sure to mention the name of the company, the department of that company, the number assigned to the complaint that you are tracking and the date on which it was filed.

Jot down the names and numbers of those with whom you speak. And keep detailed notes of your conversations, complete with dates and times.

3. Contesting an Abatement Plan

You have the right to contest an abatement plan directed to your employer by OSHA to correct a workplace hazard—for example, if you feel the suggested plan is insufficient. To do so, send a letter expressing your intent to contest the plan to your local OSHA director within 15 days after the OSHA citation and announcement of the plan is posted in your workplace. You need not list specific reasons for contesting the plan in this letter; all you need to make clear is that you think the plan is unreasonable.

There Really Is Strength in Numbers

If other employees feel the abatement plan is unfair or insufficient, encourage them to register their protests with OSHA as well.

Sample letter

April 10, 20XX

Ms. Mary Official
Regional Director
Occupational Safety and Health Administration
321 Main Street
Anycity, USA 12345

Dear Ms. Official:

As allowed by 29 U.S.C. Section 659(e), I wish to contest the abatement plan agreed to by your agency and my employer, the Oldtime Mousetrap Company. This abatement program resulted from a complaint that I filed with your office on April 3, 20XX. That complaint was assigned number A-123456 by your office.

I contest this agreement because I believe that it is unreasonable.

Sincerely,

Elmer Springmaker
456 Central Road
Anycity, USA 12340
123/555-5555

After it receives your letter, OSHA will refer the matter to the Occupational Safety and Health Review Commission in Washington, DC, an agency independent of OSHA. That commission will send your employer a notice that the abatement plan is being contested.

This notice will order the employer to post in the workplace an announcement that the plan is being contested. It will also require the employer to send a form that certifies the date on which that announcement was made back to the commission—with copies to OSHA, to you and to other employees who have contested the plan.

Then, everyone involved in the case has ten days from the date the contest notice was posted to file an explanation of their viewpoints on the abatement plan with the commission. Copies must also be sent to all others involved in the case.

Tips on Presenting Your Views

The explanation you file on the abatement plan need not be elaborate. It should be as clear, brief and precise as possible. For example, if you have made a list of employee injuries that have already resulted from the hazard in your workplace, list the date, time, location and identity of the worker injured for each incident in your explanation.

Your explanation need not be typewritten, but your odds of communicating your viewpoint effectively will be increased if it is easy to read. If you do not have access to a typewriter or computer, consider having your explanation typed by a commercial typing service. You can usually find them in the Yellow Pages of your local telephone directory.

Send your explanation by certified mail to:

Executive Secretary
Occupational Safety and Health Review Commission
200 Constitution Avenue, NW
Washington, DC 20010

Be sure to include a cover letter—and to specify in it the name of the company involved, the number assigned to the case by the review commission and OSHA and your mailing address and telephone number. Send a copy to the OSHA office where you filed your original complaint, to your employer and to any people identified in the paperwork the commission sent to you as parties in the case. Also, be sure to save a copy of your cover letter, your explanation and any supporting documents that you send with it for your personal files.

After it has gathered all the statements on the case, the commission will typically turn them over to U.S. Labor Department lawyers who will attempt to meet with everyone who submitted statements and negotiate a resolution that is agreeable to all. The commission tries to negotiate settlements whenever possible, and by this point everyone involved will have had an opportunity to read and think about each other's viewpoints. So the odds are that your complaint will be resolved at this stage.

4. Administrative Review

When attempts to reach a resolution are unsuccessful, the commission submits the case to an administrative law judge. These proceedings usually take several months—and sometimes years—depending upon the complexity of the workplace hazards involved.

Hearings before administrative law judges are very much like a trial. Much time and money can be consumed in gathering evidence, and the hearings are usually scheduled during daytime hours when most employees are at work. You will probably have to hire a lawyer to help if you decide to pursue your safety complaint at this level. (See Chapter 18, Section D.)

You also have the right to appeal a decision by an administrative law judge for the Occupational Health and Safety Review Commission to the full commission or in federal court, but you will probably have to hire a lawyer to help you at these levels as well.

5. Walking Off the Job

OSHA gives you the right to refuse to continue doing your job in extreme circumstances that represent an immediate and substantial danger to your safety.

This right is limited. You cannot walk off the job and be protected by OSHA in just any workplace safety dispute—and this tactic cannot be used to protest general working conditions. But OSHA rules give you the right to walk off the job without being discriminated against later by your employer if the situation is a true workplace safety emergency.

A walk-off will be legally merited only if your situation meets all of the following conditions.

- You asked your employer to eliminate the hazard and your request was ignored or denied. To protect your rights, it would be best to tell more than one supervisor about the hazard, or to call the danger to the attention of the same supervisor at least twice—preferably in front of witnesses.
- You did not have time to pursue normal OSHA enforcement channels. In most cases, this means that the danger must be something that came up suddenly and is not a safety threat that you allowed to go unchallenged for days, weeks or months.
- Staying on the job would make a reasonable person believe that he or she faced a threat of serious personal injury or death because of the workplace hazard. If the hazard is something that you can simply stay away from—such as a malfunctioning machine in a work area that you do not have to enter—it probably would not qualify as creating an emergency.
- You had no other reasonable alternative to refusing to work, such as asking for a reassignment to another area.

Example: *Mike is a welder in a truck building plant. Shortly after starting work one day, he noticed that a large electrical cable running along the plant's ceiling had broken overnight, was coming loose from the hardware attaching it to the ceiling and was dangling closer and closer to the plant floor. He and several of his co-workers immediately told their supervisor about the broken cable, but the supervisor did nothing about it. The group also told the supervisor's boss about the danger, but still nothing was done to correct it.*

By about 11 a.m., the broken cable had dropped to the point where it was brushing against the truck body that Mike was welding. Sparks flew each time the cable and the truck body touched. Because he had a reasonable fear that an electrical shock transmitted from the broken cable could seriously injure or kill him, Mike walked off the job. His supervisor fired him for leaving work without permission. But because the danger fit OSHA's definitions of an emergency, OSHA ordered the company to reinstate Mike to his job with back wages—after first repairing the broken and dangling cable.

If you use the extreme option of walking off a job because of a safety hazard, be sure to contact your nearest OSHA office as soon as you are out of danger. Call the agency's emergency reporting number: 800-321-6742. Jot down the name of the OSHA officer with whom you speak—and also note the time that you report the hazard. That will preserve your right to be paid back wages and other losses from the time that the hazard forced you to walk away from work.

Tracking OSHA Actions

Any citation issued by OSHA must be posted for at least three days in a conspicuous place within the workplace it affects. If the hazard specified in the citation is not corrected within three days after the citation is issued, then the citation must remain posted until it is corrected.

Compliance officers are required to advise those who originally filed a complaint of the action taken on it. If you need more information about the outcome of an OSHA investigation that affects your workplace, call, write or visit your local OSHA office.

If OSHA has given your employer an extended time to remedy a workplace hazard, then you also have a right to request a copy of that abatement plan from your employer. Your other recourse is to obtain a copy from the OSHA compliance officer who handled your complaint.

---

6. Penalties for Retaliation

Under OSHA, it is illegal for an employer to fire or otherwise discriminate against you for filing an OSHA complaint or participating in an OSHA investigation. OSHA can order an employer who violates this rule to return you to your job and to reimburse you for damages—including lost wages, the value of lost benefit coverages and the cost of searching for a new job. A number of state laws also protect against retaliation for reporting workplace health and safety violations. (See Section D below.)

How to Fight Back Against Retaliation

OSHA forbids your employer from lashing out at you—cutting your pay, demoting or firing you—because you file or help investigate a complaint about an unsafe workplace. However, the Act does not authorize you to enforce this restriction by going directly into court; you must ask OSHA to intercede.

If you suspect illegal retaliation, you have 30 days from the time the illegal action took place to file a complaint about it with your local OSHA office. The outcome of your illegal discrimination complaint may turn on whether you can prove that you were fired or demoted because you contacted authorities, not because your performance slipped or economic cutbacks made it necessary. Be sure to back up your complaint with as much documentation for your employer's action as possible. (For details on how to document a dismissal, see Chapter 10, Section C.)

Once you have filed a complaint about illegal job discrimination, OSHA has 90 days to respond. If you have shown that you were fired or otherwise punished because of complaining to OSHA, the compliance officer handling your complaint will attempt to convince your employer to take the proper action to remedy the situation. For example, if you were demoted in retaliation for your complaint, the OSHA compliance officer would probably ask your employer to reinstate you to your original position and give you the backpay to which you are entitled.

If OSHA is unsuccessful in talking your employer into reversing the effects of the illegal discrimination, it can sue your employer in federal court on your behalf.

C. Criminal Actions for OSHA Violations

As noted, the enforcement arm of OSHA has the power in some situations to pursue criminal prosecutions against employers who fail to maintain a safe workplace, but it rarely does.

However, state prosecutors are increasingly bringing criminal charges such as reckless endangerment and even murder against employers whose behavior seriously endangers workers. This trend was given a boost in 1990 when the New York Court of Appeals ruled that complaints under the Occupational Safety and Health Act do not take the place of criminal actions against employers whose actions cause workers to be injured or killed. Other state courts have ruled differently, however, so the issue may need to be resolved ultimately by the U.S. Supreme Court.

In the meantime, you may want to contact your state's attorney general about the possibility of criminal action if your work conditions pose a serious threat of injury or death to you or your co-workers and you are not able to resolve your concerns through OSHA or other civil actions.

Note that while employers can be prosecuted for criminal negligence when an employee dies as a result of violations of OSHA regulations, such convictions are rare. In fact, in the first 20 years the law was in effect, only one employer was convicted and sent to jail for such a death. The main reason for this low conviction rate is that, under OSHA, prosecutors must prove that an employer's violation of workplace safety rules was willful—that is, done on purpose—a subjective standard.

D. State and Local Health and Safety Laws

Many states and municipalities have laws that can help to ensure a certain level of safety in the workplace. These laws vary greatly in what they require, how they are enforced and even which employers they cover.

In 1991, California began enforcing the most powerful of these laws: It requires every employer in the state to have a written plan to prevent workplace injuries. A number of states have followed the lead, putting teeth and nails into the laws that protect workplace safety. For example, Texas maintains a 24-hour hotline for telephone reports of violations—and prohibits employers from discriminating against workers who drop a dime to use it.

When the Boss Doubles As a Bathroom Monitor

It wasn't big news to many when government health authorities in the summer of 1997 slapped a $332,500 fine on Hudson Foods, a poultry processing plant in the town of Noel, Missouri. The plant had been inspected by the Occupational Safety and Health Administration (OSHA) 23 times in 24 years—a healthy number for an agency notoriously backlogged and selective in carrying out its charge of ferreting out workplace health and safety violations.

A number of news sources dutifully recounted the parade of transgressions OSHA inspectors had noted: blocked and restricted fire exits, failure to provide training in and enforce use of eye protective equipment, failure to provide training and issue procedures for handling hazardous chemicals, failure to securely anchor machines.

Less widely reported was one innocuous sounding violation: Insufficient Toilet Facilities. The charge drew at least a few glib jibes: "Let My People Go," trumpeted one legal journal in a headline thumbnailing the inspection.

But few could fathom the human humiliation behind it all. Hudson workers claim they were required to ask permission before being allowed bathroom breaks—and that permission was denied as often as granted. Some say they were forced to urinate in their clothes or wear diapers to absorb the inevitable. Thom Hanson, chief regulatory compliance officer at Hudson, defended the company's position: The workers simply "need to ask supervisors to release them," he explained. "Normally, a relief person comes by and takes their place."

But relief was not always in sight, according to one woman who worked five years as a packer at Hudson. "It matters how good you get along with your supervisor. Sometimes they'll say no," she said. "And it's pretty hard to leave the line when you've got thousands of chickens coming at you."

OSHA regulations have long required that employers provide toilets in the workplace: at least six for the first 150 workers, and one more for each additional 40 workers. But in a twist of semantics defying logic, the regulations mandate only the presence of toilets on the scene—not employees' rights to use them. In considering the Hudson complaints, OSHA officials found for the first time that the company in effect denied workers toilet facilities when it denied them the right to use them.

In the wake of the *Hudson* case and the public outcry it attracted, OSHA officials dictated at last that employers must give workers prompt and reasonable access to toilet facilities, even though the regulations do not specifically require it.

An official Standards and Compliance Letter issued by OSHA on April 6, 1998, notes: "Toilets that employees are not allowed to use for extended periods cannot be said to be 'available' to those employees." In other words, employers can no longer hide behind the lacking letter of the law. Employers who do not allow employees reasonable access to workplace toilets may now be cited and sanctioned by OSHA inspectors.

1. State OSHA Laws

Nearly half the states now have their own OSHA laws—most with protections for workers that are similar to those provided in the federal law. For example, employers in some low hazard industries, such as retailers and insurance companies with fewer than ten employees, are exempt from some posting and reporting requirements. Most state laws cover all small employers, regardless of the type of business.

A number of states that do not now have OSHA laws in place are presently considering passing them—and many of the states that already have such laws are considering wholesale amendments changing their coverage and content. Check your state's particulars with a local OSHA office—or call the state department of labor to check whether your state has enacted an OSHA law recently. (See the Appendix for contact details.)

A number of state laws specifically forbid employers from firing employees who assert their rights under workplace health and safety rules. (See the chart below.)

Still another group of state laws extends beyond the workplace to protect employees who report violations of laws and rules that create specific dangers to public health and safety. These laws, commonly referred to as whistleblower statutes, generally protect good eggs—individuals who are attempting to uphold a public policy of the state. For example, typical whistleblower statutes prohibit employees from being fired for reporting toxic dumping or fraudulent use of government funds. (See Chapter 11, Section B, for an extensive discussion of these laws.)

The Knock That Never Comes

If you happen upon an OSHA official who is feeling chatty and loose-tongued, you may hear what we all suspected: There simply are not enough inspectors to go around inspecting. Perhaps the jobs are hard to fill. OSHA inspectors nestle among IRS auditors on most lists of unwelcome visitors.

Restricted budgets may be a problem, too—the agency has been forced to set staff levels low and keep them there.

All this makes for lax enforcement. For example, there are only about 250 inspectors on the California OSHA staff available to monitor businesses and dole out citations for failing to comply with the state's comprehensive law requiring health and safety plans for every employer in the state.

And California is a big state.

Chamber of Commerce officials there recently estimated that if all the inspectors started at the state's Oregon border and worked their way south through every business, it would take at least 300 years to reach Mexico.

Additional Laws May Apply

If the chart below indicates that your state has no statute, this means there is no law that specifically addresses the issue. However, there may be a state administrative regulation or local ordinance that does control. Call your state labor department for more information. (See the Appendix for contact details.)

State Health and Safety Laws

Alabama	Employees may not be fired for filing a written notice of an intentional violation of an employer's specific written safety rule. Ala. Code §25-5-11.1
Alaska	Employees may not be fired or discriminated against for filing a complaint or testifying in any proceeding under the Occupational Safety and Health Act. Alaska Stat. §18.60.089
Arizona	Employers may not discriminate against employees because they have filed complaints about or given testimony in a proceeding about violations of state workplace safety rules, and cannot be fired for filing health or safety complaints with the Industrial Commission. Ariz. Rev. Stat. Ann. §23-425 Employees may not be fired for filing a complaint or testifying under statutes regulating the control of pesticides. Ariz. Rev. Stat. Ann. §3-376

Arkansas	Public employees are protected from discharge, discipline and other forms of retaliation if they requested information, filed a complaint, instituted a proceeding or testified about any right contained in the Public Employees' Chemical Right to Know Act (Ark. Code Ann. §§8-7-1001 to 1016). Ark. Code Ann. §8-7-1010
California	Employees cannot be fired or discriminated against for reporting safety violations in the workplace, or refusing to perform any work that would be in violation of a safety standard or order. Cal. Lab. Code §§6310 and 6311
Colorado	No statute
Connecticut	Employees may not be disciplined in any manner for reporting violations of state Occupational Health and Safety laws. Conn. Gen. Stat. Ann. §31-40d
Delaware	Employees cannot be discharged or disciplined for complaining or testifying about the presence of hazardous chemicals. Del. Code. Ann. tit. 16, §2415
District of Columbia	Employees are protected for disclosing unsafe or unhealthy working conditions. D.C. Code Ann. §1-621.5
Florida	Employees cannot be fired or threatened with firing for exercising their rights under the Occupational Safety and Health Act regarding toxic substances. Fla. Stat. §442.116
Georgia	Employees of hazardous chemical manufacturers, importers or distributors are protected from retaliation for requesting a copy of the employer's material safety data sheet or for refusing to work with the chemical in question if the employer fails to provide the data sheet five days after the employee requests it. Ga. Code Ann. §45-22-7
Hawaii	Employees cannot be fired for reporting Occupational Safety and Health violations or testifying regarding such a violation or for refusing to engage in an unsafe practice that violates the law. Haw. Rev. Stat. §396-8(e)
Idaho	Employees cannot be fired or discriminated against for participating in proceedings under the Farm Labor Sanitary Protection Act. Idaho Code §44-1904
Illinois	Employees cannot be fired or in any way discriminated against for assisting in the enforcement of the state's Toxic Substances Act regarding toxic chemical exposure in the workplace. 820 Ill. Comp. Stat. 255/14
Indiana	Employees may not be fired for filing a complaint under the Occupational Health and Safety Act. Ind. Code Ann. §22-8-1.1-38.1
Iowa	Employees cannot be fired for filing a complaint or participating in a proceeding for violation of Occupational Safety and Health laws. Iowa Code §88.9
Kansas	Employees may not be fired or discriminated against for disclosing information regarding a violation of Occupational Safety and Health laws. Kan. Stat. Ann. §44-636
Kentucky	Employees cannot be fired for exercising rights under an Occupational Safety and Health claim. Ky. Rev. Stat. §338.121(3)(a)

Louisiana	Employees are protected from reprisal for reporting violations of environmental laws or regulations of state, federal or local authorities. La. Rev. Stat. Ann. §30:2027 An employer cannot take any discriminatory action or retaliation against an employee who exercises, in good faith, the rights given under the Lead Hazard Reduction, Licensure and Certification Act, including the right to report hazardous lead conditions. La Rev. Stat. Ann. §30:2351.55
Maine	Employees cannot be fired or discriminated against for filing a complaint about violations of a state health and safety law or for testifying in any proceedings relating to employee safety and health. Me. Rev. Stat. Ann. tit. 26, §570
Maryland	Employees cannot be discriminated against or fired for filing an action or complaint under the Occupational Safety and Health Act. Md. Ann. Code Lab. and Emp. art. 5, §604
Massachusetts	Employees may not be fired for exercising rights under the Toxic Substances law regarding exposure to toxic substances in the workplace. Mass. Gen. Laws Ann. ch. 111F, §13
Michigan	An employer may not discharge or discriminate against an employee who refuses to operate equipment or participate in a process that has been tagged by the department of labor as violating a health or safety rule. Mich. Comp. Laws §408.1031 An employer may not discriminate against an employee who has filed a complaint, instituted a proceeding or testified under the Occupational Health and Safety Act. Mich. Comp. Laws §408.1065
Minnesota	Employees cannot be fired for being involved in an Occupational Health and Safety case. Minn. Stat. Ann. §182.654
Mississippi	No statute
Missouri	No statute
Montana	The Community Hazardous Chemical Information Act prohibits firing or adversely acting against an employee who exercises rights under the Act regarding exposure to toxic substances in the workplace. Mont. Code Ann. §50-78-204
Nebraska	No statute
Nevada	Employees may not be discriminated against or fired because of safety and health complaints. Nev. Rev. Stat. §618.445
New Hampshire	Employees cannot be fired or in any way penalized for filing complaints or exercising rights under the Worker's Right to Know Act regarding toxic substances in the workplace. N.H. Rev. Stat. Ann. §§277-A:7
New Jersey	An employer may not penalize or discharge an employee because he has exercised his rights under the Hazardous Substances Right to Know Act, including the employee's right to report violations to the Commissioner of the Department of Labor. N.J. Stat. Ann. §§34:5A-16 to 17
New Mexico	Employees cannot be fired or in any way discriminated against because of safety and health complaints. N.M. Stat. Ann. §50-9-25

New York	Public employers cannot fire or otherwise discriminate against employees because of Occupational Safety and Health complaints. An employer cannot reduce the wages of an employee who accompanies the commissioner of labor on an inspection. N.Y. Lab. Law §27-a
	Employers may not retaliate against employees who disclose violations that create a substantial danger to public health or safety. N.Y. Lab. Law §740
North Carolina	Employees cannot be fired for making safety or health complaints under the Hazardous Chemicals Right to Know Act (N.C. Gen. Stat. §95-196) regarding exposure to toxic substances in the workplace or the Occupational Safety and Health Act. N.C. Gen. Stat. §95-241(a)(1)(b)
North Dakota	No statute
Ohio	An employer may not retaliate against an employee who reports a violation that causes imminent risk of physical harm or is a hazard to public health or safety. The employee must first file a report with the supervisor and wait 24 hours to see if corrective action is taken. Ohio Rev. Code §4113.52
Oklahoma	No employer may discharge or take any adverse personnel action against an employee who has filed a complaint, instituted or participated in a proceeding or exercised any right under the Oklahoma Occupational Health and Safety Standards Act of 1970 (tit. 40, §§401 and following). Okla. Stat. Ann. tit. 40, §403B
Oregon	Employees cannot be fired for reporting safety or health violations in the workplace. Or. Rev. Stat. §654.062
Pennsylvania	Employers may not fire employees for filing health and safety complaints or exercising rights under the Community and Worker Right to Know Act regarding hazardous substances in the workplace. Pa. Stat. Ann. tit. 35, §7313
Rhode Island	Employees may not be fired for making a complaint regarding toxic substances in the workplace. R.I. Gen. Laws §28-21-8
	Employers may not fire employees for health and safety complaints. R.I. Gen. Laws §28-20-21
South Carolina	Employees may not be fired for making safety and health complaints. S.C. Code Ann. §41-15-510
South Dakota	No statute
Tennessee	Employees may not be fired for making safety and health complaints or testifying in any proceeding brought under the Occupational Safety and Health law. Tenn. Code Ann. §50-3-106(7)
Texas	The Division of the state OSHA must maintain a 24-hour telephone hotline for reports of violations of occupational health or safety laws. An employer may not suspend, terminate or discriminate against an employee because an employee used the telephone service to report in good faith an alleged violation of an occupational health or safety law. Texas Code Ann. Lab. §§411.081 to .083

Utah	An employee cannot be fired for making an Occupational Safety and Health complaint, or because the employee has testified or is about to testify in any proceeding related to an occupational safety law, or because the employee has exercised any occupational safety right on behalf of himself or others. Utah Code Ann. §34A-6-203
Vermont	Employees cannot be fired or otherwise discriminated against for making safety and health complaints. An employee who feels he has been treated in violation of this law may file a complaint with the commissioner of labor, who may bring a legal action to compel reinstatement and back pay. The employee may, instead or in addition, sue the employer for triple the wages lost, reinstatement, damages and costs. Vt. Stat. Ann. tit. 21, §231 and 232
Virginia	Employees cannot be fired or otherwise discriminated against for making Occupational Health and Safety complaints. Va. Code §40.1-51.2:1
Washington	Employers cannot fire employees for making a complaint about workplace safety and health under the Worker and Community Right to Know Act (Wash. Rev. Code Ann. §49.70.010 and following) regarding exposure to toxic substances or the Occupational Safety and Health law. Wash. Rev. Code Ann. §49.17.160
West Virginia	An employer may not discharge or discriminate against an employee for filing a complaint or initiating or participating in any proceeding under the Occupational Safety and Health Act. W.Va. Code §21-3A-13
Wisconsin	Employers cannot fire employees for testifying about or exercising any rights regarding toxic substances in the workplace. Wis. Stat. Ann. §101.595
Wyoming	Employers cannot fire or in any way discriminate against employees for reporting safety and health conditions in the workplace, or for testifying about conditions in the workplace or exercising any right to a safe workplace. Wyo. Stat. §27-11-109

2. Sanitation Laws

Many state and local health and building codes offer quick and easy guidance in how to keep your workplace safe. While not intended specifically to ensure workplace safety, these laws often include programs designed to ensure good sanitation and public safety in general.

For example, the health department of the city in which you work probably has the power to order an employer to improve restroom facilities that are leaking and causing unsanitary workplace conditions. And your local building inspector typically can order an employer to straighten out faulty electrical wiring that presents a shock or fire hazard to people working near that wiring.

You can find state and local health and building codes at your city hall or county courthouse.

E. Tobacco Smoke in the Workplace

OSHA rules apply to tobacco smoke only in the most rare and extreme circumstances, such as when contaminants created by a manufacturing process combine with tobacco smoke to create a dangerous workplace air supply that fails OSHA standards. Workplace air quality standards and measurement techniques are so technical that typically only OSHA agents or consultants who specialize in environmental testing are able to determine when the air quality falls below allowable limits. But when asked to intercede on workplace complaints about tobacco smoke, Environmental Protection Agency (EPA) officials typically hedge that "exposures to the carbon monoxide or other toxic substances in the tobacco smoke rarely exceed current OSHA permissible exposure limits or PELs (OSHA Standards Interpretation and Compliance Letter, 10/26/98).

But the torturous effects of tobacco smoke on human health have been clearly established and even certified by the government. A recent report by the EPA, for example, estimated that secondhand tobacco smoke that emerges from exhaling and burning cigarettes causes approximately 3,000 lung cancer deaths and 37,000 heart disease deaths in nonsmokers each year. So people who smoke cigarettes, cigars or pipes at work increasingly find themselves to be an unwelcome minority—and many employers already take actions to control when and where smoking is allowed.

Workplace bans and limits on smoking are still controversial, but gaining support. According to a 1999 Gallup poll, for example, 95% of Americans—smokers and nonsmokers—now believe companies should either ban smoking totally in the workplace or restrict it to separately ventilated areas.

Although there is no federal law that directly controls smoking at work, a majority of states protect workers against unwanted smoke in the workplace. (See Section E1.) In addition, hundreds of city and county ordinances restrict smoking in the workplace, but only a few of these local laws, including San Francisco, ban it outright. (See the Appendix for contact details for organizations with current information on laws that restrict smoking in your workplace.)

In contrast, about half the states make it illegal to discriminate against employees or potential employees because they smoke during nonworking hours. (See Section E2.) And because it has much encouragement and financial support from the tobacco industry, this smokers' rights movement appears to be gaining strength.

So the ongoing legal battle boils down to a question of what is more important: one person's right to preserve health by avoiding co-workers' tobacco smoke, or another's right to smoke without the interference of others.

1. Protections for Nonsmokers

Because of the potentially higher costs of healthcare insurance, absenteeism, unemployment insurance and workers' compensation insurance associated with employees who smoke, some companies now refuse to hire anyone who admits to being a smoker on a job application or in prehiring interviews.

The sentiment against smoking in the workplace and any other space shared with others has grown so strong that many companies now increase their attractiveness to jobseekers by mentioning in their Help Wanted advertising that they maintain a smoke-free workplace.

Except in the states that forbid work-related discrimination against smokers and the states where it is illegal for employers to discriminate against employees on the basis of any legal activities outside work, there is nothing to prevent employers from establishing a policy of hiring and employing only nonsmokers.

a. State laws

While most states now protect workers from unwanted smoke on the job, they follow different approaches. Many states have laws that specifically address smoking in workplaces; they live on the books alongside regulations that apply elsewhere. A large number of states have smoking control laws that apply to everyone in public places and specified private places; nonsmoking employees in these states are protected only if they happen to work in a place that is specifically covered by the statute. A few state laws are all-encompassing—limiting or banning smoking in both public places and workplaces.

Where smoking is limited, some states prohibit it except in a designated area within the workplace. Other states take the opposite approach, requiring employers to set aside pristine areas for the nonsmokers in the work crowd.

There are also common exceptions written into anti-smoking laws. Often, their protections do not apply to:

- places where private social functions are typically held, such as rented banquet rooms in hotels; presumably, even the most sensitive nonsmoking employees must brave the smoke when they are guests in these places
- private offices occupied exclusively by smokers
- inmates at correctional facilities and hospital patients, who usually must comply with the rules of the institution while they are confined, and
- employers who can show that it would be financially or physically unreasonable to comply with the legal limitations.

Additional Protection Under the ADA

Some workers who are irked and injured by smoke on the job have brought successful claims for their injuries under the Americans With Disabilities Act, which prohibits discrimination against people with disabilities. (See Chapter 8, Section F.) You are entitled to protection under this law only if you can prove that your ability to breathe is severely limited by tobacco smoke, making you physically disabled.

Additional Laws May Apply

If the chart below indicates that your state has no statute, this means there is no law that specifically addresses the issue. However, there may be a state administrative regulation or local ordinance that does control. Call your state labor department for more information. (See the Appendix for contact details.)

Laws That Protect Nonsmokers

Alabama	No statute
Alaska	Smoking is not permitted in any state-owned or leased property or building, or in any private place of business where the employer has chosen to post a no smoking sign. If a private place of business has designated a smoking area, there must be adequate ventilation to ensure that nonsmokers are not subject to the active byproducts of smoke. Does not apply to restaurants seating fewer than 50 people, nor to correctional facilities. Ala. Code §§18.35.300(2) & (9) and §198.35.320(c)
Arizona	Smoking is prohibited in any state-owned or leased property or building, except for clients at the Arizona State Hospital, inmates in correctional facilities and residents of state-owned residences. The ban does not apply when tobacco products are used for religious or ceremonial purposes. The Department of Administration may, however, designate smoking areas as long as there is no resulting drifting smoke. The statute provides for anonymous complaint procedures. Ariz. Rev. Stat. Ann. §36-601.02
Arkansas	No statute
California	Employers may not knowingly or intentionally permit smoking in an enclosed place of employment. Exceptions include: 65% of the rooms in a hotel or motel, designated lobby areas, meeting and banquet rooms—except when food is being served—tobacco shops, warehouses, patient smoking areas in longterm healthcare facilities, truck cabs if no nonsmoking employees are present, and employee breakrooms designated for smoking, provided no air from the room circulates to other parts of the building and there are breakrooms for nonsmokers. An employer is free to designate the entire workplace as nonsmoking and is not required to establish separate smoking areas—which, if established, must be separately ventilated. Employers with five or fewer employees may permit smoking as long as no minors enter the smoking area, all employees consent and no one is required to enter the smoking area as part of his or her work responsibilities. Local ordinances may be more restrictive, but not less so. Cal. Lab. Code §6404.5
Colorado	Smoking is not permitted in most public places, hospitals, theaters and mass transit. Smoking is permitted in sections of bars and restaurants. Employers are encouraged to designate a separate nonsmoking lounge area. Colo. Rev. Stat. §25-14-103
Connecticut	State and private employers must establish nonsmoking areas on request and may designate the entire facility as nonsmoking. The employer may be exempted from compliance with the statute if the labor commissioner finds that the employer made a good faith effort to comply and further steps would constitute "an unreasonable financial burden." Conn. Gen. Stat. Ann. §31-40q(a)(4)
Delaware	Statute applies to public places and workplaces. Smoking is not allowed in many specific areas—including public meetings, elevators, mass transit and healthcare facilities. Smoking is allowed only in designated areas in public buildings, auditoria and theaters.

Every employer is directed to set aside a nonsmoking area for every employee who asks for one. There must be smokefree areas in cafeterias and lounges. Statute does not apply to bars, hotel rooms or private social functions where the host, not the proprietor, is in charge of the seating arrangements. Clean Indoor Air Act, Del. Code Ann. tit. 16, §2901 to 2905

District of Columbia | Smoking is prohibited in elevators, selling areas of retail stores, government-owned or leased meeting rooms, public transit, educational facilities, public areas of healthcare facilities and in any public or private workplace.
Restaurants seating 50 or more must designate 25% of seating capacity for nonsmoking; restaurants built or undergoing major renovation after 3/29/88 must designate 50% of seating capacity for nonsmoking.
The employer may designate an entire worksite nonsmoking, but must designate an area where smoking is allowed. The smoking area must be a separate room or have a physical barrier separating it from the rest of the workplace.
Statute does not apply to tobacco shops, stages where actors perform, restaurants seating fewer than 50, taverns and nightclubs or rooms used for private social functions where the host, not the proprietor, is in charge of the seating arrangements. D.C. Code Ann. §§6-911 to 918

Florida | In a workplace of smokers and nonsmokers, employers shall develop and implement smoking and nonsmoking areas, taking into consideration the proportion of smokers and nonsmokers. Employers may satisfy the statute's requirements by making "reasonable efforts" to do so. Florida Clean Indoor Air Act, Fla. Stat. §85-257

Georgia | No smoking is permitted on public transit vehicles and stations. Ga. Code Ann. §16-12-120

Hawaii | There is no smoking in public places except for small businesses and small retail stores less than 500 square feet.
If requested to do so, an employer shall attempt to reach a "reasonable accommodation" between the wishes of smokers and nonsmokers, using existing ventilation and partitions and without the expenditure of additional funds.
If an accommodation cannot be reached, the employer shall follow the preferences of the majority; and if the nonsmokers are dissatisfied with the arrangements, they may appeal to the director of health. The statute does not apply to federally owned or leased property, or to private enclosed workspaces occupied exclusively by smokers. Smoking In the Workplace Act, Haw. Rev. Stat. §328K, Part II

Idaho | Employees are protected under the law protecting the general public. Smoking is not allowed in any public place except in designated smoking areas. A public place means any enclosed indoor area used by the general public, including restaurants that seat over 30 patrons, retail and grocery stores, public transit, education facilities, hospitals, nursing homes, arenas and meeting rooms.

Bars, bowling alleys and halls or rooms used for a private social function—where the seating arrangements are under the control of the host, not the proprietor—may be designated smoking in their entirety. Proprietors shall make a good faith effort to minimize the effect of smoke on nonsmoking areas. Idaho Code §§39-5501 and following

Illinois	Smoking is not allowed in a public place unless that place is designated a smoking area. The rule does not apply to factories, warehouses or similar places of work not frequented by the public nor to rooms used for private functions where the seating is under the control of the sponsor, not the owner. In designing a smoking area, the state or private owner need only use existing ventilation and structures. Statute specifies that local governments may not pass laws allowing smoking in public places. Illinois Clean Indoor Air Act, Ill Comp. Stat. ch. 410 §80/1 and following.
	No person may be discriminated against because of exercising rights under the Illinois Clean Indoor Air Act.
	It is not discriminatory for an employer to offer different premiums for health policies for smokers and nonsmokers as long as the charges reflect actual differential costs paid by the employer, and employees are given statements of the insurance carriers' rates. 820 Ill. Comp. Stat. 55/5
Indiana	Smoking is not allowed in a public building—including state classrooms or health facilities, buildings occupied by a state agency and public schools—except in designated areas. The person in charge must designate a nonsmoking area and may designate smoking areas. Local governments may adopt stricter regulations. Clean Indoor Air Act, Ind. Code Ann. §16-41-37-1 and following
Iowa	Smoking is prohibited in any public place—that is, any enclosed indoor area used by the public or serving as a place of work, that is at least 250 square feet, including a restaurant serving more than 50 people.
	Smoking areas may be designated using existing barriers and ventilation to contain the smoke. Statute does not apply to warehouses, factories, private, enclosed offices occupied exclusively by smokers, tobacco shops, bars, rooms or halls rented out for private social functions where the host, not the proprietor is in control of seating arrangements, dormitory rooms, hotel rooms and each resident's room in a healthcare facility. In warehouses and factories where smoking is allowed, a nonsmoking area must be designated. Iowa Code Ann. §142B.1 and following
Kansas	Smoking is not permitted in enclosed indoor areas open to the public, including restaurants, stores, theaters, libraries, mass transit and healthcare facilities. A smoking area can be designated in a public area as long as there are physical barriers and a ventilation system that minimize the toxic effect of the smoke. Kan. Stat. Ann. §21-4009 and 4010
Kentucky	No statute
Louisiana	Every employer with more than 25 employees must have a smoking policy. If a nonsmoking employee complains about smoke in the workplace, the employer must attempt to reach an accommodation between smokers and nonsmokers using existing ventilation and structures. The employer is not required to make any expenditures or structural changes to accommodate the nonsmokers or smokers.

The statute applies to enclosed offices, hospitals, libraries, museums and office buildings.

Does not apply to private homes used as workplaces and private enclosed workspaces occupied exclusively by smokers, even though nonsmokers may visit the area.

With the exception of any local ordinances enacted prior to 9-1-93, no local laws may be more restrictive of smoking than the state law. Louisiana Office Indoor Clean Air Law, La. Rev. Stat. Ann. 40:1300.21 and following

Smoking is not permitted in schools and school buses. La. Rev. Stat. Ann. §17:240

Smoking is prohibited in elevators, public transit and child care facilities. Restaurant owners may establish nonsmoking laws according to customer demand. Smoking is permitted in bars. La. Rev. Stat. Ann. §40:1300.41 and following

Maine	Smoking is prohibited except in designated areas, and an employer may prohibit smoking entirely. If asked, the Bureau of Health will assist employers to develop a policy for designating smoking areas. Does not apply if the employer and all the employees have mutually agreed upon their own policy. Me. Rev. Stat. Ann. tit. 22, §1580-A(3)
Maryland	Smoking is permitted except in certain areas of restaurants and a percentage of hotel and motel rooms. A proprietor may restrict smoking altogether. Md. Code Ann. Lab. and Emp. §2-106(c)
Massachusetts	Smoking is prohibited in public buildings, public elevators, markets, courthouses, schools, colleges, universities, museums, libraries, daycare facilities, on public transit or transit platforms, trains, airplanes, airport waiting areas or in restaurants seating more than 75 people. Owners and employers may designate smoking areas, but only if there remains a sufficiently large nonsmoking area. Statute does not apply to completely enclosed one-person offices. Mass. Gen. Laws Ann. ch. 270 §22
Michigan	Smoking is not allowed in public places except for private educational facilities after school hours and rooms used for private functions where the seating is under the control of the sponsor. Mich. Comp. Laws §§333.12601 and following

Smoking is not permitted in child care centers, elevators and school buses. Mich. Comp. Laws §§333.12604; 408.820; 257.1853

Food service establishments that seat fewer than 50 people may designate up to 75%, and establishments that seat more than 50 may designate up to 50% of seating capacity for smokers. In retail food establishments, the only place smoking may be permitted is in a designated area for employees and the public that is isolated from the retail food area. Mich. Comp. Laws §§333.12905; 289.707a |
| Minnesota | Smoking is not allowed in an enclosed, indoor public place or area of work, except for private, enclosed offices occupied exclusively by smokers. Using existing ventilation and structures, employer may designate smoking areas which must minimize the toxic effect of smoke on adjoining areas. |

Statute does not apply to warehouses, factories or similar workplaces not frequented by members of the public, but the state commissioner shall establish rules to restrict smoking if there is smoke pollution in these structures to nonsmokers. Minn. Stat. Ann. §§144.413 and following

Mississippi	No statute
Missouri	Smoking is not allowed in a public place except in designated areas. Public places include enclosed indoor areas used by the general public or serving as a place of work and mass transit vehicles. The person in control may designate up to 30% of the available space as a smoking area.

Does not apply to a room or hall rented for a private social occasion at which the host, not the proprietor, sets the seating arrangements; to bars and restaurants that seat fewer than 50 people; to sports arenas that accommodate more than 15,000; to tobacco shops. Local ordinances may be more restrictive. Indoor Clean Air Act, Mo. Stat. Ann. §§191.765 and following

Montana	All buildings maintained by the state may be smokefree. Except in community colleges designated smokefree by the board of trustees, a state or local government agency shall designate convenient smoking and nonsmoking areas. Restrooms, bars that do not serve meals and rooms and cars with fewer than six public occupants are exempted. Mont. Code Ann. §50-40-201 to 205

In buildings not maintained by the state, the manager or owner shall designate nonsmoking areas and may designate the entire space to be nonsmoking. If smoking areas are established, they must be clearly posted. Statute does not apply to restrooms, bars that do not serve meals and rooms or vehicles seating six or fewer members of the public. Mont. Code Ann. §50-40-101 to 109

Nebraska	Smoking is not allowed in a public place—that is, an enclosed, indoor area used by the public or serving as a place of work—except in designated smoking areas. Does not apply to private, enclosed offices occupied exclusively by smokers, even though visited by nonsmokers; nor does it apply to an entire hall or room rented for a social function where the seating arrangements are under the control of the host, not the owner.

As to factories, warehouses and similar places of work not usually frequented by the public, the Departments of Health and of Labor must establish rules to prohibit or restrict smoking in workplaces where the workers' close proximity or inadequate ventilation causes smoke pollution detrimental to the health and comfort of nonsmokers. Neb. Rev. Stat. §71-5704 and following

Nevada	Smoking is prohibited, except in designated areas, in any public building—one owned and used by the state, the University of Nevada, or any county, city or school district; in any public elevator, waiting room, lobby or hall of any medical facility; and in the office of any doctor, dentist, optometrist, optician, physical therapist or psychologist. It is also prohibited in a public bus, the public area of any food market and in any child care facility room that children use; and in any hotel, motel or restaurant where the operator in charge of the facility has designated it to be a nonsmoking area.

Does not apply to gaming establishments. Retail food establishments may permit smoking if ventilation substantially removes smoke from the area. Nev. Rev. Stat. Ann. §§202.2491 and following

New Hampshire   Smoking is prohibited in all enclosed places of public access, publicly owned offices and buildings and in any enclosed workspace in which four or more people work, except in effectively segregated smoking areas. If a smoking area cannot be effectively segregated, smoking shall be totally prohibited.

The statute includes hospitals, public education facilities, elevators, public conveyances and enclosed spaces owned and operated by private social, fraternal or religious organizations when the facilities are made available to the general public, such as a church hall used as a polling place.

The statute excludes restaurants seating fewer than 50 people, public conveyances rented for private purposes, hotel and motel rooms, residents' rooms in public housing and nursing homes, and prison and detention facilities.

If an area is designated "smoking allowed," the person in charge shall develop a written policy covering the training of employees, reviewing and arbitrating of complaints and handling of violations. Special consideration shall be given to people whose proven medical condition is directly and adversely affected by smoke, as documented by an occupational physician.

The provisions of the statute may be waived if the person in charge can prove by clear and convincing evidence that compelling reasons exist to justify a waiver, for example, that compliance would cause undue hardship or interfere with other policies of the facility. A waiver must not jeopardize the health or welfare of the employees.

The statute may not be used by an employee as the basis for a refusal to discharge normal duties, including entering an area in which smoking is permitted. Indoor Smoking Act, N.H. Rev. Stat. Ann §155.64 and following

New Jersey   In workplaces with more than 50 employees, the employer shall establish written rules governing smoking to protect the health, welfare and comfort of nonsmokers. The employer may designate smoking areas within a nonsmoking facility, but must designate nonsmoking areas if smoking is otherwise allowed. Municipal ordinances may further protect the rights of nonsmokers, but may not be less protective. N.J. Stat. Ann. §§26:3D-24 to 31

Smoking is prohibited in retail food and marketing stores with more than 4,000 square feet open to the public. In enclosed public places such as theatres, libraries, museums, concert halls and auditoriums. Casinos, racetracks, sporting event facilities, dancehalls, bowling alleys and skating rinks are exempt. N.J. Stat. Ann. §§26:3D-46 and following

New Mexico   Smoking is not permitted in public places except in designated areas. A designated area can be a fully enclosed office or room occupied only by smokers although visited by nonsmokers or another area designated by the employer. Smoking is permitted at private functions where the seating is under the control of the sponsor.

At places of public employment with more than 15 employees, there is no smoking in elevators, nurse aid stations or in half of the floor space of the cafeteria or lounge. Employers must post no smoking signs and provide smokefree work areas to employees who request it but are not required to make structural changes.

Except for private offices and the house and senate lounges, no part of the state capitol shall be designated as an area in which smoking is permitted. N.M. Stat. Ann. §§24-16-1 to 11

New York Smoking is prohibited in indoor areas open to the public, including classrooms, public transit and ticketing and boarding areas. Each employer shall adopt a written smoking policy that provides nonsmokers with a smokefree work area. A work area may be designated as a smoking area as long as all employees in that area agree. There must be contiguous nonsmoking areas in cafeterias, lunchrooms and lounges. Smoking is not allowed in auditoriums, gyms, restrooms, copy machine areas or areas of other equipment used in common or meeting or conference rooms unless all present agree otherwise. An employer is not required to spend money to comply with the statute; but if an employer is unable, despite best efforts, to comply with an employee's request for a smokefree area, that area must be designated smokefree. Employers who violate the statute may defend themselves by showing that they made a good faith effort to comply. Waiver of the statute is possible if the employer can show that compliance would constitute an undue hardship, or that other factors such as the physical layout of the business make strict compliance unreasonable.

The statute does not apply to bars, tobacco shops or private social functions where the seating is under the control of the sponsor. N.Y. Pub. Health Law, Art. 13-E, §§1399 and following

North Carolina Local government entities may pass stricter legislation regulating smoking in the workplace. See the New York City Smokefree Air Act, NYC Admin. Code §§17-501 and following

North Dakota Smoking is not permitted in public places except in designated areas. Smoking is permitted in bars. N.D. Cent. Code §§23-12-9 and 10

Ohio A public place that seats more than 50 people must have a no smoking area. Does not apply to restaurants, bowling alleys and bars. Ohio Rev. Code §3791.031

Oklahoma Smoking is not allowed in a public place except in designated smoking areas. Public places include enclosed, indoor areas owned or operated by a government entity, a workplace for public employees and a privately owned, enclosed area used by the general public—including education and health facilities and restaurants that seat more than 50 patrons.

Nonsmoking and smoking areas shall be designated with signs, and the employer must ask smokers to refrain from smoking in nonsmoking areas. Nursing homes and long-term care facilities have separate regulations. Okla. Stat. Ann. tit. 63, §§1-1522 and following

Oregon Smoking is not permitted in public elevators. Smoking is permitted in bars, tobacco shops, restaurants seating fewer than 30 people, enclosed offices even if visited by nonsmokers, private functions where the seating is under the control of the sponsor. Oregon Clean Indoor Air Act, Or. Rev. Stat. §§433.835 and following; §479.015

	Smoking is not permitted in hospital rooms unless they have been designated for smoking or in other areas in which patient care is provided. Hospital administrators must designate reasonable areas in lobbies and waiting rooms for nonsmoking and a reasonable number of nonsmoking patient rooms. Or. Rev. Stat. §441.815
	Smoking is not permitted in places of state employment. The personnel division may adopt rules for the designation of smoking areas. Or. Rev. Stat. §243.345 and .350
Pennsylvania	Smoking is not allowed in a public place—an enclosed, indoor area owned or operated by a government entity; and a workplace used by the general public. Statute does not apply to private social functions in which seating arrangements are set by the host and not the proprietor, bars, public halls and lobbies, hotel and motel rooms and restaurants that seat fewer than 75 patrons. Smoking restrictions do not apply to tobacco shops or to factories, warehouses or similar places where the general public does not go. Pa. Cons. Stat. Ann. tit. 35 §1230.1 and following
Rhode Island	An employer that allows smoking must make reasonable accommodations for the preferences of both smokers and nonsmokers, particularly those employees who, as a result of a physical condition, are unduly sensitive to smoke. If a nonsmoker objects to the presence of smoke in the workspace, the employer shall use available ventilation and structures. However, no money need be spent or structural changes undertaken. The statute applies to enclosed public and private workspaces, including office spaces in federal offices where people other than federal employees are present; and factories and manufacturing plant areas. Does not apply to public lobbies; private homes used as a workplace; office space owned or rented by an independent contractor for his or her own use; or private enclosed workspaces occupied exclusively by smokers, even though nonsmokers may enter the area. Rhode Island Workplace Smoking Pollution Control Act, R.I. Gen. Laws §§23-20.7.1 and following
South Carolina	Smoking is not permitted, except in designated smoking areas, in public schools (except in the teachers' lounge), children's service facilities, healthcare facilities, elevators, mass transit, indoor arenas auditoriums and government buildings, except in enclosed private offices and employee breakrooms. S.C. Code Ann. §§44-95-10 and following
South Dakota	Smoking in nursing or medical facilities, libraries, museums, theaters, public schools, jury rooms, elevators and daycare centers is permitted in designated areas only. S.D. Codified Laws §22-36-2
Tennessee	The head of each state agency must establish a policy that protects the rights of smokers and nonsmokers and provides smoking and nonsmoking areas in the workplace. Tenn. Code Ann. §4-4-121
Texas	Smoking is permitted only in designated areas in most public places, including public primary and secondary schools, elevators, enclosed theatres,

movie houses, libraries, museums, hospitals, buses, planes and trains. Texas Code Ann. Penal §48.01

Utah

Employers must have a smoking policy restricting smoking to designated enclosed smoking areas. If the smoking area does not effectively prevent smoke from reaching the working areas of nonsmokers, as determined by the local health department, the smoking area cannot exist.

The statute does not apply to Native American ceremonies, to bars, to buildings rented or owned by religious, fraternal or social organizations and used solely by their members and guests, to private functions where the seating arrangements are under the control of the sponsor.

Smoking is not allowed in any state-owned or leased building, except in designated areas. Utah Clean Indoor Act, Utah Code Ann. §§26-38-1 and following

Vermont

Each employer must establish a smoking policy which must prohibit smoking throughout the workplace or restrict it to enclosed, designated smoking areas. Smoking may be permitted in designated unenclosed areas as long as there is no resulting smoke irritation to nonsmokers and three-fourths of the employees in the workplace agree. Areas that employees are required to visit on a regular basis may not be designated smoking. Up to 30% of a cafeteria or lounge can be designated as a smoking area.

Municipal ordinances may be more protective of nonsmokers rights, but not less so. Vt. Stat. Ann. tit. 18, §§1421-1428

Virginia

Every state and local government entity must provide nonsmoking areas in any state or locally owned or leased building.

In addition, smoking is not allowed in specific areas, including elevators, pubic school common areas and buses, indoor service and cashier lines.

The person in charge of an education or healthcare facility or a retail establishment of over 15,000 square feet, including department and grocery stores, and restaurants seating over 50 people must designate nonsmoking areas. Does not apply to retail tobacco stores, bars, or to warehouses or manufacturing facilities not open to the general public. Virginia Indoor Clean Air Act, Va. Code Ann. §15.2-2801 and following

Except for local ordinances enacted before January 1, 1990, local laws may not be more restrictive of smokers' rights. An employer may, however, further restrict the use of tobacco in the workplace as long as the policy is the subject of a written agreement between the employer and the employees. An employer may totally ban smoking in the workplace only after a majority vote of all the affected employees voting. Va. Code Ann. §§15.2-2803 and 2807

Washington

Smoking is permitted in public places only in designated areas. Smoking is allowed in a private enclosed workspace even if nonsmokers visit it. Smoking is not allowed at all in elevators, buses, streetcars, retail stores, bank lobbies, public buildings, museums, public meetings, classrooms, indoor sports arenas, hallways of healthcare facilities. Smoking is allowed in all parts of tobacco shops and bars. Wash. Rev. Code Ann. §§70.160.010 and following

West Virginia

No statute

Wisconsin	Employees are protected only to the same extent as the general public. Smoking is not allowed in indoor enclosed public places, including restaurants, buses, public buildings, and a hospital or physician's office, except in hospital areas where mentally ill or drug dependent patients are being treated. A smoking area can be designated in all places except buses, hospitals, physician's offices and day care centers. Smoking restrictions do not apply to rooms where the main occupants smoke, even if visited by nonsmokers; Type 2 secured correctional facilities, prisons; restaurants with Class B liquor licenses that make more than 50% of gross receipts from sale of alcohol; areas of facilities used to manufacture goods or products for sale; or rooms used for private functions where the seating is under the control of the sponsor. Wisconsin Clean Air Act, Wis. Code Ann. §§101.123(1)(am) and following
Wyoming	No statute

b. Taking action

If your health problems are severely aggravated by co-workers' smoking, there are a number of steps you can take.

- *Ask your employer for an accommodation.* Successful accommodations to smoke-sensitive workers have included installing additional ventilation systems, restricting smoking areas to outside or special rooms and segregating smokers and nonsmokers.

Example: *Carmelita's sinus problems were made almost unbearable by the smoke created by the people who work with her in an insurance claims processing office. Since her job involves primarily individual work on a computer terminal and no contact with people outside the company, Carmelita convinced her employer to allow her to start her workday at 4 p.m., just an hour before her co-workers leave for home.*

When Carmelita needs to discuss something with co-workers or her supervisor, she does so via electronic mail or at occasional one-hour staff meetings that begin at 4 p.m.—and at which smoking is not allowed.

- *Check local and state laws.* As indicated, a growing number of local and state laws prohibit smoking in the workplace. Most of them also set out specific procedures for pursuing complaints. If you are unable to locate local legal prohibitions on smoking, check with a smokers' rights group. (See the Appendix for contact details.)
- *Consider filing a federal complaint.* While OSHA is handling an increasing number of smoking injuries, most claims for injuries caused by second-hand smoke in the workplace are pressed and processed under the Americans With Disabilities Act. (See Chapter 8, Section F.) In the strongest

complaints, workers were able to prove that smoke sensitivity rendered them handicapped in that they were unable to perform a major life activity: breathing freely.

- *Consider income replacement programs.* If you are unable to work out a plan to resolve a serious problem with workplace smoke, you may be forced to leave the workplace. But you may qualify for workers' compensation or unemployment insurance benefits. (For details on unemployment insurance and workers' compensation benefits, see Chapters 12 and 13.)

Example: *Albert has suffered various problems with breathing since birth. The insurance agency where he has worked for five years has no policy on smoking, and his state has no law restricting smoking in the workplace. Albert has complained repeatedly to the management that the smoke-filled air in the office has often caused him to suffer spells of coughing and dizziness.*

One day several of his co-workers puffed up a thick cloud of cigarette smoke, and Albert suffered a particularly bad bout of coughing and dizziness. An ambulance had to be called to take him for emergency medical attention.

Albert's physician advised him that he would be risking serious, permanent damage to his health if he returned to the smoky environment of his job. Albert was able to qualify for unemployment insurance benefits while he looked for a new job because the cause of his unemployment was beyond his control.

Where There's Smoke, There's Ire

A California man received neither tea nor sympathy recently when he complained that bar patrons seated near him ruined his early supper with their cigarette smoking. He complained to a waiter and huffed out.

The former diner, John L. King, claimed the smokers in Ottino's Delicatessen were lighting up in violation of a local ordinance that prohibits smoking completely while the restaurant portion of the establishment is open.

King took his complaint to the city manager—which did little but prompt deli owner Roswitha Hofer to call King and let him know he was more than welcome to take his business elsewhere in the future.

In response, King sued, claiming the deli discriminated against him because he is a nonsmoker. He argued that nonsmokers as "a discrete and significant class within society, who have as a class endured oppression from public smoke and smokers" deserve legal protection.

"The argument is overblown," the court held. It reasoned that nonsmoking is not the type of personal belief that the civil rights law prohibiting discrimination includes in its protections (*King v. Hofer*, 42 Cal.App. 4th 678 (1996)).

2. Protections for Smokers

Some states protect both smokers and nonsmokers by insisting that employers provide a smokefree environment for nonsmokers and by prohibiting discrimination against an employee who smokes—either while off the job or at limited places and times in keeping with a worksite smoking policy.

Protection for smokers may be couched in laws that prohibit discrimination against employees who use "lawful products" outside the workplace before or after workhours. Wisconsin law goes an extra step and forbids employers from discriminating against both workers who use and workers who do not use lawful products.

Several of the state laws that prohibit discrimination against smoking employees do not apply if not smoking is truly a part and parcel of the job. This exception is written into the laws in a number of states—including Minnesota, Montana, North Carolina, Oregon, South Dakota, Wisconsin and Wyoming. In these states it is likely, for example, that a worker in the front office of the American Cancer Society—a group outspoken in its disdain of tobacco—could be fired for lighting up on the job.

And even in those states that offer some protection to smokers—such as Minnesota, Montana, South Dakota, Wisconsin and Wyoming—employers are free to charge smokers higher health insurance premiums than nonsmoking employees must pay.

Additional Laws May Apply

If the chart below indicates that your state has no statute, this means there is no law that specifically addresses the issue. However, there may be a state administrative regulation or local ordinance that does control. Call your state labor department for more information. (See the Appendix for contact details.)

Laws That Protect Smokers	
Alabama	No statute
Alaska	No statute
Arizona	No state employer may discriminate against a person because of the use or nonuse of tobacco products. Ariz. Rev. Stat. Ann. §36-601.02(F)
Arkansas	No statute
California	No statute
Colorado	No statute

Connecticut	No employer, state or private, may discriminate against an employee on the basis of the use of tobacco outside the job; nor can nonsmoking be a condition of employment. Statute does not apply to nonprofit organizations whose primary purpose is to discourage smoking. Conn. Gen. Stat. §31-40s
Delaware	No statute
District of Columbia	An employer may not fire or in any way discriminate against an employee on the basis of the use of tobacco. Statute does not apply if the nonuse of tobacco is a bona fide occupational requirement, reasonably related to the requirements or the responsibilities of the position. D.C. Code Ann. §6-913.3 If the employer designates an entire worksite as nonsmoking, it must also designate an area where smoking is allowed. D.C. Code Ann. §913.2
Florida	In a workplace of smokers and nonsmokers, employers shall develop and implement smoking and nonsmoking areas, taking into consideration the proportion of smokers and nonsmokers. Employers may satisfy the statute's requirements by making "reasonable efforts" to do so. Florida Clean Indoor Air Act, Fla. Stat. §85-257
Georgia	No statute
Hawaii	No statute
Idaho	No statute
Illinois	No employee may be discriminated against for lawful use of products outside of work, except for nonprofits whose primary objective is to discourage the use of such products. 820 Ill. Comp. Stat. 55/5 No person may be discriminated against because of the exercise of rights under the Illinois Clean Indoor Air Act (410 Ill. Comp. Stat. §80/1 and following). Illinois Right to Privacy in the Workplace Act, 820 Ill. Comp. Stat. §770/1 and following
Indiana	An employer cannot require, as a condition of employment, that an employee abstain from the use of tobacco products outside the course of employment nor discriminate with respect to compensation, benefits or terms and conditions of employment on the basis of such use. The statute does not apply to employers who are churches or religious organizations, or to schools or businesses operated by either. Ind. Stats. Ann. tit 22, §§5-4-1 to 5-4-4
Iowa	No statute
Kansas	No statute
Kentucky	An employer may not refuse to hire or otherwise discriminate against any person because the person is a smoker or nonsmoker, as long as the person complies with the workplace policy regarding smoking. An employer may not require abstinence from tobacco use as a condition of employment. Ky. Rev. Stat. §344.040
Louisiana	An employer may prohibit smoking entirely in an office workplace, but an employer that is a government entity must designate smoking areas. This requirement does not apply to educational or health facilities, or to courtrooms. La. Rev. Stat. Ann. §40:1300.21 and following As long as an employee complies with applicable laws and the employer's adopted workplace smoking policy, the employer cannot discriminate against the employee because the employer is a smoker or a nonsmoker, nor may the employer require abstinence during nonworking hours. La. Rev. Stat. Ann. §23:966

Maine	An employer cannot condition employment, or discriminate regarding conditions or terms of employment, on the basis of an employee's use of tobacco products outside the course of employment, as long as the employee complies with the policy regarding workplace smoking. Me. Rev. Stat. Ann. tit. 26, §597
Maryland	No statute
Massachusetts	No statute
Michigan	No statute
Minnesota	An employer cannot refuse to hire and cannot discriminate against an employee because the employee engages or has engaged in the use of lawful consumable products if done off-premises and during nonworking hours. The employer may restrict lawful use during nonworking, offsite hours if the restriction is a bona fide occupational requirement and reasonably relates to the job duties or responsibilities of the particular employee; or if a restriction is necessary to avoid a conflict of interest or the appearance of a conflict between the employee's tobacco use and the responsibilities owed by the employee to the employer. If an employer offers a healthcare plan that sets higher premiums for smokers than nonsmokers, the employer may pass that differential along to the employee. Minn. Stat. Ann. §181.938(1) & (2)
Mississippi	An employer may not require an employee to refrain from the use of tobacco products during nonworking hours, provided the employee otherwise complies with smoking policies in the workplace. Miss. Code Ann. §71-7-33
Missouri	Employers may not retaliate against employees for using tobacco products off the premises and during nonworking hours. Law does not apply to religious organizations nor to nonprofits whose principal business is healthcare promotion. Mo. Stat. Ann. §290.145
Montana	An employer may not refuse to hire or otherwise discriminate against an applicant or an employee because of the use of a lawful substance off-site and during nonworking hours. However, this protection does not apply if such use affects the employee's job performance or the safety of other employees, or if it conflicts with a bona fide occupational requirement reasonably related to the requirements of the employee's job. A personal service contract may condition the use of lawful substances, and restrictions may be imposed by a nonprofit organization whose primary purpose is to discourage the use of tobacco. An employer who restricts use off the premises based on the good faith belief that the restriction reflects the policy of an established substance abuse program does not violate this statute. If an employer offers a healthcare plan that sets higher premiums for smokers than nonsmokers, the employer may pass that differential along to the employee. Mont. Code Ann. §39-2-313(5)
Nebraska	No statute

Nevada	Employers may not discriminate against employees who lawfully use products outside the workplace as long as it does not interfere with their job performance. Nev. Rev. Stat. §613.333
New Hampshire	No statute
New Jersey	No statute
New Mexico	An employer may not refuse to hire an employee and may not discharge or otherwise discriminate against an employee based on that person's use or nonuse of tobacco, provided the person complies with smoking policies in the workplace. Does not prevent an employer from conditioning employment on the nonuse or use of tobacco if use or nonuse is a bona fide occupational requirement that is reasonably related to the particular job and its responsibilities. N.M. Stat. Ann. §50-11-3
New York	It is illegal for an employer to discriminate against an employee because of the employee's legal use of consumable products during nonworking hours away from the job. N.Y. Labor Code §201-d.2.b
North Carolina	Public employers and private employers with more than three employees may not discriminate against an employee because of that employee's lawful use of lawful products during nonworking hours and off the work premises, as long as the use does not adversely affect the employee's job performance, ability to fulfill the responsibilities of the position or the safety of other employees. The employer may restrict such use if the restriction relates to a bona fide occupational qualification and is reasonably related to the employment activities, or if it relates to the fundamental objectives of the organization. An employer whose healthcare plan costs more for smokers than for nonsmokers may pass on only the actual differential to the employee. N.C. Gen. Stat. §95-28.2
North Dakota	It is illegal to discharge or in any way disadvantage a person due to the person's participation in lawful activity off the employer's premises during nonworking hours. N.D. Century Code §14.02.4-03
Ohio	No statute
Oklahoma	An employer may not discriminate against any employee who smokes during nonworking hours; nor may the nonuse of tobacco be a condition of employment. Okla. Stat. Ann. tit 40, §500
Oregon	An employee may not be required to abstain from the use, during nonworking hours, of lawful tobacco products, except when nonuse of tobacco is reasonably related to a bona fide occupational requirement of the employee's job. Ore. Rev. Stat. §659.380
Pennsylvania	No statute
Rhode Island	An employer may not condition employment on the nonuse of tobacco products outside the course of employment. Does not apply if the employer is a nonprofit organization that attempts, as one of its primary purposes, to discourage the public's use of tobacco. R.I. Gen. Laws §23-20.7.1-1
South Carolina	The use of tobacco outside the workplace may not be the basis of any personnel action—including employment, termination, demotion or promotion. S.C. Code Ann. §41-1-85

South Dakota	An employee may not be terminated for using tobacco offsite, during nonworking hours, unless the abstention of tobacco use is a bona fide occupational requirement that is reasonably related to the employee's activities and responsibilities; or is necessary to avoid a conflict of interest or the appearance of a conflict with any responsibilities to the employer. The employer may offer a health or life insurance policy that makes distinctions between smokers and nonsmokers. S.D. Codified Laws §60-4-11
Tennessee	An employer cannot fire an employee because of the employee's use of a lawful product as long as the product is used during nonworking hours. Tenn. Code Ann. §50-1-304
Texas	No statute
Utah	No statute
Vermont	No statute
Virginia	No public employee or applicant for employment with the state or any local government agency may be required to not use tobacco products on the job or outside the course of employment. Firefighters are excepted. Va. Code Ann. §§15.2-1504; 2.1-111.1
Washington	No statute
West Virginia	No public or private employer may discharge, discriminate against or refuse to hire any employee because the employee uses tobacco products off the premises during nonworking hours. Statute does not apply to nonprofit corporations that have as one of their primary purposes the cessation of the public's use of tobacco. The law does not prohibit an employer from offering health plans that are more expensive for smokers, as long as the different rates reflect actual costs to the employer, nor does it prohibit an employer from offering programs to help smokers quit. W.Va. Code §21-3-19
Wisconsin	An employer may not discriminate against an employee on the basis of using or not using a lawful product unless such use or nonuse impairs an individual's ability to do the job or is related to a bona fide occupational requirement. The statute's protections do not apply if the employer is a nonprofit organization that attempts, as one of its primary purposes, to discourage the public's use of tobacco. Employers may offer health plans with premiums that are more expensive for smokers. Wis. Stat. Ann. §111.35
Wyoming	It is a discriminatory act or an unfair labor practice for an employer to require as a condition of employment the use or nonuse of tobacco products outside employment, unless the use or nonuse is a bona fide occupational requirement. Employers may offer health plans with premiums higher for smokers than nonsmokers, but may pass on only the exact amount of the increase, and must notify the employee in writing of the addition. Wyo. Stat. §27-9-105

F. Pesticide Laws

Misused and overused pesticides are one of the greatest safety threats to people who work on farms, in other parts of the food industry and in gardening and lawncare companies, to name just a few. Heavy exposure to some of these chemicals can cause serious health problems and even death. For people with certain types of allergies, even small doses of some pesticides can cause severe illness.

However, in 1975, a federal court ruled that the U.S. Environmental Protection Agency (EPA)—not OSHA—is responsible for making sure that workers are not injured by exposure to pesticides at work (*Organized Migrants in Community Action, Inc. v. Brennan*, 520 F. 2d 1161).

There have been some disputes between the EPA and OSHA over this ruling in recent years—and the question of enforcement responsibility remains unsettled decades later. If you believe that you or your co-workers are being exposed to dangerous doses of pesticides at work, the best thing to do is to file complaints with both OSHA and the EPA—and let them decide which agency controls your workplace. To find the nearest EPA office, look in the U.S. Government section of the white pages of the telephone book. You can also find a listing of local EPA offices at the agency's website at http://www.epa.gov under About EPA.

G. Hazardous Substances Laws

Most states now have laws that restrict or regulate the use, storage and handling of hazardous substances in the workplace. These laws vary greatly from state to state, and the identification of toxic and otherwise hazardous substances is a very technical matter that most often is the responsibility of the state's labor department.

In some cases, workers detect that they are being exposed to a hazardous substance when one or more of them notices that a health problem—a skin rash or eye irritation are common examples—coincides with work hours.

If you think that you are being subjected to hazardous substances in your workplace, follow your complaint to OSHA with a call to your state's labor department. (See the Appendix for contact details.)

Example: *Hanchung took a job as a forklift driver in a metal plating plant. After his first few hours at work, his eyes began to water and became badly reddened. On the way home from work, Hanchung visited a walk-in medical clinic, where the doctor used a cotton swab to take samples of skin residues from his face. A few days later, the doctor told Hanchung that the problem with his eyes was a reaction to sulfuric acid that apparently was in the air where he worked and had settled on his skin and eyes.*

Hanchung filed a complaint with OSHA and his state's labor department. As a result of the joint investigation, OSHA ordered his employer to construct an enclosure around processing areas that used sulfuric acid, and to provide Hanchung and his co-workers with protective clothing to wear at work while the enclosures were being built.

H. Violence in the Workplace

The numbers and pronouncements about our chances of being attacked or killed while at work are scary.

Homicide reigns as the leading cause of workplace death among women. In fact, the National Institute for Occupational Safety and Health lists homicide as a leading cause of all work-related deaths in the United States, second only to motor vehicle crashes. An average of 20 people are murdered each week in American workplaces. And an estimated one million workers suffer nonfatal assaults on the job each year. The U.S. Postal Service alone reported 500 cases of employees being violent toward supervisors in a recent period of 18 months—and an additional 200 cases of supervisors acting violently toward employees. And frightening results of a recent study claim that an employee in California is more likely to be murdered at work than to die in a car accident commuting to or from work.

Part of what makes violent behavior difficult to control is that it usually comes unannounced. But most workplace killers are disgruntled former employees who have been laid off or fired or the obsessed spouse or lover of an employee. And those who kill at work, experts say, usually give off warning signals that typically include:

- following or stalking an employee to or from the place of work
- entering the workplace
- following an employee at work, and
- telephoning or sending correspondence to the employee.

Co-workers describe many individuals who have committed violence in the workplace as: loners, not team players, having a history of interpersonal conflict and displays of anger, having made threats of violence in the past, being withdrawn, showing symptoms of current drug or alcohol abuse, being argumentative and quick to blame others for their own problems and frustrations.

Both employers and employees may be able to help ward off violence by heeding these signals of disturbed souls and taking immediate action. As an employee, you should report threatening co-workers. And encourage your employer to both refer such problem co-workers to a ready source of help and tell them, in no uncertain terms, that they will be fired if their bad behavior continues.

But realistically, employers who try to ward off violence often get caught in the conundrum of balancing employees' safety against the rights of the potential perpetrator. On one hand, employers are charged with keeping the workplace safe. Several have been successfully sued for negligent hiring, negligent supervision and wrongful death because they kept suspicious employees on staff who ultimately maimed or killed others on the job.

Increasingly, the pressure to act comes from victims of workplace violence and their survivors. And an increasing number of courts find employers directly liable for violence when they turn a deaf ear to workers' complaints about inadequate security—or a blind eye to knowledge that a worker's past actions might make him or her likely to attack co-workers and others on the job.

But employers have also felt the sting of lawsuits by employees who claim that overzealous investigations have violated laws protecting them from discrimination or invasions of their privacy.

Of late, scales are tipping in favor of keeping workplaces safe. In one recent case, for example, a Massachusetts court held that an employer, the U.S. Postal Service, was well within its rights when it fired a worker who screamed obscenities, swept the contents off a supervisor's desk, threw a typewriter and chair and knocked down several office partitions. The employee defended that he had an explosive personality disorder that entitled him to protection as a disabled employee rather than a pink slip. But the court held that a fundamental requirement of any job is that an employee must not be violent and destructive (*Mazzarella v. U.S. Postal Service,* 849 F.Supp. 89 (D. Mass. 1994)).

And a Florida court held recently that an employee—even one diagnosed with a chemical imbalance—could be fired on the spot for bringing a loaded gun to work (*Hindman v. GTE Data Services,* 4 A.D. Cas. (BNA) 182 (M.D. Fla. 1995)).

CHAPTER

8

ILLEGAL
DISCRIMINATION

It is almost always illegal for employers to discriminate against workers because of their race, skin color, gender, religious beliefs, national origin, physical handicap—or age, if the employee is at least 40 years old. In most situations, it is also illegal for employers to discriminate against workers on the basis of factors such as testing positive for the HIV virus or being pregnant, divorced, gay or lesbian.

The most powerful anti-discrimination law governing the workplace is Title VII of the federal Civil Rights Act of 1964. It originally outlawed discrimination based on race, skin color, religious beliefs or national origin, and it created the Equal Employment Opportunity Commission (EEOC) to administer and enforce the legal standards it set. (See Section A.)

Today, a number of additional federal laws—several of them amendments to Title VII—are used to fight unfair workplace discrimination.

- The Equal Pay Act of 1963 specifically outlaws discrimination in wages on the basis of gender. (See Section C below.)
- The Age Discrimination in Employment Act (ADEA) outlaws workplace discrimination on the basis of age. The law has been amended several times since it was passed in 1967, and now applies only to employees who are at least 40 years old. (See Section D below.)
- The Older Workers Benefit Protection Act is an amendment to the ADEA, passed in 1990, that specifically outlaws discrimination in employment benefit programs on the basis of employees' age, and it too applies only to employees age 40 and older. It also deters employers' use of waivers in which employees sign away their rights to take legal action against age-based discrimination. (See Section E below.)
- The Pregnancy Discrimination Act (PDA), which makes it illegal for an employer to refuse to hire a pregnant woman, to terminate her employment or to compel her to take maternity leave, was passed in 1978 as an additional amendment to Title VII. (See Chapter 5, Section C, for more on family and medical leaves.)
- In 1986, in *Meritor Savings Bank v. Vinson,* the U.S. Supreme Court held that Title VII also protects against sexual harassment, another form of illegal workplace discrimination. (See Chapter 9.)
- The Americans With Disabilities Act (ADA), enacted in 1990, makes it illegal to discriminate against people because of their physical or mental disability. (See Section F below.)
- The Labor Relations Act and amendments, passed as a patchwork of protections, generally make it illegal to discriminate against workers for belonging or refusing to belong to a labor union. (See Chapter 16.)

A. Title VII of the Civil Rights Act

Most of the workplace laws that broadly protect employees against discrimination in the workplace have been enacted through the years as amendments to the Civil Rights Act, also known as Title VII (42 U.S.C. §2000 and following).

1. Who Is Covered

Title VII applies to all companies and labor unions with 15 or more employees. It also governs employment agencies, state and local governments and apprenticeship programs.

Title VII does not cover:

- federal government employees; special procedures have been established to enforce anti-discrimination laws for them, and
- independent contractors (discussed in detail in Chapter 2, Section A).

2. Illegal Discrimination

Under Title VII, employers may not use race, skin color, gender, religious beliefs or national origin as the basis for decisions on hirings, promotions, dismissals, pay raises, benefits, work assignments, leaves of absence or just about any other aspect of employment. Title VII covers everything about the employment relationship—from pre-hiring ads to working conditions, to performance reviews, to giving post-employment references.

Counting Employees: Not As Easy As It Sounds

The Civil Rights Act is clearly written to apply to employers with 15 or more employees. But courts across the nation have been of differing minds when it comes to deciding which employees should stand up and be counted.

Most courts used a counting system in which hourly and parttime employees were considered in the total, but only on the days they were at work or on paid leave.

However, the U.S. Supreme Court recently ruled that this is a disingenuous shell game. The Court held that employees should be defined and tallied for purposes of Title VII according to the payroll method. Under the payroll method, employers are covered if they have 15 or more employees on the payroll for each working day in 20 or more weeks, regardless of the actual work the workers perform or whether they are compensated (*Walters v. Metropolitan Educational Enterprises, Inc.*, 117 S.Ct. 660 (1997)).

Knowing about this judicial clarification can be powerful information if your discrimination claim is dismissed because your employer is too small. You may be able to successfully argue that parttime workers and those on leave should be included in the final tally of employees.

3. Remedies Available

There are a number of remedies that the courts or the EEOC can provide under Title VII to an employee who suffers the effects of discrimination on the job.

Reinstatement and promotion. A court can order that the employee be rehired, promoted or reassigned to whatever job was lost because of the discrimination.

Wages and job-connected losses. A court can award any salary and benefits the employee lost as a result of being fired, demoted or forced to quit because of discrimination. This can include loss of wages, pension contributions, medical benefits, overtime pay, bonuses, backpay, shift differential pay, vacation pay and participation in a company profit-sharing plan.

Money damages. A court can award a limited amount of damages to compensate for personal injuries, which can include money to cover the actual amount of out-of-pocket losses, such as medical expenses. It can also include other compensatory and punitive damages, but the amount of such damages is limited to between $50,000 and $300,000—depending on the number of people employed by the business.

Injunctive relief. A court can direct the company to change its policies to stop discrimination and to prevent similar incidents in the future.

Attorneys' fees. If the employee wins a case, a court can order the company to pay attorneys' fees.

4. Filing a Complaint With the EEOC

Compared to most other government agencies, the EEOC has very well-defined procedures for filing complaints. But the EEOC also operates through a complex hierarchy of offices and has strict time limits for filing complaints that usually range from a few months to nearly a year. Pay particular attention to timing if you decide to take action against what you believe is illegal workplace discrimination. (See subsection b, below.)

Who Will Heed the Calls?

The EEOC is the federal agency responsible for evaluating, smoothing over and pursuing nearly all cases of workplace discrimination. The burden is burgeoning—the caseload increased nearly 40% from 1990 to 1998. But the budget is not—there has been no increase in several years.

Despite its beleaguered condition, the EEOC has historically vowed to ferret out all reported discrimination on the job. But that might be changing. The EEOC recently quietly issued a new policy setting its sights a little lower: It will deal with the worst cases; the rest are anyone's call.

The dictate will likely make EEOC staff lawyers more prone to cut deals in cases that seem weaker on their merits rather than to insist that the wrongdoers pay large amounts in damages.

As part of its rehaul, the agency will divide claims into three categories:
- A cases—those likely to result in a finding of discrimination
- B cases—those that cannot be immediately assessed one way or the other, and
- C cases—those unlikely to result in a discrimination judgment.

The claims now most likely to get attention are those that affect a large number of employees. And for better or worse, there is an early indication that the changed policy has made the agency more efficient. By the end of fiscal year 1999, the backlog of charges was down nearly 55% from its highest level of languishing charges reached in 1995.

Bear in mind that even if the EEOC deign not to take on your case, however, you are still free to sue your emplyer in federal court. (See Section A5.)

a. Where to file

Title VII complaints can be filed at:
- Local Equal Employment Opportunity agency offices. These are not federal offices, but agencies that have been designated as representatives of the EEOC. (See Chapter 9, Section C for contact information.)
- State and regional offices of the EEOC. (See the listing below.)

There are EEOC offices throughout the United States. Normally, it is best to file a complaint at the office nearest to you or your place of employment. But if there is no office nearby or in your state, you can legally file a complaint in any office. For assistance in locating the nearest office, call 800-669-4000. You can also find a list of local offices on the EEOC's website at http://www.eeoc.gov.

EEOC District Offices

Alabama	Birmingham District Office 1900 Third Avenue, North, Suite 101 Birmingham, AL 35203 205-731-0082 TDD: 205-731-0095 FAX: 205-731-2101
Arizona	Phoenix District Office 3300 North Central Avenue, Suite 690 Phoenix, AZ 85012 602-640-5000 TDD: 602-640-5072 FAX: 602-640-5071
Arkansas	Little Rock Area Office 425 West Capitol Avenue, Suite 625 Little Rock, AR 72201 501-324-5060 TDD: 501-324-5481 FAX: 501-324-5991
California	Fresno Local Office 1265 West Shaw, Suite 103 Fresno, CA 93711 599-487-5793 TDD: 599-487-5837 FAX: 599-487-5053
	Los Angeles District Office 255 East Temple, 4th Floor Los Angeles, CA 90012 213-894-1000 TDD: 213-894-1121 FAX: 213-894-1118
	Oakland Local Office 1301 Clay Street, Suite 1170 N Oakland, CA 94612 510-637-3230 TDD: 510-637-3234 FAX: 510-627-3235

San Diego Area Office
401 B Street, Suite 1550
San Diego, CA 92101
619-557-7235
TDD: 619-557-7232
FAX: 619-557-7274

San Francisco District Office
901 Market Street, Suite 500
San Francisco, CA 94103
415-356-5100
TDD: 415-356-5098
FAX: 415-356-5126

San Jose Local Office
96 North Third Street, Suite 200
San Jose, CA 95112
408-291-7352
TDD: 408-291-7374
FAX: 408-291-4539

Colorado	Denver District Office 303 East 17th Avenue, Suite 510 Denver, CO 80203 303-866-1300 TDD: 303-866-1950 FAX: 303-866-1386
Dist.of Columbia	Washington Field Office 1400 L Street, NW; Suite 200 Washington, DC 20005 202-275-7377 TDD: 202-275-7518 FAX: 202-275-0025
Florida	Miami District Office One Biscayne Tower Two South Biscayne Boulevard, Suite 2700 Miami, FL 33131 305-536-4491 TDD: 305-536-5721 FAX: 305-536-4011

	Tampa Area Office 501 East Polk Street, 10th Floor Tampa, FL 33602 813-228-2310 TDD: 813-228-2003 FAX: 813-228-2891	Kentucky	Louisville Area Office 600 Dr. Martin Luther King Jr. Place Room 268 Louisville, KY 40202 502-582-6082 TDD: 502-582-6285 FAX: 502-582-5895
Georgia	Atlanta District Office 100 Alabama Street Atlanta, GA 30303 404-562-6800 TDD: 404-562-6801 FAX: 404-562-6910	Louisiana	New Orleans District Office 701 Loyola Avenue, Suite 600 New Orleans, LA 70113 504-589-2329 TDD: 504-589-2958 FAX: 504-689-6861
	Savannah Local Office 410 Mall Boulevard, Suite G Savannah, GA 31406 912-652-4234 TDD: 912-652-4439 FAX: 912-652-4248	Maryland	Baltimore District Office 10 South Howard Street, 3rd Floor Baltimore, MD 21201 410-962-3932 TDD: 410-962-6065 FAX: 410-962-4270
Hawaii	Honolulu Local Office 300 Ala Moana Boulevard P.O. Box 50082 Honolulu, HI 96850 808-541-3120 TDD: 808-541-3131 FAX: 808-541-3390	Massachusetts	Boston Area Office 1 Congress Street, Room 1001 Boston, MA 02114 617-565-3200 TDD: 617-565-3204 FAX: 617-565-3196
Illinois	Chicago District Office 500 West Madison Street, Suite 2800 Chicago, IL 60661 312-353-2713 TDD: 313-353-2421 FAX: 313-353-7355	Michigan	Detroit District Office 477 Michigan Avenue, Room 865 Detroit, MI 48226 313-226-7636 TDD: 313-226-7599 FAX: 313-226-2778
Indiana	Indianapolis District Office 101 West Ohio Street, Suite 1900 Indianapolis, IN 46204 317-226-7212 TDD: 317-226-5162 FAX: 317-226-5571	Minnesota	Minneapolis Area Office 330 South 2nd Avenue, Suite 430 Minneapolis, MN 55401 612-335-4040 TDD: 612-335-4045 FAX: 612-335-4044
Kansas	Kansas City Area Office 400 State Avenue, Suite 905 Kansas City, KS 66101 913-551-5655 TDD: 913-551-5657 FAX: 913-551-6950	Mississippi	Jackson Area Office Dr. A. H. McCoy Federal Building 100 West Capitol Street, Suite 207 Jackson, MS 39201 601-965-4537 TDD: 601-965-4915 FAX: 601-965-5272

St. Louis District Office
Robert A. Young Building,
Room 8.100
St. Louis, MO 63103
314-539-7830
TDD: 314-539-7803
FAX: 314-539-7893

New Jersey   Newark Area Office
1 Newark Center, 21st Floor
Newark, NJ 07102
201-645-6383
TDD: 201-645-3004
FAX: 201-645-4524

New Mexico   Albuquerque Area Office
505 Marquette Street, NW;
Suite 900
Albuquerque, NM 87102
505-248-5201
TDD: 505-248-5240
FAX: 505-248-5233

New York   Buffalo Local Office
6 Fountain Plaza, Suite 350
Buffalo, NY 14202
716-846-4441
TDD: 716-846-5923
FAX: 716-551-4387

New York District Office
7 World Trade Center, 18th Floor
New York, NY 10048
212-748-8500
TDD: 212-748-8399
FAX: 212-748-8465

North Carolina   Charlotte District Office
129 West Trade Street, Suite 400
Charlotte, NC 28202
704-344-6682
TDD: 704-344-6684
FAX: 704-344-6734

Greensboro Local Office
801 Summit Avenue
Greensboro, NC 27405
910-333-5174
TDD: 910-333-5542
FAX: 910-333-5051

Raleigh Area Office
1309 Annapolis Drive
Raleigh, NC 27608
919-856-4064
TDD: 919-856-4296
FAX: 919-856-4151

Ohio   Cincinnati Area Office
525 Vine Street, Suite 810
Cincinnati, OH 45202
513-684-2851
TDD: 513-684-2074
FAX: 513-684-2351

Cleveland District Office
Skylight Office Tower
1660 West Second Street,
Suite 850
Cleveland, OH 44113
216-522-2001
TDD: 216-522-8441
FAX: 216-522-7395

Oklahoma   Oklahoma Area Office
210 Park Avenue, Suite 1350
Oklahoma City, OK 73102
405-231-4911
TDD: 405-231-5745
FAX: 405-231-4140

Pennsylvania   Philadelphia District Office
21 South Fifth Street, 4th Floor
Philadelphia, PA 19106
215-451-5800
TDD: 215-451-5814
FAX: 215-451-5767

Pittsburgh Area Office
1001 Liberty Avenue, Suite 300
Pittsburgh, PA 15222
412-644-3444
TDD: 412-644-2720
FAX: 412-644-2664

South Carolina   Greenville Local Office
15 South Main Street, Suite 530
Greenville, SC 29601
803-241-4400
TDD: 803-241-4403
FAX: 803-241-4416

Tennessee	Memphis District Office 1407 Union Avenue, Suite 521 Memphis, TN 38104 901-544-0115 TDD: 901-544-0112 FAX: 901-544-0111		San Antonio District Office 5410 Fredericksburg Road, Suite 200 San Antonio, TX 78229 210-281-7600 TDD: 210-281-7610 FAX: 210-229-4381
	Nashville Area Office 50 Vantage Way, Suite 202 Nashville, TN 37228 615-736-5820 TDD: 615-736-5870 FAX: 615-736-2107	Virginia	Norfolk Area Office World Trade Center, Suite 4300 101 West Main Street Norfolk, VA 23510 757-441-3470 TDD: 757-441-3578 FAX: 757-441-6720
Texas	Dallas District Office 207 South Houston Street, 3d Floor Dallas, TX 75202 214-655-3355 TDD: 214-655-3363 FAX: 214-655-3443		Richmond Area Office 3600 West Broad Street, Room 229 Richmond, VA 23230 804-278-4670 TDD: 804-278-4654 FAX: 804-278-4660
	El Paso Area Office The Commons Building C, Suite 100 4171 North Mesa Street El Paso, TX 79902 915-534-6550 TDD: 915-534-6545 FAX: 915-534-6552	Washington	Seattle District Office 909 1st Avenue, Suite 400 Seattle, WA 98104 206-220-6883 TDD: 206-220-6882 FAX: 206-220-6911
	Houston District Office 1919 Smith Street, 7th Floor Houston, TX 77002 713-209-3320 TDD: 713-209-3367 FAX: 713-209-3381	Wisconsin	Milwaukee District Office 310 West Wisconsin Avenue, Suite 800 Milwaukee, WI 53203-2292 414-297-1111 TDD: 414-297-1115 FAX: 414-297-4133

b. When to file

If your state has its own equal employment opportunity laws (see Section B), you will typically be allowed 300 days after the act of discrimination occurred to file a complaint. But if your state does not have its own equal employment opportunity laws, you have only 180 days to file. The safest way to proceed is to assume that 180 days is the limit in your case and file your complaint as soon as possible.

In some cases, you will not be able to recognize illegal discrimination from a single action by an employer. If you discern a pattern of illegal discrimination that extends back more than 180 days, the safest way to proceed is to assume that the EEOC time limit began with the event that caused you to recognize the pattern and file a complaint as soon as possible. Since such cases often require complicated proof, consider consulting a lawyer for help. (See Chapter 18, Section D.)

Example: *A woman who worked with Jan in a pharmaceutical lab was fired in January. Two months later, the lab fired another woman. In June, a third woman was fired.*

When the third woman was fired, Jan began to notice that the firings seemed to have nothing to do with job performance. Although the lab employed several men with less experience and whose job performance was not as good as the three women who had been fired, no men had been fired.

After consistently receiving positive performance reviews, Jan's supervisor informed her the lab staff was being reduced and she should start looking for another job. Jan took a few weeks to gather evidence to support her belief that the company was illegally discriminating against women on the basis of gender, and then filed a complaint with the EEOC in September.

c. Organizing your evidence

Because illegal discrimination rarely takes the form of one simple event, it is important to organize your evidence of incidents of illegal discrimination before contacting the EEOC to file a complaint.

Whenever possible, keep a log of the date, time, location, people involved and nature of actions that demonstrate any pattern of illegal discrimination. Keep a file of any documents that your employer gives you, such as written performance reviews or disciplinary notices. (See Chapter 1.)

If you present your evidence to the EEOC in an organized way—without yielding to the temptation to vent your displeasure with your employer's policies and practices—you will raise the chances of your complaint getting full attention and consideration from the EEOC investigators.

d. How the EEOC handles complaints

When you file a complaint, typically an EEOC staff lawyer or investigator will interview you and initially evaluate whether or not your employer's actions appear to violate Title VII. Theoretically, the EEOC has 180 days to act on your complaint. If the interviewer does not feel that the incident warrants a complaint, he or she will tell you so. You may have to think about other options, such as pursuing a complaint through your company's established complaint procedure.

If the interviewer feels you should pursue your complaint with the EEOC, he or she will fill out an EEOC Charge of Discrimination form describing the incident and send it to you to review and sign. After receiving your complaint, the EEOC is supposed to interview the employer that is the subject of the complaint and then try to mediate a settlement of the complaint between you and that employer.

That is what the EEOC's operating regulations provide. And for the most part, the EEOC does what it is supposed to do. But do not expect every claim to proceed as described. EEOC offices differ in caseloads, local procedures and the quality of their personnel. Investigations are usually slow, sometimes taking three years or more. The EEOC takes only a small portion of its cases to court—as few as 1% of those that are filed with it. These and other factors can have an impact on how a case is actually handled.

Tips for Dealing With the EEOC

There are a number of things to keep in mind when helping to shuttle your claim through the EEOC bureaucracy most efficiently.

- *Stay alert.* Do not assume that the EEOC will do everything and that you don't have to monitor what is going on. Check periodically with the EEOC to find out what is happening with your case.
- *Be assertive.* If some EEOC action—or, more likely, inaction—is causing you serious problems, call that to the attention of the people handling your case.
- *Keep your options open.* Filing a claim with the EEOC does not prevent you from taking other action to deal with your case. You still have a right to try to solve the problem on your own or use a company complaint procedure. You also have the right to hire an attorney to file a lawsuit, if that is appropriate for your situation.

e. Penalties for retaliation

It is illegal for your employer to retaliate against you either for filing a Title VII complaint, or for cooperating in the investigation of one. But to take advantage of this protection, you must be able to prove that the retaliation occurred because you filed a complaint. (See Chapter 11, Section A3.)

More often than not, an employer that wants to retaliate against you for filing a Title VII complaint will cite substandard job performance.

Example: *Hector filed a Title VII complaint because he observed that his employer never promotes anyone of his race above a certain level. To investigate Hector's complaint, the EEOC reviewed documents related to the company's hiring practices to determine whether it is, in fact, using race as the basis for hiring decisions.*

Two weeks later, Hector was dismissed from his job because, the company claimed, his performance was below its standards. If Hector decides to file an additional complaint charging the company with illegal retaliation, he will probably have to prove that his performance satisfied or exceeded the company's standards—and that the real reason he was fired was because he filed a Title VII complaint.

5. Filing a Title VII Lawsuit

In the very likely event that the EEOC does not act on your complaint within 180 days, you then have the right to request a right to sue letter that authorizes you to file a lawsuit in federal court against the offending employer. This type of lawsuit is complex, and in cases involving an employee dismissal is often packaged with other claims. (See Chapter 11, Section D.) You will probably need to hire a lawyer to help you file a lawsuit under Title VII. (See Chapter 18, Section D.) A number of specialized organizations offer legal referrals and advice on workplace discrimination. (See the Appendix for contact details.)

Once you receive a right to sue letter, you have only 90 days to file a lawsuit, so deadlines are very important at this point of the Title VII process. The EEOC has the right to file a lawsuit on your behalf, but do not expect that to happen unless your case has a very high political or publicity value—a very small percentage of the claims filed. The EEOC's out-of-pocket expenses are limited by law to $5,000 per lawsuit—many thousands of dollars less than it typically costs to take an employment discrimination case to court.

a. Class actions

For some employees, the most likely way to succeed in a Title VII case is to become part of a class action lawsuit. The courts allow lawsuits to be pursued as class actions when it is shown that a number of people have been injured by the same unlawful act. Because the potential damages from a Title VII class action lawsuit are much larger than in an individual lawsuit, some attorneys will take those cases on a contingency basis—which means that their fees will not be paid upfront but will be taken as a percentage of the amount recovered. (See Chapter 18, Section C.) The amount recovered will be divided among those certified as class members.

BFOQs: Jobs That Require Discrimination

Under Title VII and many state and local anti-discrimination laws, an employer may intentionally use gender, religious beliefs or national origin as the basis for employment decisions only if the employer can show that the job has special requirements that make such discrimination necessary.

When an employer establishes that such a special circumstance exists, it is called a bona fide occupational qualification (BFOQ).

Example: A religious denomination that employs counselors who answer telephone inquiries from those interested in becoming members of that religion would typically be allowed to limit its hiring of counselors to people who believe in that religion. Being a member of that denomination would be a BFOQ.

In general, the courts, the EEOC and state equal employment opportunity agencies prohibit the use of BFOQs except where clearly necessary. They typically require any employer using a BFOQ in employment decisions to prove conclusively that the BFOQ is essential to the successful operation of the company or organization. Typically, this type of permissible discrimination turns on gender. The classic example is the job of a wet nurse, who must be female. But theaters, cosmetic companies and modeling agencies have also succeeded in arguing that workers hired needed to be of a particular gender to get the job done.

You are most likely to encounter a BFOQ on a job application, in which case the employer must state on the application that the employment qualification covered by the questions would otherwise be illegal, but has been approved by the EEOC.

b. State and local laws

In general, employment-related lawsuits filed under state or local laws are easier to win than those filed under Title VII. And, unlike most Title VII cases, state and local anti-discrimination laws often offer the possibility of a larger judgment in favor of the worker who files the lawsuit.

B. State and Local Anti-Discrimination Laws

Nearly all state and local laws prohibiting various types of discrimination in employment echo federal anti-discrimination law in that they outlaw discrimination based on race, color, gender, age, national origin and religion. But the state and local laws typically tend to go into more detail, creating categories of protection against discrimination that are not covered by federal law.

In Louisiana, for example, it is illegal to discriminate in employment matters on the basis of a worker's sickle cell trait. In Minnesota, it is illegal to discriminate against people who are collecting public assistance. And in Michigan, employees cannot be discriminated against because of their heights or weights.

Many state anti-discrimination laws also provide faster and more effective procedures for pursuing complaints about illegal workplace discrimination than the EEOC process. An employee in New Jersey, for example, may go directly into superior court with a lawsuit based on age discrimination without first complaining to the EEOC.

State laws prohibiting discrimination in employment, along with agencies responsible for enforcing anti-discrimination laws in those states, are listed in the chart below. (See Section B3.) You can research municipal anti-discrimination laws at the headquarters of your community's government, such as your local city hall or county courthouse.

1. How to Take Action

If you wish to consider filing a complaint under your state's employment discrimination laws, you must first find out if your state has an agency empowered to process such a complaint. (The chart in Section B3 provides this information.) There are several states that have discrimination laws, but no state agency to enforce them. In these states, you must rely on the federal law or a private lawsuit to enforce your rights.

2. Time Limits for Filing

Ordinarily, a charge with the EEOC must be filed within 180 days of the date of the action about which you are complaining. State laws have their own separate time limits. And if your state has an agency that enforces its own age discrimination law, you must file your EEOC complaint within 30 days of notice that the state is no longer pursuing your case, even if the normal 180-day period is not up.

These time limits are counted from the date you get notice from your employer or union of the action that you think is discriminatory—a demotion, layoff, forced retirement. If there is no specific date you can pinpoint, file your charge as soon as you have gathered enough information to convince yourself that you have been subjected to discrimination.

3. State Laws and Enforcing Agencies

This section offers a synopsis of factors that may not be used as the basis for employment discrimination under state laws. Keep in mind that it is only a synopsis, and that each state has its own way of determining such factors as what conditions qualify as a physical disability. Many state anti-discrimination laws apply only to employers with a minimum number of employees, such as five or more.

In states where no special agency has been designated to enforce anti-discrimination laws, your state's labor department or Attorney General's office or the closest office of the federal Equal Employment Opportunity Office should direct you to the right agency or person with whom to file a complaint over illegal discrimination in employment.

In certain states or circumstances, you may have no way to pursue your complaint over illegal discrimination other than to file a lawsuit or to hire an attorney to file one for you.

Keeping the Faith at Work

In the last few years, there has been a notable increase in the number of religious discrimination lawsuits. Theologians hail this burst in litigation as a sign that Americans are returning to the fold. Pessimists say that workers are looking for just another excuse to work less.

Title VII of the Civil Rights Act and most state laws prohibit employers from discriminating on the basis of religious beliefs. Where workers articulate a need to express their religious beliefs and practice in the workplace, employers are generally required to accommodate them—unless doing so would cause the employer undue hardship.

As in all other claims where the term comes up, the meaning of undue hardship in this context gives employers and courts cause for pause. The U.S. Supreme Court has pronounced twice on the issue.

In *Trans World Airlines Inc. v. Hardison* (432 U.S. 135 (1977), an airline employee claimed that his religion, the Worldwide Church of God, forbade him from working on Saturdays. In subsequent meetings, TWA union officials argued that allowing the employee to change shifts would violate a collective bargaining agreement that banned the arrangement for workers without sufficient seniority. The Court agreed, holding that the union agreement was more sacrosanct than the religious practices.

Nearly a decade later, the Court again heard the pleas of a member of the Worldwide Church of God—this time arguing that he needed six days off per school year for religious observance. The sticking point again was a collective bargaining agreement providing only three days of paid leave for religious observation. The Court waffled some in its opinion, holding that the court below could decide whether providing unpaid leave to make up the balance was a reasonable accommodation (*Ansonia Board of Education v. Philbrook*, 479 U.S. 60 (1979)).

Since then, the lower courts that have faced the issue have reached grandly differing conclusions about what is an undue burden for employers. A Florida police officer's request for Saturdays off was denied "for public safety reasons." But a New Mexico court ruled that a truck driver was illegally denied a job because of his practice of smoking peyote during a Native American ritual. And a California court shot down an employer's order that banned religious artifacts in all workers' cubicles and prevented them from any type of "religious advocacy" on the job.

For now, employers and employees grappling with the issue would be best served to work together to reach an accommodation—and keep the issue out of the uncharted territory of court decisions.

State Laws Prohibiting Discrimination in Employment

Alabama	Age discrimination (40 years or older) for employers with 20 or more employees. (Ala. Code § 25-1-20 and following) No other anti-discrimination law, but employers are encouraged to employ people who are blind or otherwise physically disabled. (Ala. Code §21-7-1) If an employer has an affirmative action program, the term minority, in addition to an ethnic group or other classification, shall also include American Indians or Alaskan Natives, as identified by birth certificates or tribal records. (Ala. Code §25-1-10) Enforcing agency: Consult with the local EEOC office or state department of labor
Alaska	Race, religion, color, national origin, age, physical disability, gender, marital status, changes in marital status. (Alaska Stat. §18.80.220) Mental illness. (Alaska Stat. §§47.30.865, 18.80.220) Enforcing agency: Human Rights Commission 800 A Street, Suite 204 Anchorage, AL 99501 907-274-4692 http://www.gov.state.ak.us/aschr/aschr.htm
Arizona	Race, color, religion, gender, age, physical disability (excluding current alcohol or drug use), national origin. (Ariz. Rev. Stat. Ann. §41-1461 and following) Enforcing agency: Civil Rights Division 1275 West Washington Street Phoenix, AZ 85007 602-542-5263 http://www.ag.state.az.us/civilrights/index.html
Arkansas	No discrimination on basis of race, religion, national origin, gender or physical or mental disability. (Ark. Code Ann. §§16-123-107, -108) Prohibits discrimination in wages on the basis of gender. (Ark. Code Ann. §11-4-601) For state employees only: age if 40 years old or older. (Ark. Code Ann. §§21-3-201 to 203) Enforcing agency: Equal Employment Opportunity Commission 425 West Capitol, Suite 625 Little Rock, AK 72207 501-324-5060
California	Race, religious creed, religion, color, national origin, ancestry, physical disability, mental disability, medical condition, marital status, gender, age if 40 or older, pregnancy, sexual orientation, childbirth or related medical conditions. (Cal. Gov't. Code §§12920, 12926, 12940, 12941, 12945) AIDS or HIV: If an employee's participation in a research study regarding

	AIDS or HIV is disclosed, the information shall not be used to determine the employability or insurability of that person. (Cal. Health & Safety Code §121115) Political activities or affiliations. (Cal. Lab. Code §§1101, 1102 and 1102.1) Enforcing agency: Department of Fair Employment and Housing 2014 T Street, Suite 210 Sacramento, CA 95814 800-884-1684 http://www.dfeh.ca.gov
Colorado	Race, religion, color, age, gender, disability, national origin, ancestry. Fair Employment Practices Act (Colo. Rev. Stat. §24-34-401 and following) Mental disability. (Colo. Rev. Stat. §27-10-115) Sexual orientation, state employees only (Executive Order No. D0035; December 10, 1990) Enforcing agency: Civil Rights Commission 1560 Broadway, Suite 1050 Denver, CO 80202-5143 303-894-2997 http://dora.state.co.us/Civil-Rights
Connecticut	Race, color, religion, age, gender, pregnancy, marital status, sexual orientation, national origin, ancestry, present or previous mental or physical disability. (Conn. Gen. Stat. Ann. §§46a-60, 81c; Conn. Public Act 98-180) Enforcing agency: Commission on Human Rights and Opportunities 1229 Albany Avenue Hartford, CT 06112 860-566-7710 http://www.state.ct.us/chro
Delaware	Race, color, religion, gender, national origin, marital status, age if between ages 40 and 70, or physical disability as long as the cost to the employer of accommodating the employee's physical disability does not exceed 5% of that employee's annual compensation. (Del. Code Ann. tit. 19, §710 and following) Enforcing agency: Department of Labor Labor Law Enforcement Section State Office Building, 6th Floor 820 North French Street Wilmington, DE 19801 302-761-8200
District of Columbia	Race, color, religion, national origin, age if between ages 18 and 65, gender, personal appearance, marital status or family responsibilities, sexual orientation, political affiliation, matriculation or physical disability. (D.C. Code Ann. §1-2512)

	Enforcing agency: Human Rights Commission 441 4th Street, NW Washington, DC 20001 202-727-3900 http://www.ohr.washingtondc.gov/main.htm
Florida	Race, color, religion, gender, national origin, age, marital status, physical disability. (Fla. Stat. Ann. §760.10) AIDS or HIV condition. (Fla. Stat. Ann. §760.50) Enforcing agency: Commission on Human Relations 325 John Knox Road, Bldg. F, Suite 240 Tallahassee, FL 32303-4149 850-488-7082 http://www.fchr.state.fl.us
Georgia	In public employment: Race, color, national origin, religion, sex, age, disability—excluding alcohol or drug use. Fair Employment Practices Act (Ga. Code Ann. §45-19-28 and 29) In private employment: Mental or physical disability—excluding the use of alcohol or any illegal or federally controlled drug and excluding disabilities based on communicable diseases and disabilities that interfere with the person's ability to do the job. (Ga. Code Ann. §34-6A-4) Age if between 40 and 70 years old. (Ga. Code Ann. §§34-1-2) Enforcing agency: Equal Employment Opportunity Commission 100 Alabama Street, Suite 4R30 Atlanta, GA 30303 404-463-0904
Hawaii	Race, religion, color, ancestry, gender, sexual orientation, age, marital status, mental or physical disability, pregnancy, childbirth or related medical conditions, arrest and court record—except if there has been a conviction directly related to job responsibilities. (Haw. Rev. Stat. §378-1 and following) Enforcing agency: Hawaii Civil Rights Commission 830 Punchbowl Street, Room 411 Honolulu, HI 96813 808-586-8640 http://www.state.hi.us/hcrc
Idaho	Race, color, religion, national origin, gender, age, or physical or mental disability. (Idaho Code §67-5909) Enforcing agency: Commission on Human Rights Owyhee Plaza, 4th Floor Boise, ID 83720 208-334-2873 http://www.state.id.us/ihrc/ihrchome.htm

Illinois	Race, color, gender, national origin, ancestry, religion, age if over 40, marital status, physical or mental disability (excluding substance abuse). (775 Ill. Comp. Stat. 5/2-101 and following) Enforcing agency: Department of Human Rights James R. Thompson Center 100 West Randolph Street, 10th Floor Chicago, IL 60601 312-814-6245 http://www.state.il.us/dhr
Indiana	Race, color, gender, national origin, ancestry, religion, age if between 40 and 70 years old or physical or mental disability. (Ind. Code Ann. §§22-9-1-2 and 13, 22-9-2) Enforcing agency: Civil Rights Commission 100 North Senate Avenue, Room N-103 Indianapolis, IN 46204 800-628-2909 http://www.state.in.us/icrc
Iowa	Race, color, religion, age, gender, national origin, pregnancy, AIDS or physical disability. Does not apply to workers under 18 and to workplaces with fewer than four employees. (Iowa Code Ann. §216.1 and following) Enforcing agency: Civil Rights Commission 211 East Maple Street, 2nd Floor Des Moines, IA 50319 800-457-4416 http://www.state.ia.us/government/crc
Kansas	Race, color, religion, gender, age if over age 18, national origin or ancestry, or physical disability. (Kan. Stat. Ann. §§44-1001 and following) Enforcing agency: Human Rights Commission Landon State Office Building 900 SW Jackson, Suite 851 South Topeka, KS 66612-1258 785-296-3206 http://www.ink.org/public/khrc
Kentucky	Race, color, religion, national origin, gender, age if between ages 40 and 70, physical or mental disability. (Ky. Rev. Stat. §344.040) AIDS or HIV. (Ky. Rev. Stat. §207.135) In addition, no employee can be fired, refused employment or discriminated against because of being diagnosed with level 1/0, 1/1 or 1/2 pneumoconiosis (black lung disease) with no respiratory impairment. Ky. Rev. Stat. §342.197

Enforcing agency:
Human Rights Commission
332 West Broadway, 7th Floor
Louisville, KY 40202
800-292-5566

Louisiana
Race, color, religion, gender, national origin, pregnancy, sickle cell traits. (La. Rev. Stat. Ann. §§23:311 to 352)
Physical or mental disability. (La. Rev. Stat. Ann. §§46:2251, 23:323)
Age (40 to 70 years old). (La. Rev. Stat. Ann. §23:312)
Enforcing agency:
Louisiana Commission on Human Rights
P.O. Box 94004
Baton Rouge, LA 70804
225-342-6969
http://www.gov.state.la.us/depts/lchr.htm

Maine
Race, color, gender, religion, national origin, ancestry, age, or physical or mental disability, sexual orientation or pregnancy. (Me. Rev. Stat. Ann. tit. 5, §§4572 to 4575)
Enforcing agency:
Human Rights Commission
51 Statehouse Station
Augusta, ME 04333
207-624-6050
http://janus.state.me.us/mhrc/homepage.htm

Maryland
Race, color, religion, gender, national origin, age, marital status, past or current physical or mental illness or disability. (Md. Code Ann. art. 49B, §16)
Enforcing agency:
Commission on Human Relations
6 Saint Paul Street
Baltimore, MD 21202
410-767-8600
http://www.mchr.md.us

Massachusetts
Race, color, religion, gender, sexual orientation, national origin, ancestry, age or physical or mental disability. (Mass. Gen. Laws Ann. ch. 151B, §4)
Enforcing agency:
Commission Against Discrimination
One Ashburton Place
Boston, MA 02108
617-727-3990
http://www.magnet.state.ma.us/mcad

Michigan
Race, color, religion, gender, national origin, height, weight, marital status or age. (Mich. Comp. Laws §37.2202)
Physical and mental disability, including AIDS and HIV. (Mich. Comp. Laws §37.1202)

	Enforcing agency: Department of Civil Rights 1200 6th Street, 7th Floor Detroit, MI 48226 313-256-2615 http://www.mdcr.com
Minnesota	Race, color, religion, creed, gender, marital status, pregnancy, sexual orientation, national origin, age, physical disability or receipt of public assistance. (Minn. Stat. Ann. §363.03) Enforcing agency: Department of Human Rights Bremer Tower 7th Place and Minnesota Streets St. Paul, MN 55101 612-296-5663
Mississippi	State employer cannot discriminate based on race, color, religion, sex, national origin, age or physical disability. (Miss. Code Ann. §25-9-149) Small businesses may not receive assistance from the state unless they certify that they do not discriminate based on race, color, religion, sex, national origin, age or physical disability. (Miss. Code Ann. §57-10-519) Enforcing agency: Consult the local EEOC office or Mississippi Department of Labor
Missouri	Race, color, religion, gender, national origin, ancestry, age between ages 40 and 70 or physical or mental disability. (Mo. Ann. Stat. §§213.010 and .055) AIDS condition, except individuals currently contagious who pose a direct threat to the health and safety of others or who are unable to perform the duties of their employment. (Mo. Ann. Stat. §191.665) Enforcing agency: Commission on Human Rights 3315 West Truman Boulevard Jefferson City, MO 65102-1129 573-751-3325 http://www.dolir.state.mo.us/hr/index.htm
Montana	Race, color, religion, creed, gender, age, national origin, marital status, or physical or mental disability. (Mont. Code Ann. §49-2-303) Enforcing agency: Human Rights Commission P.O. Box 1728 Helena, MT 59624 406-444-2884 http://erd.dli.state.mt.us/HumanRights/Hrhome.htm
Nebraska	Race, color, religion, gender, national origin, age between ages 40 and 70, marital status or disability—excluding addiction to alcohol, other drugs or gambling. (Neb. Rev. Stat. Ann. §48-1104)

	Enforcing agency: Equal Opportunity Commission 301 Centennial Mall South Lincoln, NE 68509 800-642-6112 http://www.nol.org/home/NEOC
Nevada	Race, color, religion, gender, age if over 40 years old, national origin, pregnancy, physical disability, sexual orientation. (Nev. Rev. Stat. Ann. §613.330 and 335) Enforcing agency: Equal Rights Commission 2450 Wrondel Way, Suite C Reno, NV 89502 702-688-1288 http://state.nv.us/detr/nerc
New Hampshire	Race, color, religion, gender, age, national origin, marital status, pregnancy, sexual orientation or physical or mental disability. (N.H. Rev. Stat. Ann. §354-A:6 and 7) Enforcing agency: Human Rights Commission 163 Loudon Road Concord, NH 03301 603-271-2767 http://www.state.nh.us/hrc
New Jersey	Race, color, religion, gender, national origin, ancestry, age between ages 18 and 70, marital status, sexual or affectional orientation, genetic information, atypical hereditary cellular or blood trait, past or present physical or mental disability or draft liability for the armed forces. (N.J. Stat. Ann. §10:5-12) Enforcing agency: Division of Civil Rights 31 Clinton Street, 3rd Floor Newark, NJ 07102 609-292-4605 http://www.state.nj.us/lps/dcr
New Mexico	Race, color, religion, gender, age, national origin, ancestry, medical condition, or physical or mental disability. (N.M. Stat. Ann. §28-1-7) Enforcing agency: Human Rights Commission 1596 Pacheco Street Aspen Plaza Santa Fe, NM 87505 800-566-9471 http://www.dol.state.nm.us/dol_hrd.html

New York	Race, color, religion, creed, gender, age if age 18 or older, national origin, marital status, physical or mental disability, genetic predisposition, pregnancy, political activities. (N.Y. Exec. Law §§292, 296; Labor Law §201-d) Enforcing agency: Division of Human Rights 55 West 125th Street New York, NY 10027 212-961-8400 http://www.nysdhr.com
North Carolina	Race, color, religion, gender, age, national origin. Applies only to employers who regularly employ more than 15 employees. (N.C. Gen. Stat. §143-422.2) Sickle cell or hemoglobin C traits, genetic testing or information. (N.C. Gen. Stat. §95-28.1 to 1A) Physical or mental disability. (N.C. Gen. Stat. §§168A-1 to A-5) AIDS or HIV condition. Employers can require applicants to take an AIDS test as part of a pre-employment medical examination and can deny employment based solely on a positive test result but cannot require testing or discriminate against existing employees. (N.C. Gen. Stat. §130A-148) Enforcing agency: Workplace Retaliatory Discrimination Office Department of Labor 4 West Edenton Street Raleigh, NC 27601 800-522-6763
North Dakota	Race, color, religion, gender, national origin, age if 40 or older, marital status, status with regard to public assistance or physical or mental disability and participation in lawful activity off the employer's premises during nonworking hours. (N.D. Cent. Code §14.02.4-03) Enforcing agency: Department of Labor Division of Human Rights 600 East Boulevard Avenue, Dept. 406 Bismarck, ND 58505 800-582-8032
Ohio	Race, color, religion, gender, national origin, ancestry, age (if over 40) or physical or mental disability. (Ohio Rev. Code Ann. §4112.02 and .14) Enforcing agency: Civil Rights Commission 220 Parsons Avenue Columbus, OH 43266 http://www.state.oh.us/crc

Oklahoma	Race, color, religion, gender, national origin, age if age 40 or older, or physical disability. Applies to public employees and private employers with more than 20 employees. (Okla. Stat. Ann. tit. 25, §§1301 and 1302) Enforcing agency: Human Rights Commission 2101 North Lincoln Boulevard, Room 480 Oklahoma City, OK 73105 405-521-2360
Oregon	Race, color, religion, gender, national origin, marital status, age if age 18 or older, or because of a juvenile record that has been expunged. Protection is also extended to persons who associate with members of the protected groups. (Or. Rev. Stat. §659.030) Physical or mental disability. (Or. Rev. Stat. §659.400) Enforcing agency: Civil Rights Division Bureau of Labor & Industry 800 NE Oregon Street, Box #32 Portland, OR 97232 503-731-4075
Pennsylvania	Race, color, religion, gender, national origin, ancestry, age if between ages 40 and 70, familial status, physical or mental non-job-related handicap or disability. Human Relations Act (43 Pa. Cons. Stat. Ann §§953, 954) Enforcing agency: Human Relations Commission Riverfront Office Center 1101-1125 South Front Street Harrisburg, PA 17104 717-787-4410
Rhode Island	Race, color, religion, gender, pregnancy, ancestry, age if between ages 40 and 70, sexual orientation or physical or mental disability. (R.I. Gen. Laws §28-5-6 and 7) AIDS condition or the perception of it. (R.I. Gen. Laws §23-6-22) Enforcing agency: Commission for Human Rights 10 Abbott Park Place Providence, RI 02903 401-222-2661
South Carolina	Race, color, religion, gender, age if age 40 or older, pregnancy or childbirth and related conditions, national origin. (S.C. Code §1-13-30 and 80) Physical or mental disability. (S.C. Code §43-33-530) Enforcing agency: Human Affairs Commission 2611 Forest Drive, Suite 200 Columbia, SC 29204 803-253-6336

South Dakota	Race, color, religion, creed, gender, national origin, ancestry or disability including blindness or partial blindness. (S.D. Codified Laws Ann. §20-13-10 and 10.1) Enforcing agency: Commission on Human Relations 118 West Capitol Avenue Sioux Falls, SD 57102 605-773-4493 http://www.state.sd.us/dcr/hr/HR_HOM.htm
Tennessee	Race, creed, color, religion, gender, age if over 40, national origin. (Tenn. Code Ann. §4-21-401) Physical, mental or visual disability. (Tenn. Code Ann. §8-50-103) Enforcing agency: Human Rights Commission 531 Henley Street, Suite 701 Knoxville, TN 37902 615-594-6500 http://www.state.tn.us/humanrights
Texas	Race, color, religion, gender, pregnancy, age if 40 or older, national origin or physical or mental disability. (Texas Lab. Code Ann. §§21.051, 21.101 through 21.129) Enforcing agency: Commission on Human Rights 6330 Highway 290 East, Suite 250 P.O. Box 13493 Austin, TX 78711 512-437-3450 http://www.welcome.to/tchr
Utah	Race, color, religion, gender, age if over age 40, national origin, pregnancy, childbirth or related medical conditions or physical or mental disability. (Utah Code Ann. §§34A-5-106) Enforcing agency: Anti-Discrimination Division of the Industrial Commission 160 East Third, South, 3rd floor Salt Lake City, UT 84111 801-530-6801
Vermont	Race, color, religion, gender, national origin, ancestry, age if age 18 or older, place of birth, sexual orientation or individuals with physical or mental disabilities. Mental and psychological disorders including learning disabilities, emotional illness, drug addiction and alcoholism are afforded protection under these statutes. (Vt. Stat. Ann. tit. 21, §§495 through 495d) AIDS/HIV provision. State employees or prospective employees, including teachers, cannot be required to take an HIV-related blood test and may not be discriminated against on the basis of HIV-positive results. (Vt. Stat. Ann. tit. 3, §961) Enforcing agency:

	Attorney General's Office Civil Rights Division 109 State Street Montpelier, VT 05609 802-828-3657
Virginia	Race, color, religion, gender, national origin, age, marital status, pregnancy, or physical or mental disability. (Va. Code Ann. §2.1-714 and following) Enforcing agency: Council on Human Rights 1100 Bank Street Richmond, VA 23219 804-225-2292 http://www.chr.state.va.us
Washington	Race, color, creed, gender, age if between age 40 and 70, national origin, marital status, or the presence of any sensory, physical or mental disability. (Wash. Rev. Code Ann. §49.60.180) Enforcing agency: Human Rights Commission 1511 Third Avenue, Suite 921 Seattle, WA 98101 206-464-6500
West Virginia	Race, religion, color, national origin, gender, familial status, age if 40 or older, blindness or disability. (W.Va. Code §5-11-9) Enforcing agency: Human Rights Commission 1321 Plaza East, Room 106 Charleston, WV 25301 304-588-2616 http://www.state.wv.us/wvhrc
Wisconsin	Race, color, religion, gender, age if age 40 or older, national origin, sexual orientation, marital status, arrest or conviction record, or physical disability. (Wis. Stat. Ann. §111.321 through 11.36) Enforcing agency: Department of Industry, Labor and Human Relations Equal Rights Division 201 East Washington Avenue, Room 402 Madison, WI 53708 608-266-6860 http://www.dwd.state.wi.us/er
Wyoming	Race, color, creed, gender, national origin, ancestry, age if between ages 40 and 69, or physical or mental disability. (Wyo. Stat. §27-9-105) Enforcing agency: Department of Employment Labor Standards Division 6101 Yellowstone, Room 259C Cheyenne, WY 82002 307-777-726 http://www.wydoe.state.wy.us/labstd

C. The Equal Pay Act

A federal law, the Equal Pay Act (29 U.S.C. §206), requires employers to pay all employees equally for equal work, regardless of their gender. It was passed in 1963 as an amendment to the Fair Labor Standards Act. (See Chapter 3, Section B.)

While the Act technically protects both women and men from gender discrimination in pay rates, it was passed to help rectify the problems faced by women workers because of sex discrimination in employment. And in practice, this law almost always has been applied to situations where women are being paid less than men for doing similar jobs.

The wage gap has narrowed slowly since 1980, when women's weekly earnings were only 64% of men's; the 1999 figure has women earning about 76% as much as working men. But the Equal Pay Act likely has little to do with it. The law's biggest weakness is that it is strictly applied only when men and women were doing the same work. Since women have historically been banned from many types of work and had only limited entree to managerial positions, the Equal Pay Act in reality affects very few women.

To successfully raise a claim under the Equal Pay Act, you must show that two employees, one male and one female:

- are working in the same place
- are doing equal work, and
- are receiving unequal pay.

You must also show that the employees in those jobs received unequal pay because of their genders.

1. Who Is Covered

The Equal Pay Act applies to all employees covered by the Fair Labor Standards Act, which means virtually all employees are covered. (See Chapter 3, Section A.) But in addition, the Equal Pay Act covers professional employees, executives and managers—including administrators and teachers in elementary and secondary schools.

> ### Concerned About Equal Pay—For Good Reason
>
> According to a recent nationwide survey by the AFL-CIO, money is foremost in the minds of America's working women. Asked to cite their top workplace concerns, about 94% of the women polled rated equal pay for equal work; 33% noted childcare; 78% cited sexual harassment; 72% mentioned downsizing.
>
> The math supports the mindset. On average, according to the Institute for Women's Policy Research, women earn $24,000 annually—much less than men's $32,000 yearly average. If these figures hold, today's 25-year-old woman who puts in 40 years of work before retiring will earn about a half million fewer dollars than a male worker at the same age and stage.

2. Determining Equal Work

Jobs do not have to be identical for the courts to consider them equal. In general, the courts have ruled that two jobs are equal for the purposes of the Equal Pay Act when both require equal levels of skill, effort and responsibility and are performed under similar conditions.

There is a lot of room for interpretation here, of course. But the general rule is that if there are only small differences in the skill, effort or responsibility required, two jobs should still be regarded as equal. The focus is on the duties actually performed. Job titles, classifications and descriptions may weigh in to the determination, but are not all that is considered.

The biggest problems arise where two jobs are basically the same, but one includes a few extra duties. It is perfectly legal to award higher pay for the extra duties, but some courts have looked askance at workplaces in which the higher-paying jobs with extra duties are consistently reserved for workers of one gender.

Equal Pay v. Comparable Worth

The Equal Pay Act covers only situations where men and women are performing jobs that require equal skill, effort and responsibility and are performed under similar circumstances. Often, however, men and women are doing different jobs at different payrates, despite the fact that the value of their work is equal. Disputes over this type of situation are typically lumped under the term comparable worth.

When Congress passed the Equal Pay Act, legislators squirmed to choose their words carefully. Representative Goodell (R-NY), one of the Act's sponsors, explained: "We went from 'comparable' to 'equal,' meaning that the jobs should be virtually identical—that is, that they would be very much alike or closely related to each other."

A comparable worth case typically is not covered by the Equal Pay Act. Because they are broader in scope, Title VII or the state anti-discrimination laws (discussed in Section B) are better routes to use for pursuing comparable worth complaints.

3. Determining Equal Pay

In general, pay systems that result in employees of one gender being paid less than the other gender for doing equal work are allowed under the Equal Pay Act if the pay system is actually based on a factor other than gender, such as a merit or seniority system.

Example: *In 1980, the Ace Widget Company was founded and initially hired 50 male widgetmakers. Many of those men are still working there. Since its founding, the company has expanded and hired 50 more widgetmakers, half of them female. All of the widgetmakers at Ace are doing equal work, but because the company awards raises systematically based on seniority or length of employment, many of the older male workers earn substantially more per hour than their female co-workers. Nevertheless, the pay system at Ace Widget does not violate the Equal Pay Act because its pay differences between genders doing equal work are based on a factor other than gender.*

4. How to Take Action

The Equal Pay Act was passed one year before Title VII of the Civil Rights Act. Both laws prohibit wage discrimination based on gender, but Title VII goes beyond ensuring equal pay for equal work, as it also bars discrimination in hiring, firing and promotions. In addition, Title VII broadly prohibits other forms of discrimination, including that based on race, color, religion and national origin. (See Section A for a detailed discussion of how to take action under Title VII.)

Example: *Suzanne works as a reservations agent for an airline, answering calls on the company's toll-free telephone number. About half of the other reservations agents in her office are men, who are typically paid $1 per hour more than Suzanne and the other female agents. What's more, the company has established a dress code for female reservations agents, but not for the male agents.*

If Suzanne decides to file a discrimination complaint against her employer, the Equal Pay Act would apply to the pay difference between females and males. Title VII would apply to both the pay difference and the fact that only the female employees in her office are held to a dress code.

In cases where both Title VII and the Equal Pay Act apply, the Equal Pay Act offers one big advantage: You can file a lawsuit under the Equal Pay Act without first filing a complaint with the EEOC.

Unlikely Heroes: Look Who's Talking

The issue of pay inequity for working women has rankled since the Equal Pay Act was passed in the mid 1960s to shine light on it. Yet, while it's a constant thorn in many workers' sides—particularly minority women workers—and a periodic plank in a political platform, true reforms to bring women's wages up to par still seem far away.

Meanwhile, they're still talking.

- "Countries rarely have conditions like this. If we can't use this moment to deal with these longterm challenges, including the equal pay challenge, when will we ever get around to it?" (President William Jefferson Clinton, remarking on the nation's low unemployment and strong economy; Equal Pay Roundtable, April 7, 1999)
- "The folks at Wimbledon recently rejected a request to give female players the same amount that the male players get ... the women are carrying the promotional load and bringing fans through the turnstiles. They should be paid accordingly." (John McEnroe, *New York Times*, June 6, 1999)
- "Older male bosses at my company have said that women should not be paid as much as men because women have the option of marrying rich." (A respondent to a *Glamour Magazine* survey on whether affirmative action programs are necessary for women, 1998)
- "I have always believed that contemporary gender discrimination within universities is part reality and part perception. True, but now I understand that reality is by far the greater of the balance." (Charles M. Vest, President of the Massachusetts Institute of Technology (MIT), upon the release of a study documenting a pattern of gender discrimination at the School of Science; *New York Times*, March 23, 1999)

Source: Quotes compiled by the National Committee on Pay Equity

D. The Age Discrimination in Employment Act

The federal Age Discrimination in Employment Act, or ADEA (29 U.S.C. §§621 to 634), is the single most important law protecting the rights of older workers. Basically, it provides that workers over the age of 40 cannot be arbitrarily discriminated against because of age in any employment decision. Perhaps the single most important rule under the ADEA is that no worker can be forced to retire.

The Act also prohibits age discrimination in hiring, discharges, lay-offs, promotion, wages, healthcare coverage, pension accrual, other terms and conditions of employment, referrals by employment agencies and membership in and the activities of unions. It requires that there must be a valid reason not related to age—for example, economic reasons or poor job performance—for all employment decisions, but especially firing.

Of all the possible claims of workplace discrimination, age discrimination has the broadest potential reach; most workers will live to be over 40. And the protection is likely to become even more important. We live in a time where the life expectancy is increasing, the older population is expanding rapidly and many older workers stay in the workforce for a long time.

Generally, to win a claim under the ADEA, you must be able to prove that:

- you are 40 years old or older
- you have been discharged or demoted, and
- when you were discharged or demoted, you were performing your job in a way that met your employer's legitimate expectations.

Some courts used to require that you also prove that after you were discharged or demoted, your position was filled by someone younger than 40 years. However, the U.S. Supreme Court recently held that you need not be replaced by a whippersnapper to make your case. In one of the briefest opinions on record, the Court held that what is important is that a worker is discriminated against because of age; who takes over the job is irrelevant. The Court held that: "there can be no greater inference of age discrimination when a 40-year-old is replaced by a 39-year-old than when a 56-year-old is replaced by a 40-year-old" (*O'Connor v. Consolidated Coin Caterers Corp.*, 116 S.Ct. 1307 (1996)).

An amendment to the ADEA, the Older Workers Benefit Protection Act, sets out specifics of how and when ADEA protections can be waived. (See Section E.)

The ADEA is enforced, along with other discrimination complaints, by the EEOC. (See Section A for more on procedure.) A number of national organizations will also provide legal referrals and help in evaluating age discrimination complaints. (See the Appendix for contact information.)

The End of Mandatory Retirement

No one fought so hard or did so much to shape the law for the poor and the elderly as Claude Pepper, the Democratic Congressman from Florida. He promoted, and many say created, legal rights for the elderly—backing legislation to fight crime in housing projects for the elderly, to cut Amtrak fares for senior citizens and to provide meals for homebound older Americans. He was also widely recognized as the primary congressional advocate of Social Security and Medicare.

Elected to the House of Representatives for 14 terms, Pepper was appointed chair of the Select Committee on Aging in 1977. In that role, he orchestrated dramatic parades of witnesses to testify about the plight of the aging elderly, some of them wheeled in on hospital beds and hooked to oxygen tanks.

But the legislative reform of which Pepper was proudest was the 1978 bill abolishing the federally mandatory retirement age of 65. True to form, Pepper packed the congressional hearing room when the bill was being debated. This time, he filled it with vibrant and able-bodied septuagenarians—politicians, actors and businesspeople, including Colonel Harlin Sanders, the fried chicken magnate. That bill did away with the mandatory retirement limit for federal government workers; the retirement age for nonfederal employees was raised from 65 to 70 years.

Pepper died on May 30, 1989. He was 88 years old. On September 7, 2000, the U.S. Postal Service honored the Congressman by issuing a stamp bearing his likeness.

1. Who Is Covered

The ADEA applies to employees age 40 and older—and to workplaces with 20 or more employees. Unlike several other federal workplace laws, the ADEA covers employees of labor organizations and local and federal governments. It does not apply to state governments.

There are a number of exceptions to the broad protection of the ADEA in addition to workers employed by companies which have fewer than 20 employees.

- Executives or people "in high policy-making positions" can be forced to retire at age 65 if they would receive annual retirement pension benefits worth $44,000 or more.
- There are special exceptions for police and fire personnel, tenured university faculty and certain federal employees having to do with law enforcement and air traffic control. If you are in one of these categories, check with your personnel office or benefits plan office for details.

- The biggest exception to the federal age discrimination law is made when age is an essential part of a particular job—referred to by the legal term of bona fide occupational qualification (BFOQ). An employer that sets age limits on a particular job must be able to prove the limit is necessary because a worker's ability to adequately perform that job does in fact diminish after the age limit is reached.

2. State Laws

Most states have laws against age discrimination in employment. (See Section B.) An individual working in a state with such a law can choose to file a complaint under either state law or the federal law (ADEA), or both.

In many cases, the state law can provide greater protection than the federal law. For example, several states provide age discrimination protection to workers before they reach age 40, and other states protect against the actions of employers with fewer than 20 employees. Even if the protection offered by your state law is the same as that provided by the federal law, you may get better results pursuing your rights under state law. A state agency entrusted with investigating and enforcing its own age discrimination law may provide easier, quicker and more aggressive prosecution of your complaint than the overburdened Equal Employment Opportunity Commission does in enforcing the ADEA. (See Section B for specific information on how to enforce your rights under state law.)

E. The Older Workers Benefit Protection Act

The main purpose of the Older Workers Benefit Protection Act (29 U.S.C. §§623, 626 and 630) is to make it clearly illegal:
- to use an employee's age as the basis for discrimination in benefits, and
- for companies to target older workers for their staff-cutting programs.

The law was passed in 1990, after a controversial U.S. Supreme Court ruling (*Public Employees Retirement Sys. v. Betts,* 109 U.S. 2854 (1989)) confused the question of when and how the Age Discrimination in Employment Act applied to benefit programs. (See Section D.)

Most of the effects of this law are very difficult for anyone but a benefits administrator who is immersed in the lingo to understand. However, one provision of the law that you are most likely to use—regulating the legal waivers that employers are increasingly asking employees to sign in connection with so-called early retirement programs—is relatively clear and specific.

By signing a waiver—often called a release or covenant not to sue—an employee agrees not to take any legal action, such as an age discrimination lawsuit, against the employer. In return for signing the waiver, the employer gives the employee an incentive to leave voluntarily, such as a severance pay package that exceeds the company's standard policy. (See Chapter 3, Section C.)

This type of transaction was very popular in the early 1990s among large corporations that wanted to reduce their payroll costs. Because older workers who have been with a company a long time typically cost more in salary and benefits than younger workers, most staff-cutting programs were directed at older workers. But cutting only older workers constitutes illegal age discrimination, so companies commonly induced the older workers to sign away their rights to sue their former employers. In colloquial parlance, these deals are often referred to as Golden Handshakes—as in Thank-You-Very-Much-for-Your-Hard-Years-of-Service-and-If-You-Retire-Right-Now-This-Grand-Bunch-of-Benefits-Will-Be-Yours. This cruel squeeze play is now somewhat limited.

Under the Older Workers Benefit Protection Act, you must be given at least 21 days to decide whether or not to sign such a waiver that has been presented to you individually. If the waiver is presented to a group of employees, each of you must be given at least 45 days to decide whether or not to sign. In either case, you have seven days after agreeing to such a waiver to revoke your decision.

1. Who Is Covered

The Older Workers Benefit Protection Act applies to nonunion employees in private industry who are at least 40 years old.

2. Restrictions on Agreements Not to Sue

There are a number of other key restrictions the Older Workers Benefit Protection Act places on agreements not to sue.

- Your employer must make the waiver understandable to the average individual eligible for the program in which the waiver is being used.
- The waiver may not cover any rights or claims that you discover are available after you sign it, and it must specify that it covers your rights under the ADEA.
- Your employer must offer you something of value—over and above what is already owed to you—in exchange for your signature on the waiver.
- Your employer must advise you, in writing, that you have the right to consult an attorney before you sign the waiver.

- If the offer is being made to a class of employees, your employer must inform you in writing how the class of employees is defined; the job titles and ages of all the individuals to whom the offer is being made; and the ages of all the employees in the same job classification or unit of the company to whom the offer is not being made.
- You must be given a reasonable time in which to make a decision on whether or not to sign the waiver.

Employers are allowed no room to hedge on any one of these requirements—and a waiver that does not comply with all the absolute requirements is the same as no waiver at all. The U.S. Supreme Court reaffirmed this in a recent decision—and pointedly held that an employee who signed a deficient waiver could not only sue for age discrimination, but did not need to return severance pay she received from her former employer (*Oubre v. Entergy Operations, Inc.*, 118 S.Ct. 838 (1998)).

3. Negotiation Rights

The Older Workers Benefits Protection Act gives additional legal protections if your employer offers you the opportunity to participate in a staff reduction program. The Act indirectly puts you in a position to negotiate the terms of your departure.

The fact that your employer has offered an incentive tells you that the company wants you gone and is worried that you might file a lawsuit for wrongful discharge. (See Chapter 11, Section A.) Although company heads may say that you have only two choices—accept or reject the offer—there is nothing preventing you from making a counteroffer.

For example, after taking a week or two to think, you might go back to your employer and agree to leave voluntarily if your severance pay is doubled. There is power in numbers, so this type of negotiating is even more likely to be effective if done on behalf of a group of employees who are considering the same offer.

As in all employment transactions, it is wise to advise your employer of your decision in writing, and to keep a copy of that letter—along with copies of all documents given to you by your employer as part of the staff reduction program. If you refuse to accept such an offer and are later dismissed, you may be able to allege illegal age discrimination as a basis for challenging your dismissal.

4. How to Take Action

If you believe that an employer has violated your rights under the Older Workers Benefit Protection Act, you can file a complaint with the EEOC just as you would against any other workplace discrimination prohibited by Title VII. (See Section A4.) If the EEOC does not resolve your complaint to your satisfaction, you may decide to pursue your complaint through a lawsuit. (See Section A5.)

F. The Americans With Disabilities Act

The Americans With Disabilities Act, or ADA (42 U.S. Code §§12102 and following), prohibits employment discrimination on the basis of workers' disabilities. While debated, haggled over and honed by both employees and employers before it was passed, the law is not a panacea for either group. It is widely criticized as poorly drafted.

Generally, the ADA prohibits employers from:

- discriminating on the basis of virtually any physical or mental disability
- asking job applicants questions about their past or current medical conditions
- requiring job applicants to take pre-employment medical exams, and
- creating or maintaining worksites that include substantial physical barriers to the movement of people with physical handicaps.

The Act requires that an employer must make reasonable accommodations for qualified individuals with disabilities, unless that would cause the employer undue hardship. But those dictates are frustrating. It is unclear what disabilities qualify individuals for coverage under the law. (See Section 2 below.) And the meanings of "qualified workers," "reasonable accommodations" and "undue hardship" remain elusive. (See Sections 1 and 4 below.)

A precursor of the ADA, the Vocational Rehabilitation Act (29 U.S.C. §794), prohibits discrimination against handicapped workers in state and federal government. Its narrow protections are generally thought to be usurped by the more extensive ADA.

1. Who Is Covered

The ADA covers employers with 15 or more employees. Its coverage broadly extends to private companies, employment agencies, labor organizations and state and local governments.

The Act protects workers who, although disabled in some way, are still qualified for a particular job—that is, they would be able to perform the essential functions of a job, either with or without some form of accommodation. Whether a disabled worker is deemed qualified for a job seems to depend on whether he or she has appropriate skill, experience, training or education for the position.

To determine whether a particular function is considered essential for a job, look first at a written job description. If a function is described there, it is more likely to be considered an essential part of the job. But an employer's discretion and the reality of an individual workplace enter the fray, too. For example, if other employees would likely be available to take over some tangential part of a job, or if only a small portion of the workday is spent on the function, or if the work product will not suffer if the function is not performed—then that function may not be deemed essential to the job.

2. Definition of Disabled

The ADA's protections extend to the disabled—defined as a person who:
- has a physical or mental impairment that substantially limits a major life activity
- has a record of impairment, or
- is regarded as having an impairment.

This list makes clear why the new law provides just cause for consternation. Many of the terms used in the Act are broad—and not well-defined. Some of their intended meanings were hinted at during the congressional debates on the legislation, but many will simply have to be hammered out in the courts over time.

a. Impairments limiting a life activity

Impairment includes both physical disorders, such as cosmetic disfigurement or loss of a limb, and mental and psychological disorders. Physical disabilities which can be easily seen are those most often protected, presumably for the simple reason that they are easiest to prove to others.

Many of the conditions the ADA is intended to cover are specifically listed—a list that is sure to grow over time. In fact, the ADA requires that every year, the Secretary of Health and Human Services must provide a list of infectious and communicable diseases, as well as information on how they are transmitted.

Note, however, that several state and local public health departments have passed regulations that allow some forms of discrimination in the food handling industry. For example, several state laws provide that if a communicable disease can be transmitted through handling food, and if the risk cannot be eliminated by reasonable accommodation, then an employer may refuse to hire an individual for a food handling job. For more information on these types of laws, contact your local public health department.

In addition, testing applicants and employees for the possibility of infectious diseases raises a number of privacy issues, commonly addressed in local and state laws. (See Chapter 6.)

The ADA specifically protects workers with Acquired Immunodeficiency Syndrome (AIDS) and Human Immunodeficiency Virus (HIV) (see Chapter 6, Section B), alcoholism, cancer, cerebral palsy, diabetes, emotional illness, epilepsy, hearing and speech disorders, heart disorders, learning disabilities such as dyslexia, mental retardation, muscular dystrophy and visual impairments.

A number of other conditions can be protected under the ADA upon proper proof that they are limiting in some way. To be covered, an individual's condition must restrict a life activity—broadly defined as the ability to walk, talk, see, hear, speak, breathe, sit, stand, reach, reason, learn, work or care for himself or herself. However, the ADA does not cover conditions that impose short-term limitations, such as pregnancy or broken bones.

And in its most recent pronouncement on the issue, the U.S. Supreme Court held that health conditions that can be limiting, but may be treated through drugs or accouterments—such as diabetes and poor eyesight—are not protected disabilities under the ADA (*Sutton v. United Air Lines*, 119 S.Ct. 2139 (1999) and *Murphy v. United Parcel Service, Inc.*, 119 S.Ct. 2133 (1999)).

These Court decisions will be tied to the larger new wave of controversy in ADA claims based on conditions some workers contend limit them, but are murky for outsiders to detect. For example, some workers claim that Multiple Chemical Sensitivity, or MCS, caused by carpet, glue or furniture fumes makes them dizzy, tired and headachy. Other workers claim that mold and mildew on the job aggravate or cause respiratory problems. And some claim latex gloves and chemical coatings have given them asthma. Where the symptoms can be traced to poor ventilation in workplaces, they are commonly dubbed Sick Building Syndrome.

But linking the Syndrome to a successful ADA claim is still a gamble. A few complaints have resulted in money awards from employers—but paradoxically, most workers have had to prove they were unable to work to collect. The greater success stories come from employees and employers who work together to come up with a solution to a complaint before it produces a disabling condition—often as simple as improving ventilation or setting up an office with air filtration and without carpeting.

What's Going On

The ADA took effect in July 1992. During its first seven years, the EEOC received nearly 109,000 ADA complaints against employers. Most claims involved discriminatory firings or failures to provide accommodations.

Of the claims resolved during that time, only about 10% were resolved in favor of employees.

Disturbing statistics showed:

- nearly 40% were closed out for what was mysteriously dubbed Administrative Reasons—for example, that the EEOC could not find the employee, and
- over half were dismissed out of hand as unreasonable.

Equally disturbing to some is the type of disabilities the law is being called upon to protect. Back pain, Carpal Tunnel Syndrome and mild depression together account for over 40% of the claims. What were deemed traditional disabilities—such as blindness and deafness—account for only about 6% of the claims filed.

b. Records of impairment

Because discrimination often continues even after the effects of a disability have abated, the ADA prohibits discrimination against those who have had impairments in the past. This includes many hard to qualify groups of workers such as former cancer patients, rehabilitated drug addicts, recovering alcoholics and even those misclassified as having a condition, such as someone misdiagnosed as being HIV-positive.

c. Regarded as impaired

In recognition of the fact that discrimination often stems from prejudice or irrational fear, the ADA protects workers who have no actual physical or mental impairment, but may be viewed by others as disabled—for example, someone who is badly scarred, deaf or epileptic. An employer cannot refuse to hire a person because of the perception that others will react negatively to him or her.

So far, this legal requirement has drawn the most questions. The House Labor Committee Report that originally considered the ADA attempted to provide some guidance by stating that if an employer fires someone "because of the employer's perception that the person has an impairment which prevents that person from working, that person is covered" under the Act. In truth, the guidance has not been great enough. And judges called upon to decide ADA cases have refused to follow what guidance this offers: Most blatantly hold that a perceived limitation is simply not a handicap under the Act.

All in the Mind?
The ADA and Mental Disability Claims

In the newest wave of ADA complaints, workers claim that post-traumatic stress makes them hyperactive or short-tempered. Others claim that Attentive Deficit Disorder, or ADD, makes it difficult for them to concentrate and be productive on the job. Even where diagnosed and treated with drugs, some argue that mental conditions such as these are not true disabilities within the meaning of the law.

The EEOC issued guidelines on mental illness in March of 1997, mostly reiterating that the ADA protects workers who have mental impairments that limit "a major life activity" such as learning, thinking, concentrating, interacting with others, caring for himself or herself or performing manual tasks. The EEOC opined that protected conditions may include major depression, bipolar disorder, anxiety disorders such as panic and obsessive compulsive disorders. But the agency also emphasized that the impairment must be lasting; while a serious depression lasting a year or more might qualify under the ADA, a down spell of a month probably would not.

Despite this gentle nudge from the EEOC to heed mental disability claims, many judges and juries around the country continue to reject them out of hand. The discrepancy may be due to the problem of definition. The lack of objective criteria for assessing mental diseases often makes their diagnoses murky—and the most skeptical observers claim that some employees seek out a finding of mental disability as an excuse to shirk work.

And workers who claim mental disabilities are often faced with a Catch-22 when proving their cases: The ADA covers only those who are still able to perform their jobs; a worker who makes a convincing case of mental disability may have a tough time persuading others that he or she is still fit to work.

Finally, there may be problems getting an accommodation that realistically meets the needs of worker and workplace. Some accommodations may be effective and easy to provide—for example, moving an employee away from noisy machinery or allowing beverages in the workplace to combat a dry mouth caused by medication. But other accommodations, such as allowing more time to complete a work activity, may smack of favoritism in the hearts and minds of other workers. And in the meanest workplaces, doctors' orders not to startle or ridicule a particular employee may cause co-workers to escalate the bad behavior.

3. Illegal Discrimination

The ADA prohibits employers from discriminating against job applicants and employees who have disabilities in a number of specific situations.

a. Screening tests

Employers may not use pre-employment tests or ask interview questions that focus on an applicant's disabilities rather than skills related to the job. Although these questions used to be routine, employers can no longer ask, for example: Have you ever been hospitalized? Have you ever been treated for any of the following listed conditions or diseases? Have you ever been treated for a mental disorder? (See Chapter 6, Section B, for a discussion of privacy issues related to testing.)

However, in screening applicants to find the best match to fill a job opening, employers are free to ask questions about an individual's ability to perform job-related tasks, such as: Can you lift a 40-pound box? Do you have a driver's license? Can you stand for long periods of time?

b. Insurance benefits

Employers cannot deny health coverage or other fringe benefits to disabled workers. Before the ADA was passed, many employers railed that their insurance costs would skyrocket if they were forced to provide coverage for the special medical needs of disabled workers. The ADA does not require that all medical conditions be covered; workplace policies can still limit coverage for various treatments or design exclusions for preexisting conditions. However, employers must provide the same coverage for workers with disabilities as they do for workers without disabilities. (See Chapter 4 for a discussion of health insurance.)

c. Disabled relatives and friends

The ADA also attempts to clamp down on the invidious effects of taint by association. Employers are banned from discriminating against people who are not disabled, but are related to or associated with someone who is disabled. For example, an otherwise qualified worker cannot be denied employment because a brother, roommate or close friend has AIDS.

d. Segregation

On the job, employers cannot segregate or classify disabled workers in a way that limits their opportunities or status—for example, by placing them in jobs with different pay, benefits or promotion opportunities from workers who are not disabled.

Is Obesity a Disability? Still Too Soon to Tell

Courts that have been called upon to decide whether overweight people are disabled within the meaning of state disability laws and the ADA have split on the issue.

Some courts have held that all overweight workers are physically impaired—and entitled to be protected from discrimination under disability laws. Some courts have opined that overweight workers are protected by disability laws only if there is some medical evidence showing that the weight gain is due to a physiological condition. And a third line of legal reasoning holds that only obese workers—those 100% or more over normal weight, or by some definitions, those who weigh twice the normal weight for their height—are entitled to the laws' protections.

When asked to provide some guidance, the EEOC was noncommittal—stating only that obesity claims would be considered "on a case by case basis." It added, however, that because of the ADA requirement that a disability must substantially limit a major life activity, few individuals can meet the burden.

Watch for the next bit of legal guidance to come from the least likely of places: Hollywood. Holly Hallstrom recently sued America's quintessential television host Bob Barker and producers of "The Price Is Right." Hallstrom, 43, claims that the game show fired her illegally after she gained 14 pounds and her weight would not come on down. The gain, she argues, was due to a hormone imbalance common to pre-menopausal women—a disability—which required her to take estrogen and progesterone to correct. If the case succeeds, it will likely swell the number of claims filed under the ADA and state discrimination statutes.

---

4. Accommodations by Employers

The core of the ADA is what initially got employers up in arms over its passage; some of them felt the law wrested important workplace decisions from them. It requires employers to make accommodations—changes to the work setting or the way jobs are done—so that disabled people can work. The law also specifies what employers must do in the sticky situation where two equally qualified candidates, one of whom is disabled, apply for a job. An employer cannot reject the disabled worker solely because he or she would require a reasonable accommodation—a reserved handicapped parking space, a modified work schedule, a telephone voice amplifier—to get the job done.

In reality, a disabled individual who wants a particular job must become somewhat of an activist. Since the law does not require an employer to propose reasonable accommodations—only to provide them—the onus of suggesting workable and affordable changes to the workplace that would allow him or her to perform a job is on the employee who wants the accommodation.

a. What is a reasonable accommodation

The ADA points to several specific accommodations that are likely to be deemed reasonable—some of them changes to the physical set-up of the workplace, some of them changes to how, when or where work is done. They include:

- making existing facilities usable by disabled employees—for example, by modifying the height of desks and equipment, installing computer screen magnifiers or installing telecommunications for the deaf
- restructuring jobs—for example, allowing a ten-hour/four-day workweek so that a worker can receive weekly medical treatments
- modifying exams and training material—for example, allowing more time for taking an exam, or allowing it to be taken orally instead of in writing
- providing a reasonable amount of additional unpaid leave for medical treatment (see also, Chapter 5)
- hiring readers or interpreters to assist an employee
- providing temporary workplace specialists to assist in training, and
- transferring an employee to the same job in another location to obtain better medical care.

These are just a few possible accommodations. The possibilities are limited only by an employee's and employer's imaginations—and the reality that one or more of these accommodations might be financially impossible in a particular workplace.

It Helps to Beat Them to the Punch

As one might imagine, the ADA has spawned yet another crop of Workplace Experts, all eager to give tips to employers on what they must do to comply with the convoluted law. Most offer some type of checklist or list of steps to take to help meet the ADA's provisions.

In truth, the checklists are most valuable for disabled employees who want to get or keep a job. They will be in the best possible bargaining position if they approach a potential employer with answers to the questions.

Here are some things to ponder:

- Analyze the job you want and isolate its essential functions.
- Write down precisely what job-related limitations your condition imposes and note how they can be overcome by accommodations.
- Identify potential accommodations and assess how effective each would be in allowing you to perform the job.
- Estimate how long each accommodation could be used before a change would be required.
- Document all aspects of the accommodation—including cost and availability.

b. What is an undue hardship

The ADA does not require employers to make accommodations that would cause them an undue hardship—a weighty concept defined in the ADA only as "an action requiring significant difficulty or expense." To show that a particular accommodation would present an undue hardship, an employer would have to demonstrate that it was too costly, extensive or disruptive to be adopted in that workplace.

The Equal Employment Opportunity Commission (EEOC), the federal agency responsible for enforcing the ADA, has set out some of the factors that will determine whether a particular accommodation presents an undue hardship on a particular employer:

- the nature and cost of the accommodation
- the financial resources of the employer—a large employer, obviously, may reasonably be asked to foot a larger bill for accommodations than a mom and pop business
- the nature of the business, including size, composition and structure, and
- accommodation costs already incurred in a workplace.

It is not easy for employers to prove that an accommodation is an undue hardship, as financial difficulty alone is not usually sufficient. Courts will look at other sources of money, including tax credits and deductions available for making some accommodations and the disabled employee's willingness to pay for all or part of the costs.

5. How to Take Action

Title I of the ADA is enforced by the Equal Employment Opportunity Commission. (See Section A4 for specifics on how to file a complaint.) How efficient and responsive the agency will be and what kinds of lines it will draw in the cases it investigates remain to be seen as the relatively new law makes its presence felt in workplaces and courts.

In addition, many state laws protect against discrimination based on physical or mental disability. (See Section B for a list of laws and enforcing agencies.) An individual working in a state with such a law can choose to file a complaint under either state law or the federal law (ADA), or both.

6. Where to Get More Information

For additional information on the ADA, contact:

Disability Rights Section
Civil Rights Division
U.S. Department of Justice
P.O. Box 66738
Washington, DC 20035
800-514-0301 (voice) or 800-514-0383 (TDD)

The Disability Rights Section operates a Web page devoted to the ADA at http://www.us.doj.gov/crt/ada/adahom1.htm. There are also a number of national organizations that offer guidance and referrals in dealing with ADA problems. (See the Appendix for contact details.)

When Money Isn't Everything

According to ergonomic and job accommodation experts, the amount of money employers would need to pay to accommodate a particular worker's disability is often surprisingly low.

- 31% of accommodations cost nothing.
- 50% cost less than $50.
- 69% cost less than $500.
- 88% cost less than $1,000.

The following is a list of the problems that recently surfaced—and their inexpensive solutions:

Problem: A person had an eye disorder. Glare on the computer screen caused fatigue.

Solution: The employer purchased an antiglare screen for $39.

Problem: An individual lost the use of a hand and could no longer use a camera. The company provided a tripod, but that was too cumbersome.

Solution: A waist pod, such as is used in carrying flags, enabled the individual to manipulate the camera and keep his job. Cost? $50.

Problem: A seamstress could not use ordinary scissors due to pain in her wrist.

Solution: The business purchased a pair of ergonomically designed springloaded scissors for $18.

Problem: A receptionist, who was blind, could not see the lights on her telephone that indicated whether the telephone lines were ringing, on hold, or in use at her company.

Solution: The company bought a light probe, a penlike product that detected a lighted button, for $45.

Problem: A medical technician who was deaf could not hear the buzz of a timer, which was necessary for specific laboratory tests.

Solution: An indicator light was attached for $26.95.

Problem: A person who used a wheelchair could not use a desk because it was too low and his knees would not go under it.

Solution: The desk was raised with wood blocks, allowing a proper amount of space for the wheelchair to fit under it. Cost? Nothing.

Source: The Job Accommodation Network, 2000

G. Discrimination Against Workers With HIV or AIDS

Government polls indicate that roughly one in every 100 American workers has been infected by HIV, the virus believed to cause Acquired Immune Deficiency Syndrome (AIDS). And in some communities with high risk populations, such as San Francisco, the infection rate is reported to be as high as one in every 25 workers. Additional recent polls reveal that even these high estimates are unrealistically low.

Half of our nation's 121 million workers are in the age group of those most likely to be infected in the future—adults between the ages of 25 and 44 years old.

A growing number of employers have attempted to smooth over real and perceived problems with HIV-infected and AIDS-infected workers by holding training sessions and adopting written policies specifically prohibiting discrimination.

Nevertheless, some employers and employees have reacted to the spread of AIDS with panic—and a strong prejudice against working with people who are infected with the HIV virus. Some insurance companies have made that panic worse by restricting healthcare coverage or dramatically raising premiums for those infected. (See Chapter 6, Section B, for a discussion of privacy rights connected with AIDS testing.)

While prejudice and skittishness remain, the legal picture for workers with HIV and AIDS is more clear since the passage of the Americans With Disabilities Act or ADA. (See Section F.) Under the ADA, it is clearly illegal for any company employing 15 or more people to discriminate against workers because they are HIV-infected or have AIDS. Employers covered by the ADA must also make reasonable accommodations to allow employees with AIDS or HIV to continue working. Such accommodations include extended leave policies and reassignment to vacant positions that are less physically strenuous and/or that have flexible work schedules.

In addition, many state and local anti-discrimination laws make it illegal to discriminate in employment-related matters on the basis of HIV infection or AIDS. (See Section B.)

A number of organizations offer publications and specific information on the HIV virus, AIDS and resources on AIDS in the workplace. The organizations often provide sources of counseling and legal referrals. See the Appendix for contact details.

No One Is Immune

Although there is some hopeful news in AIDS treatments and prognosis, the epidemic continues to produce some startling statistics that affect us all.

- AIDS is the second leading cause of death among U.S. adults ages 25 to 44 years old.
- Two-thirds of large businesses have employees with HIV infection or AIDS.
- One in ten small businesses has employees with HIV infection or AIDS.
- By 1997, more than 38,000 Americans had died of AIDS.
- HIV infection and AIDS are rising among women, racial and ethnic minorities and young people.
- AIDS is the leading cause of death among young adults in 64 cities in the United States.

Source: National AIDS Fund, 1999

H. Discrimination Against Gay and Lesbian Workers

Gay men and lesbians have historically been subjected to painful measures that would legalize discrimination: initiatives barring them from teaching in public schools, local ordinances allowing private clubs to bar them from their doors, loud and heavy lobbying against same-sex marriage laws. On the job, the discrimination often continues—with homophobic comments and jokes, lectures about upholding The Company Image, promotions denied and jobs lost.

Although women, minorities, people older than 40 and people with disabilities now enjoy an umbrella of state and federal protections from discrimination in the workplace, gays and lesbians have, for the most part, been left out in the rain, at least at the national level. There is no federal law that specifically outlaws workplace discrimination on the basis of sexual orientation—in either the public or the private sector.

At the state level, however, there is more cause for hope, depending on whether the workplace is public or private. Seven states have laws prohibiting sexual orientation discrimination in public employment: Illinois, Iowa, Maryland, New Mexico, New York, Pennsylvania and Washington. Eleven states have laws prohibiting sexual orientation discrimination in both private and public jobs: California, Connecticut, Hawaii, Massachusetts, Minnesota, Nevada, New Hampshire, New Jersey, Rhode Island, Vermont and Wisconsin. The District of Columbia prohibits sexual orientation discrimination in both the public and private sectors.

If you are gay or lesbian and your state does not have a law that protects you from workplace discrimination, you may still be protected by city and county ordinances. There are 124 cities and counties that prohibit sexual orientation in the workplace—from Albany, NY, to Ypsilanti, MI. In addition, some companies have adopted their own policies prohibiting such discrimination.

According to the National Gay and Lesbian Taskforce, the hodgepodge of laws and ordinances means that approximately 62% of the population has no legislative protection from workplace discrimination based on sexual orientation, at least in the private sector. In the public sector, the percent of the unprotected population is slightly lower.

However, in states and cities that do not have laws forbidding workplace discrimination on the basis of sexual orientation, you can often take action against an employer who fires or otherwise discriminates against you because you are gay or lesbian by filing a lawsuit claiming invasion of privacy.

Example: *Janet worked at a small law firm specializing in patents. After 15 years of work filled with consistent promotions, pay raises and good performance reviews, Janet was fired the day after her supervisor saw her holding hands with her lover at a weekend movie. Janet would have a good shot at winning a lawsuit against the law firm based on invasion of privacy, because the firing amounted to the employer exerting undue control over her private life.*

Finally, a growing number of more enlightened employers have included a clause that they will not discriminate against workers based on sexual orientation.

With sufficient documentation, you may also be able to prove in specific instances that your demotion or firing was due to:
- illegal discrimination under the ADA (discussed in Section F) based on a perceived fear of HIV virus infection
- one of the other wrongful discharge strategies (discussed in Chapter 11, Section A), or
- illegal discrimination prohibited by a specific workplace policy.

Damned Either Way

Deciding whether to be openly identified at work as gay can be a grueling choice. Courts have split on whether there is legal protection for workers who do not openly identify themselves as gay but who are discriminated against because an employer believes they are gay.

For more information on the legal rights of gay and lesbian couples, see *A Legal Guide for Lesbian and Gay Couples*, by Hayden Curry, Denis Clifford, Robin Leonard and Frederick Hertz (Nolo). A number of organizations offer publications, counseling, advice and research on issues gay and lesbian workers face on the job. (See the Appendix for contact details.)

CHAPTER
9

SEXUAL HARASSMENT

In legal terms, sexual harassment is any unwelcome sexual conduct on the job that creates an intimidating, hostile or offensive working environment. Simply put, sexual harassment is any offensive conduct related to an employee's gender that a reasonable woman or man should not have to endure while at work.

The laws prohibiting sexual harassment are gender-blind; they prevent women from harassing men, men from harassing other men, and women from harassing other women. However, the vast majority of cases involve women workers being harassed by male co-workers or supervisors.

The forms that sexual harassment can take range from offensive sexual innuendoes to physical encounters, from misogynist humor to rape. An employee may be confronted with sexual demands to keep a job or obtain a promotion, known in the earliest cases as a quid pro quo form of harassment—literally, do this for that. In other forms of sexual harassment, the threat—or the trade-off—is not as blunt. When sexually offensive conduct permeates the workplace, an employee may find it difficult or unpleasant to work there. The term hostile environment was frequently used in the cases and literature to describe this form of sexual harassment.

The definition of sexual harassment is evolving as it passes through courts and legislatures. The most authoritative refinements come from the U.S. Supreme Court, which has issued a number of pronouncements on the subject.

For example, the Court held that a worker need not show psychological injury to prove a case of sexual harassment; it also intimated that one or two offensive remarks are not enough to make a case (*Harris v. Forklift Sys., Inc.*, 114 S.Ct. 367 (1993)).

And in additional recent cases, the Court has offered forth some uncharacteristically homespun advice for both employers and employees entangled in harassment issues: Act reasonably. Use your common sense.

- The Court without equivocation recognized that illegal harassment can occur between people of the same gender. It implied that drawing the line between horseplay or flirtations and discrimination on the job is not as hard as some pretend, even while acknowledging that men and women may play differently (*Oncale v. Sundowner Offshore Services, Inc.*, 118 S.Ct. 998 (1998)).

- The Court also acknowledged that the jargony labels of quid pro quo and hostile environment may be more confusing than helpful in defining sexual harassment. It held that an employer may be liable for sexual harassment even when an employee did not succumb to sexual advances or suffer diverse job consequences. But the employer can defend itself against liability and damages by showing that it used reasonable care in stopping harassment—a strong written anti-harassment policy or an investigation procedure. An employee who does not take advantage of the workplace policy by reporting the harassment has a considerably weaker case (*Burlington Industries, Inc. v. Ellerth*, 118 S.Ct. 2257 (1998)).

- And the Court resolved the question of whether an employer could be held liable for a supervisor's harassing behavior when it had no knowledge of it. It held again that an employer could defend itself against a sexual harassment charge by showing it acted reasonably to prevent it. The Court intimated that, at a minimum, acting reasonably includes establishing a policy prohibiting sexual harassment and establishing a procedure for dealing with it (*Faragher v. City of Boca Raton, Florida*, 118 S.Ct. 2275 (1998)).

For comprehensive information about sexual harassment, see *Sexual Harassment on the Job: What It Is and How to Stop It*, by William Petrocelli and Barbara Kate Repa (Nolo).

A. The Effects of Sexual Harassment

Sexual harassment on the job can have a number of serious consequences, both for the harassed individual and for other workers who experience it second-hand and become demoralized or intimidated at work. (See Section B for a discussion of legal remedies.)

1. Loss of Job

Sometimes the connection between sexual harassment and the injuries it causes is simple and direct: A worker is fired for refusing to go along with the sexual demands of a co-worker or supervisor. Usually the management uses some other pretext for the firing, but the reasons are often quite transparent.

Sometimes the firing technically occurs because of some other event, but it is still clearly related to sexual harassment. For example, if a company downgrades an employee's job and assignments because of a harassment incident and then fires him or her for complaining about the demotion, that injury is legally caused by sexual harassment.

If an employee is temporarily unable to work as a result of the harassment and the management uses that as an excuse to fire him or her, that is considered part of the harassment.

2. Loss of Wages and Other Benefits

An employee who resists sexual advances or objects to obscene humor in the office may:
- be denied a promotion
- be demoted, and
- suffer various economic losses.

That employee may also suffer harm to his or her standing within the company and have future pay increases jeopardized.

A loss of wages usually entails a loss of other job benefits as well, such as pension contributions, medical benefits, overtime pay, bonuses, sick pay, shift differential pay, vacation pay and participation in any company profit-sharing plan.

3. Forced Reassignment

Sometimes a company responds to a complaint of sexual harassment by transferring that employee somewhere else in the company and leaving the harasser unpunished. This forced reassignment is another form of job-connected injury, and it may be compounded if it results in a loss of pay or benefits or reduced opportunities for advancement.

4. Constructive Discharge

Sometimes the sexual harassment is so severe that the employee quits. If the situation was intolerable and the employee was justified in quitting, sexual harassment caused him or her to be constructively discharged—that is, forced to leave. While often difficult to prove, this is the same as an illegal firing.

Example: *A woman who worked for a film editing company received frequent threats as well as blatant sexual solicitations from the owner of the company, which culminated when he posed the ultimatum: "Fuck me, or you're fired." The owner told the woman he was leaving for a brief business trip, but his parting words were: "I'll see you when I get back." A federal court hearing the case ruled that the sexual ultimatum, combined with the explicit threat, made her working conditions so intolerable that a reasonable person in her position would be compelled to resign—the very definition of a constructive discharge. (Stockett v. Tolin, 791 F. Supp. 1536 (S.D. Fla. 1992)).*

5. Penalties for Retaliation

Employees are frequently fired or penalized for reporting sexual harassment or otherwise trying to stop it. Such workplace reprimands are called retaliation. In such cases, the injury is legally considered to be a direct result of the sexual harassment.

6. Personal Injuries

In addition to job-connected losses, a sexually harassed worker often suffers serious and costly personal injuries—ranging from stress-related illnesses to serious physical and emotional problems.

Sexual harassment also causes a great many other types of physical, mental and emotional injuries. Some of these injuries are stress-related, but others are caused by physical pranks or violent acts directed at the harassed worker.

Yes, Virgil. Men Get Harassed, Too

A few years after sexual harassment against women came out of workplace closets across America, a new whisper emerged: "I've been harassed, too. And I'm a man." At first, many people—particularly women—took a dim view of this development. Sexual harassment on the job, after all, had been diagnosed as a social ill stemming from an abuse of power, and men had long dominated the powerful positions in most workplaces. It was harder to sympathize with The Harassed Man than to see him as the poor lunk who failed to duck as the pendulum was swinging.

The popular press and the silver screen seemed titillated by the thought of the role reversal. Michael Crichton was inspired to pen yet another novel on the theme, *Disclosure*. Still, when the book surfaced inevitably in a film version, even the threat of a besuited Demi Moore pinning a hapless male underling against her mahogany desk seemed less scary than, say, being passed over for a promotion.

The reality is, of course, that abusive behavior in the workplace is not limited by stereotypes of Bad Boys and Good Girls. Sexual harassment on the job is not about sex; it's about unwanted, abusive behavior—usually repeated and often in the face of requests to cut it out. Women as well as men dish out the discriminatory behavior that is sexual harassment, and they'll do it to harass men they want to intimidate or humiliate or drive out of their workplaces.

Some believe it's worse than we fear, that nearly as many men as women are harassed on the job, but few of them are willing or able to speak up about it—as if that extra chromosome reared up and got caught in their collective throats.

The most recent statistics available show a steady increase in the percent of claims that men have filed with the EEOC—up from 7.5% in 1991 to about 12% in 1999. Many expect a greater increase given the U.S. Supreme Court's recent recognition of same sex harassment.

The exciting development is that gender may not matter in the eyes of the law. Many judges who have considered sexual harassment issues recently—including the U.S. Supreme Court justices, who took on a blockbusting number of four such cases during the 1998 term—have edged toward making it gender neutral. For example, most have stopped taking up space in their decisions over whether incidents of alleged harassment should best be viewed from the eyes of a reasonable woman or a reasonable man.

For a growing number of courts these days, the vantage point is common sense, the guiding premise that most workers, men and women, simply want to come to work and do their jobs.

B. Federal Law

Sexual discrimination in employment became illegal in the United States when the Civil Rights Act of 1964 was adopted. That Act established the Equal Employment Opportunities Commission (EEOC), which later issued regulations and guidelines on the subject of sexual harassment. (See Chapter 8, Section A, for a discussion of the EEOC.)

For several years, the EEOC took no action against sexual discrimination in employment. It was not until a long time later, however, that the agency began enforcing the law as written. In late 1991, in the wake of the well-publicized hearings to confirm Clarence Thomas as a U.S. Supreme Court Justice, Congress amended the Civil Rights Act to allow employees to sue for damages for sex discrimination, including harassment.

They'll Be Watching You, Too

Keep in mind that an important part of the definition of sexual harassment is that it is unwelcome behavior. Realistically, it is up to you, as the harassed person, to make clear that you find it objectionable.

Giving mixed signals can defeat your claim. For example, courts have suggested that telling sexual stories, engaging in sexual gestures, initiating sexual talk or soliciting sexual encounters with co-workers are all types of conduct that imply that sexual conduct was welcome.

You will also likely have a tougher time making out a claim of sexual harassment if you do not report the unwelcome behavior to others.

---

1. Who Is Covered

The Civil Rights Act extends protection against sexual harassment to employees of all public and private employers in the United States, including U.S. citizens working for a U.S. company in a foreign country. The Act also applies to labor unions—both to the workers they employ and to their members.

However, there is one major exception: The Civil Rights Act does not apply to any company that has fewer than 15 employees.

2. Remedies Available

Remedies that the courts or the EEOC can provide under the Civil Rights Act to a sexually harassed employee include: reinstatement and promotion in a job, an award of wages and job-connected losses, money damages and injunctive relief—including a court order to the employer to fashion a written sexual harassment policy and to pay attorneys' fees to the harassed employee.

Behind Open Doors: How the Battle Was Accidentally Waged

As introduced in Congress, the Civil Rights Act of 1964 only prohibited employment discrimination based on race, color, religion or national origin. Discrimination on the basis of sex was not included. It was attached to the bill at the last moment by conservative Southern opponents of the bill. They hoped that adding sexual equality was so obviously preposterous that it would scuttle the entire bill when it came to a final vote.

The very idea of prohibiting sex-based discrimination engendered mirth on the floor of Congress and on the editorial pages of major newspapers: Men, it was laughingly argued, could now sue to become Playboy bunnies. The Lyndon Johnson administration, however, wanted the Civil Rights Act passed badly enough that it decided not to oppose the amendment. The Civil Rights Act, including the ban on sex discrimination, became law. Only one of the Congressmen who had proposed the sex discrimination amendment actually voted for the bill.

C. State Laws

Some states have passed their own laws and regulations making sexual harassment illegal—usually called Fair Employment Practices (FEP) laws. But whether a harassed worker has good protection under state law depends on where he or she lives.

Some states, such as Louisiana, adopted a law prohibiting sexual discrimination but established no agency to enforce it. Others, like Georgia, set up an enforcement agency but enacted a law that only applied to public employees. Most states have done somewhat better, giving their enforcement agency or the courts the power both to reinstate a sexually harassed worker who was fired or forced out of a job, and to make the employer pay any lost wages. Alabama lags behind everyone—it has no law at all.

On the key issue of compensation for personal injuries, some states, like New York and Massachusetts, have enacted relatively good remedies that allow an employee to recover full compensation. Unfortunately, most state laws have no provision for awarding compensatory damages for personal injuries an employee suffers.

The following list includes citations of statutes on sexual harassment. In most cases, the state organization responsible for administering and enforcing the law against sexual harassment is the same as the state agency charged with enforcing state anti-discrimination laws. (See Chapter 8, Section B.) Call the state agency for information on how and where to file a claim. Where no state law or agency is available, contact the local EEOC office. (See Chapter 8, Section A.)

Additional Laws May Apply

If the chart below indicates that your state has no statute, this means there is no law that specifically addresses the issue. However, there may be a state administrative regulation or local ordinance that does control. Call your state labor department for more information. (See the Appendix for contact details.)

State Fair Employment Practices Laws	
Alabama	No statute
Alaska	Alaska Stat. §§18.80.010 to 300 and 22.10.020
Arizona	Ariz. Rev. Stat. §§41-1461 to 1465, 1481 to 1484
Arkansas	Ark. Code Ann. §§16-123-101 to 108
California	Cal. Gov't Code §§12900 to 12996
Colorado	Colo. Rev. Stat. §§24-34-301 to 406
Connecticut	Conn. Gen. Stat. §46a-51 to 99
Delaware	19 Del. Code Ann. §§710 to 718
District of Columbia	D.C. Code §1-2501 to 2557
Florida	Fla. Stat. Ann. §760.01 to .11
Georgia	Ga. Code Ann. §45-19-20 to 45
	Applies only to employees of the state of Georgia
Hawaii	Haw. Rev. Stat. §368-1 to 17, §378-1 to 9
Idaho	Idaho Code Ann. §67-5901 to 5912
Illinois	775 Ill. Comp. Stat. 5/1-101 to 5/2-105; 775 Ill. Comp. Stat. 5/7A-101 to 5/7A-104; 775 Ill. Comp. Stat. 5/8A-101 to 5/8A-104
Indiana	Ind. Code Ann. §22-9-1-1 to 18

Iowa	Iowa Code Ann. §601A.1 to .19
Kansas	Kan. Stat. Ann. §§44-1001 to 1013 and 44-1044
Kentucky	Ky. Rev. Stat. §§344.010 to .450
Louisiana	La. Rev. Stat. Ann. §23-1006
Maine	Maine Rev. Stat. Ann. tit. V, §§4551-4633
Maryland	Ann. Code of Md. Art. 49B, §§9 to 39
Massachusetts	Mass. Gen. Laws Ann. ch. 151B, §§1 to 10
Michigan	Mich. Comp. Laws §§37.2101 and following
Minnesota	Minn. Stat. Ann. §§363.01 to .15
Mississippi	Miss. Code Ann. §25-9-149 Although there is a state law prohibiting discrimination against state employees, no damages, exclusions or other specifics are mentioned in the statute.
Missouri	Mo. Ann. Stat. §213.010 to .137
Montana	Mont. Code Ann. §§49-2-101 to 49-2-601
Nebraska	Neb. Rev. Stat. §48-1101 to 1126
Nevada	Nev. Rev. Stat. Ann. §§613.310 to .430
New Hampshire	N.H. Rev. Stat. Ann. §354-A:1 to A:14
New Jersey	N.J. Stat. Ann. §10:5-1 to 28
New Mexico	N.M. Stat. Ann. §§28-1-1 to 15
New York	N.Y. Executive Law §§290 to 301
North Carolina	Gen. Stat. of N.C. §§143-422.1 to .3
North Dakota	N.D. Cent. Code Ann. §14-02.4-01 to 21
Ohio	Ohio Rev. Code Ann. §4112.01 to .99
Oklahoma	25 Okla. Stat. §§1101 to 1706
Oregon	Or. Rev. Stat. §659.010 to .990
Pennsylvania	43 Penn. Stat. Ann. §§951 to 962.2
Rhode Island	Gen. Laws of R.I. §28-5-1 to 40
South Carolina	S.C. Code Ann. §§1-13-10 to 110
South Dakota	S.D. Codified Laws §20-13-10 to 56
Tennessee	Tenn. Code Ann. §§4-21-101 to 408
Texas	Texas Code Ann. Lab. §21.001 to .259
Utah	Utah Code Ann. §34A-5-101 to 108
Vermont	21 Vt. Stat. Ann. §495h
Virginia	Va. Code Ann. §§2.1-714 to -725
Washington	Rev. Code of Wash. Ann. §49.60.010 to .330
West Virginia	W.Va. Code §5-11-1 to 19
Wisconsin	Wis. Stat. Ann. §11.31 to 39
Wyoming	Wyo. Stat. Ann. §27-9-101 to 108

D. Taking Steps to End Sexual Harassment

The alternatives described here can be viewed as a series of escalating steps in stopping sexual harassment. If a particular tactic does not end the objectionable behavior, you can switch to increasingly formal strategies until you find one that is effective.

1. Confront the Harasser

Often the best strategy for the employee sounds the simplest: Confront the harasser and persuade him or her to stop. This is not appropriate or sensible in every case, particularly when you have suffered injuries or are in some physical danger. But surprisingly often—most workplace experts say up to 90% of the time—it works.

Confronted directly, harassment is especially likely to end if it is at a fairly low level: off-color jokes, inappropriate comments about appearance, repeated requests for dates, sexist cartoons tacked onto the office refrigerator. Clearly saying no does more than assert your determination to stop the behavior. It makes clear that you find the behavior unwelcome—a critical part of the definition of sexual harassment. It is also a crucial first step if you later decide to take more formal action against the harassment.

Tell the harasser to stop. It is best to deal directly with the harassment when it occurs. But if your harasser surprised you with an obnoxious gesture or comment that caught you completely off-guard—a common tactic—you may have been too flabbergasted to respond at once. Or if you did respond, you may not have expressed yourself clearly. Either way, talk to the harasser the next day.

- Keep the conversation brief. Try to speak privately, out of the hearing range of supervisors and co-workers.
- Do not use humor to make your point. Joking may be too easily misunderstood—or interpreted as a sign that you don't take the situation seriously yourself.
- Be direct. It is usually better to make a direct request that a specific kind of behavior stop than to tell your harasser how you feel. For example, saying "I am uncomfortable with this" may be enough to get the point across to some people, but the subtlety may be lost on others. And of course, making you uncomfortable may be just the effect the harasser was after.
- Offer no excuses. Keep in mind that you're not the one whose behavior is inexcusable. Simply make the point and end the conversation. There is no need to offer excuses, such as: "My boyfriend wouldn't like it if we met at your apartment to discuss that new project."

Put it in writing. If your harasser persists, write a letter, spelling out what behavior you object to and why. Also specify what you want to happen next. If you feel the situation is serious or bound to escalate, make clear that you will take action against the harassment if it does not stop at once. If your company has a written policy against harassment, attach a copy of it to your letter.

Beware of Retaliation

In possibly volatile cases in some workplaces, do not overlook the possibility that some company witnesses may be blackmailed with the threat—often unspoken—of losing their jobs or being demoted if they cooperate with you in documenting or investigating a sexual harassment complaint. While retaliation is illegal, it is difficult to prove. If possible, try to document the harassment by talking with witnesses both inside and outside the company.

2. Use a Company Complaint Procedure

A court sometimes requires a company to write a comprehensive policy if it finds there has been a problem with sexual harassment. Many businesses are also adopting sexual harassment policies on their own, to foster a better atmosphere for employees.

If you are harassed at work, a sexual harassment policy can help you determine what behavior you can take action against and how to ensure the harassment is stopped.

Find out whether or not your employer has a sexual harassment policy by contacting the human resources department or the person who handles employee benefits. If there is no policy, lobby to get one.

And if your company does have a policy prohibiting harassment, it is more important than ever to take advantage of it. It may be some impetus to remember that prohibited sexual harassment is unwanted behavior—and showing that you complained about it is often considered part and parcel of being unwanted.

3. File a Complaint With a Government Agency

If the sexual harassment does not end after face-to-face meetings or after using the company complaint procedure, consider filing a complaint under the U.S. Civil Rights Act with the U.S. Equal Employment Opportunities Commission (EEOC) (see Chapter 8, Section A), or filing a complaint under a similar state law with a state Fair Employment Practices (FEP) agency. (See Section C above.)

Contacting these agencies does two important things:

- It sets in motion an investigation by the EEOC or the state FEP agency that may resolve the sexual harassment complaint, and
- It is a necessary prerequisite under the U.S. Civil Rights Act and under some state FEP laws if you want to file a lawsuit with the help of an attorney under the Civil Rights Act or under a state FEP law.

Sometimes an EEOC or a state FEP agency can resolve a sexual harassment dispute at no cost to the employee and with relatively little legal involvement. Almost all of these agencies provide some sort of conciliation service—a negotiation between the employer and employee to end the harassment and restore peace in the workplace. And most agencies protect the employee against retaliation for filing the complaint. Most agencies have the power to expand their investigation to cover more widespread sexual harassment within the company. A few state FEP agencies also provide an administrative hearing panel that can award money to compensate a harassed employee for personal injuries, although the EEOC and most state agencies do not have this important power.

The EEOC and state FEP agencies can resolve a lot of cases, but not all of them. Investigations sometimes drag on longer than the harassed employee is prepared to wait. Not all cases will yield to the conciliation efforts of such agencies; this is particularly true in severe cases of sexual harassment with significant personal injuries.

4. File a Private Lawsuit

If investigation and conciliation by the EEOC or a state FEP agency does not produce satisfactory results, your next step may be to file a lawsuit under the U.S. Civil Rights Act or under one of the state FEP statutes.

Even if you intend right from the beginning to file such a lawsuit, you frequently must first file a claim with a government agency, as described above. An employee must file a claim with the EEOC before bringing a lawsuit under the U.S. Civil Rights Act. Some states also require that the employee first file a claim with the state FEP agency before suing under state law. At some point after such claims are filed and investigated, the agency will issue you a document—usually referred to as a right to sue letter—that allows you to take your case to court. Going to court in such lawsuits requires getting legal advice from an attorney who is experienced in these types of cases. (See Chapter 18, Section D.)

Generally speaking, suing under the U.S. Civil Rights Act is better than relying on state law. Most state FEP laws allow you to win lost wages and benefits, but not compensation for physical and mental injuries such as stress and anxiety caused by the harassment. By contrast, the Civil Rights Act allows the employee to recover some money—out-of-pocket losses plus $50,000 to $300,000, depending upon the number of employees in the company. Its coverage, however, is limited to employers with 15 or more employees.

However, some states, such as New York and California, do better. They allow an employee to be compensated up to the full amount of damages proven without any artificial limits. Employees in those states will probably want to pursue their rights under state law or maybe a combination of state and federal law.

5. File a Tort Lawsuit

Bringing a tort action is often the last legal resort for sexually harassed workers. These legal actions provide a wider range of possible remedies than those available under the Civil Rights Act. You can sue for both compensatory damages for the emotional and physical distress suffered because of the workplace harassment, and potentially large punitive damages aimed at punishing the wrongdoer.

These lawsuits, which will usually require help from a lawyer, are based on traditional legal theories such as assault and battery, intentional infliction of emotional distress, interference with contract and defamation. These actions, called torts, are civil wrongs—and are filed in state courts like any other lawsuit based on a personal injury.

Tort actions allow, at least in theory, unlimited dollar verdicts for some of the most severe injuries wrought by the harassment: emotional and physical harm. These tort actions are particularly appropriate where a worker has suffered severe trauma from the psychological remnants of harassment—embarrassment, fright, humiliation—which can cause a permanent loss of self-esteem and take a heavy toll on emotional and physical health.

While a tort lawsuit action may be the best option for some harassed workers, it is the only possible remedy for others. As mentioned, if your employer has 14 or fewer employees, you are not covered by the U.S. Civil Rights Act and cannot file an EEOC complaint or a federal lawsuit for money.

Can You Collect If You Win?

Even a multi-million dollar court award will be worth only the paper it's written on unless the person or company found liable is able to pay. In most sexual harassment cases, collecting what is due and owing to you is not a problem because your employer as well as the harasser is liable—and either or both are likely to be solvent. Some larger employers also purchase a form of specialized insurance that covers attorneys' costs in defending against a harassment lawsuit.

As a general rule, employers are responsible for sexual harassment by supervisors and managers who work there. And they may even be held financially responsible for harassment you suffer at the hands of a co-worker if a supervisor either knew or should have known about the wrongful behavior.

Where a co-worker commits one act of harassment with no prior history or workplace pattern of such treatment, the employer may not be liable. When the employee alone is liable, it will probably be difficult to collect. And if the employer is small and has limited cash supply and no insurance to cover attorneys' fees for defending a sexual harassment lawsuit, it may be impossible to collect a large judgment.

E. Where to Get More Information

Contact the local office of the EEOC and your state FEP agency. Many will send you written materials on sexual harassment, and can provide information on local training programs, support groups and attorneys.

Some states and larger cities also have a Commission on the Status of Women or a state or local agency dealing specifically with women's issues which offer help to sexually harassed workers. The services these groups provide range from referrals to local groups, to advice and counseling, to legal referrals. Check your telephone book to see if there is such a group in your area.

Many unions and groups for union members are especially active in the fight against sexual harassment. Contact your local to find out if it offers any special services or guidance.

Also, some law schools have clinics that deal with sexual harassment or employment law. These clinics are usually staffed by students, who are assisted by experienced attorneys. Many provide in-person or telephone counseling and legal advice, and some will even represent you in court. Their services are low-cost, often free. Call law schools in your area and ask if they have such a clinic.

Finally, a number of organizations offer specialized information and guidance on evaluating sexual harassment in the workplace and many also offer legal referrals. (See the Appendix for contact details.)

Special Mention: 9to5

One group is doing so much to end sexual harassment that it deserves special mention.

9to5, National Association of Working Women, is a national nonprofit membership organization for American office workers that has local chapters throughout the country. It maintains a toll-free confidential telephone hotline, staffed by trained job counselors, and provides information and referrals on how to deal with sexual harassment and other problems on the job. Books and reports on sexual harassment are available at a discount to members, who can also get legal referrals to attorneys specializing in sexual harassment. A newsletter is published five times a year. Some 9to5 local chapters offer sexual harassment support groups and referrals to training resources.

9to5, National Association of Working Women
231 West Wisconsin Avenue, Suite 900
Milwaukee, WI 53203
414-274-0925 (General information)
800-522-0925 (Hotline)

CHAPTER

10

LOSING OR LEAVING A JOB

The truth will surprise you: No law gives you an automatic right to keep your job. In fact, most of the legal principles and practices of the workplace are indisputably on the side of the employer who fires you.

You can be fired for a host of traditional and obvious reasons: incompetence, excessive absences, violating certain laws or company rules, sleeping or taking drugs on the job. And other reasons for firings are gaining in popularity—most notably, because of economic need occasioned by a downturn in company profits or demands. In most cases, an employer does not need to provide any notice before giving an employee walking papers.

Still, there are limits. The laws do guarantee you some rights on the way out the door. And because of the grand importance of job security to the majority of Americans, employees are increasingly fighting for and slowly garnering more rights in the workplace. In fact, when a case in which a former employee challenges a firing makes it to court, jurors of late are apt to concentrate not on whether the worker committed a wrong and deserved to be fired; they look at whether the employer treated the fired soul fairly and reasonably.

Even at the tail end of your work relationship, employers do not have the right to discriminate against you illegally (see Chapter 8) or to violate state or federal laws, such as those controlling wages and hours. (See Chapter 3.) And there are a number of other more complex reasons that may make it illegal for an employer to fire you—basically boiling down to the Golden Rule that an employer must deal with you fairly and honestly.

If you lost your job—or have good reason to think you are about to lose it—it may behoove you to become familiar with the various situations in which it may be illegal to fire an employee. (See Chapter 11.)

A. The Doctrine of Employment at Will

Once again, for the value of its shock: People employed in private industry have no automatic legal right to their jobs.

That is because of the long-established legal doctrine of employment at will—a term you are most likely to hear cited by your boss or your company's lawyers if you speak up and protest your dismissal. An employer's right to unilaterally determine whether or not you should stay on the payroll stems from a 1894 case (*Payne v. Western & Atlantic RR,* 81 Tenn. 507), in which the court ruled that employers do not need a reason to fire employees; they may fire any or all of their workers at will. Even if the reason for dismissal is morally wrong, the court held, no legal wrong has occurred and the government has no basis to intervene.

The management of America's factories was still in the experimental stage in the 1890s when that case was decided. The business community successfully argued then, and in cases that followed, that factories could not be operated profitably unless employers were free to hire and fire as they chose. The employment at will doctrine has been reinforced over and over again by subsequent court rulings—and expanded to include not only factories but also virtually all other types of private industry jobs.

But the doctrine has been weakened a bit since the 1970s by rulings in wrongful discharge suits in which former employees question the legality of their firings (discussed in Chapter 11, Section A)—and by some new laws that are more favorable to employees. For example, in Montana, employees who have completed probation are protected from being fired unless there is good cause (Mont. Code Ann. §39-2-901 to 905). And some states have made it illegal to fire employees for taking time off to care for a sick child (discussed in Chapter 5, Section B) or because they are gay or lesbian (discussed in Chapter 8, Section H).

1. Exceptions to the Rule

There are a few important exceptions to the employment at will doctrine that may make it possible for employees to hang onto their jobs. And as anxieties deepen over job security, more employees are taking the time and effort to contradict their employers' assertions that it may be time for them to go.

a. Written promises

You have the easiest chance of arguing that you are not an employee at will if there is a strong written statement signifying that you are excepted from the employment at will doctrine. These statements are scarce and getting scarcer.

For example, most collective bargaining agreements that set out union members' rights state that union members can be fired only "for good cause." So while union members are still technically employees at will, their agreements often make them exceptions to the general rule, requiring that employers point to a specific, legally valid reason before firing them. (See Chapter 16.)

And some employees negotiate and sign detailed contracts with their employers—contracts which set out the specific terms of their employment, including salary and relocation rights. Employment contracts are rare—usually reserved for only the uppermost company executives and other notables such as professional athletes. Those holding employment contracts are usually not subject to the employment at will doctrine; their contracts spell out the length of their employment and specifically note when and how the employment relationship can end.

b. Implied promises

Some former employees have successfully contested their dismissals by pointing to the promising words found in the employee manuals they were handed when they were hired.

A few courts have held, for example, that where company manuals state that employees become permanent after a certain time, or that they must be given a hearing before being fired, employers must deliver on those promises. However, most savvy businesses these days are well-acquainted with this legal loophole, so few of them now include such vague promises in their employee manuals.

c. Breaches of good faith and fair dealing

Because it is an uphill battle to prove that a written or implied promise tantamount to a contract ever existed, it follows that it's even tougher to prove that one has been violated. And barring discrimination or some other egregious wrongdoing in the process, your best hope of fighting a firing is to claim that your former employer breached what is referred to as a duty of good faith and fair dealing.

Courts have held that employers have committed breaches of good faith and fair dealing by:

- firing or transferring employees to prevent them from collecting sales commissions
- misleading employees about their chances for future promotions and wage increases
- fabricating reasons for firing an employee on the basis of on-the-job performance when the real motivation is to replace that employee with someone who will work for lower pay
- soft pedaling the bad aspects of a particular job, such as the need to travel through dangerous neighborhoods late at night, and
- repeatedly transferring an employee to remote, dangerous or otherwise undesirable assignments to coerce him or her into quitting without collecting the severance pay and other benefits that would otherwise be due.

d. Violations of public policy

The employment at will doctrine also flies out the window if a worker is fired merely to be quieted from complaining about illegal conduct or a wrong an employer committed, such as failing to pay workers a minimum wage or overtime pay when it is required. Indeed, it is illegal to violate public policy

when firing a worker—that is, fire for a reason that most people would find
morally or ethically wrong. (See Chapter 11, Section B.)

2. Employees' Rights

The other side of the employment at will logic is that employees are also free to
leave a job at any time; an employer cannot force you to stay in a job you no
longer wish to keep. And while it is customary to give an employer notice
before leaving a job, it is not usually required by law. The right to leave a job at
any time feels like small recompense for most workers. Obviously, most legal
battles are fought by former employees who want their jobs back, not employers demanding that employees stay on.

B. Finding Out Why You Were Fired

Few job losses come as complete surprises. Unless you are the unfortunate heir
to a sudden unforeseen cutback in the workforce, you are likely to have seen
the end of your employment coming well before it arrived. This is particularly
true if you are fired because your employer claims your work was below par or
that you violated a particular workplace rule.

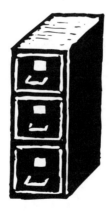

1. If You Have Been Disciplined

Although an employer has the right to fire you on the spot for substandard performance or stealing from the company coffer, most employers proceed more gingerly these days—beginning with a verbal warning and progressing to a written warning to probation to suspension, then to dismissal.

There are a number of steps you can take when you suspect the end is near. You are not legally entitled to any progressive warning system. But if you find yourself on the receiving end of a disciplinary notice, there are several steps you should take to avoid losing your job.

- Be sure you understand exactly what work behavior is being challenged. If you are unclear, ask for a specific meeting with your supervisor or human resources staff to discuss the issue more thoroughly.

- If you disagree with allegations that your work performance or behavior is poor, ask for the assessment in writing. You may want to add a written clarification to your own personnel file—but should do so only if you feel your employer's assessment is inaccurate. First take some time to reflect and perhaps discuss your situation with friends and family. If your clarification is inaccurate or sounds vengeful, your words could be twisted against you as evidence of your inability to work as a team player, take constructive criticism or some other convenient company slang.

- Look for written company policy on discipline procedures in the employee handbook or a separate document. If the policy says certain measures "must," "will" or "shall" be followed before an employee will be dismissed, then you have more clout in demanding that the steps be followed. Point out the rules and ask why they are being bent in your situation. That may help buy you more time so that you can change your work habits—or allow you to wait until a workplace controversy dies down or the situation improves in some other way.

- Read behind the lines to see whether your disciplining or firing may be discriminatory or in other ways unfair. Pay particular attention to the timing: Were you put on probation shortly before your rights in the company pension plan vested? Look also at uneven applications of discipline: Are women more often given substandard performance reviews or fired before being elevated to supervisor?

2. Finding Out the Reason

Before any holes had been punched in the employment at will doctrine, companies often refused to give employees any reasons for being fired. Since a company had the legal right to hire and fire without any justification, most opted not to invite trouble by stating a reason for firing.

Today, many companies have reversed their policies on giving reasons for dismissals. Because courts throughout the country are gradually establishing more rights for fired employees (discussed in Chapter 11), many companies, particularly large corporations that are attractive targets for wrongful discharge lawsuits, now are careful to provide at least the appearance of fair and even-handed treatment of employees who are fired. Company owners and managers typically do this by carefully documenting the employee's allegedly unacceptable work performance. Then, the employer can provide the employee—and a court, should it come to that—with specific and tangible documentation of the cause of firing.

If you are fired, make your best effort to obtain a clear statement of the employer's reasons for doing so. Office or factory rumors, your suspicions or your spouse's hunches just will not suffice. If you eventually decide to challenge your dismissal (discussed in Chapter 11, Section D), the reasons that your former employer stated for firing you will almost certainly become a major point in any legal battle that may develop.

C. Documenting Your Dismissal

Even if you decide not to challenge the legality of your firing, you will be in a much better position to enforce all of your workplace rights if you carefully document the circumstances. For example, if you apply for unemployment insurance benefits and your former employer challenges that application, you will typically need to prove that you were dismissed for reasons beyond your control. (See Chapter 12, Section D.)

There are a number of time-tested ways to document the circumstances leading to your firing.

Labels Make No Difference

People tend to think that getting fired means that you did something wrong on the job, and that when other terms are used—such as dismissal, discharge, layoff, staff cut, reduction in force, downsizing and the all-too-sane-sounding rightsizing—it somehow means something less onerous. In hopes of preventing bad community relations and wrongful discharge lawsuits, many companies use these gentler words to describe firings.

Some companies have gone so far as to announce the firing of large groups of employees by using sterile, institutional terms such as Reorganizational Incentives or Activity Analysis and Review. Still other companies have described the process of firing groups of employees as early retirement—even where the people being dismissed are not being given anywhere near enough money to continue to live the rest of their lives without working.

Whenever you are permanently dismissed from a job without being given sufficient income to continue living without working, all these terms mean the same thing: You've been fired. (For more information on layoffs, see Section G.)

1. Keeping a Paper Trail

Long before being fired, you may sense that something has gone wrong in the relationship between you and your employer, even if there has been no formal disciplinary action against you. Perhaps your first clue will be that your pay has been stuck at one level with no raises for an unusually long time. Or you may notice that none of your work assignments extend more than a few weeks. Whatever the sign that your job may be in jeopardy, use it as a reason to begin keeping a log of your interactions with your employer.

Record and date each work-related event, such as performance reviews, commendations or reprimands, salary increases or decreases and even informal comments that your supervisor makes to you about your work. Note the date, time and location for each event; which members of management were involved; and whether or not there were witnesses. Whenever possible, back up your log with written materials your employer has issued, such as copies of the employee handbook, memos, brochures and employee orientation videos.

In addition, ask to see your personnel file. (See Chapter 6, Section A, for a discussion of privacy concerns.) Make a copy of all reports and reviews in it. Because personnel administrators are notoriously covetous of employee files, you may have to make repeated requests to see your file or pay a certain amount of money to copy each page in the file. It will be money well spent.

Many former employees are startled to learn that their personnel files have been tampered with by unscrupulous former employers. If you fear this might happen, make an additional copy of your file or of relevant reports or performance reviews and mail them to yourself by certified mail. Then, should matters heat up later—or should a court battle become necessary—you will have dated proof of how the documents looked before any tampering took place.

2. Getting Written Explanations

There are a number of reasons why you might want to get a written explanation from a former employer of why you were fired: to see whether the reason your former employer gives meshes with your own hunches and, in the hardest situations, to use as documentation if you feel your dismissal was discriminatory or otherwise illegal. Written explanations may also help you in a later job search, as you will be better able to assess whether a soon-to-be-former employer is likely to give a good recommendation to your prospective employers. (See Chapter 11, Section A5 for more on employer references.)

In a rare but possible scenario, you may receive an explanation of your firing that is so shocking, so wrongheaded and so mean-spirited that it seems that its purpose is to keep you from being hired again. It may indicate that your employer is blacklisting you—a practice that is illegal in many states. (See Chapter 11, Section C.)

a. Information from former employers

Nearly half the states have laws, sometimes known as service letter laws, that require employers to provide former employees with letters describing work histories. (See the chart below.)

Service letter laws vary greatly from state to state. In Minnesota, for example, an employer must provide a written statement of the reasons for an employee's dismissal within five days after the employee requests such a statement in writing. Kansas also has a type of service letter law, but it does not require a former employer to list a reason for your dismissal. Employers in Kansas must state only your length of employment, job classification and wage rate.

You Don't Get It Both Ways

When asking a former employer for a service letter, you are asking for the truth, the whole truth and nothing but the whole truth as to why you were fired. But reasons for firing are subjective. And chances are, you may not like what you read. Note that a number of states specifically protect employers from being sued for defamation because of what they have written in a service letter. Most laws require a former employer to provide a statement that is "truthful," or "in good faith."

Did They Say Merge or Squeeze Out?

The economic uncertainty of our times has forced many formerly hardy employers to scuttle about for funds. Some pressed companies decide that the best route out of their woes is to restructure the business completely. Many of them opt to merge with or acquire other companies. This can leave all employees involved in the lurch—unsure of their rights, unsure of the security of their jobs.

The law is lurching to keep up with these corporate gyrations, too. Legal questions are just now beginning to emerge that may help shape employees' rights during mergers and acquisitions.

A few hot spots are already clear.

Imperiled personnel information. When two companies merge, the negotiation process leaves all the transitory employees vulnerable: Their salaries are disclosed to potential buying companies, their personnel files are often laid bare as part of full disclosure before the deal gets closed.

Robbed of negotiation rights. Employees who are left over after a merger are most often handed a Take It or Leave It package: They can accept the position available at the reconstituted company—or walk. The deal their employer strikes may rob them of the chance to negotiate a severance package.

Noncompete rights and wrongs. A number of employees sign noncompete agreements when they come on board, in which they typically agree not to go into the same type of business within a certain geographical region for a specified number of years. This is to prevent workers from running off with trade secrets and established clients by setting up a competing business.

But as more of the specialized companies merge to become conglomerates, this will mean that employees who quit or are fired will have fewer places to look for work.

Stay tuned for developments.

The Glowing Letter of Recommendation: Sometimes, It's Better to Remain Mum

A California court recently turned the tables and sent out a warning signal to employers who are inclined to leave an important element—the truth—out of letters of recommendation. While the full impact of the case is yet to be felt, it may signal to workers that they can expect less glowing letters of recommendation from former employers.

When Robert Gadams went looking for a job with the Livingston Union School District, he came armed with letters of recommendation from former employers—all of them painting him in no uncertain glowing terms.

One letter effused: "He is a 'perfectionist' and concentrates on 'getting the very best' from everyone. I wouldn't hesitate to recommend Mr. Gadams for any position!"

"Considering his experience at the elementary, high school and adult education levels," wrote another former employer, "I would recommend him for almost any administrative position he wishes to pursue."

Still a third letter described Gadams as "an upbeat, enthusiastic administrator who relates well to the students."

In fact, Gadams left all three of these positions after being investigated for sexual misconduct with female students.

Failing to read between the lines of the enthusiastic letters, Livingston hired Gadams as vice principal at once. Shortly after that, he was accused of sexually molesting a 13-year-old student in his new office.

The student sued, claiming that school authorities who failed to disclose their former employee's propensity for sexually molesting students were liable for the harm he caused her. The court agreed that the school districts had a duty not to misrepresent Gadams's suitability for the job as vice principal. It held that the student could base claims of negligent misrepresentation, fraud and negligence on the disingenuous letters (*Randi W. v. Livingston Union School District*, 41 Cal. App. 4th 400 (1996)).

But the final word on Gadams's future employability—and on potential liability for letters of recommendation—is still to come. While the California Supreme Court affirmed the findings of misrepresentation and fraud in January 1997, he is still contemplating an appeal.

Additional Laws May Apply

If the chart below indicates that your state has no statute, this means there is no law that specifically addresses the issue. However, there may be a state administrative regulation or local ordinance that does control. Call your state labor department for more information. (See the Appendix for contact details.)

State Laws on Information From Former Employers

Alabama	No statute
Alaska	An employer may disclose information about an employee's job performance at the request of a former employee or prospective employer without fear of civil liability, as long as the information is truthful. Alaska Stat. §09.65.160
Arizona	Employers may provide information on a former employee's education, training, experience, qualifications and job performance if another employer requests it. A copy of any written communication must be sent to the employee. Ariz. Rev. Stat. Ann. §23-1361(b)
Arkansas	Upon written consent from a current or former employee, an employer may disclose to a prospective employer information about that employee's employment history, drug or alcohol tests for the past year, most recent performance evaluation, violent or threatening behavior, reasons for leaving employment and eligibility for rehire. The written evaluation is valid for six months or as long as the employee's application is valid with the prospective employer, whichever is less. Statute does not require the former employer to provide employment history information. Ark. Code Ann. §11-3-204
California	If requested, an employer may give a truthful statement as to why an employee voluntarily left or was discharged. Employers who furnish such information without being specifically asked to do so or who use a special mark, sign or code whose meaning differs from what would be expressed by words, are guilty of a misdemeanor and may be sued for treble damages. Cal. Lab. Code §1053 Every public utility must, upon request, give a former employee a letter stating the period and type of service rendered by that person. Cal Lab. Code §1055 A former employer who misrepresents, prevents or attempts to prevent a former employee from obtaining employment is guilty of a misdemeanor and may be sued for triple damages. Cal. Lab. Code §§1050, 1053, 1054 Any person who tells another about an employee's felony conviction, with the intent of causing the employee to be fired, is guilty of a misdemeanor if the employee is in fact fired as a result. Cal. Penal Code §2947

	An employer may not give misinformation to prevent a former employee from obtaining employment. Cal. Lab. Code §1050
Colorado	If a bank or financial institution requests information about a current or former employee, it is not unlawful for another bank or financial institution to disclose information about that employee's involvement in a theft or other financial wrongdoing. Colo. Rev. Stat. §8-2-111.5
	An employer may give another person "fair and unbiased information" about a current or former employee as long as it is not knowingly false, misleading or disclosed for a malicious purpose. Colo. Rev. Stat. §8-2-114
	A former employer may provide to a prospective employer information about a current or former employee's job history, work-related skills, abilities and habits, whether the employee is eligible for rehire and the reason for separation. Upon request, the employer must either mail or give a copy of the information to the employee. Colo. Rev. Stat. §8-2-114
Connecticut	No statute
Delaware	Upon request from a healthcare or child care facility, an employer must provide a service letter for a former employee within ten days. Del. Code Ann. tit. 19, §708
	An employer may disclose the following information about a current or former employee to a prospective employer: job performance or work-related characteristics, ability to perform and actions in violation of any law. Del. Code Ann. Tit. 19, §709
District of Columbia	No statute
Florida	Employers who are required to conduct criminal record background checks as a condition of employment must release copies of current and former employees' personnel records to any other employer who requests them. Information may include any disciplinary matters or reasons for termination. Fla. Stat. Ann. §435.10
	Employers may disclose information about a current or former employee to a prospective employer, upon request from either the prospective employer or the employee. Fla. Stat. Ann. §655.51
Georgia	An employer who provides factual information about a former employee's job performance, at the request of the employee or a prospective employer, is presumed to be acting in good faith unless doing so violates a nondisclosure agreement or the information is otherwise confidential. Ga. Code Ann. §34-1-4
Hawaii	An employer who in good faith provides to a prospective employer information or an opinion about a current or former employee's job performance is immune from civil liability. Haw. Rev. Stat. §663-1.95
Idaho	An employer may provide information about the job performance, professional conduct or evaluation of a current or former employee at the request of the employee or a prospective employer. Idaho Code §44-201
Illinois	An employer who provides truthful, performance-related information or an opinion about a current or former employee in response to an employment reference inquiry is protected from civil liability. 745 Ill. Comp. Stat. §§46/5 and 46/10

Indiana	Upon written request from an employee, an employer must write a letter regarding the nature and duration of service, and truly stating the cause, if any, for the ending of employment. The prospective employer must give the prospective employee copies of any letters received from current or former employees, as long as the employee makes a written request within 30 days of applying for employment. Ind. Code Ann. §22-6-3-1 Employers may not prevent a fired employee from obtaining another job, but may state the correct reason for a former employee's dismissal to a prospective employer. Ind. Code Ann. §§22-5-3-1
Iowa	Employers who provide work-related information about a current or former employee upon request by a prospective employer or upon request or authorization from the employee are immune from civil liability unless: the information violates the employee's civil rights or the employer knowingly gives the information to a person who has no legitimate reason to receive it. Iowa Code §91B.2
Kansas	Upon written request, an employer must provide a former employee with a letter stating the former employee's length of employment, job classification and wage rate. Kan. Stat. Ann. §44-808(3)
Kentucky	No statute
Louisiana	Employers who provide accurate information about a current or former employee's job performance or reasons for separation, when requested to do so by the employee or a prospective employer, are immune from civil liability. La. Rev. Stat. §23:291(A)
Maine	Upon written request, an employer must provide a discharged employee with a written list of the reasons for being fired. An employer who fails to do so within 15 days of receiving the request may be subject to a fine of $50 to $500. Me. Rev. Stat. Ann. tit. 26 §630 Employers may provide information about a former employee's job performance or work record to a prospective employer. Me. Rev. Stat. Ann. tit. 26 §598
Maryland	No statute
Massachusetts	When asked for an employment reference, hospitals, home health agencies and hospice programs are not liable for disclosing information about a current or former employee's employment history or reasons for separation. Mass. Ann. Laws. ch. 111, §721.1/2
Michigan	An employer may not divulge a disciplinary report, letter, reprimand or other disciplinary action to a third person unless the employer gives the employee notice by first class mail on or before the day of disclosure. The employer must not disclose information about disciplinary actions that are more than four years old unless they are the subjects of a legal action. Mich. Comp. Laws §§423.506 and 507
Minnesota	Employers must provide an employee who has been fired with a written listing of the reasons for the employee's dismissal. However, the former employee must request that listing in writing within five working days after the discharge. Minn. Stat. Ann. §181.933

Mississippi	No statute
Missouri	Employers with seven or more employees must provide a discharged employee with a letter stating the length of the former employment, the nature of the job held and the reasons for the discharge. This letter must be provided to the former employee within 45 days after the company receives a request for it. Employers who do not comply with this request are liable for compensatory and possible punitive damages. Mo. Ann. Stat. §290.140 An employer may respond in writing and disclose the information contained in a service letter after receiving a written request from a prospective employer. An employer may respond in writing and disclose the information contained in a service letter. Mo. Ann. Stat. §290.152
Montana	Upon request from a discharged employee, an employer must provide that employee with a written statement of the reasons for the discharge. Mont. Code Ann. §39-2-801
Nebraska	Upon request by a discharged or quitting employee, employers in public service corporations and contractors doing business in the state must provide a statement of the nature and duration of the services rendered by the employee and the reasons for the termination. An employer who refuses or fails to issue a service letter or who provides incorrect information is guilty of a misdemeanor punishable by a $1,000 fine, up to a year in prison or both. Neb. Rev. Stat. §§48-209 to 48-211
Nevada	Former employees who held a job for 60 days or more may demand from the former employer a written statement of the reason for their departure from the job. Nev. Rev. Stat. §613.210
New Hampshire	No statute
New Jersey	No statute
New Mexico	When requested to provide a reference for a current or former employee, an employer acting in good faith is immune from liability for comments on the employee's job performance. N.M. Stat. Ann. §50-12-1
New York	No statute
North Carolina	Employers may disclose information about a current or former employee's job performance, including skills, abilities and traits related to future employment, eligibility for rehire and reasons for separation, if requested by a prospective employer or by the employee. N.C. Gen. Stat. §1-539.12
North Dakota	An employer is immune from civil liability for providing a truthful reference to a prospective employer, including dates of service, wage history and job description and duties. N.D. Cent. Code. §34-02-18
Ohio	A railroad employee is entitled to a written statement of reasons within ten days of his or her discharge. Ohio Rev. Code Ann. §4973.03.
Oklahoma	Employees of public service corporations and their contractors are entitled to a statement of the nature of service, duration and cause of discharge or quitting. No form letters are allowed, and every letter must be signed by a company official. An employer who fails to provide this letter in its correct form is guilty of a misdemeanor, punishable by a fine of $100 to $500 and by one month to one year in jail. Okla. Stat. Ann. tit. 40, §171

	An employer who gives information about an employee's job performance to a prospective employer is immune from liability if the employee requests the information. The statute does not apply if the employer knowingly transmits false information, or acts with malice or reckless disregard of the truth. Okla. Stat. Ann. tit. 40, §61
Oregon	An employer may disclose information about a former employee's job performance to a prospective employer upon request of the employee or the prospective employer. Or. Rev. Stat. §30.178
Pennsylvania	No statute
Rhode Island	No statute
South Carolina	An employer who responds to a written request concerning a current or former employee's job performance and reasons for separation is immune from liability as long as the information disclosed is truthful. S.C. Code Ann. §41-1-65
South Dakota	An employer who discloses information about an employee's job performance at the request of an employer or prospective employer is presumed to be acting in good faith. The employee is entitled to a copy of the written response. S.D. Codified Laws §60-4-12
Tennessee	An employer who provides truthful, fair and unbiased information about an employee's job performance is presumed to be acting in good faith, but he may not disclose information that is knowingly false, deliberately misleading or disclosed for a malicious purpose. Tenn. Code Ann. §50-1-05
Texas	Upon request by an employee or a prospective employer, an employer may furnish a written truthful statement of the reason for discharge. The statement cannot be used as the basis for a criminal or civil charge of libel. Tex. Lab. Code Ann. §52.031(d)
	An employer must provide an employee with a true statement of the causes for discharge within ten days of the employee's request and must give the employee a copy of any information disclosed to a prospective employer, along with the names of the people to whom it was sent. Texas Civil Stat., Art. 5196(5)
	Employers who disclose truthful information about a current or former employee's job performance, including attendance, attitudes, effort, behavior and skills are immune from civil liability, as long as the request comes from either the employee or a prospective employer. Tex. Lab. Code §§103.001 to 103.003
Utah	An employer who, upon request and in good faith, provides information about the job performance of an employee to a prospective employer, may not be held civilly liable. There is no protection if the employer acts with malice or an intent to mislead. Utah Code Ann. §34-42-1
Vermont	No statute
Virginia	No statute
Washington	Within ten days of a request by a discharged employee, former employers must furnish a signed statement of the reason for the discharge and the date it was effective. Wash. Admin. Code R. §296-126-050

West Virginia	An officer of a financial institution may provide employment information about an employee or former employee to another financial institution when that information is limited to the employee's violation of a statute, rule or regulation related to financial institutions and the violation has been reported to the proper authorities. W.Va. Code §31A-4-44
Wisconsin	An employer may tell a bondsman or a prospective employer the true reason for a former employee's discharge, but not with the intent of preventing the employee from getting work. Wis. Stat. Ann. §134.02(2) An employer who, upon request from a prospective employer or a former employee, provides a reference about the employee's job performance and employment qualifications, is immune from civil liability. Wis. Stat. Ann. §895.487
Wyoming	An employer who discloses information about a former employee's job performance to a new or prospective employer is immune from civil liability. Wyo. Stat. §27-1-113

b. Requesting an explanation

If you live in a state that has a service letter law requiring explanations of dismissals, and the employer who fired you does not provide you with one, request one in writing.

Sample Letter

June 10, 20XX

Ellen Ullentine
President
Tasteless Frozen Pizzas Inc.
123 Main Street
Anywhere, MO 54321

Dear Ms. Ullentine:

As required by Missouri Statutes Section 290.140, I request from you a letter stating the length of my employment with Tasteless Frozen Pizzas Inc., the nature of my work there and the reason I was dismissed from employment.

Please note that this law requires you to provide me with such a letter within 45 days of when you receive this request.

Sincerely,

Paul Smith
321 Front Street
Anywhere, MO 54321
234-555-6666

Some laws specify a time limit for requesting service letters. But if possible, it is usually wise to make your request within a day or two of your dismissal to make sure that you meet any such deadlines and to prevent the passing of time from affecting people's memories. Send your request for a service letter by certified mail so that you can prove, if necessary, that you made your request within any time limits specified.

c. States without laws or explanations

If you live in a state that does not have a service letter law, there is a chance that your employer will not offer you any written explanation for your firing. This is particularly likely if the company dismissing you is small or does not know much about workplace law and current legal techniques for firing employees. If no written explanation of your dismissal is given, ask the person who officially informs you of your firing for a written explanation of the company's decision to dismiss you. Be firm but polite; keep in mind that having to fire someone is an extremely stressful assignment for even the most experienced managers.

Companies usually want dismissed employees to be out of their buildings and away from the remaining employees as quickly as possible to prevent vengeful sabotage or spreading anti-company sentiment. Therefore, a person being fired exercises a substantial amount of negotiating power by merely sitting in place in front of the person doing the firing, quietly insisting on written documentation until the request is satisfied. Remember, however, that in some companies, using your posterior as a negotiating tool, if pushed too far, can get you escorted out forcibly by the corporate security force or local police.

At Long Last, Have You No Decency?

Firings rankle all around. They can devastate the fired soul. They can demoralize those left to pick up the slack. And they can turn formerly rational workplace managers into paranoid battalion chiefs.

Witness one scenario that is becoming familiar: An unsuspecting employee shows up for work and is fired on the spot, told to pack up all personal belongings in the office and escorted out of the building by a guard. Cowed co-workers are left to watch, gossip and wonder what wrong could be grievous enough to warrant such cloak and dagger behavior.

When there is no threat that an employee will make off with top corporate secrets or sabotage next season's new product line, such unwanted escorts are embarrassing. And they may now be illegal.

Courts have recently brought some sensitivity back into such scenes, recognizing that in the laden situation of a workplace firing, actions speak as least as loudly as words.

- A Minnesota social worker was fired recently after he disagreed with the proper treatment for a resident patient. On his last day of work, a treatment center director accompanied the man to his office, stayed while he packed his belongings and led him out the main entrance. The former worker won a case for defamation. The court reasoned, rather poetically, that: "Language may include gestures or actions; communication is not a captive of the voice." (*Bolton v. Dept. of Human Serv.*, 527 N.W.2d 149 (Minn. App.1995)).

- When a General Motors plant began experiencing problems with employees, it stepped up security and surveillance. One foreman, without being able to articulate why, became suspicious of a particular employee. As the employee left work that day, security guards blocked his path, twisted his arm behind his back and forced him to open his jacket, pants and shirt. No contraband was found on the employee. But he later found his way to court—and won a slander lawsuit against GM. The court reasoned that the guards' heavy-handed activities logically conveyed to passersby the thought that the employee was a thief (*General Motors Corp. v. Piskor*, 340 A.2d 767 (M.D. App. 1995)).

d. Letters of understanding

If you have done everything within the limits of civility, but your employer still refuses to give you written documentation of the reasons for your dismissal, you may be in for a wait—and some extra work—before you get it. If your state is among the majority that have no laws requiring such documentation, there is not much else you can do to force the issue at the time of your dismissal. Later, you may obtain documentation through some of the laws granting employees access to their personnel files (see Chapter 6, Section A), or by filing a wrongful discharge lawsuit (see Chapter 11, Section A) and demanding the company's internal documents concerning your employment during the course of the lawsuit.

But before that, you might want to write a letter of understanding to the person who fired you. This is especially important if you received some mixed messages upon being fired. Of course, it is to your advantage to get your employer to specify the reason for your firing that makes you seem the least culpable—and the most attractive to prospective employers.

Although you should mail your letter of understanding promptly, it is usually best to let it sit for a day or two after writing it. Then, read it over again to make sure you have kept it businesslike and to the point. Getting fired is a very emotional event—one that often generates more than a little anger and desire for revenge in even the most saintly people.

Correspondence between you and your former employer may eventually become the basis of future negotiations or even courtroom evidence, and you do not want its credibility to be tainted by ink from a poison pen.

Send your letter of understanding by certified mail so that you will be able to prove that the company received it. Using certified mail in this case may also help drive home to your former employer that you are serious about enforcing your rights concerning your dismissal.

If the company responds to your letter, you have obtained at least one piece of documentation of its reason for firing you. If the company does not respond to your letter after a month or so, you can probably assume that the reason stated in your letter of understanding is correct.

Sample Letter

August 2, 20XX

Aggie Supervisor
XYZ Company
2222 Lake Street
Anytown, CA 12345

Dear Ms. Supervisor:

I'm writing to clarify the reasons for my dismissal from employment at XYZ Company on July 29, 20XX.

My understanding is that I was dismissed because there was a sharp decline in the market for our product, seamless rolled rings, due to the recent cutback in government military spending.

If you feel that my understanding is incorrect, please advise me in writing by August 16, 20XX.

Sincerely,

John Employee
123 Any Street
Anytown, CA 12345
234-555-6666

3. Additional Documentation

Other important forms of documentation for your firing may come your way in the weeks following your dismissal. For example, if you file a claim for unemployment compensation, your former employer will have to respond to that claim. That response will eventually be translated into a document that the local unemployment insurance office will provide to you. (See Chapter 12.)

Store all such documents in a file folder, shoebox or some safe place where they will not get lost or destroyed—and where you can find and organize them easily.

D. Waiving Your Right to Sue

In large companies, the firing process may work like this: A member of the human resource management staff hands you a formal written notice that you are fired. You are then asked to sign a statement indicating that you have read the documents and that you accept what is written in them. You are given a check for a few extra months of severance pay, although this is beyond the company's legal obligations. (See Section F.) You will then be told that the check will be released to you immediately if you sign a waiver of any rights to take legal action against the company as a result of your dismissal.

This method of firing can seem cruel or unfair. But in the past, it was effective for some companies in discouraging wrongful discharge lawsuits.

It is no longer a foolproof tactic. An increasing number of employees who have signed waivers of their rights to file a lawsuit over their firing have later succeeded in having the courts throw out the waivers by arguing, for example, that the waivers were signed under duress. Whether signing such a waiver will prevent you from suing your former employer depends on the circumstances of each individual case, however, so there is no way of predicting the power of a waiver in advance.

Going along with the firing will typically mean you will get immediate severance pay. However, if you have doubts about the validity of your dismissal, withhold your signature on any waiver of your right to sue while you think over the company's offer, obtain more information and perhaps hire a lawyer. (See Chapter 18.) You take the chance of not getting the money and documentation that the company waves in front of you, but you will lower your risk of signing away essential rights.

Beware of the Early Retirement Waiver

If you are asked to sign a waiver of your right to sue in return for participation in an early retirement program offered by your former employer, the Older Workers Benefit Protection Act may give you the right to consider the company's offer for 45 days before you accept or reject it, and seven more days to revoke a decision to accept the company's offer. (See Chapter 8, Section E.)

E. Your Right to a Final Paycheck

Most state laws specify when a final paycheck must be issued to employees who are fired or resign, and some of those laws are quite powerful. (See the listing below.) For example, Wyoming law requires that an employee who is fired be paid in full within 24 hours. If not, the employee may sue for additional wages and interest on them, plus attorneys' fees and costs of the lawsuit.

If You Have a Contract, You're Outside the Law

If you are one of the rare breed who have an employment contract (see Section A1), you may be specifically excluded from the protections of the laws listed below. Your rights to pay are dictated by the terms of the employment contract you signed.

Additional Laws May Apply

If the chart below indicates that your state has no statute, this means there is no law that specifically addresses the issue. However, there may be a state administrative regulation or local ordinance that does control. Call your state labor department for more information. (See the Appendix for contact details.)

State Laws That Control Final Paychecks	
Alabama	No statute
Alaska	Within three days. (Alaska Stat. §23.05.140)
Arizona	If employee is fired: within three days or next scheduled payday, whichever is sooner. If employee quits: next scheduled payday. (Ariz. Rev. Stat. Ann. §23-353)
Arkansas	Railroad employees only: If employee is fired, immediately. All other employees: if employee is fired, within seven days after demand. If employee quits: no applicable law. (Arkansas Code §11-4-405; *Howard v. Glenn Bros. Trucking*, 609 S.W.2d 897 (Ark. 1980))
California	If employee is fired: immediately. If employee quits and does not have a contract for a definite period of employment: within 72 hours, or immediately if the employee has given 72 hours of notice. If seasonal agricultural industry employee is fired: within 72 hours. If motion picture industry employee is laid off: next pay day; if fired, within 24 hours. If oil drilling industry employee is laid off: within 24 hours. Accrued vacation benefits must be paid as wages with final paycheck. (Cal. Lab. Code §§201, 202 and 227.3)
Colorado	If employee is fired: immediately. If employee quits: next scheduled payday. (Colo. Rev. Stat. Ann. §8-4-104)

Connecticut	If employee is fired: next business day. If employee quits: next scheduled payday. (Conn. Gen. Stat. Ann. §31-71c)
Delaware	Next scheduled payday. (Del. Code Ann. tit. 19, §1103) Accrued vacation pay need not be part of final paycheck.
District of Columbia	If employee is fired: next business day. If employee quits: next scheduled payday or seven days, whichever is sooner. (D.C. Code §36-103)
Florida	No statute
Georgia	No statute
Hawaii	If employee is fired: immediately. If employee quits: next scheduled payday. (Haw. Rev. Stat. §388-3)
Idaho	Next scheduled payday or within ten business days, whichever is sooner. If written request made for earlier payment, within 48 hours. (Idaho Code §45-606)
Illinois	Next scheduled payday. (820 Ill. Comp. Stat. 115/5) Accrued vacation benefits must be paid as wages with final paycheck.
Indiana	Next scheduled payday except for railroad employees, who are covered under federal law. If an employee leaves voluntarily and his or her whereabouts are unknown, the employer need not issue the final paycheck at the next regularly scheduled payday and may wait until ten days have passed since an employee has furnished an address. (Ind. Code §§22-2-9-2 and 22-2-5-1)
Iowa	Next scheduled payday. (Iowa Code Ann. §91A.4) Accrued vacation benefits must be paid as wages with final paycheck.
Kansas	If employee leaves or is discharged, next scheduled payday. (Kan. Stat. Ann. §44-315)
Kentucky	If employee is fired: next scheduled payday or within 14 days, whichever is later. (Ky. Rev. Stat. Ann. §337.055) Accrued vacation pay need not be part of final paycheck.
Louisiana	If employee is fired: within three days. If employee resigns: on or before the next regular payday or within 15 days following the resignation, whichever comes first. La. Rev. Stat. Ann. §23:631 Accrued vacation benefits must be paid as wages with final paycheck.
Maine	Next scheduled payday or within two weeks after demand, whichever is earlier. (Me. Rev. Stat. Ann. tit. 26, § 626) Accrued vacation benefits must be paid as wages with final paycheck.
Maryland	Next scheduled payday. (Md. Lab. & Emp. Code Ann. §3-505)
Massachusetts	If employee is fired: immediately. If employee quits: next scheduled payday. (Mass. Ann. Laws ch. 149 §148) Accrued vacation benefits must be paid as wages with final paycheck.
Michigan	As soon as amount can be determined with due diligence. (Mich. Comp. Laws §408.475)

Minnesota	If employee is fired: within 24 hours. If employee quits: not later than the first regularly scheduled payday following the final day of work. If this is less than five days after the last day of work, then the paycheck may be delayed until the next regularly scheduled payday, or within 20 days of the final day of work, whichever is sooner. (Minn. Stat. §§181.13 and 181.14)
Mississippi	No statute
Missouri	If employee is fired: immediately. The employee may request in writing that the pay be sent by mail, and if it does not arrive within seven days of the request, the employee is entitled to sue for it. If employee quits: no applicable law. (Mo. Ann. Stat. §290.110)
Montana	If employee is fired for cause: immediately. If employee quits: next payday or 15 days, whichever comes first. (Mont. Code Ann. §39-3-205)
Nebraska	If employee is fired: next scheduled payday or within two weeks, whichever is sooner. If employee quits: no applicable law. (Neb. Rev. Stat. §48-1230)
Nevada	If employee is fired: immediately. If employee quits: next scheduled payday or within seven days, whichever is earlier. (Nev. Rev. Stat. §§608.020 to 608.050)
New Hampshire	If employee is fired: within 72 hours. If employee quits: next scheduled payday; or if employee gives at least one pay period's notice, within 72 hours of the last day of work. (N.H. Rev. Stat. Ann. §275:44)
New Jersey	Next scheduled payday. (N.J. Stat. Ann. §34:11-4.3)
New Mexico	If employee is fired: due immediately and payable within 5 days. However, if the pay is not based on a set amount but is calculated according to commission, task or other method of computation, it is due and payable within ten days. If employee quits and does not have a written employment contract for a definite period: next payday. (N.M. Stat. Ann. §§50-4-4 and 50-4-5)
New York	Next scheduled payday. (N.Y. Labor Laws §191) Accrued vacation pay need not be part of final paycheck.
North Carolina	Next scheduled payday. However, wages based on commissions, bonuses or other methods of calculation are due on the next regularly scheduled payday following that calculation. (N.C. Gen. Stat. §95.25.7) Accrued vacation benefits must be paid as wages with final paycheck.
North Dakota	If employee is fired: immediately; must be paid by certified mail within 15 days or the next scheduled payday, whichever comes first. If employee resigns: next scheduled payday. (N.D. Cent. Code §34-14-03)
Ohio	No statute
Oklahoma	Next scheduled payday. (Okla. Stat. Ann. tit. 40, §165.3)
Oregon	If employee is fired: immediately. If employee quits: immediately as long as he or she has given 48 hours notice. If less than 48 hours notice has been given, within five days or the next payday, whichever occurs first. For seasonal farmworkers who have given 48 hours notice of quitting: immediately; if less than 48 hours notice, 48 hours or next payday, whichever comes first. (Or. Rev. Stat. §652.140) Accrued vacation benefits must be paid as wages with final paycheck.

Pennsylvania	Next scheduled payday. (43 Pa. Cons. Stat. Ann. §260.5)
Rhode Island	Next scheduled payday. (R.I. Gen. Laws §28-14-4) Accrued vacation benefits must be paid as wages with final paycheck.
South Carolina	Within 48 hours or next scheduled payday, which may not be more than 30 days. (S.C. Codified Laws §41-10-50)
South Dakota	If employee is fired or quit: next scheduled payday. (S.D. Codified Laws §§60-11-10 and 60-11-11)
Tennessee	Next scheduled payday or 21 days, whichever occurs later. (Tenn. Code. Ann. §50-2-103) Accrued vacation benefits must be paid as wages with final paycheck.
Texas	If employee is fired: within six days. If employee quits: next regularly scheduled payday. (Texas Code Ann., Labor §61.014)
Utah	If employee is fired: within 24 hours. If employee quits and there was not an employment contract for a definite period: next regular payday. (Utah Code Ann. §34-28-5)
Vermont	If employee is fired: within 72 hours. If employee quits: next scheduled payday or, if no scheduled payday exists, the next Friday. (Vt. Stat. Ann. tit. 21, §342)
Virginia	Next scheduled payday. (Va. Code §40.1-29)
Washington	Next scheduled payday. (Wash. Rev. Code §49.48.010)
West Virginia	If employee is fired: within 72 hours. If employee quits: next regular payday; if employee has given one pay period of notice: immediately. (W.Va. Code §21-5-4)
Wisconsin	Any employee, except a salesperson paid by commission, who does not have an employment contract and who quits or is fired: next regular payday but not more than a month later. (Wis. Stat. Ann. §109.03)
Wyoming	Five business days. (Wyo. Stat. Ann. §27-4-105)

F. Severance Pay

Many people assume that when they leave a job, they have a legal right to severance pay. This is yet another bit of workplace lore that builds false hope in the newly unemployed.

Most employers do offer severance in the form of a month or more worth of salary to employees who are laid off or let go for some reason other than misconduct. The old general rule was that where severance was offered, a reasonable amount was one month's pay for every year of service—up to 24 months.

In the last couple years, the amount of severance pay has become less tied to the length of time an employee has worked with a company. Rates have also become less generous—averaging 30 weeks of pay for nonexempt employees to 39 weeks for those classified as executives.

And the cutrate severance comes with an additional pricetag, as more companies demand that departing employees sign broad severance agreements before getting a red cent. The agreements typically include provisions requiring a former employee to waive the right to file a number of legal claims against the company. And increasingly, severance agreements include clauses aimed at preventing employees who leave from complaining about the company to other employees and from talking to the media about negative experiences while on the job.

Some employment experts are quick to disparage such so-called nondisparagement clauses, fearing that disgruntled workers are being unjustly paid to zip their lips rather than shed light on larger workplace wrongs.

There is no grand guidance on the issue. If presented with the option of either signing a nondisparagement clause and getting a hefty severance sum or losing the right to vent and getting nothing, you are the only one who can evaluate which value weighs out.

But keep in mind that no law requires an employer to pay severance. Whether it is given at all now varies drastically from employer to employer, region to region, industry custom to industry custom.

However, an employer may be legally obligated to pay you some severance pay if you had good reason to believe you had it coming, as evidenced by:

- a written contract stating that severance will be paid
- a promise that employees would receive severance pay as documented in an employee handbook
- a history of the company paying severance to other employees in your position, or
- an oral promise that the employer would pay you severance—although you may run into difficulties proving the promise existed.

If your employer refuses to pay you severance or offers an amount that you find unacceptable, you have nothing to lose by asking, or asking again. Request a meeting with a company representative to discuss the issue. Remain calm and polite; do not threaten. Explain why you need the money—support while securing another job is the usual reason. In the last few years, employers' building fear of lawsuits has meant that more of them are willing to grant severance pay to departing employees and to be flexible in the amount they will award.

If you meet with no success, take another hard look at the legal reasons listed above that may entitle you to severance pay. If you feel you may have a valid claim, collect as much evidence as you can to back up your position. (See Section C above.)

Then think again. A breach of contract action, which is what you can bring against an employer that has reneged on a promise to pay severance, will likely require the help of an attorney. If the amount involved is not substantial, you could be facing more in legal fees than you would stand to gain by collecting the severance money. If you consult with an attorney about handling your case, that calculation should be one of the first questions you ask. (See Chapter 18, Section D.)

G. Temporary Job Losses

We tend to speak in euphemisms around difficult and painful events—like the death of a person or the loss of a job. This lack of directness may make it easier to get words out, but it also makes it easy to get confused when talking.

Historically, the word layoff typically was used to describe situations in which factory production workers were told not to report to work until their help was needed again on the production lines. But over time, the word has also been applied to other types of job losses—even those that obviously are permanent.

The confusion over the meaning of layoff became even worse in the early 1990s, when economic downturns meant that some companies needed to cut costs. Some of these companies decided that it was more equitable to make all of their employees take a week off from work without pay every once in a while than to fire a few employees. Ironically, many of these plans, which clearly fit the traditional definition of layoff, were euphemistically called Job Security Programs.

Ignore the name that your employer assigns to a temporary loss of employment. If you become involved in an employment cut that appears to be temporary, the strategies discussed in the preceding sections of this chapter and in Chapter 11 will not be relevant. These strategies are intended for people who have lost their jobs permanently. Typically, the only legal action available to deal with a temporary loss of employment is to file an application for unemployment insurance benefits (discussed in Chapter 12, Section D) and then wait to be recalled to your job.

However, if you believe that temporary employment cuts imposed by your employer form a pattern of illegal discrimination (discussed in Chapter 8, Section A), you may want to file what is usually called an abusive layoff complaint under anti-discrimination laws. You will probably need to hire a lawyer to help you with that kind of case. (See Chapter 18, Section D.)

Example: *John is employed as a production worker at a nonunion steel foundry in Pennsylvania, where about two-thirds of the workers are white and one-third are black. For the past three years, business has been slow for the foundry, so every few months some employees were told not to report to work for six weeks at a time.*

The employees who were laid off were allowed to collect unemployment insurance benefits, which replaced about one-half of the income they would receive if they were working.

But all the workers who have been put out of work temporarily, John notices, were black. All the white workers have been employed steadily for 40 hours or more per week. Even black workers who have been employed there longer and have more work skills were told to stay home while the white workers continued to work.

It appears that the foundry is treating its white workers better than those who are black, so John can take action against the abusive layoffs under Title VII of the Civil Rights Act of 1964 or under his state's anti-discrimination laws on the basis of racial discrimination.

H. Collecting Fringe Benefits

A number of workplace benefits, formerly known by the quaint title of "fringe benefits," need not be provided by employers, although most employers provide them—at least to fulltime employees. Fringe benefits include retirement plans, group health insurance and paid days off for vacations, holidays, personal and medical leave. (See Chapters 3, 4 and 5 for a more in-depth discussion of these topics.)

Keep in mind, however, that if your employer does have a policy of offering some or all of these job benefits, it cannot discriminate in offering them. The question that most often arises about these discretionary benefits when employees quit or are fired from a job is whether they are entitled to be paid for time that was accrued—or earned and owing—but not taken.

There is no easy answer.

First of all, just as the benefits are discretionary with each employer, so is the policy of how and when they accrue. Employers are free to apply conditions on fringe benefits. For example, it is perfectly legal for an employer to require a certain length of employment—six months or a year are common—before an employee is entitled to any fringe benefits. It is perfectly legal for fringe benefits to be prorated for parttime employees, or denied them completely. Employers are also free to set limits on how much paid time off employees may accrue before it must be lost or taken.

1. Getting the Benefits You Are Due

In evaluating whether your former employer has given you all accrued fringe benefits you are due, you have two allies: documentation and history. First, search for any written policy on benefit accrual: in an employee manual, personnel package or company memo. If the rights have been promised to you, you can enforce them just like any other contract. If the promise is in writing, you have an even better chance of succeeding in enforcing it.

Look, too, to how other employees were treated in the past. If it has become company custom to pay employees accrued fringe benefits when they leave, you may be legally entitled to them, too. You must compare apples with apples. Look to other employees who worked in jobs similar to yours and who worked the same hours.

Finding out what others were paid when they left may take some brave sleuthing on your part: You may have to hunt down past employees and ask them some uncomfortable questions, point blank. But the effort may be worth it. If other former workers with jobs similar to yours were given benefits you were denied, you may be able to claim that your employer discriminated against you when it denied them. (See Chapter 8.)

2. Continuing Healthcare Coverage

Most workplace disputes and misunderstandings over fringe benefits concern healthcare coverage. Ironically, workers have more rights to healthcare insurance coverage after they lose their jobs than while employed because of a 1986 law, the Consolidated Omnibus Budget Reconciliation Act, or COBRA. Under COBRA, employers must offer former employees the option of continuing to be covered by the company's group healthcare insurance plan at the workers' own expense for some time after employment ends. Family coverage is included.

In general, COBRA gives an employee who quits or is dismissed for reasons other than gross misconduct the right to continue group healthcare coverage for 18 months. In some other circumstances, such as the death of the employee, that employee's dependents can continue coverage for up to 36 months. (See Chapter 4, Section C.)

I. Outplacement Programs

Each year, many thousands of workers are permanently dismissed by corporations that are shrinking or dying. And as they bid adieu, some former employers offer outplacement services to workers to help ease the sting of being out of work.

Outplacement services are not employment agencies. They are not executive search firms. They are not employee leasing companies. They do not find a new job for you, but they do help and encourage you in finding one for yourself.

Although some outplacement firms offer packages of services that can be purchased by individuals, outplacement counselors are most often brought in and paid for by employers who want to diminish their risks of being sued for wrongful discharge. Outplacement benefits have even been negotiated into union contracts.

The theory underlying the popularity of outplacement in the corporate world is that fired employees who move quickly and smoothly into a new job typically do not sustain grudges against the company that fired them. Nor do they experience the kind of financial problems that can inspire job-related lawsuits. If a person goes through outplacement, cannot find a replacement job and decides to file a wrongful discharge lawsuit, the company can show a court that it has done all it can to limit the damage done to the employee by the firing.

An outplacement program typically begins with classes or individual counseling on how to take an inventory of your marketable job skills. Then, you are assigned a furnished office space from which to launch your search for a new employer. These offices are usually equipped with a telephone and an extensive library of business directories, and they have a central typing service that will pump out resumes and letters for you.

Many outplacement firms even provide the people passing through them with business cards that carry only the person's name and a daytime telephone number, but no business title. Outplacement offices are frequently equipped with a switchboard operator to answer telephone calls in a corporate style, but without indicating any company affiliation. These props typically get a lot of use, because many outplacement participants are required to turn in daily or weekly logs of potential employers they have contacted to inquire about possible job openings.

Periodic counseling and encouragement sessions with the outplacement firm's staff continue until you have found a new job, or until your former employer's willingness to pay for the outplacement services runs out. There is no standard duration. Some people spend only a few days in outplacement, but some stay for a year or more. Because some people have a difficult time finding a new job even with the support of an outplacement firm, some of these firms now offer programs that teach new work-related skills.

An employer cannot force you to participate in an outplacement program. However, most large employers will continue to pay your salary and benefits for at least a few weeks or months after you are fired on the condition that you actively participate in the outplacement services provided. Drop out—and you are on your own financially.

Your refusal to participate in an outplacement program might also weaken any lawsuit you might later file against your former employer because you could be depicted as contributing to your loss of employment income. Your participation in outplacement might, on the other hand, provide additional verification that you were competent and professional while at the job from which you were fired.

Where the Jobs Are: It Computes

According to Department of Labor projections, total employment will increase by 14% in the decade from the year 1998 to2008. If DOL predictions hold true, most of the 20.3 million new jobs will be concentrated in the areas of business, healthcare and social service—led by the continuing surge in positions in computers and health.

DOL first began issuing its crystal ball guide to the job market in 1946, in a handbook for World War II veterans returning to the workforce. The public clamored for more—prompting the agency to publish updated editions of the *Occupational Outlook Handbook* in years ending in even numbers.

The slogan of yesteryear, To Get a Good Job, Get a Good Education, still holds credence. For while employment is expected to grow in jobs at all levels of education and training, jobs requiring an associate degree or more will grow the fastest. But experience on the job will likely win new respect, too.

The most recent predications about the top ten fastest growing occupations summarize the best training required and tag the job changes by both number and percent.

Fastest Growing Occupations, 1998 to 2008

Occupation	Number	Percent	Training
Computer engineers	323,000	108	Bachelor's degree
Computer support specialists	439,000	102	Bachelor's degree
Systems analysts	577,000	94	Bachelor's degree
Database administrators	67,000	77	Bachelor's degree
Desktop publishing specialists	19,000	73	Long term on-the-job training
Paralegals and legal assistants	84,000	62	Associate degree
Medical assistants	146,000	58	Moderate term on-the-job training
Home health aides	433,000	58	Short term on-the-job training
Social and human service assistants	141,000	53	Moderate term on-the-job training
Physician assistants	32,000	48	Bachelor's degree

J. Replacing Your Income

When your employment is interrupted, it is important to act quickly to replace as much of your income as you can. Each day that passes without money earned puts you and those who rely on you for financial support in greater risk of running into money troubles. In some states, for example, the gap between the time that a person files for unemployment insurance and the time he or she receives the first unemployment check averages six weeks. And applying for the wrong income replacement program can waste many more precious days, weeks or even months.

Here is a brief breakdown of what is covered by each of the three major income replacement programs.

- *Unemployment insurance.* This program may provide some financial help if you lose your job, temporarily or permanently, through no fault of your own. (See Chapter 12.)
- *Workers' compensation.* When you cannot work because of a work-related injury or illness, this is the program that is most likely to provide you with replacement income promptly. It may also pay the medical bills resulting from a workplace injury or illness; compensate workers for a permanent injury, such as the loss of a limb; and provide death benefits to the survivors of workers who die from a workplace injury or illness. (See Chapter 13.)
- *Social Security disability insurance.* This is intended to provide income to adults who, because of injury or illness, cannot work for at least 12 months. Unlike the workers' compensation program, it does not require that your disability be caused by a workplace injury or illness. (See Chapter 14.)

Once you have decided which of these programs fits your situation, read the more detailed description of that program in the chapters noted and then apply for the appropriate benefits.

Dual Payments for Disabled Workers

Many disabled employees qualify for benefits under both workers' compensation and Social Security disability insurance. There is nothing illegal about collecting from both at the same time if the claims you file are valid.

However, if you qualify for benefits from both programs, the total benefits you receive from both programs cannot equal more than 80% of your average earnings prior to becoming disabled.

Some states also allow disabled workers to collect both unemployment and workers' compensation benefits at the same time. When in doubt, file truthful claims for any program for which you might logically qualify and let the system decide if you are eligible for benefits.

K. Other Income Replacement Options

Although the government insurance programs covering unemployment, workplace injuries and permanent disability are the most substantial sources of replacement income for people who are out of work, there are other options.

1. Private Disability Insurance

While you were working, you or your employer may have been paying into a private disability insurance program. If you were paying for it through payroll withholdings, or if all the premiums were being paid by your employer, you may have forgotten that you have this coverage.

Coverage and eligibility for benefits differ among policies and companies. Review the employee policy manual or packet that your employer gave you when you took the job to see whether any private disability coverage is described there. If not, the people who handle benefits for your employer should be able to help you determine whether you have such coverage.

2. State Disability Programs

A few states—including California, New Jersey, Rhode Island, New York and Hawaii—offer disability benefits as part of their unemployment insurance programs. Typical program requirements mandate that you submit your medical records and show that you requested a leave of absence from your employer. Some may also require proof that you intend to return to your job when you recover. Call the local unemployment insurance and workers' compensation insurance offices to determine whether your state is one that maintains this kind of coverage. (See Chapters 12 and 13.)

3. Withdrawals From Retirement Plans

Some retirement plans allow withdrawals prior to retirement for emergency purposes. The administrator of your plan can advise you on whether you have this option. (For more on pensions, see Chapter 15, Section B.)

4. Food Stamps

Although many people incorrectly think that the federal food stamp program is a form of welfare, it is actually financed by the U.S. Department of Agriculture as a way of increasing the demand for food products. You do not have to be receiving welfare to qualify for food stamps. In fact, the eligibility formula for food stamps makes them available to many people who are not all that poor. If your income is eliminated or significantly reduced for several months because you are not working, check on whether you are eligible for food stamps.

To locate the agency in your area that issues food stamps, scan the county government offices listings in the telephone directory. Typically, you will find a listing for food stamp information under a category such as Human Services. If not, call your local office of the U.S. Department of Agriculture. Or get more information online at http://www.fns.usda.gov.

5. Veterans' Benefits

There are programs that provide income to veterans of the U.S. military who become unable to work because of a disability, even if that disability is not a result of military service. Additional specialized laws may also provide veterans returning from service with the right to return to their jobs without losing seniority or benefits.

However, laws protecting veterans' rights, particularly their job rights, are subject to be passed and repealed with the changing of the political winds—making it tough to keep current. Your local Veterans' Administration office, listed in the federal government agency section of the telephone directory, can give you details. Local offices are also listed on the VA's website at http://www.vba.va.gov.

6. Supplemental Social Security Income

Usually known as SSI, this program provides money to disabled people who have low incomes and very few assets. Unlike Social Security disability insurance, it does not require you to have worked under and paid into the Social Security program. If the circumstances surrounding your inability to earn income are so unusual that you have fallen between the cracks of the larger programs, SSI may be the one program that provides you with some income.

You can get details and file a claim at your local Social Security Administration office. Look in the federal government section of the telephone directory for contact details. Or look for information and contact details at http://www.ssa.gov.

7. Black Lung Benefits

The Social Security Administration also runs a federal program that provides money benefits to victims of anthracosilicosis—an occupational disease often suffered by miners. Typically known as Black Lung, the disease is caused by long exposure to coal particles in the air. It frequently leaves miners unable to work because they cannot breath properly.

The benefits under this program are also payable to dependents of Black Lung victims, so the best way to research your eligibility for those benefits is to investigate details of the program at your local Social Security office. (See Section 6, above, for contact information.)

8. Disaster Benefits

When a flood, earthquake, hurricane or other natural disaster tears through an area, the president or governor will often declare it a disaster area and special unemployment benefits will become available to people who lost their jobs because of the disaster. These special unemployment benefits are usually handled by the same offices that handle regular unemployment claims.

9. Medicare

Like Social Security, most people think that Medicare is reserved solely for elderly people. But in fact, it also covers disabled people, and can be a good way of coping with medical bills when an injury or illness prevents you from working. For more details on this program, call the Medicare information line: 800-952-8627.

However, you should be aware that the federal government has been tightening the restrictions for Medicare for those less than 65 years old, so this type of coverage may be difficult to secure.

L. Agreements Not to Compete

A growing number of employers are straining to stretch out controls beyond the office compounds by asking employees to sign noncompete agreements promising that they will not work for a direct competitor.

These concerns and attempts to control the future are more understandable and more often enforced where workers have access to sensitive business information or trade secrets. A trade secret is information that gives you a competitive advantage because it is not generally known and cannot be readily learned by other people who could benefit from it. It can be a formula, pattern, compilation, program, device, method, technique or process that you've made reasonable efforts to keep secret.

When employees with access to trade secrets leave—either because they quit or have been fired—their former employers may be concerned that they will use the information gleaned on the job to their personal advantages. For example, a former employee may open a competing business or may go to work for a competitor and unwittingly or wittingly divulge hard-won keys to success.

Whether a judge will enforce a covenant not to compete is always an iffy question. The legal system puts a high value on a person's right to earn a living. Covenants not to compete will not be enforced if they're found to be unreasonable. A covenant may be held unreasonable because it:
- lasts for too long a time
- covers too wide a geographic area, or
- is too broad in the types of business it prohibits.

The biggest and most often raised bone of contention with noncompete agreements is how long a time an employee can be restrained from competing in a similar business. While there is no dyed in the wool guidance on what will and will not pass muster, courts and legislatures are beginning to set out some bounds as to what is reasonable. A good example is Florida's statute (Fla. Stat. §542.335), which sets out specific guidance as to the type and length of business matters that can be restrained after an employee leaves.

Subject Matter of Agreement	Reasonable	Iffy	Unreasonable
Trade secrets	Up to 5 years	5-10 years	10 years
Sale of a business	Up to 3 years	3-7 years	7 or more years
Other	Up to 6 months	6 months to 2 years	2 or more years

A covenant may also be held unreasonable because the information revealed to the worker isn't all that sensitive, so the restriction doesn't serve a valid business purpose.

Judges are more likely to enforce restrictive covenants against high-level managers who truly are given inside information, on the theory that such former employees are in a position to do real harm.

If pressed, a judge may order an employee not to use the information even if he or she didn't sign a secrecy agreement—if the former employer can show that what the employee took is truly a trade secret. This often involves establishing two things: that the information was not readily obtainable elsewhere, and that precautions were taken to keep it secret. For example, an employer who put together a valuable customer list that includes customers' buying history and buying habits, must also be able to show that the list was painstakingly built up over several years and that only a limited number of employees were allowed to see it.

Former employees who have signed noncompete agreements may face special hardships, as their job searches may become even more limited. And even those with solid job offers may face lawsuits by former employers—often accompanied by a damaging court order forbidding them from working until the case is resolved.

Next Time, I'll Know Better

When initially faced with signing a noncompete agreement, your first best step may be to negotiate some of the finer print with your employer.

There are a few pointers for crafting your arguments.

- If you are promoted to a new job that carries with it a new request to sign a noncompete agreement, it is not too cheeky to ask for money to compensate you for signing. Keep in mind, though, that this will almost certainly prevent you from later claiming that the clause should not be enforced against you. Courts will likely point to your fattened wallet and conclude that you should not take in money for a condition, then claim it does not apply to you.

- If presented with a noncompete clause, demand to have it worded to take effect only if you leave the job voluntarily. This may make a job search less daunting for an employee who is fired or laid off.

- Ask for the prohibited competition to be clearly specified. Many employers, for example, will fear competition with only one or two specific companies —and will readily name their names in your agreement.

CHAPTER

11

CHALLENGING A JOB LOSS

The legal doctrine of employment at will rules the workplace, so the dire truth remains that your employer can fire you.

On the spot.

Any time.

Without notice.

And the odds are that you will not be able to use the legal system to completely reverse your firing and get your job back. (See Chapter 10, Section A for a detailed discussion of employment at will.)

However, if you have lost your job or think you may soon lose it, do not despair. There are some laws that may protect you against suddenly joining the ranks of the unemployed without money or other help to ease the impact.

Depending on your situation, you may have the legal right to:

- protection from being denied a promotion, demoted or fired from your current job
- fair treatment during and after you are fired
- a truthful reference from your former employer to help in future job hunting, or
- continuing coverage under your former employer's benefit programs.

You may even be able to get some compensation if the firing causes you severe economic hardship, or to win a court judgment against your former employer in a wrongful discharge lawsuit.

At the very least, understanding how and when laws may protect job security and other workplace rights should help you determine whether your dismissal may justify taking legal action, in which case you may want to consult a lawyer. (See Chapter 18, Section D.)

A. When a Firing Is Illegal

New legal theories that challenge an employee's dismissal are being developed constantly. In general, these actions are lumped under the label of wrongful discharge.

The most common ground for a wrongful discharge claim is that there has been some form of discrimination in hiring, employing or firing an individual worker. A number of local, state and federal laws prohibit discriminating against an individual worker because of race, gender, age, national origin or sexual orientation. (See Chapter 8 for a thorough discussion of discrimination in employment and how to take action against it.)

There are also strong state and federal protections prohibiting individuals from being fired in violation of public policy—or for a reason most people would find morally wrong, such as for reporting mishandling of government funds. (See Section B.)

Several additional legal theories are frequently used in challenging employee firings:

- breach of good faith and fair dealing
- breach of contract
- retaliation
- fraud, and
- defamation.

In some situations, more than one of these theories may be used in the same legal action. (See Section D below.)

1. Breach of Good Faith and Fair Dealing

The most flexible way to challenge a job dismissal is to show that there has been a breach of good faith and fair dealing—simply that the employer did not follow that Golden Rule about doing unto others and should now be required to do the right thing.

This type of claim is based on the legal principle that an employer has an inherent responsibility to deal with employees fairly and in good faith. However, employers often commit breaches of good faith and fair dealing by:

- firing or transferring employees to prevent them from collecting sales commissions
- misleading employees about their chances for future promotions and wage increases
- contriving reasons for firing an employee on the basis of on-the-job performance when the real motivation is to replace that employee with someone who will work for lower pay
- soft pedaling the bad aspects of a particular job, such as the need to travel through dangerous neighborhoods late at night, and
- repeatedly transferring an employee to remote, dangerous or otherwise undesirable assignments to coerce him or her into quitting without collecting the severance pay and other benefits due.

The legal claim of breach of good faith and fair dealing is so broad and flexible that, no matter what other claims you use as a basis for a wrongful discharge action, you will likely include a claim of breach of good faith and fair dealing as well. (See Section D.)

2. Breach of Contract

There are two types of employment contracts that your employment might violate: a written contract or an implied contract. Proving that a written contract existed and was broken is easy; you can pick up the contract and point to its terms. But proving that an implied contract existed and should be legally protected can be an uphill road.

a. Written contracts

If you have a written employment contract setting out the terms of your work, pay and benefits, you may be able to get it enforced against an employer who ignores any one of its terms. But written employment contracts are rare—reserved mostly for top level executives and professional athletes. (See Chapter 10, Section A.)

A legal contract—covering employment or anything else—is created when three things occur:

- an offer is made by one person to another
- that offer is accepted, and
- something of value is exchanged based on the agreement.

Two Wrongs May Mean No Rights

Many jobseekers inflate their resumes by exaggerating their experience or credentials. A recent study revealed that:

- 9% of job applicants falsely claimed they had a college degree, listed false employers or identified jobs that didn't exist
- 4% listed incorrect job titles
- 11% misrepresented why they left a former employer, and
- nearly 33% listed dates of employment that were off by more than three months.

Employers have always been free to fire employees who lie about a significant qualification. Now they may be able to use this misinformation to defend against lawsuits for wrongful termination or discrimination. Courts reason, in essence, that employees who lied to get a job cannot later come to court and claim the employer did them wrong.

The emerging tactic even has a name: the After-Acquired Evidence Theory. Conduct that has been held sufficiently serious to be admitted as after-acquired evidence has included:

- 150 instances of falsifying company records
- failing to list a previous employer on a resume
- failing to admit being terminated for cheating on timecards
- failing to reveal a prior conviction for a felony
- lying about education and experience on a job application
- fabricating a college degree during an interview, and
- removing and copying the company's confidential financial statements.

If you did lie on your job application or resume, however, you may not be completely out of luck. Your employer can use the misinformation as a defense only if it was truly related to your job duties or performance. The employer must be able to show that you would have been fired—or not hired in the first place—if he or she had known the truth. Proving this type of second guessing may not be easy.

b. Implied contracts

Most breach of contract actions these days are based on the theory that you and your employer have an implied contract. This is one more way employees have to chip away at the doctrine of employment at will, which holds that an employer can fire you at any time. (See Chapter 10, Section A.) But chipping is not easy. An implied contract assumes that words and things of value exchanged between a former employer and employee created a legal contract governing their relationship.

Until legal challenges to employee dismissals began to be filed with fervor in the early 1980s, many employers used terms such as "permanent employment" in their employee manuals, on job application forms or orally when offering a position to a prospective employee.

Today, employees who challenge their firings sometimes argue that when an employer referred to permanent employment in the hiring process, that created an implied contract between them. They claim that this implied contract means that the company can only fire them for just cuase, such as bad behavior on the job. An employer who fires for less than that, the theory goes, has breached the implied contract.

In determining whether you have a binding implied employment contract with a former employer, courts will look at a number of factors that might have led you to believe your employment was rooted in solid ground, including:

- the duration of your employment
- whether you have received regular promotions
- whether you have consistently received positive performance reviews
- whether you were assured that you would have continuing employment
- whether your employer violated a usual employment practice in firing you—such as neglecting to give a required warning, or
- whether promises of permanence were made when you were hired.

Example: *In 1983, Marguerite took a job as an accountant with EZ Ink Printing. EZ Ink's employee manual stated that employees were not considered permanent until they completed a 90-day probationary period.*

For more than 17 years, Marguerite built her life around EZ Ink—assuming that she would be able to keep her job there until she reached retirement age. However, in 2000, the head of EZ Ink unexpectedly fired Marguerite, claiming her quarterly reports were incomplete.

Marguerite would likely be able to win a lawsuit against EZ Ink based on breach of an implied contract. The three elements required to create an implied employment contract were there:

- *an offer—the employee manual's implication that all employees who remained with the company more than 90 days were permanent employees*
- *an acceptance of that offer—Marguerite's more than 17 years of employment by the company*
- *an exchange of value—the wages that EZ Ink had paid Marguerite and her labor for them.*

Beware of Job Loss Insurance Policies

As the concept of long-term job security fades, some businesses are trying to exploit employees' fears of job loss by offering insurance policies that claim to cover certain bills during periods of unemployment.

Flyers urging you to buy job loss insurance are often included with your monthly credit card statement. The glitzy ads usually offer to make the payments on that worrisome credit card account should you lose your job. And mortgage companies frequently offer job loss insurance as a part of the process of closing the purchase of a home, arguing that your mortgage payments would be made by the insurance company should you become unemployed.

Such insurance usually is not a wise buy for most people. Look closely at the fine print of most job loss insurance policies and you will see a long list of situations in which benefits are not available. Typical exceptions: you are out of work for less than several weeks, you volunteered for an early retirement program, you were fired because of something you did at work or you are involved in a labor dispute.

Most job loss policies only provide coverage in limited situations—for example, if your employer suddenly went bankrupt.

3. Retaliation

Various types of laws—notably, those protecting whistleblowing (see Section B) and prohibiting discrimination (see Chapter 8)—specifically forbid employers from retaliating against employees who avail themselves of legal protections. But a lawsuit alleging retaliation need not always be pegged to a specific statute. An increasing number of cases are now based on the time-tested ban against getting even, legally known as retaliation.

The broad claim of retaliation is a little more complicated, but somewhat easier to prove, than a charge of workplace discrimination. The reason is that evidence supporting retaliation claims is usually less subjective, more obvious than for cases of discrimination. To make out a case of retaliation, you must prove that:

- you were engaged in a legally protected activity—such as filing a complaint with the Equal Employment Opportunity Commission or formally complaining to your own company officials about harassment or discrimination

- your employer then took adverse action against you—by firing you, denying you a promotion, giving an unwarranted bad work performance review, increasing job duties or responsibilities, scrutinizing your work very closely or giving an inaccurate poor reference, and
- your actions were the cause of your employer's actions—for example, you were demoted just after your employer found out that you filed a charge of sexual harassment.

The employer or former employer is then free to show that there was some legitimate reason—other than retaliation—for its actions. If such evidence is presented, you get one more shot at winning by showing that the employer would not have acted—that is, fired or demoted you—if you had not acted first. This last is a tad tricky. In seeing whether this link exists, courts are most likely to look at:

- who made the job decision against you—he or she must likely have known about the action you took
- your prior work record—especially important if you were fired, demoted or given poor job performance evaluations following your action, and
- the timing of the employment decision—the shorter the time between them, the more likely they are related.

4. Fraud

In extreme cases, an employer's actions are so devious and wrong-hearted that they constitute fraud. Fraud can be found at various stages of an employment relationship—most commonly in the recruiting process, where promises are made and broken, or in the final stages, such as when an employee is induced to resign.

By dint of its devious nature, fraud is tough to track and expose. And harder still to prove fraud in court. To win, you must show that:

- the employer made a false representation
- someone in charge knew of the false representation
- your employer intended to deceive you or induce you to rely on the representation
- you relied on the representation as the truth, and
- you were harmed in some way by your reliance.

The hardest part of proving fraud is connecting up the dots to show there was purposefulness in the bad behavior. That requires good documentation of how, when, to whom and by what means the false representations were made. If your employer is a large corporation, the task of collecting and proving this information is all the more difficult, since you must usually work through layers of bureaucracy and many individuals. You must be able to name the people who made the fraudulent representations, their authority to speak, to whom they spoke, what they said or wrote and why you relied on it.

If you are sufficiently lucky and resourceful to present this cogent puzzle after your employer defrauds you, you may be entitled to be reimbursed for a surprising array of costs, including the costs of uprooting your family to take the job and the loss of income and security that resulted from leaving your former employer.

Dream Job Delivers Rude Awakening

Native New Yorker Andrew Lazar uprooted his family to take a California dream job only after a long and agonizing courtship instituted by Rykoff, a restaurant supply and equipment firm.

When Rykoff first set its eyes on Lazar in 1990, he was working in the same family-owned restaurant in which he had worked for over 18 years—and bringing home about $120,000 each year to help cover living expenses for himself, his wife and their two teens. Rykoff promised him more: a $130,000 salary to start, ample chances for bonuses and increases, a sure shot at becoming department head in a few years, a job with a lifetime guarantee.

Lazar bit—after being assured that Rykoff was fiscally strong and growing. The company resisted entering a written contract, however, assuring Lazar that "in the Rykoff family, our word is our bond."

But Rykoff's financial picture was not as rosy as painted. While wooing Lazar, it had just experienced its worst year in a long time and was planning to merge with another company—a move that would mean cutting many employees from its staff.

Lazar worked hard and well, exceeding sales goals, increasing sales and lowering operating costs. But after two years on the job, he was shown the door. Out of work, out of money for home payments, out of touch with New York job contacts, Lazar sued. He claimed that Rykoff never intended to make him a permanent part of the staff, never intended to pay the wages and bonuses it promised—and so was guilty of fraud. The court agreed (*Lazar v. Superior Court of Los Angeles County*, 12 Cal. 4th 631 (1996)).

---

5. Defamation

Defamation is a legal action with the chivalrous-sounding intent of protecting a person's reputation and good standing in the community. There are a lot of opportunities in the typical firing process for an employer to sully an employee's reputation, so it is increasingly common for former employees to bring a defamation charge when they are fired.

A defamation claim is not a challenge to the legitimacy of an employee's dismissal. Rather, it is a way of getting monetary revenge on the employer who was sloppy, insensitive or downright mean in firing you or in dealing with your need for references in obtaining a new job.

a. Proving the case

Defamation is usually difficult to prove. Typically, you must show that, in the process of dismissing you from your job or subsequently providing references to potential new employers, your former employer significantly damaged your good name and, usually, that this reduced your chances for gaining new employment. This commonly entails much legal hair-splitting over the facts surrounding a firing. Most disputes involve whether the employer may legitimately communicate the facts surrounding a dismissal to other people. And a number of defamation claims center on whether or not the distribution of the damaging information was intentional and malicious—that is, meant to harm you.

To sue for defamation, you must show that your former employer:

- made a false or damaging statement about you
- told or wrote that statement to at least one other person
- was negligent or intentional in communicating the statement, and
- harmed you in some way by communicating the statement, such as by causing others to shun you or causing you to lose a job or promotion.

Company Makes a Very Expensive Call

Don Hagler had just finished a shift at a Dallas office of Proctor & Gamble Co. when a burly security guard stopped him at the front gate, searched a bag he was toting and confiscated a telephone inside it.

Hagler, who had worked at the detergent plant for 41 years, claimed he had paid for the phone out of his own pocket. But P&G management members saw the phone as their own. They began an intensive investigation, which included posting notices on 11 bulletin boards throughout the plant and over the company e-mail system that read: "It has been determined that the telephone in question is Proctor & Gamble's property and that Don had therefore violated Work Rule #12 concerning theft of company property."

Then Hagler was fired.

He sued for defamation, claiming that P&G used him as an example, to stem a tide of property pilfering. At trial, a co-worker testified that he was with Hagler at a mall when he bought the phone. Hagler testified that he had applied for more than 100 jobs, but no employer would take him on after learning he was fired for theft.

After deliberating for five hours, the jury returned a verdict for Hagler—and awarded him $15.6 million in damages.

Hagler became richer, but wistful. "I'm not proud of the fact that I had to sue the company I was dedicated to for 41 years," he told *The Wall Street Journal* just after the verdict. "I sued because they called me a thief and put it on 11 bulletin boards in the plant. I think P&G's a good company. But I think they've changed. They're not as nice to people as they used to be."

To win a case of defamation, you must prove that the hurtful words were more than petty watercooler gossip. The words must also be more than a personal opinion. It is ordinarily legal for anyone to voice an opinion, no matter how unflattering.

Statements that have been ruled to sufficiently harm a worker and qualify as defamation are false claims that he or she:

- committed a crime
- performed job duties incompetently
- improperly used drugs or alcohol, or
- acted in some other way that clearly implied unfitness for a particular job.

Because a few unflattering comments or even a small dose of mean-spiritedness do not usually qualify as defamation, it is extremely important to scrupulously document cases where false or damaging statements are made. You can do this by writing down not only the exact offensive words that were said and who said them, but when and where they were said and whether there were any witnesses. Securing this type of documentation may be difficult if you have lost your job and are no longer in the workplace.

Keep in mind that courts will generally be most persuaded by words that clearly damage your work reputation. For example, a former employer's false statement that you stole money would probably qualify as defamation because most people would probably not hire you because of it. But a false statement that you had stayed on your last job only two months would probably be defamatory only if you could prove that it damaged you severely—such as by preventing you from getting a new job, causing a landlord to refuse to rent an apartment to you and otherwise causing you social embarrassment and emotional distress.

b. Negative job references

Employers contacted for references about former employees often find themselves caught between the desire to be truthful and their fear that, if they say anything unflattering, they will be sued. The number of costly defamation lawsuits filed in the last decade over negative references makes this fear a real one. And the U.S. Supreme Court added fuel to the fire when it ruled recently that former employees who sue their employers for retaliatory negative job references are protected by the Civil Rights Act (*Robinson v. Shell Oil Co.,* 519 U.S. 337 (1997)).

These days, conventional legal wisdom cautions all employers to stick to the barest bones. Many companies have steel-clad policies to supply only the dates of employment, job title and final salary to prospective employers.

Some cautious companies even require that employees who leave must sign releases allowing them to give reference information in the future. And some employers ask even prospective employees to sign the same sort of release. Courts have upheld these releases of late, holding that employees who sign away rights to this information have also signed away their rights to bring a lawsuit for defamation based on what beans get spilled. In some states, employers are protected by law from defamation lawsuits if they answer questions about former employee truthfully. (See Chapter 6, Section A.)

The broad warning for employers giving references is that they should give out only easily documented facts—your attendance record or production record, for example.

But this closed approach seems to unfairly penalize prize employees, who may depend on good references to snag their next jobs. And many employers who think that an employee has done a poor job or has blatantly violated company rules feel that they have a responsibility to let prospective employers know about the problem. There is nothing inherently illegal about this, unless you can prove that an employer told a bald-faced lie about you—for example, that you raided the company till when you did not. However, gathering proof of an intentional lie is nearly impossible. And a seemingly noncommital "no comment" in response to a prospective employer's probe about your strengths and weaknesses may be the most damaging of all—yet its evasiveness makes it a poor candidate for the basis of a defamation lawsuit.

If you suspect your former employer would give a negative review of your work, it is best to have a strategy on hand. Try to secure a letter of recommendation from someone in the company who would praise your work. Perhaps you can persuade your employer to keep certain employment matters confidential—such as the reason for your dismissal. If not, it might be best not to list the employer as a reference. But have a ready reason to explain the circumstances that has no acrimonious ring to it—for example, you believe it was time to move on to a new challenge.

B. Violations of Public Policy

An employer may not violate public policy when he or she fires you—that is, fire you for a reason that most people would find morally or ethically wrong.

Discovering what a court would decide is morally wrong can, of course, be an exasperating exercise. Before allowing an action for a violation of public policy, most courts strictly require that there be some specific law setting out the policy. Many state and federal laws oblige and take some of the guessing out of this issue by specifying employment-related actions that clearly violate public policy, such as firing an employee for:

- disclosing a company practice of refusing to pay employees their earned commissions and accrued vacation pay (see Chapter 3, Section B)

- taking time off work to serve on a jury (see Chapter 3, Section E2)
- taking time off work to vote (see Chapter 3, Section E3)
- serving in the military or National Guard (see Chapter 3, Section E4), or
- notifying authorities about some wrongdoing harmful to the public—generally known as whistleblowing (see the listing below).

In addition, a number of state laws protect employees from being fired for asserting a number of more arcane rights—including serving as an election officer, serving as a volunteer firefighter, having certain political opinions, appearing as a witness in a criminal case or even being elected to the general assembly. Many of these laws, passed as kneejerk reactions to assuage particular workplace disputes, have become all but dead letters. Few people know they exist; they are seldom violated. And very few workers attempt to claim their protections. Still, if you feel that your firing may have violated one of these prohibitions, doublecheck the laws in your state. (See Chapter 18, Section E, for guidance on how to do your own legal research.)

Courts have also held that it violates public policy for an employer to fire you because you took advantage of some legal remedies or exercised a legal right. For example, it is illegal for your employer to fire you because you:

- file a workers' compensation claim (see Chapter 13, Section D)
- file a complaint under the Fair Labor Standards Act (see Chapter 3, Section H)
- report a violation of the Occupational Safety and Health Act or state safety law (see Chapter 7, Section B)
- claim your rights under Title VII of the Civil Rights Act (see Chapter 8, Section A and Chapter 9, Section D)
- exercise your right to belong or not to belong to a union (see Chapter 16)
- exercise your right to take a leave from work that was available under state or federal law (see Chapter 5)
- refuse to take a lie detector test (see Chapter 6, Section B)
- refuse to take a drug test given without good reason (see Chapter 6, Section B2), or
- have your pay subject to an order for child support or a wage garnishment order (see Chapter 3, Section F).

The High Cost of Whistleblowing

The story of one of the most famous whistleblowers, Karen Silkwood, was the inspiration for hundreds of articles, several books—and a heavily bankrolled motion picture.

In the early '70s, Silkwood worked as a lab analyst in an Oklahoma Kerr-McGee plant which manufactured plutonium pins used as fuel for nuclear reactors. Plutonium, a radioactive chemical element, is known to be highly toxic and carcinogenic. Silkwood, an elected union official and outspoken critic of Kerr-McGee's health and safety practices, began collecting and recording information to substantiate her charges that employees at the plant were dangerously exposed.

In early November 1974, Silkwood was found to be contaminated with the chemical. Nine days later, while enroute to meet with a *New York Times* reporter and union leader to turn over her documentation of Kerr-McGee's unsafe work conditions, Silkwood was killed in a car accident with suspicious overtones. The damning documentation she was alleged to have had with her was not recovered from the accident scene.

Silkwood's estate sued Kerr-McGee for the injuries caused by the escaping plutonium. After several appeals involving esoteric issues of state and federal legal authority, the U.S. Supreme Court affirmed the award to the Silkwood estate of $10 million in punitive damages—damages designed to punish the wrongdoer and act as a deterrent—and an additional $5,000 in property damages to cover the cost of sanitizing her contaminated apartment (*Silkwood v. Kerr-McGee,* 464 U.S. 238 (1984)).

1. State Whistleblower Laws

While states differ in the details, whistleblowing laws generally protect individuals who report to proper authorities any activity that is unlawful or that is against the public interest. One unique feature about whistleblowing is its foul-crying kind of aspect. The whistleblower is protected for doing the civic duty of pointing out the misdeeds of powers that be. Many of the whistleblower statutes apply only to public employees.

Who Ya Gonna Call?

Some statutes are quite specific as to the ear that the whistleblower should seek.

In California and Washington, for example, you must report the wrongdoing to the State Auditor; and in Delaware, you must contact the State Office of Auditor of Accounts. In Colorado, the report made be made to "any person," and Tennessee employees are protected if they simply "speak out."

The law in Utah mentions using broadcast media. Many statutes list prosecuting attorneys, legislative or public bodies or state watchdog agencies as the proper recipients of the information. Some statutes simply do not specify to whom the report is to be made.

A play fair provision in a number of state laws requires employees to tell your employer about the wrongdoing first—and allow him or her to straighten up.

State Whistleblower Laws

Alabama	No employer may discriminate against anyone who has opposed, reported or testified about an act or practice made illegal under the child labor laws. Ala. Code §§25-8-32 to 61
	A public employee is protected from discharge, demotion, transfer or other discrimination for reporting a violation, or what the employee believes in good faith is a violation, of the Code of Ethics for public employees, or for reporting a violation of a state law or local government law, rule or regulation to a public body. Ala. Code §§36-25-24, 36-26A-1
Alaska	State and local employees are protected for reporting any violation of a law, regulation, danger to public health and safety, gross mismanagement, waste, abuse of authority or a matter for investigation by the office of the ombudsman to a public body.
	Employers may require employees to give notice prior to making a report, but notice is not required if the employee believes it would not result in prompt action, the employer already knows about the activity, the situation is an

	emergency or the employee fears discrimination or reprisal. A person who violates this law may be liable for a civil fine of up to $10,000. Alaska Stat. §§39.90.100 through 39.90.150
Arizona	Public employees are protected against reprisal for reporting violations of law, mismanagement, abuse of authority or gross waste of funds to the attorney general, legislature, governor, county attorney or any federal, state or local law enforcement agency. Ariz. Rev. Stat. Ann. §38-532
Arkansas	It is illegal to discharge, threaten or otherwise discriminate or retaliate against a public employee who, in good faith, reports a waste of public funds, a violation of state or local law, rule or regulation, or a breach of a code of ethics or standard of conduct. The employee must have personal knowledge of the facts in the policy violation and must give the public employer reasonable notice and time to correct it. Ark. Code Ann. §§21-61-601 to 609
California	State employees are protected from reprisal for reporting violations of state or federal laws or regulations, economic waste, gross misconduct, incompetence or inefficiency to the State Auditor. University of California employees are also protected from reprisal for reporting similar improper activities by the university or its employees, officers or faculty. California Whistleblowers Act, Cal. Gov't. Code §§8547 and following Employees are protected from reprisal for reporting violations of a federal or state statute or regulation to a government or law enforcement agency. Cal. Lab. Code §1102.5
Colorado	State employees are protected from reprisal for disclosing information to any person or testifying before any committee of the general assembly regarding any practice, including waste of public funds, abuse of authority or misman-agement. Employees must make a good faith effort to provide information to their supervisor before disclosure. Colo. Rev. Stat. §§24-50.5-101 through 24-50.5-105
Connecticut	Employees are protected from reprisal for reporting or testifying to a public body about a violation of federal, state or local statutes, regulations or ordi-nances. Conn. Gen. Stat. Ann. §§31-51; Conn. Public Act 97-47, §48 State government employees are protected from reprisal for reporting corrup-tion, unethical conduct, violation of state or federal law, gross waste of funds, mismanagement, abuse of authority, or danger to public health and safety to a public body. Conn. Gen. Stat. Ann. §4-61dd; Conn. Public Act 97-55 Employees of utility or utility holding companies or nuclear power plant facilities are protected from retaliation for reporting misconduct to the Department of Public Utility Control. The Department of Public Utility Control will not inform the employer of the identity of the person making the report. Conn. Public Act 97-60
Delaware	Public employees are protected from reprisal for reporting to the State Office of Auditor of Accounts violations of state or federal laws or regulations. Del. Code Ann. tit. 29, §5115

District of Columbia	All District employees, including those working for independent agencies and contractors, are protected against reprisal for disclosing information concerning illegal or unethical conduct that threatens public health or safety. D.C. Code Ann. §§1-616.11 and 1-616.19
Florida	State employees and independent contractors for the state are protected against reprisal for reporting violations of law or regulations that create danger to the public or constitute gross waste or mismanagement of public funds. Fla. Stat. §112.3187
	It is illegal to discriminate against, discharge or in any manner harass an employee who has acted lawfully under the False Claims Act by reporting violations, helping an investigation and participating in proceedings under the Act. Fla. Stat. §68.088
	An employer may not take retaliatory action against an employee because that employee has disclosed or threatened to disclose any violation of law, or gave information to any governmental agency or objected to an illegal act, provided that he first told the employer and gave him a reasonable time to correct the problem. Fla. Stat. §§448.101 to 103
Georgia	A public employee is protected from reprisal in the reporting of the possible existence of fraud, waste and abuse regarding state programs and operations. The employee may remain anonymous unless the employer decides that disclosure is necessary to the report. Public employees are also protected against retaliation for complaining or testifying about discriminatory employment practices. Ga. Code Ann. §§45-1-4; 45-19-45
	Retaliation is not permitted against employees of longterm care facilities because of making a complaint to the state or community ombudsman. Ga. Code Ann. §31-8-60
Hawaii	Employees are protected against reprisal for disclosing violations of state or local laws or rules to public bodies. Haw. Rev. Stat. §§378-61 through 378-69
Idaho	An employer may not take any adverse action against a public employee who, in good faith, reports the existence of waste of public funds or a violation of law. The reporting employee must give the employer a reasonable opportunity to correct the problem.
	The reporting privilege extends to objecting to or refusing to carry out a directive that the employee reasonably believes is a violation of law. The employer cannot set policies that unreasonably restrict an employee's ability to document waste or violations. Protection of Public Employees Act, Idaho Code §6-2101 to 2109
Illinois	State employees are protected from reprisals for disclosing waste, mismanagement, abuse of authority, substantial and specific danger to public health and safety, or violation of a law, rule or regulation. 5 Ill. Comp. Stat. 395/1
Indiana	State employees are protected from reprisals for reporting in writing violations of state or federal laws or regulations, or misuse of public resources. Employees must first disclose to their supervisors and give a reasonable time to

correct the problem before reporting it to anyone else. Ind. Code Ann. §4-5-10-4
An employee of a private employer under contract with the state is protected
for reporting violations of the law or misuse of public resources to the agency
involved. Unless the employer is the suspected violator, the employee must
first tell the employer. If the state agency does not make a good faith effort to
correct the violations within a reasonable time, the employee may submit a
written report to any person or organization. Ind. Code Ann. §22-5-3-3
Employees of political subdivisions of the state enjoy the same protections as
state employees. Ind. Code Ann. §31-1-8-8

Iowa
State employees are protected against reprisal for disclosing information
regarding violations of any law or rule, mismanagement, gross abuse of funds,
abuse of authority, or substantial and specific danger to public health and safety
to a member of the General Assembly, legislative service bureau, legislative
fiscal bureau or caucus staff of General Assembly. Iowa Code §70A-28

Kansas
It is unlawful to discharge or discriminate against any employee who testifies
before the secretary of human resources, or files a complaint or in any way
brings to the secretary's attention any matter of controversy between the
employee and the employer. Kan. Stat. Ann. §44-615
State employees are protected from reprisal for discussing the operations of
any state agency with any member of the legislature. The statute specifically
prohibits any requirement of notification of supervisor prior to reporting.
Kan. Stat. Ann. §75-2973

Kentucky
State government employees are protected against reprisal for reporting
violations of any state or federal law or regulation, or mismanagement, waste,
fraud, or endangerment of public health or safety to judicial, legislative, or
law enforcement agencies. Employees need not give employers prior notice.
Ky. Rev. Stat. §§61.102 through 61.103

Louisiana
Employees are protected from reprisal for reporting violations of environmental laws or regulations of state, federal or local authorities. La. Rev. Stat. Ann.
§30:2027
Employees may not be discharged or discriminated against for testifying or
disclosing information to an investigation of labor law enforcement. La. Rev.
Stat. Ann. §23:964
Public employees are protected for reporting to an agency head, Board of
Ethics for Elected Officials or the Commission on Ethics for Public Employees
anything that the employee reasonably believes is a violation of government
ethics or any alleged act of impropriety within any government entity. La.
Rev. Stat. Ann. §42:1169
An insurer may not penalize an employee for reporting in good faith to the
commissioner of insurance or other appropriate authority a suspected
violation of law, including illegal discrimination against an individual. La.
Rev. Stat. Ann. §22:13

Maine	Private sector employees are protected from reprisal for reporting information concerning violations of state or federal law or regulation. To be protected, the employee must first disclose the violation to a supervisor and give the employer an opportunity to correct the problem, unless the employee has specific reason to believe that such notice is futile. State employees are protected for giving any information to legislative committees. Me. Rev. Stat. Ann. 26, §§831 to 840
	It is unlawful to discharge, discipline or otherwise discriminate against an employee who has assisted in the supervision or enforcement of the law regulating smoking in the workplace Me. Rev. Stat. Ann. tit. 22, §1580-A(6)
Maryland	State employees are protected against reprisal for disclosing what they reasonably believe are violations of any law, rule or regulation, gross misman-agement, gross waste of funds, abuse of authority or substantial and specific danger to public health and safety. Md. Code Ann., State Personnel and Pensions, art. 5, §305
Massachusetts	Public employees are protected from retaliation for disclosing or threatening to disclose an activity, policy or practice that the employee reasonably believes violates the law or poses a risk to public health or safety or the environment. Providing information, testifying or refusing to participate in an illegal or unsafe activity are also protected. The employee must first bring the issue to the supervisor's attention, with certain exceptions enumerated in the statute. Mass. Gen. Laws Ann. ch. 149 §185
Michigan	Employees are protected against reprisal for reporting to a public body violations of a federal, state, or local statute or regulation. Mich. Stat. Ann. §§15.361 and 17.428
Minnesota	Employees are protected for reporting violations of any federal or state law or rule to the employer or to any governmental body or law enforcement official. The employee's identity must be kept confidential. A good faith belief that a violation has occurred is protected. Employers must give written notice of the reason for employee's termination. Minn. Stat. Ann. §§181.931 through 181.935
Mississippi	State employees cannot be dismissed or penalized because they provided information to or testified before an investigative body. Miss. Code Ann. §§25-9-173 to 175
	Employees of longterm care facilities, hospitals and home health agencies cannot be retaliated against because they report abuse or exploitation of a patient or resident. Miss. Code Ann. §43-47-370
Missouri	State employees are protected from reprisal for disclosing violations of any law, rule or regulation, gross mismanagement, gross waste of funds, abuse of authority, or substantial and specific danger to public health and safety to the state auditor or any member of the legislature. Employees are not required to notify their supervisors before making disclosures. Mo. Rev. Stat. §§105.0550 and 105.058

	Employees of hospitals and ambulatory surgical centers are protected from reprisal for disclosing, in good faith: mismanagement or fraudulent activity; violations of federal or state laws or rules of patient care or of patient and facility safety; employee incompetence. Mo. Stat. Ann. §197.285
Montana	A public or private employer may not fire an employee because that employee reported a violation of public policy or refused to violate public policy. Employees who have completed probation are protected from discharge unless it is done for good cause. An employee who reports that the employer violated provisions of its own personnel policy is also protected. The Wrongful Discharge From Employment Act. Mont. Code Ann. §39-2-901 to 905
Nebraska	Employees of the state and its political subdivisions and of private employers with 15 or more employees are protected against reprisal for opposing an unlawful practice or refusing to carry out any unlawful action under federal or state law. Neb. Rev. Stat. §48-1114
Nevada	No retaliatory action may be taken against a state employee for reporting improper governmental action. Reprisals include denial of adequate personnel to perform duties, frequent staff replacements, frequent and undesirable changes in office location, refusal to assign meaningful work, a demotion, pay reduction, promotion denial, transfer and other acts. Employees who suspect reprisal may request a hearing within two years of their disclosure. Nev. Rev. Stat. §§281.611 to .671
New Hampshire	Employees are protected from reprisal for reporting violations of any state or federal law or rule or for participating in an investigation. Employees may refuse to participate in any unlawful activity or any activity which is fraudulent or incompatible with public policy concerning public health, safety and welfare and the protection of the environment. The employee is required to give prior notice to the employer and to give him or her reasonable time to correct unless the employee has specific reason to believe that such notice is futile. N.H. Rev. Stat. Ann. §275-E:1 to 275-E:7
New Jersey	Public and private sector employees are protected from reprisal for reporting any violation of law or regulation, improper patient care, or any action that is incompatible with public health, safety or welfare or the protection of the environment, to a supervisor, a public body, or to another employer with whom there is a business relationship. Employees are required to give written notice to supervisors unless the violation is known to supervisors, or the situation is an emergency and the employee fears physical harm. N.J. Stat. Ann. §34:19-1 to 19-8
New Mexico	Retaliatory discharge against an employee who reports or who refuses to commit a violation of state public policy is unlawful. N.M. Jury Instructions, Civil §13-2304; *Vigil v. Arzola*, 699 P.2d 613 (1983)
New York	Public and private employees are protected from reprisal for reporting to a public body violations of state, federal or local statutes or regulations which create a substantial and specific danger to the public health and safety.

	Written prior notice to supervisors with reasonable opportunity to correct the problem must be given. Employees may refuse to participate in the violation. N.Y. Lab. Law §740
North Carolina	State employees are protected from reprisal for reporting violations of any state or federal law or regulation, fraud, misappropriation of state funds, or danger to public health and safety to a supervisor or other appropriate authority. Employees are also protected for refusing to carry out any order which constitutes a violation of law or poses a substantial danger to public health and safety. N.C. Gen. Stat. §§126-84 to 88
North Dakota	Public employees are protected from reprisal for reporting violations of state or federal laws or rules or misuse of public resources to their agency head, state's attorney, attorney general or an employee organization. N.D. Cent. Code §34-11.1-04
	All employees are protected from reprisals for reporting to their employer, government body or law enforcement official a suspected violation of law; or for participating upon request in an investigation or hearing; or for refusing to perform an action that the employee objectively believes is a violation of law. The employee may ask the commissioner of labor for assistance. N.D. Cent. Code §34-01-20
Ohio	Employees are protected against reprisal for disclosing to supervisors or any appropriate public official violations of any federal or state law or regulation which is either criminal or likely to cause imminent risk of physical harm to persons or is a hazard to public safety.
	Employees must give an employer immediate oral notice of the violation followed by a written report. The employer has 24 hours to remedy the situation. If the violation is not corrected, the employee may report to the appropriate public officials. Ohio Rev. Code Ann. §§4113.51 through 4113.53
	State civil service employees are protected for reporting in writing violations of laws or misuse of public resources to their supervisors. If the employee reasonably believes that the violation or misuse is a criminal offense, he may also report it to a prosecuting attorney or a peace officer. Ohio Rev. Code §124.34.1
Oklahoma	Employees of state agencies are protected from reprisal for disclosing to any member of the legislature, legislative committee, administrative hearing or court of law violations of laws or policies, gross waste of public funds, abuse of authority and substantial and specific danger to public health or safety. There is no need to give notice. Employees may discuss the operations of the agency with the governor, members of the legislature or others. Okla. Stat. tit. 74,§840-2.5
Oregon	Employees who report criminal activity or bring or participate in a civil or criminal proceeding are protected from retaliation. Or. Rev. Stat. §659.550
	Public employees are protected from reprisal for disclosing, in response to an official request, activities of the agency or state and for disclosing violations of laws or rules, improper actions or inefficiency of superior officers or fellow

	employees, gross waste of funds, abuse of authority, specific danger to public health and safety. There is no requirement that the employee give notice to his or her superior before disclosure. Or. Rev. Stat. §659.510
Pennsylvania	State and local government employees are protected against reprisal for disclosing to their superiors or to appropriate federal, state or local agencies violations of any federal or state law or regulation; or of a code of ethics that protects the public's or employer's interest. Pa. Cons. Stat. Ann. tit. 43, §§1421 to 1428 An employer may not discharge or discriminate against any person who has refused to operate a commercial motor vehicle that does not comply with safety laws; or who has filed a complaint, testified or is about to testify in a proceeding regarding carrier safety. 43 Pa. Cons. Stat. §1431
Rhode Island	Employees who report a violation of a law or regulation or are required by a public body to participate in a hearing or inquiry are protecting from reprisals. Whistleblower Protection Act, R.I. Gen. Laws §28-50-1 and following
South Carolina	State and local government employees are protected from reprisal for disclosing violations of any federal or state law or regulation, or criminality, corruption, waste, fraud, gross negligence or mismanagement to an appropriate public body. S.C. Code Ann. §§8-27-10 through 8-27-50
South Dakota	Public employees who believe they have been retaliated against for reporting a violation of state law may file a grievance with the career service commission. S.D. Codified Laws Ann. §3-6A-52
Tennessee	Employees are protected from termination for speaking out about or refusing to participate in an activity that is in violation of a state or federal law or regulation that is intended to protect public health and safety. Tenn. Code Ann. §50-1-304 State employees are encouraged to report violations of state or federal laws or regulations, fraud, misuses of resources or acts that are a danger to the health and safety of the public or other employees. No employee may be discharged, disciplined, threatened or otherwise discriminated against for making such reports. Tenn. Code Ann. §§8-50-1
Texas	State employees are protected against reprisal for reporting violations of state or federal statutes or rules or local ordinances or rules, to an appropriate law enforcement authority. Texas Code Ann., Gov. §554.002
Utah	State or local government employees are protected from reprisal for reporting in any fashion, including verbal, written, broadcast or otherwise, a violation of any federal, state or local law or rule, or the waste of public funds, property or human resources. An employer may not implement policies that unreasonably restrict an employee's ability to document waste or violations. Utah Code Ann. §§67-21-1 through 67-21-9

Vermont	An employer may not discharge, discipline or discriminate against any employee who files a complaint against or testifies about violations of the state's law prohibiting an employer from requiring an employee to take a lie detector test, anti-discrimination laws, smoking in the workplace laws or unfair labor practice laws. Vt. Stat. Ann. tit. 21, §§494(d), 495; tit. 18, §427; tit. 3, §961
Virginia	A nursing facility or assisted living facility may not retaliate against a person who provides information to a government agency or to another entity responsible for protecting patients' or residents' rights. Va. Code Ann. §32:1-138.4 Employers may not penalize or discriminate against employees who report violations of lead abatement laws and regulations. Va. Code Ann. §54.1-515
Washington	State and local government employees are protected from reprisal for reporting to the State Auditor any violation of state laws or rules, abuse of authority, waste of public funds, or a substantial and specific danger to public health and safety. Wash. Rev. Code Ann. §§42.40.010 to .900, 42.41.010 to 902 Employees who oppose discriminatory labor practices are protected from reprisal. Wash. Rev. Code Ann. §49.60.210 Employees who complain to the department of social and health services of abuse, neglect or exploitation of a person in a hospital or other facility licensed by the Department of Health are protected from retaliation. Wash. Rev. Code Ann. §§70.124.100; 70.34.180. Employees who complain to the department of health about improper quality of care by a healthcare provider or facility are protected from retaliation. Wash. Rev. Code Ann. §43.70.075
West Virginia	State or local government employees are protected from reprisal for reporting to government bodies or agencies violations of any federal or state law or regulation, or of a code of ethics or standard of conduct or of a waste of public funds. W.Va. Code §6C-1-1 and following It is against public policy for private employers to retaliate against employees for whistleblowing. *Harless v. First National Bank in Fairmount*, 246 S.E.2d 270 (1978)
Wisconsin	State employees are protected from reprisal for disclosure of violations of any state or federal statute, rule or regulation, mismanagement, abuse of authority, substantial waste of public funds, or a danger to the public health and safety to the appropriate law enforcement agency or to any person. Employee must first disclose the information in writing to a supervisor. Wis. Stat. Ann. §§230.80 through 230.89
Wyoming	Licensed hospitals, care facilities and service providers may not harass or discriminate against any resident, patient or employee for reporting to the Department of Health a violation of state or federal law. Wyo. Stat. Ann. §35-2-910 State employees may not be terminated or retaliated against for making a written report of a violation of a state or federal law, regulation or rule or a condition that threatens public or employee health or safety. Wyo. Stat. §9-11-103

2. Using Other State Laws

Even if the reason for your dismissal is not specifically outlawed by a public policy law in your state or a provision within one of your workplace laws, you may have another convincing legal argument to raise. Courts often play Follow the Leader—adopting the public policy holdings from other states. If you can point to a well-reasoned opinion with facts similar to yours, you may be able to convince a court that conduct that was against public policy in another state should be illegal in your state, too.

Example: *Horatio, a salesperson in a clothing store in Virginia, was fired because he reported to police that the manager of the store was buying stolen wristwatches and selling them to customers on the sly. Virginia does not have a law that specifically prohibits firing an employee who reports a crime. Nevertheless, Horatio might be able to argue successfully in court that his firing violated public policy because other states, such as South Carolina, have laws that specifically forbid such firings.*

Tips for Telling Whether You Are Protected

Whistleblower statutes attempt to protect against the too-common occurrence of employees who are fired just after speaking to authorities about some wrongdoing.

Coincidence? Maybe.

What makes the firing questionable—and possibly covered by a whistleblower statute—is often the timing. Pay strict attention to when you were fired. Note whether it was soon after your employer found out that you reported the wrongful behavior. The shorter the time, the more likely that you are protected by a whistleblower statute.

There are also a number of other questions you should ask to help determine whether you may be covered by a whistleblower statute.

- Did you complain to anyone at your own workplace about the wrongful behavior before going outside? If so, what was the response? Were you threatened? Were you offered special benefits for not filing a complaint?
- If your company has a policy of progressively disciplining employees—reprimand, probation, suspension, dismissal—was it speeded up or ignored in your case?
- Were your whistleblowing activities specifically mentioned to you by your supervisor? By company management? By other employees?
- Have other employees been fired for whistleblowing?
- Did you notice management or co-workers treating you differently after you complained about the illegal behavior? Were you suddenly ostracized or ignored, passed over for promotions, given a less attractive job assignment?

The more documentation you can produce—memos from management, dated notes summarizing conversations with co-workers, signed statements from other former employees—the stronger your case will be. (For other advice on documenting your dismissal, see Chapter 10, Section C.)

C. Blacklisting

As archaic and barbaric as it may seem, there are still some companies, labor unions and people working within them that are not content to merely fire you or force you out of your job. They seem unwilling to rest until they have squelched all hope that you will work again.

The danger of losing a defamation lawsuit does not seem to dissuade some vengeful people from trying to put former employees on a list of people that no one else will hire. So some states have passed laws that expressly allow former employees to take legal action—criminal, civil or both—against those who try to sabotage efforts to secure new employment. (See the chart below for state blacklisting laws.)

Although in many cases, you could sue instead for defamation for this type of wrong, the advantage of using the blacklisting statute is that you do not have to prove that you were harmed—often a difficult task at trial. (See Section A5.)

1. Detecting Blacklisting

The mere fact that you have to work hard at finding a new job usually is not sufficient evidence to suggest blacklisting. But a strong signal would be a series of situations in which potential new employers seem to be on the verge of hiring you, then suddenly lose all interest. This indicates that, when a prospective employer checks your references just before hiring you, the blacklister is tipped off to where you have applied for work and is able to ding you.

2. State Laws on Blacklisting

This is a synopsis of state laws prohibiting blacklisting. Note also that nearly half the states have additional laws that specifically make it illegal for an employer to defame an employee in words or writing.

Additional Laws May Apply

If the chart below indicates that your state has no statute, this means there is no law that specifically addresses the issue. However, there may be a state administrative regulation or local ordinance that does control. Call your state labor department for more information. (See the Appendix for contact details.)

State Blacklisting Laws	
Alabama	Employers may not keep or use a blacklist to prevent any person from gaining employment. Violations are punishable as misdemeanors. Ala. Code §13-A-11-123
Alaska	No statute
Arizona	Blacklisting is forbidden by the state constitution. Ariz. Const. Art. XVIII, §9 It is also considered unlawful by statute. Ariz. Rev. Stat. Ann. §23-1361(A)

Arkansas	Employers may not distribute writing containing false statements or any other information about the employee for the purpose of getting that employee fired or to prevent a hiring. Violations are punishable as misdemeanors, by fines of $100 to $500 and jail for up to one year. Ark. Stat. Ann. §11-3-202
California	Any person who tells another about an employee's felony conviction, with the intent of causing the employee to be fired, is guilty of a misdemeanor if the employee is in fact fired as a result. Cal. Penal Code §2947 An employer may not give misinformation to prevent a former employee from obtaining employment. Cal. Labor Code §1050
Colorado	Employers may not blacklist or cause a discharged employee to be blacklisted. Violators are subject to a fine, imprisonment or both. Colo. Rev. Stat. §§8-2-110 and 8-2-111 If a bank or financial institution requests information about a current or former employee, it is not unlawful for another bank or financial institution to disclose information about that employee's involvement in a theft or other financial wrongdoing. Colo. Rev. Stat. §8-2-111.5 An employer may give another person "fair and unbiased information" about a current or former employee as long as it is not knowingly false, misleading or disclosed for a malicious purpose. Colo. Rev. Stat. §8-2-114
Connecticut	Employers may not blacklist, publish an employee's name with the intent of preventing the employee from getting employment or conspire to prevent an employee from getting other employment. Employers may make truthful statements to prospective employers. Violations are punishable by fines of from $50 to $200. Conn. Gen. Stat. Ann. §31-51
Delaware	No statute
District of Columbia	No statute
Florida	An agreement or conspiracy to prevent any person from procuring work or to cause his or her firing is prohibited. Communications threatening injury to life, property or business for the purpose of procuring the firing of any person or to prevent a person from getting hired is also prohibited. Violations are punishable as misdemeanors. Fla. Stat. §448.045
Georgia	No statute
Hawaii	It is illegal to make, circulate or cause a blacklist to be circulated. Haw. Rev. Stat. §377-6(11)
Idaho	It is unlawful for an employer to maintain a blacklist or to notify another employer than an employee has been blacklisted. Idaho Code §44-201
Illinois	No statute
Indiana	Employers may not prevent a fired employee from obtaining another job, but may state the correct reason for a former employee's dismissal to prospective employers. Employers found guilty of blacklisting are liable for compensatory, and possibly exemplary damages. Ind. Code Ann. §§22-5-3-1 and 22-5-3-2
Iowa	Employers may not prevent or try to prevent a fired employee from obtaining other employment either by oral or written communication of any kind, blacklisting or making false charges concerning the employee's honesty.

	Employers who blacklist are liable for treble damages. Iowa Code §§730.1 through 730.3
Kansas	Employers may not prevent a discharged employee from obtaining employment except by furnishing in writing, upon request, the cause of such discharge. Kan. Stat. Ann. §§44-117 through 44-119
Kentucky	An employer cannot blacklist any person for failing to use the company store of a mining company. Ky. Rev. Stat. §352.550
Louisiana	An employer may not disclose false or misleading information about an employee's job performance or reasons for separation. La. Rev. Stat. Ann. §23:291
Maine	A person may not prevent—by intimidation, force or a blacklist—a wage earner from gaining employment. Violators may be fined up to $500 and jailed for up to two years. Me. Rev. Stat. Ann. tit. 17, §401
Maryland	No statute
Massachusetts	No person shall, by intimidation or force, prevent another from entering into or continuing employment. Mass. Gen. Laws ch. 149 §19
Michigan	No statute
Minnesota	Employers may not prevent former employees from obtaining employment elsewhere. Violations are punishable as misdemeanors. Minn. Stat. §179.60
Mississippi	Public service corporations—telegraph, phone and railroad companies—that employ telegraphers may not blacklist a telegrapher that is affiliated with a lawful trade or labor union. Miss. Code Ann. §§77-9-725 - 727 and 77-9-33
Missouri	No statute
Montana	Employers may not blacklist a discharged employee or an employee who voluntarily left the company's service. Employers may give a prospective employer a truthful statement regarding the reason for discharge. Employers who violate blacklisting laws may be punished by six months in jail, a $500 fine or both. If an employee is prevented from obtaining employment, punitive damages will be assessed. Mont. Code Ann. §§39-2-801 through 39-2-803
Nebraska	No statute
Nevada	Employers may not prevent former employees from engaging in or securing other employment. Violations are punishable as misdemeanors. However, when employees are discharged, employers may give truthful written reasons for the discharge. Nev. Rev. Stat. §613.210
New Hampshire	No statute
New Jersey	No statute
New Mexico	An employer who prevents or tries to prevent a former employee from obtaining other employment is punishable by six months to one year in prison. However, employers may give an accurate report or honest opinion of the qualifications or performance of a former employee upon request. N.M. Stat. Ann. §30-13-3

New York	It is an unfair labor practice to circulate a blacklist to prevent an individual from securing employment because he exercised rights to unionize. N.Y. Labor Law §704(2)
North Carolina	Employers may not prevent, attempt to prevent or conspire to prevent a discharged employee from obtaining other employment. N.C. Gen. Stat. §§14-355 and 356
North Dakota	Any person who maliciously interferes with or hinders a person in obtaining or enjoying employment is guilty of a misdemeanor, punishable by up to one year in prison, a $12,000 fine or both. N.D. Cent. Code §34-01-06 Corporations may not exchange blacklists. Const., Article XII §17
Ohio	An employer cannot disclose false information concerning the employment of a former employee with the intent to mislead a prospective employer. Ohio Rev. Code §4113.71
Oklahoma	Employers may not blacklist or require a "letter of relinquishment"— basically, a letter of resignation—for the purpose of preventing the employee from obtaining other employment. Violators are subject to a fine of $100 to $500, and a blacklisted employee may sue for damages. Okla. Stat. Ann. tit. 40, §§172 and 173
Oregon	Employers may not prevent former employees from engaging in or securing other employment. Or. Rev. Stat. §659.230
Pennsylvania	No statute
Rhode Island	An employer cannot blacklist any employee who engages in legal union activities, including organization. R.I. Gen. Laws §§28-7-12
South Carolina	No statute
South Dakota	No statute
Tennessee	No statute
Texas	Employers may not blacklist an employee who quits or is discharged to prevent the former employee from getting similar or other employment. Blacklisting is punishable by a fine of $50 to $250, 30 to 90 days in prison or both. Texas Code Ann., Lab. §52.031 It is unlawful discrimination to blacklist or to prevent an employee from obtaining new employment. An employer that receives any communication that could be considered a form of blacklisting must give the affected employee a copy of it within ten days, if he or she requests it. Tex. Civil Stat. art. 5196(1)(4)
Utah	Employers may not blacklist someone who is fired or voluntarily quits to prevent that person from obtaining similar employment. Violations are punishable as felonies by a fine of $55 to $1,000 and imprisonment for 60 days to one year. Utah Code Ann. §§34-24-1 and 34-24-2 Anyone who "maliciously hinders" another from obtaining or enjoying employment shall be guilty of a crime (Utah Const., Art. XII §19), and the exchange of blacklists by railroads, corporations, associations or people is prohibited. (Art. XVI §4)

Vermont	No statute
Virginia	Blacklisting is a misdemeanor which carries a fine of $100 to $500, but the employer may tell other employers the true reason for a discharge or give a true statement regarding the character and ability of an employee who voluntarily quit employment. Va. Code §40.1-27
Washington	Employers may not blacklist employees or former employees to prevent their employment or cause their discharge. Violations are misdemeanors and punishable by a fine of from $100 to $1,000 and imprisonment for 90 days to one year. Wash. Rev. Code Ann. §49.44.010
West Virginia	No statute
Wisconsin	Employers are prohibited from blacklisting discharged or voluntarily quitting employees to prevent them from obtaining other employment. Violations are punishable by fines of from $100 to $500. Wis. Stat. §134.02
Wyoming	No statute

D. Taking Action Against Your Dismissal

Once you become familiar with how employee dismissals are successfully challenged, compare those legal strategies to your firing and decide:
- which legal principle used to challenge a job loss best fits your situation
- whether you are willing to expend the effort, money and time it usually takes to fight a firing, and
- whether or not you will need a lawyer to help you challenge your firing.

Look first to local specialized resources for affordable help. For this, your telephone book can be a godsend. Check the topic index in the yellow pages under Community Services, Employment or similar headings. You are likely to find a number of listings for groups that deal with specialized workers—younger workers, older workers, immigrants, blue collar workers. Steel your nerves and give them a call. Many organizations now offer legal counseling or referrals. A growing number also offer the invaluable help of support groups or workplace counselors—people in like situations or with specialized training who can help you discover what your options might be.

Also check the Appendix to this book; it lists a number of specialized organizations that may offer advice, publications or referrals.

If you were fired for reasons that appear to violate public policy (see Section B) or were discriminated against in some way (see Chapter 8), you may be able to get government help in challenging your dismissal. For example, if you were fired for filing a complaint under the Fair Labor Standards Act, you can ask the

Labor Department to help you fight that dismissal. But be forewarned. These agencies are swamped with complaints—and are able to pursue only a fraction of the claims that have merit.

Look into possibilities less drastic than going to court—such as arbitration or mediation. (See Chapter 18, Section A.)

Finally, consider getting a lawyer's help in filing a lawsuit to challenge your dismissal. (See Chapter 18, Section D.) If you do consult a lawyer, he or she will likely urge you to package two or more legal claims in a single lawsuit. This may be your strongest bet in a wrongful discharge case because, if a judge or jury decides against you on one of the claims, you still have another leg to stand on. It is especially difficult to base an entire successful case on a breach of contract or public policy violation, since there are limits on what you can collect even if you do win such cases.

For example, damages awarded in a lawsuit based only on a breach of an implied employment contract would typically be limited to:

- reinstatement to the job—not a desirable thing, in many cases, because there are often bad feelings between the employee and employer, and
- lost wages, which do not often amount to much—particularly if you find a new job soon after being fired.

In contrast, a breach of good faith and fair dealing is a tort—an intentional or careless act of a person or institution that directly harms another person or institution. And in tort actions, you typically can ask for actual damages based on such things as emotional suffering, and for punitive damages—an amount of money that the wrongdoer is ordered to pay as a form of punishment and as a deterrent to repeating the behavior that gave birth to the lawsuit.

Punitive damages are usually based not on the size of the injury, but on the court's estimate of how large a financial penalty would be needed to make a former employer feel the sting. In the case of many large corporations, the size of the penalty needed to make the company hurt can be quite large.

Example: *Elmer was a salesperson for a building supply company whose employee manual stated that employees were considered permanent after completing a 90-day probation period. Elmer had been employed by the company for 14 years and was about to qualify for more than $50,000 in commissions from accounts he had sold years before.*

He was fired just a week before qualifying for those commissions—but he found an equivalent new job just a few weeks later. Elmer sued the company that had fired him for breach of implied contract (the employee manual's statement on permanent employment) and breach of good faith and fair dealing (the company's use of dismissal as a way to avoid having him qualify contractually for the commissions).

On the breach of implied contract count, the court awarded him only the wages he lost while unemployed—which, because he quickly found a replacement job, totaled less than $5,000. But on the breach of good faith and fair dealing claim, the court awarded Elmer the $50,000 in commissions that he would have qualified for had he not been fired, $250,000 for the emotional stress he suffered because of the ordeal of being fired and another $250,000 in punitive damages to deter his ex-employer from using that commission-avoidance trick again.

E. Plant Closing Laws

The statutes typically known as plant closing laws apply only to mass dismissals of employees. They are the poor cousins of wrongful discharge lawsuits.

These laws sometimes offer a way to challenge a job loss that is much quicker, easier and less expensive than filing a lawsuit. But the amounts of money and other relief that workers can seek under plant closing laws typically are minuscule compared with the recoveries available via the wrongful discharge lawsuit route.

Also, keep in mind that neither the federal plant closing law nor the state and local laws in the same category actually forbid closing worksites and dismissing the people who work there. All these laws really do is require that companies give employees a little advance notice that their jobs are going to go away, like it or not.

At most, plant closing laws can provide some income between jobs for employees of companies that fail to provide a warning that they're going to make a mass staff cut—and some punishments that might persuade a company that does not comply with the advance notice requirements of the plant closing laws not to repeat that behavior.

1. Federal Law

The federal plant closing law—more properly, the Worker Adjustment and Retraining Notification, or WARN Act (29 U.S.C. §§2101, 2102 to 2109)—requires employers with 100 or more fulltime employees to provide 60 days' advance written notice that they are going to lose their jobs before closing a facility—and before putting into effect any other mass staff reduction that will last six months or more.

Employers are also required to provide 60 days' notice of the staff reduction to the chief local elected official, such as the mayor of the city in which the cut will take place, and to the Dislocated Worker Unit of the state in which the cut will occur. The agency designated as the Dislocated Worker Unit varies from state to state, but your state's labor department should be able to direct you to the agency responsible for assisting workers who lose their jobs in mass dismissals. (See the Appendix for contact information.)

2. Exceptions

The federal plant closing law does not apply if:
- fewer than 50 workers are cut from the payroll
- the cut takes away the jobs of less than 500 workers and represents less than one-third of the employer's workforce
- the workers affected are parttime; this law defines parttime workers as those who average fewer than 20 hours of work per week, or who have been employed by the company for less than six of the 12 months preceding the staff cut
- the employees left voluntarily or were discharged for good cause, such as performance that does not meet the company's standards
- the staff cut is the result of a natural disaster
- the employees affected were working on a project that was considered temporary and were told that when they were hired
- waiting 60 days to let the workers go would put the company in danger of going out of business
- the employer could not have foreseen the circumstances that make the staff cut necessary
- the employer offers the workers being cut new jobs at another site within reasonable commuting distance, and the new jobs start within six months of when the old ones ended, or the workers being cut are offered new jobs at another site anywhere and they agree to the transfers within 30 days of when the employer offers them
- the employer voluntarily offers severance pay, not required under any contract or other agreement, that is equal to or greater than the number of days that the company is short on the 60-day notice requirement, or
- more than 90 days pass between two mass dismissals which would require advance notice if added together but which fall under the minimum size rules when counted separately.

3. Penalties for Violations

Obviously, the plant closing law has almost as many holes as fabric. But employers who manage to violate it despite all the exceptions can be made to pay the following penalties:

- backpay to each employee affected by the violation, up to a maximum of 60 days of pay
- reimbursement of the employees' benefit costs that would have been paid by the company had the illegal staff cut not occurred
- a fine of up to $500 per day for each day of the violation, up to a maximum of $30,000, and
- any attorneys' fees incurred.

This last penalty—requiring that legal fees be paid—is important because, if you have received your walking papers as part of a mass firing that violates the federal plant closing law and the government refuses to go to bat for you, you and your co-workers will probably have no recourse but to file a lawsuit to enforce your rights.

The Math May Be Tricky

Counting the days may be more difficult than you would assume. At least one court has ruled recently that backpay was based on 60 workdays rather than calendar days (*Saxion v. Titan-C-Mfg.*, 86 F.3d 553 (6th Cir. 1996)).

Help From the Government

Before you hire a lawyer to take action under the federal plant closing law, you may want to write or call the highest elected official of the municipality where the staff cut took place and ask him or her to pursue your complaint. The federal plant closing law specifies that a unit of the local government aggrieved may sue the employer involved in the federal district court where the incident occurred or in any district where the employer does business.

In general, governmental bodies are not very aggressive in pursuing complaints against businesses. But because largescale staff cutting may be a high profile political issue, your local mayor may surprise you by suddenly becoming your legal advocate.

4. State and Local Plant Closing Laws

A growing number of states have their own plant closing laws. (See the chart below.) Even a few cities, such as Vacaville, California, and Philadelphia, Pennsylvania, have laws restricting companies that order mass dismissals. Most of these laws merely add a minor restriction or two to the rules of the federal plant closing law, such as requiring that the corporation planning a mass staff cut notify another level of government of its plans in advance.

However, some of the state plant closing laws do provide substantial benefits for the workers they cover. For example, Hawaii's version requires an employer, under certain conditions, to make up the difference between a worker's regular pay and the unemployment compensation the worker will receive for up to four weeks after the staff cut.

Each of these laws specifies different restrictions, penalties and methods of enforcement. You can usually learn the details of any state or local law governing mass dismissals by calling your state's labor department.

Additional Laws May Apply

If the chart below indicates that your state has no statute, this means there is no law that specifically addresses the issue. However, there may be a state administrative regulation or local ordinance that does control. Call your state labor department for more information. (See the Appendix for contact details.)

State Plant Closing Laws	
Alabama	To lessen the financial burden of closure or layoffs, the Commissioner of Labor shall provide seminars on dealing with employee debts and must meet with the employees and management. The commissioner may communicate directly with creditors. If there is a substantial layoff, any state-chartered credit union may expand its membership into the general area. A credit union shall give its members additional time in which to satisfy their debts. Ala. Code §25-3-5
Alaska	No statute
Arizona	No statute
Arkansas	No statute
California	Private industry councils and the state Employment Development Department and its Dislocated Worker Unit shall provide training and assistance for workers who have lost their jobs due to a plant closure. Cal. Unemp. Ins. Code §§15076 and 15077.5

Colorado	Workers who have lost their jobs because of plant closings or technology are eligible to receive training for new jobs through a customized training program established by the Board of Education. Colo. Rev. Stat. §23-60-306
Connecticut	When an employer with 100 or more workers closes or relocates, the employer must continue to pay for employees' health insurance for 120 days after the closing or relocation, or until the employees become eligible for replacement group coverage. Conn. Gen. Stat. Ann. §31-51o
Delaware	No statute
District of Columbia	No statute
Florida	No statute
Georgia	No statute
Hawaii	Employers with 50 or more employees must give at least 45 days notice of impending job loss due to mass dismissal or business relocation. Haw. Rev. Stat. §394B-9 Employers must pay each former employee an allowance for the difference between the former wage and unemployment benefits for four weeks after termination. Haw. Rev. Stat. §394B-10 Employers who do not follow notice and severance requirements are liable to each employee for three months of compensation. Haw. Rev. Stat. §394B-12
Idaho	No statute
Illinois	No statute
Indiana	No statute
Iowa	Workers who have lost their jobs due to plant closures, and who are eligible for assistance under the federal Job Training Partnership Act, can receive job training, job search assistance and funds for education through the state job training partnership program. Ia. Code §7B.1 to .5
Kansas	The state Secretary of Human Resources must give prior approval to mass dismissals within certain industries such as public utilities and public transportation companies. Kan. Stat. Ann. §44-616
Kentucky	No statute
Louisiana	No statute
Maine	Employers must give employees at least 60 days advance notice before relocating a plant. An employer who relocates or terminates a work facility with over 100 employees must pay severance pay of one week per year worked at that site to employees who have been employed for more than three years—to be paid within one regular pay period of the employees' last work day. The statute does not apply to an employee who accepts relocated work, if the closure is caused by a physical calamity or the employment contract expressly provides for severance pay. Me. Rev. Stat. tit. 26, §625B
Maryland	Employers should follow guidelines established by the Work Force Investment Board covering issues such as advance notice to employees when planning a mass dismissal or relocation. Whenever possible, employers should give at least 90 days of notice to employees who are terminated because of a reduction in operations. Violators may be fined up to $1,000. Md. Code Ann. Lab. & Emp., Art. 11 §§301 to 304

Massachusetts	Employers who receive assistance from certain state agencies must make a good faith effort to give advance notice to employees who will lose their jobs in a mass dismissal and to help them maintain their income and health insurance benefits; the Commonwealth expects at least 90 days' continuance of each. Mass. Gen. Laws Ann. ch. 149 §182
	If a company with 50 or more employees is sold, employees who have worked there at least three years and who lose their jobs within two years after the sale are entitled to severance pay equal to two weeks of compensation for every year of service, due within one regular pay period after the employee's last day of work. Those terminated within one year after a sale are entitled to the same amount of severance, due within four pay periods after the sale. This statute does not apply to businesses sold within a family or where there is a more generous severance provision in an employee's contract. Mass. Gen. Laws Ann. ch. 149 §183
	All HMO and health insurance contracts must guarantee 90 days of continued coverage to employees terminated due to a plant closure. Mass. Gen. Laws Ann. ch. 176G, §4A and ch. 175, §110D
	Employees who have worked for a company for at least one year are eligible for reemployment assistance of up to $97/week for 13 weeks if they are laid off due to a plant closing or partial closing. Mass. Gen. Laws Ann. ch. 151A §71A-I
Michigan	The Department of Labor is directed to encourage businesses that are closing or relocating to give notice as soon as possible to the Department, employees, the unions and the community. If requested, the Department may study the feasibility of the employees establishing an employee-owned corporation to continue the business and may provide technical and financial assistance. Mich. Comp. Laws §§450.732 and following
Minnesota	Employers are encouraged to give notice of a planned plant closing or substantial layoff to the commissioner of economic security, to the employees and to the local government where the plant is located.
	The commissioner may initiate feasibility studies as to alternatives to closings and layoffs, including employee ownership, other new ownership, new products or public financial or technical aid. Dislocated workers and affected communities are eligible for assistance; employees may receive basic readjustment services for up to 90 days. Minn. Stat. Ann. §268.978 and following
Mississippi	No statute
Missouri	The company making the offering in a business takeover must disclose to the state securities commission and plant closures or relocations, significant layoffs or changes to the economic conditions for employees of the target company. Mo. Ann. Stat. §409.516
Montana	No statute
Nebraska	No statute
Nevada	No statute
New Hampshire	No statute

New Jersey	State agencies must assist workers who want to establish employee ownership options to save jobs threatened by plant closure. N.J. Stat. Ann. §34:1B-30 and following.
	If the plant closure would cause significant employment loss to an economically distressed municipality, the Commissioner of Commerce may grant funds for studying the benefits of employee stock ownership plans. N.J. Stat. Ann. §52:27H-95
New Mexico	No statute
New York	The Department of Labor, in coordination with the Department of Economic Development and the Dislocated Worker Unit, provides basic readjustment services after a plant closure, including: onsite intervention within 48 hours of notification of a closing or substantial layoff and resources and technical assistance to study employee ownership. N.Y. Lab. Law, §§835 and following
	Employees at plants that are about to be closed are encouraged to continue to operate them as employee owned enterprises; state assistance is available. N.Y. Pub. Auth. Law §§1836a and following
	A corporation registering a takeover offering must disclose to the state securities commission any plant closings or relocations, significant layoffs or material changes in compensation or employment conditions for workers at the target company. N.Y. Bus. Corp. Law. §1603
North Carolina	No statute
North Dakota	No statute
Ohio	No statute
Oklahoma	No statute
Oregon	Employers with 100 or more fulltime employees must notify the state's Economic Development Department whenever plant closings or mass layoffs are planned. There are programs, projects, expenditures and other forms of assistance available to communities, employers and workers under the Job Training Partnership Act. Or. Rev. Stat. §§285A.510 to .522
	Dislocated workers, including those laid off due to permanent plant closings or substantial layoffs, are entitled to unemployment compensation and related benefits while they are receiving professional technical training so that they can continue to care for their families and obtain employment. Or. Rev. Stat. §§657.335 to .340
Pennsylvania	Workers who are laid off due to plant closings are eligible for assistance to support them in job training programs. 43 Pa. Stat. §§690.a.1 and following
	Dislocated workers are also eligible for job training available through state programs established by the Department of Education. 24 Pa. Cons. Stat. Ann. §§6201 and following
Rhode Island	No statute
South Carolina	Employers who require employees to give notice of quitting must give those employees the same amount or at least two weeks of advance notice of a closing. Notice must be in writing and posted in every room of the work building. S.C. Code Ann. §41-1-40

South Dakota	No statute
Tennessee	Employers with 50 to 99 fulltime employees within the state must notify state labor officials of a mass dismissal after notifying those employees who will lose their jobs. State officials will then notify various state agencies, including welfare, health and education. Statute does not apply if the reduction or closing results solely from a labor dispute or from typical industry seasonal factors. Tenn. Code Ann. §50-1-601 to 604
Texas	No statute
Utah	Workers in defense or defense-related jobs who are laid off may apply to the Office of Job Training for assistance in retraining or re-education for job skills in demand. Utah Code Ann. §67-1-12
Vermont	No statute
Virginia	No statute
Washington	No statute
West Virginia	No statute
Wisconsin	Employers must give at least 60 days of notice of a permanent or temporary business closing or mass dismissal in which 25 or more fulltime employees or 25% of the workforce, whichever is greater, lose their jobs. Wis. Stat. §109.07
Wyoming	Workers displaced by plant closures or by substantial layoffs are eligible for occupational transfer and retraining programs and for other services. Wyo. Stat. §§27-13-101 to 103

CHAPTER

12

UNEMPLOYMENT INSURANCE

Unemployment insurance, often called UI or unemployment compensation, is intended to provide you with regular financial support when you are out of work.

Unemployment insurance programs are run jointly by the federal government and the states and are paid for primarily by a tax on employers. There are differences among the states in how the programs are administered, in who qualifies to receive benefits—and, importantly, in how much is available in benefits.

This chapter discusses unemployment insurance in general and explains some specific state nuances. For more information on your state's program, check with the nearest Unemployment Insurance Office or Employment Security Division, usually part of the state department of labor. (See the Appendix for contact details.)

A. Who Is Covered

Unemployment insurance covers nearly 97% of the workforce—employees of nearly every stripe, including parttimers and temporaries.

To be covered, you must meet a number of qualifications.

- You must have worked as an employee for a substantial period and earned a minimum amount in wages before becoming unemployed. In most states, you must have been employed for at least six months during the year before your job loss. The amount you are required to have earned to qualify for unemployment insurance benefits varies by state, and is frequently changed to reflect inflation and the cost of living.

- You must be a U.S. citizen or have the documents required by the U.S. Immigration and Naturalization Service to legally work in the United States. (See Chapter 17.)

- You must be available to be recalled to your old job or to work in a similar one. For example, you may become ineligible if you take a new job or if you take a long vacation during which you cannot be reached by your former employer or a new one.

- You must be physically and mentally able to perform your old job or a similar one. The requirement that workers must be physically able to work can be confusing when applied to pregnant women. In general, the courts have ruled that unemployment insurance benefits cannot be denied simply because an employee is pregnant, but can be denied if the pregnancy makes the employee physically unable to perform her normal job or one similar to it.

    Workers who are physically unable to perform their jobs usually have to apply for financial help under workers' compensation or Social Security disability insurance programs. (See Chapters 13 and 14.) However, a few states pay unemployment insurance benefits during periods of temporary disability. Your local unemployment insurance agency should help you determine whether your state is one of them.

    The requirement that a worker must be mentally able to work has reduced the number of unemployment claims filed because a job was too stressful.

B. Being Disqualified for Benefits

A few categories of employees are specifically listed as ineligible to receive unemployment insurance benefits. And a great many more employees are disqualified because of their own behavior or actions—such as quitting a job without a legally recognized reason.

1. Employees Excluded

The categories of employees not covered by unemployment insurance usually include people employed by small farms, those who are paid only through commissions, casual domestic workers and babysitters, newspaper carriers under age 18, children employed by their parents, adults employed by their spouses or their children, employees of religious organizations, some corporate officers and elected officials.

2. Disqualifying Behavior

Even if you are covered by unemployment insurance and otherwise eligible to receive it, you may be disqualified from receiving benefits. The reasons for disqualification vary from state to state, but the most common ones are discussed here.

- You were fired from your job for deliberate and repeated misconduct. That includes chronic absence or tardiness without a good explanation, sleeping on the job or violating clear and reasonable workplace rules. Note that it is not enough that you were careless or negligent on the job, that you arguably used poor judgment or that you accidentally damaged some of your employer's property. Your misconduct must have been purposeful and, unless it is very serious, must usually have happened more than one time.
- You refused to accept a similar job without good reason. In these economically strapped times, courts have been especially hard-pressed to find legally sufficient grounds for you to reject a valid job offer. The few reasons that have succeeded are that the employee was not physically able to do the work required, that the job was too far from his or her home and family or that the job would have required the employee to violate a firmly held religious belief, such as working on days his or her religion prohibits work.

- You are unemployed because you went on strike or are not working because you refused to cross a picket line. In some states, you will be entitled to unemployment benefits if there is a lockout at work—that is, your employer closes down because there is a contract dispute or refuses to let you work until you agree to accept changed work conditions.
- You quit your job without a good reason. (See the discussion below.)

Independent Contractors: A Gray Area

Independent contractors are not usually eligible for unemployment insurance. But in some cases, people treated as independent contractors by companies are found to be legal employees—and therefore eligible for unemployment benefits. (See Chapter 2, Section A.)

In fact, the legal controls are somewhat relaxed in allowing independent contractors to be covered by unemployment benefits. If your employment status is somewhat uncertain, you may need to provide proof that you qualified as an employee of a company rather than as an independent contractor before you can collect benefits from your state's unemployment system.

Persuasive proof would be that:

- your work was supervised by employees of the company
- your work was considered a normal part of the company's course of business—for example, an integral part of the quarterly financial review, rather than a one-time consulting job
- you worked in the company office, rather than from your own home, workshop or studio, or
- you used company-owned equipment—computers, machining tools, construction equipment—to get the work done.

---

3. Acceptable Reasons for Quitting

The last reason to be shut off from benefits—quitting your job—is particularly troublesome. Disputes over unemployment insurance claims often occur when the employee believes that his or her reason for quitting a job was a good one, and the employer disagrees.

Of course, the definition of a good reason to quit a job varies with each person and each circumstance. In most situations, you must first have informed your employer that there was a change in the job or working conditions that make it impossible for you to stay on. A number of reasons are usually considered good enough for you to quit your job and still be eligible for unemployment insurance.

- Some form of fraud was involved in recruiting you for the job. For example, employers sometimes offer a certain level of wages and benefits, but then try to cut back on that offer once the employee shows up for work.
- Your life or health was endangered by the employer's failure to maintain workplace safety. You will need to have some evidence that a doctor has examined you and confirmed that your health was jeopardized by the chemical discharge or other condition in the workplace. (See Chapter 7 for additional workplace safety concerns.)
- The nature of your work was changed dramatically from what you had originally been hired to do, or your wages and benefits were substantially reduced without your consent. Keep in mind that you may have to tolerate small changes in your job duties or conditions due to work restructuring or simple economics. However, if your job changes so substantially that it begins to look and feel different from the position you were offered originally, that may mean you are legally allowed to quit and still collect unemployment benefits.
- You were subjected to some intolerable or illegal condition on the job, such as discrimination or sexual harassment, and your employer refused to correct the situation after learning of it.
- A change in the location of your work made it impractical for you to continue in the job. A change of only a few miles would not likely be sufficient. But if the move is so far that it adds a substantial increase to your commuting time—several hours—or the company relocates to another state, that may be considered sufficient reason for you to leave the job and collect unemployment benefits.
- Your spouse had to relocate to take a new job. This reason, however, will not hold up in all states. In a number of cases, former employees argued that because women most often leave their jobs when a spouse gets transferred, it is discriminatory to deny unemployment benefits to them. The courts so far have disagreed and held that because men could be affected, too, there is no sex discrimination in denying benefits to workers who must move to stay with their mates.

Several states may also award you unemployment benefits if you can prove you quit for a compelling personal reason. But beware that you must usually back such claims with substantial evidence. For example, if you quit your job to care for a sick spouse, you will probably be asked to show that no alternative care arrangements were feasible, and that your employer was unwilling to grant you a paid or unpaid leave of absence.

If you have the luxury, do a little research on your eligibility for benefits before you leave your job. You can quit your job for other reasons and still file a claim for unemployment insurance benefits. True—filing for unemployment benefits requires perseverance, time, wading through paperwork and waiting in lines to speak with—and sometimes be berated by—unemployment office personnel. But you have little to lose by filing a claim you consider to be valid and hoping for a favorable decision. As the system is set up, employees who file for unemployment benefits are presumed to be entitled to them. Be forewarned that if your former employer challenges your claim, you will need to prove through the appeal process described below that your reason was good enough.

C. Calculating Your Benefits

Each state sets its own maximum and minimum limits on the amount of benefits you can collect. Whether you are entitled to the high end or the low end of the benefit amount allowed depends on the amount of money you earned in your last position.

Under normal circumstances, unemployment insurance benefits are limited to 26 weeks. However, this period is extended by legislative whim—especially during periods of high unemployment. In most states during most times, you will be entitled to an additional 13 weeks of benefit payments on top of the 26 weeks you already have coming.

To calculate your benefits, the unemployment insurance office will typically use one of three rather complicated formulas premised on the wages you recently earned. Then, depending on your state's law, you will be given more or less than half that amount. In addition, each state has minimum and maximum benefit limits within which it must abide.

Severance Pay: It May Not Compute

As protection against wrongful discharge lawsuits, employers increasingly offer an unearned severance payment—usually several months' worth of the employee's normal pay—to get an employee to quit a job rather than be fired. (See Chapter 10, Section F.) In such situations, severance pay can delay the start of unemployment insurance benefits—or even make a worker ineligible for them.

Example: *Raj worked for a company that wanted to economize by cutting 500 employees. He accepted the company's offer of six months' severance pay—four months more than the two months' severance pay he had earned through the benefits program—in return for a signed statement that he had not been dismissed, but had volunteered to quit his job.*

When Raj filed a claim for unemployment insurance benefits, he was shocked and disappointed when it was turned down. His former employer contested the claim, arguing that Raj had made a decision to quit voluntarily.

Raj appealed the denial of his claim, and he won because he proved that he was coerced into quitting. But the appeal office also ruled that Raj could not begin collecting unemployment insurance benefits until the four months covered by the unearned severance package had expired.

Regulations and rulings covering the effects that severance pay has on unemployment insurance vary greatly from state to state, and are changing rapidly. In some cases, groups of workers who have been cut from company payrolls through offers of severance packages have created enough political pressure to have the rules in their state changed in their favor.

If you quit your job in exchange for severance pay, protect your rights by filing a claim for unemployment insurance benefits. If that claim is denied, you will then have the right to explain during the appeals process what really happened—or to benefit from any changes in your state's unemployment insurance rules covering severance pay.

1. Average Weekly Wages

In Florida, Michigan, New Jersey, New York and Ohio, benefits are based on the average weekly wage, which is then cut in half to determine the weekly unemployment benefit amount.

Example: *Marika worked as a sales clerk, earning a weekly salary of $600, which was increased to $800 mid-year. Her average weekly wage was $700 ($600 + $800 divided by 2). The weekly unemployment benefit to which she is entitled is $350—$700 divided in half.*

2. Total Wages

In Alaska, Kentucky, Montana, New Hampshire, Oregon and West Virginia, unemployment benefits are computed by taking the annual wage and multiplying it by a set percentage, which varies by state and with time.

Example: *Blaine earned an annual wage of $36,500 as an assistant furniture buyer at a department store in Lexington, Kentucky. Multiplying his total annual wages by the state multiplier—.01185—yields a weekly unemployment benefit amount of $433.*

3. Highest Quarter of Earnings

All other states compute unemployment benefits using a slightly more complicated formula—based on the highest earnings you made during a certain period. In most states, this is calculated by quarters or three-month periods. The period in which an employee had the highest wages is the one most states use to calculate the amount of weekly unemployment insurance benefits. And the crucial quarters in most states are the first four of the last five quarters you worked before losing your job, but the period varies.

Example: *Bart worked for 26 weeks as a mechanic in an auto repair business, earning $350 per week. He then got a raise to earn $400 weekly—and worked an additional 26 weeks before being laid off. Bart's benefits will be based on the $5,200 ($400 x 13 weeks) that he earned during the quarter of his highest earnings. That amount will then be divided by 26, to get the $200 in weekly unemployment benefits Bart will be allowed.*

Some states also pay partial benefits to people whose workhours slip below their normal level for a substantial period. These programs vary widely, so when in doubt, it is wise to inquire at the unemployment insurance office if you think you may qualify for coverage.

Parttime Work: Throwing It Into the Mix

The bottom line is that unemployment benefits are based on the amount you used to earn. If your former job was parttime, you still may be eligible to collect unemployment benefits if you lose that job. This is true even if you hold down several parttime jobs—and lose only one of them. Keep in mind, however, that the amount to which you are entitled in unemployment benefits will be offset by the amount you still earn—and by any amounts you receive from workers' compensation and other sources.

The same is true if you secure a parttime job after losing other work. Your unemployment benefits will be reduced by the amount of income you earn in the new parttime job. You will have to weigh the drawbacks of this income loss against the benefits the parttime work may afford: a boost to your confidence, camaraderie of co-workers, increased visibility and contacts in the work world, added work experience.

D. Filing a Claim

Claims for unemployment insurance benefits are accepted and paid by the states through thousands of offices throughout the country. Tales of difficult dealings with the unemployment office are legion—long waits, surly officeworkers, piles of paperwork—all coming your way at what is likely to be an emotionally shaky time for you. Keep in mind that you are merely pursuing your legal right. And arm yourself with the mantle of patience.

Finding the right office is the first hurdle. The names for the agencies that handle the claims vary, but are typically something that sounds more upbeat than unemployment—such as Bureau of Employment Security, Job Service Office or State Employment Service.

Whatever your local version is called, you can locate the office closest to you by checking the state government section of your local telephone directory. Because of the varying names used and the fact that there are many other government programs relating to jobs, it is wise to call to confirm that you have the right place. There are also links to all of the state unemployment offices' websites at http://www.doleta.gov/programs/uimap.htm.

In most states, there is a waiting period of one week between the time you lose your job and the time you can collect unemployment insurance benefits. But it is a good idea to visit the nearest unemployment office as soon after you lose your job as possible. You can then present your documentation, complete the required paperwork and convince agency representatives to begin investigating your claim—all the initial steps needed to get the bureaucratic ball rolling.

The Taxman Will Cometh

Unlike workers' compensation benefits (discussed in Chapter 13), unemployment insurance benefits are taxed as income. Because the benefit amounts paid are often below the taxable annual earning level, however, many states will not take the automatic step of deducting any taxes from your unemployment benefit check.

However, the state will—almost unfailingly—take the leap of reporting the unemployment benefit amount you were paid to the Internal Revenue Service and to your state taxing authority.

If you were receiving unemployment benefits during part of the year during which you got a new job, you may want to increase the amount your employer withholds in taxes from your paycheck. Otherwise, you may be unpleasantly surprised at tax time when you either owe more or receive less of a refund than anticipated.

---

1. Required Documentation

You claim will get processed more quickly if you bring the proper documentation when you visit the local office. You will need a number of documents, including:

- a detailed work history covering at least a few years prior to your unemployment, including accurate names, addresses, telephone numbers and IRS employer identification numbers of your previous employers. You should find these numbers on your paystubs or on employment-related IRS forms, such as your W-2 or 1099-Miscellaneous
- recent pay stubs and other wage records, such as the W-2 form on which your employer reports your income to the Internal Revenue Service
- your Social Security card, or another document that shows your Social Security number, and
- any documentation you have that proves you are unemployed, such as a layoff or dismissal notice from your employer, and your employer's unemployment insurance account number, if you know it. (For more on how to document a job loss, see Chapter 10, Section C.)

Typically, your first visit to the unemployment insurance claims office will include some type of orientation—ranging from simple instructional signs hanging from the ceiling to explanatory pamphlets to sophisticated video productions. In any case, you will be required to fill out forms explaining your unemployment. This is where your documentation will be especially useful.

What to Say, and What Not to Say

When completing your unemployment forms, one of the first questions posed will be something like: Explain in your own words the reason for leaving your last job. You will see first that there is little room for long-worded explanations. Take the clue and keep your responses simple and noncommittal.

Unless you were clearly dismissed from your job because of something you did wrong, avoid using the word "fired" in filing out any forms or answering any interview questions at the unemployment insurance office. There are many unspecified words thrown around concerning the end of employment, but fired is the one most often taken to mean that you did something wrong and were dismissed because of it.

If you lost your job because business was slow, note that you were laid off. "Laid off" is an equally vague term, but it is less likely to raise questions about the validity of your claim.

If you were discharged by your employer, take pains to note: "Discharged without any misconduct" or "Quit for good cause personal reason." Leave out any qualifying details, such as: "My supervisor never liked me from the first day I walked in, so naturally, I was the first to be laid off."

2. The Investigation

Once you have handed in your completed forms, the rituals that follow vary somewhat from state to state. You may be interviewed the same day or told to come back for an interview. If a second visit is required, be sure to take your employment document collection with you.

Whatever the ritual in your locale, the goal of the unemployment insurance claim filing process is to determine whether you are entitled to benefits, and what the amount of those benefits should be. The interviewer will likely concentrate on why you left your last job. Keep your explanations helpful but as brief and objective as possible.

In some states, you may be approved to receive benefits immediately. If your employer later challenges the award, you should continue to get those benefits during the time the appeal is processed.

But in most states, the clerks at the unemployment insurance office will use your first interview to launch an investigation of your claim by sending inquiries to your former employers. The employers then must respond, either verifying or disputing your version of the circumstances surrounding your unemployment, the wages you received and other relevant information. The process usually takes at least a few weeks, and sometimes more.

While waiting for your claim to go through this verification process, you will probably be required to visit the unemployment insurance office once each week or two to sign a statement affirming that you still meet all the legal requirements of the program—and that you are looking for a new job. It is important to comply with this reporting requirement even before receiving unemployment insurance checks. If you have not yet received a cent in unemployment benefits, once your claim is verified, you will usually be paid after the fact for all the weeks for which you did qualify.

If your claim is approved, you will typically receive your unemployment benefit check in the mail every two weeks after your claim is verified and your benefit level is determined.

3. Continuing Your Benefits

Once you have qualified for unemployment insurance benefits, you are not free to simply sit back and welcome the checks each week. You must continue to comply with the state program's rules and rituals to keep them coming.

You must visit the unemployment insurance office as frequently as your state requires it. During each visit, you must verify that you remain unemployed but available for work, that you remain physically able to work and that you are actively looking for work. The documents you sign on your visits to the unemployment insurance office will typically ask you to certify that you continue to meet these requirements, and it is usually a criminal offense to lie about any of your answers.

In some states, you are also required to list a minimum number of potential employers to whom you have applied for work since the last time you signed for benefits. This requirement may vary according to economic conditions. If the lines at the unemployment insurance offices get too long in your area, for example, you may be allowed to merely mail in your information every two weeks.

The unemployment insurance program cannot require you to take a job that varies much from your normal field of work and your normal wage level. But these ranges are subject to interpretation, so exercise care in deciding where to apply for a new job. Some unemployment insurance offices maintain and post listings of jobs that are available locally. Apply only for jobs that are similar to your normal type of work and wage levels so that you will not run the risk of having your unemployment insurance claim discontinued because you refused to accept substitute employment.

Where to File If You Move

If you become unemployed in one state and then move to another, you can file your claim in your new state, but your benefits will be determined by the rules used by your former state. Although your new state administers your claim, the cost of your benefits is charged back to the state in which you became unemployed. A move will also add time to processing your claim—usually increasing the delay by several weeks.

Keep in mind that even when you relocate, you still must meet all the requirements of the unemployment insurance program to qualify for benefits. Your new location must be one to which you were required to move by family circumstances, or in which it is logical for you to expect to find a new job. For example, you cannot decide to move to a small seacoast town with virtually no business activity because you like the countryside there, quit your old job for no other reason, and then expect to be eligible for unemployment insurance when you get to your new home and cannot find work.

E. Appealing Benefit Decisions

If your claim is approved, your former employer will have the right to appeal it. If you are denied benefits, you are legally entitled to appeal the decision.

1. If Your Employer Appeals

There are cases, of course, where some former employees begin to collect unemployment insurance benefits to which they are not legally entitled—and the employer justifiably appeals the decision.

However, some employers have an outrageous policy of appealing all unemployment insurance claims filed against them. Typically, they use tactics such as claiming that workers quit when, in fact, they were fired because business became slow.

These employers often hire lawyers or agencies that specialize in frustrating unemployment insurance claims—hired gunslingers who make a living by fighting employees' claims until the employees find new jobs and drop their complaints. Money is usually their motivation: The higher turnover a company has, the higher the company's unemployment premiums.

If your claim is approved but your employer appeals it, you will be notified of that appeal in writing. In general, an appeal by your former employer of an approved claim will be conducted in the same way as your appeal of a denied claim. (See Section 2, below.)

You will be able to continue collecting your benefits until a decision is issued on your former employer's appeal. You may, however, be required to repay all or part of the benefits if your ex-employer wins the appeal. Typically, your ability to repay is the deciding factor in such circumstances.

2. Appealing a Denied Claim

If your claim is denied, you will be notified in writing of why that decision was made, and informed of the procedure and time limits for filing an appeal. Depending on your state, you will have from one to four weeks to file an appeal from the time that the notice of denial of an unemployment insurance claim is mailed to you.

A hearing will likely be scheduled within a few weeks after you advise the unemployment insurance office of your intention to appeal its decision, and you will have the option of representing yourself or hiring a lawyer for help. If you want a lawyer but cannot afford one, check with your local Legal Aid Society or a clinic at a nearby law school to see if someone there can represent you. If you are unemployed and without benefits, chances are good that they will help. (See Chapter 18, Section D.)

Your former employer also has the option of being represented by a lawyer or an agency that specializes in challenging unemployment insurance claims. Typically, the appeal hearing will be conducted informally before a hearing examiner, referee or administrative law judge. At the hearing, you and your former employer will be allowed to bring witnesses, such as co-workers and medical experts—and most of the formal rules of evidence that apply to formal courtroom proceedings will not apply or will be only loosely enforced.

Mind the Time

Most states have strict rules about the time limits within which appeals must be filed—and they are doggedly enforced. You should find the appeal limit clearly marked on the notice of the determination or ruling. And late appeals will be accepted only if you can show that you have extremely good cause for being late: that circumstances beyond your control that you could not have anticipated caused you to file late. Excuses such as you forgot or did not note the filing due date will not pass legal muster.

Representing Yourself

If you can clearly document the reasons that you are unemployed and present them in an organized manner, you can do a good job of representing yourself in all but the most complex situations. At this level, the appeal process is intended to resolve disputes rather than to take on the look of a formal court action, so do not be afraid to ask questions at the unemployment insurance office or at your hearing.

Well before the hearing is scheduled to begin, write down the reasons that you feel you are entitled to unemployment insurance benefits in as few words as possible; then practice presenting those reasons to a friend or family member. Do not give in to the human temptation to use the hearing as an opportunity to insult or get revenge on your former employer.

Do a thorough and thoughtful job of researching, organizing, documenting and presenting your case. Keep your argument focused, because it is at this level that you are most likely to win a decision that will quickly start your benefit checks flowing. (For details of how to document your job loss, see Chapter 10, Section C.)

If you win this appeal, you will soon begin receiving benefits, typically including back payments from the date on which you first became eligible.

Both you and your former employer will have the option of appealing the ruling on your appeal to the state courts. However, only a tiny percentage of unemployment insurance cases continue up into the state courts or higher. Those that do typically require help from a lawyer. (See Chapter 18, Section D.)

Many Unemployment Insurance Appeals Boards publish pamphlets or other publications explaining the state's appeal process. These publications vary in comprehensiveness and helpfulness. But if you plan to appeal, it is certainly worth your while to call the local UI office and ask whether a publication is available.

CHAPTER

13

WORKERS' COMPENSATION

The workers' compensation system provides replacement income and medical expenses to employees who are injured or become ill as a result of their jobs. Financial benefits may also extend to workers' dependents and to the survivors of workers who are killed on the job. In most circumstances, workers' compensation also protects employers from being sued for those injuries or deaths.

> ### Other Laws on Work-Related Illness and Injury
>
> Workers' compensation covers some aspects of work-related injuries, illnesses and deaths. But injured workers should be aware of other laws that may give them rights or entitle them to compensation. Some laws work in tandem, providing individuals with different options; some may provide the exclusive remedy for a workplace wrong.
> - Social Security disability insurance provides some income for people who are unable to work because of a physical or mental disability. (See Chapter 14.)
> - Unemployment compensation provides individuals with some financial benefits when they are out of work. (See Chapter 12.)
> - The Americans With Disabilities Act prohibits discrimination against workers who have some types of physical limitations or illnesses. (See Chapter 8, Section F.)
> - The Family and Medical Leave Act allows an employee to take up to 12 weeks of unpaid leave in a year due to a serious health condition that makes the employee unable to do his or her job. (See Chapter 5.)
>
> Other lawsuits for injuries or job loss may help redress some additional workplace injuries, particularly where workers have lost their jobs. For example, workers' comp claims filed by workers who have been fired are often paired with wrongful termination actions. (See Chapter 11, Section A.)

The benefits paid by workers' compensation are almost always limited to relatively modest amounts. The system is financed primarily by insurance premiums paid by employers. In some states, employers may opt to self-insure—meaning that they can pay for any claims themselves.

Contrary to popular misconception, filing a workers' comp claim does not involve suing the employer. Unless the employer has committed some serious wrong or is illegally uninsured or underinsured, filing for workers' comp is more like submitting a claim to a car insurer following an accident.

The idea behind the workers' comp system is that employers and employees can settle their potential differences over money and liability privately and quickly. Injured employees are compensated for the costs of workplace injuries and illnesses. In return, employers can run their businesses free from the constant threat of negligence lawsuits filed by their employees. In reality, however, the system is fraught with difficulties—high premiums for employers and grindingly slow claim processing for injured employees. Doctors and lawyers are often thrown into the fray to make the system painfully costly and complicated.

Like unemployment insurance (discussed in Chapter 12) and Social Security disability insurance (discussed in Chapter 14), the workers' compensation system is national, but is administered by the states. The laws and court decisions governing it follow a pattern throughout the country, but vary significantly from state to state on everything from eligibility for benefits to the proper process for filing claims.

A. Who Is Covered

In general, anyone who qualifies as a parttime or fulltime employee under the Internal Revenue Service guidelines (discussed in Chapter 2, Section C) is covered by workers' compensation insurance. There are a few exceptions to this rule—notably harbor workers, seafarers, railroad employees and federal employees—all of whom must file lawsuits to get disputed compensation rather than use the workers' comp system.

But coverage details vary from state to state, so certain categories of employees may be excluded from coverage in some locales. For example, in some states, companies with fewer than five employees are not required to carry workers' compensation coverage, and many states exclude volunteers, farmworkers, federal employees and domestic workers from coverage.

Workers who are not covered by workers' comp but who suffer work-related illnesses or injuries are usually relegated to getting compensation from their employers through:

- a company-backed policy, such as paid time off for sick days
- a settlement reached through arbitration or mediation (see Chapter 18, Section A), or
- a lawsuit filed against an employer or former employer—for negligence or breach of contract, for example.

Many states require employers to post an explanation of workers' compensation coverage in a prominent place within the work area. If your employer keeps such a notice on your workplace bulletin board, you are probably covered. If you are unsure whether your employer is covered, your state workers' compensation agency should tell you. (See the listing in Section G for contact details.)

Independent Contractors Lose Out

Independent contractors are not covered under the workers' comp systems in most states. However, workers who are categorized as independent contractors may in reality be employees. (See Chapter 2, Section A.) If you are unclear about your status as a worker, file a workers' comp claim for your injuries, anyway. It will then be up to your employer to prove that you are not eligible because you qualify legally as an independent contractor rather than an employee.

B. Conditions Covered

Workers' compensation provides a claim and benefit system for workers who become ill, are injured or die on the job.

1. Injuries

To be covered by workers' compensation, an injury need not be caused by a sudden accident such as a fall. Equally common claims are for injuries due to the repeated use of body parts—backstrain from lifting heavy boxes, for example. Also covered may be a physical condition that was aggravated by workplace conditions—such as emphysema made worse by airborne chemicals. And increasingly, workers are being compensated for the effects of psychological stress caused by the job.

With a few exceptions, any injury that occurs in connection with work is covered. The legal boundary is that employees are protected by workers' comp as long as they are "in the course of employment." For example, a computer repair technician would be covered by workers' comp while making service calls on customers, but not while traveling to and from work or going to a purely social dinner later that evening.

From the employee's standpoint, workers' comp is a no-fault system. It does not matter whether a worker was careless while injured—although claims from employees hurt while drunk or fighting have traditionally been rejected as outside the bounds of "work-related activity." Some states restrict coverage for injuries caused by employees' own "willful misconduct"—a term given differing spins by differing courts. And a number of states expressly restrict or eliminate benefits when an employee's claim is based on injuries caused by nonprescription, illegal drugs.

Injuries that can be shown to have been intentionally self-inflicted by the employee, or to have been caused by substance abuse, generally are not covered. However, the courts have often sided with the injured worker when such cases are disputed—ruling that the injury is covered as long as the employee's behavior was not the only thing that caused the injury. Another questionable area is injuries caused by a co-worker's violent behavior—although the workers' comp law in a few states, including California, specifically covers them.

The legal definition of when you are working, for workers' compensation purposes, also has expanded in recent years, so that a great number of injuries are covered. For example, employees who were injured playing baseball or football on a company-affiliated team have been allowed to collect workers' compensation benefits for those injuries.

Avoiding Injuries Caused by Repetitive Motion

In a typical year, more than six million work-related injuries and illnesses occur in the United States. The most rapidly growing and widely publicized category of workplace injuries is caused by repetitive motions of the body. These occupational pains of the information age go by many names and acronyms: Repetitive Stress Injuries (RSIs), Cumulative Trauma Disorders (CTDs), Repeated Motion Injuries (RMIs).

When they primarily afflict the wrists, hands and forearms, these injuries are called Carpal Tunnel Syndrome—the bane of a growing number of office workers who spend their days in front of computer terminals.

And many other parts of the body are susceptible to injury from being used repeatedly to perform motions that exceed the specifications for which nature designed them. People working on auto factory and meat processing production lines, for example, often suffer repetitive motion injury to their elbows, fingers, shoulders, backs, knees, ankles and feet.

Our bodies were simply not made to withstand the demands of making the same motion thousands of times in a short time period. Pay attention to this, too: A recent study found that employees who were dissatisfied with their jobs were most likely to develop repetitive stress injuries.

Typical symptoms of repetitive stress injuries include swelling and redness near bone joints; extreme sensitivity of the affected body part to movement and external touch; pain, both sharp and dull, in the overused area that may radiate into other parts of the limb, abdomen, head or back; and numbness of the affected body part or those near it. If detected early, injuries caused by repeated motions can often be cured by a short period of rest, light medication and rehabilitative exercise. The most serious and neglected cases, however, can escalate to a lifelong physical disability.

Work-related cumulative motion injuries are typically covered by workers' compensation insurance. But the best workers' compensation claim is the one that you never have to file, so here are a few of the steps that health experts recommend to avoid becoming afflicted with a work-related repetitive motion injury:

- Take frequent, short breaks from repetitive, physically stressful work whenever possible. This allows your muscles and joints to recover a bit from unnatural tensions that may result from your work.
- Do gentle stretching exercises at work regularly, paying particular attention to the parts of your body that are likely to be used most often. This reduces the muscle tightening that is believed to contribute to the illness.
- Watch for early symptoms, such as stiffness or other discomfort in heavily used body parts. Quick and complete recovery is much more likely if the symptoms are recognized early.
- Redesign your work tools or your typical work position and movements—or ask your employer to help do so. Good examples of redesigning are wrist rests for use with personal computer keyboards and ergonomic lines of office furniture.
- Remember that heart-pounding physical exertion is not necessary for dangerous body stress to occur. Just as you can wake up with a sore shoulder after sleeping all night in an awkward position, you can subject yourself to the dangers of muscle and tendon injury even in jobs that involve very limited exertion. (For more on preventing workplace injuries, see Chapter 7, Section B.)

2. Illnesses

An illness becomes an occupational illness—and is covered under the workers' compensation system—when the nature of a job increases the worker's chances of suffering from that disease. In fact, in some states, certain illnesses such as heart attacks and hernias are presumed to be covered for high stress jobs such as police work and firefighting. There must, however, be a clear connection between the job and the illness. Also, in examining a claim, investigators will look into nonwork factors—such as diet, exercise, smoking and drinking habits and hobbies—that may affect or aggravate a particular condition.

Illnesses that are the gradual result of work conditions—for example, emotional illness and stress-related digestive problems—increasingly are being recognized by the courts as covered by workers' compensation insurance. Perhaps not coincidentally, such stress injury claims are on the rise, too.

The American medical profession, traditionally slow to acknowledge the interworkings of mind and body, no longer ignores the effects of job-related stress on general health. According to the American Institute for Preventative Medicine, stress is at the root of nearly two-thirds of all office visits and plays a major role in heart disease and cancer. Currently, only about half the states recognize stress as a valid basis for workers' comp claims. But in every state, if you show that stress has disabled you from doing your job, employers must accommodate your work to your condition—by reducing work hours or providing a quieter atmosphere, for example. (See Chapter 8, Section F.)

3. Deaths

Dependents of workers—usually a spouse, children or other family members—who are killed on the job or die as a result of a work injury or illness are almost always eligible to collect workers' compensation benefits.

Even if an employee is found dead in the workplace, no one witnessed the death and no cause of death is obvious, the death is usually covered by workers' compensation. The possibilities of suicide or murder are usually ignored by courts unless there is strong evidence that the death qualifies as one or the other.

The Expanding and Shrinking Compensation World

One of the most dramatic expansions of the definition of illness caused by work occurred in a 1990 Michigan appeals court ruling. In that case, a brewery worker was found eligible for workers' compensation benefits because his tendency toward alcoholism—he typically drank 15 to 20 bottles of beer at work each day, and more at home—had been made worse by the fact that his employer gave employees free beer to drink during their breaks (*Gacioch v. Stroh Brewery Co.*, 466 N.W. 2d 302).

However, the courts do set some limits, as demonstrated by a California case. There, a workers' compensation claim was filed by a lawyer who fell off his bicycle while pedaling to a weekly meeting of workers' compensation attorneys. He argued that because he is a lawyer, much of his work involves thinking and analyzing. And because "his office is in his head," he claimed he should remain covered by workers' comp around the clock.

In rejecting the claim, the workers' comp board referee injected a bit of common sense: "Would claimant be covered if he woke in the middle of the night with an idea regarding a case and injured himself falling out of bed to write it down?" he asked. "Common sense tells me that the employment relationship, no matter how all-consuming it may appear to the claimant, must have limits. When claimant fell from his bicycle ... while thinking of client calls to be made, he was pedaling beyond those limits" (WCB Case No. 90-18674).

C. The Right to Medical Care

When you are injured at work, the workers' comp system usually entitles you to receive immediate medical care.

> ### Laws Regulating Work Injuries: Both a Blessing and a Curse
>
> Most employers make every effort to get injured workers back on the job as soon as possible. In some situations, this may mean modifying an employee's job somewhat—eliminating the requirement of hand-delivering hourly reports, for example, until a broken leg heals.
>
> Making such accommodations is sanctioned and even required by the Americans With Disabilities Act, a federal workplace law that protects most workers who are disabled by injuries. (See Chapter 8, Section F.)
>
> However, these well-meaning plans may conflict with yet another workplace law, the Family and Medical Leave Act. (See Chapter 5.) The FMLA allows employees to take up to 12 weeks of unpaid leave in a year due to a serious health condition that makes them unable to do their jobs.
>
> Legal experts fret that the FMLA serves as a disincentive for workers to come back to a modified job while they heal completely—and an incentive to keep them out of work until their allotment of leave time expires. What the experts might be forgetting is that FMLA leave is unpaid time off—a luxury many workers cannot afford.

1. Treating Physician

If you have a regular doctor, inform your employer in writing that if you are injured at work, you wish to be treated by that doctor. Keep a copy of that letter should problems arise later.

If you make no such written request—and you intend to have an injury claim handled under the workers' comp system—either your employer or the insurance company will usually be free to dictate which doctor will treat you for the first 30 days after your injury or work-related illness. After that time, you may be free to receive treatment from the doctor of your choice. But by that time, the company-referred doctor, who is likely to give a conservative diagnosis of the extent of your injury, may have already jeopardized your benefit claim.

2. Continuing Treatment

The insurance company is responsible for paying for all treatment you are diagnosed to require, even if that treatment must continue after you return to work. Your ongoing treatment should be paid for life, but you can trade away future medical payments for cash when you settle your case.

If you are uncertain about whether settling makes good financial sense for you—and that uncertainty is more likely if your work-related illness or injury is quite severe—then you may want to consult an experienced workers' comp attorney. (See Chapter 18, Section D.)

D. Filing a Workers' Compensation Claim

Get immediate medical care if your injury requires it. You must then inform your employer of your injury as soon as possible. This is a tricky part of processing a workers' comp claim, since states have wildly different limits on the number of days you have to notify your employer; in most states, the limit is one month, but the range is from a few days to two years.

In the unlikely event that your employer refuses to cooperate with you in filing a workers' compensation claim, a call to your local workers' compensation office will usually remedy the situation.

Typically, your employer will have claim forms for you to fill out and submit, or can obtain a form quickly. It then becomes your employer's responsibility to submit the paperwork to the proper insurance carrier. Depending on state law, you—rather than your employer—may need to file a separate claim with your state's workers' compensation agency. There is a time limit on this, too—often a year after injury. But your state may have a shorter limit.

If your claim is not disputed by your employer or its insurance carrier, it will be approved and an adjuster for the insurance company will typically contact you or your employer with instructions on how to submit your medical bills for payment. But be prepared. Things do not always go smoothly. The employer, in an attempt to keep workers' comp rates from skyrocketing, may fight your right to benefits. The best way you can counteract such disputes is by producing good documentation, including complete medical records, of your injury and treatment.

If your injury is not permanent and does not cause you to lose income, the payment of your medical bills will probably be the extent of your claim, and there will not be much else for you to do. If you are temporarily unable to work because of your injury, you will also begin receiving checks to cover your wage loss—typically within a week or two after your claim is approved. Your employer will notify the insurance company to stop sending you wage-replacement checks as soon as you recover and return to work.

E. Calculating Benefits

Your workers' compensation benefits may take several forms. The following are the most common, although some states may provide additional benefits.

1. Costs of Medical Care

The bills for medical care you required because of your workplace injuries will be paid. Theoretically, at least, there is no limitation on medical coverage for illnesses and injuries that are covered. Medical coverage includes costs of:

- doctors
- hospitals
- nursing services, including home care
- physical therapy
- dentists
- chiropractors, and
- prosthetic devices.

2. Temporary Disability

This is the most common disability compensation paid under workers' compensation, awarded if you are unable to work, but are expected to recover and return to work.

You will receive tax-free temporary disability payments that substitute for the income you would have earned had you not been injured. If you cannot work at all, typically you will be paid two-thirds of your average wages, with state-set minimums and maximums. People with unusually low incomes may actually experience an income increase while receiving workers' compensation—and those with high incomes will probably experience an income cut.

In most states, workers become eligible for wage loss replacement benefits as soon as they have lost a few days of work because of an injury covered by workers' compensation. The number of days required to qualify varies by state—and some states allow the payments to be paid retroactively to the first day of wage loss if the injury keeps the employee out of work for an extended period.

3. Vocational Rehabilitation

If your injury prevents you from returning to your job, but you are physically able to do some work, you may be entitled to vocational rehabilitation, which may include additional job training or schooling. Since the early '90s, when workers' comp costs skyrocketed, most states have put severe limits on the sensible benefit of rehabilitation. At a minimum, your treating physician and a workers' comp board staffer or judge must agree to your need for vocational rehabilitation. Injured workers who qualify for state-sponsored rehabilitation programs will usually be entitled to receive temporary disability payments—at a somewhat reduced rate.

4. Permanent Disability

If you have a partial or complete disability, you may receive a lump sum payment in workers' compensation benefits. The lump sum payments that you are eligible to receive will vary greatly with the nature and extent of your injuries. If your injuries fall into one of the following categories, you may qualify for lump sum benefits.

- *Permanent total disability*: You are unable to work at all, and you are not expected to be able to work again.
- *Permanent partial disability*: Although you are able to perform some types of work, you are not expected to be able to fully regain your ability to earn money. This type of disability is usually divided into two groups, schedule and nonschedule injuries.
- *Schedule injuries*: These are injuries for which a set lump sum payment has been prescribed by law in your state. It is the injury that is assigned a value, not the employee, so former earnings levels are irrelevant.
- *Nonschedule injuries*: These are injuries for which no such lump sum amount has been specified, so a settlement must be negotiated. In Florida, for example, there is no law specifying the benefit to be paid to an employee who loses a foot in a work-related accident.

5. Death Benefits

Weekly compensation benefits are paid to surviving dependents of workers—usually children and spouses—who are killed in the course of employment or as the result of a work-related injury or occupational disease. The amounts paid typically equal about two-thirds of the deceased worker's weekly salary. About a third of the states limit the total amount of the death award given; a few states limit the number of weeks or years survivors may receive death benefits.

Death benefits to surviving spouses usually come to an end if they remarry—and some states provide for a lump sum to a former spouse upon remarriage. Death benefits for surviving children usually end when they reach majority—or somewhat later for fulltime students.

In addition, if an employee dies from a workplace accident, then the employee's estate receives burial expenses in the amount specified by law in the state where the accident occurred.

Complex Cases Require Expertise

If your workers' compensation claim is denied, you have the right to appeal it at several levels. If your work-related injury is a permanent or long-term one, then pursuing your claim for workers' compensation benefits to its fullest extent will likely be a complicated task.

And there may be added complications: If you have previously filed a separate workers' compensation claim, the cost of your benefits may have to be distributed between your current employer's insurance carrier and a special state fund that covers workers' compensation injuries beyond the first one.

If your claim falls into any of these categories, you will probably need to hire a lawyer who specializes in workers' compensation cases to help. (See Chapter 18, Section D.)

F. Penalties for Retaliation

In many states, employers may not retaliate against an employee for filing a workers' compensation claim. Some states prohibit all forms of retaliation—for example, firing, disciplining, discriminating in any way; other statutes mention only discharge.

Additional Laws May Apply

If the chart below indicates that your state has no statute, this means there is no law that specifically addresses the issue. However, there may be a state administrative regulation or local ordinance that does control. Contact your state workers' compensation office department for more information. (See section G, below, for contact details.)

State Retaliation Laws	
Alabama	Employees may not be fired for filing a workers' compensation claim. Ala. Code §25-5-11.1
Alaska	An employer may not discriminate in hiring, retention or policies because an employee has in good faith filed a claim for workers' compensation benefits. Alaska Stat. §23.30.247
Arizona	Employees cannot be fired for filing a workers' compensation claim. Arizona Const., Art. 18, §3, as interpreted by *Daniel v. Magma Copper Co.,* 620 P.2d 699 (Ariz. Ct. App., 1980)
Arkansas	Discrimination against an employee because of the employee's claim for benefits under the workers' compensation scheme subjects the employer to a fine of up to $10,000. Ark. Stat. Ann. §11-9-107
California	Employees cannot be fired, threatened or otherwise discriminated against for filing a workers' compensation claim. Employers who violate this law are guilty of a misdemeanor, and the employee's compensation award will be increased by one-half, but not to exceed a $10,000 increase. Employees are also entitled to reinstatement and back wages. Cal. Lab. Code §132a
Colorado	An employer may not retaliate against an employee who files a claim or exercises rights under the Colorado Workmen's Compensation Act. Colo. Rev. Stat. §§8-40-101 and following The employee may sue for wrongful discharge. *Lathrop v. Entenmann's Inc.,* 770 P.2d 1367 (1989)
Connecticut	Employees cannot be fired or discriminated against for filing a workers' compensation claim. Conn. Gen. Stat. Ann. §31-290a
Delaware	An employer may not discharge or discriminate against an employee who files a workers' compensation claim, reports an employer's noncompliance with the workers' compensation law or testifies in any proceeding related to workers' compensation. Del. Code Ann. tit. 19, §2365
District of Columbia	Employees may not be fired for claiming workers' compensation benefits. An employer that violates this law is subject to a fine of up to $1,000 which the employer alone, and not the insurance carrier, must satisfy. D.C. Code Ann. §36-342

Florida	Employees cannot be fired for filing a workers' compensation claim. Fla. Stat. §440.205
Georgia	No statute
Hawaii	Employees cannot be fired, suspended or discriminated against for suffering a compensable work-related injury. Haw. Rev. Stat. §378-32(2)
Idaho	No statute
Illinois	Employees cannot be fired or discriminated against for exercising rights under the Workers' Compensation Act. 820 Ill. Comp. Stat. 305/4(h)
Indiana	Employers may not retaliate against an employee for filing a workers' compensation claim. *Frampton v. Central Indiana Gas Co.*, 297 N.E. 2d 425 (Ind. 1973)
Iowa	Employers may not discharge or interfere with an employee who claims benefits under workers' compensation law. No contract requiring an employee to waive rights to file a workers' compensation claim is valid. *Springer v. Weeks*, 429 N.W. 2d 558 (1988)
Kansas	It is against public policy for employers to retaliate against employees who file workers' compensation claims and employees may sue employers who do so. *Chrisman v. Philips Industries, Inc.*, 751 P.2d 140 (Kan. 1988)
Kentucky	Employees cannot be fired or discriminated against for filing a workers' compensation claim. Ky. Rev. Stat. §342.197
Louisiana	Employees may not be fired or refused employment for filing workers' compensation claims. La. Rev. Stat. Ann. §23:1361
Maine	Employees cannot be fired or discriminated against for filing workers' compensation claims. Me. Rev. Stat. Ann. 39A §353 It is unlawful for an employer to refuse to hire an applicant or otherwise discriminate against an employee or applicant on the grounds that the individual has asserted a claim or right under the workers' compensation law. Me. Rev. Stat. 5 §4572
Maryland	Employees cannot be fired for filing claims under workers' compensation. Md. Code Ann. Lab. Emp. Law §9-1105
Massachusetts	Employees cannot be fired or discriminated against for filing or participating in a workers' compensation claim or proceeding. Mass. Gen. Laws Ann. ch. 152, §75B
Michigan	An employer cannot discharge or in any way discriminate against employees for filing complaints or instituting proceedings under the workers' compensation laws. Mich. Comp. Laws §418.125
Minnesota	An employer who discharges or threatens to discharge an employee for seeking workers' compensation benefits is liable in a civil lawsuit for any loss of benefits and for costs, reasonable attorneys' fees and punitive damages up to three times the amount of compensation. Minn. Stat. Ann. §176.82
Mississippi	No statute
Missouri	Employees cannot be fired or discriminated against for filing workers' compensation claims. Mo. Ann. Stat. §287.780

Montana	An employer cannot fire an employee because he or she filed a workers' compensation claim. Mont. Code Ann. §39-71-317 If an injured employee is able to return to work within two years, he or she must be given employment preference over other applicants. Mont. Code Ann. §39-1-317
Nebraska	No statute
Nevada	An employer who discharges an employee in retaliation for filing a workers' compensation claim violates state public policy. The fired employee may sue for damages. *Hansen v. Harrah's*, 675 P.2d 394 (1984)
New Hampshire	No statute
New Jersey	It is unlawful for an employer to discharge or discriminate against an employee because he or she claimed workers' compensation benefits or testified in any proceeding. The employer is subject to a fine from $100 up to $1,000 or a sentence up to 60 days in prison or both, and must also reinstate the employee and pay any lost wages. N.J. Stat. Ann. §34:15-39.1
New Mexico	An employer may not discharge or threaten to discharge an employee, or retaliate in any way on account of the employee seeking occupational disease disablement benefits or workers' compensation benefits. N.M. Stat. Ann. §§52-3-54.2 and 52-1-28.2
New York	Employees cannot be fired or otherwise discriminated against for filing workers' compensation claims. Employers are liable for fines from $100 to $500. N.Y. Work. Comp. Law §120
North Carolina	Employees may not be discharged, suspended, demoted or in any way discriminated against for filing workers' compensation claims. N.C. Gen. Stat. §§95-240 and 241
North Dakota	Retaliating against an employee seeking workers' compensation by firing him or her violates public policy and the employee may sue the employer for wrongful discharge. *Krein v. Marian Manor Nursing Home*, 415 N.W. 2d 793 (N.D. 1987)
Ohio	Employees cannot be fired or disciplined for filing workers' compensation claims. Ohio Rev. Code Ann. §4123.90
Oklahoma	An employee who has, in good faith, filed a workers' compensation claim or testified before a proceeding may not be fired and is entitled to reinstatement and reasonable damages. The employer may also be assessed exemplary or punitive damages of not more than $100,000. Okla. Stat. Ann. tit. 85, §§5 and 6
Oregon	An employee cannot be fired or discriminated against for filing a workers' compensation claim. Or. Rev. Stat. §659.410 State employees may not be discriminated against by having their health benefits discontinued if they are absent from work for an illness or injury for which a workers' compensation claim has been filed. Or. Rev. Stat. §659.455
Pennsylvania	It is a violation of public policy to retaliate against an employee who files a workers' compensation claim. The employee may sue for wrongful discharge. *Shick v. Shirey*, 716 A.2d 1231 (Pa. 1998)

Rhode Island	No statute
South Carolina	Employers may not retaliate against employees who institute or participate in workers' compensation proceedings. S.C. Code Ann. §41-1-80
South Dakota	An employee may not be terminated for filing a lawful workers' compensation claim and may sue for wrongful discharge. S.D. Codified Laws Ann. §62-1-16
Tennessee	An employee who is terminated for filing a workers' compensation claim may sue for retaliatory discharge. *Clanton v. Cain-Sloan Co.*, 677 S.W. 2d 411 (1994)
Texas	An employer may not discharge or in any way discriminate against an employee because the employee filed a workers' compensation claim in good faith, hired a lawyer to represent him or her in a claim or instituted a proceeding or testified in a proceeding relative to the workers' compensation laws. Texas Code Ann., Lab. §451.001
Utah	No statute
Vermont	An employer may not discharge or discriminate against an employee or refuse to hire an applicant because the employee or applicant has filed a workers' compensation claim. Vt. Stat. Ann. tit. 21, §710
Virginia	No employer shall discharge an employee solely because the employee intends to file or has filed a workers' compensation claim or has testified or is about to testify in a workers' compensation proceeding. Va. Code Ann. §65.2-308
Washington	No employer may discharge or in any way discriminate against an employee who has filed or intends to file a workers' compensation claim. Employers who violate the law will be ordered to rehire or reinstate with backpay. Wash. Rev. Code Ann. §51.48.025
West Virginia	An employer may not discriminate in any manner against present or former employees because they receive or attempt to receive workers' compensation benefits. W.Va. Code §23-5A-1
Wisconsin	Employers may not discharge or refuse to hire someone for filing a workers' compensation claim. Violation of this law carries a fine of $50 to $500. Wis. Stat. Ann. §102.35
Wyoming	An employee who is terminated for exercising rights under the workers' compensation statutes may sue for damages. *Griess v. Consolidated Freightways Corp.*, 776 P.2d 752 (1989)

G. State Workers' Compensation Offices

Alabama
Workers' Compensation Division
Department of Industrial Relations
Industrial Relations Building
649 Monroe Street
Montgomery, AL 36131
334-242-2868
FAX: 334-242-3960
http://www.dir.state.al.us/

Alaska
Alaska Department of Labor
Alaska Workers' Compensation Board
P.O. Box 25512
Juneau, AK 99802-5512
907-465-2790
FAX: 907-465-2797
http://www.labor.state.ak.us/wc/wc.htm

Arizona
State Compensation Fund
3031 North 2nd Street
Phoenix, AZ 85012
602-631-2050
FAX: 602-631-2213

Arkansas
Arkansas Workers' Compensation Commission
4th & Spring Streets
P.O. Box 950
Little Rock, AR 72203-0950
501-682-3930
FAX: 501-682-2786
TTY: 800-285-1131
http://www.awcc.state.ar.us/

California
Department of Industrial Relations
Division of Workers Compensation
45 Fremont Street, Suite 3160
San Francisco, CA 94105
415-975-0730
FAX: 415-703-3971
http://www.dir.ca.gov

Colorado
Colorado Department of Labor and Employment
Division of Worker's Compensation
1515 Arapahoe Street, Tower 2
Suite 500
Denver, CO 80202-2117
303-7575-8814
FAX: 303-575-8881
http://workerscomp.cdle.state.cp.is/default.htm

Connecticut	Workers' Compensation Commission 21 Oak Street Hartford, CT 06106 860-493-1500 FAX: 860-247-1361 http://wcc.state/ct/us/index2.htm
Delaware	Division of Industrial Affairs Office of Workers Compensation 4425 North Market Street Wilmington, DE 19802 302-761-8200 FAX: 302-761-6601 http://www.delawareworks.com/division/industrialaffairs/diaindex.html
District of Columbia	Department of Employment Services Office of Workers' Compensation 500 C Street, NW Room 600 Washington, DC 20011 202-724-7000 FAX: 202-541-3595 http://www.washingtondc.gov/agencies
Florida	Division of Workers' Compensation 250 East Park Avenue Lakewales, FL 33853 800-394-2767 FAX: 863-676-1041 http://www.fdles.state.fl.us/wc/
Georgia	State Board of Workers' Compensation Claims Assistance Office 270 Peachtree Street, NW Atlanta, GA 30303-1299 404-656-2034 FAX: 404-651-9467 http://www.ganet.org/sbwc
Hawaii	State Department of Labor & Industrial Relations Disability & Compensation Division 830 Punchbowl Street, Room 209 P.O. Box 3769 Honolulu, HI 96812 808-586-9151 FAX: 808-586-9099 http://www.dir.state.hi.us/

Idaho	Industrial Commission of Idaho
	317 Main Street
	Boise, ID 83720
	208-334-6000
	FAX: 208-334-2321
	TTY: 800-950-2110
	http://www2.state.id.us/iic/
Illinois	State Industrial Commission
	100 West Randolph, Suite 8-200
	Chicago, IL 60601
	312-814-6556
	FAX: 312-814-6523
	TTY: 312-814-2959
	http://www.state.il.us/agency/iic
Indiana	Workers' Compensation Board of Indiana
	402 West Washington Street, W-196
	Indianapolis, IN 46204
	317-232-3809
	FAX: 317-233-5493
	http://www.state.in.us/wkcomp/index.html
Iowa	
	Industrial Commission
	1000 East Grand Avenue
	Des Moines, IA 50319
	515-281-8335
	FAX: 515-281-4698
	TTY: 800-562-4692
	http://www.state.ia.us/government/wd/index.htm
Kansas	State Department of Human Resources
	Division of Workers' Compensation
	Claims Advisory Office
	401 SW Topeka Boulevard
	Topeka, KS 66612-1227
	785-296-3441
	800-332-0353
	FAX: 785-296-0179
	TTY: 785-296-5044
	http://www.hr.state.ks.us
Kentucky	Workers' Compensation Board
	403 Wapping Street, Suite 340
	Frankfort, KY 40601
	502-564-6209
	FAX: 502-564-6117
	http://www.state.ky.ys/agencies/labor/labrhome.htm

Louisiana	Department of Employment & Training
	Office of Workers' Compensation
	1001 N. 23rd
	P.O. Box 94040
	Baton Rouge, LA 70804-9040
	225-342-7561
	FAX: 225-342-5665
	http://www.idol.state.la.us/
Maine	Workers' Compensation Board
	Station 27, Deering Building
	Augusta, ME 04333
	207-287-7096
	FAX: 207-287-7198
	http://janus.state.me.us/wcb/
Maryland	Workers' Compensation Commission
	6 North Liberty Street
	Baltimore, MD 21201
	410-767-0829
	FAX: 410-333-8122
	TTY: 800-735-2258
	http://www.charm.net/~wcc/
Massachusetts	Department of Industrial Accidents
	600 Washington Street, 7th Floor
	Boston, MA 02111
	617-727-4900
	FAX: 617-727-6477
	http://www.magnet.state.ma.us/dia/
Michigan	Department of Labor
	Workers' Disability Compensation Office
	7150 Harris Drive
	Box 30015
	Lansing, MI 48909
	517-322-1296
	FAX: 517-322-1808
	http://www.ag.state.mi.us/
Minnesota	Minnesota Department of Labor & Industry
	Workers' Compensation Division
	443 Lafayette Road
	Street Paul, MN 55155
	612-296-6490
	800-342-5354
	FAX: 612-282-5405
	http://www.doli.state.mn.us/

Mississippi	Workers' Compensation Commission P.O. Box 5300 Jackson, MS 39296-5300 601-987-4258 FAX: 601-987-4233 http://www.mwcc.state.ms.us/
Missouri	Department of Labor Division of Workers' Compensation 3315 West Truman Boulevard P.O. Box 504 Jefferson City, MO 65102-0504 573-751-4231 800-775-2667 FAX: 573-751-4135 http://www.dolir.state.mo.us/
Montana	Department of Labor & Industry Division of Workers' Compensation P.O. Box 537 Helena, MT 59624 406-444-7794 FAX: 406-444-7798 http://dli.state.mt.us/
Nebraska	Workers' Compensation Court Old Federal Courthouse 129 North 10th Street Lincoln, NE 68509 402-471-2525 FAX: 402-471-2800 http://www.nol.org/home/WC/
Nevada	Employers' Insurance Company 888-682-6671 http://www.employersinsco.com/index.htm
New Hampshire	Department of Labor 95 Pleasant Street Concord, NH 03301 603-271-3176 FAX: 603-271-6852 http://www.state.nh.us/dol/dol-wc/
New Jersey	Division of Workers' Compensation Department of Labor P.O. Box 110 135 East State Street, CN 381 Trenton, NJ 08625-0381 609-292-2414 FAX: 609-633-9271 http://www.state.nj.us.labor/

New Mexico	Workers' Compensation 1820 Randolph, SE P.O. Box 27198 Albuquerque, NM 87125-7198 505-841-6006 FAX: 505-841-6866 http://www.state.nm.us/wca/
New York	Workers' Compensation Board 20 Park Street Albany, NY 12207 518-474-6670 FAX: 518-473-1415 http://www.wcb.state.ny.us/
North Carolina	Industrial Commission 4319 Mail Service Center Raleigh, NC 27699-4319 919-733-4820 FAX: 919-715-0282 http://www.comp.state.nc.us/
North Dakota	Workers' Compensation Bureau 500 East Front Avenue Bismarck, ND 58504-5685 701-328-3800 FAX: 701-328-3820 TTY: 701-328-3786
Ohio	Ohio Bureau of Workers' Compensation 30 West Spring Street Columbus, OH 43266-0581 614-466-8751 FAX: 614-752-8428 http://www.bwc.state.oh.us/home/home.htm
Oklahoma	Workers' Compensation Department of Labor 4001 North Lincoln Boulevard Oklahoma City, OK 73105 405-528-1500, ext. 259 FAX: 405-528-5751 http://www.state.ok.us/~okdol/workcomp/
Oregon	Department of Consumer & Business Services Workers' Compensation Division Benefits Section 350 Winter Street, NE, Room 27 Salem, OR 97301-3879 503-947-7810 800-452-0288 FAX: 503-373-1684 TTY: 503-378-4100 http://www.cbs.state.or.us/external/wcd/index.html

Pennsylvania	Bureau of Workers' Compensation Labor & Industry Building Harrisburg, PA 17120 717-783-5421 FAX: 717-787-8826 http://www.dli.state.oa.us/bwc/index.html
Rhode Island	Department of Workers' Compensation 610 Manton Avenue Providence, RI 02909 401-457-1800 FAX: 401-277-2127 TTY: 401-457-1888
South Carolina	Workers' Compensation Commission 1612 Marion Street P.O. Box 1715 Columbia, SC 29201 803-737-5744 FAX: 803-737-5768 http://www.state.sc.us/wcc/
South Dakota	Division of Labor and Management Department of Labor Kneip Building 700 Governors Drive Pierre, SD 57501-2291 605-773-3681 FAX: 605-773-4211 TTY: 605-773-3101 http://www.state.sd.us/dol/dlm/dlm-home.htm
Tennessee	Department of Labor Division of Workers' Compensation 710 James Robertson Parkway Gateway Plaza, 2nd Floor Nashville, TN 37243 615-741-2395 FAX: 615-741-5078 http://www.state.tn.us/labor-wfd/wcomp.html
Texas	Workers' Compensation Commission 4000 South I-H 35 Austin, TX 78704 512-804-4000 FAX: 512-804-4001 http://www.twcc.state.tx.us/

Utah	Division of Industrial Accidents P.O. Box 146610 Salt Lake City, UT 84114 801-530-6800 FAX: 801-530-6804 http://www.ind-com.state.ut.us/indacc/indacc.htm
Vermont	Division of Workers' Compensation Department of Labor and Industry National Life Building, Drawer 20 Montpelier, VT 05620-3401 802-828-2286 FAX: 802-828-2195 http://www.state.vt.us/labind/wcindex.htm
Virginia	Workers' Compensation Commission 1000 DMV Drive Richmond, VA 23220 804-367-8600 FAX: 804-367-9740 http://www.vwc.state.va.us/index.htm
Washington	Department of Labor and Industries Insurance Services Division P.O. Box 44100 Olympia, WA 87504-2401 360-902-4252 FAX: 360-902-4940
West Virginia	Workers' Compensation Fund 4700 MacCorkle Avenue, SE Box 3151 Charleston, WV 25332 304-926-5048 FAX: 304-926-5372 http://www.state.wv.us/bep/wc/default.HTM
Wisconsin	Division of Workers' Compensation 201 East Washington Avenue P.O. Box 7901 Madison, WI 53707 608-266-1340 FAX: 608-267-0394 http://www.dwd.state.wi.us/wc/
Wyoming	Workers' Safety and Compensation Division Herschler Building 122 West 25th Street Cheyenne, WY 82002 307-777-7441 FAX: 307-777-6552 http://wydoe.state.wy.us/wcsd/

H. Related Lawsuits for Work Injuries

The workers' compensation system is the normal remedy for work-related injuries and illness. But in a growing number of situations, an injured worker will have the option of filing a lawsuit against another responsible person or company in addition to filing a claim for workers' compensation. For example, an injured worker might sue the manufacturer of a defective machine for negligence.

Employers who fail to maintain the workers' compensation coverage required in their state, or who otherwise violate the laws of the workers' compensation system, generally can be sued over work-related injuries. You will probably need to hire a lawyer to help with this type of lawsuit. (See Chapter 18, Section D.)

Nearly half the states also allow employees to sue employers who fired them in retaliation for filing a workers' compensation claim or for testifying on someone else's behalf in a workers' compensation case. (See Section F.)

SOCIAL SECURITY DISABILITY INSURANCE

Social Security disability insurance is one component of the federal Social Security system. The benefits it provides are intended to prevent people from becoming paupers because an injury or illness has left them completely unable to earn a living—something that affects a surprisingly large portion of the population. In fact, one out of every four people in America can expect to become disabled for an extended period before reaching age 65; one in ten of them will have a disability lasting two years or more. And over five million workers and their families currently draw Social Security disability benefits.

When you and your employer pay into the Social Security program, you are buying long-term disability insurance coverage. Once you have paid into the program for a period specified by the Social Security program, you are eligible for benefits should you become unable to earn a living.

Disability program payments are not intended to cover temporary, short-term or partial disability. The benefits were sanctioned by Congress with the assumption that working families have other support resources during short-term disabilities—such as workers' compensation, insurance, savings and investment income.

For a complete explanation of the Social Security system and more detail on filing and appealing Social Security disability insurance claims, see *Social Security, Medicare & Pensions: Get the Most Out of Your Retirement and Medical Benefits*, by Joseph L. Matthews with Dorothy Berman Matthews (Nolo).

Workers' Comp and Social Security: Separate and Unequal

In contrast to the workers' compensation program (see Chapter 13), the Social Security disability insurance system does not recognize degrees of wage-earning capability. Under Social Security eligibility rules, you are either able to work—in which case you do not qualify for its benefits. Or you are not able to work—in which case you may qualify. Also, unlike workers' comp eligibility requirements, a disability need not be work-related under the Social Security benefit system.

However, if you receive workers' comp payments, your Social Security benefit may be reduced. The law states that the sum of all your disability payments cannot exceed 80% of your earnings averaged over a period of time shortly before you became disabled. (See Section F3, below.)

A. Who Is Covered

Disability benefits are only paid to workers and their families when the worker has enough work credits to qualify.

The definition of what is required for a work credit changes over time. Currently, workers accumulate credits based on income, length of time worked and whether your job was covered by Social Security. You can earn up to four work credits per year. The number of work credits needed to qualify for disability benefits depends on your age when you become disabled.

Timing is important, too. You must have earned at least 20 credits of the required amount within the ten years immediately before you became disabled—unless you qualify under one of the special rules explained below. The amount of your monthly disability check is based on your age and earnings record. (See Section D2.)

Age of Disability and Work Credits Required

If you were born before 1930, and you became disabled before age 62 in:	You need this many work credits:
1980	29
1981	30
1982	31
1983	32
1984	33
1985	34
1987	36
1989	38
1991 or later	40

If you were born after 1929, and you became disabled at age:	You need this many work credits:
42 or younger	20
44	22
46	24
48	26
50	28
52	30
54	32
56	34
58	36
60	38
62 or older	40

1. Young Workers

If you were disabled when still young, you need fewer work credits to qualify for benefits. The Social Security formula recognizes that you obviously did not have the opportunity to acquire many quarters of work.

2. Blind Individuals

If your vision is not better than 20/200 even with glasses, or if your field of vision is limited to 20 degrees or less, you are considered blind under Social Security rules.

If you are disabled by blindness, there is no requirement that any of your work credits must have been earned within the years immediately preceding your disability. Your work credits can be from any time after 1936—the year the Social Security law went into effect. The only requirement is that you have enough cumulative work credits, based on your age, as shown in the chart above.

3. Widows and Widowers

If you are a widow or widower, age 50 or over, and disabled, you may receive disability benefits even though you do not have enough work credits of your own to qualify—as long as your deceased spouse had enough work credits for his or her age at the time of death.

The rules are as follows.

- You must be disabled. Your age, work experience and training are not considered in whether you are disabled.
- You must be age 50 or older.
- Your spouse must have been fully insured at death—meaning he or she had enough work credits considering his or her age.
- Your disability must have begun before your spouse's death or within seven years after the death.
- If you already receive Social Security benefits as a surviving widow or widower with children, you will be eligible for disability benefits if you are age 50 or older and you become disabled before those payments end or within seven years after they end.
- Even if you were divorced before your former spouse died, you may still be eligible for these benefits if you had been married to him or her for ten years or more.

The amount of these benefits will depend entirely upon your spouse's work record and average earnings. And these special disability benefits may end if you remarry.

B. Disabilities Covered

Many injuries and illnesses are obviously disabling. There are others, however, such as chronic illnesses which become acute with age, or residual conditions which deteriorate over time, that become disabling even though they were not initially too severe. For example, a worker may have had a previous injury that is aggravated through the years to the point where work is extremely difficult or impossible. He or she may become eligible for disability benefits even though the original illness or injury was not disabling.

Social Security disability is a government program—and so it carries with it a grand amount of qualifying rules and regulations. To receive Social Security disability benefits:

- You must have a physical or mental impairment

- The impairment must prevent you from doing any substantial gainful work, and
- The disability must be expected to last, or has lasted, at least 12 months, or must be expected to result in death.

Of course, these terms are subject to different interpretations. There are guidelines developed by Social Security and the courts regarding qualifications for disability. But proving a disability is often a difficult task. In preparing your claim for a disability, examine these guidelines carefully, discuss the matter with your doctor or doctors and plan your claim thoroughly.

1. Physical or Mental Impairments

The basic rule regarding disability is that the condition preventing you from working must be a medical one—meaning that it can be discovered and described by doctors. To prove this, when you file your disability claim, you should bring with you letters from doctors, or from hospitals or clinics where you have been treated, describing the medical condition that prevents you from doing any substantial gainful work. The letters should also state that your disability is expected to last for 12 months or is expected to result in death.

2. Substantial Gainful Work

Social Security will first consider whether your condition prevents you from doing the job you had at the time you became disabled, or the last job you had before becoming disabled. If your disability prevents you from performing your usual job, Social Security will next decide whether you are able to do any other kind of substantial gainful work—defined as any job that pays $500 per month or more.

Your age, education, training and work experience will be considered in making this determination—as will the practicality of learning new job skills for another work position. Social Security will evaluate whether you are able to perform any kind of work for pay, whether or not there are actually any such jobs available in the area in which you live. However, it is up to Social Security to prove that there is gainful employment you can perform. You need not prove there is no work you can do.

Example: *Arnold has been a longshoreman for 40 of his 58 years. Weakened by an early injury, Arnold's back has grown slowly but steadily worse over the past decade, causing him to miss several months of work in the past two years. His doctor has told him that his back will not get better, and Arnold decides to apply for disability benefits.*

As Arnold's back prevents him from standing for long periods of time and restricts the movement of his arms, Social Security determines he is unable to do any physical labor. The next question would be whether he is able to do any other kind of work. It is possible that his back would be too bad for him to do even a job which required him to sit at a desk; if so, and Arnold proved this to Social Security through his doctor or by trying and being unable to do a desk job, he would probably get his disability payments. On the other hand, if his back were not quite that bad, he might be forced at least to try other work.

3. Disability Must Be Lasting

No matter how serious or completely disabling your illness or injury is, you will not qualify for disability benefits unless your condition has lasted, or is expected to last, for 12 months—during which time you are unable to perform substantial gainful work. The disability will also qualify if it is expected to result in death. Even though the disability must be expected to last 12 months, you do not have to wait for 12 months to apply.

As soon as the condition is disabling and a doctor can predict that it is expected to last a year, you may qualify for disability benefits. And if, after you begin receiving benefits, it turns out that your disability does not last 12 months, Social Security cannot ask for its money back. You are not penalized for recovering sooner than expected, as long as the original expectation that the illness would last 12 months was a legitimate one.

Listing of Impairments Social Security Considers Disabling

To simplify things a bit, the Social Security Administration has developed a list of conditions which it usually considers disabling without giving much of an argument. In other words, if you prove, through medical records or doctors' reports, that you have one of the conditions on Social Security's Listing of Impairments—paralysis of an arm and a leg, for example—you will probably be considered disabled without having to convince Social Security that you cannot perform substantial gainful work. But each claim for disability is considered separately; having a condition on this list does not automatically qualify you for disability benefits.

Impairments certified by Social Security include:

- diseases of the heart, lung or blood vessels which have resulted in a serious loss of heart or lung reserves as shown by X-ray, electrocardiogram or other tests; and, in spite of medical treatment, there is breathlessness, pain or fatigue
- severe arthritis which causes recurrent inflammation, pain, swelling and deformity in major joints so that the ability to get about or use the hands is severely limited
- mental illness resulting in marked constriction of activities and interests, deterioration in personal habits and seriously impaired ability to get along with other people
- damage to the brain or brain abnormality which has resulted in severe loss of judgment, intellect, orientation or memory
- cancer which is progressive and has not been controlled or cured
- Acquired Immune Deficiency Syndrome (AIDS) or any of its related secondary diseases causing an inability to perform work
- diseases of the digestive system which result in severe malnutrition, weakness and anemia
- loss of a leg or a disease or injury which have caused it to become useless
- loss of major function of both arms, both legs or a leg and an arm
- serious loss of function of the kidneys, and
- total inability to speak.

Timing May Be Everything

Social Security disability benefits may be discontinued if you are able to earn your own living. If you are legally disabled but are earning too much money to qualify for Social Security benefits, you may still be able to claim something if your earnings are significantly lower than they were before the onset of your disability.

You may qualify because in some circumstances, the Social Security Administration can put a disability freeze on your earnings record.

The amount of your ultimate retirement benefits or of your disability benefits if you later qualify is determined by your average income over the years. If, after your disability, you are earning considerably less than you were before, the years of those earnings would pull your average income lower, which could result in a lower ultimate Social Security payment. The disability freeze permits you to work and collect your lower income without having it figured into your lifetime average earnings.

C. Dependents Entitled to Benefits

If you are disabled, your spouse and children under age 18 may also be eligible for dependents' benefits. If so, your combined family benefits—the total amount you, your spouse and your children receive—will be limited to a maximum of either 85% of what you were earning before you became disabled, or to 150% of what your monthly individual benefit would have been, whichever is lower. (See Section D2 for an explanation of how monthly individual benefits are calculated.)

Example: *Juan Menendez was making $2,200 a month when he was disabled. At the time he became disabled, Juan's total Social Security earnings record would have given him an individual disability benefit of $600 a month. But Juan's wife, Theresa, and their two teenage children, Angela and Bobby, were also eligible to collect dependents' benefits. Their total family benefits would be the lower of 85% of Juan's $2,200 monthly salary, which comes out to $1,870, or 150% of what Juan's individual disability benefit ($600) would be, which comes out to $900. The Menendez family would receive $900 a month, the lower of the two amounts.*

In addition, certain family members may qualify for benefits if a disabled worker dies. They include:

- a disabled widow or widower 50 or older, and
- a disabled ex-wife or ex-husband who is 50 or older if the marriage lasted ten years or longer.

D. Filing a Social Security Claim

It is extremely important to file your claim for Social Security disability benefits as soon as you become disabled, because there is a waiting period of five months after filing before you can begin receiving payments. If you wait a long time to file, you may be disappointed to learn that back payments are limited to the 12 months before the date on which you file.

You must file your claim at one of the Social Security Administration offices located in most cities, listed in the government section of the telephone book. If your disability prevents you from visiting a Social Security office, you can usually file your claim by mail or over the telephone.

1. Documentation Required

Social Security staff will complete the forms and other paperwork necessary to file a disability claim. You will need to provide documentation, including:
- a copy of your birth certificate
- your Social Security number
- names, addresses and telephone numbers of doctors, clinics and hospitals—and the dates on which they treated you
- a summary of your work history for the past 15 years, and
- dates of any military service.

If you have dependents who may be eligible for benefits under your Social Security disability insurance claim, you will have to present similar documentation for them when filing a claim.

The Social Security Administration will then investigate your claim—and will pay for any examinations and reports it requires to verify your claim. The Social Security staff will also help you with the paperwork and procedures required for payment.

The results of those examinations and reports will usually be sent to your state's vocational rehabilitation agency, which is responsible for determining whether or not you are considered sufficiently disabled to qualify for benefits. In some cases, the vocational rehabilitation office will conduct its own examination, tests and personal interviews as well, before providing the Social Security Administration with a decision on your case.

The Social Security Administration provides emergency funds for disabled people who need financial help during the long waiting period during which their claims are being processed. The Social Security employees handling your claim can give you details of how to qualify for emergency funds.

Trial Runs at Returning to Work

Social Security disability insurance is more friendly than other income-replacement programs because it allows you to try going back to work without canceling your claim. You can participate in a total of nine months of trial work without losing any benefits—and the nine months need not be consecutive or in one job. Of course, you must still technically qualify as disabled to take advantage of this trial period.

You could, for example, continue to receive Social Security disability checks while trying different jobs for a week or two every few months, until you find one you can do with your disability. Any months in which you do not earn more than $200—or spend more than 40 hours in self-employment—do not count as trial months.

After a trial work period, Social Security will review your case to see whether you have become able to work gainfully. The first key is whether you are able to earn $500 per month in gross wages. (See Section F1.)

If you succeed in returning to work after qualifying for Social Security disability benefits, the checks will keep coming for two months after your period of disability has ended to help ease your transition back into the workforce.

---

2. Calculating Benefits

Like other Social Security benefits, the amount of your monthly disability check is determined by your age and earnings record. The amount of your benefits will be based upon your average earnings for all the years you have been working—not just on the salary you were making most recently. Although the amount will be substantial, it alone will not equal your pre-injury income.

Monthly payments for individuals qualifying for disability benefits average about $1,000. The average disability payment for a disabled worker with a spouse and child is about $1,500. There is also a yearly cost of living increase if the Consumer Price Index rises over 3% for the year. For those who first became disabled in 1982 or later, there is no minimum benefit amount.

Some people—generally only those with high total incomes—may have to pay federal income taxes on their Social Security disability benefits. At the end of the year, you will receive a Social Security Benefit Statement showing the amount of benefits you received.

Contact the Internal Revenue Service's toll-free number for forms and publications, 800-829-3676, and ask for IRS Publication 915 if you need additional information on the tax. You can also download the publication from the IRS website at http://www.irs.gov.

Your monthly check will be based entirely on your earnings record, with no consideration given to a minimum amount needed to survive. If you receive only a small disability benefit, however, and you do not have a large amount of savings or other assets, you may be eligible for some other benefits in addition to your Social Security disability benefits. (See Section F.)

Getting Help With Estimating Benefits

The best way to determine your specific benefit level is to file a copy of the Social Security Administration's Form SSA-7004-PC-OP1, entitled Request for Earnings and Benefit Estimate Statement. You can obtain one at your local Social Security Administration office or download it from the SSA website at http://www.ssa.gov. You need not be planning to file a claim to do this—you can file the form any time you are merely curious. The Social Security staff will calculate benefits to which you are entitled and notify you by mail of its determination.

3. Continuing Your Claim

Although many people who suffer total disabilities remain disabled for life, that is not always the case. So the Social Security disability insurance program includes various efforts to rehabilitate workers and get them back to work.

If at First You Don't Succeed, Try Again

Some disabilities experts estimate that only about 35% of all Social Security disability claims are approved the first time they are submitted. Another 13% of applicants win benefits after appealing.

They'll Be Keeping Tabs

If your medical condition improves and you go back to work, your disability eligibility will end. Even if you do not go back to work voluntarily, Social Security will review your case periodically—or at least once every three years—to determine whether, in its opinion, your condition has improved enough for you to go back to work. From time to time, therefore, Social Security may ask for updated medical evidence from your doctor, or may even require that you be examined by another doctor or undergo additional medical tests—arranged and paid for by Social Security.

You must cooperate with these periodic reviews or run the risk of losing your disability benefits. You have the right, however, to insist on being given enough time to gather necessary information from your doctor, and enough notice to meet the appointment for the examination or test. If you are unable to keep an appointment scheduled for you by the Social Security office, do not hesitate to ask for a rescheduling.

E. Appealing a Denied Claim

The greatest number of Social Security disability claims are denied because an individual is deemed to be able to do some kind of work, in spite of a disability. If your claim is denied, there are four levels of appeal available to you. At each step of the appeal process, you have 60 days from the date of the previous decision to take action to move up to the next appeal level.

With the exception of the fourth option, filing a lawsuit in federal court, the staff at the Social Security Administration office will supply you with the proper forms for pursuing an appeal and will assist you in completing them.

Request for reconsideration. You ask to see the Social Security Administration's files concerning your claim, and then submit corrections or additional information that you hope will cause the agency to reconsider your claim and approve it.

Administrative hearing. You request a hearing by an administrative law judge who has never looked at your case before. You can ask to have the judge issue a ruling based on the evidence you have already submitted, or you can ask for a ruling without a hearing but with consideration of additional written evidence. You can also request a hearing at which new or more detailed evidence can be presented. These hearings are usually informal and held in the same locale where you filed your claim.

Review by appeals council. You ask to have the Social Security Appeals Council, based in Washington, DC, consider your claim. If the council decides to hear your appeal, you can submit a written argument in support of your evidence. Or you can elect to appear before the council to argue your case.

Federal court. If you do not win approval of your claim at any of the previous levels, or if the appeals council refuses to hear your appeal, you can file a lawsuit in federal court to try to get the courts to order the Social Security Administration to approve your claim. You will probably have to hire a lawyer to help you at this appeal level. (See Chapter 18, Section D.)

F. Collecting Other Benefits

Since disability payments are often not enough to live on, it is important for you to collect all the other benefits to which you may be entitled and even try to supplement your income by working a little if you are able.

You May Qualify for State Benefits

Note that a few states—including California, Hawaii, New Jersey, New York and Rhode Island—offer disability benefits as part of their unemployment insurance programs. (See Chapter 12.) Call the local unemployment insurance and workers' compensation insurance offices to determine whether your state is one that maintains this kind of coverage. (See Chapters 12 and 13.)

1. Earned Income

If you earn any regular income, you might not be considered disabled any longer and you could lose your disability eligibility altogether. You are only officially disabled if you are unable to perform any substantial gainful work.

However, Social Security usually permits you to earn up to about $500 a month, or $940 if you are blind, before you will be considered to be performing substantial gainful work—its buzzword for disability eligibility. But this income limit is not an absolute rule; other facts will be considered—your work duties, the number of hours you work and, if you are self-employed, the extent to which you run or manage your own business. In deciding how much you are earning, the Social Security office can deduct from your income the amounts of any impairment-related work expenses such as medical devices or equipment—a wheelchair, for example—attendant care, drugs or services required for you to be able to work.

2. Other Social Security Benefits

You are not permitted to collect more than one Social Security benefit at a time. If you are eligible for more than one monthly benefit—disability and retirement, for example, or disability based on your own work record and also as the disabled spouse of a retired worker—you will receive the higher of the two benefit amounts, but not both.

For the purposes of this rule, though, Supplemental Security Income (SSI)—a program jointly run by federal and state governments to guarantee a minimum income to elderly, blind and disabled people—is not considered a Social Security benefit. You may collect SSI in addition to a Social Security benefit.

3. Other Disability Benefits

You are permitted to collect Social Security disability payments and, at the same time, private disability payments from an insurance policy or coverage from your employer. You may also receive Veterans' Administration disability coverage at the same time as Social Security disability benefits. And you may collect workers' compensation benefits at the same time as Social Security disability benefits.

However, the total of your disability and workers' compensation payments cannot be greater than 80% of what your average wages were before you became disabled. If they are, your disability benefits will be reduced to the point where the total of both benefits is 80% of your earnings before you became disabled. If you are still receiving Social Security disability benefits when your workers' compensation benefits run out, you can again start receiving the full amount of your Social Security benefits.

> **Example:** *Minnie became disabled while working for the telephone company in the computer analysis department. At that time she was making $1,400 a month. Her Social Security disability benefits were $560 a month; she also applied for and began receiving workers' compensation benefits of $625 a month. Because the total of the two benefits was more than 80 percent of her prior salary (80% of $1,400 is $1,120, and she would be getting $1,185), her disability benefits were reduced by the extra $65 down to $495 a month.*
>
> *If Minnie were still disabled when her workers' compensation benefits ran out, her Social Security disability benefits would go back up to $560 a month, plus whatever cost of living increases had been granted in the meantime. If Minnie also had private insurance which paid disability benefits, she could receive those benefits as well as all of her Social Security.*

4. Medicare

After you have been collecting disability benefits for 24 months—not necessarily consecutive months—you become eligible for Medicare coverage even though you are not old enough to be covered by Medicare under the regular rules of the program. Medicare Part A hospitalization coverage is free after you pay a deductible. Like everyone else, though, you must pay a monthly premium if you want to be covered by Medicare Part B medical insurance that partially covers doctor bills, lab work, outpatient clinic care and some drugs and medical supplies.

For more information on Medicare, contact the Medicare information line: 800-952-8627. Or go to the Medicare website at http://www.hcfa.gov/medicare/medicare.htm.

CHAPTER

15

RETIREMENT PLANS

There is no law requiring private employers to offer their employees retirement plans. In fact, only about half of the country's total private workforce are employed by companies that have some kind of pension plan.

Those employers that do offer pension plans are not required to pay any minimum amount of money—and an increasing number of individuals who invested in saving for their futures are disappointed and disillusioned to learn their retirement plans simply do not deliver what they promised.

The old standby, Social Security—the government's income system for people 55 and over created by the passage of the Social Security Act in 1935—was not meant to be a pension program as much as insurance against extreme poverty in the later years of life. Although Social Security benefit checks for retirees have increased some in recent years, they still do not provide enough income for most people to maintain their preretirement lifestyles. Consequently, many people rely on some form of private pension—however small—to enhance their incomes after they retire.

This chapter cannot begin to cover all aspects of pension law, which has evolved into a complex morass of legal exceptions, exemptions and loopholes and is controlled by individual plan agreements. It discusses the most important laws concerning your right to collect the pension benefits you have earned and provides resources for more help.

A. Social Security Retirement Benefits

There are many ins and outs to the Social Security retirement benefit system—most of them dependent on factors such as the type of job you work, the length of time you work and the age at which you retire.

For more information on Social Security programs and benefits and how to file for them, see *Social Security, Medicare & Pensions: Get the Most Out of Your Retirement and Medical Benefits*, by Joseph L. Matthews with Dorothy Berman Matthews (Nolo).

1. Who Is Qualified

As with other Social Security benefits, to be eligible for any amount of retirement benefits, you must have accumulated enough work credits. Work credits are measured in quarters (January through March, April through June, and so on) in which you earned more than the required amount of money. The number of work credits you need to be eligible for benefits depends on your age when you apply.

In addition, certain dependents of retired workers are eligible for monthly benefits if the worker has amassed enough work credits to qualify for benefits. Dependents who may qualify for these derivative benefits include:

- a spouse age 62 or older
- a spouse under age 62 who cares for the worker's young or disabled children
- a divorced spouse age 62 or older, if the marriage lasted ten years and if two years have passed since the divorce
- unmarried children under 18 or who are severely disabled, and
- grandchildren under the care and custody of the worker.

Work Credits Required for Social Security Retirement Benefits

If you reach age 62 in:	*You need this many quarters of employment:*
1980	29
1981	30
1982	31
1983	32
1984	33
1985	34
1990	39
1991 or later	40

2. Calculating Your Benefits

Note that when the term retire is used by the Social Security Administration, it only refers to the time you claim your retirement benefits. It does not necessarily mean you have reached a particular age or that you have stopped working.

The average benefit for a person who retires at age 65 is about $750 per month; for a couple, the monthly average is about $1,280. Whatever the amount of your retirement benefit, you will receive an automatic cost of living increase on January 1 of each year. This increase is tied to the rise in the Consumer Price Index—the cost of basic goods and services.

Help With Estimating Benefits

Even if you have not worked for many years, and you did not make much money in the few years you did work, check your earnings record. You may be surprised to find you have quite a few quarters of credit from years gone by. If you want to estimate the amount of Social Security benefits you are entitled to receive after you have retired from your job, complete and submit the Social Security Administration's Form SSA-7004-PC-OP1, Request for Earnings and Benefit Estimate Statement. You can obtain one from the Social Security Administration office closest to you or download one from the SSA website at http://www.ssa.gov.

3. Taxes on Your Benefits

Most Social Security retirement benefits are not considered taxable income by the Internal Revenue Service—although you do have to pay income tax on any interest you earn from saving your benefits. But if your adjusted gross income—from a parttime job, for example—plus one-half of your year's Social Security benefits adds up to $25,000 or more, then you must pay income tax on one-half of your Social Security benefits. The income and benefit limit is about $34,000 for an individual; $44,000 for a couple. In January of each year, you will receive a statement from the Social Security Administration showing the amount of benefits you received in the previous year and an IRS form explaining how to report this income, if necessary.

Medicare and Disability: Not-So-Distant Cousins

The Social Security system wears many hats.

Another one of them is Medicare—a federal government program run by the Department of Health and Human Services, set up to assist senior and some disabled people in paying for some hospital and medical costs. If you become sick or disabled and unable to work, you and your dependents may qualify for additional benefits that are part of the broader Social Security system. (See Chapter 14, Section F.)

---

4. Working After Retirement

In addition to the need for more income, many people keep their jobs or take new ones after a planned retirement so that they can stay active and stay ahead of the bills. People who have reached full retirement age—currently 65 years of age by Social Security's count—may work and earn any amount without losing any of their benefits.

However, people who collect Social Security benefits before they reach the age of 55 will lose one dollar of those benefits for every two dollars they earn over a set yearly limit. For the year 2000, that limit is $10,080. The limit applies only to earnings from work; it does not apply to income from such things as savings, investments, pensions or rental property.

Retirement Benefits: Keep an Eye on the Calendar

The Social Security law permits you to retire and claim benefits as early as age 62. If you do, you will receive a lower monthly amount—one that Social Security figures will total, over your lifetime, the same amount you would have received if you retired at 65.

Monthly benefits for retirement at age 62 are about 20% less than if you wait until age 65—about 13% less if you retire at 63, 6.6% less at age 64. The reduction in monthly benefits is permanent. They do not increase to the full amount when you turn 65.

Not only do you have the option of claiming early retirement, you can also wait until after age 65 and claim a higher delayed retirement benefit. For example, if you wait until age 72 to claim retirement, your benefits would permanently be 7% higher than if you retired at age 65.

For an unconventional look at retirement, see *Get a Life: You Don't Need a Million to Retire Well,* by Ralph Warner (Nolo).

B. Private Pensions

Pensions, according to many workplace experts, are a good idea run amok.

Pension plans became popular during the Second World War at a time when there were more jobs than workers. Employers used fringe benefits, such as pensions, to attract and keep workers without violating the wartime wage freeze rules. Since the early 1950s, unions and employers have both recognized pension plans as crucial elements in labor negotiations.

But until the mid-1970s, having a pension plan and collecting a pension benefit check were two different animals. Many people were promised a pension as part of the terms of their employment, and many workers contributed to pension funds through payroll deductions, but relatively few actually received much in the way of benefits at retirement. There were several reasons for the failure of pensions to deliver what they promised: people changed jobs and had to leave their pension rights behind; workers were not-so-mysteriously let go just before they reached retirement age; and pension plans, or whole companies, went out of business.

1. Legal Controls on Pensions

Since the passage of a federal law, the Employee Retirement Income Security Act of 1974 (29 U.S.C. §§301 and following), commonly called ERISA, at least some of the worst sorts of disappearing pension acts have been halted. ERISA sets minimum standards for pension plans, guaranteeing that pension rights cannot be unfairly denied or taken from a worker. ERISA also provides some protection for workers in the event certain types of pension plans cannot pay all the benefits to which workers are entitled. But while ERISA does provide the protection of federal law for certain pension rights, its scope is limited.

The Incredible Shrinking Pension Check

Inflation is an old enemy of your right to receive a decent retirement pension. The figures an employer shows you as your potential pension benefit may seem decent when you are hired, and may even pay a reasonable amount when you first retire. But because few private pension plans are indexed to the rising cost of living, an amount sufficient at the time you retire will seem smaller and smaller as inflation cuts into the value of your pension dollar. In other words, the cost of living will go up, but your pension check will not. Unfortunately, ERISA does not require pension plans to respond to inflation's bite into your retirement benefits.

Pension Terms Defined

Jargon dominates the pension industry. However, the following definitions of some of the common terms involving plans and benefits will get you on the road to understanding your pension rights and wrongs.

Defined benefit plan. The employer promises to pay the employee a fixed amount of money, usually monthly, after the employee retires. Although a defined benefit plan is what usually comes to mind when people think about pensions, this plan has become less common than the defined contribution type.

Defined contribution plan. The employer promises to pay a certain amount into the employee's retirement account while the employee is working, but does not promise a specific amount of income for the employee after retirement. Your employer may promise to pay $50 per month per employee into the company's pension plan, for example, but the size of the monthly pension check you would receive after retirement would vary according to the interest rate paid on your pension account and other economic factors.

Defined contribution plans can take several different forms, such as 401(k) plans through which your employer and you can contribute jointly to retirement savings. (See Section D.) For the most part, defined contribution pension plans are individual savings accounts that have some tax advantages—but also some limitations on withdrawals and reinvestment—that regular savings accounts do not have.

Employee Retirement Security Act (ERISA). The most important federal law governing pensions and other employee benefit programs. Administered by the U.S. Department of Labor, the Internal Revenue Service and the Securities and Exchange Commission, ERISA sets minimum standards for pensions and attempts to guarantee that pension rights cannot be unfairly taken from or denied to workers.

Pension Benefit Guaranty Corporation. An organization that insures many pension plans in the United States, the PBGC is half private and half public. It is supposed to get its money from insurance premiums paid by the pension plans it covers, but it regularly turns to the federal government for money when it runs short.

Plan administrator. The person or organization with the legal authority and responsibility for managing your pension program.

Vesting. Getting a legal right to collect from a benefit program. For example, some pension plans require you to work a certain number of years for a company before you have any right to a pension. Once you are vested, you continue to have rights to the pension plan even if you no longer work there.

2. Eligibility for Pension Coverage

There is no law that requires an employer to offer a pension plan. However, if a company chooses to do so, ERISA requires that the pension plan spell out who is eligible for coverage. Pension plans do not have to include all workers, but they cannot legally be structured to benefit only the top executives or otherwise discriminate—for example, by excluding older workers. The plan administrator for your company's pension program can tell you whether or not you are eligible to participate.

If you are eligible to participate in your employer's pension program, the administrator must provide you with several documents needed to understand the plan.

- *A summary plan description.* Explains the basics of how your plan operates. ERISA requires that you be given the summary plan within 90 days after you begin participating in a pension plan, and that you must be given any updates to it.

  This document will also tell you the formula for vesting in the plan—if it is a plan that includes vesting—the formula for determining your defined benefits or the defined contributions that your employer will make to the plan and whether or not your pension is insured by the Pension Benefit Guaranty Corporation or PBGC. (See Section B7, below.)
- *A summary annual report.* A yearly accounting of your pension plan's financial condition and operations.
- *Survivor coverage data.* A statement of how much your plan would pay to any surviving spouse should you die first.

Your plan administrator is also required to provide you with a detailed, individual statement of the pension benefits you have earned, but only if you request it in writing or are going to stop participating in the plan because, for example, you change employers. Note, however, that ERISA gives you the right to only one such statement from your plan per year.

3. Early Retirement and Pension Benefits

Each pension plan has its own rules on the minimum age for filing benefits. Most private pension plans consider 65 to be the normal retirement age. However, some private pensions also offer the option of retiring early, usually at age 55. If you elect early retirement, however, expect your benefit checks to be much smaller than they would be if you waited until the regular retirement age.

Many corporations now use the early retirement option of their pension plans to cut staff. By making a temporary offer to increase the benefits available to those who opt to retire early, these corporations create an incentive for employees to voluntarily leave the company's payroll before turning age 65. Sometimes companies make the early retirement offer even more attractive by throwing in a few months of extra severance pay.

Some early retirement offers are very lucrative, and some are not. Before accepting one, study the details carefully, keeping in mind that the offer you accept may have to serve as your primary income for the rest of your life. (See Chapter 8, Section E, on the Older Workers Benefit Protection Act.)

Because pension law is so specialized and complex, you may also consider consulting a lawyer who specializes in it if the terms of your employer's early retirement offer to you are not clear. (See Chapter 18, Section D.)

Integrated Plans: Innovation or Deviation?

In the past few years, the popularity of integrated plans, a somewhat devious form of pension plan, has grown among employers. When a pension plan is integrated with Social Security retirement benefits, your actual monthly or yearly pension benefit is reduced by all, or some percentage of, your Social Security check. One type of integrated plan operates by setting up what is called a benefit goal for your retirement. This means the plan sets a goal for the amount of money you should have from a combination of pension and Social Security retirement income. The figure the plan arrives at as your benefit goal is usually a percentage of your average pre-retirement income. Your pension amount is then only what is needed to make up the difference between your Social Security benefits and this pre-determined benefit goal.

One small—very small—consolation about integrated plans is that once they have reduced your pension to fit it into the benefit goal along with Social Security benefits, they cannot further reduce your pension amount when Social Security benefits rise because of cost of living increases.

4. Filing for Benefits

Although ERISA does not spell out one uniform claim procedure for all pension plans, it does establish some rules which must be followed when you retire and want to claim your benefits. All pension plans must have an established claim procedure and all participants in the plan must be given a summary of the plan which explains the plan's claim procedure. When your claim is filed, you must receive a decision on the claim, in writing, within a "reasonable time." The decision must state specific reasons for the denial of any claimed benefits and must explain the basis for determining the benefits which are granted.

From the date you receive a written decision on your pension claim, you have 60 days to file a written appeal of the decision. The details for where and how this appeal is filed must be explained in the plan summary. In presenting your appeal, the claim procedures must permit you to examine the plan's files and records and to submit evidence of your own. ERISA does not, however, require the pension plan to actually give you a hearing regarding your appeal. Within 60 days of filing, the pension plan administrators must file a written decision on your appeal. If your claim is still denied, in whole or in part, you then have a right to press your claim in either state or federal court.

When Retirement Does Not Mean Retirement

If your benefits have vested when you reach the retirement age established by your pension plan—usually 65—you are free to leave a job with the employer who pays your pension and work for someone else, or open your own business, while collecting your full pension.

However, if you return to work for the employer that is paying your pension benefits, ERISA permits the employer to suspend payment of your pension for as long as you continue working for that employer. Some workers are covered by a multi-employer pension plan, such as those through an industrywide union contract. Also, your pension benefits can be suspended if you return to work for a different employer whose employees are covered by the same pension plan.

---

5. Appealing a Denial of Benefits

Each pension plan has its own system for appeals. If your pension plan denies you benefits to which you are entitled, its administrator is required to advise you about how to appeal that decision. You will have 60 days to request such an appeal, and the group that reviews your appeal will, in most cases, have 120 days after you file it to issue its decision. ERISA requires that you be given a plain English explanation of the decision on your appeal.

If your pension plan's internal review system also rules against you, you are entitled to appeal that decision by contacting:

Pension and Welfare Benefits Administration
1730 K Street, NW; Suite 556
Washington, DC 20006
202-254-7013

In addition, the rules of ERISA permit you to file a specific ERISA enforcement lawsuit in federal court to enforce any rule or provision of the ERISA law or of a pension plan covered by ERISA rules. In particular, you may file a federal court lawsuit under ERISA to:

- recover benefits which have been unfairly denied
- change a ruling made by the pension plan that would affect your future benefits—such as a ruling regarding eligibility, accrual or vesting
- force the plan to provide information required by ERISA
- correct improper management of the plan or its funds, and
- protect any other right established by the rules of your particular pension plan or by ERISA itself.

Lying Doesn't Pay, Liars Do

The U.S. Supreme court has made it clear to employers that they cannot be sneaky when dealing with employee benefit rights.

The definitive case taking on the issue arose when Varity Corporation, a farm equipment manufacturer with a branch based in Iowa, began experiencing financial woes in the mid-1980s. In desperation, it developed a new business plan—perkily dubbed Project Sunshine—with the master plan of transferring the money-losing divisions and other company debts into a new subsidiary. One of the debts it hoped to eliminate in the reorganization was its promise to pay medical and other benefits.

To cover its asset-shifting, Varity painted the new company as financially sound—and offered longtime employees the alleged opportunity to switch over to the new company. Many leaped at the chance.

In reality, Project Sunshine did not offer a bright future at the new company, which started out $46 million in debt, ended the first year $88 million in debt and went under shortly after—leaving 1,500 employees and 4,000 retirees without promised benefits. They sued—and won the right to have benefits restored.

Varity appealed to the U.S. Supreme Court, arguing that under ERISA, employees could not sue the company on their own behalf and that, when describing the rosy future of the new company at a meeting with employees, it was acting as a regular employer, not in its capacity as plan administrator under ERISA.

The Court found these arguments disingenuous, holding that: "Making intentional representations about the future of plan benefits is an act of plan administration" (*Varity Corp. v. Howe*, 116 S.Ct. 1065 (1996)).

6. Terminated Plans

Your employer may simply decide to terminate your plan, even if it is financially sound; about 10,000 firms do just that every year—mostly in the name of cutting back on corporate costs. If your employer terminates your pension plan, your plan administrator is required to notify you in writing of the approaching termination at least 60 days before the plan ends.

If the termination is a standard one, that means that your plan has enough assets to cover its obligations. Your plan administrator is required to notify you in such cases of how the plan's money will be paid out and what your options are during the pay-out period.

If the termination is being done under distress, the Pension Benefit Guaranty Corporation may become responsible for paying your pension benefits. (See Section 7, below.) If your plan is not insured by the PBGC and it is terminated, your pension rights may be reduced—or you may lose them.

7. Mismanaged Plans

In recent years, a number of pension funds have gone broke, through mismanagement, fraud or overextended resources. The future is likely to bring with it an increasing number of pension plan failures. Under ERISA, there is some insurance against pension fund collapses. ERISA established the Pension Benefit Guaranty Corporation, a public, nonprofit insurance fund, to provide coverage against bankrupt pension funds. Should a pension fund be unable to pay all its obligations to retirees, the PBGC may, under certain conditions, pick up the slack and pay much of the pension fund's unfulfilled obligations.

However, the PBGC does not cover all types of pension plans and does not guarantee all pension benefits of the plans it does cover. Only defined benefit plans are covered—through insurance premiums they pay to the PBGC—and only vested benefits are protected by the insurance. Also, PBGC insurance normally only covers retirement pension benefits; other benefits, such as disability, health coverage and death benefits, are not usually covered.

If you have a question about termination of benefits because of failure of your pension plan, contact:

Pension Benefit Guaranty Corporation
Case Operations and Compliance
1200 K Street, NW
Washington, DC 20005
202-326-4000
800-400-7242
TDD: 202-326-4179
FAX: 202-326-4016
http://www.pbgc.gov

If you think you can prove that the people managing your pension plan are not handling your pension money in your best interests—for example, they are making questionable investments—ERISA gives you the right to file a lawsuit against them in federal court. You will probably need to hire a lawyer to help you with this type of lawsuit. (See Chapter 18, Section D.)

C. Where to Get More Information

If you want more details on your rights to receive benefits from a private pension plan, there are a number of free brochures available from:

American Association of Retired Persons (AARP)
601 E Street, NW
Washington, DC 20049
800-424-3410
TDD: 202-434-6554
FAX: 202-434-2320
http://www.aarp.org

Another organization that offers a number of publications relating to pensions is:

The Pension Rights Center
918 16th Street, NW; Suite 704
Washington, DC 20006
202-296-3776
FAX: 202-833-2472

D. 401(k) Deferred Compensation Plans

Many employers that offer retirement benefits do so through a 401(k) deferred compensation plan—the name taken from the number of an IRS regulation that provides the plan with its tax-deferred status. 401(k) plans are deferred compensation programs in which employees invest part of their wages, sometimes with added employer contributions, to save on taxes; they are not actually pension programs that establish a right to retirement benefits. This section explains the basics of 401(k) plans.

1. Structure of 401(k) Plans

In a 401(k) plan, an employee contributes out of his or her salary to one of several retirement investment accounts set up by the employer and administered by a bank, brokerage or other financial institution. Depending on the rules of the particular plan, the employer often makes some additional contribution in addition to the amount the employee sets aside. However, unlike traditional pension plans, the employer has no obligation to contribute anything and can change the contribution amounts from year to year. These plans are cheaper for the employer than more traditional pension plans because employees make the primary contributions from their salaries, the employer has no fixed obligation to contribute and when the employer does contribute, it does so as a tax-deductible business expense.

2. Investment Choices

401(k) plans do not require either the employee or the employer to contribute any set amount each year. An employee can contribute a limited part of his or her wages each year. That amount is limited by the IRS each year. The maximum permissible contribution amount goes up each year with the rise in the cost of living. There is no legal limit on the amount an employer may contribute, but the amounts are usually a percentage of the amount of the employee's contribution.

A 401(k) plan usually offers the employee a choice among different investments for the deferred income. Some plans offer a selection of pre-approved savings accounts, money market funds, stocks and bonds and mutual funds. Other plans permit employees to select their own investment funds or even to buy individual stock shares on the open market. However, there are usually some limits on the number of investments offered and on the frequency and amount of changes in investments that can be made in a given period of time.

Tax Advantages of 401(k) Plans

401(k) plans have two tax advantages for the employee.

The first is that income taxes on the amount of wages invested in the plan are not paid in the year of earning but are deferred until you withdraw the money from the plan after retirement. Most people have significantly lower income tax brackets after they stop working, and so the total tax paid on the income is lower.

The second advantage is that taxes on income earned by the investments of the 401(k) plan are likewise deferred until the money is withdrawn after retirement.

401(k) Investments May Be Risky

Along with a choice of investments for the employee comes the risk of poor returns. Unlike traditional pension plans that sink or swim on the total pension fund's portfolio and are backed up by the government's Pension Benefit Guaranty Corporation, the amount of an employee's 401(k) plan fund at retirement depends entirely on how well the plan's individual investments do over the years. An employee who makes particularly risky investments could wind up with less in 401(k) funds than he or she invested.

3. Withdrawing Money

One of the advantages of most 401(k) plans is that they permit you to withdraw your deferred compensation earlier than pension plans. Most 401(k) plans permit withdrawal without any tax penalty at age 59½, or at age 55 if you have stopped working. Funds may be withdrawn in a lump sum or in monthly allotments. Money that remains in the account, including future earnings, will not be taxed until withdrawal. 401(k) plans also allow your beneficiaries to withdraw the 401(k) funds without tax penalty if you die at any age.

If you withdraw funds before the age permitted by the rules of your plan, you will pay a 10% penalty on the amount withdrawn, plus all income taxes at your current tax rate. And IRS rules require that you begin withdrawing funds by age 70½ at the latest. The amount you must withdraw to avoid a tax penalty is determined by the IRS based on your age and the year you were born. The administrator of your plan can tell you your minimum withdrawal amount.

Some 401(k) plans also permit withdrawing funds without penalty if needed for a family emergency, such as for medical expenses or for investment in a home. And in some plans, you can take out a loan from your own 401(k) funds, up to 50% of the total in the account or $50,000, whichever is less, if you have sufficient collateral and you repay it within five years. There are strict rules applying to such withdrawals and loans. Check with your 401(k) plan administrator or a financial advisor.

For an explanation of how to take money out of your retirement plan, see *IRAs, 401(k)s & Other Retirement Plans*, by Twila Slesnick and John C. Suttle (Nolo).

Sniffing Out the Bad Apples

As 401(k) plans have become more common, so have incidents of 401(k) fraud. According to financial experts, most problems occur in plans at smaller companies—those with 500 employees or fewer.

You might need to become a bit more watchful, too, if your employer runs into hard times financially. A number of employers down on their luck have been tempted to delve into 401(k) reserves, leaving their employees out of retirement funds.

In addition, there are a few precautions that every employee invested in a 401(k) plan should take.

- *Carefully read your account statements.* Most problems with 401(k)s occur before employers hand over the money to the investment manager—a bank, mutual fund or insurance company. Make sure the amount that your investment manager has received matches the deduction on your paystub. Watch for late statements, inaccurate balances and unusual transactions—such as loans to your employer. Also, be wary of frequent changes in investment managers.

- *Ask for interim statements.* Some plans distribute statements only once a year—not often enough for you to keep a vigilant eye on what is happening with them. Many companies will be willing to give you a statement more often, although no law requires them to do so. And most plans have 800-numbers you can call to check on your balance.

- *Talk with former employees.* If former employees are having trouble getting their benefits paid correctly and on time, chances are you will, too.

- *Read your plan's description.* This document will tell you how long your employer may hold your money before giving it to the investment manager. And it identifies the plan trustee and administrator who are responsible for the plan.

Adapted from Kiplinger's Personal Finance Magazine; *March 1996*

CHAPTER

16

LABOR UNIONS

Labor unions are organizations that deal collectively with employers on behalf of employees. Their best-known role is negotiating group employment contracts for members that spell out workplace essentials such as mandatory procedures for discipline and firing. But unions also often perform other workplace chores such as lobbying for legislation that benefits their members and sponsoring skill training programs.

Today, fewer than 15% of all American workers are union members—half as many as belonged in 1946, when membership was at a fever pitch. If you belong to a union, the specifics of your work relationship are covered in a collective bargaining agreement. That means nearly everything—work schedules, wages and hours, time off, discipline, safety rules, retirement plans—is spelled out in that contract. If you have a workplace problem, the process available to resolve it is spelled out in your collective bargaining contract, too. Usually, you are required to discuss your problem first with a designated union representative, who will then take it up with union officials. If your complaint is found to be a reasonable one, the union reps will guide you through a complaint or grievance procedure. If you disagree with the union's assessment of your situation, you can follow the steps provided for appealing the decision.

Some labor unions also operate benefit programs, such as vacation plans, healthcare insurance, pensions and programs that provide members with discounts on various types of personal needs, such as eyeglasses and prescription drugs.

Most unions are operated by a paid staff of professional organizers, negotiators and administrators, with some help from members who volunteer their time. In general, the money to pay unions' staffs and expenses comes from dues paid by their members—which typically total about $50 per member per month. There is no law that specifically regulates the amount of money that unions can charge their members—but it may not be excessive. Courts have provided little guidance in defining this, but have held that a union initiation fee equal to one month's salary by a starting worker would likely be considered excessive.

The laws and court decisions governing labor unions and their relationships with employers are so complex and separate from the rest of workplace law that this chapter can give you only an overview.

If you are already a member of a labor union and want to continue as one, the information provided here can help you to doublecheck on the performance of your union's leaders.

If you are not represented by a union and would like to be, or if you are a member of a union and want out, this chapter will help you become familiar with the basic laws labor unions must follow and alert you to your rights in dealing with unions.

A. Federal Laws

The federal laws broadly regulating unions—and the copious amendments to those laws—have dramatically changed the look and function of unions over time. The changing laws have also acted as political mirrors—alternately protecting employees from unfair labor practices and protecting employers from unfair union practices as unions' influence in the workplace has ebbed and flowed. Several of the most important federal controls are discussed here.

1. The National Labor Relations Act

Labor unions secured the legal right to represent employees in their relationships with their employers when the National Labor Relations Act, or NLRA (29 U.S.C. §§151 and following), was passed in 1935. That federal Act also created the National Labor Relations Board (NLRB) to police the relationships among employees, their unions and their employers.

Under the NLRA, an employer may not:

- interfere with or restrain employees who are exercising their rights to organize, bargain collectively and engage in other concerted activities for their own protection
- interfere with the formation of any labor organization—or contribute financial or other support to it
- encourage or discourage membership in a labor organization by discriminating in hiring, tenure or employment conditions
- discharge or discriminate against employees who have filed charges or testified under the NLRA, or
- refuse to bargain collectively with the employees' majority representative.

a. Who is covered

The NLRA requires most employers and unions to negotiate fairly with each other until they agree to a contract that spells out the terms and conditions of employment for the workers who are members of the union. The NLRB enforces this requirement by using mediators, negotiators, administrative law judges, investigators and others.

b. Who is excluded

Certain groups of employees are not covered by the NLRA. They include:

- managers, supervisors and confidential employees such as company accountants
- farm workers
- the families of employers
- government workers
- most domestic workers, and
- certain industry groups, such as railroad employees, whose work situations are regulated by other laws.

The NLRA also contains some special exemptions for specific groups of workers within industries that are otherwise covered. Contact your local NLRB office for more information on whether your job is covered by the NLRA.

2. The Labor Management Relations Act

In the dozen years following enactment of the NLRA, Congress was progressively bombarded with pleas to rein in the unions' power in the workplace. Both employers and employees contended they needed protection from union overreaching, such as coercing workers to join by using threats and violence. The public joined in the outcry—complaining about work stoppages that increasingly threatened health, safety and food supply.

In 1947, the Labor Management Relations Act, popularly known as the Taft-Hartley Act (29 U.S.C. §141 and following), was passed. It was aimed at preventing unfair union practices and banned unions from:

- restraining or coercing employees who were exercising their rights under the NLRA, including the right to select a bargaining representative
- causing or influencing an employer to discriminate against an employee because of membership or nonmembership in a union
- refusing to bargain in good faith with an employer if a majority of employees have designated a union bargaining agent
- inducing or encouraging employees to stop work to force special treatment of union matters, and
- charging excessive fees to employees and employers.

3. The Labor Management Reporting and Disclosure Act

In a third attempt to right the balance among employees, employers and unions, Congress passed the Labor Management Reporting and Disclosure Act of 1959 (29 U.S.C. §153 and following). The most important contribution of that law is that it imposes a code of conduct for unions, union officers, employers and management consultants—holding each to a standard of fair dealing.

4. Enforcing Your Rights

You can sue unions and employers over violations of the National Labor Relations Act (NLRA), and many people have won such lawsuits. However, you will probably need a lawyer's help to file a lawsuit under the NLRA. (See Chapter 18, Section D.)

Also, there are a number of organizations that may provide free or low-cost help in pursuing union problems and complaints. (See Section H and the Appendix for contact information.)

B. State Laws

Section 14(b) of the NLRA authorizes each state to pass laws that require all unionized workplaces within their boundaries to be open shops—and nearly half the states have passed such laws. (See the chart below.) In each of these states, you have the right to hold a job without joining a union or paying any money to a union, so they are usually called right to work laws.

One boon for employees in right to work states is that the NLRA requires that a union give fair and equal representation to all members of a bargaining unit, regardless of whether they are union members. If you are employed in a right to work state and are a member of a bargaining unit represented by a labor union, you can refuse to join the union or to pay any money to it—and the union still must represent you the same as your union co-workers.

If the union representing your bargaining unit fails or refuses to represent you in such situations, you can file an unfair labor practices charge against it with the NLRB.

The states listed below have right to work laws—which prohibit making union membership or nonmembership a condition of employment.

Additional Laws May Apply

If the chart below indicates that your state has no statute, this means there is no law that specifically addresses the issue. However, there may be a state administrative regulation or local ordinance that does control. Call your state labor department for more information. (See the Appendix for contact details.)

State Right to Work Laws	
Alabama	Ala. Code §25-7-12
Alaska	Alaska Stat. §23.40.110
Arizona	Ariz. Rev. Stat. Ann. §23-1302
Arkansas	Ark. Stat. Ann. §11-3-303
California	Cal. Lab. Code §§921 and 922

Colorado	No statute
Connecticut	No statute
Delaware	Del. Code Ann. tit. 14, §4007 (public schools) Del. Code Ann. tit. 19, §1307 (all public employers)
District of Columbia	No statute
Florida	Fla. Stat. Ann. §447.17
Georgia	Ga. Code Ann. §34-6-21
Hawaii	No statute
Idaho	Idaho Code §44-2003
Illinois	No statute
Indiana	No statute
Iowa	Iowa Code §731.1
Kansas	Kan. Stat. Ann. §44-808
Kentucky	No statute
Louisiana	La. Rev. Stat. Ann. §§23:983 (all workers) and 23:881 (agricultural workers)
Maine	Me. Rev. Stat. Ann. tit. 26, §1324 (agricultural workers)
Maryland	Md. Lab. and Emp. Code Ann. §4-304
Massachusetts	Mass. Gen. Laws Ann. ch. 149 §20
Michigan	Mich. Comp. Laws §423.16
Minnesota	Minn. Stat. Ann. §179.60
Mississippi	Miss. Const. Art. 7, §198-A
Missouri	No statute
Montana	Mont. Code Ann. §39-31-401
Nebraska	Neb. Rev. Stat. §48-217
Nevada	Nev. Rev. Stat. §250
New Hampshire	N.H. Rev. Stat. Ann. §275.1
New Jersey	No statute
New Mexico	N.M. Stat. Ann. §50-2-4
New York	No statute
North Carolina	N.C. Gen. Stat. §§95-78 to 95-84
North Dakota	N.D. Cent. Code §34-01-14
Ohio	Ohio Rev. Code Ann. §§4113.02 and 4973.03
Oklahoma	No statute
Oregon	If at least 40% of the members of a bargaining unit covered by a closed shop agreement sign a petition to rescind the agreement, there will be an election by secret ballot, unless there was an election within the past 12 months. Or. Rev. Stat. §663.035
Pennsylvania	43 Pa. Cons. Stat. Ann. §211.6
Rhode Island	R.I. Gen. Laws §28-7-13

South Carolina	S.C. Code Ann. §41-7-30
South Dakota	S.D. Codified Laws Ann. §60-8-3; Const., Art. VI, §2
Tennessee	Tenn. Code Ann. §§50-1-201 to 204
Texas	Texas Code Ann., Lab. §101.052
Utah	Utah Code Ann. §§34-34-8 to 34-34-10
Vermont	Vt. Stat. Ann. tit. 3, §961 (state employees)
	Vt. Stat. Ann. tit. 21, §1621 (all employees)
Virginia	Va. Code §§40.1-60 to 40.1-62
Washington	Wash. Rev. Code Ann. §41.56.122 (public employees)
West Virginia	No statute
Wisconsin	Wis. Stat. Ann. §134.02(f)
Wyoming	Wyo. Stat. §27-7-109

C. The Bargaining Unit

The basic union building block under the NLRA is the bargaining unit: a group of employees who perform similar work, who share a work area and who could logically be assumed to have shared interests in such issues as pay rates, hours of work and workplace conditions.

A bargaining unit may be only a part of a larger union, or it may constitute a whole union itself. And a bargaining unit is not always limited to people who work in one building or for one company. For example, the workers in several small, independent sheet metal shops in a specific city will often be members of the same union bargaining unit.

On the other hand, a bargaining unit may include only part of a company. So it is possible—and quite common—for only a small portion of a company's workforce to be unionized, or for various departments in one company to be represented by different unions.

Something that is frequently misunderstood about bargaining units is that they are composed of jobs or job classifications—not of individual workers. For example, if Wilda Samano retires, and her former position as machinist is then filled by Sam Alvarez, the bargaining unit does not change—only the personnel.

D. Types of Union Work Situations

If you take a job that is covered by a contract between the employer and a labor union, a representative of the union will typically approach you about membership requirements shortly after you are hired.

Unionized work situations generally fall into one of three categories: open shop, agency shop and union shop. The type of shop that exists within a unionized bargaining unit will be spelled out in the contract between the union representing that unit and the employer. Ask the union representative for a copy of the contract governing your job before you sign up for union membership.

1. The Open Shop

Here, a union represents the bargaining unit of which you are a member—but you are not required to join the union or pay dues to it. Open shops are most commonly found in states that have passed right to work laws. (See Section B.)

2. The Agency Shop

You can make your own decision about whether or not to join the union. But, whether you join or not, you will have to pay the union the same dues and other fees that other members of your bargaining unit are required to pay. In return for your dues, the union must represent you if labor problems develop, just as it protects members of a bargaining unit. However, you will not be able to take advantage of the broader protections and disciplinary processes included in union contracts. This type of arrangement is legal in any state that has not passed a right to work law. (See Section B.)

3. The Union Shop

Although you are not required to be a union member when you take the job, you will be forced to join after a specified grace period—usually within 30 days after starting your new job—if a union shop clause is included in the contract covering your bargaining unit. Whether or not union shops are legal is a matter of controversy because the controlling law, Section 8(a)(3) of the NLRA, seems to contradict itself.

The law specifies that it is legal for a contract to require an employee to join a union within 30 days of starting a job. But it also states that an employer may fire you because of your lack of union membership only if the union rejected or expelled you for not paying the union's regular fees and dues.

In 1963, the U.S. Supreme Court ruled that the second clause is the one that controls. That decision, widely considered to be the landmark on the legality of union shops, is *NLRB v. General Motors* (373 U.S. 734).

If you take a job in a company in which the union contract calls for a union shop but you refuse to join the union, the employer and the union will usually overlook your refusal to join as long as you pay the union's fees and dues. You can, however, expect to be subjected—at the very least—to cold shoulder treatment by union officials and members.

E. Union Elections

When a union files a petition with the NLRB to be recognized as the representative of a bargaining unit, the petition includes the union's description of what group of workers it would like to have included in that bargaining unit. The employer usually contests these descriptions and tries to have the size of the bargaining unit trimmed down. Negotiations follow, and if the union and the employer cannot agree on the exact shape and size of a bargaining unit, the NLRB decides.

Bargaining units are little democracies, in which the majority rules and the minority must comply. For example, if you work in an office and more than half of the people who work there vote to be represented by a union, the entire office is likely to be designated as a bargaining unit. You will be represented by that union. Even if you do not want to be.

Except in a few circumstances, the NLRB generally will conduct an election for a bargaining unit to decide whether or not it wants to be represented by a certain union whenever at least 30% of the members of that bargaining unit indicate they want an election to be held. The members of the bargaining unit may express their wishes for an election by signing a group petition—or by signing individual cards that state, in essence, the same thing—and presenting that evidence of their wishes to their local NLRB office.

1. Types of Union Elections

NLRB-supervised elections generally fall into three categories:
- Certification elections, in which the employees who make up a bargaining unit vote on whether to have a union begin representing them.
- Decertification elections, in which the employees who make up a bargaining unit vote on whether to end their representation by a specific union.
- Situations where the employees who make up a bargaining unit want to switch unions. The existing union must be voted out through a decertification election and the new union voted in through a certification vote.

2. Restrictions on Union Elections

The courts have reached different conclusions about whether a union-related election can be held. But there are three NLRB policies on union-related elections that you can usually count on. The NLRB will not conduct an election:

- during the first year that a bargaining unit is represented by a particular union
- within a year of the last election held for that bargaining unit, or
- during the period covered by a union contract.

If the contract lasts more than three years, the NLRB will conduct an election at the end of the first three years of the contract if that is what the bargaining unit's members want.

Union-Free Policies May Violate Your Rights

In companies where the employees are not represented by unions, it is common practice for the employer to openly state its wish to remain union-free. In general, companies have the right to make such statements under Section 8(c) of the National Labor Relations Act, as well as under the freedom of speech provisions of the First Amendment to the U.S. Constitution.

However, recent rulings by the National Labor Relations Board indicate that employers must be very careful about where and how they express their wishes for a workplace free of unions. They run the risk of violating the employees' right to unionize under the National Labor Relations Act.

An older, but one of the most significant, rulings restricting union-free statements was issued by the NLRB in 1989, after a union that hoped to organize the employees of a hotel chain filed an unfair labor practices charge against the chain.

The hotel company's management had violated the NLRA, the NLRB ruled, by positioning a union-free statement in the policy manual that it gave to all new employees. The page following the one on which the union-free statement appeared asked employees for their signatures, verifying that they accepted the terms of employment set out in the manual.

The sequence of those pages in the employee manual, the NLRB decided, could lead employees to believe that adhering to the company's union-free policy was a condition of continued employment. And making employees believe that would violate Section 8(a) of the NLRA, which makes it illegal for an employer to coerce employees away from pursuing their rights to union representation (293 NLRB No. 6, 130 LRRM 1338 (1989)).

F. The Right to Unionize

Sections 7 and 8 of the National Labor Relations Act guarantee employees the right to create, join and participate in a labor union without being unfairly intimidated or punished by their employers.

1. Employee Rights

Generally, the courts have ruled that Section 7 of the NLRA gives employees the right to:

- discuss union membership and read and distribute literature concerning it during nonwork time in nonwork areas such as an employee lounge
- sign a card asking your employer to recognize your union and bargain with it, to sign petitions and grievances concerning employment terms and conditions and to ask your co-workers to sign petitions and grievances, and
- display your pro-union sentiments by wearing message-bearing items such as hats, pins and T-shirts on the job.

Religious Objections to Unions

Some employees are members of religions with beliefs that conflict with membership in a labor union. If your religion prohibits you from taking oaths, for example, having to swear allegiance to a labor union might force you to violate your religious beliefs.

In general, the courts have recognized an employee's right to refuse to join a union on religious grounds. However, you can still be required to pay union dues and fees if you work in an agency or union shop in a state that has not passed a right to work law. (See Section B.)

2. Employer Limitations

Most courts have also ruled that Section 8 of the NLRA means that an employer may not:

- grant or promise employees promotions, pay raises, desirable work assignments or other special favors if they oppose unionizing efforts
- close down a worksite or transfer work or reduce benefits to pressure employers not to support unionization, or
- dismiss, harass, reassign or otherwise punish or discipline employees—or threaten to—if they support unionization. (See Chapter 11, Section C, for a related discussion of blacklisting laws.)

3. Deducting Union Dues From Paychecks

One thing on which labor unions and the government agree is that it is easier to get money from people who never get to touch that money in the first place. To ease their operations, many union contracts include a check-off clause.

Much like income tax withholding, the check-off clause requires your employer to withhold your union dues from your pay and then forward the money to the union. By voting to approve a contract between your union and your employer, you also signify approval of any check-off clause in that contract. So unions' practice of having employers withhold dues from a paycheck is generally legal.

How Unions Are Born

If a group of employees wishes to campaign for unionization of their jobs, the best place to begin is by contacting a union they think would be interested and proposing the idea.

Unions are usually listed in the Yellow Pages of your local telephone directory under Labor Organizations. Don't let their names discourage you. It is not unusual for meatpackers to belong to the United Steel Workers, for example, or for office workers to belong to the Teamsters union, which originally represented freight drivers. The only practical way to determine which unions might be interested in unionizing your workplace is to call and ask.

If the union you approach is interested, it will assign professional organizers who will guide you through the rest of the process. If it is not interested—perhaps because your employer is too small or because you work in an industry with which it is not comfortable—that union should be able to suggest another one that would be more appropriate for you to contact. If not, contact:

The American Federation of Labor and Congress
    of Industrial Organizations (AFL-CIO)
815 16th Street, NW
Washington, DC 20006
202-637-5000
FAX: 202-637-5058
http://www.aflcio.org/home.htm

The National Labor Relations Act allows you to form your own, independent union to represent only the workers at your place of employment without affiliating with any established union. Such unions exist, but the complexities of labor law and the cost of running an independent union typically make them unfeasible in all but the largest companies

G. The Right to De-Unionize

Just as it gives employees the right to unionize, the NLRA gives them the right to withdraw from union membership.

1. How to De-Unionize

There are two basic ways to de-unionize.

One way is to conduct a campaign among the members of your bargaining unit to get them to petition the NLRB to conduct a de-certification election. If you are able to bring about an election, you will probably also have to campaign hard against the union for the votes of other members of the bargaining unit.

Another way to de-unionize is simply to resign your individual membership. The courts have ruled that informing your employer that you want check-off deductions for union dues and fees stopped is not sufficient to quit a union; you must advise the union in writing of your decision to quit.

In right to work states, such a resignation leaves you free and clear of the union altogether—no membership, no dues, no fees. In other states, you may be required to continue paying fees and dues to your bargaining unit's union if the contract there calls for a union or agency shop, as described in Section D.

2. Limitations on Unions

The NLRA also prohibits unions from interfering with your right to reject or change union membership. Unions may not:

- restrain or coerce employees from exercising their rights under the NLRA; this includes the violence and threats of violence that some unions use against people who reject union membership
- cause or encourage an employer to discriminate against an employee or group of employees because of their de-unionization activities
- interfere in any way with an employee's right to freely express opinions on union membership
- fail or refuse to bargain in good faith with an employer on behalf of a bargaining unit that has designated the union as its bargaining agent, even if the union and the bargaining unit are at odds, or
- prevent you from going to work by using such tactics as mass picketing.

H. Where to Get More Help

It is easier to get free legal advice and help with labor union matters than on any other aspect of workplace law.

The place to start is your local office of the National Labor Relations Board (NLRB), listed in the Federal Government section of your telephone directory. The NLRB also maintains a list of local offices on its website at http://www.nlrb.gov. If the NLRB considers your union-related problem to be a serious one, it will pay for all the costs of the investigations and hearings required to take your complaint through the legal process.

If the NLRB cannot or will not help, you can turn to several other sources. If you consider yourself to be pro-union, contact AFL-CIO headquarters:

> The American Federation of Labor and Congress
>   of Industrial Organizations
> 815 16th Street, NW
> Washington, DC 20006
> 202-637-5000
> Internet: http://www.aflcio.org

If you consider yourself to be anti-union, contact:

> The National Right to Work Committee
> 8001 Braddock Road
> Springfield, VA 22160
> 703-321-9820
> 800-325-7892
> FAX: 703-321-7342
> http://www.nrtwc.org

If you are unsure about what your opinion on unions is, call both places. These organizations maintain legal staffs to answer union-related questions. They may even provide you with free legal representation.

CHAPTER

17

IMMIGRATION ISSUES

Many immigrants, even those with the documentation required to stay in the United States, may incorrectly believe they have fewer legal rights than American-born citizens. In fact, the Constitution of the U.S. protects everyone, regardless of citizenship or immigration status. It guarantees the same freedoms—to practice religion, to say what you want, to get due process of law, to live and work free from discrimination.

A. Federal Law

The Immigration Act and Naturalization Act of 1990, also known as the Immigration Act (8 U.S.C. §§1323a and b), marked the most comprehensive overhaul of immigration law since legal controls were passed in the early 1900s. It sets out a complex system of quotas and preferences for determining who will be allowed to permanently live and work in the United States.

For a complete explanation of immigration laws, including step-by-step guidance and forms required to enter and stay in the United States legally, see:

- *How to Get a Green Card: Legal Ways to Stay in the U.S.A.,* by Loida Nicolas Lewis and Len T. Madlansacay (Nolo), and
- *U.S. Immigration Made Easy,* by Laurence A. Canter and Martha S. Siegel (Nolo).

The Immigration Act covers all employers and all employees hired since November 6, 1986, except employees who provide occasional, irregular domestic services in private homes. Independent contractors are not covered. (See Chapter 2, Section A for details on independent contractor status.)

Under the Immigration Act, it is illegal for an employer to:

- hire or recruit a worker who the employer knows has not been granted permission by the Immigration and Naturalization Service (INS) to be employed in the United States
- hire any worker who hù£ not completed an INS Form I-9, the Employment Eligibility Verification Form, proving the worker's identity and legal right to work in the United States, or
- continue to employ an unauthorized worker—often called an illegal alien or undocumented alien.

Employers may continue to employ workers who were on their payrolls before November 6, 1986—regardless of their immigration status—as long as those workers continue in essentially the same jobs they had before the law went into effect.

Your employer is not required under the Immigration Act to fire you if you lack employment authorization from the INS but have been in the same job since before the law took effect. However, this provision does not exempt employees from complying with other requirements of U.S. immigration law.

B. Documentation Required to Work in the U.S.

Only legally authorized employees may work in the United States. When you take a new job, you are required to fill out the employee's section of INS Form I-9 by the end of your first day on the job. You then have three business days to present your new employer with documents that prove:

- that you are who you say you are, and
- that you are legally authorized to work in the United States.

If you use forged, counterfeit or altered documents to prove your identification or authorization to work, you may be fined from $250 to $2,000—and up to $5,000 for each false document if there is a second offense (8 U.S.C. §1324c).

1. When One Document Is Sufficient

The INS recently changed rules for documents it deems sufficient to prove both identity and eligibility to be employed in the United States. The following will now be accepted:
- a United States passport—either expired or unexpired
- an unexpired foreign passport with an I-551 stamp
- an alien registration receipt card or permanent resident card
- an unexpired employment authorization card
- an unexpired employment authorization document issued by the INS which contains a photograph, or
- an unexpired foreign passport with Form I-94 containing an endorsement of nonimmigrant status.

2. When Two Documents Are Required

An employee who does not have any of that evidence must produce two documents: one establishing that he or she is authorized to work in the United States and another verifying identity.

As documents proving employment authorization, the INS will accept:
- a Social Security card
- a U.S. birth or birth abroad certificate
- a Native American tribal document
- a U.S. citizen ID card
- a resident citizen ID card, or
- unexpired employment authorization documents issued by the INS.

As documents proving identity, the INS will accept:
- a current U.S. or Canadian driver's license
- a federal, state or local identification card with a photograph on it
- a school ID card with a photograph
- a voter's registration card
- a U.S. military card or draft record
- a military dependent's ID card

- a U.S. Coast Guard Merchant Mariner card, or
- a Native American tribal document.

For workers age 16 and younger, the INS considers a school report card or a hospital record such as a birth certificate acceptable as proof of identity.

3. Time Limits

New employees have three days in which to complete the I-9 Form. However, when you require some extra time to pull together the documents proving your identity and authorization—for example, if you need to obtain a certified copy of a birth certificate from another state—your employer can give you an additional 18 business days to produce the required documents. To get an extension of time, however, you must show proof that you have applied for the documents by producing, for example, a receipt for fees charged for a certified birth certificate.

Your Employer May Copy and Keep the Forms

Your new employer is required to note the type of documents you produce and any expiration dates on your Form I-9. Although employers are not required to photocopy such documents, they have the right to do so. If they do, the copies must be kept on file with your Form I-9. Employers who do not keep completed forms on file can be fined $100 for a first violation—and more if the violations persist.

C. Illegal Discrimination

The Immigration Act makes it illegal for an employer with three or more employees to:
- discriminate in hiring and firing workers—other than unauthorized immigrant workers, of course—because of their national origin
- discriminate in hiring and firing workers because of their citizenship, or
- retaliate against employees for exercising any rights under immigration laws.

To be successful in charging an employer with a violation of the Immigration Act, you must prove that the employer knowingly discriminated against you because of your citizenship or national origin, or that the employer had a pattern of committing the same offense against others.

1. Enforcing Your Rights

If a prospective or current employer violates your rights under the Immigration Act, you have 180 days from when the violation occurred to file a complaint with the Office of the Special Counsel for Unfair Immigration-Related Employment Practices. The most common violation of the anti-discrimination laws protecting immigrants occurs when employers refuse to hire someone because they suspect—incorrectly—that the person is not legally authorized to work in the United States.

2. The Complaint Process

To begin the complaint process, you can write a letter summarizing the situation to the following address:

Special Counsel
Immigration-Related Unfair Employment Practices
P.O. Box 27728
Washington, DC 20038-7728

If you need legal advice, call the special counsel office to discuss your situation with a staff attorney: 202-616-5594; there is also a hotline at 800-255-7688.

The special counsel has 120 days from the day it receives your complaint to investigate and decide whether it will pursue a charge against the employer before an administrative law judge.

If the special counsel does not bring a charge against the employer within the 120 days, or notifies you that it has not found sufficient evidence to support your charges, you have the right to plead your case directly before an administrative law judge. But you must request your hearing within 90 days of the end of the original 120-day period allowed for the special counsel to take action.

Immigration law is a world all its own. You will probably need the help of an attorney with experience in immigration law if you decide to pursue an antidiscrimination complaint after the special counsel has failed to do so. (See Chapter 18, Section D.)

The Appendix also contains contact information for a number of groups that may provide advice and legal referrals. Since the Immigration Act specifically outlaws immigration-related discrimination only in hiring and firing decisions, but not in other employment-related actions such as promotions and wage increases, you may want to file your immigration-related complaint under Title VII of the Civil Rights Act or your state's anti-discrimination laws. (For details on those laws and how to take action under them, see Chapter 8, Sections A and B.)

D. English-Only Rules

The U.S. Census Bureau predicts that by the year 2050, 24% of the population of the United States will be Hispanic—and Asians and Pacific Islanders will make up nearly 10% of it. Facing this future, American workplaces will need better direction on the legality of rules that limit or prohibit employees from speaking languages other than English on the job.

The debate about English-only rules is already boiling.

Supporters of English-only rules claim they are essential so that employers can assure that workers are obeying company rules and being polite and respectful to co-workers and clients. Opponents denounce the rules as punishing and demeaning to workers who are not fluent in English, and they claim the rules are a thinly veiled method to target and discriminate against immigrant workers. Some also point up that in parts of the country such as southern California that have a workforce rich in immigrants, it is a boon to businesses to train new hires or deal with customers in their native languages.

The Equal Employment Opportunity Commission has found many English-only workplace rules to be wrongful discrimination on the basis of national origin under the Civil Rights Act. (See Chapter 8, Section A.) It reports that it is currently processing nearly 200 cases claiming discrimination based on English-only policies—and the list is growing.

In most situations, employees must be allowed to speak among themselves in their own language while working or during breaks. In fact, EEOC guidelines, issued to clarify the suspiciousness with which courts must approach English-only rules, expound that such rules are presumed to be illegal—unless there is a clear business necessity for speaking only English.

The same skepticism applies to workplace screening tests that seem to exclude or disqualify a disproportionate number of applicants of a specific national origin.

Exceptions have been allowed only in cases where there is a clear business necessity, such as for air traffic controllers or for those who must deal with company customers who speak only English. Whenever there is some stricture requiring that employees speak only English on the job, employers must first:

- notify all employees of the rule
- inform all employees of the circumstances under which English is required, and
- explain the consequences of breaking the rule.

This is the law of the land. But in recent years, courts and a number of employers have been pushing the bounds of these guidelines—or ignoring them altogether. The tug and pull in these cases is on the definition of whether or not the English-only policy has a valid business purpose or is downright discriminatory. And while there is a theoretical difference between rules that ban languages other than English altogether and those that have bans under limited circumstances, that line is not always clear.

In recent legal challenges, courts have upheld some form of English-only rules when they were passed:

- so that supervisors could better manage employees' work, or because customers might object to hearing conversations in a language they could not understand
- to promote racial harmony after non-Spanish-speaking employees claimed that hearing Spanish spoken distracted them.

Courts in many of the cases have intimated, however, that employers must exempt employees who do not speak any English from the requirements of English-only rules—or provide training in English so that they may learn to speak it.

Now You Say It, Now You Don't

The war of the words that has developed over English-only rules prompted the Equal Employment Opportunity Commission recently to issue examples of when it might and might not be permissible to require that only English be uttered on the job. Even this guidance might appear to offer some distinctions without differences.

Possibly Permissible

- A chemical refining plant requires English for employees working directly with dangerous chemicals.
- All workers on the deck of an oil rig are required to speak English because they need to communicate quickly and respond effectively to emergencies.
- A factory requires English of workers who must share tools on an assembly line and are paid according to the number of components they assemble.

Possibly Not Permissible

- A chemical refining plant requires English for clerical workers who do not work directly with dangerous chemicals.
- A retailer requires English at all times during the workday because its customers object to employees speaking Spanish.
- An insurance company orders English only after employees argue in Spanish and are openly subordinate to their supervisor.

Source: Compliance Manual for EEOC investigators

CHAPTER

18

LAWYERS AND LEGAL RESEARCH

In workplace disputes, more than any other area of possible legal dispute, there are specialized agencies to advise and assist you with legal problems. If your problem is a matter of wage and hour law, for example, you can call the Labor Department's investigators directly for assistance. If your problem involves illegal discrimination, you can call the Equal Employment Opportunity Commission and talk over your case with a compliance officer or staff attorney. A number of specialized agencies are noted throughout the book—and a list of additional resources and contact information is contained in the Appendix.

With some types of workplace problems, however, you are on your own. If you need help getting your former employer to continue your healthcare benefits after you have lost your job, for example, no one is quite sure where to call. If you have been denied workers' compensation benefits, you may want to doublecheck your rights before deciding whether to file an appeal. In some unsettled legal areas, you may need to decide the best course of action: an alternative to court such as mediation, a small claims court claim, hiring a lawyer to help you through or doing some of your own legal research. This chapter gives you guidance in using and choosing among your options.

A. Mediation and Arbitration

At least partly because of how the legal world is portrayed on television and in movies, some people think that a courtroom is the best—and only—place to resolve any legal dispute. In fact, mediation and arbitration can be faster, less expensive, more satisfying alternatives than going to court. Workplace experts are hailing these less confrontational methods of solving workplace disputes as the hallmark of forward-thinking companies. And many employers are jumping on the bandwagon by adding clauses to their written employment agreements and employee manuals requiring that workplace disputes be resolved by arbitration or mediation.

Although mediation and arbitration are often lumped together under the general heading of alternative dispute resolution, there are significant differences between the two.

Mediation. Two or more people or groups get a third person—a mediator—to help them communicate. The mediator does not represent either side or impose a decision, but helps the disagreeing parties formulate their own resolution of their dispute.

Arbitration. Both sides agree on the issue but cannot resolve it themselves. They agree to pick an arbitrator who will come up with a solution. Essentially, the arbitrator acts as an informal judge, but at far less cost and expense than most legal proceedings require.

Mediation and arbitration are sometimes used to help work out the terms of an agreement to end a work relationship, but they are most effective when those involved have a continuing relationship and want to find a mutually acceptable way to work together.

1. When Mediation Works Best

Mediation offers benefits to many employers and employees, since the resolution to a particular problem is reached quickly and creatively. And because all involved feel they have a stake in fashioning the agreement, they are more likely to abide by the solution.

Mediation is not the best solution for all types of disputes, since success depends on both sides being willing to meet in the middle and deal directly with one another. However, many workplace experts have found that mediation is particularly effective in resolving a number of common workplace conflicts.

- *Disputes between employees.* Many disputes fester because two people are not able to talk with one another. By setting up a nonjudgmental, nonconfrontational way for them to air their differences, mediation may offer a way for them to change their behavior so they can work together more effectively.
- *Deteriorating performance.* Good employees may stop performing well for any number of reasons. Encouraging judgment-free discussion, mediation can help remove the dynamics of browbeating and defensiveness that often result when a supervisor confronts an employee about a slipping work record.
- *Sexual harassment complaints.* Many such problems involve an initial misperception about what is and what is not considered acceptable workplace behavior—and are made worse by an inability to discuss the differences openly. Mediation can open communication and help ease the hostility that may pollute a work environment.
- *Termination.* While a firing is usually unpleasant for both employers and employees, mediation can help an employee receive a fair hearing of differences when that deck is so often stacked in favor of the company. For the employer, mediation can offer hope for a peaceful parting, free from the threat of future litigation.

2. Where to Get More Information

Leading sources of professional arbitrators and mediators and of information on how to use these approaches to resolve disputes are:

American Arbitration Association
335 Madison Avenue
New York, NY 10017
212-716-5800
800-778-7879
FAX: 212-716-5905
http://www.adr.org

American Bar Association
Standing Committee on Dispute Resolution
740 15th Street, NW
Washington, DC 20005
202-662-1680
FAX: 202-662-1683
Internet: http://www.abanet.org

National Institute for Dispute Resolution
1726 M Street, NW, Suite 500
Washington, DC 20036
202-466-4764
FAX: 202-466-4769

For more information on how to choose a mediator, prepare a case and go through the mediation process, see *How to Mediate Your Dispute*, by Peter Lovenheim (Nolo).

The Times They Have A-Changed

Courts used to look with disfavor on resolving workplace disputes through arbitration and mediation rather than in front of juries. Their reasoning was somewhat murky, but usually hinted that while arbitrators did fine at handling black-and-white problems such as contract disputes, they were universally less adept at enforcing legislation, which lies at the root of many workplace disputes.

But courts' gradual willingness to enforce arbitration clauses was boosted recently by a strong directive from the U.S. Supreme Court. In the 1991 case of *Gilmer v. Interstate Johnson Lane Corp.* (500 U.S. 20 (1991)), the Court upheld the clause in a stock exchange agreement requiring disputes to be arbitrated. A host of state courts followed suit—upholding arbitration clauses in age and physical handicap discrimination, sexual harassment and wrongful termination claims.

In light of this new judicial attitude, Congress is considering an amendment to the Civil Rights Act—the federal law that broadly prohibits discrimination. The proposed legislation "encourages alternative means of dispute resolution" in resolving discrimination claims.

The changed wind is not universally welcomed. Some plaintiffs' attorneys question the fairness of taking issues such as sexual harassment and racial discrimination out of the courtroom. They say that mandatory arbitration agreements can be coercive if employees feel that they have to agree to arbitration to get or keep a job.

B. Small Claims Court

Some disputes over workplace law, such as wages owed to you by a former employer, involve only relatively small amounts of money. In many of those cases, you can file your own lawsuit in small claims court to collect the money that is owed to you.

The hallmark of small claims court is that it is inexpensive and easy to file a case there, and court procedures are simplified. You do not need to hire a lawyer to represent you, and in some states, lawyers are not even allowed. The small claims hearing is held before a judge, magistrate, commissioner or volunteer attorney, who will usually decide the case on the spot or within a few days.

The amount you can sue for is limited—usually to between $2,000 and $5,000, depending on your state. But these limits increase regularly, so check first with the local court clerk if you decide to use small claims court.

For more information on using small claims court, see *Everybody's Guide to Small Claims Court*, by Ralph Warner (Nolo).

C. Class Action Lawsuits

The federal courts sometimes allow lawsuits to be filed jointly by groups of people who have all been injured by the same or similar conduct of an employer. These are called class actions. Because they spread the legal costs among many people who are injured, class actions can make it feasible to sue an employer or former employer where the expense would be too great for an individual. Of course, all those who join in the lawsuit will also share in any judgment.

The legal requirements for pursuing a class action are complex, and almost always require a lawyer's help. But keep this option in mind if a number of other workers suffered similar wrongs or injuries to yours.

Your local office of the American Civil Liberties Union (ACLU) should be able to direct you to lawyers who specialize in civil rights class action lawsuits. (See the Appendix for contact details of the national headquarters.)

There Really Is Strength in Numbers

About 14,000 current and former female grocery store employees in northern California emerged a little richer and a lot more satisfied recently when they shared in a multi-million dollar class action settlement .

The lawsuit began in 1988 when five women sued Lucky Stores, Inc. in a San Francisco federal court, alleging the store discriminated against female employees by denying them advancement opportunities. The store at first defended that women were "not as interested in promotions as men."

But the plaintiffs in the case disagreed. Loudly. One of them, Reba Barber-Money, claimed that she was hired as a checker in 1979 and made to stay in the position—bypassed for more than ten years by male employees who were given management training and then promoted. Diane Skillsky, another plaintiff, claimed she was also denied training necessary for a promotion—training that Lucky urged upon her teenage son while he was employed at the same store.

After a ten-week trial, a California district court in 1992 found Lucky liable for sex discrimination against its female employees in job assignments, promotions and allocating work hours. Women who had worked at Lucky Stores for three months or more and who earned average salaries less than male employees were considered eligible to join in the class action.

After much legal wrangling and years of heated negotiations to determine appropriate damages, Lucky agreed in early 1994 to a $107 million settlement. It included $60 million to settle all damage claims and $20 million to pay for affirmative action programs aimed to bring more women into top management positions at Lucky.

D. Hiring a Lawyer

If your workplace problem involves a complex or ambiguous area of law—negotiating a complicated settlement, filing a claim of blacklisting or a violation of public policy—you will probably need to hire a lawyer for help. Depending on your circumstances and location, a number of places may provide referrals to lawyers with special expertise in workplace law.

- Try local legal clinics. Some may only make referrals to lawyers with appropriate knowledge and experience. And some may have lawyers on staff who will handle your case for a low cost or free of charge. Locate your community's legal aid clinics by looking in the telephone directory under Legal Aid Society or Legal Services—or check with the nearest law school.

- Organizations in your area that serve as advocates for the legal rights of minority groups, such as gay rights coalitions and local chapters of the National Association for the Advancement of Colored People (NAACP) may also make lawyer referrals.
- National organizations that deal with specific types of workplace rights, such as the National Association of Working Women or the National Coalition Against Sexual Assault may know of competent lawyers for referrals.
- Groups of specialized employees may have access to legal help offered by special interest groups. Union workers, for example, can contact the Coalition for Labor Union Women for legal guidance and referrals to experienced attorneys.

See the Appendix for listings of organizations that provide legal referrals and additional information on specialized workplace problems.

Beware of Lawyer-Run Referral Services

Bar associations and other lawyer groups often maintain and advertise lawyer referral services. Usually, there is little or no screening before a lawyer can get listed in these services. While it is always possible you will find a good lawyer through one of these services, your chances are hit and miss.

1. Comparison Shopping for a Lawyer

Take detailed notes on each lawyer mentioned during your research, and you should soon have your own small directory of lawyers with employment-related expertise from which to choose.

Be careful that people do not merely give you the names of lawyers they have heard of—or one who handled an entirely different kind of case, such as a divorce or a house closing. Any lawyer can become well-known just by buying a lot of advertising time on television or a large block in the Yellow Pages. Beware that in many states, lawyers can advertise any area of specialization they choose—even if they have never before handled a case in the area.

a. Questions to ask

Keep in mind that individual preferences for a particular lawyer are guided by intangibles such as personality or your comfort level with the person. Here are a few questions you may want to ask a person who gives you a glowing review of a particular employment law lawyer.

• Did this lawyer respond to all your telephone calls and other communications promptly?

• Did the lawyer take the time to listen to your explanation and understand your situation fully?

• Were all the bills you received properly itemized and in line with the cost projections you got at the start of your case?

• Did this lawyer personally handle your case, or was it handed off to a younger, less experienced lawyer in the same firm?

• Did the lawyer deliver what he or she promised?

It may be slightly more difficult to evaluate a lawyer referral you get from an agency or special interest group. Reputable organizations will strike from their referral lists the names of lawyers about whom they have received negative reviews. You can help groups that make referrals keep their information accurate and useful to others if you let them know of both your good and bad experiences with a particular individual.

b. Deciding on a lawyer

Once you have a referral to a lawyer—or even better, several referrals—contact each one and see whether he or she meets your needs.

Come forearmed with some inside knowledge.

Most lawyers are guided by the principle that Time Is Money. And time and money should also be your guiding concerns in deciding whether to hire a lawyer to help with your workplace claim.

Even the simplest problems can take a long time to be resolved through the legal system. And potential legal problems in the workplace do not often present themselves in straightforward issues. Unless a case is settled—most cases are—a court proceeding can take from five to eight years before a final judgment is reached.

A lawyer's help rarely comes cheap. Legal organizations estimate that workplace rights cases eat up an average of between $8,000 to $30,000 in lawyers' time and other legal costs such as court filings and witness interviews.

Lawyers often take on workplace cases for little or no money upfront. They depend on court-ordered fees and often a percentage of your recovery, or a contingency fee. (See Section 3.) This means that a lawyer will be assessing whether your case is likely to pay off, so that he or she will be compensated.

Given these hapless circumstances, you will want to be as certain as possible that any lawyer you hire will be doing the utmost to represent you fairly and efficiently—and that you are comfortable with his or her representation. Keep in mind that lawsuits can get dirty; the other side may try to probe deeply into your private life to gain the upper edge. A lawyer can represent you best if you are willing and able to speak candidly and comfortably to him or her about your case.

2. The Initial Interview

Start by calling for an appointment. Some lawyers will try to screen you over the phone by asking you to discuss the basics of your case. A little of this can be helpful to you both. You can begin to assess the lawyer's phoneside manner; he or she can begin to assess whether you truly need expert legal advice.

Many lawyers will agree not to charge you for an initial consultation to decide whether your situation requires legal action. But be prepared to pay a reasonable fee for legal advice. A charge of between $75 and $250 for a one-hour consultation is typical. Organize the facts in your case well before going to your consultation and be clear about what you are after—whether it is a financial settlement or reinstatement to your old job. An hour should be more than enough to explain your case and obtain at least a basic opinion on how it might be approached and what it is likely to cost. If you find the right lawyer and can afford the charge, it can be money well spent.

Keep in mind that very few employment law disputes actually end up in a courtroom. Most are settled or resolved in some other way. So you need not be swayed by a lawyer's likely effect on a jury alone. A good lawyer may also offer the valuable advice that you do not have a good case—or may suggest a good strategy for negotiating a settlement.

3. Paying a Lawyer

Some words to the wise about legal bills: Get Them In Writing.

After you have interviewed a few lawyers and decided which one can best handle your case, do not just turn the case over to the lawyer of your choice. Most disagreements between lawyers and clients involve fees, so be sure to get all the details involving money in writing—including the per-hour billing rate or the contingency fee arrangement, the frequency of billing and whether you will be required to deposit money in advance to cover expenses.

Most workplace cases are handled under some form of contingent fee arrangement in which a lawyer agrees to handle a case for a fixed percentage of the amount finally recovered in a lawsuit. If you win the case, the lawyer's fee comes out of the money awarded to you. If you lose, neither you nor the lawyer will get any money.

A lawyer's willingness to take your case on a contingent fee is a hopeful sign of faith in the strength of your claim. A lawyer who is not firmly convinced that your case is a winner is unlikely to take you on as a contingency fee client. Be very wary of a lawyer who wants to take your case on an hourly payment basis. That usually signals that he or she does not think your case is very strong in terms of the money you might be able to recover. It could also mean financial disaster for you, as your legal bills are likely to mount up with no useful results. At the very least, insist that the lawyer write down some specific objectives to be accomplished in your case—and put a limit on how high the fees can accumulate.

Although there is no set percentage for contingency fees in most types of cases, lawyers demand about 35% if the case is settled before a lawsuit is filed with the courts, and 40% if a case has to be tried. Keep in mind that the terms of a contingency fee agreement may be negotiable. You can try to get your lawyer to agree to a lower percentage—especially if the case is settled quickly—or to absorb some of the court costs.

Sometimes, a lawyer working for you under a contingency agreement will require that you pay all out-of-pocket expenses, such as filing fees charged by the courts and the cost of transcribing depositions—interviews of witnesses and others involved in a lawsuit who may provide additional information about the facts and circumstances. If this is so, the lawyer will want you to deposit a substantial amount of money—a thousand dollars or more—with the law firm to cover these expenses. From your standpoint, it is a much better arrangement for the lawyer to advance such costs and get repaid out of your recovery. A common sense arrangement might involve you advancing a small amount of money for some costs, with the attorney advancing the rest.

In some types of workplace lawsuits, such as Civil Rights Act violations, there is also the possibility of the court awarding you attorneys' fees as part of the final judgment. However, this award may not be large enough to cover the entire amount owed to your attorney under the legal fee contract. Therefore, the contingency fee contract should spell out what happens to a court award of attorneys' fees. One approach is to have the fees paid to the attorney in their entirety—and subtract that amount from the contingency fee to which you have agreed.

4. Managing Your Lawyer

Most complaints against lawyers have to do with their failure to communicate with their clients. Your lawyer may be the one with the legal expertise, but the rights that are being pursued are yours—and you are the most important person involved in your case. You have the right to demand that your lawyer be reasonably available to answer your questions and to keep you posted on your case.

You may need to put some energy into managing your lawyer.

Carefully check every statement. Each statement or bill should list costs that the lawyer has paid or that you are expected to pay. If you question whether a particular bill complies with your written fee agreement, call your lawyer and politely demand that a new, more detailed version be sent before you pay it. Don't feel as though you are being too pushy: The laws in many states actually require thorough detail in lawyers' statements.

Learn as much as you can about the laws and decisions involved in your case. By doing so, you will be able to monitor your lawyer's work and may even be able to make a suggestion or provide information that will move your case along faster. Certainly if the other side offers a settlement, you will be in a better position to evaluate whether or not it makes sense to accept it.

Keep your own calendar of dates and deadlines. Note when papers and appearances are due in court. If you rely on your lawyer to keep your case on schedule, you may be unpleasantly surprised to find that an important deadline has been missed. Many a good case has been thrown out simply because of a lawyer's forgetfulness. Call or write to your lawyer at least a week before any important deadline in your case to inquire about plans to meet it.

Maintain your own file on your case. By having a well-organized file of your own, you will be able to discuss your case with your lawyer intelligently and efficiently—even over the telephone. Being well-informed will help keep your lawyer's effectiveness up and your costs down. Be aware that if your lawyer is working on an hourly basis, you will probably be charged for telephone consultations. But they are likely to be less expensive than office visits.

Disagreeing on a Settlement Offer

In many cases, your employer may offer a cash amount to settle the case. The problem is that you and your lawyer may have different interests at heart.

If your lawyer is rushed or needs money, he or she may be ready to settle your case quickly for an inadequate amount. You, on the other hand, may want to hold out for an amount that you consider to be more adequate. At this critical juncture, you may wish to get a second legal opinion as to whether the amount offered is realistic given the facts of your situation.

5. Firing a Lawyer

Change lawyers if you feel it is necessary. If your relationship does not seem to be working out, or if you feel that your case is not progressing as it should, consider asking another lawyer to take over. Be clear with the first lawyer that you are taking your business elsewhere, and immediately put your decision in writing. Otherwise, you could end up receiving bills from both lawyers—both of whom will claim they handled the lion's share of your case.

Before you pay anything, be sure that the total amount of the bills does not amount to more than you agreed to pay. If you have a contingency fee arrangement, it is up to your new lawyer and former lawyer to work out how to split the fee.

Take prompt action against any lawyer whose behavior appears to be deceptive, unethical or otherwise illegal. A call to the local bar association, listed in the telephone directory under Attorneys, should provide you with guidance on what types of lawyer behavior are prohibited and how to file a complaint.

Most state attorney regulatory bodies are biased toward lawyers. Unless the lawyer's conduct is plainly dishonest or he or she has abandoned your case, you will probably not get much satisfaction. However, sometimes the threat of filing a complaint can move your lawyer into action. And if worst comes to worst, filing a formal complaint will create a document that you will need if you later file a lawsuit against a lawyer for malpractice.

E. Legal Research

This book gives you a general understanding of the legal principles involved in common workplace disputes. However, in negotiating with your employer, presenting your workplace problem to government investigators, preparing for mediation or arbitration, or working with a lawyer you hire, you may gain additional power and speed the resolution of your dispute by having detailed and specific legal knowledge.

In these situations, you may want to do some legal research of your own. If you have been laid off or fired, you likely have some time on your hands—and may even find it surprisingly therapeutic to get to work doing your own research.

This book explains the more traditional form of legal research—using books and law libraries (see Section E1)—and the newer-fangled method of research through online services (see Section E2).

Don't Start From Scratch

For more general information about specific workplace issues, check the Appendix. Many legal and special interest groups publish helpful bibliographies and pamphlets on the legal aspects of workplace issues such as sexual harassment and age discrimination. Before you do extensive research on your own, take a look at what others have done.

1. Library Research

The reference sections in most larger public libraries contain a set of local and state laws, as well as a set of the federal statutes. The reference librarian should be able to help you look up any laws that might affect your situation. However, if you want to look up a court case or a ruling by a government agency such as the Equal Employment Opportunity Commission, you will probably have to visit a law library.

In many states, county law libraries are free and open to the public. You can also try the library of the nearest law school, particularly if it's affiliated with a public university funded by tax dollars. Law school libraries offer one big advantage: They are usually open from early in the morning until late at night— even on weekends and some holidays. Whatever library you choose, you will find that most librarians are not only well-versed in legal research techniques, but also are open to helping you through the mazes of legal citations.

a. Where to begin

There are several types of research materials concentrating on employment law that you may find useful: secondary sources such as books and law review articles, and primary sources such as statutes and cases. These resources serve different purposes.

Secondary sources—general books and scholarly articles—are usually used to get an overview of a particular topic. If you find a good article or chapter on a topic you're interested in, it will give both an explanation of the law and citations to other materials—especially cases—that may prove helpful.

Primary sources—statutes (state and federal laws) and cases (published decisions of state and federal courts)—tell you the current status of the law. Very often, your goals in doing legal research are first to find the statutes that apply to you, and then to find the court cases that interpret the statutes in situations similar to yours. There may be cases with similar facts—for example, a supervisor who persistently asked a female employee to go out with him after she repeatedly said no. Or there may be a court case that raises a similar issue or legal question—for example, whether an employer is legally responsible for paying for an independent contractor's commuting costs. These court decisions may give you some indication of how a government agency or court is likely to decide your case.

The best place to begin your research depends on your situation. If you want some additional general information about a particular workplace issue, or an update on the law since this book was published, you will probably find a recent book or article more than adequate. However, if you want very specific legal information—for example, whether wrongful discharge is a valid legal theory in your state—you will probably need to look at both your state fair employment practice law and any judicial decisions dealing with the issue. The sections that follow describe how to find and use several types of resources to learn about the law that applies to your situation.

For more on the specifics of legal research, see *Legal Research: How to Find and Understand the Law*, by Steve Elias and Susan Levinkind (Nolo).

b. Statutes

When people refer to The Law, they are usually talking about statutes—the written laws created by state and federal legislatures.

Federal statutes are contained in the United States Code. For example, if you are looking for the Civil Rights Act, 42 U.S.C. 2000, locate Title 42 of the United States Code and turn to Section 2000.

Finding state statutes is a bit trickier, because states use slightly different systems to number and organize their statutes. Most states use one of the following methods:

- *By topic*. California uses this type of organization. To find Cal. Gov't. Code §12900, locate the volumes that contain the state's government code and turn to Section 12900.

- *By number.* Florida, for example, lists statutes numerically, without flagging the topics the laws cover. To find Fla. Stat. §760.01, turn to Section 760.01.
- *By title.* Vermont, for example, divides its statutes into titles, similar to the federal citation system. To find 21 Vt. Stat. §495, locate Title 21 of the Vermont Statutes—and turn to Section 495.

Inside the back cover of the volume, you will find an unbound supplement called a pocket part. This material updates the information in the main volume, including any amendments or changes to the law that have happened since the main volume was published. It is organized just like the main volume, using the same numerical system. Be sure to check the pocket part every time you use a statute. If you forget this crucial step, you may be relying on law that is no longer valid.

The Two Research Tracks: Federal and State

Two separate sets of laws control the workplace—federal law and state law. Each has separate statutes, regulations and court cases, so you must decide which law you are relying on before you start to research.

The U.S. Civil Rights Act, for example, is a federal law, and the court decisions which interpret it—including those involving the EEOC—are federal cases. However, not all federal decisions carry equal weight. The cases which will be most persuasive in federal court are those from the highest court in that jurisdiction: the United States Supreme Court. On the second level in the hierarchy are the federal courts of appeal. You should look first for cases in the same judicial circuit or geographical region as yours, since these will be more authoritative. And finally, on the lowest level are the federal district courts—again, look first for cases in your geographical area.

If you are researching your state's laws, you will be looking at state court cases. Most state court systems are similar to the federal system, in that there are three hierarchical levels of courts. The most authoritative cases will be those from your state's highest court—usually called the supreme court—followed by decisions issued by your state appellate court, followed by decisions issued by your state trial court.

---

c. Regulations

In some situations, you may also want to consult the regulations that pertain to a statute. Regulations are the rules created by administrative agencies for carrying out legislation. If, for example, a statute requires an agency to investigate complaints about workplace safety hazards, there will probably be regulations that give more detail about what form the investigation will take, who will conduct it and how it will be done.

Federal regulations can be found in the Code of Federal Regulations—usually abbreviated as CFR.

Don't Forget Local Laws

Many major cities and some counties also have their own laws on illegal workplace practices, such as discriminating against gay and lesbian workers, and regulations detailing how these laws should be carried out. Do not neglect these in your research. Sometimes a local law will contain the best protections against workplace problems or provide the best remedies. Ask your law librarian how to find and use your city or county code.

d. Cases

Sometimes, you will find all the information you need in the statutes and regulations. However, laws can be deceptively straightforward, impossibly complex—or somewhere in between. To be sure you get the point, it is wise to also look at court cases that involve the statute and see how the courts apply and interpret it. Courts have been known to take a law with an apparently obvious meaning and turn it on its head.

And sometimes, there will be no statute that applies to your situation. For example, when you are researching whether a legal theory such as the intentional infliction of emotional distress applies to your situation, you will absolutely need to look at some court decisions, since these issues are decided on a case-by-case basis.

Many court cases are cited throughout this book. Be sure to look at them as possible leads. If the discussion here makes a case seem similar in some way to your situation, you might want to look up the case and read the court's ruling. For information on how to interpret case citations, see Subsection e, below.

Finding a case interpreting a statute. If you want to track down how a certain statute has been referred to by the courts in a case, your research task will be fairly simple: All you have to do is consult an annotated code. An annotated code is a version of the state or federal statutes that contains summaries of cases that have interpreted various provisions of a statute. There are two sets of federal annotated codes: the United States Code Service and the United States

Code Annotated. Most states also have annotated codes. Ask the law librarian where you can find them.

To use an annotated code, look for the numbered section of the statute that is relevant to your situation. If there have been any court cases interpreting that statute, they will be listed after the specific section of the statute, along with a sentence or two describing the case. If the summary of the case leaves you wanting to know more about it, you can track down the case and read it by following the citation given there.

Finding a case using secondary sources. In some situations, you will want to find court decisions on a particular topic without referring to a statute. For example, if you want to find out whether some uncomfortable situation at work might form the basis of a tort action in your state, you should probably not begin your research with a statute. Common law tort actions were developed almost exclusively by case decisions. Sometimes these torts are also written into code—such as a state criminal statute defining and setting out the punishment for assault—but more likely, you will have to hunt down a few cases.

One good way to find relevant cases is through secondary sources (discussed in Section E1). Quite often, a law review article or book—including this one—will discuss key cases and give citations for them. If you find a source that analyzes an issue that is important in your case, you will likely get some good leads there.

Digests. Another good resource for finding cases is the digest system. These digests, published by the West Publishing Company, provide brief summaries of cases organized by topic. There are many sets of digests, divided by geographic region.

To use the digest system to find cases, first choose the relevant volumes—regional, state or federal. Next, look in the descriptive word index. You will find a number of categories listed under each heading. Look in the digest under topics that are relevant to your search—for example, Wrongful Discharge, Employer Negligence, Blacklisting. Under each topic, there will be short summaries of cases, arranged chronologically. If a case interests you, you can find the complete decision in the state or regional reporter by using the case citation.

The digests have a handy feature: the key number system. All of the digests use the same headings to categorize cases. Topics are divided into subtopics; each subtopic is given a number. If you find a topic in the state digest that seems relevant, and want to find federal cases on the same point, look in the federal practice digest under the same key number.

Employment law reporters. Perhaps the best way to find cases is through one of two specialized legal publications that gather both state and federal cases on employment law issues:

- *Fair Employment Practices Cases* (Fair Empl. Prac. Cas.), published by the Bureau of National Affairs, and
- *Employment Practices Decisions* (Empl. Prac. Dec.), published by Commerce Clearing House.

To use these publications, look in the index volumes and glance through for specific topics that interest you. Then use the case citations listed to look for relevant court decisions in the reporter volumes.

Finding similar cases. Once you find a case that seems relevant to your situation, you can determine if there are more by using a publication called *Shepard's Citations.* Shepard's collects and lists every reference to a particular case. In other words, you can look up any case—state or federal—in the Shepard's volumes, and get a list of every case decided after it that has mentioned your case. This is very valuable for finding cases on the same subject, as well as for determining whether the original case you found has been influential or discredited.

e. Treatises

There are several books—sometimes called treatises—that cover workplace issues. The drawbacks of most treatises is that nearly all of them are written by and for lawyers—with little effort made to translate legalese into English. Also, these books oftentimes devote many pages to lawyerly concerns, such as how to plead and prove picayune points of law. Still, these volumes will often provide you with helpful background information—and will also often lead you to cases that pertain to your situation. When using a legal treatise, be sure to check the back inside cover; most publishers update the books periodically by issuing pocket parts, bound pamphlets noting changes and additions to the text.

How to Read a Case Citation

There are several places where a case may be reported. If it is a case decided by the U.S. Supreme Court, you can find it in either the United States Reports (U.S.) or the Supreme Court Reporter (S.Ct.). If it is a federal case decided by a court other than the U.S. Supreme Court, it will be in either the Federal Reporter, Second Series (F.2d) or the Federal Supplement (F. Supp.).

Most states publish their own official state reports. All published state court decisions are also included in the West Reporter System. West has divided the country into seven regions—and publishes all the decisions of the supreme and appellate state courts in the region together. These reporters are:

A. and A.2d. Atlantic Reporter (First and Second Series), which includes decisions from Connecticut, Delaware, the District of Columbia, Maine, Maryland, New Hampshire, New Jersey, Pennsylvania, Rhode Island and Vermont.

N.E. and N.E.2d. Northeastern Reporter (First and Second Series), which includes decisions from New York*, Illinois, Indiana, Massachusetts and Ohio.

N.W. and N.W.2d. Northwestern Reporter (First and Second Series), which includes decisions from Iowa, Michigan, Minnesota, Nebraska, North Dakota, South Dakota and Wisconsin.

P. and P.2d. Pacific Reporter (First and Second Series), which includes decisions from Alaska, Arizona, California*, Colorado, Hawaii, Idaho, Kansas, Montana, Nevada, New Mexico, Oklahoma, Oregon, Utah, Washington and Wyoming.

S.E. and S.E.2d. Southeastern Reporter (First and Second Series), which includes decisions from Georgia, North Carolina, South Carolina, Virginia and West Virginia.

So. and So.2d. Southern Reporter (First and Second Series), which includes decisions from Alabama, Florida, Louisiana and Mississippi.

S.W. and S.W.2d. Southwestern Reporter (First and Second Series), which includes decisions from Arkansas, Kentucky, Missouri, Tennessee and Texas.

A case citation will give you the names of the people or companies on each side of a case, the volume of the reporter in which the case can be found, the page number on which it begins and the year in which the case was decided. For example:

Smith v. Jones Internat'l, 123 N.Y.S.2d 456 (1994)

Smith and Jones are the names of the parties having the legal dispute. The case is reported in volume 123 of the New York Supplement, Second Series, beginning on page 456; the court issued the decision in 1994.

*All California appellate decisions are published in a separate volume, the California Reporter (Cal. Rptr.), and all decisions from New York appellate courts are published in a separate volume, New York Supplement (N.Y.S.).

f. Law Review Articles

Law reviews are periodicals containing articles written by lawyers, law professors and law students—usually covering a unique or evolving legal topic. Since workplace law is of great current interest, you will find lots of articles about it. The inside joke about law review articles is that they are made up mostly of footnotes. While annoying to many readers, these footnotes—which contain references or citations to other relevant cases, statutes and articles—can be goldmines for researchers. Look especially for articles that are published in law reviews from schools in your state, since these will be most likely to discuss your state's law and court decisions.

There are two tools in every law library that can help you find law review articles on topics that interest you: the *Current Law Index* and the *Index to Legal Periodicals*. These volumes are published annually, except for the most recent listings, which are published every month. Both list articles by subject, by author and by the cases and statutes referred to in the article. If you don't have a case name or a specific statute in mind to guide you, turn to the index and peruse the listings of articles there.

How to Read Law Review Citations

Both the *Current Law Index* and the *Index to Legal Periodicals* will give you the author, title and citations of law review articles. The citations will give the title of the publication and the volume and page numbers of the articles you want to look at. For example, if you look under Sexual Harassment—Analysis, you will see a listing for Susan Estrich's article "Sex at Work." The citation reads:

43 Stan. L. Rev. 813 (1991)

This article can be found in volume 43 of the *Stanford Law Review*, beginning on page 813; 1991 is the year of publication. If you have trouble deciphering the law review names, check the listing of abbreviations in the index—or ask a law librarian for help.

---

2. Online Resources

Many readers have discovered the wildly varied and rich resource known as the Internet, and it is only a matter of time before even the most stubborn technophobe will be drawn into its web. There are many sites—maintained by the government, law schools or libraries, law firms and individuals—that can be useful to employees. These sites are not a substitute for a law library; nothing on the Internet is as complete and systematic as a library. But they may have just what you are looking for—and they certainly are convenient.

- **Nolo's Legal Encyclopedia**
  http://www.nolo.com
  Sorry to toot our own horn too loudly, but this one is tootable. Loads of free information for consumers interested in finding out more about rights in the workplace. Topics covered include: discrimination, sexual harassment, fair pay and time off, health and safety, independent contractors, losing or leaving a job and privacy.
- **The Legal Information Institute at Cornell Law School**
  http://fatty.law.cornell.edu/topics/employment_discrimination.html
  Provides information about discrimination in the workplace, including relevant codes and regulations.
- **Employment Discrimination Laws**
  http://www.coloradolawyer.com/discrim.html
  Summarizes the major federal laws that prohibit employment discrimination. A good place to begin your search if you're looking for an overview.
- **AHI's Employment Law Resource Center**
  http://www.ahipubs.com/FAQ/index.html
  Aimed at managers and human resource personnel, this site offers common sense packaged as frequently asked questions about many aspects of employment, from benefits to safety and health concerns. Of course, the information is helpful to Just Plain Workers, too.
- **Work Doctor—Employee Advocates**
  http://www.workdoctor.com
  Offers candid advice for dealing with bothersome workplace behavior that does not quite rise to the level of a legal infraction: bullying, power plays, other displays of insecurity. Includes an e-mail advice column and timely tips for bullybusting.
- **LaborNet**
  http://www.labornet.org
  LaborNet is a group of labor unions, activists and organizations using computer networks to share information about workers' rights. There is lots of information here about pending and recent legislation, labor movements and disputes and international labor issues. Includes links to other employment sites.

APPENDIX RESOURCES

The organizations listed here can give you additional information or assistance on specific workplace issues. Some groups offer a wide variety of services—including publications and written materials, telephone counseling and hotlines for advice, support groups or in-person counseling for workplace problems, attorney referrals and workplace training resources, including onsite training programs and written and video training materials.

Some organizations offer only limited services or restrict services to their members or to a limited geographic area. Be sure to ask whether you are eligible to use their services. Also, ask for an additional, more appropriate referral if the group you contact is not able to help.

AIDS-HIV

See also organizations listed under Gay and Lesbian.

ACLU AIDS Project
See American Civil Liberties Union under Civil Rights.

AIDS Action Council
1875 Connecticut Avenue, NW; Suite 700
Washington, DC 20009
202-986-1300
FAX: 202-986-1345
e-mail: hn3384@handsnet.org
http://www.aidsaction.org
National advocacy organization working for more effective AIDS policy, education and funding. No direct service for individuals. Promotes and monitors legislation on AIDS research and education and on related public policy issues.

American Foundation for AIDS Research (AmFAR)
1828 L Street, NW; Suite 802
Washington, DC 20036
202-331-8600
800-392-6327
FAX: 202-331-8606
http://www.amfar.org

Nonprofit public foundation funds programs for AIDS research, education for AIDS prevention and public policy development.

American Red Cross
17th and D Streets, NW
Washington, DC 20006
202-737-8300
FAX: 202-783-3432
http://www.redcross.org
Humanitarian relief and health education organization chartered by Congress. Conducts public education campaign on AIDS.

Centers for Disease Control
National Prevention Information Network
National Center for HIV, STD and TB Prevention
P.O. Box 6003
Rockville, MD 20849-6003
800-458-5231
FAX: 888-282-7861
e-mail: Info@cdcnpin.com
http://www.cdcnpin.org
The CDC National Prevention Information Network (NPIN) provides information about HIV/AIDS, sexually transmitted diseases (STDs), and tuberculosis (TB) to people and organizations working in prevention, healthcare, research, and support services. All of NPIN's services are designed to facilitate the sharing of information about education, prevention, published materials and research findings and news about HIV/AIDS-, STD-, and TB-related trends.

National Minority AIDS Council
1931 13th Street, NW
Washington, DC 20009
202-483-6622
FAX: 202-483-1135
http://www.nmac.org
Works to encourage leadership within minority communities responding to the HIV and AIDS epidemic. Monitors legislation and provides AIDS programs with technical assistance. Distributes information on AIDS—especially information concerning the impact of the disease on minorities.

Civil Rights

American Civil Liberties Union (ACLU)
125 Broadway
New York, NY 10036
212-549-2500

Advocates individual rights through litigation and public education on a broad range of issues affecting individual freedom. Legal advice and counseling, as well as attorney referrals, provided by state offices. Check your phone book for the nearest location. The ACLU's National Task Force on Civil Liberties in the Workplace (in New York office, address above) answers questions on drug testing, discrimination, privacy, unjust dismissal and whistleblowing and has information on special projects on AIDS and on lesbian and gay rights.

Asian-American Legal Defense and Education Fund
99 Hudson Street, 12th Floor
New York, NY 10013
212-966-5932
http://www.janet.org/~ebihara/aavn/aav_org.html

Free legal advice, counseling and attorney referrals for Asians and Asian-Americans. Focus on issues of immigration, family, employment and anti-Asian violence.

Disabled Workers

ABLEDATA
8455 Colesville Road, Suite 200
Silver Spring, MD 20910
800-346-2742 or 800-227-0216
FAX: 301-608-8958
http://www.abletodo.com

A consumer referral service that maintains a database of more than 17,000 adaptive devices from 2,000 companies.

Job Accommodation Network (JAN)
918 Chestnut Ridge Road; Suite 1
West Virginia University
P. O. Box 6080

Morgantown, WV 26506-6080
800-232-9675 or 800-526-7234
Computer bulletin board: 800-342-5526
http://janweb.icdi.wvu.edu

Provides free consulting services to people with disabilities seeking accommodation information under the Americans With Disabilities Act (ADA) and to employers seeking to accommodate employees with disabilities. Maintains a database of companies nationwide that have accommodated workers and organizations, support groups, government agencies and placement agencies that assist the disabled.

National Organization on Disability
910 16th Street, NW; #600
Washington, DC 20006-2988
202-293-5960
800-248-2253
TDD: 202-293-5968
FAX: 202-293-7999
http://www.nod.org

Administers the Community Partnership program, a network that works to address educational, employment, social and transportation needs of people with disabilities. Provides members with information and technical assistance, makes referrals, monitors legislation.

Office on the Americans With Disabilities Act
Civil Rights Division
U.S. Department of Justice
P.O. Box 66118
Washington, DC 20035-6118
202-514-0301
TDD: 202-514-0383
http://www.usdoj.gov/crt/ada/adahom1.htm

Government agency specialists answer your questions about the ADA—except on federal government holidays. Publishes a number of free booklets, including information on how to file a complaint under the ADA. Publications are also available in alternate formats for the disabled—Braille, computer disk, audiocassette and large print.

Pacific Disability and Business Technical Assistance Center
2168 Shattuck Avenue, Suite 301
Berkeley, CA 94704
510-848-2980
Hotline: 800-949-4232
TDD: 510-848-1840
FAX: 510-848-1981
http://www.pacdbtac.org

Provides information, materials and assistance to those covered by the ADA.

President's Task Force on Employment of Adults with Disabilities
U.S. Department of Labor
200 Constitution Avenue, NW, Suite S-2220
Washington, DC 20210
202-693-4939
TTY: 202-693-4920
FAX: 202-693-4929
http://www.disability.gov

Independent federal agency facilitates employment of people with disabilities and enforces Americans With Disabilities Act (ADA). Provides education, information, training and technical assistance.

Social Security Administration
Disability Office
6401 Security Boulevard, #560
Baltimore, MD 21235
410-965-3424
FAX: 410-965-6503
http://www.ssa.gov

Administers and regulates the disability insurance program and disability provisions of the Supplemental Security Insurance (SSI) program.

Discrimination

Equal Employment Opportunity Commission
1801 L Street, NW
Washington, DC 20507
800-669-4000 to file charge or reach field office
800-669-3362 information and publication center
TDD: 800-800-3302

FAX: 202-663-4110
In Washington, D.C., metropolitan area, call:
202-663-4900
TDD: 202-663-4141
http://www.eeoc.gov

Federal agency working to ensure equality of opportunity by enforcing federal laws prohibiting employment discrimination and sexual harassment through investigation, conciliation, litigation, coordination, education and technical assistance.

National Committee on Pay Equity
1126 Sixteenth Street, NW, #411
Washington, DC 20036
202-331-7343
FAX: 202-331-7406
e-mail: fairpay@aol.com
http://www.feminist.com/fairpay.htm

Provides information and technical assistance to those interested in eliminating wage discrimination based on gender and race. Members receive updates and mailings on pay equity activity; NCPE's newsletter, NEWSNOTES; discounts on NCPE publications; and access to pay equity networks.

Family Issues

See also organizations listed under Women's Issues.
Families and Work Institute
330 Seventh Avenue
New York, NY 10001
212-465-2044
FAX: 212-465-8637
http://www.familiesandworkinst.org

Operates a national clearinghouse of information on work and family life; advises business, government, and community organizations, and conducts management training on work and family issues.

Formerly Employed Mothers at the Leading Edge
(FEMALE)
P.O. Box 31
Elmhurst, IL 60126
630-941-3553
http://www.femalehome.org
Nationwide, membership-based support and
advocacy group for women dealing with transition
between paid employment and staying at home.
Publishes monthly newsletter.

Initiatives: Center for Workforce Diversity
300 Welsh Road, Building 4
Horsham, PA 19044
215-659-5911
Corporate consulting firm providing an array of
services on work/family issues—including employee
workshops on balancing work and family, management training programs and resource and referral
services.

New Ways to Work
785 Market Street, Suite 950
San Francisco, CA 94103
415-995-9860
Educational and advocacy organization devoted to
promoting flexible work arrangements. Serves as a
clearinghouse for information, has an extensive
publications list and offers seminars and training to
companies.

Work/Family Directions
928 Commonwealth Avenue West
Boston, MA 02215-1212
617-264-3200
800-447-0543
FAX: 617-582-0935
http://www.wfd.com
Consulting company offering services to companies
including workplace surveys and help with
planning and implementing work and family
programs.

Workplace Options
109 South Bloodworth Street
Raleigh, NC 27601
800-874-9383
919-834-6505
http://www.workplaceoptions.com
Corporate consulting firm specializing in helping
employers design and deliver work and family
benefits. Offers training workshops, needs assessment and resource and referral services.

Gay and Lesbian

ACLU National Lesbian and Gay Rights Project
See American Civil Liberties Union under Civil
Rights.

Gay and Lesbian Advocates and Defenders (GLAD)
294 Washington Street, Suite 740
Boston, MA 02108
617-426-1350
800-455-4523
http://www.glad.org
Publishes information and provides general advice
on sexual orientation and HIV status. Provides
lawyer referrals.

Lambda Legal Defense and Education Fund
120 Wall Street, Suite 1500
New York, NY 10012
212-809-8585
FAX: 212-809-0055
http://www.lambdalegal.org
Provides publications, advice and legal information
on gay and lesbian job discrimination and HIV
discrimination issues. Phone-in service for lawyer
referrals.

National Center for Lesbian Rights
870 Market Street, Suite 570
San Francisco, CA 94102
415-392-6257

Offers publications, advice, counseling and lawyer referrals.

National Gay and Lesbian Task Force Policy Institute
2320 17th Street, NW
Washington, DC 20009-2702
202-332-6483
TTY: 202-332-6219
FAX: 202-332-0207
http://www.ngltf.org

Political advocacy group. Publishes organizing manual for implementing domestic partnership benefit plans and nondiscrimination policies. Provides referrals for counseling and lawyers.

Working It Out
The Newsletter for Gay and Lesbian Employment Issues
Ed Mickens
P.O. Box 2079
New York, NY 10108
212-769-2384
FAX: 908-280-3016

Quarterly publication for corporate human resource departments, management and others concerned with gay and lesbian issues in the workplace.

Health Insurance

International Foundation of Employee Benefit Plans
18700 West Bluemound Road
P.O. Box 69
Brookfield, WI 53008-0069
262-786-6710
FAX: 262-786-8670
http://ifebp.org

Publishes report *COBRA Continuation Coverage* on individual's rights to continue health insurance coverage.

Immigration

Immigration and Naturalization Service (INS)
425 I Street, NW
Washington, DC 20536
202-514-4316
FAX: 202-514-4623
http://www.usdoj.gov/ins

Federal agency responsible for overseeing and enforcing visa and lawful permanent resident applications and procedures.

Center for Immigrants Rights
48 Saint Marks Place
New York, NY 10003
212-505-6890

Provides advocacy and organizing advice for immigrant workers. Also gives advice and legal counseling on discrimination and compensation issues.

Labor Departments

Federal Labor Department

U.S. Department of Labor
200 Constitution Avenue, NW
Washington, DC 20210
202-219-7316
FAX: 202-219-8822
Internet: http://www.dol.gov

State Labor Departments

Alabama   Labor Department
649 Monroe Street
Post Office Box 303500
Montgomery, AL 36131
334-242-8990
FAX: 334-242-8843
Internet: http://www.dir.state.al.us

Alaska   Labor Department
1111 West Eighth Street, Room 304
Post Office Box 21149
Juneau, AK 99801-1145
907-465-2700
Internet: http://www.state.ak.us/lss/lss.htm

Arizona   Industrial Commission
800 West Washington Street, Suite 102
Phoenix, AZ 85007-2922
602-542-4411
http://www.ica.state.az.us/ADOSH/oshatop.htm

Arkansas   Labor Department
10421 West Markham Street
Little Rock, AR 72205
501-682-4500
Internet: http://www.state.ar.us/labor

California   Industrial Relations Department
455 Golden Gate Avenue, 10th Floor
San Francisco, CA 94102
415-703-5050
Internet: http://www.dir.ca.gov

Colorado   Department of Labor and Employment
1515 Araphoe Street
Denver, CO 80202
303-572-2241
Internet: http://cdle.state.co.us/

Connecticut   Labor Department
200 Folly Brook Boulevard
Wethersfield, CT 06109
860-566-5123
Internet: http://www.ctdol.state.ct.us

Delaware   Labor Department
4425 North Market Street
Wilmington, DE 19802
302-761-8000
Internet: http://www.delawareworks.com

District of Columbia   Labor Relations Office
441 4th Street, NW
Washington, DC 20001
202-724-8052
Internet: http://www.dccouncil.washington.dc.us

Florida   Labor and Employment Security Department
303 Hartman Building
2012 Capitol Circle, SE
Tallahassee, FL 32399-2189
904-488-4398
Internet: http://www.fdles.state.fl.us/

Georgia   Labor Department
148 International Boulevard, NE, Suite 600
Atlanta, GA 30303-1751
404-656-3017
Internet: http://www.dol.state.ga.us

Hawaii   Labor & Industrial Relations
Department
830 Punchbowl Street, Room 321
Honolulu, HI 96813
808-586-8844
Internet: http://www.state.hi.us/dlir/
hiosh

Idaho   Labor & Industrial Services
Department
317 Main Street
Boise, ID 83735
208-334-6100
Internet: http://www.doe.state.id.us

Illinois   Labor Department
160 North LaSalle Street, 13th Floor
Chicago, IL 60601
312-793-2800
FAX: 312-793-2800
Internet: http://www.state.il.us/
agency/idol

Indiana   Labor Department
402 West Washington, Room W-195
Indianapolis, IN 46204-2751
317-232-2378
Internet: http://www.state.in.us/
labor/iosha/iosha.html

Iowa   Workforce Development
1000 East Grand Avenue
Des Moines, IA 50319-0209
515-281-3447
Internet: http://www.state.ia.us/
government/wd/index.htm

Kansas   Labor Management Relations
Employment Standards Division
401 SW Topeka Boulevard
Topeka, KS 66606
913-296-5000
Internet: http://www.state.ks.us

Kentucky   Labor Cabinet
U.S. Highway 127, South Building
Frankfort, KY 40601
502-564-3070
http://www.state.ky.us/agencies/
labor/labrhome.htm

Louisiana   Labor Department
Post Office Box 94094
Baton Rouge, LA 70804
504-342-3011
Internet: http://www.ldol.state.la.us

Maine   Labor Department
45 State House Station
Augusta, ME 04333-0045
207-624-6400
Internet: http://janus.state.me.us/
labor/

Maryland   Labor, Licensing and Regulation
Department
1100 North Eutaw Street, Rm. 613
Baltimore, MD 21201-2206
410-767-2999
Internet: http://
www.dllr.state.md.us

Massachusetts   Division of Employment & Training
19 Staniford Street
Boston, MA 02114
617-727-6560
Internet: http://www.detma.org

Michigan   Michigan Consumer & Industry
Services
525 W. Ottawa
Lansing, MI 48909
517-373-1820
Internet: http://www.cis.state.mi.us

Minnesota   Labor & Industry Department
443 Lafayette Road North
St. Paul, MN 55155-4307
651-296-2342
Internet: http://
www.doli.state.mn.us

Mississippi	Employment Security Commission 1520 West Capitol Post Office Box 1699 Jackson, MS 39215 601-354-8711 Internet: http:// www.mesc.state.ms.us
Missouri	Labor & Industrial Relations Department 3315 West Truman Boulevard Jefferson City, MO 65102 314-751-3403 Internet: http:// www.dolir.state.mo.us
Montana	Labor & Industry Department 1327 Lockey Avenue Post Office Box 1728 Helena, MT 59624 406-444-9091 Internet: http://dli.state.mt.us
Nebraska	Labor Department Post Office Box 94600 Lincoln, NE 68509 402-471-9000 Internet: http://www.dol.state.ne.us
Nevada	Labor Commission 400 West King Street, Suite 400 Carson City, NV 89703 775-687-3032 Internet: http://www.state.nv.us/ b&i/ir/
New Hampshire	Labor Department 95 Pleasant Street Concord, NH 03301 603-271-3176 Internet: http://www.state.nh.us/dol

New Jersey	Labor Department Post Office Box 110 John Fitch Plaza Trenton, NJ 08625 609-292-2323 FAX: 609-633-9271 Internet: http://www.state.nj.us/labor
New Mexico	Department of Labor Post Office Box 1928 1596 Pacheco Street Albuquerque, NM 87502 505-827-6875 Internet: http://www3.state.nm.us/ dol/dol_home.html
New York	Labor Department State Campus, Building 12 Albany, NY 12240 518-457-2741 FAX: 518-457-6908 Internet: http:// www.labor.state.ny.us
North Carolina	Labor Department 4 West Edenton Street Raleigh, NC 27601-1092 919-807-7166 Internet: http://www.dol.state.nc.us/ DOL
North Dakota	Labor Department 600 East Boulevard, Dept. 406 Bismarck, ND 58505 701-328-2660 Internet: http://www.state.nd.us/ labor
Ohio	Industrial Commission 125 East Court Street, Suite 600 Cincinnati, OH 45202-1211 513-357-9750 Internet: http://www.ic.state.oh.us
Oklahoma	Labor Department 4001 N. Lincoln Boulevard Oklahoma City, OK 73105 405-528-1500 Internet: http:// Iwww.oklaosf.state.ok.us/~okdol

Oregon	Labor & Industries Bureau	**Texas**	Texas Workforce Commission
	800 NE Oregon, Suite 32		101 E. 15th Street
	Portland, OR 97232		Austin, TX 78778
	503-731-4200		512-463-2222
	Internet: http://www.boli.state.or.us		Internet: http://www.twc.state.tx.us
Pennsylvania	Labor & Industry Department	**Utah**	Labor Commission
	7th and Forster Street		160 East 300 South, 3rd Floor
	Harrisburg, PA 17120		Post Office Box 146650
	717-787-5279		Salt Lake City, UT 84114-6650
	Internet: http://www.li.state.pa.us		801-530-6901
Rhode Island	Labor and Training		Internet: http://www.labor.state.ut.us
	101 Friendship Street		
	Providence, RI 02903-3740	**Vermont**	Labor & Industry Department
	401-222-3600		National Life Building, Drawer 20
	Internet: http://www.det.state.ri.us/		Montpelier, VT 05620-3401
South Carolina	Labor Department		802-828-5098
	Post Office Box 11329		Internet: http://www.state.vt.us/labind
	110 Centerview Drive		
	Columbia, SC 29210	**Virginia**	Labor & Industry Department
	803-896-4300		13 South 13th Street
	FAX: 803-896-4393		Richmond, VA 23219
	Internet: http://www.llr.state.sc.us/		804-786-2377
			Internet: http://www.dli.state.va.us
South Dakota	Labor Department	**Washington**	Labor & Industries Department
	700 Governors Drive		Post Office Box 4401
	Pierre, SD 57501		Olympia, WA 98504-4001
	605-773-3681		360-902-4200
	Internet: http://www.state.sd.us/dol		Internet: http://www.lni.wa.gov
Tennessee	Labor Department	**West Virginia**	Labor Division
	710 James Robertson Parkway, 2nd Floor		State Capitol Complex, Room 319
	Nashville, TN 37243-0659		Charleston, WV 25305
	615-741-2582		304-558-7890
	Internet: http://www.state.tn.us/labor		Internet: http://www.state.wv.us/labor

Wisconsin Workforce Development
Department
201 E. Washington Avenue GEF-1
Madison, WI 53702
608-266-3131
Internet: http://
www.dwd.state.wi.us

Wyoming Labor Standards Division
Herschler Building, 2nd Floor East
122 West 25th Street
Cheyenne, WY 82002
307-777-7672
Internet: http://wydoe.state.wy.us

Legal Referrals

National Employment Lawyers Association
600 Harrison Street
San Francisco, CA 94133
415-227-4655
http://www.nela.org

National directory of employment law attorneys, including brief descriptions of their practices. Send a stamped, self-addressed envelope for more information.

National Resource Center for Consumers of Legal Services
6596 Main Street
P.O. Box 340
Gloucester, VA 23061
804-693-9330
FAX: 804-693-7363
http://www.nrccls.org/

Nationwide legal referrals to attorneys experienced in employment law. Publishes materials on how to choose a lawyer and articles about job rights. Send a stamped, self-addressed envelope for more information.

Mediation and Arbitration

American Arbitration Association
365 Madison Avenue
New York, NY 10017
212-716-5800
800-778-7879
http://www.adr.org

National nonprofit organization offering mediation and arbitration services through local offices across the country. Also conducts neutral investigations of workplace disputes. Provides education and training in alternative dispute resolution. General information about out-of-court settlements, negotiation opportunities, rules and procedures of mediation.

National Institute for Dispute Resolution
1726 M Street, NW, Suite 500
Washington, DC 20036-4502
202-466-4764
FAX: 202-466-4769
e-mail: nidr@igc.apc.org

Provides publications, advice and referrals on alternative dispute resolution.

Miscellaneous Workplace Issues

Bureau of National Affairs BNA-Communications
1231 25th Street, NW
Washington, DC 20037
202-452-4200
http://www.bna.com

Special reports, audio-video materials and manuals in many areas of employment, including disabilities, discrimination, diversity and management training.

Business and Legal Reports, Inc.
141 Mill Rock Road East
Old Saybrook, CT 06475
800-727-5257
FAX: 860-510-7220
http://www.blr.com

Publishes booklets on numerous workplace issues including safety, workers' compensation, sexual harassment, family leave, drug testing and stress management.

Center for Working Life
503-287-5561
National nonprofit organization providing training and consultation for development of programs to assist in relocating displaced workers and workplace education.

Employee Benefit Research Institute
2121 K Street, NW, #600
Washington, DC 20037-1896
202-659-0670
FAX: 202-775-6312
http://www.ebri.org
Researches proposed policy changes to employee benefits. Sponsors studies on retirement income and on health, work, family leave and other workplace benefits.

National Employee Rights Institute
414 Walnut Street, Suite 911
Cincinnati, OH 45202
513-241-5157
800-469-6374
FAX: 513-241-7863
http://www.net.nerinet.org/
National nonprofit organization providing information, education and assistance to individual employees and promoting public policies to advance their rights. Gives advice to employees via hotline, through e-mail, by mail and through publications.

Older Workers

American Association of Retired Persons
601 E Street, NW
Washington, DC 20049
202-434-2277
800-424-3410
FAX: 202-434-2320
http://www.aarp.org
Nonprofit membership organization of older Americans open to people age 50 or older. Wide range of publications on retirement planning, age discrimination and employment-related topics. Networking and direct services available through local chapters.

National Senior Citizens Law Center
1101 14th Street, NW, Suite 400
Washington, DC 20005
202-289-6976
FAX: 202-289-7224
http://www.nslc.org
Litigates on behalf of legal services and elderly poor clients. Interests include Social Security and Supplemental Security Income (SSI), Medicare, Medicaid, nursing home residents' rights, home health care, public and private pensions and protective services.

Older Women's League
666 Eleventh Street, NW, Suite 700
Washington, DC 20001
202-783-6686
800-825-3695
FAX: 202-638-2356
http://owl-national.org/
Organization concerned with the social and economic problems of middle-aged and older women. Interests include health care, Social Security, pension rights, housing, employment, women as caregivers, effects of budget cuts and issues related to death and dying.

Retirement Plans and Pensions

American Association of Retired Persons
See listing under Older Workers.

Pension Benefit Guaranty Corporation
Coverage & Inquiries Branch
1200 K Street, NW
Washington, DC 20005-4026
202-326-4010
TDD: 202-326-4179
FAX: 202-326-4016
e-mail: pnsn@aol.com
http://www.pbgc.gov
Government agency established to protect pension benefits. Collects premiums from participating companies. Investigation with Labor Department. Provides insolvent multi-employer pension plans with financial assistance to enable them to pay guaranteed benefits.

Pension Rights Center
918 16th Street, NW; Suite 704
Washington, DC 20006-2902
202-296-3776
FAX: 202-833-2472
Nonprofit organization and service network providing pension advice or lawyer referral. Publications list available.

Safety and Health Issues

American Psychological Association
750 First Street, NE
Washington, DC 20002-4242
202-336-5500
TDD: 202-336-6123
FAX: 202-336-6069
http://www.apa.org
Information on career training, stress and well-being at work, counseling and psychotherapy for work dysfunctions. Monitors federal legislation on mental health issues.

Americans for Nonsmokers' Rights
2530 San Pablo Avenue, Suite J
Berkeley, CA 94702
510-841-3032
FAX: 510-841-3060
http://www.no-smoke.org
Nonprofit advocacy group that campaigns for legislation to assure that nonsmokers can avoid involuntary exposure to secondhand smoke in the workplace, restaurants, public places and public transportation. Offers educational programs for children on smoking prevention and the right to smokefree air.

National Institute for Occupational Safety and Health (NIOSH)
200 Independence Avenue, SW
HHH Building, Room 715-H
Washington, DC 20201
Information hotline: 800-356-4674
http://www.cdc.gov/niosh/homepage.html
Research institute offering publications on various workplace health and safety issues. Maintains database on indoor air quality, carpal tunnel, workplace homicide and other current topics. Conducts evaluations of individual worksites. Also makes available training programs, materials and videos.

National Safety Council
1121 Spring Lake Drive
Itasca, IL 60143-3201
630-285-1121
FAX: 630-282-1315
http://www.nsc.org
Conducts research and provides education and information on occupational safety; encourages policies that reduce accidental deaths, injuries and preventable illnesses; monitors legislation and regulations affecting safety.

Occupational Safety and Health Administration
200 Constitution Avenue, NW
Washington, DC 20210
202-693-1999
Emergency hotline: 800-321-6742
http://www.osha.gov
Federal agency responsible for establishing and overseeing workplace health and safety standards.

White Lung Association
P.O. Box 1483
Baltimore, MD 21203-1483
410-243-5864
http://www.whitelung.org
National nonprofit organization of asbestos victims. Teaches consequences and effect, removal and disposal of asbestos. Provides literature.

Unions

American Federation of Labor and Congress of Industrial Organizations (AFL-CIO)
815 16th Street, NW
Washington, DC 20006
202-637-5000
FAX: 202-637-5058
http://www.aflcio.org
Voluntary federation of 86 unions with over 14 million members. Printed materials on all aspects of union employment. Information and assistance for union-related issues at local levels.

Association for Union Democracy
500 State Street
Brooklyn, NY 11217
718-855-6650
FAX: 718-885-6799
http://www.uniondemocracy.com
Nationwide attorney referrals, legal advice, counseling and organizational assistance for union members.

Coalition of Labor Union Women (CLUW)
1126 16th Street, NW
Washington, DC 20036
202-466-4610
FAX: 202-776-0537
http://www.cluw.org
National organization with 75 local chapters. Provides education, organizes conferences and workshops, lobbies for legislation, supports strikes and boycotts. Newsletter and written materials. Provides referrals to attorneys and legal rights groups for union workers.

National Right to Work Committee
8001 Braddock Road
Springfield, VA 22160
703-321-9820
800-325-7892
FAX: 703-321-7342
http://www.nrtwc.org
Citizens' lobbying organization to pass more right to work legislation and combat compulsory unionism.

National Right to Work Legal Defense Foundation
8001 Braddock Road
Springfield, VA 22160
703-321-8510
800-336-3600
FAX: 703-321-9319
e-mail: info@nrtw.org
http://www.nrtw.org
Nonprofit charitable organization which offers free legal aid to employees whose rights are violated by compulsory unionism abuses.

Women's Issues

Business and Professional Women, USA
2012 Massachusetts Avenue, NW
Washington, DC 20036
202-293-1100
FAX: 202-8611-0928
http://www.bpwusa.org
Seeks to improve the status of working women through education, legislative action and local projects. Sponsors Business and Professional Women's Foundation, which awards grants and loans, based on need, to mature women reentering the workforce or entering nontraditional fields.

Equal Rights Advocates
1663 Mission Street, Suite 550
San Francisco, CA 94103
415-621-0672 (General information)
415-621-0505 (Advice and counseling hotline)
FAX: 415-621-6744
http:///www.equalrights.org
Nonprofit public interest law firm providing legal advice and counseling in both English and Spanish.

Federally Employed Women, Inc.
P.O. Box 27687
Washington, DC 20038
202-898-0994
FAX: 202-898-0998
http://www.few.org
Membership group for women and men who work for the federal government. Works to eliminate sex discrimination in government employment and to increase job opportunities for women. Offers training programs, monitors legislation and regulations.

Federation of Organizations for Professional Women
1825 I Street, NW; #400
Washington, DC 20006
202-328-1415
FAX: 202-328-1415
Telephone advice and counseling on sexual harassment and discrimination. Publishes written materials. Support groups in Washington, D.C. area.

Feminist Majority Foundation
1600 Wilson Boulevard, #801
Arlington, VA 22209
703-522-2214 (General information)
703-522-2501 (Sexual harassment hotline)
FAX: 703-522-2219
e-mail: femmaj@feminist.org
http://www.feminist.org

The Fund is political and does lobbying, seeking to increase the number of feminists running for public office. The Foundation with which it is associated is a nonprofit research organization which provides public information about battered women, sexual harassment and international women's issues.

9to5, National Association of Working Women
614 Superior Avenue, NW
Cleveland, OH 44113
216-566-9308 (General information)
800-522-0925 (Hotline)
http://www.9to5.org

National nonprofit membership organization for working women. Counseling, information and referrals for problems on the job, including family leave, pregnancy disability, termination, compensation and sexual harassment. Newsletter and publications. Local chapters throughout the country.

National Partnership for Women and Families
(Formerly Women's Legal Defense Fund)
1875 Connecticut Avenue, NW
Suite 710
Washington, DC 20009
202-986-2600
FAX: 202-986-2539
http://www.nationalparternship.org

A nonprofit, nonpartisan organization that uses public education and advocacy to promote fairness in the workplace, quality healthcare and policies that help women and men meet the dual demands of work and family.

National Women's Law Center
11 Dupont Circle, NW; Room 800
Washington, DC 20036
202-588-5180
FAX: 202-588-5185
http://www.nwlc.org

Works to expand and protect women's legal rights through litigation, advocacy and public education. Interests include reproductive rights, health education, employment discrimination and sexual harassment, women in prison, income security and family support.

NOW Legal Defense and Education Fund
99 Hudson Street, 12th Floor
New York, NY 10013
212-925-6635
http://www.now.org

A non-profit advocacy organization that strives to eliminate discrimination and harassment in the workplace and other sectors of society; secure abortion, birth control and reproductive rights; end violence against women; eradicate racism, sexism and homophobia, and promote equality and justice. NOW pursues its goals through direct mass actions (including marches, rallies, pickets counter-demonstrations, non-violent civil disobedience) intensive lobbying, grassroots political organizing and litigation (including class action lawsuits).

U.S. Department of Labor, Women's Bureau
200 Constitution Avenue, NW; #S3002
Washington, DC 20210
800-827-5355
202-219-6611
FAX: 202-219-5529
http://www.dol.gov/dol/wb/

Monitors women's employment issues. Promotes employment opportunities for women; sponsors workshops, job fairs, demonstrations and pilot projects. Offers technical assistance, conducts research and provides publications on issues that affect working women.

Wider Opportunities for Women (WOW)
815 15th Street, NW; #916
Washington, DC 20005
202-638-3143
FAX: 202-638-4885
http://www.wow.org

National nonprofit organization, primarily focusing on economic opportunities for women and girls. Publishes reports and other materials.

Women in Community Service
1900 North Beauregard Street, Room 103
Alexandria, VA 22311
703-671-0500
800-442-9427
FAX: 703-671-4489
http://www.wics.org

Contracts with the Labor Department for outreach, support services and job placement for the Job Corps. Sponsors the Lifeskills Program to assist at-risk women in such areas as job training and money management.

Women Work!
The National Network for Women's Employment
1625 K Street, NW, #300
Washington, DC 20006
202-467-6346
800-235-2732
FAX: 202-467-5366
http://www.womenwork.org

Fosters development of programs and services for former homemakers reentering the job market and provides information about public policy issues that affect displaced homemakers.

INDEX

CATALOG

BUSINESS

	PRICE	CODE
Avoid Employee Lawsuits (Quick & Legal Series)	$24.95	AVEL
⊙ The CA Nonprofit Corporation Kit (Binder w/CD-ROM)	$49.95	CNP
▣ Consultant & Independent Contractor Agreements (Book w/Disk—PC)	$24.95	CICA
▣ The Corporate Minutes Book (Book w/Disk—PC)	$69.95	CORMI
The Employer's Legal Handbook	$39.95	EMPL
Firing Without Fear (Quick & Legal Series)	$29.95	FEAR
▣ Form Your Own Limited Liability Company (Book w/Disk—PC)	$44.95	LIAB
▣ Hiring Independent Contractors: The Employer's Legal Guide (Book w/Disk—PC)	$34.95	HICI
▣ How to Create a Buy-Sell Agreement & Control the Destiny of your Small Business (Book w/Disk—PC)	$49.95	BSAG
▣ How to Form a California Professional Corporation (Book w/Disk—PC)	$49.95	PROF
▣ How to Form a Nonprofit Corporation (Book w/Disk —PC)—National Edition	$44.95	NNP
⊙ How to Form a Nonprofit Corporation in California (Book w/CD-ROM)	$44.95	NON
▣ How to Form Your Own California Corporation (Binder w/Disk—PC)	$39.95	CACI
▣ How to Form Your Own California Corporation (Book w/Disk—PC)	$39.95	CCOR
▣ How to Form Your Own New York Corporation (Book w/Disk—PC)	$39.95	NYCO
⊙ How to Form Your Own Texas Corporation (Book w/CD-ROM)	$39.95	TCOR
How to Write a Business Plan	$29.95	SBS
The Independent Paralegal's Handbook	$29.95	PARA
Leasing Space for Your Small Business	$34.95	LESP
Legal Guide for Starting & Running a Small Business, Vol. 1	$29.95	RUNS
▣ Legal Guide for Starting & Running a Small Business, Vol. 2: Legal Forms (Book w/Disk—PC)	$29.95	RUNS2
Marketing Without Advertising	$22.00	MWAD
▣ Music Law (Book w/Disk—PC)	$29.95	ML
Nolo's California Quick Corp (Quick & Legal Series)	$19.95	QINC
Nolo's Guide to Social Security Disability	$29.95	QSS
Nolo's Quick LLC (Quick & Legal Series)	$24.95	LLCQ
⊙ Open Your California Business in 24 Hours (Book w/CD-ROM)	$24.95	OPEN
▣ The Partnership Book: How to Write a Partnership Agreement (Book w/Disk—PC)	$39.95	PART
Sexual Harassment on the Job	$24.95	HARS
Starting & Running a Successful Newsletter or Magazine	$29.95	MAG
Tax Savvy for Small Business	$34.95	SAVVY
Wage Slave No More: Law & Taxes for the Self-Employed	$24.95	WAGE
▣ Your Limited Liability Company: An Operating Manual (Book w/Disk—PC)	$49.95	LOP
Your Rights in the Workplace	$29.95	YRW

CONSUMER

	PRICE	CODE
Fed Up with the Legal System: What's Wrong & How to Fix It	$9.95	LEG
How to Win Your Personal Injury Claim	$29.95	PICL
Nolo's Everyday Law Book	$24.95	EVL
Nolo's Pocket Guide to California Law	$15.95	CLAW
Trouble-Free Travel...And What to Do When Things Go Wrong	$14.95	TRAV

ESTATE PLANNING & PROBATE

	PRICE	CODE
8 Ways to Avoid Probate (Quick & Legal Series)	$16.95	PRO8
9 Ways to Avoid Estate Taxes (Quick & Legal Series)	$24.95	ESTX
Estate Planning Basics (Quick & Legal Series)	$18.95	ESPN
How to Probate an Estate in California	$39.95	PAE
⊙ Make Your Own Living Trust (Book w/CD-ROM)	$34.95	LITR
Nolo's Law Form Kit: Wills	$24.95	KWL
▣ Nolo's Will Book (Book w/Disk—PC)	$34.95	SWIL
Plan Your Estate	$39.95	NEST
Quick & Legal Will Book (Quick & Legal Series)	$21.95	QUIC

▣ Book with disk   ⊙ Book with CD-ROM

	PRICE	CODE

FAMILY MATTERS

	PRICE	CODE
Child Custody: Building Parenting Agreements That Work	$29.95	CUST
Child Support in California: Go to Court to Get More or Pay Less (Quick & Legal Series)	$24.95	CHLD
The Complete IEP Guide	$24.95	IEP
Divorce & Money: How to Make the Best Financial Decisions During Divorce	$34.95	DIMO
Do Your Own Divorce in Oregon	$29.95	ODIV
Get a Life: You Don't Need a Million to Retire Well	$24.95	LIFE
The Guardianship Book for California	$34.95	GB
⊙ How to Adopt Your Stepchild in California (Book w/CD-ROM)	$34.95	ADOP
A Legal Guide for Lesbian and Gay Couples	$25.95	LG
⊙ The Living Together Kit (Book w/CD-ROM)	$34.95	LTK
Nolo's Pocket Guide to Family Law	$14.95	FLD
Using Divorce Mediation: Save Your Money & Your Sanity	$21.95	UDMD

GOING TO COURT

	PRICE	CODE
Beat Your Ticket: Go To Court and Win! (National Edition)	$19.95	BEYT
The Criminal Law Handbook: Know Your Rights, Survive the System	$29.95	KYR
Everybody's Guide to Small Claims Court (National Edition)	$18.95	NSCC
Everybody's Guide to Small Claims Court in California	$24.95	CSCC
Fight Your Ticket ... and Win! (California Edition)	$24.95	FYT
How to Change Your Name in California	$34.95	NAME
How to Collect When You Win a Lawsuit (California Edition)	$29.95	JUDG
How to Mediate Your Dispute	$18.95	MEDI
How to Seal Your Juvenile & Criminal Records (California Edition)	$34.95	CRIM
Mad at Your Lawyer	$21.95	MAD
Nolo's Deposition Handbook	$29.95	DEP
Represent Yourself in Court: How to Prepare & Try a Winning Case	$29.95	RYC

HOMEOWNERS, LANDLORDS & TENANTS

	PRICE	CODE
California Tenants' Rights	$24.95	CTEN
▣ Contractors' and Homeowners' Guide to Mechanics' Liens (Book w/Disk—PC)—California Edition	$39.95	MIEN
The Deeds Book (California Edition)	$24.95	DEED
Dog Law	$14.95	DOG
⊙ Every Landlord's Legal Guide (National Edition, Book w/CD-ROM)	$44.95	ELLI
Every Tenant's Legal Guide	$26.95	EVTEN
For Sale by Owner in California	$29.95	FSBO
How to Buy a House in California	$29.95	BHCA
The Landlord's Law Book, Vol. 1: Rights & Responsibilities (California Edition)	$44.95	LBRT
⊙ The California Landlord's Law Book, Vol. 2: Evictions (Book w/CD-ROM)	$44.95	LBEV
Leases & Rental Agreements (Quick & Legal Series)	$24.95	LEAR
Neighbor Law: Fences, Trees, Boundaries & Noise	$24.95	NEI
⊙ The New York Landlord's Law Book (Book w/CD-ROM)	$39.95	NYLL
Renters' Rights (National Edition—Quick & Legal Series)	$19.95	RENT
Stop Foreclosure Now in California	$34.95	CLOS

HUMOR

	PRICE	CODE
29 Reasons Not to Go to Law School	$12.95	29R
Poetic Justice	$9.95	PJ

IMMIGRATION

	PRICE	CODE
How to Get a Green Card	$29.95	GRN
U.S. Immigration Made Easy	$44.95	IMEZ

MONEY MATTERS

	PRICE	CODE
▣ 101 Law Forms for Personal Use (Quick & Legal Series, Book w/Disk—PC)	$29.95	SPOT
Bankruptcy: Is It the Right Solution to Your Debt Problems? (Quick & Legal Series)	$19.95	BRS
Chapter 13 Bankruptcy: Repay Your Debts	$29.95	CH13
▣ Credit Repair (Quick & Legal Series, Book w/Disk—PC)	$18.95	CREP
▣ The Financial Power of Attorney Workbook (Book w/Disk—PC)	$29.95	FINPOA
How to File for Chapter 7 Bankruptcy	$29.95	HFB
IRAs, 401(k)s & Other Retirement Plans: Taking Your Money Out	$24.95	RET

▣ Book with disk   ⊙ Book with CD-ROM

	PRICE	CODE
Money Troubles: Legal Strategies to Cope With Your Debts	$24.95	MT
Nolo's Law Form Kit: Personal Bankruptcy	$16.95	KBNK
Stand Up to the IRS	$29.95	SIRS
Surviving an IRS Tax Audit (Quick & Legal Series)	$24.95	SAUD
Take Control of Your Student Loan Debt	$24.95	SLOAN

PATENTS AND COPYRIGHTS

	PRICE	CODE
⊙ The Copyright Handbook: How to Protect and Use Written Works (Book w/CD-ROM)	$34.95	COHA
Copyright Your Software	$24.95	CYS
Domain Names	$24.95	DOM
▣ Getting Permission: How to License and Clear Copyrighted Materials Online and Off (Book w/Disk—PC)·	$34.95	RIPER
How to Make Patent Drawings Yourself	$29.95	DRAW
The Inventor's Notebook	$34.95	INOT
Nolo's Patents for Beginners (Quick & Legal Series)	$29.95	QPAT
▣ License Your Invention (Book w/Disk—PC)	$39.95	LICE
Patent, Copyright & Trademark	$29.95	PCTM
Patent It Yourself	$49.95	PAT
Patent Searching Made Easy	$29.95	PATSE
The Public Domain	$34.95	PUBL
⊙ Software Development: A Legal Guide (Book w/ CD-ROM)	$44.95	SFT
Trademark: Legal Care for Your Business and Product Name	$39.95	TRD
The Trademark Registration Kit (Quick & Legal Series)	$19.95	TREG

RESEARCH & REFERENCE

	PRICE	CODE
Legal Research: How to Find & Understand the Law	$34.95	LRES

SENIORS

	PRICE	CODE
Beat the Nursing Home Trap: A Consumer's Guide to Assisted Living and Long-Term Care	$21.95	ELD
The Conservatorship Book for California	$44.95	CNSV
Social Security, Medicare & Pensions	$24.95	SOA

SOFTWARE

**Call or check our website at www.nolo.com
for special discounts on Software!**

	PRICE	CODE
⊙ LeaseWriter CD—Windows	$129.95	LWD1
⊙ Living Trust Maker CD—Windows	$89.95	LTD3
⊙ LLC Maker—Windows	$89.95	LLPC
⊙ Patent It Yourself CD—Windows	$229.95	PPC12
⊙ Personal RecordKeeper 5.0 CD—Windows	$59.95	RKD5
⊙ Small Business Pro 4 CD—Windows	$89.95	SBCD4
⊙ WillMaker 8.0 CD—Windows	$69.95	WP8

▣ Book with disk   ⊙ Book with CD-ROM

Call 800-992-6656 • www.nolo.com • Mail or fax the order form in this book

Order Form

Name

Address

City

State, Zip

Daytime Phone

E-mail

Our "No-Hassle" Guarantee

Return anything you buy directly from Nolo for any reason and we'll cheerfully refund your purchase price. No ifs, ands or buts.

☐ Check here if you do not wish to receive mailings from other companies

Item Code	Quantity	Item	Unit Price	Total Price

Subtotal	
Add your local sales tax (California only)	
Shipping: RUSH $8, Basic $3.95 (See below)	
"I bought 3, Ship it to me FREE!"(Ground shipping only)	
TOTAL	

Method of payment

☐ Check ☐ VISA ☐ MasterCard
☐ Discover Card ☐ American Express

Account Number

Expiration Date

Signature

Shipping and Handling

Rush Delivery-Only $8

We'll ship any order to any street address in the U.S. by UPS 2nd Day Air* for only $8!

* Order by noon Pacific Time and get your order in 2 business days. Orders placed after noon Pacific Time will arrive in 3 business days. P.O. boxes and S.F. Bay Area use basic shipping. Alaska and Hawaii use 2nd Day Air or Priority Mail.

Basic Shipping—$3.95

Use for P.O. Boxes, Northern California and Ground Service.

Allow 1-2 weeks for delivery. U.S. addresses only.

For faster service, use your credit card and our toll-free numbers

Order 24 hours a day

Online	www.nolo.com
Phone	1-800-992-6656
Fax	1-800-645-0895
Mail	Nolo.com
	950 Parker St.
	Berkeley, CA 94710

Visit us online at

www.nolo.com

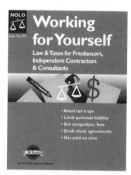

Take 2 minutes & Give us your 2 cents

Your comments make a big difference in the development and revision of Nolo books and software. Please take a few minutes and register your Nolo product—and your comments—with us. Not only will your input make a difference, you'll receive special offers available only to registered owners of Nolo products on our newest books and software. Register now by:

PHONE
1-800-992-6656

FAX
1-800-645-0895

EMAIL
cs@nolo.com

or **MAIL** us
this registration card

REMEMBER:
Little publishers have big ears. We really listen to you.

fold here

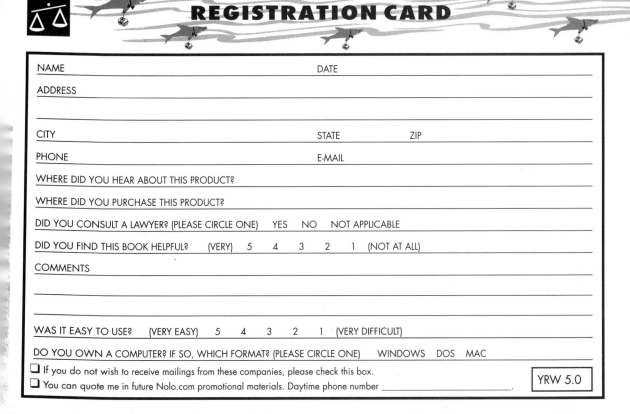

NOLO
REGISTRATION CARD

NAME		DATE	
ADDRESS			
CITY		STATE	ZIP
PHONE		E-MAIL	

WHERE DID YOU HEAR ABOUT THIS PRODUCT?

WHERE DID YOU PURCHASE THIS PRODUCT?

DID YOU CONSULT A LAWYER? (PLEASE CIRCLE ONE)   YES   NO   NOT APPLICABLE

DID YOU FIND THIS BOOK HELPFUL?   (VERY)   5   4   3   2   1   (NOT AT ALL)

COMMENTS

WAS IT EASY TO USE?   (VERY EASY)   5   4   3   2   1   (VERY DIFFICULT)

DO YOU OWN A COMPUTER? IF SO, WHICH FORMAT? (PLEASE CIRCLE ONE)   WINDOWS   DOS   MAC

☐ If you do not wish to receive mailings from these companies, please check this box.

☐ You can quote me in future Nolo.com promotional materials. Daytime phone number _____.

YRW 5.0

NOLO IN THE NEWS

"Nolo helps lay people perform legal tasks without the aid—or fees—of lawyers."

—USA TODAY

Nolo books are ..."written in plain language, free of legal mumbo jumbo, and spiced with witty personal observations."

—ASSOCIATED PRESS

"...Nolo publications...guide people simply through the how, when, where and why of law."

—WASHINGTON POST

"Increasingly, people who are not lawyers are performing tasks usually regarded as legal work... And consumers, using books like Nolo's, do routine legal work themselves."

—NEW YORK TIMES

"...All of [Nolo's] books are easy-to-understand, are updated regularly, provide pull-out forms...and are often quite moving in their sense of compassion for the struggles of the lay reader."

—SAN FRANCISCO CHRONICLE

fold here

- -

Place
stamp here

nolo
950 Parker Street
Berkeley, CA 94710-9867

Attn: YRW 5.0